SIFTING THE SOIL OF GREECE

BULLETIN OF THE INSTITUTE OF CLASSICAL STUDIES SUPPLEMENT 111

GENERAL EDITOR: MIKE EDWARDS

MANAGING EDITOR: RICHARD SIMPSON

SIFTING THE SOIL
OF GREECE

THE EARLY YEARS OF THE BRITISH SCHOOL AT ATHENS (1886-1919)

DAVID W. J. GILL

INSTITUTE OF CLASSICAL STUDIES
SCHOOL OF ADVANCED STUDY
UNIVERSITY OF LONDON

2011

The front cover image shows the east coast of the Methana peninsula in the Peloponnese. Photo: author.

ISBN 978-1-905670-32-1

Designed and computer typeset at the Institute of Classical Studies.

Printed by Short Run Press Limited, Bittern Road, Exeter EX2 7LW.

to Caroline

TABLE OF CONTENTS

ABBREVIATIONS

ABSA	*Annual of the British School at Athens*
AJA	*American Journal of Archaeology*
AJP	*American Journal of Philology*
ASAE	*Annales du Service des Antiquités de l'Égypte*
BCH	*Bulletin de Correspondance Hellénique*
CQ	*Classical Quarterly*
CR	*Classical Review*
DBA	*Dictionary of British Architects 1834-1900* (1993).
DBC	Robert B. Todd (ed.), *Dictionary of British Classicists* (Bristol: Thoemmes Continuum, 2004).
DSA	*Dictionary of Scottish Architects.* Available at www.scottisharchitects.org.uk
Faces of archaeology	Rachel Hood, *Faces of archaeology in Greece: caricatures by Piet de Jong* (Oxford: Leopard's Head Press, 1998).
G&R	*Greece and Rome*
JEA	*Journal of Egyptian Archaeology*
JFA	*Journal of Field Archaeology*
JHS	*Journal of Hellenic Studies*
JRAI	*Journal of the Royal Anthropological Institute of Great Britain and Ireland*
JRIBA	*Journal of the Royal Institute of British Architects*
JRS	*Journal of Roman Studies*
JTS	*Journal of Theological Studies*
NC	*Numismatic Chronicle*
ODNB	*Oxford Dictionary of National Biography* (Oxford: Oxford University Press, 2004).
PBA	*Proceedings of the British Academy*
PBSR	*Papers of the British School at Rome*
PCPS	*Proceedings of the Cambridge Philological Society*
Venn	J. Venn, *Alumni Cantabrigienses; a biographical list of all known students, graduates and holders of office at the University of Cambridge, from the earliest times to 1900* (Cambridge: Cambridge University Press, 1922-).
WWW	*Who Was Who.*

ACKNOWLEDGEMENTS

This work would have been impossible without the practical assistance of members of the British School at Athens (BSA). The Council of the BSA kindly granted me access to the Minute Books and gave permission for them to be cited. Dr Amalia Kakissis, Archivist, has allowed me to work in the Archives. She answered questions and offered comments on an early draft. Helen Fields, the London Secretary, has also been accommodating, even to the point of sharing her office with archive boxes. However this is not an official history of the BSA and it does not necessarily reflect the views of the School and its Officers.

I am particularly grateful to my Swansea colleague, Dr Christopher Stray, who encouraged me to write this account of the early years of the School. He has assisted with queries, suggested new areas to explore, and commented on early drafts. Richard Simpson made helpful suggestions, and Anne Chippindale kindly read and commented on the text, though any remaining mistakes are mine alone.

I am indebted to the patient and generous help of an army of archivists who have supplied me with dates, obituaries and snippets of information about the students at the British School. In particular:

Cambridge

Fiona Colbert (St John's College), Jacqueline Cox (University Archives), Adam C. Green (Assistant Archivist, Trinity College), Janet Morris (Archivist, Emmanuel College), Kate Perry (Archivist, Girton College), Jonathan Smith (Archivist, Trinity College), Elizabeth Stratton (Edgar Bowring Archivist, Clare College), Anne Thomson (Archivist, Newnham College), and Dr Frances H. Willmoth (Archivist, Jesus College).

Oxford

Juliet Chadwick (Sub-Librarian, Exeter College), Judith Curthoys (Archivist, Christ Church), Dr Robin Darwall-Smith (Archivist, Magdalen College, and University College), Clifford S.L. Davies (Archivist, Wadham College), Clare Hopkins (Archivist, Trinity College), Andrew Mussell (Archivist, Lincoln College), Rob Petre (Archivist, Oriel College), Julian Reid (Archivist, Corpus Christi College), Michael Riordan (Archivist, St John's College, and The Queen's College), Anna Sander (Lonsdale Curator of Archives and Manuscripts, Balliol College), Jennifer Thorp (Archivist, New College), Debbie Usher (Archivist, Middle East Centre Archive, St Anthony's College), and Lucie Walker (Librarian, Pembroke College).

Other University Archives

Adrian Allan (University Archivist, Liverpool University), Stephanie Clarke (Archivist and Records Manager, British Museum), Laura Dyer (Archives Assistant, Royal Holloway College, University of London), June Ellner (Special Libraries and Archives,

THE BRITISH SCHOOL AT ATHENS

University of Aberdeen), Irene Ferguson (Special Collections, University of Edinburgh), Anna Floor (Archives Assistant, Royal Holloway, University of London), Peter Keelan (Head of Special Collections & Archives, Cardiff University Library), Sylvia Lassam (Rolph Bell Archives, Trinity College, Toronto), Loryl MacDonald (University of Toronto Archives), Moira Mackenzie (Special Collections, University of St Andrews), Clare McVeigh (University Archivist, Queen's University, Belfast), Dr James Peters (University Archivist, The John Rylands Library, University of Manchester), Mark Smith (Archives Assistant, King's College, London), Sheila Turcon (archivist, McMaster University), Susannah Waters (Mackintosh Research Centre for Archives and Collections, Glasgow School of Art), and the staff of the Glasgow University Archive.

Schools

John Bever and Carole Pemberton (Manchester Grammar School), Rita Boswell (Harrow School), C. Charter (Old Reptonians), Charles Colquhoun (Clifton College), John Edwards (Wellington), Suzanne Foster (Winchester), Andrew Hambling (Archivist, Haileybury), P. Hatfield (College Archivist, Eton College), Alison Heath (Archivist, Wycombe Abbey School), Calista M. Lucy (Dulwich College), Dr T.E. Rogers (Marlborough College), and Roland Symons (Monkton Combe School).

Institutional Archives

Rachel Bowles (BBC), Felicity Cobbing (Palestine Exploration Fund), and Natalia Vogeikoff (archivist, American School of Classical Studies at Athens).

I would also like to acknowledge the help and encouragement (sometimes unknowingly) of Paul Bahn, Susan Barber (New Zealand; for information on Henry A. Tubbs), Caroline Barron, William M. Calder III, Christopher Chippindale, Getzel Cohen, Mark Curthoys, Robert Drake, Philip W.M. Freeman, Robert Frost (Yorkshire Archaeological Society), Nicholas Griffin, Nicholas Hodgins (Society of Antiquaries of Newcastle upon Tyne), Rachel and Sinclair Hood, Charles E. Jones, Rachel Maxwell-Hyslop, Evelyn Lord (Cambridge Antiquarian Society), Nicoletta Momigliano, Paul Naiditch, Tim Schadla-Hall, David Shankland, Pamela Jane Smith, David Traill, Michael Vickers, Peter Warren, Paul Woudhuysen, and the late Helen Waterhouse.

Chapter 5 is a revised version of '"The passion of hazard": women at the British School at Athens before the First World War,' *BSA* 97 (2002) 491-510; chapter 10 is a revised version of 'The British School at Athens and archaeological research in the late Ottoman Empire', in D. Shankland (ed.), *Archaeology, Anthropology and Heritage in the Balkans and Anatolia: the Life and Times of F. W. Hasluck, 1878-1920*, vol. 1 (Istanbul: The Isis Press, 2004) 223-55.

Finally I must thank family members. My parents, Denis and Caroline Gill, first introduced me to the archaeology of the Greek world and have taken an interest in my research over many years. My father-in-law, Bishop Timothy Dudley-Smith, has granted me access to his array of Cambridge memoirs. He has been a constant encouragement for this research, along with his late wife, Arlette. My wife, Caroline, has supported me through the project and has made tactful and appropriate suggestions to improve the text.

INTRODUCTION

The British School at Athens has been a significant influence on archaeology in the Mediterranean world and beyond. This study seeks to map the development of the institution from its formal foundation in 1886 to the end of the First World War. During this period some 130 individuals were admitted as students of the BSA working on a range of research topics that included sculpture, pottery, dialects, embroideries, and Byzantine architecture. Major excavations were conducted at Megalopolis, Sparta, and Phylakopi, as well as the series of digs on Crete that included Knossos.

There have been three previous studies of the School. George Macmillan prepared a short history to celebrate the Silver Jubilee in 1911.[1] Helen Waterhouse prepared a longer study to celebrate the Centenary in 1986, though this lacked a bibliography.[2] Both have been essential starting points for this study. The third work was prepared to coincide with the 2004 Athens Olympics.[3] These have been joined by a focused study on the history of British archaeological work on Crete.[4] Such research joins histories of the American School of Classical Studies at Athens (ASCSA), the Ecole française d'Athènes (EfA), the German Archaeological Institute (DAI), as well as the British School at Rome.[5] Together they provide an insight into the history of classical archaeology.[6]

The emphasis in this study is on the students, many barely mentioned in the official histories, rather than on the higher profile and more celebrated directors and members of the Managing Committee. The impetus for this project has been provided by the publication in 2004 of two key works: *The Oxford Dictionary of National Biography* (*ODNB*) and *The Dictionary of British Classicists* (*DBC*). All seven directors of the period up to the First World War appear in *ODNB* as well as 21 of the students.[7] Five of the directors and 30 of the students appear in *DBC*.[8] The research presented in these two works has allowed the students to be placed in a wider educational, social and cultural context. Interest was first stimulated by work on the collections of the Fitzwilliam Museum: the Greek and Roman

---

[1] Macmillan 1910/11.

[2] Waterhouse 1986. See also Hunt 1988.

[3] Calligas and Whitley 2005.

[4] Huxley 2000.

[5] Lord 1947; Meritt 1984; Radet 1901; Duchêne and Straboni 1996; Étienne 1996; Marchand 1996; Wallace-Hadrill 2001. See also Dyson 1998. The 1996 fascicule of the *BCH* contains a series of papers on the history of EfA.

[6] Dyson 2006. See also Bahn 1996; Stray 2002.

[7] A convenient list of entries as well as index for the students can be found in Gill 2008.

[8] F. C. Penrose and C. Harcourt-Smith do not appear in *DBC*.

collections contain a selection of material derived from BSA excavations (such as Phylakopi, Artemis Orthia, Palaikastro) as well as donations from those who were admitted as students.[9]

A number of biographical studies have also appeared. Jane Harrison was a key influence on the Managing Committee supporting the growing role of women at the BSA.[10] Eugénie Sellers (Strong) was the first woman to be admitted as a student; she was later Assistant Director of the British School at Rome.[11] The work on Crete has been covered by biographies of Sir Arthur Evans and Duncan Mackenzie.[12] There have also been a number of institutional histories considering the place of classics (and classical archaeology) especially at Oxford and Cambridge.[13]

A major source for developments at the BSA can be derived from the Minute Books for the Managing Committee.[14] The Minute Books provide information about appointments, the admission of students, excavations, finance as well as the health and welfare of the students. Sadly the first volume covering the period of the directorships of Penrose and Gardner is missing.[15] Information for this period is derived from contemporary reports in newspapers, primarily *The Times*. The BSA archive holds material from the major excavations.

The title alludes to Ernest Gardner's report to the 1890 Annual Meeting of the BSA when he described the start of the Megalopolis excavations.[16]

---

[9] For further details: Gill 1992a; Gill 1992b. See also Gill 2000a.

[10] Beard 2000; Robinson 2002. See also Gill 2002.

[11] Dyson 2004.

[12] MacGillivray 2000; Momigliano 1999. See also Brown and Bennett 2001.

[13] Stray 1999; Stray 2007. See also Stray 1998.

[14] I am grateful to the Managing Committee of the BSA for granting me permission to consult this part of the archive.

[15] The present Director and Archivist of the BSA inform me that the minute book has been missing since the 1920s.

[16] 'British School at Athens', *The Times* 3 July 1890, 6. Gardner used 'attack' rather than 'explore'.

PART 1:
THE SCHOOL

CHAPTER 1
THE ORIGINS OF THE SCHOOL

British archaeological work in the Aegean

By 1883 it was accepted that classical archaeology was 'the material foundation of all our knowledge of classical antiquity, and is as essential to the vitality of classical studies as any other branch of inquiry connected with them'.[1] The subject of this editorial from *The Times* was the proposed creation of a 'British School of Archæological and Classical Studies at Athens'.

The inspiration for such a foundation was derived from the interest in the classical world that had developed during the eighteenth century.[2] The travels of English gentleman on the Grand Tour had developed a largely amateur interest in the physical remains of the classical world. Many of the Grand Tourists visited Italy which was accessible with relative ease. Others looked further east and the site of Troy with its Homeric resonances was a draw. Richard Pococke (1704-65) visited the Troad in 1740 as part of an extensive tour that included Egypt and Palestine.[3] Robert Wood (1716/17-1771), best known for his work at Palmyra, visited the Troad in 1742 and made a study of the topography during a two-week stay in 1750.[4] Sir William Gell (1777-1836) visited the Troad in 1801,[5] and then joined Edward Dodwell (1776/7-1832) for a journey in the Peloponnese, visiting Epidauros, the Mycenaean sites of Mycenae and Tiryns, as well as the late classical fortified city of Messene.[6] Dodwell is credited with the discovery of Lykosura.

The amateur interest in classical sites is reflected in the creation of the Society of Dilettanti 1734.[7] The Society published a record of the monuments of Athens by James Stuart (1713-88) and James Revett (1720-1804).[8] The pair worked together in Athens from March 1751; Stuart was forced to leave the city in the autumn of 1753 due to rioting. They travelled through the Aegean before returning to London where they prepared their

---

[1] Editorial, *The Times* 27 June 1883, 11.

[2] For the 'Protohistory of Classical archaeology': Dyson 2006, 1-19.

[3] Baigent 2004b.

[4] Allen 1999, 41; White 2004.

[5] Wroth and Thompson 2004.

[6] Dodwell 1819; Foote 2004; Dyson 2006, 68-69.

[7] Cust and Skedd 2004.

[8] Watkin 2004b; Tony Brothers in Brothers, *et al.* 2006, 9-19; Purchas 2004. Stuart had become interested in classical art through a visit to Naples in 1748 with the dealer in antiquities, Gavin Hamilton. Stuart and Revett used their study of Augustan architecture to design a London club house for the Society in Cavendish Square. The building was never built.

Antiquities of Athens, which appeared in three volumes over the next four decades.[9] In 1764 Revett joined the Society's expedition to Ionia directed by Richard Chandler (1737-1810), who had recently concluded his study of classical sculpture and inscriptions in Oxford.[10] From 1811 to 1813 the Society sponsored a second survey of Ionia, this time under the direction of William Gell.[11] The team based at Smyrna made a study of classical sites, architecture and inscriptions of the cities of the region that appeared as *The Antiquities of Ionia*.[12] Smyrna was also the base for the antiquarian explorer Thomas Burgon (1787-1858) until 1814.[13]

Travels were seen as an opportunity for collecting, and several of the Grand Tourists had formed collections of – largely Roman – sculpture to place in their country houses. But the idea of public display also developed. The collection of Charles Townley (1737-1805), a member of the Dilettanti, was acquired by the British Museum after his death.[14] Travels were seen as an opportunity for collecting. Edward Daniel Clarke (1769-1822), who had been educated at Jesus College, Cambridge, served as tutor to a series of landed families.[15] In 1799 he set off with one of his pupils, John Marten Cripps (1780-1853), for Scandinavia and then from St Petersburg travelled through Russia to the Crimea, and thence to Constantinople and Troy.[16] After a period in Egypt and the Levant, they arrived in Greece where Clarke removed one of the caryatids from the Roman propylon at Eleusis.[17] His collection was presented to the University of Cambridge and put on display in the University Library.

Some new graduates in effect completed their study of classics at university by travelling in classical lands. Robert Pashley (1805-59) held a travelling fellowship from Trinity College, Cambridge and visited Anatolia and Crete. He visited Greece in 1833-34, shortly after the establishment of the new kingdom.[18] Among Pashley's trophies was a large marble sarcophagus from Arvi on Crete, presented to the University of Cambridge in 1835.[19]

---

[9] Vol. 1, 1762; vol. 2, 1787 [1790]; vol. 3, 1795.

[10] Wroth and Eagles 2004. For Chandler's study of the Oxford material: Chandler 1763.

[11] A third volume of *The Antiquities of Ionia* appeared in 1840, a fourth in 1881, and a fifth in 1915. A second edition of the first volume (1769) was published in 1821.

[12] 2 vols. 1769-97.

[13] Corbett 1960. Burgon conducted excavations on the island of Melos as well as at Athens (1813). Some of his collection is in the British Museum.

[14] Jenkins and Sloan 1996; Cook 1985. The collection was partly formed in Italy.

[15] McConnell 2004.

[16] Goodwin and Baigent 2004; Allen 1999, 45, 47.

[17] This, along with other sculptures, was presented to the University of Cambridge: Budde and Nicholls 1964, 46-49, pls. 24-25, no. 81.

[18] Garnett and Baigent 2004. See also Warren 2000, 7.

[19] Cambridge, Fitzwilliam Museum GR. 1. 1835. Budde and Nicholls 1964, 98-102, pls. 53-55, no. 161. The 'Pashley Sarcophagus' was presented by Admiral Sir Pulteney Malcolm, the commander-in-chief of the Mediterranean fleet (and whose services were required for transport): Laughton and Morriss 2004.

The emergence of national museums at the end of eighteenth century – stimulated in particular by the revolutionary development of the Louvre – created a desire for travellers and those linked to diplomatic missions to be alert to the possibilities of major acquisitions that could be put on display. In May 1801, Thomas Bruce, Seventh Earl of Elgin, ambassador to the Sublime Porte, obtained his controversial *firman* to remove sculptures from the Parthenon that were subsequently sold to the British Government.[20] In the summer of 1802, as the sculptures were being removed from the Athenian acropolis, William Martin Leake (1777-1860), comptroller of accounts for the British army, visited Athens and the Peloponnese as part of the British mission to the Ottoman Empire.[21] Leake made further travels though Greece from 1804 to 1807 surveying possible sites for an expected French invasion; he was arrested in February 1807, following the Ottoman Empire's alliance with France. He returned to Greece in 1809 to negotiate with Ali Pasha.[22] Leake was elected to the Society of Dilettanti in 1814. During his travels he made a built up a significant collection of coins, now in the Fitzwilliam Museum, as well as other minor antiquities.[23] One of Leake's lasting contributions was his set of topographical notes of Greece.[24]

A further collector-traveller was James Theodore Bent (1852-97), who had been educated at Wadham College, Oxford.[25] He was in the Cycladic islands of the Aegean in the mid-1880s, making a study of the Early Cycladic marble figures, and encouraging the study of Aegean prehistory.[26] Some of the material collected by him was presented to the British Museum.[27] He subsequently served on the Managing Committee of the BSA until his death.

In Greece Charles Robert Cockerell (1788-1863) visited the temple of Aphaia on Aegina and then the temple of Apollo at Bassai in 1811.[28] He arranged for the removal of the frieze from Bassai that was subsequently presented to the British Museum.[29] The pedimental sculptures from the temple of Aphaia were not acquired for Britain; they went, instead, to Munich.

---

[20] St. Clair 2004; Hitchens 2008.

[21] Wagstaff 2004; Dyson 2006, 70. On his return to England, Leake's ship, the *Mentor*, carrying part of the collection of antiquities formed by Elgin, was wrecked off the island of Kithera.

[22] For a convenient background to Ali Pasha's situation: Mazower 2001, 90-91.

[23] Babington 1867. See also Nicholls 1982.

[24] These were part of the collection of the Fitzwilliam Museum, but were transferred to the library of the Classics Faculty.

[25] Baigent 2004a.

[26] Bent 1884; Bent 1885. See also Brothers, *et al.* 2006. For the context of his work: Gill and Chippindale 1993.

[27] Fitton 1995.

[28] Wilson 2002, 68-69; Jenkins 2006, 130-50. See also Tzortzi 2000. Cockerell's interest in classical sculpture lived on in the design for the Ashmolean Museum, Oxford.

[29] Watkin 2004a.

Athens as a new centre for archaeology

One of the issues to emerge as plans were made to establish a British School of Archaeology in the Mediterranean was to be its location. One of the reasons why Athens has deemed to be a suitable location was British involvement in the Greek War of Independence which started in 1821. The focus for British philhellenes switched from antiquities to the fight for independence.[30] The defeat of the Ottoman fleet at Navarino in October 1827 helped to realise the dream, and the first president of Greece was elected.[31] In 1832 a monarchy was established in Greece. A study of the ancient ruins of Greece soon became a priority and Ludwig Ross was given charge of archaeological remains (until 1836).[32]

In Greece a Central Archaeological Museum was established in 1834 and the Archaeological Society of Athens was formed in 1837.[33] British scholars continued to visit Greece, among them Francis Cranmer Penrose (1817-1903), a member of the Society of Dilettanti, who arrived in Athens in January 1845 supported by a grant from Cambridge University.[34]

The amateur British approach to the study of the archaeology of Greece was in marked contrast to other countries. The French also had a long-standing interest in Greece and played their part in the War of Independence. In the closing stages of the War they had mounted the 'Expédition de Morée' (1829-31) which included a study of ancient remains. The French started a formal School at Athens in 1846, in part to counter British political influence in Greece.[35] Its role was to develop the study of Greek language, ancient history, and the study of antiquities. Its foundation was noted briefly in *The Times*:[36]

> The *Moniteur* publishes a Royal ordinance instituting at Athens a finishing school for the study of the Greek language, history, and antiquities, under the special surveillance and authority of the French Minister in Greece. The members of that school are to remain there two years, and during that period they will continue to enjoy their salaries as professors of the University of France. The French school may give, with the authorization or at the request of the King of Greece, public and gratuitous lectures on the French and Latin languages and literature. The director of the school, who is to be a professor of the university or a member of the Institute of France, will continue in functions during three years. His mission, however, may be prolonged two years more by a special decision of the Minister of Public Instruction.

Britain, in contrast, was not interested in developing a formal cultural presence in Athens. One of the reasons for supporting archaeology may have been the desire to acquire major monuments for display in the British Museum. 'Trophies' such as the

---

[30] Clogg 1992, 33-42.

[31] Clogg 1992, 42-43.

[32] Dyson 2006, 73-74.

[33] Dyson 2006, 75, 78.

[34] Penrose 1847.

[35] Duchêne and Straboni 1996; Étienne 1996. See Radet 1901, 9: 'l'École française est une creation de l'Angleterre'.

[36] *The Times* 14 September 1846, 5. For the French text: Étienne 1996, 7.

Parthenon sculptures or the Bassai frieze could no longer be exported from Greece after 1842.[37]

Samuel Birch (1813-85), keeper of Oriental Antiquities in the British Museum, rejected plans for the 'emotional archaeology' of the Egypt Exploration Society because it would not generate objects for the Museum.[38] With the view that collecting was important, British interest in 'Greek lands' extended well beyond the newly formed political state of Greece. There had been a long-standing interest in Anatolia through visits to the Troad. The British Museum had started to acquire significant classical material during the 1830s and 1840s.[39] Charles Fellows (1799-1860) travelled though Anatolia in 1838 and reached Lycia.[40] The British Museum was keen to acquire material from the region, though French and Austrian expeditions were also looking at the possibility.[41] A *firman* was obtained, and sailors from the Royal Navy assisted with the removal of sculptures from Xanthos from December 1841 to March 1842; Fellows returned to Xanthos in December 1843.

In 1845 the British Museum acquired a number of slabs from the Mausoleum of Halikarnassos that had been reused in the castle at Bodrum.[42] Charles Newton (1816-94), who had joined the Department of Antiquities in 1840, became interested in the possibility of working in the eastern Aegean and in particular on the Anatolian mainland.[43] He was appointed British vice-consul at Mytilene in 1852, and conducted excavations on Kalymnos. Newton was a member of the Society of Dilettanti. In 1854 he visited the newly established French School in Athens and saw the possibilities of a more investigative approach to excavation.[44] Two years later in 1856 he started excavations at Bodrum, and with assistance from the crew of HMS *Gorgon,* recovered further fragments of the Mausoleum. These were acquired by the securing of a *firman.*[45] Further pieces of ancient sculpture were recovered from Didyma (Branchidae) and Knidos.[46] Newton was also aware of other work in the area and in 1859 managed to acquire material from the excavations by Auguste Salzmann and Alfred Biliotti on Rhodes.[47] Newton was appointed Keeper of Greek and Roman Antiquities at the British Museum in 1861, a position he held until 1888.

Ephesus soon became a focus for investigation. The architect Edward Falkener first conducted research there in 1845 as part of a wider tour in the eastern Mediterranean.[48]

---

[37] Gardner 1894/5, 68. This prohibition is overlooked by Marthari 2001, 163.

[38] Drower 1982, 14.

[39] Jenkins 1992, 140-45.

[40] Challis 2008, 23-39. See also Jenkins 2006, 151-202.

[41] Wiplinger and Wlach 1996.

[42] Wilson 2002, 125.

[43] Jebb 1894; Gardner 1894/5; Jebb 1895; Cook 1997. See also Challis 2008, 55-56.

[44] Gardner 1894/5, 69.

[45] Wilson 2002, 125; Challis 2008, 55-72. See also Jenkins 2006, 203-35.

[46] Challis 2008, 72-75.

[47] Gardner 1894/5, 74. Material from excavations by Salzmann and Biliotti at Camirus on Rhodes was acquired by the British Museum in 1864.

[48] Falkener 1862. See also Aitchison and Ward 2004; Challis 2008, 118.

More sustained work was conducted in 1863 by John Turtle Wood (1821-90).[49] Wood's work, which led to the identification of the Artemision, continued until 1874. Richard Popplewell Pullan (1825-88), who had worked under Newton's direction at Knidos, explored Priene in the same period (1868-69) with the support of the Society of Dilettanti.[50] Fragments of the temple of Athena Polias were subsequently presented to the British Museum.[51] Pullan also excavated the temple of Dionysos at Teos, and his work was to appear as volume 4 of the Society of Dilettanti's *Antiquities of Ionia* (1881). In June 1868 George Dennis, best known for his surveys of Etruria, settled in Smyrna where he resided until 1870. He explored several sites in the hinterland including Sardis.[52] There was also a formal British survey of Crete by Commander Thomas A. B. Spratt (1811-1888) of the Royal Navy in 1851-53.[53] A number of inscriptions collected during the survey were presented to the Fitzwilliam Museum.[54]

Public interest in archaeology changed during the 1870s. Heinrich Schliemann, assisted by Frank Calvert, worked at Troy (1871, 1878, and 1890).[55] In 1874 there was even a possibility of major British involvement when Schliemann asked the Society of Antiquaries of London to assist with the work at Troy.[56] Lord Stanhope (1805-75),[57] president of the Society, put in an application to the Treasury which was blocked by Robert Lowe – Viscount Sherbrooke from 1880 – of the Treasury:

> Is not the literary enthusiasm of wealthy England equal to the enterprise of exploring scenes which are ever recurring to the imagination of every one who has received a classical education?[58]

France, humiliated by her defeat at the hands of Prussia in 1870-71, asserted her position in the archaeological field through developing a major programme of excavations on the island of Delos which started in 1873.[59] This pre-empted the foundation of the German Archaeological Institute (DAI) at Athens in 1874, and the initiation of its high profile excavations at Olympia, that brought much interest from the academic community.[60] This work started to uncover remains of the temple of Zeus and the surrounding sanctuary.

[49] Wood 1877. See also Higgins 2004; Challis 2008, 119-39.

[50] Aitchison and Elliott 2004; Challis 2008, 141-46.

[51] Jenkins 1992, 212; Jenkins 2006, 236-49.

[52] Rhodes 1973, 100-09; Challis 2008, 148. The rights for these excavations were later offered to the BSA.

[53] Spratt 1865; Laughton and Lambert 2004. See also Warren 2000, 7. Spratt, promoted to Captain, returned to Crete in 1858-59 after service in the Crimean War.

[54] Babington 1855.

[55] Allen 1999; Traill 1995. See also Challis 2008, 149-55.

[56] Traill 1995, 137.

[57] Matthew 2004.

[58] Quoted in *The Times* 27 June 1883, 11. See also Allen 1999, 178.

[59] Étienne 1996, 11.

[60] Marchand 1996, 77-91.

Forming the School

The high profile French and German excavations at Delos, Olympia, and Troy left British archaeology in their shadow and national pride dented. It was explicitly recognised that the presence of permanent institutions in Athens allowed the development of such major projects. Sidney Colvin (1845-1927), the Slade professor of Fine Art in Cambridge, and Newton – both were members of the Society of the Dilettanti – realised that action needed to be taken to restore Britain's position place in the archaeological field. First of all they needed to gather information and thus in the spring of 1875 they visited Olympia.

> We … rode to the village of Druva, where the German scientific expedition was installed, were hospitably received, and spent some days studying with intense interest the results of the excavations so far as they had then been carried. From the mere configuration of the ground, with the brook Kladeos, its course marked at that season by flowering Judas-trees, running at an acute angle into the broad shingle-bed of the Alpheios near the foot of the hill Kronion, it was easy enough to recognize the general plan of the site, the great common centre of ancient Greek Zeus-worship and of athletic and poetic contests and glories.[61]

Newton, accompanied by Percy Gardner, went out again in the spring of 1877 on behalf of the British Museum.[62] Gardner recalled the discovery of the Apollo from the west pediment of the temple of Zeus:

> I realized something of the keen delight which excavators feel when there gradually reveals itself to them in the ground the outline of a great work of art, which has been for ages hidden from the world and now comes back from the grave to take its place among historic monuments, and to reveal to the modern world something of the art and the history of a great bygone-civilization.[63]

Other travellers in Greece during the spring of 1877 included a party consisting of John Pentland Mahaffy (1839-1919), Oscar Wilde (1854-1900) and George Augustin Macmillan (1855-1936). It was reported that Macmillan, who was by then working in the family firm of publishers, on his return to London

> was introduced by [Mahaffy] to John Gennadius, the Greek Chargé d'Affaires … From Gennadius he learnt of the recently formed French *Association pour l'Encouragement des Etudes Grecques*, and discussed with him the prospects of founding a similar society in England. A year later he found in Sayce a scholar who was ready to help him to carry the idea into effect.[64]

In London itself Heinrich Schliemann lectured to the Society of Antiquaries on his finds at Mycenae in March 1877.[65] This prominent profile for archaeology coincided with the

---

[61] Colvin 1921, 218-19.

[62] Gardner 1933, 31-34.

[63] Gardner 1933, 33-34.

[64] *The Times* 4 March 1936. See also Macmillan 1878; Morgan 1943, 167.

[65] Traill 1995, 166.

large growth in local archaeological societies in Britain,[66] as well as with the pioneering archaeological excavations of Augustus Henry Lane Fox Pitt-Rivers (1827-1900) through the 1870s.[67]

One of the first hints of interest in a British institution abroad was raised by the Oxford-educated William Wolfe Capes (1834-1914) writing in an article for *Fraser's Magazine* in July 1878.[68] Capes had studied at The Queen's College, Oxford, and then been a Fellow (1856-70) and then Reader in Ancient History in Oxford (1870-87).[69] One of his interests was the use of Greek epigraphy for the study of ancient history.[70] Capes' proposal did not envisage the creation of buildings to house a school; indeed his model was one that was later used effectively by the Egypt Exploration Society.[71]

In May 1878 Richard Claverhouse Jebb, Professor of Greek at Glasgow, went to Greece for the first time. He claimed that his trip to Athens was 'primarily to study the schools of archaeology established there by other countries'.[72] In particular he was interested in the work of the French and German schools. He visited the French excavations on Delos[73] and travelled across the Peloponnese, visiting Corinth, Sparta, and the German excavations at Olympia. This trip seems to have spurred Jebb into action.

> He came home convinced that England lagged far behind France and Germany in appreciation of the study of ancient life and art in its bearing on classical scholarship. In other branches of archaeology the English were by no means negligent. English historians highly valued its discoveries within their own borders and largely availed themselves of its results; and the museums of local antiquities are to be found in almost every town. Bible students appreciate the assistance given to their studies by explorations in Palestine and found money and men without stint for the excavations carried on in Bible countries. But in regard to the study of ancient Greek and Roman life as revealed in contemporary monuments there had been a singular apathy.[74]

He was clearly alluding to the Society for Biblical Archaeology founded in 1870 and supported by Samuel Birch of the British Museum along with other Egyptologists and Assyriologists.[75]

---

[66] Levine 1986, 51, 182-83.

[67] Bowden 1991. Amelia Edwards' travels in Egypt during the 1870s helped to give rise to the formation of the Egypt Exploration Society in 1882: Drower 1982; Rees 1998.

[68] Capes 1878. Quoted in Beard and Stray 2005, 375. For Capes: Magrath and Baigent 2004.

[69] Capes was succeeded in his ancient history role by Henry Francis Pelham. Capes was also Rector of Bramshott in Hampshire (from 1869) and a Fellow and Tutor of Hertford College (1876-86).

[70] Capes 1877.

[71] Janssen 1992; James 1982. The EES was formed in 1882.

[72] Jebb 1907, 210.

[73] Jebb 1880.

[74] Jebb 1907, 211-12.

[75] See Drower 1982, 24.

In September 1878 Jebb wrote to *The Times*.[76] He drew on his experiences of earlier in the year, reviewing the finds from the German excavations at Olympia, including the Nike of Paionios of Mende and the Hermes by Praxiteles. He also considered the French exploration of Rheneia near Delos. Such productive work, the fruit of established institutes in Athens and Rome, raised the question, 'Why should there not be a British school of archaeology at Athens and at Rome?' He then outlined the structure of the *École française*, which had six members who spent one year in Italy followed by two years in Greece. Jebb emphasised the training element of the French system: 'The discipline provided by the French system is exact and complete; it is peculiarly well fitted to train an able student for that which is often his destination – a Chair of Faculty in France.' He noted differences with the German school, noting the advanced levels of Greek and Latin required. Jebb proposed that Oxford and Cambridge should dedicate their existing travelling fellowships towards those students demonstrating 'proficiency in archaeological studies … on the condition that these studies should be pursued for a certain time in Italy and Greece'. Jebb anticipated the change in the Cambridge Classical Tripos with the inclusion of classical archaeology at Part 2 by noting that such a scheme 'pre-suppos[ed] adequate classical scholarship'.[77] He built on Capes' proposal from earlier in the year by suggesting the formation of a committee. Significantly he saw the central place of the British Museum, and no doubt Newton ('distinguished archaeologists on its staff are among the first whose advice and co-operation would be sought'),[78] in such a scheme; in part this was linked to exposing potential students to the material culture of the Greek world.

It is curious that this initial proposal did not necessarily include the provision of a permanent residence for the School. However Jebb felt that the school would need 'a resident officer' who would be an 'archaeologist of eminence'. He estimated that the annual cost of running such a school, based on the French model, would be approximately £2,400. He concluded:

> If English schools and Universities encourage students to read the life of the Greek and Roman world in its monuments as well as in its books, there will be no lack either of inclination or of trained capacity for original work in Greece and Italy, and Englishmen will take their due place in a province of scientific research which has long been left chiefly to the scholar on the Continent.[79]

Jebb followed up this letter with an article in *The Contemporary Review* also in 1878.[80]

The formation of a steering committee

Although there was no initial response to Jebb's proposal, public attitudes to archaeology were changing. Developments in archaeology advanced with the foundation of the Egypt

---

[76] Jebb 1878. Quoted in Jebb 1907, 212.

[77] Jebb 1878.

[78] Jebb 1878.

[79] Jebb 1878. Quoted in Jebb 1907, 212.

[80] Beard and Stray 2005, 374. For the context of this period: Stray 2002.

Exploration Fund (the Society for the Promotion of Excavation in the Delta of the Nile) in 1882.[81] Among its supporters were those who were to feature in the development of the BSA including Charles Newton and Percy Gardner.[82] In the same year the Ancient Monuments Act was passed providing protection to designated ancient monuments in Britain, and on 1 January 1883 the first Inspector of Ancient Monuments was appointed, Pitt-Rivers.[83]

A further impetus to the creation of a British School was the creation of the American School of Classical Studies at Athens (ASCSA). Charles Eliot Norton had initiated the foundation of the Archaeological Institute of American and ASCSA in a letter of April 1879.[84] Norton was also driven in part by nationalism:

> France and Germany have their schools at Athens, where young scholars devote themselves, under the guidance of eminent masters, to studies and research in archaeology. The results that have followed from this training have been excellent; and it is greatly to be desired, for the sake of American scholarship, that a similar American School may before long enter into honorable rivalry with those already established.[85]

There was swift movement on the project and by April 1882 a Managing Committee for ASCSA has been formed and the School opened in October.[86]

In the spring of 1882 Jebb received a visit from Professor William Watson Goodwin, the first Director of ASCSA.[87] Jebb and the Goodwins arranged to visit the site of Hissarlik, the supposed site of Troy, in the autumn of 1882 with Frank Calvert as their guide.[88] It is perhaps significant that Calvert at this time had serious doubts about Schliemann's interpretation of the site.[89] Jebb had been raising questions about the excavations, to which his opponent John P. Mahaffy had responded.[90] Jebb, too, was suspicious of Schliemann's discoveries: 'His own knowledge of classical literature made him certain that in many points Dr Schliemann was hopelessly wrong'.[91] Jebb had reviewed *Ilios* anonymously for the *Edinburgh Review* (May 1881) and this was an opportunity to look at the site itself.[92] Jebb was persuaded by Dörpfeld's interpretation of the strata and this was the position he took in a lecture to the Hellenic Society on the

---

[81] Levine 1986, 40. For detail: Drower 1982.

[82] Drower 1982, 15.

[83] Bowden 1991, 95-96.

[84] Lord 1947, 3-4.

[85] Quoted in Lord 1947, 4 (May 1880).

[86] Lord 1947, 8-10.

[87] Lord 1947, 33.

[88] Jebb 1907, 242; Traill 1995, 225. Goodwin also wanted to visit Assos and Lesbos.

[89] Allen 1999, 212.

[90] Jebb 1881; Mahaffy 1882. See also Walker 2004.

[91] Jebb 1907, 242.

[92] Traill 1995, 208.

19 October, 'Troy based on a recent visit to the Troad'.[93] The debate continued in *The Times* with Sayce translating (and apparently adapting) Dörpfeld's view of Schliemann's stratigraphy; Sayce and Jebb continued the debate in the *Journal of Hellenic Studies*.[94]

Jebb had seen for himself the value of excavation, most recently at Troy but earlier at Olympia and on Delos, and so he decided to make a concerted effort to establish a British School of Archaeology at Athens similar to the one newly opened by the Americans. He sought the support of Newton, who had assisted Goodwin with the creation of a library for ASCSA. The Council of the Hellenic Society was apparently unreceptive to the idea,[95] and yet there were clearly moves afoot in Athens. In a review of the developments of the School, a report in *The Times* noted: 'In the autumn of 1882 the Greek Government had generously offered, through the English Foreign Office, to give a piece of ground at Athens for the proposed British school'.[96] The site was located on the southern slope of Lykabettos, and the gift was estimated at *c.* £2,700. Newton and Jebb enlisted in their support Francis Clare Ford, British minister in Athens (March 1881-December 1884).[97] Ford gained the help of the then Prime Minister, Charilaos Trikoupis (1832-96), who was attempting to place Greece on an international footing.[98]

This offer of land seems to have been the impetus for a correspondence through the winter of 1882/83. Jebb contacted Professor Sidney Colvin who replied to him on Tuesday 6 December 1882,[99] significantly the day after the Annual Meeting of the Cambridge Branch of the Hellenic Society that had met in Colvin's rooms. Newton and Jebb had clearly indicated to Colvin that they needed to raise the sum of £20,000 that they hoped could be done by subscription. Colvin suggested that Jebb and Newton should appeal to national pride:

> I do not know the history of the fund for the Celtic chair: but should imagine that zeal for philology, or archaeology contributed but a small proportion of the sum, and that zeal for the honour of a quasi-national cause was the powerful instrument of extraction.[100]

The original idea to establish a school without a building seems to have been dropped, especially following the offer of land by the Greek Government. The proposal was that British students should be admitted to one of the other foreign schools such as the French:

---

[93] Jebb 1882. The meeting of the Hellenic Society was chaired by Newton.

[94] Sayce and Jebb 1883. For the debate in *The Times:* Traill 1995, 229-30. Schliemann joined the attack on Jebb, 'my persistently bitter critic', in *Troja,* commenting: 'no courtesy on my part can save Professor Jebb from the fate on which an eminent classical scholar rushes when he mingles in an archaeological debate in ignorance of the first principles of archaeology': Schliemann 1884, 236-41. For the context: Sayce 1923, 224.

[95] See Jebb 1907, 244.

[96] 'Proposed British School of Archaeology at Athens', *The Times* 3 February 1885, 7.

[97] Seccombe 2004.

[98] For the immediate context: Clogg 1992, 67.

[99] The letter is quoted in Beard and Stray 2005, 377. The original is in the BSA archive.

[100] Quoted in Beard and Stray 2005, 377, who suggested that the context is the Edinburgh Chair established in 1882.

Jebb was strongly opposed. In a letter to George Macmillan, Honorary Secretary of the Hellenic Society, on 12 December 1882 he wrote:[101]

> It would be scarcely a worthy manner for England's first appearance at Athens, and would bring into strong relief the comparative deadness of archaeological interest in this country, the wealth of which is even exaggerated by foreigners.

The nationalistic appeal was clearly designed to be emotive as the School could just as easily have been the French, the German or the American.[102] There continued an urgent plea:

> Make up your minds first whether you are going to try for an English School now. If you are, then drop the mevtoikoi scheme ... My own belief is that by a really vigorous effort we could get an English School started in (say) two or three years from now. I should prefer, then, to refrain from the other plan till such an effort had been made, and had failed.

Jebb was a clear strategist trying to ensure that there was a single plan placed before the Council.

Among those consulted was Frederick Pollock, a member of the Hellenic Council (from 1882/83), and significantly one of the auditors for the Society (1880-82).[103] Pollock had been a student at Trinity where Jebb had been elected a Fellow in 1863, and had been placed second in the Classical Tripos of 1867. In 1883 he was elected to the Corpus chair of Jurisprudence at Oxford. The timing of the correspondence with Pollock is interesting as there was due to be a meeting of the Hellenic Society on 15 February 1883. Pollock had clearly been asked questions about raising funds, and advised that a grant from the Treasury was unlikely at that point, 'especially as there is a great deal still to be done for the proper care and housing of our own national collections'.[104] It may have been for this reason that Jebb wrote to William Ewart Gladstone (1809-98), the Liberal prime minister, who advised that funding should be sought from the universities.[105]

A key proposal was formulated a week after the February meeting of the Hellenic Society. Macmillan, in a letter of 22 February 1883, played a key part in suggesting that the planned School needed a patron such as the Prince of Wales.[106] The suggestion was inspired: Edward Prince of Wales was married to Princess Alexandra of Denmark, and her brother was Prince Christian William Ferdinand Adolphus George, better known as King George I of Greece (from 1864).[107] The Prince of Wales had been a trustee of the British Museum from 1881. In August of the previous year Jebb had become acquainted with

---

[101] Jebb 1907, 244-46.

[102] For the archaeological rivalry between France and Britain in this period: Challis 2008, 20.

[103] Cosgrove 2004.

[104] Letter of 2 February 1883, quoted in Beard and Stray 2005, 377.

[105] Letter of 6 February 1883, quoted in Beard and Stray 2005, 377-78.

[106] Beard and Stray 2005, 378.

[107] Clogg 1992, 59, 61.

Thomas Hay Sweet Escott (1844-1924), who had read classics at The Queen's College, Oxford, and had then lectured at King's College, London (1866-73). In 1882 Escott had become editor of the *Fortnightly Review* and he was prepared to publish Jebb's account of his trip to the Troad.[108] Escott 'agreed to make the *Review* a means of communication between [Jebb] and the public'.[109] Jebb constructed an article calling for the creation of a British School; this had been completed by 3 April when Jebb asked Escott to show the text to Lord Carnarvon, so that it could be passed to the Prince of Wales.[110]

It is perhaps significant that the official history of the School saw May 1883 as 'the first definite impetus towards the foundation of the School'.[111] This was when Jebb published 'A plea for a British Institute at Athens' in the *Fortnightly Review*.[112] Macmillan suggested that it was this article which 'came under the notice of the Prince of Wales' that led to the meeting in June of the same year; however it is clear that in February 1883 Macmillan was already suggesting the Prince of Wales to Jebb.

Jebb started his article with an anecdote about the Homeric scholar Joshua Barnes (1654-1712). Barnes had argued that the origins of the *Iliad* lay with King Solomon, so that he could obtain access to funds from his wife to allow publication. The point that Jebb was making was clear: find a project with Biblical links and there would be public support and funding. He noted,

> The British taxpayer can be induced to tolerate the application of public money to researches, such as the exploration of Sinai or Palestine, which can in any way be associated with the Bible.

The allusion was to the Palestine Exploration Fund, founded in 1865, which had been excavating at Jerusalem (1867-70) and undertaking the survey of western Palestine (1871-78).[113] Jebb then noted the lack of government support for the Society of Antiquaries' proposed excavations at Troy. Finally he turned to the creation of the British School, making public the sum of £20,000 and calling for a benefactor to create 'a living monument of the most splendid and enduring kind'.[114]

Things moved swiftly. Jebb was invited to meet the Prince of Wales to go through the resolutions for a meeting to establish the School and to approve 'the names of those selected to propose and second them'.[115] The scene was set for the Annual Meeting of the Hellenic Society on 14 June 1883, which was chaired by Newton.[116] Jebb reported on the

---

[108] Jebb 1883.

[109] Jebb 1907, 246.

[110] Beard and Stray 2005, 378.

[111] Macmillan 1910/11, ix.

[112] Beard and Stray 2005, 375-76.

[113] King 1983, 7-8. The Egypt Exploration Society also had Biblical studies as part of its early agenda: Drower 1982.

[114] Beard and Stray 2005, 375-76.

[115] Jebb 1907, 248.

[116] Hellenic Society 1883b, xl-xliii.

'position and prospects of the scheme for the establishment of a British School at Athens', alluding to the article in the *Fortnightly Review*.[117] Jebb continued:

> The Prince of Wales and the Duke of Albany had promised support, and so had the Chancellors of the two Universities, the President of the Royal Academy, the President of the Society of Antiquaries, the Bishop of Durham, and others.

Gladstone, the Prime Minister, had already contributed to the fund. Jebb was clearly expecting to hold a general meeting in July at which he hoped a general committee would be appointed. It was suggested that various institutions and societies be represented on the executive committee: the Hellenic Society, the Society of Dilettanti, the Society of Antiquaries, and the universities of Oxford and Cambridge. The purpose of the School was outlined as follows:[118]

> 1. The School would be not exclusively of archaeological science, but more widely of Greek studies in Greek lands ...
> 2. There must be a director with a salary of not less than £500;
> 3. A library of which the director would take charge, and a house – it had been estimated that a good house could be built for £3,000 – a site on Mount Lycabettus would probably be granted by the Greek Government;
> 4. Membership would be open to all persons accredited by the Universities or other responsible bodies, and, possibly, on payment of a small fee, to travellers residing in Athens only for a few weeks;
> 5. It was proposed that the director should give guidance and advice to students, and possibly encourage the occasional reading of papers, but it was desirable to leave him as free as possible.

A major step forward was made on Monday 25 June 1883 when a meeting was held at Marlborough House, the London home of the Prince, to discuss the foundation of the School. Its object was 'to promote all researches and studies which can advance the knowledge of Hellenic history, literature, and art from the earliest age to the present day'.[119] Among those present were Gladstone, the Prime Minister and authority on Homer; the Marquess of Salisbury (Robert Arthur Talbot Gascoyne-Cecil), the leader of the Conservative opposition; and the Earl of Rosebery (Archibald Philip Primrose), the Liberal Under-Secretary at the Home Office. This led to the formation of a small committee. Jebb and Escott were appointed as honorary secretaries. Leaf, who had been taught by Jebb at Trinity College, Cambridge, served as honorary treasurer; he had been elected a Fellow of Trinity the year that Jebb went to Glasgow.

The meeting was endorsed in a leader in *The Times* on Wednesday 27 June. Again the fund-raising aspect was emphasised with 'the modest sum of £20,000' that was intended 'to purchase or build a suitable home for the school at Athens, to establish and maintain an adequate library, and to furnish the endowment of a resident Director'. It was intended

---

[117] Hellenic Society 1883b, xlvi.

[118] The points appear in Hellenic Society 1883a.

[119] Reported in *The Times* 27 June 1883, 11.

that that 'its membership would be open without payment to any person accredited by a University or College of the United Kingdom, or by the authorities of the British Museum or of the Royal Academy'. The leader also drew attention to the growing role of classical archaeology as a discipline:

> Classical archaeology is hardly a bread-winning study in England, and it requires special aptitudes and a genuine enthusiasm for its successful pursuit. But we live in an archaeological age, as our own columns are frequently showing, and it can hardly be doubted that students fit, though few, will in time be found to whom the advantage of pursuing Greek studies in Greek lands will prove to be most inestimable.[120]

Classical archaeology was being transformed in Britain. In Cambridge, the Disney Chair of Archaeology had been established in 1851 through the generosity of John Disney, whose collection of classical sculpture had been presented to the university in the previous year.[121] The chair was first held by John H. Marsden from 1851-65, and he was succeeded by Churchill Babington (1821-89), who had a strong interest in papyrology, and in 1880 by Percy Gardner (until 1896). Sidney Colvin (1845-1927), Slade Professor of Fine Art (1873-85) and director of the Fitzwilliam Museum (1876-84), had visited the German excavations at Olympia in 1875. He was a near contemporary of Jebb's at Trinity. A further influence in Cambridge was Robert Burn (1829-1904), praelector in Roman literature and archaeology at Trinity College. In 1885 Newton was able to comment on the Cambridge situation and 'the apparatus of archaeology', noting in particular the development of the cast collection.[122] In London the Yates Chair of Classical Archaeology was created in 1880 with (Sir) Charles Newton as the first holder. He was succeeded in 1889 by Reginald Stuart Poole (1832-95), keeper of Coins and Medals at the British Museum, and in 1896 by Ernest Gardner (by then a former Director of the BSA). In Oxford, the Lincoln and Merton Chair of Classical Archaeology was held initially for one year (1885-86) by (Sir) William Mitchell Ramsay (1851-1939). He was succeeded in 1887 by Percy Gardner (1846-1937). Elsewhere in Britain there was some interest in classical archaeology at Aberdeen through Ramsay's work, and Edward Lee Hicks (1843-1919) developed the study of classical archaeology, and especially epigraphy, at Owens College, Manchester (1886-90).

Thus in 1883 the proposed British School was supported by the three key representatives of classical archaeology in Britain: Newton in London, and Sidney Colvin and Percy Gardner in Cambridge. In fact Colvin moved to be Keeper of Prints and Drawings at the British Museum in 1883.[123] The editorial in *The Times* tried to demonstrate that the subject was moving away from its antiquarian roots to a more professional approach: 'Classical archaeology … is a serious study, and no mere *dilettante* pursuit'.[124] It went on to examine the position of archaeology:

---

[120] *The Times* 27 June 1883, 11.

[121] Gill 2004h.

[122] 'Proposed British School of Archaeology at Athens', *The Times* 3 February 1885, 7. For the cast collection: Beard 1993.

[123] Wilson 2002, 183.

[124] See a similar theme in 'Ancient Art and Archæology', *The Times* 14 December 1883, 4.

It is … the material foundation of all our knowledge of classical antiquity, and is as essential to the vitality of classical studies as any other branch of inquiry connected with them. Exactly in proportion, therefore, as we value classical studies as an element in a liberal education, we must value the study of classical archaeology as one of the scientific bases on which a liberal education rests. It is to take a narrow and antiquated view of a classical education to confine it exclusively to the study of the works of Greek and Roman authors. These must be illustrated and elucidated by all the collateral knowledge which it is in our power to bring to bear upon them. It is only, however, in comparatively modern times that this elucidation has been possible or this vital importance has been perceived. The study itself has grown by the accumulation of its materials, and its materials have been rendered accessible by the facilities of modern travel and intercourse. It is possible, of course, to learn a great deal of Greek archaeology without going beyond the wall of the British Museum; but, notwithstanding the freedom with which Western nations have heretobefore helped themselves to the portable remains of classical antiquity, it must be obvious that the material relics of ancient civilization will always be most profitably studied in the very lands in which that civilization flourished. Climate and other physical conditions do not count for everything in the growth of a nation, but they still count for something, and in art especially they count for something essential.[125]

The School was distancing itself from 'the sort of archaeological pillage which found favour with former generations'. The aim was not to build up a national collection, but rather to add to the treasures displayed in Greece: 'Whatever is now found in Greece will belong to Greece'. *The Times* acknowledged that the Parthenon marbles ('the Elgin marbles') had been obtained under 'the laxer archaeological conscience of former times', although it also noted that such acquisitions had 'kindled among us a zeal for a serious, intelligent, and sustained study of classical archaeology'.[126]

The American journalist William James Stillman (1828-1901), writing to *The Times* from Italy on 11 July 1883, supported the project.[127] Stillman's second wife, Marie, was the daughter of Michael Spartali, the Greek consul-general in London.[128] Stillman drew attention to the difference between Ottoman rules governing excavation and the less liberal regulations governing archaeological work in Greece. On 25 July 1883 Jebb could report to his mother:

This morning's post brought me good news. A despatch from the Greek Government has been received at the Foreign Office in London saying that they will *give* us the best site at their disposal for our school.[129]

---

[125] *The Times* 27 June 1883, 11.

[126] For the continuing issue: Howland 2000; Hitchens 2008.

[127] Stillman 1883.

[128] Nunn 2004. Stillman's son-in-law (from 1892) was John H. Middleton, Slade Professor of Fine Art in Cambridge, and also director of the Fitzwilliam Museum.

[129] Jebb 1907, 248.

Clearly the support from Trikoupis and his government was significant. He had also received support from William Cavendish (1808-91), the Seventh Duke of Devonshire, who was also the Chancellor of the University of Cambridge, promising to subscribe to the project.[130] By the autumn the plans for the School were moving ahead and at the October 1883 meeting of the Hellenic Society Newton and Macmillan were elected to represent the society on the BSA's steering committee.[131]

By the following year a measure of progress had been made. At the Annual Meeting of the Society for the Promotion of Hellenic Studies in June 1884, the President of the Society, the Rt Rev. J. B. Lightfoot, Bishop of Durham made this plea:

> It was satisfactory to note that the society had taken an active part in promoting the scheme for a British School at Athens. It was hardly creditable that England should be so far behind her neighbours in the establishment of such a school, considering her close political connexion with Greece and her really wide interest in Greek literature. Until there was such a centre of work established on Greek soil Hellenic studies in England would be at a decided disadvantage. Referring to the society's work in the field of exploration, the Bishop of Durham said that, perhaps, to most scholars Hellas proper presented greater attractions, but for his own part he ventured to think that the ground which had actually fallen to the lot of the society would yield even richer results. Beneath the soil of Asia Minor lay hidden the key to many an interesting problem in history and ethnology. As an example might be cited the light recently thrown upon the remarkable extension of the Hittite Empire. Referring to his own special line of study, the president dwelt in some detail upon the value of Mr Ramsay's discoveries as illustrating the early history of the Christian Church in Phrygia, and showed by several examples how much might be learnt even from the finding of an inscription of a single name. Mr. Ramsay had still before him important and numerous discoveries, and it was greatly to be hoped that his work would not be hindered by lack of funds. The president, in conclusion, threw out two suggestions for the society's work in the future. In the first place might be undertaken by competent persons the thorough investigation of the monastic and other libraries in the East. The investigators should be competent in every branch of Hellenic study, or some manuscripts of great value might escape if they chanced not to belong to their special department. … another work that might usefully be undertaken by the society was the mapping out of subjects to be worked upon by competent young scholars, who would devote time and labour to their solution. Many vexed questions might be cleared up in this way.[132]

At the same time arrangements for the construction of the School were put in hand. In May 1884 the transfer of land from the monastery of Ayios Asomatos was approved by

---

[130] Letter of 26 July 1883, reported in Jebb 1907, 249.

[131] Hellenic Society Annual Report (1884) xli. The Secretary was James Gow (1854-1923), a former student at Trinity College, Cambridge. For further details: Hopkinson 2004. Gow was elected to the Council of the Hellenic Society (1884/85).

[132] *The Times* 28 June 1884. See also Hellenic Society 1884, xli-xliii. Lightfoot had overlapped with Jebb at Trinity College, Cambridge. For their friendship: Jebb 1907, 119 (5 February 1872).

the Greek government, and a formal contract was signed on 3 November 1884.[133] This was witnessed by the three trustees appointed by the School's committee: James Tynte Agg-Gardner (who is likely to have come into contact with Jebb when a student at Trinity College, Cambridge), Pandeli Ralli, and Charles Waring.[134] Arthur Nicolson (1849-1928), the British *Chargé d'Affaires* at Athens (1884-85) acted as attorney.[135] The support of the staff at the British Legation was widely acknowledged, and not least that of Sir Horace Rumbold (1829-1913) who returned to Greece in 1884 as envoy-extraordinary, a post he held until 1888.[136]

The first meeting of the Subscribers of the BSA was held on 2 February 1885. It was reported that the committee had already raised over £4,000.[137] It was felt that this was sufficient 'to build a house of the kind contemplated – viz., containing accommodation for a resident director, and affording one good-sized room to serve as the library of the school. Besides building such a house, the sum of £4,000 would also, it was believed, suffice to provide a library of reference for the school, or at any rate the nucleus of such a library'.[138] It was a matter of urgency that the project moved forward. The chairman, Lightfoot, commented:

> It now touched our honour as Englishmen very nearly that this scheme should be carried out without delay. France and Germany had long been in the field. France had her school, and Germany her institute, and now America likewise forestalled us in this race. That new country notwithstanding the vast and absorbing interests of the present, notwithstanding the boundless hopes of the future, had been eager to claim her part in the heritage. While all the civilized nations of the world, one after another, had established their literary councils at Athens, should England alone be unrepresented at the centre of Hellenic culture? It might have been expected that England would have been foremost in the field. No country had taken so direct an interest in the revival of down-trodden Hellas or had so close a political sympathy with Greece as England; no country claimed a greater share for Hellenic study in her higher education; and lastly, no country possessed in a greater degree the wealth and resources necessary for carrying out such a scheme as this. All this might have led to the reasonable expectation that England would have been first in the field.

After acknowledging the generosity of the Greek Government, the chairman returned to the place of classics in British higher education.

> There was indeed every need for such an institution. He had spoken already of the large place which Hellenic studies had in our higher education; he had no doubt that

---

[133] 'Proposed British School of Archaeology at Athens', *The Times* 3 February 1885, 7. See also Lord 1947, 30; Kakissis 2004, 206.

[134] The Trustees are discussed in Chapter 3.

[135] Neilson 2004.

[136] Gilbert 1973; Chirol and Matthew 2004.

[137] 'Proposed British School of Archaeology at Athens', *The Times* 3 February 1885, 7.

[138] 'Proposed British School of Archaeology at Athens', *The Times* 3 February 1885, 7.

they did produce a very sensible effect throughout England. They stimulated our literary imagination and they influenced our practical politics. But when we looked at their direct and tangible results in the direction of history and archaeology we must confess they were somewhat disappointing. It so happened that his own particular studies led him across some question of classical archaeology almost from day to day. When he wanted his difficulties solved he had to go, not to any English source, but to some monograph in German, French, or sometimes in Italian; it was very rarely that he could find what he required in English. That was a state of things with which we ought not to be content. It was a great satisfaction to know that the Universities were taking up the study of archaeology, making it part of their examination system, and so endeavouring to promote its spread. But what we wanted was to connect ourselves directly with the heart of Hellenic culture so that its very lifeblood might flow through our veins, and this we should gain by the establishment of the school at Athens.[139]

There was, however, continuing concern about the finances, with the suggestion that £600 per year was needed.[140] Among those supporting the project were two men who had been educated at Balliol College, Oxford: the Rev. Dr James John Hornby (1826-1909), provost of Eton; and William Sandys Wright Vaux (1818-85), Secretary of the Royal Asiatic Society and a former Keeper of Coins and Medals at the British Museum (1861-70).[141] The latter proposed that the 1883 general committee be entrusted with the funds raised. In supporting this proposal Mr Argyropoulos commented 'that the news of the meeting at Marlborough House had been received most enthusiastically, not only at Athens but everywhere in Greece'.[142] Certainly a contemporary report was able to note,

> A marked feature of the new British School is its comprehensiveness: it has from the start sought to excite the national sympathies of the Greek people, and its aim is proclaimed to be the study of Greece, during not only its classic but also its modern history.[143]

Charles T. Newton (1816-94), still Yates Professor of Classical Archaeology at University College London, proposed a formal resolution that consisted of the following items which set the agenda for the early years of the School:

> 1. The first aim of the school shall be to promote the study of Greek archaeology in all its departments. Among these shall be (1) the study of Greek art and architecture in their remains of every period; (2) the study of inscriptions; (3) the exploration of ancient sites; (4) the tracing of ancient roads and routes of traffic.
> 2. Besides being a school of archaeology, it shall be also, in the most comprehensive sense, a school of classical studies. Every period of the Greek language and literature,

---

[139] 'Proposed British School of Archaeology at Athens', *The Times* 3 February 1885, 7.

[140] For the year 1894/95, the expenditure was £550, against subscriptions of £471.

[141] See also Wilson 2002, 93.

[142] 'Proposed British School of Archaeology at Athens', *The Times* 3 February 1885, 7.

[143] Frothingham 1885, 219.

from the earliest age to the present day, shall be considered as coming within the province of the school.

3. The school shall be under the care of a director, whose primary duties shall be (1) to guide the studies of the members, and to exercise a general supervision over the researches undertaken by them; (2) to report at least once a year on the work of the school, to record from time to time for the information of scholars at home any important discoveries which may come to his knowledge, and to edit any publications of the school.

4. It shall further be the duty of the director to afford information and advice to all properly accredited British travellers in Greece who may apply to him.[144]

Sir Frederick Pollock, speaking on behalf of the Society of Dilettanti, emphasised the foundation as 'one of the most important steps yet taken towards realizing the study of a classical language'.

One of the other decisions made at the February meeting was to begin work on the new building. This was to provide accommodation for the Director, as well as space for a library and a communal room for meetings. The proposal was made by Jebb:

That the executive committee be authorized for the purpose of the school in erecting a suitable building on the site granted to the school by the Greek Government.[145]

Jebb then proceeded to outline the plan for construction. He noted that Nicolson, the *Chargé d'Affaires* in Athens 'had recommended that the plans of a house should be prepared in London and sent to Athens, where he thought that he would be able to place the execution of the work in proper hands'. The building itself was designed by Penrose, the surveyor for St Paul's Cathedral in London and a member of the Society of Dilettanti, who then showed his plans, and explained the possible areas for later expansion; the outlined cost was around £3,000. The proposal was supported by Charles Waring, one of the trustees.

The idea of finding funds to complete the project was left to Ford, who had negotiated with the Greek Government for the land. The appeal was nationalistic, as he reminded those present:

On revisiting Athens, [Ford] had been astonished to find the existence of an American school, about which he had known nothing. On asking how they had managed to start it, and to get funds, he had been told that they had no funds. People who looked at the French school, and the German and American schools, asked how it was that England, the richest country in the world, had none, even when the land had been given to them. It was difficult for people to understand the obstacles in the way of funds that stopped enterprises of this sort.[146]

---

[144] The resolution was also published by the Archaeological Institute of America: Frothingham 1885, 218.

[145] 'Proposed British School of Archaeology at Athens', *The Times* 3 February 1885, 7.

[146] 'Proposed British School of Archaeology at Athens', *The Times* 3 February 1885, 7.

The report was a little misleading as ASCSA had in fact opened on 2 October 1882 in rented rooms on Odos Amalias while Ford was minister in Athens; though the permanent site, adjacent to the location assigned to the British School, was not assigned until the autumn of 1884.[147] The appeal to other institutions was made by the Rev. Henry Fanshawe Tozer (1829-1916).[148] He had been educated at Winchester and Oxford, and had travelled widely in Greece and Anatolia; from 1869 he had been curator of the Taylorian Institution in Oxford. His resolution, backed by Colvin who expressed Cambridge support for the project, was 'that a formal appeal in aid of the school be made to the Universities, the Royal Society, the Society of Antiquaries, the Hellenic Society, the Royal Academy, the Institute of British Architects, and other public bodies'. Wider academic support for the enterprise was reflected in letters sent by Professor Samuel Henry Butcher (1850-1910) who held the chair of Greek at Edinburgh and Dr Robert Yelverton Tyrrell (1844-1914), Regius Professor of Greek at Dublin. Both, like Jebb, were from Ireland; Butcher had been a student at Trinity College, Cambridge under Jebb.

There was still some lingering concern that classical archaeology was, as reported in 1883, a *dilettante* pursuit. This is perhaps reflected in the account of the developments made for the Archaeological Institute of America.

> It is to be hoped that the impetus given to classical archaeology by this movement will lead to the foundation in England of a school of genuinely scientific archaeologists, who may rival their co-workers on the continent. The uncritical school headed by Mr J. H. Parker will probably cease to occupy so prominent a position, and their writings which have hitherto been accepted will be displaced by works of critical and scholarly value. Probably only a few persons in this country [sc. North America] are aware of the existence for many years in Rome of a "British and American Archaeological Society," founded by Mr Parker, whose principal work consisted in procuring two or three gentlemen of some archaeological acquirements to arrange "personally conducted" parties to the principal sites. Perhaps at some future time this Society, which has at present no scientific value, may be reorganized on a totally different basis, and do some valuable work; for it will some day seem indispensable, that the English school at Athens, as well as the French and German schools, should be supplemented by a similar establishment at Rome. The library of the society at Rome contained, not long ago, many works of importance, and would form a good nucleus of a working library.[149]

John Henry Parker (1806-84), the target for this piece, had died in January 1884. He had been a bookseller in Oxford and London, and in 1870 he became the first keeper at the Ashmolean Museum, a post which he himself had endowed. The British and American Archaeological Society had been founded by Parker in 1865.[150]

---

[147] Lord 1947, 10, 21.

[148] Fraser and Baigent 2004.

[149] Frothingham 1885, 219.

[150] Hodges 2000, 31.

Jebb was firmly in favour of a School based in Athens. Arguments were, however, put forward that it would make more sense to install a base in Smyrna. Such an establishment would give British archaeologists access to sites in the Ottoman Empire rather than creating yet another foreign institute in Athens. Such a view is hardly surprising given the activity of Fellows and Newton in recent decades. Among those in favour of a Turkish base was Archibald H. Sayce. He expressed the view:

> The archaeology of Greece was being well looked after by the French and German schools at Athens as well as by the Greek Government itself; what we had to do was to carry on a similar work in Asia Minor and eventually establish a school at Smyrna.[151]

In 1885 William R. Paton (1857-1921) wrote to *The Times* supporting an Anatolian base.[152] Paton had read classics at University College, Oxford, and had been studying inscriptions in the eastern Aegean. He wrote:

> It is perhaps too late to ask the question, Why should our archaeological school be at Athens? But as there may be others like myself who would be more ready to make sacrifices for its support if they saw more clearly the necessity for its existence, I hope you may find it possible to publish these few remarks. It has appeared to me that the cause of archaeological research would receive for greater benefit from the establishment of a school on the other side of the Aegean, say at Smyrna.
>
> The objects of such an institution may be said to be three – (1) the study of existing monuments; (2) the verification of discoveries; (3) exploration.
>
> For the first a library is, of course, required. There are in Athens at least two libraries, those of the German and French schools, which foreign students properly introduced are kindly allowed to consult. It seems rather absurd that foreign archaeologists in Athens, numbering not more than a score, should require three libraries, presumably identical in their contents. In Smyrna there is not, as far as I am aware, any adequate library, and there can be no doubt that it would be a better return for the courtesy we have met with in the past, and a more valuable service to the cause of science, if we founded a library there which archaeologists of other nations could consult. The second object is more important. The staff of *savants* already at Athens is, or ought to be, adequate to the task of keeping a register of the antiquities discovered in Greece. Any one acquainted with Athenian dealers knows that they get many of their most beautiful objects from Asia Minor, but they never have any record of the exact place where they were discovered. It would be most desirable to have a few competent men, constantly resident at Smyrna, whither objects of art from all parts of the peninsula find their way. Only thus can we hope to localize the different styles of Asiatic art.[153]
>
> Lastly, as regard exploration and excavation, there is little to be done in Greece, where the Greek Society has of late taken everything into its own hands. In Asia

---

[151] Sayce 1923, 172.

[152] Paton 1885.

[153] Gill 2004n. Paton married Irene, the daughter of the mayor of Kalymnos, in 1885 and they settled on the mainland of Turkey near the ancient city of Myndus.

Minor the unexplored sites are countless, and there is no national society to do the work.

It was perhaps telling that a letter from John Turtle Wood was published immediately beneath Paton's making a plea for funds to support the excavation of the temple of Artemis at Ephesus.[154]

Macmillan responded in a letter to *The Times* and while acknowledging 'that a School at Smyrna would be a most useful institution' raised the key issue of financial support for the project. He continued:

> It is difficult, as it has hitherto been found, to raise sufficient money for a school at Athens, with all the associations of that almost sacred name, how much more difficult would it have been to interest the English public in a school at Smyrna? At the present stage of interest in classical archaeology, I believe that it would have been simply impossible. This objection, then, seems to me fatal, even if we grant Mr. Paton's proposition that a School at Smyrna is in itself more desirable than a school at Athens.

He returned to the *metic* argument of Jebb about the undesirability of British students using facilities provided by the existing institutions in Athens.

> It is true that there are already good libraries at Athens to which English students may already have access. But I cannot think it would be a very dignified thing for a great and wealthy country like England thus to depend for the needs of her students upon the charity of her neighbours. Neither Germany nor America have thought that the existence of the library of the French School or of the National University rendered such as addition to their own institutions unnecessary. Besides, the work of a British School would surely be more effectively carried on in concert under its own roof than if the students were scattered among the various foreign libraries in Athens.

Macmillan argued that Athens would provide a natural base of museum and library resources to prepare students for 'expeditions' outside 'the Greek kingdom'. He explained:

> From Athens as a base of operations expeditions may very easily be sent to any place that seems to call for exploration. Such expeditions have always formed part of the work of the French, German, and latterly of the American School. Witness the French excavations of Delos, and the recent very important excavations of the Americans at Assos. It would be the natural duty of the Director of the British School at Athens to send his students from time to time on missions of exploration to all parts of the Greek world. But in the museums and libraries of Athens they could both obtain, before starting, the best equipment of previous knowledge, and work out, on their return, the practical result of their explorations. Later on it might perhaps be possible to establish a small branch at Smyrna. But in the meantime it seems clear that a school at Athens will fully meet all the objects in view.[155]

---

[154] Wood 1885.

[155] Macmillan 1885.

Macmillan's prophecies were correct as major expeditions of Asia Minor and Cyprus were mounted, although it was not until after the Second World War that a British Institute of Archaeology was founded in Ankara.[156] Macmillan closed his letter with a clinching argument: plans for a British School at Athens were so advanced, with a site offered by the Greek Government, that it was impossible to change plans. He urged that 'all friends of classical archaeology in England should henceforth agree to sink minor differences, and support with hearty and undivided effort the project which has already been carried to so far towards success'.

By the annual meeting of the Hellenic Society, on 25 June 1885, plans for the BSA were being finalised. Finance seemed to be assured and it was reported that the University of Oxford had agreed to give an annual grant of £100 to the School along with £3,000 from the Society over the first three years.[157] Private scholars also rallied to help. Jane Harrison offered to donate her fees from a series of lectures on Greek vase-painting to the School. These had been due to be given at the Chelsea High School.[158] However there continued to be difficulties to address. A report in *The Times* for October 1885 continued:

> It was hoped that … a large number of men interested in these studies might have an opportunity of hearing a lecturer who by study and travel is recognized generally as an authority on the mythology of the *Iliad*. At the eleventh hour, however, the chairman of the Girls' Public Day Schools Association has, apparently without any reference to the council, placed his veto upon the admission of men to these lectures. As one of the original supporters of the movement which led to the establishment of the Girls Public Day Schools, and as an original shareholder and worker when the movement was still fighting its way, I desire to protest through *The Times* against an act which is wholly at variance with the broad principle upon which the association was founded – the extension of knowledge, not only to girls, but through women. But, after all, it will be the women themselves who will be the chief sufferers should this ill-advised ukase not be at once withdrawn. The chairman, who lives nearly all the year in the country, does not probably realize that he practically cuts off from every lady, married or single, who does not keep a carriage, the possibility of attending these lectures, for few parents would venture to allow their daughters or other female members of their households to be abroad alone in the streets on the dark November evenings.[159]

[156] Gill 2004c. It is perhaps significant that one of the founders of the British Institute of Archaeology at Ankara was Winifred Lamb, a former student of the British School at Athens: Gill 2000b; Gill 2004r. For French work in Anatolia: Le Roy 1996.

[157] Hellenic Society 1885, xlvi. *The Times* 20 May 1885, 10, reported from Oxford: 'A decree is to be proposed authorizing an annual contribution of £100 for three years towards the maintenance of the British School of Archaeology at Athens'.

[158] I am grateful to Dr C. A. Stray for this information. The school was incorrectly identified as the South Kensington High School.

[159] *The Times* 3 October 1885, 9.

Building work on the project progressed through 1885 although an American plan for 'a library wing in common was no longer feasible'.[160]

Among the other fund-raising activities was the staging of 'Helena in Troas' by John Todhunter (1839-1916) at Hengler's Circus, Argyll Street, during May 1886.[161] The performance, under the patronage of the Prince of Wales, was directed by Edward William Godwin (1833-86). The lead of Helen was taken by Alma Murray (1854-1945), 'far in advance of her companions'.[162] Among the actors was Herbert Beerbohm Tree (1852-1917) who appeared as Paris, and his wife Maud (1863-1937) as Oenone. Constance (1858-98), the wife of Oscar Wilde, played a minor part.[163] The music was composed by B. Luard Selby. The interior of the Circus was transformed into a Greek theatre complete with an altar of Dionysos; the architectural elements were based on the frieze from the temple of Apollo at Bassai.[164] One review described the production as 'a curiosity of archaeological research and conscientious reproduction of the past'.[165] Within five years students of the BSA would be excavating the theatre of Megalopolis.

At the Annual Meeting of the Hellenic Society on 24 June 1886, at which Jebb was lecturing on the Homeric house at Tiryns, it was reported that the construction of the School building had been completed.[166] The Society had committed itself to supporting the School with a grant of £100 for the first three years. The School was ready to open.

---

[160] Lord 1947, 31.

[161] 'London theatricals', *The Scotsman* 18 May 1886, 5. For an advertisement: *The Times* 14 May 1886, 12. The BSA is also mentioned in the satirical review, 'Athenians at Hengler's', *Punch* 29 May 1886, 262.

[162] 'London theatricals', *The Scotsman* 18 May 1886, 5.

[163] Wilde reviewed the play, 'Helena in Troas', reproduced *The Prose of Oscar Wilde* (2005) in 272-77.

[164] 'A Greek theatre in London', *Daily News* 15 May 1886. The model was the theatre at Syracuse. See also '"Helena in Troas" at Hengler's', *The Pall Mall Gazette* 18 May 1886; 'Helena in Troas', *The Era* 22 May 1886 (with cast list).

[165] 'Helena in Troas', *The Era* 22 May 1886.

[166] Hellenic Society 1886, xlvii.

CHAPTER 2
THE DIRECTORS OF THE SCHOOL

There were seven directors of the British School from its opening in 1886 until the outbreak of the First World War. Five had been students at Cambridge, and only one at Oxford (Hogarth).[1] One of them, Harcourt-Smith, was not a graduate and had been seconded from the Department of Greek and Roman Antiquities at the British Museum.[2] It is perhaps significant that three of the first four directors (Penrose, Harcourt-Smith, and Hogarth) had been educated at Winchester College; Thomas Ashby, Director of the British School at Rome had also been educated there. Not all were classicists by background: Penrose had read Mathematics at Cambridge, and Dawkins had studied electrical engineering at King's College London, before a legacy had allowed him to study classics at Emmanuel College, Cambridge. With the exception of the initial director, all but one of the directors – Harcourt-Smith – had been students at the BSA.

Their duration in office ranged from a single year for the initial director, Penrose, through to the eight years of Ernest Gardner; Wace held office for ten years but the war years disrupted his tenure. The youngest director to take up office was Gardner at the age of 25, followed by Bosanquet at 29. Harcourt-Smith, Hogarth, Dawkins and Wace were all in their mid-thirties. In contrast Penrose was 69 when he became director.

Francis Cranmer Penrose (1886-87)

Penrose was born in 1817 at Bracebridge in Lincolnshire, where his father, John, was the vicar.[3] His mother was a published author writing under the name Mrs Markham.[4] Francis' paternal aunt was Mary, wife of Thomas Arnold, later headmaster of Rugby. Penrose was educated at Bedford Modern School (1825-29) and Winchester (1829-35). After leaving Winchester he worked for the architect Edward Blore.[5] Blore was famous as an architect of Country Houses, though he was also commissioned to undertake ecclesiastical commissions. Blore was interested in archaeology and was a founder member of the British Archaeological Association (1843).[6]

---

[1] Contrast this with the British School at Rome where all three Directors in the same period had been educated at Oxford: Gordon NcNeil Rushforth, Henry Stuart-Jones and Thomas Ashby. See Wallace-Hadrill 2001, 22-34.

[2] Harcourt-Smith was known as Cecil Smith before his knighthood. However to save confusion the hyphenated surname is used.

[3] Waterhouse and O'Donnell 2004. For his father: Hinings 2004. Francis was the fourth son, though the second was stillborn.

[4] Mitchell 2004.

[5] Port 2004.

[6] Levine 1986, 48.

Penrose left Blore in 1839 and was admitted, at the age of 22, to read mathematics at Magdalene College, Cambridge. After graduating in 1842 Penrose was awarded a grant from Cambridge. This allowed him to embark on an architectural tour of Europe which brought him into direct contact with classical architecture. During a six-month stay in Rome he was able to study the Pantheon. He made his first visit to Athens early in 1845, and became interested in fifth-century BC architecture. He returned to Athens the following year with the architect Thomas Willson (1824-1903) on behalf of the Society of Dilettanti.[7] He made a substantial study of Athenian architecture in 1851 (and reissued in 1888),[8] and became increasingly interested in astronomy and studied the orientation of temples in relation to the sun.

When the BSA was founded, Penrose was commissioned to build the School on land granted in June 1884.[9] In the spring of 1886 he visited Schliemann's excavations at Mycenae and Tiryns with members of ASCSA, and W. J. Stillman, the Athens Correspondent for *The Times*.[10] The comments that some of the architecture was Hellenistic brought a sharp response from Wilhelm Dörpfeld.[11] This led to a public debate under the auspices of the Hellenic Society at the Society of Antiquaries in London that July; *The Times* noted, 'the combat was truly heroic'.[12] Schliemann and Dörpfeld, supported by Middleton and Newton, were on one side; Penrose was on the other. Stillman's paper was read by Henry Francis Pelham (who had accompanied Stillman to Mycenae and Tiryns).

Penrose was appointed the first Director and, aged 69, took up residence in November 1886. He was accompanied to Athens by his daughter Emily, then aged 28.[13] She was later admitted to read *literae humaniores* at Somerville College, and became its principal in 1907. Penrose initiated the report of archaeological work in Greece that became a regular feature of the *Journal of Hellenic Studies*.[14] Following his retirement in the autumn of 1887, Penrose revisited Tiryns and Mycenae with Dörpfeld.[15] This resulted in a letter which was published in the *Athenaeum* in November (and reprinted as an adjunct to a letter from Schliemann in *The Times* in December).[16]

---

[7] Penrose 1847.

[8] Penrose 1851; Penrose 1888.

[9] Waterhouse 1986, 7.

[10] 'The excavations at Mycenae and Tiryns', *The Times* 24 April 1886, 10; 29 April 29 1886, 4; 23 June 1886, 4. See also Traill 1995, 254.

[11] Dörpfeld 1886. The party also suggested that the palace at Tiryns was Byzantine in date. For the details: Traill 1995, 254.

[12] *The Times* 3 July 1886, 11. For the text of papers: 'The remains at Tiryns', *The Times* 3 July 1886, 12. Stillman added further comments: 'The Tiryns case', *The Times* 16 July 1886, 3. See also Traill 1995, 255.

[13] Adams 2004.

[14] Penrose 1887.

[15] Schliemann 1887.

[16] Penrose 1887.

Penrose continued to work on Athenian architecture in his retirement,[17] and was elected a Fellow of the Society of Antiquaries (1898). He returned to Athens in 1890/91 as acting director while Gardner was in Cambridge.[18] He continued as a member of the Managing Committee until his death in 1903. The library was named in his honour as Macmillan and Harcourt-Smith explained:

> This form of memorial seemed to be peculiarly appropriate, because Mr. Penrose had first made his reputation by his great work on 'The Principles of Athenian Architecture'; he had been the first director of the school, and had remained until his death an active member of its managing committee; and had, moreover, been called in more than once of late years by the Athenian authorities to advise as to the preservation of the Parthenon.[19]

Ernest Arthur Gardner (1887-95)

Gardner was born at Clapton in London in 1862. His father Thomas was a member of the London stock exchange, and his mother was Ann Pearse. Thomas had come from Coggeshall in Essex, and Ann's family were London merchants. Ernest was the youngest of six children who included Percy (1846-1937), later Lincoln Professor of Classical Archaeology at Oxford, and Alice (1854-1927), the Byzantine historian.[20] The family were brought up with Christian convictions as members of the Congregational Church, where they came under the influence of John Pye Smith (1774-1851), whose wife Mary was from Hackney.[21] Ernest, like Percy before him, was educated at the City of London School, where Edwin A. Abbott (1838-1926) was headmaster (1865-89) as successor to Dr Mortimer.[22]

In 1880 Ernest was admitted to Gonville and Caius College, Cambridge. One of the fellows at the college was the Cicero scholar James Smith Reid (1846-1926), an exact contemporary of Percy Gardner at the City of London School, and then at Christ's College, Cambridge.[23] In 1872 Reid had married Ruth, one of the Gardner sisters, and in 1874 Percy married Agnes, Reid's sister. Percy himself had been elected to the Disney Chair of Archaeology at Cambridge in 1880, although this was, at this particular time, little more than a visiting lectureship. One of the other influences at Caius was the Rev. Ernest Stewart Roberts (1847-1912), the epigraphist. Ernest Gardner took a first in both parts of the new classical tripos (1882 and 1884). His interest in classical archaeology is seen as early as 1882, when he published his first article on the Athena in the west

---

[17] Penrose 1892; Penrose 1895.

[18] 'The British School at Athens', *The Times* 6 July 1891, 13.

[19] Macmillan and Harcourt-Smith 1904.

[20] The two eldest children were girls; the other brother was described by Percy as 'a man of business … an authority on Gothic architecture'. The older children were born in Hackney.

[21] Gardner 1933, 3.

[22] Farnell and Jann 2004. Abbott was himself a former pupil of the school and had read classics at Cambridge.

[23] Adcock and Smail 2004.

pediment of the Parthenon, drawing on representations in late classical pottery and early drawings, in the *Journal of Hellenic Studies*, edited by his brother Percy.[24] In 1882 he took part in the production of the *Ajax*, the first Cambridge Greek play, under the direction of J. Willis Clark (1833-1910) and Charles Waldstein.[25]

Ernest developed a strong interest in classical archaeology, publishing Greek material from the northern shores of the Black Sea, as well as an iconographical study of small-scale classical sculptures showing a boy and a goose.[26] One of his interests was in Greek epigraphy. Charles Newton's request for records of inscriptions had brought to light a manuscript volume of inscriptions copied by Charles R. Cockerell, and Ernest was invited to publish these at the invitation of the editors of the *Journal of Hellenic Studies*.[27] Newton's support for Ernest is also shown in the way that he entrusted to him the publication of squeezes from Kos and the adjacent Anatolian mainland.[28] Ernest was appointed a fellow of Caius in 1885, and was invited to join Flinders Petrie for his excavation, under the auspices of the Egypt Exploration Fund, of the Greek settlement at Naukratis in the western Delta.[29] Gardner's specific role was to work on the Greek inscriptions from the site, though he also excavated in the temenos of Aphrodite.[30]

Ernest continued to work on epigraphy publishing a new inscription found at Chalcedon and in a private collection in Constantinople; and as a result of his work at Naukratis went on to publish a study of the Ionic alphabet.[31] These studies culminated in the joint publication with E. S. Roberts from Caius.[32] On 4 November 1886 a letter signed by George Macmillan invited individuals to apply to be one of the students at the newly established School; Ernest took advantage of this opportunity, and by December was resident in Athens under Penrose. Early the following year David Hogarth joined them as the first Oxford student. Gardner continued to publish pottery from Naukratis,[33] and an inscription from Laconia (that had been noted by the Rev. H. J. Bidder).[34] Gardner's interest in Greek sculpture and epigraphy was stimulated by the discovery in February 1886 of deposits of archaic sculpture on the Athenian acropolis; the pieces could be matched with dedicatory inscriptions that gave the names of the sculptors.[35] His position to review developments in Greece and share them with the wider

---

[24] Gardner 1882.

[25] Easterling 1999.

[26] Gardner 1884; Gardner 1885d.

[27] Gardner 1885a; Gardner 1885b.

[28] Gardner 1885c.

[29] Petrie 1885.

[30] Petrie and Gardner 1886. See also Gardner 1886b.

[31] Gardner 1886c; Gardner 1886a.

[32] Roberts and Gardner 1887.

[33] Gardner 1887d.

[34] Gardner 1887a. Bidder was Bursar of St John's College, Oxford; see 'An Oxford bursar', *The Times* 20 October 1923, 12.

[35] Gardner 1887b.

world is seen in his significant review article on sculpture and epigraphy in Greece – a companion to Penrose's review of excavations[36] – a format that was to evolve into the familiar reports on 'Archaeology in Greece'.[37]

Penrose retired, aged nearly 70, from the directorship after one year and Gardner took his place. His position was funded by his Caius fellowship and by his appointment as Craven student (1887-90). He married Mary, daughter of Major John Wilson, of the Scots Greys, in 1887; and in May the following year their first son was born back in London.[38] Gardner immediately became involved with the work of the Cyprus Exploration Fund, supported by Francis Henry Hill Guillemard who was also a fellow of Caius.[39] Gardner continued Penrose's tradition of an annual report for the Hellenic Society on archeologically developments in Greece, initially by Jane Harrison, and then subsequently by himself.[40]

Gardner was sensitive to other developments in archaeology. He welcomed Flinders Petrie to Athens in 1891, and together they inspected the remains at Mycenae.[41] Petrie was by this time recognising that Greek pottery was turning up in Middle and New Kingdom levels in Egypt.[42] After four years Gardner's post was renewed through the generosity of the Master and Fellows of Caius who agreed to extend the fellowship for a further three years (to 1894) if it 'was of consequence to the cause of archaeology'.[43] This allowed Gardner to turn his attention to excavations on the Greek mainland, at Megalopolis in the Peloponnese.

One of the features of Gardner's directorship was the introduction of tours, broadening the appeal of the BSA to a wider public. These became extremely popular and led to his publication of a handbook for travellers which first appeared in 1933.[44] According to *The Times* the first trip appears to have been in 1892. The party of fourteen travelled on a 400 ton steamer under the care of 'three well-known dragomans resident at Athens', Weale, Apostolis and Melssinos, with Ernest Gardner as a guide. Among the party was Dr Jex-Blake. The ten day voyage included visits to Marathon, Thermopylae and Salamis; the Cyclades; the excavations on the island of Delos; Tinos, Naxos and Melos; and Thera.

> They have personally tested and satisfied themselves of the identity of famous sites. They have assisted at revered national festivals, and traced the course of Hellenic splendour, classical and mediaeval, with the melancholy testimonies of its long interval of decay, down to the modern, if partial, revival of life and prosperity.

The advantages of such tours was presented as follows:

---

[36] Penrose 1887.

[37] Gardner 1887c.

[38] *The Times* 25 May 1888, 1, 'at the house of her father-in-law, Thomas Gardner, of Oak Hill Park, Hampstead'. The couple were to have two more daughters.

[39] See chapter 7.

[40] Harrison 1888a; Gardner 1889.

[41] Drower 1995, 182-83.

[42] Petrie 1890.

[43] *The Caian* 1 (1891-92) 82, quoted in Gill 2004j. It should be noted that Cambridge University was not a direct donor to the finances of the BSA.

[44] Gardner 1938.

On a well-appointed yacht the traveller is independent of unclean inns and unpalatable food. With moderate care, he is safe from the danger of typhoid and malaria, not to speak of brigands or footpads. He has seldom to trust to the ignorance of local guides.[45]

These trips continued for many years and by 1906 were considered to be a 'legitimate' part of the work of the BSA.[46]

In 1894 Gardner's fellowship came to an end, and in 1895 he resigned as Director of the BSA.[47] The following year he was elected as Yates Professor of Classical Archaeology at University College London.[48] He was an editor of the *Journal of Hellenic Studies* (1897-1932). Gardner retired in 1929 at the age of 67, but retained a lectureship at University College London until 1933. He died at Maidenhead in 1939.

During the period of Gardner's directorship there was an increase in the level of archaeological activity in Greece. Members of the BSA had taken part on major excavations on Cyprus, and at Megalopolis. In addition there had been a survey in Aetolia and smaller excavations undertaken at Abae in Phocis: assistance had been given to exploratory work at Alexandria.

In Athens, work on the Athenian acropolis included the discovery of further archaic free-standing and architectural sculptures.[49] This allowed attempts to reconstruct the pedimental sculptures from the archaic temple of Athena. There was also discussion of how to clean the bronzes and stone sculpture.[50] Gardner raised concern that Frankish and Turkokratia architectural remains were being removed.[51] The Central Museum changed its name to the National Archaeological Museum.[52] The central part of Athens was a hive of activity including work in the Diplyon cemetery.[53] Significantly the building of the railway from Athens to the Piraeus cut across the north edge of the agora, revealing a number of finds.[54] The epigraphic evidence led to test excavations by Dörpfeld in the area of the agora to find the location of the Enneakrounos.[55] Excavations were also undertaken in the valley leading up to the Pnyx.[56] In Attica there was a wide range of work that

---

[45] *The Times* 13 April 1892.

[46] BSA Minute Book 5, Meeting of 16 October 1906.

[47] For his farewell speech: *The Caian* 6 (1896-97), 4-5.

[48] See also Calder III 1991.

[49] Harrison 1888a, 119-27; Gardner 1889, 255-70; Gardner 1890a, 210-11.

[50] Gardner 1889, 275; modified at Gardner 1892/3, 152.

[51] Gardner 1889, 256.

[52] Gardner 1889, 276.

[53] Harrison 1888a, 127-28; Gardner 1891, 388; Gardner 1892/3, 143.

[54] Gardner 1891, 386-88; Gardner 1892/3, 142-43.

[55] Gardner 1892/3, 139-41. For wider excavations in the area: Gardner 1894a, 224-26.

[56] Gardner 1895, 202-04.

included the excavations of Dionyso (the ancient Ikaria),[57] archaic tombs at Velanideza,[58] the *soros* at Marathon,[59] Eleusis,[60] and the temple of Nemesis at Rhamnous.[61]

One of the main developments in the archaeology of Greece was the excavation of Delphi by the French School. There had long been expectation of an announcement,[62] but the site was finally ceded to the French in April 1891.[63] Work began in 1892 and has continued ever since.[64] ASCSA used the money it had raised in the hope of excavating at Delphi for work at the Argive Heraion.[65] Their teams were also active at, among other places, Plataia in Boeotia dismantling Byzantine churches in the search for classical inscriptions.[66] ASCSA was working at Eretria, where Waldstein claimed to have found the grave of Aristotle.[67] The excavations focused on the theatre and the layout of its stage.[68]

Given the debate about the use of the ancient theatre, there was much interest in this topic during the 1880s and 1890s. The Germans excavated in the theatre of Dionysos at Athens,[69] and the Americans at Sikyon and Eretria;[70] the theatre at Sikyon was later reinvestigated by Dörpfeld.[71] Further work was conducted on the theatre at Argos.[72] The French were excavating the theatre on Delos,[73] and the Greek Archaeological Society at Gytheion.[74]

Schliemann had generated an interest in the prehistory of the Aegean, and the Greek Archaeological Service was excavating at Mycenae.[75] Other significant finds in this period included the discovery of Vapheio cups during an excavation by the Greek Archaeological Service.[76] Work at Troy had also resumed under the direction of Dörpfeld.[77]

---

[57] Harrison 1888a, 130-31; Lord 1947, 70-72.

[58] Gardner 1891, 388-89.

[59] Gardner 1891, 390.

[60] Harrison 1888a, 132.

[61] Gardner 1891, 391-92; Gardner 1892/3, 144.

[62] Harrison 1888a, 133.

[63] Gardner 1891, 385. The initial length of the contract was ten years.

[64] Gardner 1892/3, 139, 144-45; Gardner 1894a, 227-29; Gardner 1895, 206-08.

[65] Gardner 1892/3, 139, 145-46; Gardner 1894a, 230-31; Gardner 1895, 205-06.

[66] Gardner 1890a, 214; Gardner 1891, 395; Lord 1947, 73-74.

[67] Gardner 1891, 394; Lord 1947, 75-76.

[68] Gardner 1892/3, 146-47. See also Gardner 1894a, 231.

[69] Gardner 1889, 270; Gardner 1895, 204.

[70] Harrison 1888a, 129-30.

[71] Gardner 1892/3, 147.

[72] Gardner 1892/3, 147.

[73] Gardner 1892/3, 147; Gardner 1894a, 229-30.

[74] Gardner 1892/3, 147-48.

[75] Gardner 1889, 272; Gardner 1891, 392; Gardner 1892/3, 148-49; Gardner 1894a, 231. See also Petrie 1891.

[76] Gardner 1890a, 213.

Other archaeological fieldwork included projects in the Argolid, with extensive work at Epidauros,[78] and French exploration at Troezen,[79] and the sanctuary of Apollo Ptous.[80] The Greek excavation at Lycosura uncovered fragments of sculpture that were likely to have been made by Damophon of Messene.[81] These finds were later to be studied by Guy Dickins of the BSA.[82]

Cecil Harcourt-Smith (1895-97)

Cecil Harcourt-Smith was born in Staines, Middlesex in 1859, the son of a solicitor.[83] He was a scholar at Winchester (1873-78), and a year later joined the department of Greek and Roman antiquities at the British Museum under Charles Newton. Cecil Smith, as he was then known, regularly researched and published on Greek painted pottery;[84] he helped to prepare the catalogue of Greek Vases for the British Museum.[85] His interests were not confined to pottery, for he also published Greek inscriptions from Rhodes, and a gold tablet from Petelia in southern Italy.[86] Apart from his museum work Harcourt-Smith was a founder editor of the *Classical Review* (1887), and he had taken part in a diplomatic mission to Persia in 1887.

Harcourt-Smith succeeded Gardner as Director in 1895 at a time when the BSA was looking for more public funding; Smith was in fact seconded for two years. A financial crisis had been developing. In February 1895 the Prince of Wales had discussed with Charles Waldstein, then Slade Professor of Art in Cambridge, the possibility of a merger between the BSA and ASCSA.[87] Although this proposal does not appear to have been explored any further, the financial problem was presented to the meeting of the BSA at the annual meeting in July 1895 and underlined by the Prince of Wales.

> It is sufficient for me to say that, whereas the French School has an assured income of over £3,000 a year and the German School more than £2,000 a year, our own school last year had a precarious income of less than £500 a year. I am sure you will

[77] Gardner 1894a, 232.

[78] Gardner 1892/3, 148; Gardner 1895, 205.

[79] Gardner 1891, 393.

[80] Gardner 1889, 272-73.

[81] Gardner 1890a, 213; Gardner 1891, 390-91.

[82] Dickins 1904/05a; Dickins 1905/06a; Dickins 1906/07a; Dickins 1910/11.

[83] Laver and Farr 2004; Gill 2004k. He adopted the hyphenated name Harcourt-Smith in 1909 when he was knighted. For convenience the hyphenated form has been used in the text: footnote references to his publications use the form appropriate to the date of publication.

[84] Smith 1880; Smith 1881b; Smith 1881a.

[85] Smith 1896b.

[86] Smith and Comparetti 1882; Smith 1883a; Smith 1883b. The inscriptions had been found by Alfred Biliotti.

[87] Lord 1947, 31-32. The suggestion had apparently been made by the German Kaiser, Friedrich Wilhelm.

agree with me that this is a state of affairs which ought not to be allowed to continue, and there are hopeful signs that matters will at length be placed on a different and more satisfactory footing. A petition for support addressed to her Majesty's late Government was extensively signed by representatives of all classes of her Majesty's subjects. I have much pleasure in informing you that this petition met with a ready response, and that before leaving office Sir William Harcourt, as Chancellor of the Exchequer, had taken steps to use some portion of the public funds devoted to the encouragement of scientific investigation for the support of our school, and I understand that the present Ministers are willing to confirm the action of their predecessors.[88]

The Prince of Wales also noted financial support from one Cambridge college (Caius had effectively paid the salary for Gardner), and three Oxford colleges, and then appealed directly for private individuals to come forward. The timing could not have been worse. The Liberal government lost a vote on 21 June 1895 and the country was due to go to the polls later in the summer. However Sir William Harcourt (1827-1904), who was to lose his seat in the election, honoured the agreement.

Harcourt-Smith was only on secondment from the British Museum. This consisted of a six-month period of special leave which he combined with 'the month of vacation' that was due to him from the Museum. This allowed him to be in Athens for a seven-month period, from November until the end of May.[89] Harcourt-Smith and his wife, Alice Edith, arrived in Athens in November 1895. He felt that there were underlying problems at the BSA which had been allowed to develop under Gardner. He wrote to George Macmillan:

We steamed into Piraeus at daybreak on Monday, the Acropolis looking its best in a perfect dawn. Hill, who has been most kind, sent one of his clerks down to help us through the customs and launch us off to the School: and we found the house all ready to receive us. The repairs, repainting &c were all completed, with the exception of the kitchens, but that has now received the final touches and seems to be in working order.

As you will suppose, there has been a great deal to see to and arrange in the house: in fact, so much so that we have really had little time for anything else as yet: I am anxious to get this into thorough working order at once, so that I may be free when the time comes to wander off in search of a site. I do not know what we should have done without the Richardsons, who have been kindness itself. Mrs R. and her daughter have been in every morning helping my wife, as of course she cannot as yet talk with the servants, and I cannot always be there. As to the servants we are at present somewhat unsettled: the principle our predecessors went on was to hand over every thing to the butler Demetri who was evidently a thorough despot; and being, in his habits, also a thorough Oriental, you may imagine the result. I am at present occupied in trying to show him (what every Oriental has to learn sooner or later) what is the exact significance of the word master. Between you and me, the state of affairs we found here was nothing less

---

[88] 'The British School at Athens', *The Times* 10 July 1895, 10.

[89] British School at Athens 1895/96, 17.

than deplorable – it is no exaggeration when I tell you that the household arrangements, or rather want of arrangement, have been disgraceful. Of course I shall say nothing of this to anybody else, and I can't go into the details with you for it would take too long – but you would scarcely believe the condition of things we found. So far we have been going into the inventories, and have begun the purchases which are necessary: according to the proposal sanctioned by the Committee, we shall endeavour to restore the School to a reasonable standard of efficiency, using as a basis the Penrose's lists; I shall then draw up a fresh inventory, and it will be understood that in future each Director must be responsible (barring a fair allowance for wear and tear) for keeping it up and handing it over in this condition to his successor.[90]

The intimacy with which Harcourt-Smith wrote is suggestive of Macmillan's support. Clearly things had been bad, 'the School has been a common laughing stock'.[91]

Harcourt-Smith's experience of the *Classical Review* allowed him to initiate the *Annual of the British School at Athens* that was intended to publish the work of students at the School. It was designed to match the *Bulletin de Correspondence Hellénique* that was first published in 1877, and the *Athenische Mitteilungen*.[92] Up to this point research from the students as well as excavation reports had been published in the *Journal of Hellenic Studies* and other journals. Harcourt-Smith attempted to transfer the annual report on 'Archaeology in Greece' to the *Annual* from its previous home in the *Journal of Hellenic Studies*, but this was short-lived.[93]

He also developed the BSA by starting work on a new hostel for male students.[94] Macmillan reported to the Annual Meeting of July 1897:

> The students' hostel … had now become an accomplished fact. The total cost would probably be around £1,500. The subscriptions to the building fund amounted to rather more than £1,000, and the committee invited further aid in order that the scheme might be carried through without trenching upon the ordinary funds of the school.[95]

The work was, in fact, completed in time to allow students to be admitted for the next year's session (under the directorship of David Hogarth).

---

[90] Letter of 13 November 1895 (Macmillan archive). I am grateful to C. A. Stray for sharing this letter with me.

[91] Letter to George Macmillan, 13 December 1895 (Macmillan archive). Clearly he felt that the fault lay with Gardner.

[92] Étienne 1996, 10.

[93] Smith 1895/6a; Smith 1896.

[94] The estimate in July 1896 was for 80,000 dr: BSA Minute Book 2, Meeting of 26 July 26 1896. By December the tender was at 45,000 dr: BSA Minute Book 2, Meeting of 15 December 1896.

[95] In the annual meeting of the BSA in July 1897 the chairman noted, 'The hostel would be a great boon to students, and Mr. Smith's work raising the funds deserved their gratitude': 'British School at Athens', *The Times* 17 July 1897, 18.

The fabric of the new students' hostel, which is to be known as the "Macmillan Hostel", was completed before the opening of the session, and has been in use throughout the year.[96]

The hostel was 'where students could be housed, but the unlearned traveller might be enabled to make the best of his visit to Athens'.[97]

Apart from excavations on Cyprus and Megalopolis, and smaller digs in Phocis and the Megarid, the BSA had not been involved in large-scale fieldwork. Indeed the Megalopolis excavations had been surrounded by controversy and the BSA's reputation had been tainted. Harcourt-Smith considered the possibility of excavating at Pylos, at the suggestion of George Beardoe Grundy (1861-1948), who had conducted a survey in August 1895.[98] Harcourt-Smith explored Pylos in mid-December 1895 with Eugene Andrews of ASCSA.

The result of a close inspection of the visible ancient remains at Pylos led us to the conclusion that the cost of any excavation on that site would be considerable, and results not very startling. There is not a great deal of soil covering any part of the island of Sphacteria or of the ground to the north; all the materials and labour required would have to be shipped daily from New Pylos across the bay, a work of some difficulty when the wind blows; of this truth we had practical experience, suffering shipwreck on the return journey.[99]

In November 1896 Robert Carr Bosanquet, then a student, revisited Pylos clearly with an eye for the potential of excavating.[100] Harcourt-Smith also explored the possibility of excavating at Patras. During his travels in the Peloponnese with Bosanquet and Charles R. R. Clark in November 1896 the party observed a new copy of the Athena Parthenos.[101] Harcourt-Smith reported the refusal of his offer to excavate in a critical way, perhaps reflecting a tense working relationship with the Greek archaeological authorities:[102]

It is highly probable that a small and inexpensive excavation on the site at Psilalonia would result in the discovery of further fragments of this important figure; on behalf of the School I offered M. Cavvadias to undertake the necessary researches: the offer was declined, M. Cavvadias alleging as his reason that the Greek Government would itself carry out the work. Up to the time when we left Greece, nothing had been done, and the statuette so far as I know still remains in the Demarcheion at Patras, subject to the handling of officials who, if not wantonly careless, are at least wholly inexperienced in the proper treatment of delicate works

---

[96] 'British School at Athens', *The Times* 21 October 1898, 10.

[97] 'British School at Athens', *The Times* 21 October 1898, 10. Harcourt-Smith expanded on the usefulness of the hostel at the opening of the Penrose Library: Macmillan, *et al.* 1903/04, 236-37.

[98] Grundy and Burrows 1896 and 1897.

[99] British School at Athens 1895/96, 21.

[100] Bosanquet 1898b.

[101] Harcourt-Smith 1896/7. For details of the proposed excavations: British School at Athens 1896/97, 229.

[102] British School at Athens 1896/97, 229.

of art. Fortunately the Greek Government have at last been persuaded to have the statuette moulded; and a cast has been presented by M. Cavvadias to the British Museum, and is now exhibited in the Elgin room.

This tension with the ephor was brought to a head early in 1897, when the regulations for excavation in Greece were changed. This had an immediate impact on the work on Melos and several of the exploratory digs had to be curtailed. Harcourt-Smith explained the changes:

> At the beginning of 1897 ... the General Ephor promulgated a new law of excavation; henceforward all those who designed to excavate on private property must first *buy*, and then excavate, the land at their own cost; then hand over all objects found; and finally hand over the land itself, to the Greek government. This law, as will be seen at once, is a model of simplicity; and since it is not burdened with any cumbersome arrangement for the forced valuation and sale of likely sites, the fortunate excavator is provided by it with a capital opportunity of acquiring a first-hand experience of Greek notions of the price of land. Now it is not likely that the average peasant proprietor is going to be turned out of his homestead for its mere money value; and when it is remembered that the fact of your wishing to excavate his field confirms him in the conviction that gold statues are lying thick within it, it is not difficult to perceive that his notions of its value become extensive and peculiar.[103]

In spite of the frustrations Harcourt-Smith was able to open a small training excavation at Kynosarges in Athens.[104] This prepared the students for the main project at the Bronze Age site at Phylakopi on Melos.[105]

The value of Harcourt-Smith as Director was recognised quite quickly. In the summer of 1896 there was a strong possibility that he would not be granted leave of absence from the British Museum. Bosanquet, then a student at the BSA, wrote to the committee, 'We feel that his resignation at this moment would be a very serious blow to the welfare of the School'.[106] Moreover it was felt that such a quick change of director would suggest the unstable nature of the BSA.

Harcourt-Smith returned to the British Museum in 1897 as Assistant Keeper, and in 1904 became Keeper in succession to Alexander Stuart Murray (1841-1904).[107] He remained associated with the BSA, helping to publish inscriptions from Bosanquet's excavations at Kyzikos.[108] In 1909, the year he was knighted, he became Director of the South Kensington Museum (better known as the Victoria and Albert Museum). He served as honorary secretary of the Society of Dilettanti.[109] Harcourt-Smith died in Surrey in 1944.

---

[103] Smith 1896/7, 2. This was noted at the meeting of 17 June 1896: BSA Minute Book 2.

[104] Rodeck 1896/7; Edgar 1897. For later publication of the finds: Droop 1905/06a.

[105] Smith 1895/6b; Smith 1896/7; Atkinson, *et al.* 1904.

[106] BSA Minute Book 2, 23 July 1896. This took place shortly after the Annual Meeting. The situation was resolved by the meeting of 26 July.

[107] For Murray: Thompson 1903/4.

[108] Smith and de Rustafjaell 1902. He also continued to serve on the Managing Committee.

[109] Harcourt-Smith and Macmillan 1932.

Assistant Director: John George Smith (1895/96)

A key development under Harcourt-Smith was the creation of the post of Assistant Director. One of the reasons was that Harcourt-Smith was only seconded from the British Museum for six months (plus his one month of leave entitlement).[110] Thus he needed somebody to help with affairs in Athens if he wanted to develop a major excavation.

It was decided to appoint John George Smith (b. 1869) for the session 1895/96. He had been educated at Eton (where he was an exact contemporary of two other BSA students, Vincent W. Yorke (1869-1957) and Robert J. G. Mayor (1869-1947)) and Magdalen College, Oxford. Smith had been admitted as a student at the BSA for the session 1891/92, under Gardner, before he had completed his studies at Oxford. In 1894 he had married Pauline Flora, daughter of Major James St. John Munro, late Consul-General at Montevideo, although there is no apparent mention of her in Athens. Smith accompanied Harcourt-Smith to Melos in January 1896 to look at the possibilities for excavation.[111] Back at Athens he worked with Duncan Mackenzie on a topographical index of sites in Greece,[112] as well as providing 'invaluable help in the Library'.[113] Harcourt-Smith paid special tribute to Smith:

> With his help I was enabled to set about the necessary preparations for the serious work of the session, while my time was free for making the necessary study of the topography and antiquities of Athens, and for the preparation of lectures.[114]

Wider Excavations

There was much activity on the Athenian acropolis with ongoing reconstruction of the sculptures.[115] Excavations continued in the heart of the historic city of Athens, in particular around the area of the Pnyx. The search for the Enneakrounos continued.[116] Harcourt-Smith highlighted the problem of excavating in urban Athens in connection with the German School's search for the *Stoa Basileios*:

> unfortunately, the purchase and destruction of houses in a populous quarter of Athens is a costly affair, but it is pleasant to know that a third house is already doomed for the coming season.[117]

Such urban clearance was a feature of the later American work in the Athenian agora during the 1930s.[118] Expense was a major issue for the BSA and Harcourt-Smith decided to open a training excavation at Kynosarges.[119]

---

[110] British School at Athens 1895/96, 17-18.

[111] British School at Athens 1895/96, 21.

[112] British School at Athens 1895/96, 20. See also Momigliano 1999, 19.

[113] Letter To George Macmillan, 13 December 1895 (Macmillan archive).

[114] British School at Athens 1895/96, 17-18.

[115] Smith 1896, 338-39.

[116] Smith 1896, 335-37.

[117] Smith 1896, 337.

During the time of Harcourt-Smith's directorship ASCSA started work at Corinth in 1896,[120] and the French School at Delphi.[121] The Greek Archaeological Society were excavating at Mycenae, a site that the BSA was to work on after the First World War.[122] There was a move to excavate in the Cyclades: the German School on Thera,[123] and with the BSA on Melos.[124] A key development in the study of Byzantine Greece was the French School's survey of Mistra.[125]

Other developments

Harcourt-Smith's directorship was a time of serious upheaval. In April 1897 Greece mobilised her troops that were gathered on the frontier between Thessaly and Macedonia (then part of the Ottoman Empire).[126] Turkish forces crossed the frontier on Sunday 18 April and after four weeks of fierce fighting a truce was signed in May. On Crete there was another serious uprising against Ottoman authority that led to the intervention of the Great Powers.[127] In archaeological terms this was crucial as it opened up the possibility of excavation on the island; Arthur Evans quickly moved to form a Cretan Exploration Fund. A further result of the wars was the abandonment of excavations in Greece, in part due to the scarcity of workmen.[128]

In April 1896 the first modern Olympic Games were held in Athens. These had been proposed back in 1894 and had been generously supported by the Greek community in England.[129] Harcourt-Smith used the opportunity to draw attention to the restoration of the Parthenon and encouraged donations that would be forwarded to the Archaeological Society of Athens.[130] The games were to include a production of the *Antigone* in the newly restored stadium; Harcourt-Smith noted, 'By this arrangement the necessity will be obviated of tampering with either of the existing ancient theatres of Athens and so

[118] Mauzy 2006. For other overviews of the work: Thompson and Wycherley 1972; Camp II 1986.

[119] See chapter 8.

[120] Smith 1896, 340. See also Williams and Bookidis 2002.

[121] Smith 1896, 343.

[122] Smith 1896, 340-41; Smith 1895/6a, 54-55. For a convenient overview: French 2002.

[123] Smith 1896, 342.

[124] Smith 1896, 347-56.

[125] Smith 1896, 346; Spieser 1996.

[126] Clogg 1992, 70. For some contemporary views by Dorothy Boyd who served as a nurse: Allsebrook 1992, 40-63.

[127] For a convenient summary: Clogg 1992, 69-71.

[128] Lord 1947, 90.

[129] 'The proposed Olympic Games', *The Times* 26 December 1894, 3. The sum of £400 was reported (*The Times* 26 December 1894, 7).

[130] Harcourt-Smith 1896a.

detracting from their interest for those visitors who prefer antiquity unalloyed'.[131] Edward F. Benson, one of the BSA students, recalled the build-up to the games.

> Athens took up the notion very warmly, for athletes of all nations would certainly flock there, in order to have the honour of competing with the Hellenes, whose forefathers had been the originators of contests in bodily prowess … Strings of young men in shorts trotted about the streets of Athens all day, occasionally bursting into sprints … one day I saw two stout and elderly gentlemen solemnly wrestling together, by the columns of Zeus Olympios.[132]

Harcourt-Smith's directorship marked a major change in direction for the BSA with a commitment to scientific approach to excavation as well as a more streamlined administration.

David George Hogarth (1897-1900)

Hogarth was the son of the Rev. George Hogarth, the vicar of Barton-on-Humber.[133] He had been educated at Winchester and Magdalen College, Oxford, and was admitted to the BSA in January 1887 under Penrose; his fellow student was Ernest Gardner. His initial interest was in Alexander the Great, but he was soon involved with William M. Ramsay's expeditions through Anatolia.[134] Hogarth continued his association with the BSA through Ernest Gardner's excavations for the Cyprus Exploration Fund.[135]

After the term of his fellowship at Magdalen in 1893, Hogarth became involved in archaeological work with Flinders Petrie in Egypt. One of the projects was to explore Alexandria in 1895 with Edward F. Benson, one of the BSA students.[136] Hogarth then turned to the exploration for new papyri in the Faiyum alongside Bernard Pyne Grenfell and Arthur Surridge Hunt.[137]

In August 1896, as Harcourt-Smith's secondment from the British Museum was drawing to a close, the BSA Managing Committee invited Hogarth to be the next director starting in the autumn of 1897 for a period of three years.[138] In the meantime Hogarth was asked to report on the Cretan Revolt for *The Times*. In February 1897 British warships had opened fire on positions held by 'insurgents'.[139] Hogarth, as the 'Special Correspondent' from *The Times* at Canea, wrote of the 25,000 Muslim refugees on the island,[140] and of

---

[131] Harcourt-Smith 1896a.

[132] Benson 1930, 165-66.

[133] Gill 2004l; Lock 1990.

[134] Hogarth 1897. For his travels in Anatolia: Hogarth 1910; see also Gill 2004c.

[135] Gardner, *et al.* 1888; Hogarth 1889.

[136] Hogarth and Benson 1896.

[137] Grenfell, *et al.* 1900. See also Montserrat 1996.

[138] BSA Minute Book 2, Meeting of 6 August 1896. He was offered a salary of £500.

[139] 'Greece and Crete. The bombardment by the powers', *The Times* 23 February 1897, 5.

[140] 'Greece and Crete', *The Times* 13 March 1897, 7 (dated 12 March). He was conferring with Sir Alfred Biliotti (who as a younger man had excavated for the British Museum on Rhodes).

the intervention at Spinalonga.[141] Crete was not the only point of tension with the Ottoman Empire. Hogarth travelled to Thessaly to observe the troops massing on the frontier. In early April he was back on Crete working alongside men of the Seaforth Highlanders.[142]

Hogarth took up office in a Greece bruised from the defeat in Thessaly. He inherited the Phylakopi excavations from Harcourt-Smith, though Duncan Mackenzie was employed to take charge of the work.[143] Hogarth soon started to look for an alternative site to excavate when the work at Phylakopi was complete. By January 1898 he was considering Hermione in the Argolid, Elis, and the temple of Artemis at Lusi; the latter was no longer available as it was to be excavated by the Austrians who had just established their institute in Athens.[144] Hogarth also pressed for Daphne in Egypt, and the Carpass peninsula on Cyprus.[145] In the end Hogarth returned to Egypt to excavate at Naukratis from February to May 1899 with the support of the Managing Committee and the Society of Dilettanti.[146] This was as a result of news reaching Hogarth that 'very serious encroachments were being made upon the mounds of Gaif'.[147] He was assisted by two BSA students, Campbell C. Edgar and Charles D. Edmonds. Hogarth returned to Naukratis in 1903.[148]

One of the delays in choosing a site is likely to have been due to the events in Crete. In the spring of 1899 he joined Arthur Evans for a visit to Knossos, which French archaeologists had been hoping to claim.[149] Crete had been placed under the control of the Great Powers and it was possible for sites to be earmarked for excavation. With a new law in place restricting the acquisition of antiquities, the time was right for excavation permits to be issued on the island. A Cretan Exploration Fund was established, although it did not raise the sum that had been projected.[150]

A further site became available in the autumn of 1899. The BSA was offered the title deeds to the temple of Cybele at Sardis by the brother of George Dennis.[151] Dennis had

[141] 'The Powers and Greece', *The Times* 15 March 1897, 7.

[142] 'The situation in Crete', *The Times* 20 April 1897, 3.

[143] Hogarth 1897/98; Mackenzie 1898/9.

[144] BSA Minute Book 3, Meeting of 20 January 1898. Elis was also excavated by the Austrians in 1910.

[145] BSA Minute Book 3, Meeting of 3 February 1898. Hogarth was familiar with the area from his work with CEF excavations: Hogarth 1889.

[146] Hogarth 1898/9.

[147] Hogarth 1898/9, 26.

[148] Hogarth, *et al.* 1905.

[149] MacGillivray 2000, 163-65.

[150] MacGillivray 2000, 166.

[151] BSA Minute Book 3, Meeting of 12 October 1899. The deeds were accepted: Meeting of 30 October 1899.

hoped to excavate at the site in 1867.[152] In the end Crete rightly claimed the attention of the School, and the Sardis project was left untouched.

The BSA had been transformed during Harcourt-Smith's directorship. Hogarth's era benefited from the newly opened hostel that allowed students to reside on site.[153] In the session 1899/1900 the BSA was presented with the library and collection of George Finlay by W. H. Cooke, Finlay's surviving executor.[154] This was displayed in a room in the Macmillan hostel.

Hogarth stepped down as Director in 1900 to take a paid position from the Cretan Exploration Fund. He was partly responsible for encouraging the American Harriet Boyd to work on Crete.[155] Hogarth later excavated for the British Museum at the Artemision at Ephesus (1904-05), Asyut in Egypt (1906-07), and finally Carchemish (1911).[156] He also had a settled job in Britain as Keeper of the Ashmolean Museum (November 1908), where he was able to develop his interest in the Hittites. During the First World War he served in the Arab Bureau in Cairo. Hogarth returned to Oxford after the war and died in 1927.

Assistant Directors

Hogarth, perhaps drawing on Harcourt-Smith's experience, decided that he needed the help of an Assistant Director to remove some of the educational load from his shoulders. At the time of Hogarth's appointment as Director in August 1896 it was discussed that Robert Carr Bosanquet, the then Craven Student (1895-97), should be appointed as assistant to Hogarth when he took up office in October 1897.[157] Bosanquet had earlier been admitted as a student at the BSA in the spring of 1893 under Ernest Gardner, as he was preparing for Part 2 of the Classical Tripos at Trinity College, Cambridge. He had worked with Harcourt-Smith on the excavations at Kynosarges and on Melos. One of the ideas was that Bosanquet would hold 'a lectureship at the School'.[158]

However it was not to work out as planned. In November 1896 Bosanquet travelled to Pylos to investigate the possibility of excavating there.[159] He succumbed to malaria and, after a spell in the Evangelismos Hospital in Athens, left Greece to convalesce at Vevey. Although in the spring of 1897 he was willing to accept the 'lectureship' at the BSA for the following year, the post was considered unsuitable for him at that time.[160] As a result,

---

[152] Rhodes 1973, 101; Challis 2008, 148.

[153] The Upper House had previously been used for students. I am grateful to Amalia Kakissis and Catherine Morgan for this observation.

[154] British School at Athens 1899/1900, 131. See also Kakissis 2004, 207. For an inscription: Wilhelm 1900/01.

[155] Allsebrook 1992.

[156] For this phase in his career: Gill 2004l.

[157] BSA Minute Book 2, Meeting of 6 August 1896.

[158] BSA Minute Book 2, Meeting of 26 October 1896.

[159] Bosanquet 1898b. See also Bosanquet 1938, 60-67 for letters that cover the period 27 November 1896, to 26 February 1897.

[160] BSA Minute Book 2, Meeting of 8 April 1897.

a decision was taken in July 1897 to employ a former BSA student, George Chatterton Richards, as Assistant Director.[161] Richards was expected to assist with museum lectures to the students for a four-month period from the end of December 1897,[162] as well as providing supplementary lectures for Ernest Gardner's tours to Greece.[163] A further duty was to prepare the report on 'Archaeology in Greece'.[164] Hogarth paid the salary of £150 himself, from his own stipend.

Richards was born in Churchover, Warwickshire in 1867.[165] He was educated at Rugby, where he was influenced by T. W. Jex-Blake, and then read classics at Balliol College, Oxford. His interest in archaeology was stimulated by Percy Gardner, Professor of Classical Archaeology, and after the award of a Craven University Fellowship Richards was admitted to the BSA (1889/90, 1890/91) under the direction of Ernest Gardner. Richards took part in Gardner's excavations at Megalopolis and became embroiled, along with Loring and Woodhouse, in the debate about the nature of the theatre.[166] In this he was ranged against Eugénie Sellers, who was also a student at the BSA.[167] In 1891 Richards resigned his fellowship at Hertford College, married, and was elected Professor of Greek at the University College of South Wales and Monmouthshire at Cardiff. In 1895 he was ordained and in effect served as university chaplain alongside his academic duties. In 1898, after his time in Athens, Richards resigned as Professor in Greek at Cardiff; and the following year was appointed fellow, chaplain and tutor at Oriel College, Oxford. In later life he was appointed Professor of Greek at the University of Durham (1927). He died in 1951.

The issue of the Assistant Director appears to have been controversial as it drew attention to the role of the Director. In the summer of 1898, after Richards' time as assistant, there seems to have been a disagreement in the Managing Committee about the duties of the Director. William Loring, who had just replaced George Macmillan as Honorary Secretary, seems to have confronted Hogarth 'as regards the nature and extent of the education duties' of the Director.[168] Richards had clearly been responsible for the 'educational role' of lecturing to the students as well as providing support for Ernest Gardner and his tours. One of the issues with Loring seems to have been over the role of the Assistant Director whose duties Hogarth perceived to be 'mainly educational'. The result was a resolution:

> Mr Hogarth is not expected to give instruction to Students in Sculpture, Painting, or Architecture.[169]

---

[161] BSA Minute Book 2, Meeting of 29 July 1897.

[162] It was also suggested that he assist with lectures to supplement those of Ernest Gardner: BSA Minute Book 3, Meeting of 20 January 1898.

[163] BSA Minute Book 3, Meeting of 20 January 1898.

[164] Richards 1898. See also 'British School at Athens', *The Times*, 21 October 1898, 10.

[165] Gill 2004o.

[166] Gardner, *et al.* 1890; Gardner, *et al.* 1892.

[167] Dyson 2004.

[168] BSA Minute Book 3, Meeting of 28 July 1898.

[169] BSA Minute Book 3, Meeting of 28 July 1898.

It is likely that that Loring, who knew the BSA under Ernest Gardner, had not understood the demands of the post if the BSA was to take an active role in the field. The result was that Hogarth had no assistant for 1898/99,[170] although plans were made to select one for the coming year. At the Managing Committee of 4 May 1899 Hogarth sent a letter (reported by Robert Carr Bosanquet)

> proposing that during next year he should have a co-Director, to whom he should hand over part of his salary, Hogarth to be responsible for excavations, the other man for teaching and running the School in Athens. He named me in connection with the proposal, and it is possible that it may lead to some sort of offer being made to me, perhaps next month …[171]

In fact the issue was not discussed until the Managing Committee of May 18 at which it was reported that Bosanquet was willing to become Assistant Director in 1899/1900 at a salary of £300, of which £150 would be derived from Hogarth.[172] Bosanquet would be required to reside in Athens from 1 January to 30 June. The minutes indicated that Bosanquet's appointment was 'on the understanding that he should thus succeed' Hogarth. Bosanquet's appointment was confirmed in July.[173]

These arrangements were revealed at the Annual Meeting of Subscribers in October.[174] Hogarth specifically 'explained the reasons which had led him to desire the appointment of an Assistant Director', and Loring reported:

> Mr R. C. Bosanquet, formerly a Student of the School, and for the past year a member of the School Committee, has been appointed to the post of Assistant-Director, which has been created for this year only. The principal reason for this appointment is Mr Hogarth's strong desire to be released from the responsibility of educational work in Athens itself, and to be able to devote the whole of his energies to excavation and research. Mr Hogarth will be required to reside in Greek lands for six months only, the bulk of which will be spent in Crete, while Mr Bosanquet will reside eight months, taking charge of the School and its Students in Athens. The Committee attach great importance to maintaining the more purely educational work of the School alongside of the exploratory work; and they trust that the arrangement that have made will ensure that neither side shall be neglected.[175]

In the meantime Bosanquet excavated at Housesteads on Hadrian's Wall in the summer of 1898.[176] Among the duties for Bosanquet in Athens was the preparation of the report for

---

[170] BSA Minute Book 3, Meeting of 18 August 1898. It was decided that it would be 'undesirable' to have an Assistant Director for 1898/99.

[171] Bosanquet 1938, 69 (letter of 5 May 1899). For the Meeting of 4 May 1899 see BSA Minute Book 3, where this issue was not raised in detail.

[172] BSA Minute Book 3, Meeting of 18 May 1899.

[173] BSA Minute Book 3, Meeting of 3 July 1899.

[174] British School at Athens 1898/99.

[175] British School at Athens 1898/99, 102-03, 106.

[176] Bosanquet 1904.

'Archaeology in Greece'.[177] He also worked on the finds from Phylakopi while Hogarth was excavating on Crete.

Robert Carr Bosanquet (1900-06)

Hogarth's three year term of office came to a close in 1900 and he left to work for the Cretan Exploration Fund. Bosanquet, as had been agreed the previous year in the Managing Committee, became Director. Bosanquet had been born in 1871 in London. His father, Charles, was the secretary of the Charity Organization Society; his younger brother was the philosopher Bernard Bosanquet. Robert's mother, Eliza Isabella, was a Carr, who was descended from the Newcastle merchant and banker Ralph Carr (1711-1806).

In 1880 Bosanquet's grandfather, Rev. William Robert Bosanquet, died, and Charles inherited the family home at Rock near Alnwick. Robert was educated at the newly established Aysgarth School in Bedale, Yorkshire, from where he went to Eton College as a holder of a Newcastle scholarship. One of his tutors was Arthur C. Benson, son of the Archbishop of Canterbury.[178] Bosanquet won a scholarship to Trinity College, Cambridge. Bosanquet grew up against the backdrop of investigations of the Hadrian's Wall; his sister recorded that at the age of seven he had been looking at John Collingwood Bruce's *Handbook to the Roman Wall*.[179]

In the spring of 1893, after completing Part 1 of the Classical tripos, Bosanquet first visited Greece. One of his travelling companions was Robert J. G. Mayor; they visited Tenos in the Cyclades accompanied by a 'Miss Dawes' (surely the classical scholar Elizabeth A. S. Dawes).[180] In May of that year Bosanquet took part in the excavation of Aegosthena working with Edward F. Benson (brother of Bosanquet's tutor, Arthur C. Benson, at Eton) and Mayor.[181] After completing Part 2 of the classical tripos in the spring of 1894, Bosanquet went out to Greece in the January of 1895.[182] He was able to travel widely visiting the Peloponnese,[183] as well as the American excavations at Assos in Anatolia.[184] At Corinth Bosanquet witnessed the elections in which Charilaos Trikoupis was defeated:

> ... there are perhaps 6 places, 20 candidates in the district: they set up 20 petroleum tins in a row (for petroleum tins serve all purposes there) and attach to each a long spout of rolled tin up which a man's arm can just go: a partition is placed in each box: one side elects, one rejects. Opposite each candidate's box sits a representative of his interests: a number of lawyers are about the room to see fair

[177] Hogarth and Bosanquet 1899. See also Bosanquet 1938, 72 (letter of 10 July 1900).

[178] Bosanquet 1938, 19.

[179] The original edition appeared in 1851.

[180] Bosanquet 1938, 23-28. Dawes had studied at Bedford College, London, and at Girton College, Cambridge.

[181] Bosanquet 1938, 28-29.

[182] Bosanquet 1938, 34.

[183] Bosanquet 1938, 35.

[184] Bosanquet 1938, plate opposite p. 39. See also Dyson 1998, 71.

play. At each box the voter is given a bullet: as he cannot read, the candidate's friend sitting opposite shouts the name in his ear: he is further helped by the party badge and the candidate's photograph stuck over the box. He puts his arm up the spout, and in theory no one sees in which side he throws his bullet or bullets, for in most cases there are more bullets than there were voters, found in each box: if the excess is absurdly great, they halve the candidate's total![185]

Afterwards he visited Francis (Frank) Edward Noel who lived at Achmetaga (Achmét Aga) on Euboea.[186]

Bosanquet was by now committed to classical archaeology and in the winter of 1895 worked in Dresden on Attic white-ground lekythoi and finds from Roman Germany.[187] In Mannheim he went to hear Adolf Fürtwangler lecture on Greek terracotta plaques.[188]

> … there is no doubt that he's a genius. A lean haggard man with a high colour and thick black hair streaked with grey; tho' he is only 40; so slight that he looks tall; scrupulously dressed in clinging dark blue. Like many great men's, his eyes are the feature that haunt one. They are generally dull and half-closed, but when he is roused they open wide and *flash*. And very few people have eyes that really flash.[189]

Bosanquet was able to discuss the *lekythoi* with Fürtwangler and was invited to study the examples in Mannheim. Bosanquet also alluded to the support Furtwängler received from his pupils: 'one Englishman in particular, who translated his great book'.[190] The pupil was not male, but female: Eugénie Sellers had translated his *Masterpieces of Greek Sculpture* (1895).[191] Bosanquet then continued to St Germain to work on Roman bronzes, the very collection which had been reviewed by Sellers in 1895.[192]

Bosanquet continued to develop the work of the School through the preparation of a 'suggested work and teaching scheme' for BSA students which he prepared in February 1901.[193] This was mapped onto the view that a student would hold one of the studentships for two years allowing him (at least at this date) to devote 'the first year to general studies, the second to some special subject'. It was suggested that students should travel out via Germany – Berlin, Munich and Dresden were named – to improve their German in order

---

[185] Bosanquet 1938, 35.

[186] Bosanquet 1938, 36 (29 May 1895). Noel's daughter Irene married Philip John Baker (later Noel-Baker). Bosanquet noted that she was being educated in England: Bosanquet 1938, 38. See Winifred Lamb's visit to Achmetaga in 1921: Gill 2007.

[187] Bosanquet 1938, 42 (20 November 1895). See also Bosanquet 1896.

[188] Bosanquet 1938, 43.

[189] Bosanquet 1938, 43-44.

[190] Bosanquet 1938, 43.

[191] Dyson 2004, 66. Significantly in 1895 Sellers was also advocating the study of Roman provincial art and archaeology: Dyson 2004, 118.

[192] Bosanquet 1938, 44.

[193] Published in *BSA* 6 (1899/1900), 153. It was later entitled as 'Suggested plan of study' in subsequent *Annuals*.

to benefit from lectures given by the German and Austrian schools in Athens. During October students were recommended to travel in the Peloponnese (Olympia, Mycenae, Epidauros, the Argive Heraion) and to Delphi.[194] From early November to the middle of March students were expected to be in Athens while pursuing a topic of study. In the spring it was suggested that students should join one of the island cruises led by Ernest Gardner or W. Dörpfeld. Finally in May or June students could be involved in some form of field work or travel back to Britain via Italy where 'he will do well to attach himself to the newly founded British School at Rome'.[195]

Bosanquet took up office with the work of the Cretan Exploration Fund in full swing; Evans was at Knossos and Hogarth at Psychro. Bosanquet developed an excavation at Praesos in eastern Crete, and due to the chance discovery of Minoan remains at Palaikastro by John H. Marshall, he was able to obtain a permit to work there.[196] In 1904, much to Evans' irritation, the BSA decided to transfer its interests from Crete to mainland Greece and specifically to Laconia. Initial excavations in the Mani were switched to Sparta itself and the excavation of the sanctuary of Artemis Orthia.

In July 1902 Bosanquet married Ellen Sophia, the daughter of the historian and antiquarian Thomas Hodgkin of Northumberland, who then became a donor of the BSA until his death.[197] In 1903 Bosanquet was reappointed as Director at the continuing salary of £500.[198] However in 1905 Bosanquet's father died and he decided to resign his position to be closer to the family estate in Northumberland;[199] he actually stayed in post until 1906. Bosanquet left Athens to become professor of classical archaeology in Liverpool where he was able to develop an active programme of fieldwork. He stepped down from the chair in 1920 and lived in Northumberland; he died in Newcastle upon Tyne in 1935.

Other developments

The BSA had been transformed under Harcourt-Smith and Hogarth. In February 1903, F. C. Penrose, the BSA's first Director died.[200] He had continued to contribute to the life of the BSA through his work on the Managing Committee. Soon afterwards plans were made for a library, as it was considered that the present library in the Director's house was by that time running out of shelf space.[201] A decision was taken to start work. The building was in effect complete by early November 1904 and the revised cost was put at £1,150. In November 1904 the Managing Committee launched a formal appeal for the Penrose

---

[194] This pattern was still used after the First World War: Gill 2007.

[195] Published as 'Suggested plan of study' in *BSA* 6 (1899/1900), 153.

[196] These events are discussed in Gill 2000a.

[197] See also Freeman 2007.

[198] BSA Minute Book 4, Meeting of 11 June 1903.

[199] BSA Minute Book 5, Meeting of 25 July 1905.

[200] Waterhouse and O'Donnell 2004.

[201] Macmillan, *et al.* 1903/04, 236. See also Kakissis 2004, 207.

Memorial Library so that the building could be opened 'free of debt'.[202] At that point the Fund had received some £400 and the Managing Committee felt that it could afford a further £600 from its own funds, including a gift of £150 from the sisters of Lord Leighton (who had served on the original Managing Committee). The Athenian Archaeological Society offered to present 'a bust of Mr. Penrose to be executed by a Greek sculptor, as a mark of the high esteem in which he was held by Greek archaeologists'.[203] The library itself was expected to open 'in the course of the Archaeological Congress which is to take place in Athens next spring'. The formal opening was undertaken in April 1905 by HRH The Crown Prince of Greece in his capacity as president of the Greek Archaeological Society.[204] A signed portrait of King Edward VII, patron of the BSA, was arranged to be hung,[205] and Jebb composed some 'elegant lines' to celebrate the moment.[206]

The First International Archaeological Congress was held in Athens in April 1905.[207] This was presented as the result of collaboration between the University of Athens, the Greek Archaeological Society, and five foreign archaeological schools. It was opened on April 7, the anniversary of Greek Independence, in the Parthenon. *The Times* reported:

> The noble columns of the Parthenon, mellowed by the tints of ages, looked down from a background of deep blue sky upon a distinguished but unpicturesque throng, arrayed in the hideous cylinder and piteous swallow-tail coat of modern civilization; and one could but not regret that the eminent scholars present had failed to lend dignity to this unique occasion by appearing in their University robes. The authorities, with excellent taste, refrained from supplying the paraphernalia which usually disfigure such celebrations; there was a happy absence of flags, wreaths, and devices – to decorate the Parthenon would be a crime; only a few chairs were provided for the members of the Royal family, and the Crown Prince and the other speakers delivered their addresses standing on a fallen fragment of the ancient building.

Bosanquet was specifically reported for his speech in which he praised 'the early pioneers of research … and … the philhellenes who shed their blood for its independence'. As part of the Congress the *Antigone* was performed in the Stadion (as it had been for the 1896 Olympics), and it was observed that the actors 'were incomparably superior to most of those who have interpreted the Greek drama at Oxford and Cambridge'. The choice of venue was criticised:

---

[202] Macmillan and Harcourt-Smith 1904. The committee consisted of representatives from the BSA, the Hellenic Society, the Royal Institute of British Architects; Harcourt-Smith was one of the secretaries.

[203] Macmillan and Harcourt-Smith 1904.

[204] Macmillan, *et al.* 1903/04. This contains the speeches given at the opening.

[205] *The Times* 6 March 1905, 6. The opening was noted: 'The Archæological Congress at Athens', *The Times* 25 April 1905, 5.

[206] They are mentioned in a letter by Jebb of 22 January 1905: Jebb 1907, 409.

[207] Reported in 'The Archæological Congress at Athens', *The Times* 25 April 1905, 5.

The enormous Stadion, on the restoration of which immense sums have been spent and much magnificent material wasted, was never a beautiful structure and can hardly be adapted to any useful purpose in modern times, least of all to a dramatic representation.

The contrast was made with the Oxford and Cambridge plays 'in which every detail was scientifically worked out in accordance with the ascertained usage of the Greek stage'. The report noted

the incorrectness of the costumes, the inartistic arrangement of the drapery, the negligent grouping of actors and chorus, and the inadequate decoration of the architectural background. There was, in fact, a total absence of the picturesque and the sculpturesque, although Athens abounds in ancient models and in archaeologists whose advice might have been sought to ensure accuracy in drapery and architectural detail. Thus Ismene wore a chiton like a modern petticoat, and the armed attendants, who resembled Roman legionaries rather than Greek hoplites, wore, like the other actors, *opéra comique* "tights" – how different the bare limbs of the stalwart British undergraduates! – while no attempt was made at polychrome decoration of the architectural *scena*.

The Congress was seen as an opportunity for an appeal for more government money.

It is to be hoped that as a result of the congress which has now come to a close increased attention will be paid to the progress of British archaeology in the East and that the interests of the British School will not be neglected.[208]

Indeed the opening of the Penrose Library as part of the Congress had given Macmillan the opportunity to review the work of the School and to highlight the annual grant of £500 made by the British Government.[209]

One of Bosanquet's last tasks was his involvement with the Olympic Games in April 1906.[210] He recalled:

The Games have been fun and rather hard work. Today the Marathon race. Our team of four went to Marathon yesterday. We had two of them sleeping at the Hostel and have sent our cook to take care of them, and a hamper of provisions – I hope they may do well – 1 Australian, 1 Canadian, 1 South African Scot, and 1 glorious Galway bhoy …

One further aspect of Bosanquet's directorship was the growing concern about the health of students at the BSA. In 1905 there was alarm about typhoid in Athens;[211] it was reported 'there have been two cases of typhoid in the School during the last two years, and this in

---

[208] 'The Archaeological Congress at Athens', *The Times* 25 April 1905, 5.

[209] Macmillan, *et al.* 1903/04, 233.

[210] Bosanquet 1938, 164-65. A decision about his role was taken at the meeting of 13 March 1906 (BSA Minute Book 5).

[211] BSA Minute Book 5, Meeting of 17 October 1905.

spite of special precautions'.[212] Concerns had been expressed in 1904 that members of the American Mediterranean Fleet had contracted typhoid at Athens through the use of contaminated ice.[213] The issue was still present in 1908 when it was suggested that the hostel should use imported water.[214]

Assistant Directors

Bosanquet had been Assistant Director to Hogarth and had seen the way that the role shared the administrative load. He was assisted initially by Marcus Niebuhr Tod. Tod, the son of a Scottish tea merchant and a German mother,[215] was educated at Merchant Taylors' School in London (1892-97) and then read classics at St John's College, Oxford where he was a scholar; he took a double first in Classical Moderations (1899) and Literae Humaniores (1901). He was awarded the BSA's two year studentship worth £150 per year;[216] a new title of Senior Student was created. In February 1903 Tod was formally appointed Assistant Director.[217] The sum of £150 is also significant as this was the salary for Richards and Bosanquet in their role as Assistant Director. Loring, the Honorary Secretary, was known to have strong views about the role of the Assistant Director; in 1903 he resigned to become Director of Education in Yorkshire.

Tod excavated with Bosanquet at Palaiokastro in the spring of 1903, but that autumn returned to Oxford to take up a fellowship and tutorship in Ancient History at Oriel College (to which he had been elected in 1903). He then served as Assistant Director for two years (1903-05). In 1904/05 he was in Athens from October to early March where he had responsibilities for the Hostel and the Library.[218] He was also involved in an epigraphic survey of Laconia, found time to travel in Boeotia, and helped to prepare the report on 'Archaeology in Greece'.[219]

Tod's return to Oxford in March 1905 left the BSA without an Assistant Director just as the Penrose Memorial Library was about to open. Henry Julius Wetenhall Tillyard, who had completed Part II of the Classical Tripos at Caius in 1904, was appointed acting librarian of the newly opened Penrose Memorial Library.[220] Tillyard, like Tod, had a strong interest in epigraphy, and had been working on the boundary stones of Attica, as well as taking an active part in the Laconia project.

---

[212] BSA Minute Book 5, Meeting of 9 October 1906.

[213] 'The American fleet in the Mediterranean', *The Times* 28 July 1904, 9.

[214] BSA Minute Book 5, Meeting of 17 March 1908.

[215] Meiggs 1974.

[216] BSA Minute Book 4, Meeting of 13 December 1901.

[217] BSA Minute Book 4, Meeting of 12 February 1903. He was due to hold the position until the end of the 1903/04 Session.

[218] British School at Athens 1904/05, 313.

[219] Bosanquet and Tod 1902.

[220] 'The British School at Athens', *The Times* 26 October 1905, 13.

Bosanquet's Resignation

Bosanquet resigned as Director in July 1905 (though he did not leave for another year).[221] The Managing Committee was then faced with a dilemma. Clearly Tod, who had returned to his fellowship in Oxford, had been expected to succeed Bosanquet, in the same way that Bosanquet had been selected to follow Hogarth. In the view of the Managing Committee:

> if Mr Tod would stand his would be perhaps the most desirable and natural appointment.[222]

Other candidates also came to mind including Henry Stuart-Jones, presently the Director of the British School at Rome, as well as former students, among them John A. R. Munro (1864-1944), Fellow of Lincoln College, Oxford, and John L. Myres (1869-1954), Student and Tutor of Christ Church. Among the younger students were Richard M. Dawkins (1871-1955), Alan J. B. Wace (1879-1957) and Frederick W. Hasluck (1878-1920).

Bosanquet had made a case for a new librarian (to replace Tod and the temporary position of Tillyard); and in October 1905 the Managing Committee appointed Hasluck, Tod's exact contemporary at the School, with a salary of £150.[223] Hasluck was simultaneously holding a fellowship at King's College, Cambridge. Of the other candidates considered for the post, Wace was appointed librarian at the British School at Rome to work with Henry Stuart-Jones on the sculpture catalogue.[224]

With the Assistant Director in place, the committee then turned to the question of replacing Bosanquet. In the case of Hogarth and Bosanquet, the appointments had been made one year in advance; however for the new Director deliberations were still going on in the spring of 1906, months before Bosanquet was due to leave. By the following spring the short list was down to three main candidates: Dawkins, Wace, and Duncan Mackenzie.[225] Other candidates, among them John L. Myres, were considered 'ineligible'; indeed Mackenzie wrote of 'the existence of a Cambridge combine to keep out Myres or any other candidate from Oxford'.[226] The minutes summarised the characteristics of each candidate.

> Mr Dawkins had the advantage (as compared with Mr. Wace) of years and experience. He was a capable worker in widely varied directions and had an adequate literary style. He was also a fellow of a well endowed college. Against this he might be considered a better worker than an inspirer of work in others, and not likely to be strong on the social side, though Miss Dawkins it was understood would probably fill the position of Director's sister adequately.

---

[221] BSA Minute Book 5, Meeting of 25 July 1905.

[222] BSA Minute Book 5, Meeting of 25 July 1905.

[223] BSA Minute Book 5, Meeting of 17 October 1905. It is perhaps telling that Hasluck was considered 'senior' to Dawkins and Wace (both admitted 1902/03). For Hasluck: Kakissis 2004.

[224] Gill 2004q; Gill 2004m.

[225] BSA Minute Book 5, Meeting of 13 March 1906. The election is discussed in Momigliano 1999, 75-79.

[226] Letter to Evans, 6 March 1906; quoted in Momigliano 1999, 76.

Mr Duncan Mackenzie had had a long acquaintance with the practical side of archaeology of the prehellenic era and had also studied the art of the 'classical' age. He had also an exceptional experience of life in Greek lands. Against this it was doubted how far he would be d'accord either with the type of students ordinarily sent out or with the Managing Committee. His literary style was also against him.

Mr Wace had the merits and defects of his years. He was a competent and keen worker and capable of extracting work from others & probably a good teacher of the ordinary student in Museums. He had most of the qualities summed up in the word 'frank' to a marked degree, and would probably do fairly well on the social side. On the other hand he lacked at present the experience requisite for the handling of a delicate situation and his literary style was slovenly.[227]

At the last minute the Managing Committee also considered Burrows, a possibility explored by Harcourt-Smith. The reference that seemed to have won the day was from Dr James Adam (1860-1907) of Emmanuel College:

strongly advocating the claims of Mr. Dawkins not only as a Scholar and archaeologist but as a teacher and for his personal and social qualities.[228]

Although Evans tried to appoint Dawkins on a temporary appointment for one year, it was agreed to offer him the Directorship for three years at £500. The issue was then who to appoint as assistant; Mackenzie had made it clear that he would not serve under Dawkins.[229] It was felt that Hasluck's work in the library had so far been 'markedly successful', but wisely the decision was left to Dawkins; Hasluck was appointed. Hasluck remained as librarian, on the same stipend of £150, until 1915.[230] For one year, 1910/11, he was on leave of absence and was replaced by Arthur M. Woodward (1883-1973). During Richard M. Dawkins' leave of absence (1911/12) Hasluck served as acting Director.

Richard MacGillivray Dawkins (1906-14)

Richard Dawkins was born in 1871 at Surbiton, Surrey. His father, Richard, had been a captain in the Royal Navy, and his mother, Mary Louisa McGillivray, was the granddaughter of Sir John Easthope (1784-1865), the Liberal MP for several constituencies including St Albans, Banbury and Leicester.[231] Dawkins' father had commanded the ironclad HMS *Vanguard* that was accidentally rammed by HMS *Iron Duke* and sank off Kingstown (Dun Laoghaire) in 1875. In spite of this unfortunate

---

[227] BSA Minute Book 5, Meeting of 13 March 1906; quoted in Momigliano 1999, 77-78.

[228] BSA Minute Book 5, Meeting of 13 March 1906.

[229] Momigliano 1999, 79.

[230] *E.g.* for the salary, BSA Minute Book 5, Meeting of 20 October 1908. For the decision not to reappoint Hasluck: BSA Minute Book 8, Meeting of 22 June 1915. See also Kakissis 2004, 216.

[231] Boase and McConnell 2004.

episode he retired to Stoke Gabriel in Devon in 1878 with the rank of Rear-Admiral. Dawkins had three sisters and one brother.[232]

Dawkins was educated at Totnes Grammar School (1881-84) and then Marlborough College (1884-90). He studied electrical engineering at King's College, London from where, in 1892, he joined the firm of electrical engineers at Chelmsford managed by Rookes Evelyn Bell Crompton (1845-1940).[233] It was in this period that Dawkins developed a strong interest in languages including Sanskrit, Icelandic and Finnish. The deaths of his parents in 1896 and 1897 brought Dawkins a legacy. This allowed him, in 1898 at the age of 26, to enter Emmanuel College, Cambridge to read classics. One of the fellows at Emmanuel was Peter Giles (1860-1935) who had a strong interest in comparative literature.[234] One of the other influences at Emmanuel was James Adam (1860-1907) who lectured on Plato and philosophy.[235] Dawkins was granted a scholarship at Emmanuel in 1899 and was awarded a first in both parts of the classical tripos (1901, 1902). Among his Cambridge contemporaries were Alan Wace (1879-1957) at Pembroke College, and Percy Ure (1879-1950) at Caius; all three later excavated in Greece. In 1902 Dawkins was awarded a Craven studentship and was admitted to the BSA where Bosanquet was Director; Wace was a fellow student. Dawkins was attracted to the Dodecanese including Karpathos working on local dialects.[236] He was involved with Bosanquet's excavations at Palaikastro on Crete.[237] Dawkins was elected a Fellow of Emmanuel College in 1904.

In 1906 Dawkins was appointed Director to succeed Bosanquet; the other candidates were Wace and Duncan Mackenzie.[238] That summer Dawkins and Wace, who had developed an interest in Greek embroidery, toured the southern Sporades. Evans had probably backed Mackenzie in the hope that the BSA would commit itself to working on Crete, thereby supporting his project at Knossos. However Bosanquet had already moved the main project to Laconia which Dawkins inherited. Dawkins directed four seasons of work in Laconia, with a focus on the sanctuary of Artemis Orthia.[239]

By late 1909 Greece was dominated by the Military League.[240] Kavvadias was the target of some hostility, and the League called for his resignation.[241] Among the

---

[232] Annie (b. c. 1873), Mary (b. c. 1875), Edith (b. c. 1879), and John (b. c. 1888). By 1901 John was at a Naval academy in Kent.

[233] Randell and McConnell 2004.

[234] Dawkins and Pickles 2004.

[235] Giles and Schofield 2004.

[236] Dawkins 1902/03e; Dawkins 1903/04i.

[237] Dawkins 1902/03a.

[238] Momigliano 1999, 77. The decision was taken on 27 March 1906.

[239] Dawkins 1906/07b; Dawkins 1907/08; Dawkins 1908/09b; Dawkins 1909/10b; Dawkins 1929.

[240] Clogg 1992, 75-76.

[241] 'Greece. Attack on the Ephor of Antiquities', *The Times* 24 November 1909, 5; 'The Greek Military League. A policy of proscription', *The Times* 25 November 1909, 5. The formal attack on Kavvadias was by Svornos, Director of the Numismatic Museum.

accusations was that he had 'restricted the operations of the Greek Archæological Society and of having furnished subsidies to foreign archæologists for the purpose of excavations'.[242] The League then issued a response, accepting 'the services which they [*sc.* the foreign archaeological institutes] have rendered to scientific investigation in Greece, and stating that its former observations referred only to the management of the Greek Archæological Society'.[243] Dawkins was among the directors of the archaeological institutes who prepared a protest that was delivered via the Legations.[244] It was reported:

> Replying to the charge that the foreigners have used the money of the Greek Archaeological Society in the interests of their own Governments and their own science, the directors declare formally that all their undertaking have been paid for from their own funds, and that Greece has only contributed by assuming the superintendence of the excavations, the preservation of the objects found, and in some cases the expropriation of the land, all these measures being taken in the interests of Greece herself.
>
> In regard to the charge of having stifled Greek archæological activity with the complicity of M. Kavvadias, and of having secured the best sites for excavation to the humiliation of Greek science and the greater glory of foreign research the directors, while thanking M. Kavvadias and the Greek Archæological authorities for the facilities accorded them, point out that their authorization to undertake excavations is derived from the Greek Government and the Chamber. There can, therefore, be no question of favouritism displayed towards foreigners …
>
> Finally, the directors rebut the statement that foreigners have requited the complacence of M. Kavvadias with honours and decorations, pointing out the absurdity of supposing that the distinctions conferred upon him by the Academies of Berlin and Paris and by the Universities of Cambridge and Leipsig could thus be bought. Far from despising Greece, as has been asserted, foreign archæologists chose Athens as the seat of their first Congress – at which M. Kavvadias played so important a part – thus restoring her ancient prestige as the metropolis of antiquarian studies.

The protest was published in the Greek press and *Embros* acknowledged 'the great services rendered to Greece by the [archaeological] schools, which have made Athens the principal archaeological centre of the world'.[245] It continued to comment on the foreign archaeologists working in Greece: 'Their high position in the world of science and their great services placed them beyond all reach of any misconception.' The accusation centred round the collaborative work between the Greek Archaeological Society and

---

[242] 'Greece. Attack on the Ephor of Antiquities', *The Times* 24 November 1909, 5.

[243] 'The Greek Military League. A policy of proscription', *The Times* 25 November 1909, 5.

[244] 'Greece. The Military League and foreign archaeologists', *The Times* 26 November 1909, 5.

[245] 'Greece. The Chamber and military service', *The Times* 29 November 1909, 5.

A. Brückner of the DAI in the Kerameikos.[246] Kavvadias was forced to step down and Christos D. Tsountas took his place.[247]

Once the work at Sparta had been completed, Dawkins hoped to initiate an excavation at Datcha in Anatolia and the tholos tomb at Kirik Kilissa. Both plans were disrupted by the outbreak of Italo-Turkish War and the Balkans War.[248] As a result Dawkins returned to Melos in 1911, where he re-excavated Phylakopi.[249] Excavations continued to be thwarted by the volatile political situations in the Aegean. Salonica had fallen to Greek troops in November 1912, and the eastern Aegean islands of Lesbos, Chios and Samos had changed hands. The island of Rhodes had been occupied by the Italians during the hostilities. Against this background Dawkins was reappointed for a further year in 1913.[250] Unable to work in Anatolia, Dawkins excavated at the Kamares Cave in 1913.[251] Alongside the expected fieldwork, Dawkins developed his long-standing interest in philology and dialect. From Karpathos he looked to Anatolia and the Greek communities in Cappadocia, which he researched in three journeys in 1909, 1910 and 1911.[252]

Dawkins' personal situation changed in 1907 when John Andrew Doyle (1844-1907), historian and fellow of All Souls, Oxford, died. Doyle was a grandson of Sir John Easthope and cousin of Dawkins' mother. Dawkins inherited Plas Dulas in Denbighshire, North Wales, and Penderren near Crickhowell in Breconshire, South Wales. This gave Dawkins the means to resign the directorship in 1914, although he continued his research and was in Trebizond as the First World War broke out.

The health of Dawkins' sister was giving concern and as a result he asked for a year's leave of absence from October 1911.[253] In 1911 Dawkins was due to be on research leave and Hasluck was appointed temporary Director at a salary of £300.[254]

After war service in naval intelligence, working largely on Crete, Dawkins was appointed to the Bywater and Sotheby chair of Byzantine and modern Greek at Oxford in 1920. A fellowship at Exeter College (1922) followed. Dawkins died in Oxford in 1955.

---

[246] 'Greece. King George and the situation', *The Times* 6 December 1909, 5. For the Kerameikos excavations: Knigge 1991, 166.

[247] 'Greece. Officers and the Military League', *The Times* 3 December 1909, 5.

[248] 'British School at Athens. Effect of the war on research', *The Times* 30 October 1912, 11. Kirik Kilissa, to the east of Edirne (Adrianople), was occupied by Bulgarian troops on 14 October 1912: Forster 1941, 50.

[249] Dawkins 1910/11b.

[250] BSA Minute Book 7, Meeting of 22 July 1913. He indicated that he would not continue after October 1914: Meeting of 7 October 1913.

[251] Dawkins and Laistner 1912/13.

[252] Dawkins 1910c; Dawkins 1910b; Dawkins and Halliday 1916; Dawkins 1934. See also Mackridge 1990.

[253] BSA Minute Book 6, Meeting of 4 October 1910.

[254] BSA Minute Book 6, Meeting of 28 February 1911.

The Assistant Directors: Arthur M. Woodward

Hasluck continued as Librarian and Assistant Director. Arthur M. Woodward had been admitted as a student in 1906/07 during Dawkins' first year of office. He had studied at Magdalen College, Oxford and had completed Greats in the summer of 1906. He had been involved in the Laconia project and had taken particular responsibility for the inscriptions.[255] He also became involved in the Asia Minor Exploration Fund travelling in Lycia.[256] When Hasluck was given leave of absence in 1910/11, Woodward was a natural choice to fill the gap as Assistant Director.[257] At the end of the year he was appointed Assistant Lecturer at Liverpool, and in 1912 a Reader at Leeds. War intervened and he served in military intelligence in Salonica. In 1923 he succeeded Wace as Director of the BSA.

Alan John Bayard Wace (1914-23)

By November 1913 the Managing Committee was considering the replacement for Dawkins.[258] Guy Dickins was clearly being considered but he had declined to stand, no doubt as he had a fellowship at St John's College, Oxford as well as the position of University Lecturer in Ancient History. In the event Wace was appointed Director from 1914 for three years for £500.[259]

Alan Wace was born in Cambridge in 1879.[260] His father Frederic Charles Wace (1836-93) was a mathematician at St John's College and Mayor of Cambridge (1890-91). His mother, Fanny, was the daughter of John Campbell Bayard, a former army officer, and the family had New York links. Wace's father died in 1893, and the family returned to Shropshire, close to the Bayard family home. Wace was educated at Shrewsbury School and subsequently admitted to Pembroke College, Cambridge in 1898. He was awarded a first in both parts of the classical tripos (1901, 1902). One of the key influences on Wace was his tutor, Robert Alexander Neil (1852-1901), who had a strong interest in philology and Sanskrit.[261]

In 1906 Wace had been a candidate for the directorship of the School as Bosanquet's successor.[262] In the meantime he had been librarian at the British School at Rome, and had

[255] Woodward 1906/07; Tod, *et al.* 1906/07; Woodward 1907/08; Woodward 1908/09a; Woodward 1909/10a.

[256] Woodward and Ormerod 1909/10.

[257] Woodward was discussed at the meeting of 25 May 1909 (BSA Minute Book 6). This was accepted at the meeting of 13 July 1909. Droop was considered as a substitute if Woodward was unable to take up the post.

[258] BSA Minute Book 7, Meeting of 18 November 1913.

[259] BSA Minute Book 7, Meeting of 18 November 1913. Wace accepted at the meeting of 24 March 1914. For the announcement: 'British School at Athens. New director', *The Times* 23 December 1913.

[260] Gill 2004q.

[261] Giles and Hardy 2004.

[262] Minutes of the management committee, 13 March 1906, quoted in Momigliano 1999, 78. The decision was taken on 27 March 1906.

been working on prehistoric sites in Thessaly and Macedonia. He was particularly interested in the debate about the connection between the Aegean (especially Crete) and Central Europe in the Bronze Age.[263] Wace had become an authority on the prehistoric Aegean and classical sculpture. He was appointed a lecturer in Ancient History and Archaeology at the University of St Andrews in 1912.

Wace took up office in the autumn of 1914 but by then Britain was at war with Germany.[264] An attempt was made to continue the work of the BSA, and Wace was joined in Greece by V. Gordon Childe of The Queen's College, Oxford, who had been admitted as an Associate.[265] Childe, supported by Myres and Hogarth, worked on the prehistoric pottery of the mainland; the Balkans were a focal point in his later work.[266] Wace was invited to work with Bert Hodge Hill on ASCSA's excavation at Corinth.[267] Wace had to cope with the presence of Duncan Mackenzie, who had been hoping to excavate in Thessaly in 1915.[268] Administrative pressure was increased on Wace when the Managing Committee decided not to reappoint Hasluck.[269]

In 1916 the BSA and ASCSA considered the purchase of an extra piece of land on Odos Spevsippou, perhaps for the construction of a hostel for women.[270] The initial offer was for 40,000 francs, though this was raised to 50,000, against an asking price of 65,000.[271] The BSA was evacuated in December 1916 and the keys formally handed over to ASCSA. The vacated School was then the subject of a burglary, and as a result iron bars had to be placed in the windows.[272]

In 1917 Wace was reappointed as Director for three years though he continued to work with the British Legation until 1919. In 1919 Stanley Casson was appointed as Assistant Director and Librarian at a salary of £200,[273] and Wace's position as Director was renewed for a further term of three years partly as he had had no 'opportunity of

---

[263] Peet, *et al.* 1908; Thompson and Wace 1909.

[264] For more detail see chapter 13, below.

[265] BSA Minute Book 8, Meeting of 16 February 1915.

[266] Childe 1915.

[267] BSA Minute Book 8, Meeting of 23 November 1915. See Lord 1947, 300 (October-Christmas 1915).

[268] BSA Minute Book 8, Meeting of 10 December 1914. For the concerns among the members of the Managing Committee: Momigliano 1999, 123-24.

[269] BSA Minute Book 8, Meeting of 22 June 1915: 'to express the warm appreciation of the committee of his long and valuable service to the School'.

[270] BSA Minute Book 8, Meeting of 20 June 1916. For full details: Lord 1947, 121; Waterhouse 1986, 57.

[271] BSA Minute Book 8, Meeting of 21 November 1916; November 27, 1917. The 50,000 was divided between ASCSA (27,777. 80) and the BSA (22,222. 20). The purchase was completed in 1919: BSA Minute Book 8, Meeting of 20 May 1919.

[272] BSA Minute Book 8, Meeting of 12 June 1917.

[273] BSA Minute Book 8, Meeting of 20 May 1919.

archaeological work' during the war years.[274] Wace continued as Director until 1923 when he was replaced by Woodward. This then marked a period of marked hostility with Evans. Wace accepted the post of Deputy Keeper in the Department of Textiles at the Victoria and Albert Museum until he succeeded A. B. Cook as Laurence Professor of Classical Archaeology in Cambridge.

The British Legation

The success of the School was partly to do with the support it received from the British Legation in Athens.[275] This was especially noted by the Prince of Wales in his speech to the meeting of the BSA in July 1895.[276] Negotiations for the plot of land and the construction of the BSA had been handled by Sir (Francis) Clare Ford (1828-99) who had been in Athens from March 1881 until December 1884.

In 1885 there had been a change of political direction in Greece with the defeat of Trikoupis and the election of Theodoros Deliyannis. This led to Sir Horace Rumbold (1829-1913), the British Envoy-Extraordinary in Athens (1884-88), presenting the Greek government with a threat that the Royal Navy would be sent to the Aegean.[277] The situation was eased by the resignation of Deliyannis, but it left the country with an economic crisis. Some of the negotiations for the BSA were left to Arthur Nicolson (1849-1928), the *Chargé d'Affaires* in Athens (1884-85). James Rennell Rodd (1858-1941) was second secretary at Athens from 1888 to c. 1890. As Baron Rennell of Rodd (from 1933) he pursued his interest in archaeology through the support of the BSA's work on Ithaca.[278]

Rumbold was replaced by Sir Edmund (John) Monson (1834-1909). He had been educated at Eton and Balliol College, Oxford. He was in Athens until 1892 when he was succeeded by Sir Edwin (Henry) Egerton (b. 1841). He was supportive of the work of Harcourt-Smith, Hogarth and Bosanquet, although Harcourt-Smith did not find him easy:[279]

> Between you and me, my chief difficulty is Egerton – he is a most extraordinary individual – with the best intentions in the world (and I know that he is only too anxious to help me) he is really very difficult. He never meets me but what he lectures me by the hour about Gardner's good qualities, and is for ever advising me to do nothing without consulting Gardner. Of course I do not mind in the least, but I tell you because it is well that you should known what Egerton is.

---

[274] BSA Minute Book 8, Meeting of 17 June 1919.

[275] Macmillan 1910/11, xxxvi.

[276] 'The British School at Athens', *The Times*, 10 July 1895, 10.

[277] 'The Eastern Crisis', *The Times* 25 January 1886, 5. It was left to Louisa Rumbold to appeal to readers of *The Times* (1 March 1886) to send financial support to Greece to support the families of reservists.

[278] Waterhouse 1986, 32. *E.g.* Heurtley and Lorimer 1932/33.

[279] Letter to George Macmillan, 13 December 1895 (Macmillan Archive). I am grateful to C. A. Stray for drawing my attention to this letter.

Egerton, a nephew of Lord Egerton of Tatton (a benefactor of the BSA), had entered the diplomatic service in 1859 and had been a secretary at Athens in 1881 (under Ford). He had subsequently seen service in Egypt, Constantinople and Paris. In 1903 he was appointed British Ambassador to Madrid; *The Times* noted

> Sir Edwin took the warmest interest in the progress of antiquarian research in Greece, and especially in the work of the British School of Archaeology, to which he rendered important services. [280]

Egerton was replaced by Sir Francis (Edmund Hugh) Elliott, the son of the diplomat Sir Henry George Elliott (1817-1907) who had served in Athens (1862-63). He supported Bosanquet, Dawkins and Wace. Stanley Casson describes him at Athens during the aftermath of the Gallipoli campaign:

> Alone in a wilderness of honest men striving to be dishonest because it was fashionable, of dishonest men in lamb's clothing, of incompetent spies, of blasé secretaries, and of archaeologists thrilled to be in the limelight dressed as diplomats, stood the figure of Sir Francis Elliot, the only just man. He, as British Minister of long standing, the doyen of the Diplomatic Corps, knew not only Greece but Constantine like a book. He knew exactly where the Royal family was wrong and exactly how far they were right. A man of immaculate impartiality he tried to do justice to all. But a Foreign Office that would not take his advice and could not in any case understand it, made all his endeavours futile. He was driven in the end to do his best simply to hold the ring and try to get fair play. [281]

The pressure of the events of the winter of 1916/17 meant that he was withdrawn to London and he was elected to the BSA Managing Committee. He was replaced at Athens by Lord Granville.

---

[280] *The Times* 30 December 1903.

[281] Casson 1935, 122-23.

CHAPTER 3
THE BSA MANAGING COMMITTEE

The London base for the BSA was initially the Royal Asiatic Society at 22 Albemarle Street in London. The Managing Committee consisted of four distinct groups: the Trustees, the Officers (Treasurer and Secretary), the members elected by the subscribers, and the members nominated by the corporate bodies.[1] The role was defined as:

> The Committee shall have control of all the affairs of the School, and shall decide any dispute that may arise between the Director and Students. They shall have power to deprive any Student of the use of the school-building.[2]

The original members of the Committee consisted of 'five members . . . appointed by the general body of subscribers': Professor Percy Gardner (1846-1937), John Gennadius (1844-1932; the Greek Minister in London), Professor Richard Claverhouse Jebb (1841-1905), Sir Frederic Leighton (1830-96) and Mr John Edwin Sandys (1844-1922).[3] This reflected influences from Oxford (Gardner), Cambridge (Sandys), and the Royal Academy of Arts (Leighton), as well as the political dimension of the Greek Minister. Gardner had been editor of the *Journal of Hellenic Studies*, an assistant in the Department of Coins and Medals at the British Museum, and (from 1880) Disney Professor of Archaeology at Cambridge; in 1887 he was elected to the Lincoln and Merton Chair of Classical Archaeology at Oxford. Sandys was a Fellow of St John's College, Cambridge, as well as the university's orator. Leighton was a painter and member of the Royal Academy. The influence of Cambridge was further strengthened on the committee when Jebb, who had been holding the chair of Greek at Glasgow, moved back to Cambridge and the Regius Chair of Greek in 1889.

The Trustees

The regulations of the School allowed for three Trustees 'who shall be appointed for life'. The three original trustees, in place for the formal setting up of the School in 1884, were (Sir) James Tynte Agg-Gardner, MP; Pandeli Ralli; and Charles Waring.[4] All three had served as Members of Parliament: Agg-Gardner as a Conservative, Ralli and Waring as

---

[1] For an overview: Waterhouse 1986, 53-55.

[2] 'Rules and Regulations', no. xiv (1910/11).

[3] Macmillan 1910/11, xxviii. Details of the early decisions and workings of the committee are unclear due to the loss of the crucial first volume of minutes. For Gennadius: *The Times* 8 September 1932.

[4] Agg-Gardner: Davenport-Hines 2004. Ralli: *The Times* 1 July 1880, 12. Obituary: *The Times* 23 August 1928, 14. Waring: *Pall Mall Gazette* 1 September 1887.

Liberals. However, their seats were far from secure: Agg-Gardner lost his seat for Cheltenham in 1880 but was re-elected in 1885; Ralli had been MP for Wallingford from 1880 until the constituency disappeared in 1885; Waring had been MP for Poole but had been disqualified from standing due to charges including bribery. Thus their political influence was not as influential as it might at first seem.

Agg-Gardner had studied at Trinity College, Cambridge, and probably knew Jebb. Ralli had been educated at London. His family originated from Chios and he was part of the successful London-based trading company, the Ralli Brothers, that had close links with William Gladstone. Ralli had been elected a Fellow of the Royal Geographical Society in 1870 and was a founder member of the Hellenic Society; he was elected to its Council along with Walter Leaf.[5] Ralli attended the 1883 meeting at Marlborough House,[6] and was supportive of the reforms of the School in 1895.[7] Waring was a successful railway contractor not just in Britain but also in North and Central America, continental Europe, and Sri Lanka.

By the time of the reforms of 1895/96 only Ralli remained as a trustee. Agg-Gardner appears to have resigned and Waring died in 1887. They had been replaced by Edwin Freshfield (1858-1918), and Richard Jebb. Freshfield was a well-respected solicitor among whose clients included William Gladstone and The Bank of England.[8] Freshfield's cousin Douglas was one of the original auditors for the Hellenic Society.[9] Edwin Freshfield had been educated at Winchester and Trinity College, Cambridge, and was a Life Member of the Hellenic Society; he was also the treasurer of the Society of Antiquaries. In 1861 he had married Zoë Charlotte Hanson, daughter of J. F. Hanson of the Levant Company. Freshfield was a strong supporter of the excavations at Silchester, sponsoring the excavation of one of the insulae for £300.[10] He developed a strong interest in Byzantine architecture, supporting work of students in the early years of the BSA, and in 1908 helping to establish the Byzantine Research Fund.[11]

Ralli resigned as Trustee in 1900 'on the ground that constant absence from London prevents him from taking any active part in the management of the School'.[12] The position was taken by George Macmillan, who had previously served as Honorary Secretary of the School. The vacancy created by Jebb's death in 1905 was filled by Walter Leaf who had served as Honorary Treasurer from 1886.

---

[5] Hellenic Society 1880, xxiii. See also Macmillan 1929, 3. Election to Council: Hellenic Society 1882, xliv. Ralli retired from Council in 1887 on Rotation.

[6] *The Times* 26 June 1883, 8.

[7] *The Times* 10 July 1895, 11.

[8] Obituary in *The Times* 2 September 1918, 10.

[9] Hellenic Society 1880, xv. See Brown and Butlin 2004.

[10] 'Discoveries at Silchester', *The Times* 1 September 1890, 5; 'Recent excavations at Silchester', *The Times* 1 January 1891, 7.

[11] *E.g.* Freshfield 1881b; Freshfield 1881a; Freshfield 1890; Freshfield 1908.

[12] British School at Athens 1899/1900, 132.

The Treasurer and Secretary

Walter Leaf (1852-1927) and George Augustin Macmillan (1855-1936) were the original treasurer and secretary, both in an honorific capacity. Leaf had been appointed treasurer to the small working party formed in 1883. He had been educated at Harrow, and taught by Jebb in Cambridge when he was a classical scholar of Trinity.[13] Leaf had subsequently been elected a Fellow of Trinity (1875), although he returned to London to help with the family silk and ribbon business. He later became a director of the London and Westminster Bank (1891), and a founder of the London Chamber of Commerce. He had continued his interest in classical scholarship, publishing on Homer including a two-volume edition of the *Iliad* (1886-88); he was elected to the Council of the Hellenic Society in 1882 (at the same time as Ralli).[14] Leaf was awarded a LittD from Cambridge in 1889.[15] He served as Honorary Treasurer to the BSA until 1905 when he was elected a Trustee to replace Jebb.

Leaf was replaced as Honorary Treasurer by Vincent Wodehouse Yorke (1869-1957) (who continued in this capacity until 1955). He had been educated at Eton and then King's College, Cambridge, before being admitted as a student to the BSA under Ernest Gardner (1892-94).[16] He was elected a Fellow of King's in 1895, and worked on the epigraphy of eastern Asia Minor.[17] Yorke was a director of National Provident Institution, a director (like Leaf) of the London and Westminster Bank (1903), and subsequently chairman of the Mexican Railway Ltd. Yorke was key in helping to raise funds for the excavations in Laconia,[18] and the Macedonian Exploration Fund.[19]

The first Honorary Secretary of the BSA was George Augustin Macmillan (1855-1936) who served for ten years (1886-97).[20] He had been educated at Eton (King's Scholar) and had then entered the family publishing business in 1874. He held this position alongside the same role for the Society for the Promotion of Hellenic Studies.[21]

Macmillan was replaced by William Loring (1865-1915).[22] Loring, like Yorke, had been educated at Eton and King's College, Cambridge. He had been admitted to the BSA under Ernest Gardner (1889-93), and took part in the Megalopolis excavations.[23] He was elected a

---

[13] Lubenow 2004.

[14] Hellenic Society 1882, xliv.

[15] Leaf 1910/11; Leaf 1911/12a; Leaf 1911/12b; Leaf 1914/16.

[16] Bather and Yorke 1892; Yorke 1892; Yorke 1896a.

[17] Yorke 1896b; Yorke 1898.

[18] Yorke 1907.

[19] 'Macedonian Exploration Fund', *The Times* 15 March 1911, 5. Yorke was the treasurer of this fund.

[20] Discussed in Arsdel 2004. For his obituary: *The Times* 4 March 1936.

[21] Macmillan 1929.

[22] The decision was taken at the meeting of 8 April 1897, and Loring accepted on 27 May 1897 (BSA Minute Book 2).

[23] Gardner, *et al.* 1890; Loring 1890; Dörpfeld, *et al.* 1891; Gardner, *et al.* 1892; Loring 1892/1893; Loring 1895b; Loring 1895a.

Fellow of King's (1891-97). Prior to his appointment as Honorary Secretary Loring had served on the Managing Committee. As well as his academic interests, Loring was an Examiner for the Board of Education (1894-1903). Loring clearly held strong opinions and at the end of Hogarth's first year as director expressed a view on the 'educational duties' of the director.[24] In 1899 Loring enlisted to fight in the Boer War and during his absence, Macmillan filled the gap. When Ralli resigned as a Trustee in 1900 Macmillan took his place. Macmillan became chairman of the Managing Committee in 1903 (until 1933).[25]

With Loring still in South Africa, Robert J. G. Mayor (1869-1947) was appointed temporary Honorary Secretary.[26] Mayor, like Loring, had been educated at Eton and King's, had been admitted to the BSA under Gardner (1892/93), and had been awarded a fellowship at King's (1894). Like Loring, he was also a member of the Education Department. Loring returned to England and continued to serve as Honorary Secretary for the BSA until 1903 when he was appointed Director of Education under the West Riding County Council (1903-05).

Loring's place was taken by John ffoliot Baker Penoyre (1870-1954) who had been a student at Keble College, Oxford, an Assistant Master at Chigwell School (1896-1900), and had then been admitted to the BSA in 1900/01: he also acted as an extension lecturer on classical art and archaeology at Oxford University. The previous holders of the post had held honorary positions, but the situation had changed. The position of Secretary attracted a salary of £40 per year split between the BSA (£25) and the British School at Rome (BSR) (£15).[27] Like Loring, Penoyre acted as Secretary to the BSR (1904-12).[28] In 1904 Baker Penoyre was appointed Secretary for the Hellenic Society at £80 per year (where he also served as Librarian at £60 per year). In January 1907 Penoyre was granted a year's leave of absence for 'travel and research', and was re-admitted to the BSA.[29] He was replaced by Katherine Raleigh (the translator of *The Gods of Olympus* [1892]) at a salary of £20. Due to 'serious illness' Penoyre's leave was extended to March 1.[30] He returned to duties but by February 1909 it was minuted:

> The Committee urged Mr Penoyre to cultivate the art of saying 'No' to requests which seemed to go beyond his reasonable function as Secretary and Librarian.[31]

From 1911 (to 1920) Caroline Amy Hutton, another former BSA student (1896/97), served as acting Honorary Secretary. She had served as joint editor of the *Annual* from 1906.

[24] BSA Minute Book 3, Meeting of 28 July 1898.

[25] Waterhouse 1986, 53.

[26] BSA Minute Book 3, Meeting of 25 April 1901. This was confirmed at the meeting of 20 June 1901 (BSA Minute Book 4).

[27] BSA Minute Book 4, Meeting of 29 July 1903.

[28] For the background: Wiseman 1990; Wallace-Hadrill 2001.

[29] BSA Minute Book 5, Meeting of 8 January 1907. The leave would be from 16 January 1907, at half salary. During this time he worked on Thasos: Baker-Penoyre and Tod 1909; Baker-Penoyre 1909.

[30] BSA Minute Book 5, Meeting of 21 January 1908.

[31] BSA Minute Book 6, Meeting of 2 February 1909.

The Members Elected by the Subscribers

The elected part of the committee grew steadily from at least nine members in 1894/95 to twelve by the outbreak of the First World War.[32] There was a rotating retirement that allowed a period of office of three years. Those elected could stand for re-election (which many committee members did). One of the reasons for the expansion was due to the custom of inviting the outgoing Director to join the committee: Penrose (from 1887 until his death in 1903), Ernest Gardner (from 1895), Harcourt-Smith (from 1897), Hogarth (who had earlier served on the committee), Bosanquet (from 1906), and Dawkins (from 1914). The committee was dominated by Cambridge and Oxford academics with an interest in the classical world.

Cambridge was well represented on the committee, in addition to the former directors. Sandys had been an elected member before he became the representative for the University of Cambridge. Other permanent members included Jane Harrison, Fellow of Newnham College, who had supported the School from the early negotiations. She was also a key champion for women at the BSA. James S. Reid, Fellow of Gonville & Caius College and Professor of Ancient History (1899-1925), was also the brother-in-law to Percy and Ernest Gardner (and was particularly close to Ernest). He was co-opted on to the working-party for the creation of the British School at Rome.[33] Charles Waldstein had a distinguished career with experience of excavating in Greece (through ASCSA).[34] He had been appointed lecturer in Classics (1880), Reader in Classical Archaeology (1883-1907), simultaneously holding the directorship of the Fitzwilliam (1883-89), and the Slade Chair of Art (1895-1901, 1904-11). A further influence was Leonard Whibley, Fellow of Pembroke College (1889) and University Lecturer in Ancient History (1899-1910).[35] He was a donor to the Macedonian Exploration Fund, probably to support his former student, Alan Wace.

One of the early Cambridge members of the committee was Sir Thomas Clifford Allbutt (1836-1925).[36] He had been educated at Caius (1855), where he was awarded a classical scholarship (1856), although he subsequently turned to medicine; in 1892 he was appointed the Regius Professor of Physic at Cambridge. It was during this Cambridge period that he served on the Managing Committee. It is likely that he served on the Committee because of the college's financial support for Ernest Gardner as Director. Several Cambridge educated students served on the committee: Penrose, Gardner, Bosanquet, and Dawkins as former directors; Vincent Yorke as Honorary Treasurer; William Loring and Robert Mayor as Honorary Secretaries. Wace served on the committee before becoming Director.

Oxford was represented by Henry Francis Pelham (1846-1907), the Camden Professor of Ancient History (from 1889). From 1882 he served on the committee of the Asia Minor Exploration Fund (which supported William Ramsay); his colleagues on the committee included David B. Monro, Provost of Oriel College, who was the nominated member for

---

[32] 'Rules and Regulations' (1894/95) xiii [9]; (1910/11) xiii [12]; (1914/15) xiii [12].

[33] Wiseman 1990, 3.

[34] Lord 1947, 51.

[35] Roberts and Pottle 2004.

[36] Rolleston and Bearn 2004. He was knighted in 1907.

Oxford on the BSA's Managing Committee. A third member of the Asia Minor Committee was George Macmillan. Pelham was a key person in the development of the British School at Rome.[37]

Three Oxford men were a major force on the committee and were key in developing the work on Crete. John Linton Myres (1869-1954) had been a student at the BSA (1892-95) alongside a fellowship at Magdalen College (1892-95). He returned to Oxford as a Student of Christ Church (1895-1907) and University Lecturer in Classical Archaeology. It was at this point he joined the Managing Committee. He travelled on Crete with Arthur John Evans (1851-1941), who had been appointed Keeper of the Ashmolean Museum in 1884; Evans joined the Managing Committee in 1900, once the Cretan Exploration Fund had been established.[38] Myres, after a spell in Liverpool, returned to Oxford as the Wykeham Professor of Ancient History (1910-39); he later served as the chair of the Managing Committee from 1933 to 1947 as a successor to Macmillan.[39] Evans continued as a member of the Managing Committee and was partly responsible for the unhappiness surrounding Wace after the First World War. Francis J. Haverfield (1860-1919) briefly served on the Committee when he was Senior Student and Tutor at Christ Church.[40]

David George Hogarth (1862-1927) had been the first Oxford student at the BSA (1886/87). He served on the Managing Committee before being appointed as Director (1897-1900). He subsequently worked with Evans on the Cretan Exploration Fund, and in 1908 succeeded Evans as Keeper of the Ashmolean Museum. A further influential figure from Oxford was Marcus Niebuhr Tod (1878-1974). He was a student at the BSA (1901/02) and then Assistant Director (1902-04). He was elected a fellow of Oriel College in 1903 (although he was allowed to remain in Greece) and became Tutor in Ancient History in 1905. In 1907 he was appointed University Lecturer in Greek Epigraphy. A later Oxford member of the committee was Sir Alfred Eckhard Zimmern (1879-1957).[41] Like several of the BSA students he was educated at Winchester and New College (Lit. Hum. 1902), becoming a Fellow and Tutor (1904-09). He worked on political aspects of Greek history and was admitted as an associate of the BSA in 1910.[42] He was later an Inspector of the Board of Education (1912-15). Among the Oxford trained students was James Theodore Bent (1852/97; Wadham), the explorer of the Cyclades in the days prior to the founding of the BSA.

The committee always had a balancing act between members from Oxford and Cambridge. The representative for the Royal Academy was Sir Reginald Theodore Blomfield (1856-1942).[43] He was educated at Haileybury and Exeter College, Oxford. He was Professor of Architecture at the Royal Academy (1906), and President of RIBA (1912). He was involved with the setting up of the BSR which had a strong architectural interest.

---

[37] Wiseman 1990; Wallace-Hadrill 2001.

[38] In April 1899 Evans introduced himself (incorrectly) to the authorities on Crete as a representative of the BSA's Managing Committee: MacGillivray 2000, 164.

[39] Waterhouse 1986, 53.

[40] For Haverfield: Freeman 2007.

[41] Markwell 2004.

[42] Zimmern 1911.

[43] Briggs and Fellows 2004.

Several of the architectural students served on the committee: Theodore Fyfe, who worked with Evans on Crete, Walter S. George, of the Byzantine Fund, and Harry Herbert Jewell. Sir Francis Elliot, the head of the British Legation in Athens, joined the committee towards the end of the War after he had left Greece.

Nominated members

The 'Rules and Regulations' specified that 'A corporate body subscribing not less than £50 a year, for a term of years, shall, during that term, have the right to nominate a member of the Managing Committee'.[44] In the first period of the School both the Hellenic Society and Oxford University gave an annual grant of £100. The Hellenic Society was represented by Sidney Colvin (1845-1927).[45] He had been Slade Professor of Fine Art in Cambridge (1873-85) and Director of the Fitzwilliam Museum (1876-84), but had moved to be Keeper of Prints and Drawings at the British Museum. The University of Oxford's nominee on the Managing committee was David Binning Monro (1836-1905), Provost of Oriel College (from 1882).[46] In 1896 the University of Cambridge became an active supporter of the School (also with a £100 grant) and was thus given the right to nominate a member of the committee, Professor William Ridgeway.[47]

All three nominees were changed. In 1904/05 Ridgeway was replaced by Sandys as the nominated member for Cambridge. Sandys was a Fellow of St John's College (1867) and lecturer (1867-1907) and had been one of the original members of the Managing Committee. Monro died in 1905; he was succeeded by Professor Percy Gardner (1846-1937), who held the Lincoln and Merton chair in Classical Archaeology (from 1887). Gardner had served on the original Managing Committee when he held the Disney chair of archaeology in Cambridge. Gardner was a regular member of the committee but during the First World War the Oxford Grant lapsed and the university had no right of representation on the committee.[48] Oxford's donation was increased to the crucial £50 in 1917 and that allowed Gardner to return in June 1917.[49] Colvin was replaced by Jane Harrison of Newnham College. She had earlier served on the Managing Committee as one of those elected by the subscribers. The Hellenic Society reduced its grant to £50 for the duration of the War.[50]

Finance

Support for the BSA was initially through subscription. For the first ten years the income of the BSA was around £450 per year, though there was additional support from Gonville &

[44] 'Rules and Regulations', no. VI (1894/95).

[45] Mehew 2004. For Colvin's nomination: Hellenic Society 1887, xlvii (21 October 1886).

[46] Phelps and Smail 2004.

[47] Macmillan incorrectly cites Sandys as the first Cambridge nomination: Macmillan 1910/11, xxix. The Cambridge grant came from the Worts Fund, initially for three years: *The Times* 30 October 1895, 6.

[48] BSA Minute Book 8, Meeting of 12 October 1915. The grant was eventually reduced to £25 for 1915, and £25 for 1916 (Meeting of 23 November 1915).

[49] BSA Minute Book 8, Meeting of 20 June 1916. Percy Gardner returned for June 12, 1917.

[50] BSA Minute Book 8, Meeting of 3 April 1917.

Caius, which paid for Gardner's salary as Director. Oxford University and the Hellenic Society had also given £100 each during this period. By the summer of 1898 there was a realisation that the BSA needed an income of some £600 to £700.[51] A grant of £200 had been awarded the school from the Royal Bounty Fund in 1893/94.[52] However Cecil Harcourt-Smith realised that the funds were inadequate for an active research institute that sought to develop field projects. There were three main changes. First, he encouraged a larger number of subscribers. Second, he developed the number of corporate subscribers; Cambridge University matched Oxford's contribution of £100, and various Oxford and Cambridge colleges provided another £50 or so a year. Third, he persuaded the government to provide a grant of £500 from 1896/97 that in effect paid for the Director. This formed just over a quarter of the income for the BSA from 1894 to 1918. The government grant was a continuing matter of concern and open for renewal at regular five year intervals.

The income rose from £450 for 1887/88 to over £3,000 for 1907/08 (although this was in part to fund the Laconia project). However there were recognised issues about fund raising. As the BSA developed its work on Melos (and in particular at Phylakopi) and anticipated further excavations at Colophon and possibly Xanthus in the spring of 1897, it was reminded that not only was it trying to raise money for the new hostel, but that the public was giving to other funds such as the Indian Famine Fund, in addition to the preparations for the 60th anniversary for Queen Victoria.[53] Overall some 13% of the income of the BSA in the period 1894 to 1918 was earmarked for excavations.

The war years saw increasing concern though the BSA was helped by the decision of Christ Church, Oxford to renew its grant for three years.[54] It is likely that John G. C. Anderson had a hand in the decision. The BSA also decided to invest around £1,000 in the War Loan that in the end gave a good return.[55] In 1917 the Government Grant was suspended. However after an appeal it was decided to transfer the grant from 'the Science and Art List' to 'The Foreign Office Vote'.[56] The Government Grant was re-instated in 1919.[57]

Donors

The BSA was always looking for further sources of income. The 'Rules and Regulations' allowed for a category of Subscribers who gave £10 or more to be defined as 'donors'. This was later changed to exclude corporate bodies. The main corporate body in mind was Macmillan & Co. which regularly gave £20. One of the most generous and long-standing

[51] 'British School at Athens', *The Times* 3 July 1890, 6. For the financial background see also Waterhouse 1986, 55-61.

[52] 'The British School at Athens', *The Times* 12 July 12 1894, 11.

[53] BSA Minute Book 2, meeting of 15 March 1897. For the India Famine Fund see *The Times* 12 March 1897, 12 (although there were almost daily mentions in *The Times*).

[54] BSA Minute Book 8, Meeting of 27 October 1914.

[55] BSA Minute Book 8, Meeting of 16 February 1915.

[56] BSA Minute Book 8, Meeting of 12 June 1917. Memorandum: Kew, National Archives, Foreign Office T 1/12049.

[57] BSA Minute Book 8, Meeting of 26 February 1919.

donors was Walter Leaf who served as treasurer to the BSA and was a bank director. His earliest recorded 'subscription was for £100' (1894/95), then a regular £20 until 1899/1900, when his regular subscription was £50. George Macmillan was also a generous supporter initially with 10 guineas, rising to £20 (1898/99), £25 (1899/1900), and then £50 until the outbreak of the First World War when it was reduced to £25. Among the most generous givers was the chemical manufacturer Ludwig Mond, who gave a regular £100. Baron Ferdinand de Rothschild gave a regular £50 until his death. Rev. Henry Fanshawe Tozer (1829-1916) was one of the founding Vice-President of the Hellenic Society.[58]

Sir William Reynell Anson (1843-1914), Warden of All Souls, Oxford; vice-chancellor (1898); MP for Oxford University (£10, annually from 1899/1900 to 1913/14)

Colonel O. Chambers (£10, annually in 1899/1900 and 1900/01)

Lord Egerton of Tatton / Rt. Hon. Earl Egerton (Wilbraham Egerton) (1832-1909) (£10.10.0, annually from 1895/96 to 1906/07)

Sir Arthur J. Evans (1851-1941) (£10, annually from 1894/95 to 1917/18)

Douglas William Freshfield (1845-1934) (£10, annually from 1895/96 to 1917/18)

Lord Hillingdon (Charles Henry Mills, first Baron Hillingdon [1830–1898]) (£10, annually from 1895/96 to 1897/98)

Thomas Hodgkin (1831-1913) (£10, annually from 1902/03 to 1912/13)

Lady Howard de Walden (Lady Lucy Joan Cavendish-Scott-Bentinck) (d. 1899); widow of Charles Augustus Ellis, sixth Baron Howard de Walden and second Baron Seaford (1799–1868) (£20, annually from 1896/97 to 1898/9)

Walter Leaf (1852-1927) (£100, 1894/95; £20, annually from 1895/96 to 1898/9; £50, annually 1899/1900 and 1900/01; £20, 1901/02; £50, annually from 1902/03 to 1917/18)

William Loring (1865-1915) (£15, 1899/1900; £10, 1900/01)

Sir Thomas Lucas (1822-1902) (£10, 1895/96; £10. 10. 0, 1897/98 and 1898/9)

George A. Macmillan (£10. 10. 0, from 1894/95 to 1897/98; £20, 1898/9; £25, from 1899/1900 to 1902/03; £50, from 1904/05 to 1914/15; £25, from 1915/16 to 1917/18)

Macmillan & Co. (£20, from 1895/96 to 1898/9)

C. W. Mitchell (£10, from 1895/96 to 1902/03)

Ludwig Mond (1839-1909) (£100, from 1895/96 to 1908/09)

Walter Morrison (1836-1921); a founder of the Palestine Exploration Fund (£10, from 1911/12 to 1914/15)

Mrs J. W. Pease (£10.10.0, 1902/03)

Baron Ferdinand de Rothschild (1839-1898) (£50, from 1895/96 to 1897/98)

Sir Lawrence Alma Tadema (1836-1912) (£20, from 1895/96 to 1899/1900)

Mrs Hedwig Tod, Edinburgh (£10, from 1904/05 to 1912/13)

Rev. Henry Fanshawe Tozer (1829-1916) (£10, from 1894/95 to 1915/16)

Sir Julius (Charles) Wernher (1850-1912) (£25, from 1899/1900 to 1911/12)

Table 1. Donors to the BSA until the First World War.

---

[58] Hellenic Society 1880, xv.

Publications

From the opening of the BSA the main home for publication by its students was the *Journal of Hellenic Studies.*[59] It was here that reports from the early excavations and surveys appeared – Cyprus,[60] Megalopolis,[61] Aegosthena,[62] and the survey of Aetolia[63] – as well as overviews of 'Archaeology in Greece'. [64] However with the major reorganisation of the BSA in 1895 at the end of Gardner's directorship, a decision was taken to launch an *Annual* that would specifically reflect the work of the students. It was proposed that the new *Annual* would also be sent to the subscribers to keep them informed. A 'Prefatory note' to volume 1 made the point:

> It has, for some time past, been felt that Subscribers to the School ought to receive some more adequate return for their subscription than the Reports previously issued. The same kind of matter is here set forth in more attractive form, while the papers which follow either present an account of researches recently carried on in Greece by workers of various nationalities, or throw light on the work of individual archaeologists, or on special problems which can best be studied on Greek soil.[65]

The volume contained research articles by members of the BSA as well as details of the annual report, the accounts, a list of subscribers, the rules and regulations of the School, and a list of directors and students. It may also have been felt that the other Schools in Athens had their publications – *Bulletin de Correspondence Hellénique*, *Athenische Mitteilungen*, and the *Papers of the American School of Classical Studies at Athens* – and that the BSA should not be left out.

One of the key individuals behind the *Annual* was George Macmillan, who had persuaded his family business to publish the *Journal of Hellenic Studies* from 1880. He was Honorary Secretary both to the Hellenic Society and to the BSA. However Macmillan acknowledged the 'initiative' for the *Annual* to Harcourt-Smith, the incoming Director. Harcourt-Smith had been one of the founder editors of *Classical Review* that first appeared in March 1887. The first volume of the *Annual* reviewed the last year of Gardner's directorship. Harcourt-Smith joined the *Journal's* newly formed editorial consultative committee as an *ex officio* member.

The intention for the *Annual* had not been of competition with the *Journal*. Harcourt-Smith made it clear in the 'Prefatory note' to volume 1 on the *Annual*,

> It is intended that these more elaborate papers shall still find a place in that periodical [sc. *JHS*], while the School *Annual* may give an opportunity for publishing more

---

[59] See Waterhouse 1986, 61-63.

[60] Gardner, *et al.* 1888; Munro and Tubbs 1890; Munro, *et al.* 1891.

[61] Gardner, *et al.* 1890; Benson 1892; Loring 1892/1893.

[62] Benson 1895a.

[63] Woodhouse 1893.

[64] *E.g.* Penrose 1887; Harrison 1888a; Gardner 1889.

[65] 'Prefatory note', *BSA* 1 (1984/95) vii.

popular accounts of travel and research, or preliminary statements of problems which may be dealt with more fully hereafter. The two periodicals, therefore, will supplement one another, without any thought of rivalry between institutions whose interests are obviously identical.[66]

However by 1897 there was a crisis. The *Annual* was attracting articles away from *JHS*. The issue seems to have been first raised at the meeting of July 29, 1897, when a resolution was passed:

> it be an instruction to the Editor of the School annual to confer as occasion may arise with the Editorial Committee of the Journal of Hellenic Studies as to the distribution of paper between the two periodicals.[67]

This continued to be an issue and in October Ernest Gardner asked for the resolution to be changed, although this had to be deferred as Leaf was not present.[68] Leaf and Myres tried to find a solution by proposing that the editors of *JHS* 'should be *ex officio* Editors of the "*Annual*", and the Editor of the "*Annual*" *ex officio* Editor of the *Journal*'.[69] However the resolution merely called for a 'mutual understanding' between the two periodicals. The issue was debated at the Council meeting of the Hellenic Society in January 1898. One of the outcomes was that the results from Kynosarges were published in *JHS* and the monograph for Phylakopi was to be published as a supplement to *JHS*.[70]

This coincided with the resignation of Arthur Smith and Percy Gardner as editors of the *Journal* over a row related to the delay in publishing William Ridgeway's article on the Mycenaeans, which had been submitted in 1895.[71] In a letter to the Council of the Hellenic Society Ridgeway noted, 'It is therefore useless to blame the Annual as the cause why material is lacking for your *Journal*, for you have deliberately turned it into an organ for the expression of a particular (and moribund) set of doctrines concerning the early age of Greece'.[72] From 1896 the Director of the BSA seems have been part of the *Journal's* editorial, or consultative editorial committee.[73]

The close link between the *Journal* and the BSA was reflected in the publication of major monographs by the Hellenic Society on Megalopolis, Phylakopi, and (after the First World War) Artemis Orthia.[74] However the publication of finds from Palaikastro

---

[66] 'Prefatory note', *BSA* 1 (1984/95) viii.

[67] BSA Minute Book 2.

[68] BSA Minute Book 3, Meeting of 19 October 1897. The debate continued on 18 November 1897. It was suggested that expenditure on the annual be restricted to £80. A year later it was proposed to restrict the cost of volume 4 to £100: BSA Minute Book 3, Meeting of 15 December 1898.

[69] BSA Minute Book 3, Meeting of 2 December 1897.

[70] Edgar 1897; Atkinson, *et al.* 1904.

[71] This appeared as Ridgeway 1896.

[72] William Ridgeway, letter to the Council of the Society for the Promotion of Hellenic Studies, 26 January 1898 (Macmillan archive).

[73] *E.g.* Harcourt-Smith and Hogarth were on the editorial board.

[74] Gardner, *et al.* 1892; Atkinson, *et al.* 1904; Dawkins 1929.

appeared as the first supplementary volume for the *Annual*.[75] The growth of work in Asia Minor (especially by the Oxford students) meant that an arrangement for the publication of the work needed to be made.[76]

Harcourt-Smith continued as editor of the *Annual* until 1909. He gained the services of an assistant, Amy Hutton, first in 1904 when he was promoted to Keeper of the Department of Greek and Roman Antiquities at the British Museum, and then from 1906. He relinquished the role to Hutton in 1909 when he became Director and Secretary of the renamed Victoria and Albert Museum in South Kensington.[77]

The old issue between the *Journal of Hellenic Studies* and the *Annual* took a new form in 1910, when the newly founded Roman Society issued its own *Journal*.[78] The Roman Society wanted to include the research of BSA students, presumably if it was Roman in character.[79] No doubt one of the people behind this request was Francis Haverfield, perhaps with his student G. L. Cheesman in mind, although John G. C. Anderson is another possibility.

---

[75] Bosanquet and Dawkins 1923.

[76] BSA Minute Book 3, Meeting of 14 March 1901.

[77] BSA Minute Book 6, Meeting of 19 October 1909. This gave Hutton a place on the Managing Committee.

[78] Taylor 1960.

[79] BSA Minute Book 6, Meeting of 28 February 1911.

PART 2:
STUDENTS OF THE BRITISH SCHOOL AT ATHENS

CHAPTER 4:
OXFORD AND CAMBRIDGE STUDENTS

Defining a 'Student'

Over 130 students were admitted to the BSA in the period up to the outbreak of the First World War. Students of the BSA have a specific meaning under the Rules and Regulations of the School. The wording was as follows:

> XIX. The Students shall consist of the following: –
> (1) Holders of travelling fellowships, studentships, or scholarships at any University of the United Kingdom or of the British Colonies.
> (2) Travelling Students sent out by the Royal Academy, the Royal Institute of British Architects, or other similar bodies.
> (3) Other persons who shall satisfy the Managing Committee that they are duly qualified to be admitted to the privileges of the School.
> XX. Students attached to the School will be expected to pursue some definite course of study or research in a department of Hellenic studies, and to write in each season a report upon their work ....
> XXI. ... No person shall be enrolled as a student who does not intend to reside at least three months in Greek lands.[1]

Studentships were made available from both Oxford and Cambridge, with the School Studentships alternating between Cambridge and Oxford.

The decision to admit students was taken by the Managing Committee. There are instances when an application was turned down, often because of the candidate's insufficient academic ability. In one instance the Director, Richard M. Dawkins, was criticized for admitting Harry Pirie-Gordon as a student as he had not made an application; Pirie-Gordon's estate near Crickhowell in Wales was close to Dawkins' inherited estate.[2] In another, Solomon Charles Kaines-Smith failed to settle his account, run up during his war-time stay at the School; and the privileges of being a former student were withdrawn.

Students from Oxford and Cambridge were able to apply to a range of funds to support them in Athens. Some of these were for two years. The BSA sometimes offered other funds to support students. Thus Duncan Mackenzie was supported by a studentship worth £50 on condition that he placed 'his services at the disposal of the director for the current

---

[1] The regulations were published in the *BSA*.

[2] They also shared a friendship in Baron Corvo (Frederick William Rolfe): Benkovitz 1977. For the background to this admission: Gill 2006a.

session'.[3] In addition a Sachs Studentship was established in 1913 in memory of Gustav Sachs who had died in Athens on 19 April 1912.[4]

Cambridge students at the School

Some 52 Cambridge men and women went out to Athens as students of the BSA between 1886 and the outbreak of the First World War. Most of the students, with a handful of notable exceptions, had graduated in the 1880s or later, and were thus part of the new classical tripos which included archaeology.[5] The average age for Cambridge students when they went out to the BSA was about 25, and most had completed Part 2 of the Classical Tripos. Three men were admitted after completing Part 1. A. G. Bather was admitted in 1889, R. C. Bosanquet in 1892, and J. H. Marshall in 1898. In all three cases they were awarded a first class for Part 2, and subsequently appointed to a studentship.

A number of older students were admitted. J. G. Frazer was admitted for the session of 1889-90. At the age of 35, he was eight years senior to the Director. Frazer had been elected a Fellow of Trinity College, Cambridge in 1879. He had recently completed *The Golden Bough* (1890), and was preparing his work on Pausanias (1898). Hercules Henry West, who had been a student at Trinity, went to the BSA at the age of 40. Roandeu Albert Henry Bickford-Smith, who had been called to the bar in 1886, used the School as a base for the study of modern Greece, publishing *Greece Under King George* (1893) and *Cretan Sketches* (1898).[6] Wynfrid Laurence Henry Duckworth (1870-1956) had studied natural sciences in Cambridge, and after election as a Fellow of Jesus College, was University Lecturer in Physical Anthropology (1898-1920). He was admitted to the BSA in the 1902-03 session, at the age of 32. He worked with Bosanquet on the excavations at Palaikastro in eastern Crete, publishing studies on the human remains.[7] He later collaborated with Ridgeway to set up a Board of Anthropological Studies at Cambridge in 1904. He subsequently published a skull from a prehistoric context at Tsangli in Thessaly. The Rev. William Ainger Wigram (1872-1953) had worked in eastern Anatolia and Persia (1902-12) at the encouragement of Oswald H. Parry who was Archbishop's Missioner to the Nestorian Christians and also a former BSA student (1889-90). He moved to the Anglican chaplaincy in Constantinople in 1912, and spent part of the academic year 1913-14 in Athens where he was admitted as a student.

The academic standard of the students was also high. Twenty-six of the thirty-six male students examined under the new degree classifications were awarded a first in both Part 1 and Part 2 of the Tripos. Most had taken the Classical Tripos. The exceptions were Wynfrid L. H. Duckworth who had taken Natural Sciences, and Arthur C. Sheepshanks who took Law for Part 2 (although he had taken Part 1 of the Classics Tripos). At Part 2 there were at least thirteen distinctions in Archaeology, despite the fact that some of the students clearly concentrated in other areas such as Language (Richard M. Dawkins) and

---

[3] BSA Minute Book 3, Meeting of 18 November 1897.

[4] BSA Minute Book 7, Meeting 1913; British School at Athens 1912/13, 267.

[5] Stray 1999. See also Beard and Stray 2005: 382.

[6] Bickford-Smith 1893; Bickford-Smith and Prior 1898. See also Clogg 2000, 20.

[7] Duckworth 1902/03a; Duckworth 1902/03b.

History (Charles D. Edmonds). The women from Girton and Newnham performed less well in the tripos, although Hardie, Lorimer, and Welsh were notable exceptions who obtained firsts. One of the reasons for the discrepancy was the poor teaching the women had received before going up to Cambridge.[8]

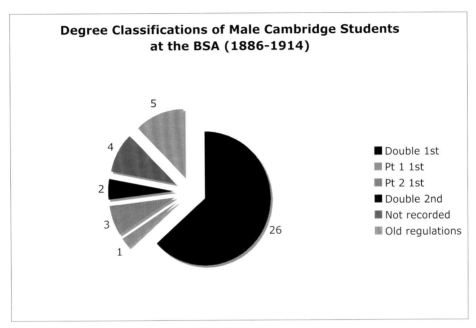

Fig. 1. Degree classifications of Cambridge students at the BSA.

Classical archaeology in Cambridge

The steady stream of Cambridge students reflects the strong interest in classical archaeology. The Laurence chair of Classical Archaeology was not established until 1931,[9] and until then there were a number of positions with an archaeological element. Archaeology had been introduced to Cambridge through the benefaction of Dr John Disney of the Hyde, near Ingatestone in Essex. In March 1851 Disney wrote to the Vice-Chancellor of the University of Cambridge, Dr James Cartmell, Master of Christ's College, that he wished to offer £1,000 to endow the Disney Professorship of Archaeology.[10] The offer was gratefully accepted and passed by the university Senate in late May 1851. The deed of trust made the purpose of the Chair quite clear. The professor 'shall deliver Lectures on the subject of Antiquities and other matters and things connected with Antiquarian research and the Fine Arts'.[11] The deed of endowment showed Disney's breadth of vision for the Chair: 'the said Disney Professor of Archaeology to deliver in the course of each

---

[8] See the comments on Sellers: Dyson 2004, 22.

[9] The first holder was A. B. Cook (1868-1952): Gill 2004e.

[10] Gill 2004h.

[11] Gill 2004h.

Academical year … Six Lectures at least on the subject of Classical Mediaeval and other Antiquities the Fine Arts and all matters and things connected therewith'.[12] The Chair was to be held for five years, and the holder could be reappointed. It was also stipulated that the holder of the chair should be 'a member of the University of Cambridge who has taken the Degree of Master of Arts or some higher Degree in the same University'.[13] One of the stipulations of Disney's endowment was that he should reserve the right to make the appointment during his own lifetime.

The first few holders of the position were more antiquarians than scientific archaeologists. The first appointment, made at Disney's prompting, was Rev. J. H. Marsden (1803-91) of St John's College in 1851. He fulfilled Disney's requirements in that he had taken his BA in 1826, his MA in 1829 and his BD in 1836. He was well known in Cambridge, serving as select preacher to the university in 1834 and 1837. In 1840 he had been appointed by St John's College to the living of Great Oakley near Harwich in Essex which was in the college's patronage. He served as Hulsean lecturer on divinity (a bequest of Rev. John Hulse of St John's College) in 1843 and 1844, and which were published as *The Evils which have resulted at various times from a Misapprehension of Our Lord's Miracles* (London 1845). Marsden's links with Disney were in part through the Colchester Archaeological Association that had emerged from the Archaeological Branch of the Colchester Literary Institution. Marsden was appointed to the committee of the Colchester Archaeological Association on 1 September 1852. This saw the transformation into the Essex Archaeological Society in December. Disney was appointed as the first president of the Society, with Marsden as one of the Vice-Presidents. Lord Braybooke had been the intended president but had declined.

Marsden's first lectures were published as *Two Introductory Lectures upon Archaeology, delivered in the University of Cambridge* (Cambridge 1852).[14] He was reappointed in 1856 – clearly Disney was pleased because he increased the size of his bequest in his will that November.[15] Through the autumn of 1856 Disney was unable to take his role as president of the Essex Archaeological Society. His will, dated 7 November 1856, had made further provision for the Chair:

> I give and bequeath to the Chancellor Masters and Scholars of the University of Cambridge the sum of two thousand and five hundred pounds in the Bank Three Pounds per Cent. Annuities in Trust nevertheless and as an augmentation of the Disney Archaeological Professorship for ever.[16]

In 1858, Marsden was appointed rural dean of Eccles, and became a chaplain to the Rt. Rev. James Prince Lee, Bishop of Manchester. Marsden was reappointed to the chair in 1861, but in 1865 he resigned. One of his tasks was to write a memoir on Colonel William Leake, whose collection of Greek figure-decorated pottery was acquired for the Fitzwilliam

---

[12] Quoted in Gill 2004h.

[13] Quoted in Gill 2004h.

[14] Marsden 1852.

[15] Disney died on 6 May 1857.

[16] Will, unpublished, of Dr John Disney.

Museum, developing the sculptural collection based on Disney's gift, and the earlier material presented to Cambridge by E. D. Clarke.[17]

Marsden was replaced in 1865 by Churchill Babington (1821-89), also of St John's College.[18] Both Marsden and Babington could be seen as antiquarians, though Babington had made his name for his publication of the speeches of Hyperides derived from papyri recently acquired in Egypt. Although Babington took the living of Cockfield in Suffolk in 1866, his office was renewed at five-yearly intervals in both 1870 and 1875, before he resigned in 1880, and was succeeded by Percy Gardner in 1880. In 1880 Babington was appointed an honorary fellow of St John's College. He made a number of benefactions to the Fitzwilliam Museum during the 1860s.[19]

A more academic approach to the material culture of the classical world came with Robert Burn (1829-1904), a Fellow of Trinity College, and from 1873 to 1885 praelector in Roman literature and archaeology. He overlapped with three of the mature students, all from Trinity, who were admitted as students to the BSA: James George Frazer (1854-1941), Hercules H. West (1856-1937), and Roandeu A. H. Bickford-Smith (1859-1916). Burn was instrumental in the reforms of the Classical Tripos and the introduction of archaeology to Part 2.[20]

An interest in the archaeology of the Greek world came from (Sir) Sidney Colvin (1845-1927) who was appointed Slade Professor of Fine Art in 1873. Two years later he was struck by the work of the German Institute at Olympia, which became a key element in his Cambridge lectures.[21] A. B. Cook was to note that Colvin 'had been virtually the first to attempt any systematic teaching of Classical Archaeology'.[22] He was to make a major impact on the teaching of classical art at Cambridge through the creation of a cast gallery after his appointment as Director of the Fitzwilliam Museum in 1876.[23] Colvin recalled:

> In the years (1876-84) when I had charge of the Fitzwilliam Museum at Cambridge, my main endeavour had been not so much to enrich its collection of miscellaneous original objects of art as to save out of its revenue a fund for providing the first and indispensable apparatus for archaeological study in the shape of a gallery of casts from antique sculpture. The new gallery was built and stocked, and in April 1884 a representative company came to the ceremony of its formal opening. The Prince of Wales was present … But far the most effective speech of the day, despite its somewhat antiquated style and stiff delivery, was Newton's. For many years of his life he had laboured in vain to get his beloved

---

[17] Marsden 1864. Marsden continued as Rector of Great Oakley until 1889, when he resigned at the age of 86. He retired to Grey Friars in Colchester where he died on 24 January 1891.

[18] Babington 1865.

[19] These included Corinthian alabastra from Camirus on Rhodes, a Rhodian stemmed dish from Camirus, an Attic head vase, an Attic Nolan amphora from 'Mr Holland's collection', an Apulian hydria, a Campanian pyxis. For benefactors to the Fitzwilliam: Gill 1992a.

[20] Beard 1999.

[21] Gardner 1933, 51.

[22] Cook 1931, 46. Cook matriculated in 1887.

[23] Cook 1931, 46. See also Beard 1993.

studies officially recognized and admitted into the curriculum of his own university of Oxford. To see that object achieved at Cambridge, with the certainty that Oxford must soon follow, was to him like a view from Pisgah.[24]

Colvin resigned his positions in 1884/5 following his move to the British Museum.

Percy Gardner (1846-1937) was appointed to the Disney chair in 1880,[25] while continuing to hold a position in the British Museum where he had been working on a series of coin catalogues. Like Colvin he had been greatly impressed by the German excavations at Olympia that he visited in 1877. A major development in the teaching of classical archaeology at Cambridge came with the appointment of Charles Waldstein (1856-1927), first as lecturer (1880) and then as Reader (1883) in Classical Archaeology.[26] Greek sculpture was among his interests. He also served as Director of the Fitzwilliam Museum (1883-89), Director of ASCSA (1889-93), and Slade Professor of Art at Cambridge (1895-1901, 1904-11). Waldstein was active in the field excavating at Plataia (1889-90), Eretria (1891), and the Argive Heraion (1892-95);[27] he served as a member of the Managing Committee of the BSA. Bosanquet recalled Waldstein's influence in a letter from Cambridge in the January of 1894:

> I am more than usually hungry for the blazing skies and the garlic and the dust (to take the worst features by way of antidote to my desires) this evening, because Waldstein (Head of the American School) has just come back and told me of all that is going on: my friends are busy, and knowledge is growing out there – but why talk?[28]

Waldstein was an influence on the Greek plays, as E. F. Benson recalled, 'continually interrupting the chanting of Athenian elders, in order to show them how to stand and move in truly Pheidian attitudes'.[29] He resigned from the Readership in Classical Archaeology in 1907.

John Henry Middleton (1846-96) was appointed Slade Professor of Art in 1886 in succession to Colvin. He held this position in conjunction with the Directorship of the Fitzwilliam Museum (1890-92). In 1892 he moved to the South Kensington Museum, while retaining his positions in Cambridge. E. F. Benson recalled his influence: 'instead of lecturing [Middleton] gave me Greek gems and fragments of red-figured vases to examine'.[30] Cook likewise recalled the interest in technical aspects: 'The curvature of a stylobate, the setting out of an Ionic volute, the use of *Pozzolana* in hydraulic cement, the

---

[24] Colvin 1921, 221-23.

[25] Gardner suggested that it was due to the influence of Colvin and Sidgwick: Gardner 1933, 52.

[26] Gardner noted the involvement of Colvin and Sidgwick: Gardner 1933, 51.

[27] Lord 1947. Waldstein retained his Cambridge position as Reader in Classical Archaeology during his appointment to Athens: Frothingham 1889, 401.

[28] Bosanquet 1938, 31.

[29] Benson 1930, 139. Waldstein provoked a response from (Sir) Charles Stanford (1852-1924), then professor of music at Cambridge.

[30] Benson 1930, 153.

cire perdue method of bronzecasting – these things appealed to the craftsman in his veins'.[31] Waldstein also held the Slade Professorship in 1895 and 1904, but in 1901 the chair was held by William Martin Conway (1856-1937). Conway was particularly frustrated by Jane Harrison's influence on the study of ancient art. He expressed this to his daughter Agnes, then a student at Newnham: 'it seems to me you're doing more Classics than Archaeology … when archaeology gets into the hands of literary students it's all up with it'.[32]

William Ridgeway (1858-1926) was appointed to the Disney chair in 1892 in succession to Percy Gardner (who had resigned in 1887 in order to move to Oxford). He was to become a major influence on classical archaeology at Cambridge, giving a strong interest in prehistory that was to continue until after the First World War.[33] He articulated the relationship between classical texts and the material culture, and saw archaeology as 'an invaluable servant, for it enables us to grasp the meaning of the ancient writers, to comprehend allusions otherwise obscure, to enhance our enjoyment of the scenes which they describe, and to realize, in a way impossible for the mere pedant, the conditions under which the ancients lived and moved and had their being'.[34]

Waldstein was succeeded in his readership by Arthur Bernard Cook (1868-1952), who had been a lecturer in classics at Queens' College, Cambridge (1900).[35] Cook worked specifically on Greek religion, notably Zeus, though was sensitive to the use of material culture.[36] He subsequently because the first Laurence Professor of Classical Archaeology at Cambridge (1931).[37] Jane Harrison exerted a key influence on women students at Newnham and Girton.[38] Six Newnham women, beginning with Margery Katherine Welsh (1903/04) and ending with Agnes Ethel Conway (1913/14), were admitted as students.

Other archaeological influences in Cambridge included Frederick Henry Marshall (1878-1955), Fellow of Emmanuel College, Cambridge.[39] He had worked in the Department of Greek and Roman Antiquities before returning to Cambridge to take up his fellowship (1912-19).[40] He also served as the first honorary keeper of Greek and Roman Antiquities at the Fitzwilliam Museum, a post that was developed by Winifred Lamb after the First World War.[41] Another was Ernest Stewart Roberts (1847-1912), college lecturer at Gonville and Caius (1870-1903) who had a strong interesting Greek epigraphy. He was

---

[31] Cook 1931, 52.

[32] Quoted in Evans 1966, 200.

[33] Ridgeway 1901. For his continuing influence on prehistory see Lamb 1936/37.

[34] Ridgeway 1915. Quoted in Cook 1931, 55-56.

[35] Gill 2004e.

[36] *E.g.* Cook 1914.

[37] Cook 1931.

[38] Robinson 2002.

[39] Marshall 1920.

[40] For the confusion between the two unrelated but contemporary Cambridge, archaeological Marshalls: Gill 2000a.

[41] Gill 1999.

a significant influence on Ernest Gardner and they later published together.[42] Henry Tillyard was also at Caius and was involved with the publication of inscriptions from the Laconia project.[43] Walter Headlam was remembered as a surprising archaeological influence on E. F. Benson, though the impression may have been on the way that archaeology could retrieve lost texts on papyri.[44] Finally, but far from least, there was the presence of Jebb, encouraging the use of the BSA until his death in 1905.

Educational background

The educational background of the former Cambridge students shows some clear trends. Eton was represented by six students: four from King's (Rhodes James, Loring, Yorke, and Mayor), and Trinity College (Bosanquet and Sheepshanks). The Provost of Eton, James John Hornby (1826-1909), had supported the formation of the BSA,[45] and had recognised the value of archaeology in the school curriculum.[46] Marlborough was represented by five students at a much wider spread of colleges: Emmanuel (Dawkins), King's (Benson), Trinity College (Bickford-Smith, West, Droop). The City of London School, well known for producing classicists, was represented by three students. Percy Gardner, the older brother of Ernest, recalled:

> In those days the School ... was in Milk Street, within a stone-throw of Cheapside, and we boys had to pass through the heart of London daily, and, since there was no play-ground, spent the half-hour allowed for lunch in roaming about the precincts of the Guildhall. ... there was on every side a stirring and an energy which acted upon the minds of boys at an impressionable age, perhaps rather below than above consciousness.[47]

Percy Gardner's contemporary was James Smith Reid (1846-1926) who was a Tutor at Caius College (where Ernest Gardner studied). Ruth Gardner, sister of Percy and Ernest, was married to Reid; and Percy Gardner was married to Agnes, Reid's sister.[48] Both Gardners and Reid served on the BSA Managing Committee.

College backgrounds

Some 14 colleges were represented by the Cambridge students. Twenty of the 52 Cambridge students (and 41 men) who were admitted to the BSA came from just two colleges (with ten each): King's and Trinity.

---

[42] Roberts and Gardner 1887.

[43] Tillyard 1904/05; Tillyard 1905/06a; Tillyard 1905/06b; Tod, *et al.* 1906/07.

[44] Benson 1930, 153.

[45] 'Proposed British School of Archaeology at Athens', *The Times* 3 February 1885, 7.

[46] *The Times* 20 October 1886, 9. Eton and Winchester were mentioned together.

[47] Gardner 1933, 7.

[48] Alice Gardner (1854-1927) was director of studies in history at Newnham (1884-1914). See Sutherland 2004.

The first student from King's was Montague Rhodes James. Like four of the other King's BSA students he had been educated at Eton, which had strong historic links with the college. James had just been elected to a fellowship at King's and he went out to Greece to take part in the excavations of the Cyprus Exploration Fund. The award of fellowships to former students of King's allowed them to go out to Greece: eight of the ten held fellowships. One of the exceptions was Edward F. Benson who consecutively held four awards to work in Greece: the Worts Fund (1891/92), the Cambridge Studentship (1892/93), the Craven Studentship (1893/94), and the Prendergast Greek Studentship (1894/95). He later recalled:

> but for the present archaeology was the passion and for three years in succession Cambridge most amiably gave me grants and travelling studentships for the pursuit of antiquity.[49]

One of the influences from King's is likely to have been Charles Waldstein, elected fellow in 1894. Benson (though completing Part 2 in 1890) noted his presence.[50] But Gutch, Marshall and Hasluck were all students while Waldstein was there; and indeed all the other King's students overlapped with them. Rhodes-James as Fellow and Provost is also likely to have been a benign influence. Two of the King's students held office in the BSA: Yorke and Loring were the honorary treasurer and secretary respectively.

Ten students from Trinity College went out to Athens. Five of them were mature students (and one was a Fellow): James G. Frazer, Hercules H. West, and Roandeu A. H. Bickford-Smith. Frazer and Bickford-Smith were admitted in 1889/90 under Ernest Gardner, West (then aged 40) in 1896/97 under Cecil Harcourt-Smith. Frazer had been elected to a fellowship at Trinity in 1879 and was working on his commentary on Pausanias.[51] Bickford-Smith was a land-owner in Cornwall and was writing a history of Greece.[52] Charles H. Hawes, who had been admitted to Trinity in 1896, after the death of his first wife, was admitted in 1904/05 under Bosanquet.[53] Arthur C. Sheepshanks was admitted in 1907/08 under Dawkins when he was an assistant master at Eton, in order to enhance his knowledge of Greece and Italy. Two of the Trinity students practised as architects. Christian C. T. Doll was subsequently awarded an architectural diploma from University College London and then became supervising architect at Knossos from 1905 (after Theodore Fyfe). Robert D. Wells was admitted with an architectural studentship and worked with Bosanquet on Crete.

Only three of the Trinity students were admitted immediately after their studies; indeed Robert Carr Bosanquet went to the BSA before he had completed Part 2. John P. Droop was first admitted under Bosanquet in 1905/06 and then repeatedly until the outbreak of the First World War; his experiences on excavations in Laconia, Thessaly and at Phylakopi, were turned into one of the first archaeological manuals.[54] Arnold W. Gomme went to Greece in

---

[49] Benson 1930, 152.

[50] Benson 1930, 139.

[51] Ackerman 1987.

[52] Bickford-Smith 1893.

[53] Further information on Hawes can be found in Allsebrook 1992.

[54] Droop 1915. Droop was even entrusted to prepare the report 'Archaeology in Greece' under Dawkins: Droop 1913.

1908/09 under Dawkins to work on the topography of Boeotia. All three later taught in Liverpool. Bosanquet resigned as Director to become the Professor of Classical Archaeology; Gomme joined Liverpool in 1910 for a year as an assistant lecturer; and Bosanquet resigned after the war to make way for Droop.

Jesus College was represented by five students, though one of them Wynfrid L. H. Duckworth had studied Natural Sciences in Cambridge and was elected a Fellow of Jesus in 1893; he then studied medicine at St Bartholomew's in London. He was admitted to the BSA in 1902/03 to work on the human remains from Bosanquet's excavations at Palaikastro on Crete. [55] Duckworth became, with William Ridgeway, an advocate for the study of anthropology at Cambridge.[56]

Eleven of the 52 Cambridge students were represented by women from Girton (five) and then Newnham (six). Amy Hutton and Eugénie Sellers were contemporaries at Girton, both completing Part 1 in 1882. Essentially the Girton women were replaced by ones from Newnham from Margery Welsh to the contemporaries, Dorothy Lamb and Evelyn Radford. Jane Harrison was a member of the BSA Managing Committee, first elected by the subscribers, and then as the nominated representative of the Hellenic Society; she was an advocate for women students in her attempts to gain greater access on their behalf to the facilities at the BSA. Some of the women were admitted when they were older – Sellers was 30 and Hutton 35 – although others went straight from their studies to Athens.

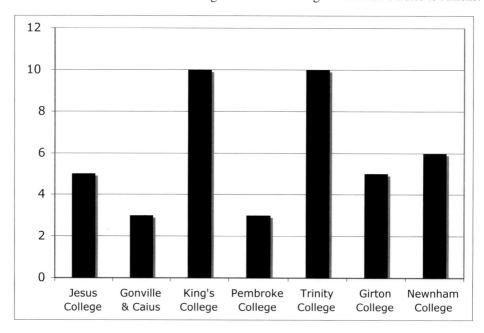

Fig. 2. The main Cambridge colleges represented by BSA students.

[55] Duckworth 1902/03a; Duckworth 1902/03b.

[56] Duckworth, *et al.* 1906.

Cambridge Studentships

There were three main sources of funds for Cambridge: the Craven studentships, the Cambridge studentships and the Prendergast studentships. Craven studentships was created from the surplus from the Craven Fund:

> devoting £200 a year to the endowment of a studentship for the purpose of facilitating advanced study or research away form Cambridge in the languages, literature, history, archaeology, or art of ancient Greece or Rome, or the comparative philology of the Indo-European languages.[57]

This was clarified, 'The studentship shall be of the annual value of £300 and shall be tenable for one year, one student being elected annually at such time as the University may from time to time determine, but a Craven student shall not be eligible for reelection on more than two occasions'.[58] These valuable awards were often granted after the student had been given a smaller grant for a previous year's study.

The Cambridge studentships, worth £50, were made on the recommendation of the Vice-Chancellor on an annual basis. The Cambridge studentship was not awarded in October 1900 due to 'the difficulty of finding suitable candidates'.[59] From 1900/01 it was decided to offer the studentship in alternate years (with Oxford),[60] and to increase it to £100.[61] Margaret Hardie was the first woman to hold the Cambridge studentship.[62]

The alternating Cambridge studentship was timed so that it did not coincide with the studentship established in January 1889 by Mrs Elizabeth Sophia Prendergast and named after Colonel William Grant Prendergast (1815-58), formerly of Trinity College. Thus Cambridge studentships were offered in odd numbered years, and Prendergast studentships in even numbered years.[63] A student with promise could apply for the award of higher value after holding the studentship. The electors for the Prendergast studentship invited:

> applications from any member of the University who has passed some final examination for the degree of B. A. in any year provided not more than four years have elapsed since December 19 next following the said final examination. The student is to devote himself to study or research in the Greek language, literature, history, philosophy, archaeology or art, according to a course proposed by himself and approved by the electors. The student will receive £200 for one year. He will be

---

[57] *The Times* 19 June 19 1885, 7.

[58] *The Times* 8 October 1886, 11.

[59] BSA Minute Book 3, Meeting of 30 October 1900.

[60] Macmillan 1910/11, xxxi. Cambridge studentships included: Loring (1889/90), Sikes (1890/91), Bather (1891/92, 1893/94), Benson (1892/93), Gutch (1898/99), Kaines Smith (1899/1900), Hasluck (1901/02), H. J. W. Tillyard (1905/06), Droop (1907/08), Growse (1909/10), Hardie (1911/12), Laistner (1913/14).

[61] The award to Kaines-Smith in 1899/1900 was at the old rate of £50.

[62] See Waterhouse 1986, 134.

[63] Thus the Oxford studentships were offered in the same year as the Cambridge Prendergast studentships.

required to conduct his research away from Cambridge for a considerable portion of the year. The studentship is not tenable with the Craven studentship.[64]

The first holder was Charles Alexander MacLean Pond (1864-93) of St John's College for the period 1890/92. He held this alongside the chair of Classics and English at Auckland, New Zealand (1890-3).[65]

A smaller grant of £40 from the Craven fund was made, in effect a Craven studentship.

The annual sum of £40 shall be paid to the managers for the time being of a fund to be called the Craven Fund, by whom grants may be made from time to time for the furtherance of research in the languages, literature, history, archaeology, and art of ancient Greece and Rome, and the comparative philology of the Indo-European languages.[66]

Craven studentships were awarded from the first Cambridge student, Ernest Gardner (1886/87).[67] The Craven Fund additionally made smaller grants such as the £40 awarded to M. R. James, a Fellow of King's College, 'for the purpose of archaeological work on Cyprus',[68] Clement Gutch, £40, 'to carry out the exploration of certain necropoleis in the Greek Cyclades',[69] or Francis Brayne Baker, £40, 'for archaeological study in connexion with the British School at Athens' (1891).[70] Other holders included F. R. Earp, £40,[71] H. J. W. Tillyard,[72] P. N. Ure (not a student), £40,[73] M. Laistner, £40,[74] and R. M. Dawkins, £50.[75]

A further source of funding for Cambridge students was the Worts Fund. Benson was admitted to the School with a grant of £100 from this source (1891/92). The Fund was then used from 1895 to give the BSA £100 per year initially for three years 'with a view to encouraging archaeological research in Hellenic lands'; the result was that Cambridge

---

[64] Cambridge University Regulations.

[65] Nine Cambridge students held an award to go out to Athens; Wace held the studentship twice. The Prendergast studentship was held by Bather (1892-93), between two Cambridge studentships, Benson (1894/95), after holding Cambridge and Craven studentships, and Marshall (1900/01), prior to a Craven studentship.

[66] Cambridge University Regulations.

[67] Cambridge Craven studentships included: Gardner (1886/87), Loring (1890/91), Benson (1893/94), Bosanquet (1894/95, 1895/96, 1896/97), Earp (1896/97), Lawson (1898/99), Marshall (1901/02), Dawkins (1903/04), E. M. W. Tillyard (1911/12), and Laistner (1912/13).

[68] *The Times* 20 January 1888, 10.

[69] *The Times* 21 June 21 1899, 12.

[70] *The Times* 29 June 29 1891, 7.

[71] *The Times* 27 June 27 1896, 16.

[72] *The Times* 30 October 1907, 8.

[73] *The Times* 5 December 1907, 10.

[74] *The Times* 17 June 1913, 4.

[75] *The Times* 24 June 1903.

was granted the right to nominate a position on the Managing Committee. The Fund also awarded Alan J. B. Wace and John P. Droop £30 'towards defraying the expense of an excavation to be undertaken in Southern Thessaly' (December 1907).

Other funds that were used by Cambridge students included the Marion Kennedy Studentship awarded to Margery Katharine Welsh of Newnham College in 1903/04, and the Prior Scholarship from Pembroke College to John Laurence Stokes in 1903/04. Other university grants were used to assist excavations, such as the £100 given to Montague Rhodes James for work on Cyprus; and £90 to Bosanquet 'to be used for the expenses in excavations at Cyzicus'.[76]

Oxford students at the School

47 students from Oxford were admitted as students at the BSA between 1886 and the outbreak of the First World War. 17 colleges were represented, Magdalen College with 11 students, and New College with 7. Many of the students were admitted to the School directly after completing *literae humaniores* (including John George Clark Anderson and William Moir Calder who had previously studied in Scotland); only three were admitted after taking classical moderations: Rupert Charles Clarke, Oswald Hutton Parry and John George Smith (Piddington). Only two students were much older: Herbert Awdry was admitted in his early forties as an Assistant Master at Wellington, and John Penoyre was 30 and had been granted leave of absence from his job as Secretary to the BSA and the Hellenic Society. Many of these students were supported through the Craven Fund.

Classical archaeology in Oxford

Sir Charles Newton was one of the most influential Mediterranean archaeologists to emerge from Oxford in the first half of the nineteenth century. He had studied at Christ Church (in 1833) where he had been influenced by Thomas Gaisford (1779-1855) and Henry George Liddell (1811-98).[77] Newton went on to be Keeper at the British Museum and to promote the foundation of the BSA.[78]

One of the key people for the development of the study of classical archaeology at Oxford was Edward Lee Hicks (1843-1919), Classical Tutor at Corpus (1866-73).[79] He developed an interest in Greek inscriptions and was invited by Newton to work on the collections in the British Museum.[80] His *Manual of Greek Historical Inscriptions* (1882) became a standard reference work.[81] Hicks was ordained in the Church of England in 1870; in 1873 he left Corpus to become incumbent of a parish. He subsequently became Principal of Owens College in Manchester (1886), and lectured on classical

---

[76] *The Times* 25 December 1901, 8.

[77] Jebb 1894, xlix; Jebb 1895, 82. See also: Gardner 1894/5; Cook 1997.

[78] A point stressed in Gardner 1894/5. For New ton's contribution to the British Museum: Jenkins 1992; Wilson 2002.

[79] Curthoys 2004.

[80] Newton, *et al.* 1874.

[81] Hicks 1882.

archaeology.[82] He became Bishop of Manchester and then Bishop of Lincoln. It was Hicks' legacy that saw so many Oxford students at the BSA opting to concentrate on epigraphy, especially in the great surveys of Anatolia.[83] Among them was Paton, who had read classics at University College, and encouraged various BSA students from his homes on Kalymnos and the Anatolian mainland.[84]

Perhaps more influential was Henry Francis Pelham (1846-1907), Classical Tutor and Lecturer at Exeter College (1870-89). His main interest lay in the Roman Empire although this extended to historical geography. He was clearly a supporter of the proposed BSA,[85] later serving on the Managing Committee as the nominated representative from Oxford. However one of his favourite projects was the work of the Asia Minor Exploration Fund, with which so many Oxford students were involved. In 1889 he was elected to be the Camden Professor Ancient History. Pelham was a moving force behind the establishment of the BSR.[86]

A further archaeological development was the endowment in 1869 of a keepership at the Ashmolean Museum by the Oxford bookseller, John Henry Parker.[87] Parker had developed a strong interest in Roman archaeology in the late 1860s and founded the British Archaeological Society at Rome; his published work on Rome drew criticism from Pelham. In spite of this, Parker was appointed the first Keeper at the Ashmolean (in 1870); his death in 1884 made way for the keepership of Arthur Evans, who was to be a major influence on the institution.

One of Pelham's students at Exeter College was Lewis Richard Farnell (1856-1934).[88] After completing his studies he travelled in Europe, and developed an interest in classical archaeology after a period of time in Berlin (1881-82). He was appointed classical lecturer at Exeter in 1883, and later Senior Tutor (1893-1913). He continued to travel in Greece[89] and Anatolia as research for his five volume work on the *Cults of the Greek States*.[90] He became university lecturer in classical archaeology (1903-14).[91] It is significant that two of his students, Rupert Charles Clarke (1866-1912) and John Arthur Ruskin Munro (1864-1944) were among the first students to be admitted to the BSA. Clarke was admitted after classical moderations in the spring of 1887 under Penrose, and Munro in 1888/89 for excavations on Cyprus.

The establishment of the BSA coincided with the development of Classical Archaeology in Oxford through the creation of the Lincoln and Merton Professorship. The first holder was William M. Ramsay (1851-1939), who held the chair for a year (1885-86) before becoming

---

[82] He continued to publish inscriptions: *e.g.* Hicks 1887b; Hicks and Bent 1887; Hicks 1888.

[83] Gill 2004c.

[84] Gill 2004n.

[85] A sent his apologies to the meeting in June 1883: 'Proposed British School at Athens', *The Times* 26 June 1883, 8.

[86] Wallace-Hadrill 2001.

[87] Riddell 2004.

[88] Farnell 1934.

[89] For a visit to the Athenian Acropolis with Eugénie Sellers: Dyson 2004, 50.

[90] Farnell 1896.

[91] Farnell 1934. Farnell, like Percy Gardner, had been educated at the City of London School.

Regius Professor of Humanity at Aberdeen. Ramsay had been supported by the Asia Minor Exploration Fund, and supported by Pelham (and George Macmillan). It is perhaps significant that two of Ramsay's Aberdeen students continued their studies in Oxford before going to Athens, namely John G. C. Anderson and William M. Calder.

Ramsay was succeeded by Percy Gardner, who moved from the British Museum and the Disney Chair at Cambridge to take the Lincoln and Merton professorship in classical archaeology in 1887 (which he held until 1925). He argued for the inclusion of classical archaeology as an integral part of the study of the classical world. Gardner recalled his emphasis as follows:

> It was the historic rather than the aesthetic side of the monuments of Greek and Roman antiquity which interested and impressed me.[92]

Gardner soon concentrated on the classical Greek period: 'its Arts and Antiquities, and tried to shew by teaching and writing how Greek history, Greek literature, Greek sculpture and vases bear one on the other, and throw light one on the other'.[93] Gardner was supported by university lecturers in classical archaeology. The first of these was Farnell (1903-14), who, like Gardner, had been educated at the City of London School. Farnell was due to be succeeded in 1915 by Guy Dickins, but Dickins was killed during the First World War. Dickins, a former student of the BSA, had been a fellow of St John's College (1909-16). His place was taken by (Sir) John Davidson Beazley (1885-1970), a Student of Christ Church (1908-25) (a former student of the BSR); he later succeeded to the chair of Classical Archaeology.[94] His interest in Greek pottery balanced Gardner's interest in sculpture.

Other influences included John A. R. Munro who became a fellow at Lincoln College, bursar from 1904, and rector from 1919. Lincoln was also Percy Gardner's college. One of the Lincoln students was Stanley Casson who was to play a crucial part in the life of the BSA between the wars.[95]

Oxford also had a growing interest in Aegean prehistory. (Sir) Arthur John Evans (1851-1941) was appointed keeper at the Ashmolean Museum in 1884.[96] While retaining an interest in the Museum, he was succeeded as Keeper in 1908 by David Hogarth.[97] The excavations on Crete, and specifically at Knossos, gave additional momentum to the study of archaeology, and specifically Aegean prehistory, in Oxford.[98] This was supplemented by John Linton Myres, a former pupil of Gardner,[99] who was also influenced by William Paton with whom he travelled in western Anatolia. Myres was a Student of Christ Church (1895-1907) and university lecturer in classical archaeology (1903-07) with a special

---

[92] Gardner 1933, 53.

[93] Gardner 1933, 59.

[94] Gill 2004a. See also Kurtz 1985.

[95] Myres 1940/45b. For Winifred Lamb's view of Casson: Gill 2007.

[96] MacGillivray 2000.

[97] Gill 2004l.

[98] Huxley 2000.

[99] Gardner 1933, 59.

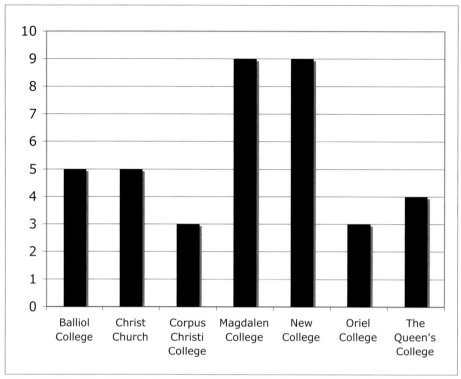

Fig. 4. BSA students and Oxford colleges

emphasis on prehistory.[100] After a spell in Liverpool (1907-10), he returned to Oxford in 1910 as Wykeham Professor in Ancient History (until 1939). Topography and geography were to be his themes, marked out by his inaugural lecture, 'Greek lands and the Greek people'. Hilda Lorimer also had a strong interest in prehistory or 'Homeric archaeology'.[101] She had been educated at Girton College, Cambridge, and was appointed fellow and classical tutor at Somerville in 1896. She was subsequently admitted to the BSA in 1901/02 under Bosanquet. She was supported by Myres, but had clashed with Pelham early on in her Oxford career. Her interest in prehistoric Greece brought about her involvement with the excavations on Ithaca in the 1930s.

The interest in epigraphy developed by Hicks was continued by Marcus Tod, who began his epigraphic career while a student at the BSA, publishing inscriptions from the Laconia survey.[102] Tod returned from Athens in 1905, where he was clearly being prepared as the successor to Bosanquet, to a tutorship in ancient history at Oriel College. In 1907 Tod was appointed university lecturer in Greek epigraphy.

Roman archaeology developed alongside Greek archaeology, in part under the influence of Francis John Haverfield (1860-1919), from 1892 Senior Student at Christ

[100] Gardner 1933, 59.

[101] Benton 1954; Hartley 1954. For her work on prehistory: Lorimer 1950.

[102] Tod 1905; Tod, *et al.* 1906/07.

Church, and from 1907 Camden Professor of Ancient History.[103] It is perhaps significant that Haverfield had been educated at Winchester like so many of the early influences on the BSA, among them Penrose, Hogarth and Harcourt-Smith. Among Haverfield's students at the School were John G. C. Anderson and Arthur M. Woodward. Anderson himself was to become Student and Tutor at Christ Church (1900-27), and later Reader in Roman Epigraphy, and Camden Professor in Ancient History.[104] Another of Haverfield's students was G. Leonard Cheesman (at New College), who was admitted to the BSA in 1908. His main interest was in the Roman provinces of the Greek east, working at Pisidian Antioch.[105] After teaching at Christ Church (1907-08), he was elected a Fellow of New College, lecturing on Roman archaeology from 1910. He was killed within days of landing at Suvla Bay in the Gallipoli campaign.

Educational background

The educational background of the Oxford students is dominated by Winchester, with ten students. The School seems to have produced a strong group of archaeologists, and three of the first four directors of the School (Penrose, Harcourt-Smith and Hogarth) had been educated there. The School itself had been a strong supporter of the BSA and its Headmaster, W. A Fearon, had attended the meeting of the BSA in October 1886.[106] Fearon certainly saw the advantages of archaeology. Writing for the Quincentenary celebrations for Winchester in 1895:

> The range of education and culture has happily so largely widened during the last generation that new machinery and new opportunity are required to satisfy modern ideals. Even classical study has gained a new reality by the fresh interest that is felt in ancient life, and by the varied discoveries of archaeology.[107]

The first former Winchester pupil to be admitted as a student was David G. Hogarth, followed by John F. R. Stainer. Both went on to Magdalen. The growing interest in archaeology is perhaps reflected in the opening of a museum at the school.[108] Among the contemporaries were Guy Dickins, Alexander C. B. Brown, George L. Cheesman and William R. Halliday, all of whom subsequently went up to New College to read Classics. It is perhaps significant that they were all at Winchester when Arthur George Bather was Assistant Master (1898 to 1928). Bather had been admitted to the School in 1889-90 under Ernest Gardner, and in subsequent years to 1893/94. He had excavated at Megalopolis. Bather had been preceded by another former BSA student, Edward Ernest Sikes who had been an Assistant Master in 1890-91. A further assistant master at the School was Rev. Alfred Hamilton Cruikshank (1862-1927), an exact contemporary of

---

[103] Freeman 2007. For Haverfield within the context of Roman archaeology: Hingley 2000.

[104] Anderson 1897/8. He assisted Haverfield in teaching epigraphy: Freeman 2007, 170.

[105] Haverfield 1915a; Haverfield 1915b.

[106] 'The British School at Athens', *The Times* 20 October 1886.

[107] Fearon 1895.

[108] Hodges 2000, 21.

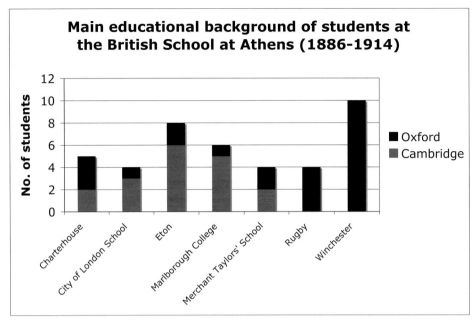

Fig. 3. The main Public Schools represented by BSA students.

Hogarth at Winchester. He had returned to Winchester (from Harrow) as an assistant master in 1894 (and chaplain from 1896); he left for Durham in 1910. He visited the Meteora in 1895/96 and was made an associate student of the BSA.[109] This period also saw the reorganisation of the BSA under Harcourt-Smith (b. 1859, a Wykehamist) and ten assistant masters as well as the Headmaster, Fearon, were signatories in support of a government grant.[110] The last student to be elected for admission as a student before the First World War was Cyril B. Moss-Blundell, a pupil at Winchester. He never went to Athens and was killed at Loos in 1915. Other Wykehamist archaeologists of this era included Arthur Hamilton Smith (1860-1941), Keeper at the British Museum and later Director of the BSR; Francis John Haverfield (1860-1919), Camden professor of Ancient History at Oxford; and Thomas Ashby (1874-1931), Director of the BSR.[111]

The next best represented schools were Rugby with four students, Charterhouse, with three, and Eton, Haileybury, Harrow and Merchant Taylors' with two each. Each of these schools had responded to the 'Memorial' appeal for the establishment of a government grant towards the work of the BSA. The Provost of Eton, Hornby, had attended meetings prior to the opening of the BSA.

[109] Cruickshank 1895/6.

[110] *BSA* 1 (1894/95), xx.

[111] Kenyon and Cook 2004; Freeman 2007; Hodges 2000.

Oxford Studentships

Students were supported by two grants from the Craven Fund. The Craven University Fellowship permitted students to study abroad and was worth £200. At least 15 of the Oxford students were Craven University Fellows, from Hogarth (1886/87), the first Oxford student at the School,[112] through to Roger M. Heath (1913/14).[113] The fellowships were awarded to graduates:

> The Fellowships shall be open to all who shall have passed the examinations required for the degree of Bachelor of Arts and who shall not have exceeded the 28th term from their matriculation. They shall be of the annual value of £200, and shall be tenable for two years. One Fellow shall be elected annually in Michaelmas Term by a committee of five persons appointed for the purpose by the Board of the Faculty of Arts (Literae Humaniores). The committee shall have power to elect either without examination or after such examination in Greek and Latin literature, history and antiquities, or in some part of these subjects, as they shall think fit. … He shall be required as a condition of his becoming entitled to the emoluments of his Fellowship to spend at least eight months of each of the two years of his tenure thereof in residence abroad for the purpose of study at some place or places approved by the selecting committee.[114]

The fact that students could spend a period of time in residence abroad made the fellowships ideal for Oxford students wishing to work in Greece.

Two of the Craven University Fellows simultaneously held Derby Scholarships which were intended for study abroad with an emphasis on classical languages and literature: Halliday (awarded 1909; 1910/11), which allowed him to study in Berlin (1909/10), and Stuart-Jones (1891/92). The Sir Charles Newton Studentship was awarded to Woodhouse.[115] Thompson was awarded the Charles Oldham University Scholarship which allowed him to be admitted to the BSA prior to the holding of a Craven University Fellowship (1907/08), and Arnold J. Toynbee was awarded the Jenkins Prize which permitted him to travel to the Mediterranean (1911/12).

Oxford also offered Craven studentships that were nominated by the Committee of the Craven Fund. They were initially worth £50, but were then offered in alternate years worth £100. The Committee of the Craven Fund was initially allowed to nominate an

---

[112] A letter, signed by George Macmillan, advertising the studentships appeared in *The Times* on 4 November 1886.

[113] The Craven University Fellows were: Hogarth (1886/87), Tubbs (1888/89), Richards (1889/90), Stuart-Jones (1890/91), Myres (1892/93), Woodhouse (1892/93), Anderson (1896/97), Edgar (1896/97), Welch (1898/99), Hopkinson (1900/01), Tod (1901/02), Peet (1906/07), Thompson (1908/10), Halliday (1910/11, awarded 1909), Heath (1913/14).

[114] *The Times* 29 June 1886, 10.

[115] For the advertisement for the studentship: *The Times* 4 November 1891, 7 ('University Intelligence').

Oxford student on an annual basis,[116] although this was changed to a more valuable School Studentship (held in alternate years by a Cambridge student).[117] Moss-Blundell, the holder of the School Studentship for 1914/15, enlisted before he was admitted to the BSA, and was killed in the Battle of Loos, September 1915.

The new studentship, worth £150 a year and to be held for two years, was discussed in December 1901.[118] It was decided that 'Candidates must be of first-class University standing or its equivalent, with special knowledge in some branch of Greek archaeology or in Greek history'.[119] Marcus Tod held the newly established 'Senior Studentship' that in effect was the equivalent of being Assistant Director.

Student projects at the School

Students at the BSA took an active part in field-projects and were encouraged to travel in Greece and the islands. However the informal arrangements were tightened by Cecil Harcourt-Smith who was keen to assign research projects to each of the students admitted to the School.[120]

Topography

The first group of Oxford students developed an active series of field projects and topographical studies across the eastern Mediterranean. David G. Hogarth initially worked on Alexander the Great, but he soon developed a keen interest in epigraphy, first in Macedonia (still part of the Ottoman Empire), and then through travels in Anatolia with William Ramsay.[121] Under Gardner, Hogarth worked on the projects of the Cyprus Exploration Fund, where he was joined for two seasons by two other Oxford students, J. Arthur R. Munro and H. Arnold Tubbs. Munro and Tubbs published their work at Polis (1889), and some of the finds from the tombs were presented to the Ashmolean Museum.[122] In the second season they were part of the team at Salamis. Munro was also to become involved in the extensive fieldwork in Asia Minor, initially in the east, and then in the north, specially in Mysia and Pontus. Tubbs became Professor of Classics in the University of Auckland. John G. C. Anderson also worked

---

[116] Macmillan 1910/11, xxxi. The Oxford students included: Woodhouse (1889/90), Milne (1890/91), Inge (1891/92), Cheetham (1892/93), Crowfoot (1896/97), Spilsbury (1897/98), Fotheringham (1898/99), Frost (1900/01), and Forster (1902/03).

[117] The Oxford School students included: Dickins (1906/07), Robinson (1910/11), Casson (1912/13) and Moss-Blundell (1914/15). The change to alternate years was proposed at the meeting of 30 October 1900 (BSA Minute Book 3). The Cambridge year would avoid the times when the Prendergast studentship was offered.

[118] BSA Minute Book 4, Meeting of 13 December 1901.

[119] BSA Minute Book 4, Meeting of 13 December 1901.

[120] British School at Athens 1896/97, 229.

[121] Gill 2004l.

[122] Munro and Tubbs 1890; Munro, *et al.* 1891.

in Asia Minor,[123] and William R. Halliday toured through Cappadocia and Pontus.[124] Such work was also extended to Cyprus.[125]

These regional surveys of Anatolia, in part encouraged by Ramsay, also encouraged work in Greece. William John Woodhouse, a student of Percy Gardner, was admitted to the BSA in 1889-90 as the first holder of the Sir Charles Newton Studentship. Apart from helping with excavations at Megalopolis, Woodhouse undertook a survey of Aetolia from 1892, publishing a study of newly identified inscriptions and in 1897 a monograph on the region.[126] Perhaps one of the most important proponents of topography and geography for archaeological study was John Linton Myres who was admitted to the BSA in 1892-93. His studies on 'Prehistoric influences on prehistoric Greece' were assisted by William Paton, a former Oxford classicist, who had married the daughter of the mayor of Kalymnos and had settled on the Turkish mainland. Maurice Thompson and Alan Wace worked together on the survey of Thessaly, and the excavation of a number of sites.[127] In this project they were joined by Arnold J. Toynbee who recalled their 'maghoula hunting' in northern Greece. Edward S. Forster worked on the topography and history of south-west Laconia,[128] as part of a wider series of excavations in Laconia.

Historical geography became especially important, and was encouraged as a subject by Myres.[129] Norman Whatley of Hertford College, Oxford 'made a series of tours, studying the influence of Greek geography on its history, and in particular tracing the ancient, military, and commercial routes'.[130] The topography of military campaigns was a specific area. Herbert Awdry worked on the topography of Plataea in response to research by George B. Grundy.[131] In 1896 and 1897 there was a major dispute between two Oxford educated scholars, Grundy who was interested in historical geography, and Ronald M. Burrows, then an assistant to Gilbert Murray in Glasgow, over the topography of the battle of Pylos and Sphacteria. Bosanquet worked on the topography of Pylos to clarify issues raised by the debate that raged between the *Classical Review* and the *Journal of Hellenic Studies*.[132] Other topographical issues include the location of the fort of Rhoduntia at Thermopylai by Wilfrid J. Farrell,[133] and a study of the Long Walls of Megara by Stanley Casson.[134]

[123] British School at Athens 1896/97, 230.

[124] British School at Athens 1910/11, 286.

[125] British School at Athens 1894/95, 25.

[126] Woodhouse 1893; Woodhouse 1897.

[127] *E.g.* Wace and Thompson 1912. For Thompson's topographical work in the Balkans: British School at Athens 1910/11, 287.

[128] British School at Athens 1903/04, 245.

[129] Myres 1910.

[130] British School at Athens 1907/08, 427.

[131] Grundy 1894; Awdry 1894/5. For Grundy's work in Boeotia: Gardner 1892/3, 150.

[132] British School at Athens 1896/97, 230. See Grundy 1896; Burrows 1896; Grundy 1897a; Grundy 1897b; Burrows 1897; Bosanquet 1898b; Burrows 1898b; Burrows 1898a.

[133] Farrell 1910.

[134] Casson 1912/13b.

Students are frequently mentioned as studying 'topographical passages'.[135] Such work had begun under Gardner. Loring had worked on the topography of routes in the Peloponnese,[136] and Woodhouse on Aetolia.[137] This was formalised by Harcourt-Smith who started to create a systematic index of sites. Among his helpers was the able linguist Hercules West,[138] Duncan Mackenzie, and J. G. Smith. These studies were crucial to the planning of major projects.

Prehistory

The excavations on Melos gave prehistory an important place in the research of the BSA. Bosanquet published a study of prehistoric graves on Syra,[139] and Charles T. Currelly worked on 'the prehistoric period in the Levant'.[140] Evans and Myres made tours through Crete and brought to light the importance of Bronze Age sites; and perhaps most importantly for the chronology of the Aegean, the pottery from the Kamares Cave.[141] Francis B. Welch, who had worked at Phylakopi, went to the Levant in 1899/1900 'to report on the Aegean pottery found in the excavations of the Palestine Exploration Fund and practically established the fact that not only Cypriote but genuine Mycenaean vases were freely imported by the cities of the Philistine seaboard'.[142] The opening of Bronze Age sites at Knossos and Palaikastro on Crete meant that prehistory became a mainstream research area. Prehistory was encouraged by William Ridgeway in Cambridge, and this is reflected in the research topics conducted by Alan Wace. Wilfrid J. Farrell of Jesus College 'continued his researches in connection with the prehistoric age in Asia Minor, visiting Yortan near Gelembeh, the prehistoric fort in the district of Calloni and other sites in the neighbourhood of Mytilene'.[143] Farrell's work of connecting the Aegean islands, and in particular Lesbos, with mainland Anatolia was continued after the First World War by another Cambridge student, Winifred Lamb.[144]

Greek pottery

As students arrived in Athens they were faced with quantities of unpublished pots and fragments from excavations, chance finds and old collections. As George C. Richards expressed the situation in relation to his study of fragments from the Athenian acropolis,

---

[135] *E.g.* J. G. Smith, C. C. Edgar, C. A. Hutton.

[136] Loring 1895b.

[137] Woodhouse 1897.

[138] British School at Athens 1896/97, 230.

[139] Bosanquet 1895/6b.

[140] British School at Athens 1903/04, 245.

[141] Myres 1895.

[142] British School at Athens 1899/1900, 130.

[143] British School at Athens 1907/08, 425.

[144] Lamb 1936/37; Gill 2000b.

there is 'enough to satisfy the most ardent enthusiast for Greek ceramography'.[145] Richards had studied under Percy Gardner at Oxford,[146] and went to Athens as Craven University Fellow (1889/90). He was invited to work on the fragments from the Akropolis Museum by Kavvadias, the Ephor of Antiquities; Jane Harrison had earlier worked on part of the same collection.[147] The drawings were prepared by Gilliéron (who was to have a long association with members of the BSA).[148] One of the pieces included a pot fragment from under the layer of poros chips east of the Parthenon which he associated with the Persian destruction level. [149]

Richards was followed to Athens by Henry Stuart-Jones (best known for his work on the *Greek Lexicon*), also from Balliol and a pupil of Percy Gardner, who held a Craven University Fellowship. One of the pieces he studied was a red-figured cup in the National Museum found at Tanagra which carried the inscription *Phintias epoiesen* and this was discussed in a paper read to a meeting of the BSA in March 1891.[150] However, as this was due to be published by P. Hartwig, Stuart-Jones changed the focus of his final version.[151] He was able to discuss a range of material linked to Phintias and discuss the complex chronological issues including the use of *kalos* names.

Eugénie Sellers published three white-ground lekythoi excavated at Eretria in 1888.[152] Ernest Gardner bought a white-ground lekythos, said to be from Eretria, for the BSA's collection in 1893.[153] The next BSA student to work on figure-decorated pottery was the Cambridge-educated Robert Carr Bosanquet. He went to Athens in the spring of 1895 to work on Attic white ground lekythoi.[154] In November of the same year he was in Dresden working on 'the Athenian white-ground vases of the fifth century'.[155] In December he was in Mannheim discussing his project with Adolph Furtwängler.

> After the lecture I caught him in the passage – a German lecturer enters at a run, begins at once, and utters his last words as he bangs the door at the end – and explained that I was working at *Lekythi* and wanted to photograph some of his vases. He answered me … with a test question – I suppose they want to see whether one is only an amateur or serious. '*Lekythi*' he said, "you have some interesting *lekythi* in the British Museum – the "Orestes" and the "Patroclus, Farewell" for instance." Now

---

[145] Richards 1892/3, 281.

[146] For Gardner on Greek pottery: Gardner 1933, 55.

[147] Harrison 1888b.

[148] For Gilliéron: Butcher and Gill 1993.

[149] Richards 1894a, 186-87.

[150] Athens, NM 1628, from Tanagra.

[151] Stuart-Jones 1891. For a discussion of Hartwig's work: Rouet 2001, 30-34. There is mention of Hartwig's 'belief that he alone had the right to talk about a vase that he owned …' (p. 33).

[152] Sellers 1892/3.

[153] Gardner 1894b.

[154] British School at Athens 1894/95, 25. Bosanquet 1896; Bosanquet 1899.

[155] Bosanquet 1938, 42 (20 November 1895, to his sister Amy).

those are just the two about whose genuineness – at least as far as their inscriptions go – I have always had doubts. And F. is one of the most unerring – and, I must say, positive authorities on the question of forgeries, and I knew he had been in London lately – I saw him in the Museum – and must know the truth. So I plunged, sink or swim, and said I believed the inscriptions to be false. His whole face changed. All the fire in his eyes flashed up and he said – 'Ja! Ich halte die Beide für falsch' – then quiet and dry again – 'Sie können ruhig studieren und photographieren.' So I was saved.[156]

This research was published in 1896.[157] Bosanquet included a series of lekythoi from Eretria in the National Museum.[158] Like Richards and Stuart-Jones, the starting point for Bosanquet was the inscriptions. He published a further study based on a white-ground lekythos discovered at Eretria in 1889.[159]

John H. Hopkinson, another student of Percy Gardner, went to Athens as Craven University Fellow in 1899/1900 to work on 'the history of vase-painting'.[160] He worked with John Baker-Penoyre (Keble College) on a study of the figure-decorated pottery of Melos.[161] This had been prompted by the discovery of 'Melian' pottery in the Rheneia deposits in 1898. The interest in this fabric had been prompted by the BSA work on Melos, and Harcourt-Smith had purchased a piece for the BSA's collection. This interest in pottery from the islands was continued by John L. Stokes (Pembroke College, Cambridge) who worked on Rhodian relief pithoi in 1903/04.[162]

Economic issues were addressed by Gisela M. A. Richter in her study of the distribution of Attic pottery.[163] She later worked on Protoattic pottery, based on a new acquisition at the Metropolitan Museum of Art in New York.[164] A further student to work on figure-decorated pottery was John P. Droop (Trinity College, Cambridge). He excavated in Laconia and became interested in the archaic Laconian pottery. This pottery had gained the name 'Cyrenaic' due to the frequency of the type in North Africa.[165] The focus of his study was a Laconian cup said to have been found at Corinth and subsequently acquired by the Fitzwilliam Museum, and another in the National Museum, Athens, which had been acquired on the Athenian market. Following further 'stratified'

[156] Bosanquet 1938, 43-44 (10 December 1895, to his mother).

[157] Bosanquet 1896.

[158] For Waldstein's work at Eretria and his search for white-ground lekythoi: Lord 1947, 75.

[159] Bosanquet 1899.

[160] British School at Athens 1899/1900, 130.

[161] Hopkinson and Baker-Penoyre 1902. Hopkinson wrote the main study, and Baker-Penoyre added 'Three early island vases recently acquired by the British School at Athens'.

[162] British School at Athens 1903/04, 245; Stokes 1905/06.

[163] Richter 1904/5.

[164] Richter 1912.

[165] Schaus 1985. As Droop noted, it was thanks to the BSA's work in Laconia that made it possible to ascertain that the pottery was made in Laconia: Droop 1910.

excavations at Sparta by the BSA, Droop developed a chronological structure for this type of Laconian pottery.[166] He further revised this scheme after the First World War.[167]

There were two other Cambridge students working on figure-decorated pottery. Eustace M. W. Tillyard, who was admitted in 1911/12, was subsequently awarded a prize fellowship at Jesus College to work on the catalogue of the Hope Collection of Greek pottery.[168] Evelyn Radford (Newnham College) was admitted to the BSA in 1913/14 and published a study on Euphronios.[169] Max L. W. Laistner, another Cambridge student, worked on Geometric pottery found at Delphi.[170]

One of the interests in the study of Greek pottery painting was the recovery of lost Greek paintings known from descriptions in ancient writers such as the Elder Pliny. This was probably the motivation of F. R. Earp who studied Greek painting at Pompeii and Naples.[171]

Sculpture

Ernest Gardner was the first Cambridge student at the BSA (1886/87). One of the tasks for his first year was a survey of Greek sculpture including a description of Kavvadias' installation in the Athenian Central Museum (later known as The National Archaeological Museum).[172] Gardner mentioned works from Tegea, Delos, and Epidauros now on display in Athens; and then reviewed the displays in the Acropolis Museum, noting the newly discovered archaic statues, and the museum at Olympia. The archaic sculptures from the Athenian acropolis were the subject of a longer, separate study.[173]

Gardner researched the technique of ancient Greek sculpture through the study of unfinished pieces.[174] These included an unfinished kouros from Naxos, an unfinished late classical piece from Rheneia, and other unfinished pieces in the Archaeological Museum. A further study published from Gardner's time as Director was a head from his excavations at Paphos on Cyprus, and the stela of Kephisodotos, possibly from Lerna, in the museum at Argos.[175] After his move to University College London, Gardner prepared a *Handbook of Greek Sculpture*.[176]

There was a Cambridge interest in classical sculpture, perhaps as a result of Charles Waldstein. Gardner's approach to sculpture is reflected in E. F. Benson's study of a

---

[166] Droop 1910.

[167] Droop 1932. He revised this in the light of Ure 1932.

[168] Tillyard 1923.

[169] Radford 1915.

[170] Laistner 1912/13.

[171] Earp was prevented from arriving in Athens due to ill health.

[172] Gardner 1887c. For the sculpture collection in the National Archaeological Museum: Kaltsas 2002.

[173] Gardner 1887b.

[174] Gardner 1890b. For the unfinished kouros from Naxos: Athens NM14, Kaltsas 2002, no. 67.

[175] Gardner 1890c.

[176] Gardner 1896; Gardner 1897.

fourth-century head in the National Museum that had been found at Laurion. This issue was whether it was a representation of Praxiteles' head of Apollo from the Lyceum.[177] Frederick A. C. Morrison of Jesus College worked on polychromy in Greek sculpture, almost certainly inspired by the recently discovered archaic korai from the Athenian acropolis.[178] His death in 1899 stopped him from completing this work. Vincent W. Yorke of King's College spotted three fragments of relief on the Athenian Acropolis that he linked to the sculpted balustrade of the temple of Athena Nike.[179]

Perhaps one of the strongest students of Hellenistic sculpture to emerge from Cambridge was Alan Wace.[180] In his first year he made a study of the Apollo seated on the omphalos.[181] This coincided with Henry Stuart-Jones' project on ancient sculpture in Rome, and Wace spent part of each subsequent years at the BSR.[182] His initial project was a study of Hellenistic royal portraits, then historical reliefs in collections in Italy.[183] Wace later published a study of Hellenistic sculpture.[184] Wace also worked on Laconian sculpture in connection with the catalogue of the Museum at Sparta.[185]

Several Cambridge women worked on sculpture. They were restricted from working on excavations; museum-based projects were considered more suitable. Margery K. Welsh of Newnham College worked on 'portrait and honorary statues'.[186] Eugénie Sellers (Mrs Arthur Strong), of Girton College, worked on Greek sculpture after her time in Athens.[187] Ethel B. Abrahams of Bedford College, University of London was a pupil of A. B. Cook and had then studied Greek dress as her MA dissertation with Ernest Gardner; she drew on the recently discovered archaic statues from the archaic acropolis.[188]

Only a handful of Oxford students worked on sculpture. Edgar studied the Greek stelae found in the Kynosarges excavations.[189] Henry Stuart-Jones developed a major project on sculpture in the collections in Rome which involved several of the BSA students in including Alan Wace and Guy Dickins.[190] Dickins, a student of Percy Gardner, was admitted to the BSA in 1904/05 and started to work on Damophon (alongside his

---

[177] Athens NM 183. Benson 1895b; Kaltsas 2002, 247, no. 514. See also British School at Athens 1894/95, 25.

[178] British School at Athens 1896/97, 230.

[179] Yorke 1892.

[180] British School at Athens 1903/04, 245.

[181] Wace 1902/03.

[182] Gill 2004q; Gill 2004m.

[183] Wace 1905b; Wace 1906c; Wace 1906a; Wace 1907; Wace 1910; Stuart-Jones 1912.

[184] Wace 1935.

[185] British School at Athens 1903/04, 245.

[186] British School at Athens 1903/04, 245; Welsh 1904/5.

[187] Sellers 1894; Strong 1907.

[188] Abrahams 1908.

[189] British School at Athens 1896/97, 230; Edgar 1897.

[190] Stuart-Jones 1905; Stuart-Jones 1910; Stuart-Jones 1912; Stuart-Jones 1926.

contribution to excavations in Laconia).[191] During his second year at the BSA the Greek Government invited Dickins to 'help in the re-erection of the colossal group at Lycosura' in Arcadia.[192] Excavations had been conducted at the site by the Greek Archaeological Service under P. Kavvadias in 1889 and 1890. Further excavations continued in 1895. The statues were found in the summer of 1889 and were quickly reported as the cult statues described by Pausanias in the temple of Despoina. These colossal statues, created by Damophon of Messene, represented Despoina and Demeter, seated on a throne, with Artemis and Anytos alongside. Waldstein wrote:

> Of these statues, nearly all the fragments apparently have been recovered. There are over a hundred fragments, most of which have already been brought here, though not unpacked and not visible to the public, while some of the torsos were so large that they could not be transported on the roads that exist there. Special arrangements will be made for transporting them soon.[193]

What Waldstein stressed was that this was the discovery of an original cult statue *in situ*.

Interest was stirred in Damophon by an article written by Augustus M. Daniel, an associate student of the BSA, who restated a case for the fourth century.[194] Waldstein responded in a short note arguing in favour of a date in the early fourth century BC.[195] The case for a second century BC date was presented by Ida Carleton Thallon, who had been a student at ASCSA in 1899-1901.[196] Dickins developed these earlier speculations, and at the annual meeting of the Hellenic Society in June 1908 it was reported that he had reconstructed 'out of unnumbered fragments, of the great group by Damophon of Messene … giving us for the first time satisfactory evidence in regard to monumental sculpture in Greece in the second century BC '[197] He continued this work in the study of the sculptures in collections at Rome.[198] One of the consequences of Dickins' work on Damophon was that he was invited to prepare the *Catalogue of the Acropolis Museum*.[199] Kavvadias had invited the BSA to take part in the project in 1906.[200]

---

[191] Dickins 1904/05a.

[192] 'British School at Athens', *The Times* 31 October 1906, 11.

[193] Pausanias 8. 37. 1-6. See Stewart 1990, 94-96, 304 (T 156), figs. 788-92. Charles Waldstein reported on the statues: 'Greek archaeological discoveries' *The Times* March 6, 1890, 3; the fuller report by Waldstein was quoted in Frothingham 1890, 209-11. Waldstein lectured on the discoveries at the Royal Institution in London: 'Recent excavations in Greece', *The Times* 26 May 1890, 10. See also Gardner 1890a, 213-14; and for later excavations: Gardner 1891, 389-90. For the pieces in the National Archaeological Museum, Athens: Kaltsas 2002, 279-81, nos. 584-91.

[194] Daniel 1904. Daniel had studied Natural Sciences at Cambridge.

[195] Waldstein 1904.

[196] Thallon 1906.

[197] 'The Hellenic Society', *The Times* 24 June 1908, 18. For Dickins' studies: Dickins 1905/06a; Dickins 1906/07a; Dickins 1910/11.

[198] Dickins 1911, esp. 313-14.

[199] Dickins 1912.

[200] BSA Minute Book 5, Meeting of 16 October 1906.

Numismatics and Gems

Surprisingly few students studied ancient coins, especially given the interest expressed by Percy Gardner. Francis Brayne-Baker of Christ's College, Cambridge, worked on coins of Asia Minor.[201] Sidney W. Grose also of Christ's College worked on the McClean coins in the Fitzwilliam Museum and subsequently became Honorary Keeper there.[202] Alan Wace published a coin hoard of Hellenistic coins found at Sparta.[203] Among the Oxford students, Joseph G. Milne had excavated in Egypt (publishing coins from the Faiyum), and subsequently became deputy keeper of coins in the Ashmolean Museum (1931-51).[204] John W. Crowfoot worked on the iconography of Thracian coins, linking them to specific inscriptions from Athens.[205] E. S. G. Robinson worked on numismatics in the museums at Athens,[206] and collected coins on his journey through Lycia and Pamphylia.[207] He subsequently became Assistant Keeper, and then Keeper, in the Department of Coins and Medals at the British Museum. Two Cambridge students worked on gems: John L. Stokes of Pembroke College on Melian gems in the collection held by the BSA,[208] and S. C. Kaines-Smith of Magdalene College, on 'the relationship between certain types of engraved gems and the grave-*stelae*'.[209]

Museum studies

Gardner was able to declare that Athens was 'an indispensable place of study for archaeologists' due to the development of its museums and collections.[210] Among the Cambridge students working in Athenian museums were C. A. Hutton,[211] Robert J. G. Mayor, Eugénie Sellers, and Edward E. Sikes. Oxford students who worked on material in the museums in Athens included G. C. Richards (1889-91), O. H. Parry (1889-90), J. F. R. Stainer (1889-90), J. L. Myres (1892/93, 1893/94, 1894/95), and E. R. Bevan (1893/94). Henry Stuart Jones, another pupil of Gardner, was inspired to go to Athens to work on Greek pottery.

Students helped to research several museum catalogues. Wace and Tod prepared *A Catalogue of the Sparta Museum* (1906) as part of the wider BSA work in Laconia. Its success led to an invitation being extended to the BSA to prepare a catalogue, in two volumes, on the Akropolis Museum. As early as 1890 Gardner regretted the lack of a

---

[201] Baker 1892; Baker 1893.

[202] Grose 1916; Grose 1923.

[203] Wace 1907/08.

[204] Grenfell, *et al.* 1900; Milne 1917; Milne 1920; Milne 1922a.

[205] British School at Athens 1896/97, 230; Crowfoot 1897.

[206] British School at Athens 1910/11, 287.

[207] British School at Athens 1910/11, 287; Robinson 1914.

[208] British School at Athens 1903/04, 245.

[209] British School at Athens 1899/1900, 130.

[210] Gardner 1891, 397.

[211] Hutton 1896/7.

'scientific catalogue for the Acropolis Museum'.[212] Some of the students studied material from the excavations. Arthur G. Bather worked on bronze fragments,[213] Hutton on terracottas,[214] Woodward on inscriptions,[215] and G. C. Richards on fragments of pottery.[216] This project was under the direction of Guy Dickins, whose main interest lay in sculpture.[217] Droop 'did some preliminary work on the minor antiquities of the Acropolis Museum, in connection with the Catalogue now being compiled by the members of the School'.[218] Dorothy Lamb, assisted by Lilian Tennant,[219] prepared the catalogue section on terracottas.[220] The Acropolis project was completed by Stanley Casson following Dickins' death in the First World War.[221] A further museum project was undertaken by J. L. Myres on the catalogue of the Cyprus Museum.[222]

Epigraphy

During the nineteenth century there had been a concerted attempt to collect and publish Greek and Latin inscriptions. The Oxford educated William Paton had travelled widely in the Aegean and lived on the Anatolian mainland.[223] Although he was not a member of the BSA, he actively encouraged students to engage with fieldwork. Ernest Gardner had a developed interest in epigraphy and published studies on new material from Petrie's excavations at Naukratis,[224] Cockerell's texts from Greece, as well as squeezes supplied by Newton from Kos.[225] He collaborated with E. S. Roberts, the master of Gonville and Caius College, on an *Introduction to Greek Epigraphy*.[226] As student and Director he continued this interest, publishing a text from Chalcedon in a private collection,[227] and a

[212] Gardner 1890a, 211.

[213] Bather 1892a; Bather 1892b.

[214] Hutton 1897.

[215] British School at Athens 1907/08, 427. This was published as Woodward 1908.

[216] Richards 1892/3; Richards 1894a; Richards 1894b.

[217] British School at Athens 1907/08, 425.

[218] British School at Athens 1907/08, 425.

[219] British School at Athens 1910/11, 287.

[220] British School at Athens 1910/11, 286-87.

[221] Casson 1921.

[222] Ohnefalsch-Richter and Myres 1899.

[223] *E.g.* Paton 1894; Paton and Myres 1896. For his life: Gill 2004n.

[224] Petrie and Gardner 1886; Gardner 1888.

[225] Gardner 1885a; Gardner 1885b; Gardner 1885c.

[226] Roberts and Gardner 1887.

[227] Gardner 1886c.

text from Neapolis (ancient Boiai) in the Malea peninsula in Laconia,[228] and offered a new reading of the Archermos inscription from Delos.[229]

New inscriptions were uncovered during BSA excavations and these formed part of the final reports: for example, Geraki[230] and Thalamai in Laconia,[231] Sparta,[232] Megalopolis,[233] Knossos,[234] and Praesos.[235] Students also observed new texts during their travels. Hogarth, during his first visit to Salonica, made a note of new inscriptions.[236] Loring saw three new inscriptions on the site of ancient Tegea in 1893 and transferred them to a local museum; he also copied a previously unknown inscription at Livadhia.[237] Forster published texts from the preliminary surveys in Laconia.[238] Woodhouse considered inscriptions as part of his wider study of Aetolia.[239] Wace and Thompson published a Latin inscription from the reign of Trajan during their travels in Macedonia.[240] On a later journey Wace and Woodward published further texts from upper Macedonia.[241] Other inscriptions noted by Wace and Thompson in Macedonia and Thessaly were published by Woodward.[242] Baker-Penoyre noted inscriptions on Thasos and at Kavalla.[243] Tod published a fragment of the Edict of Diocletian from Asine.[244] He also made a journey through south-western Messenia looking for new texts.[245] Roger M. Heath published three proxeny decrees from the Megarid,[246] and Amy Hutton published new texts from Suvla Bay.[247]

---

[228] Gardner 1887a. For the site: Cavanagh, *et al.* 1996, 312-13, NN251.

[229] Gardner 1893.

[230] Tillyard 1904/05.

[231] Dickins 1904/05c.

[232] Tillyard 1905/06a; Tillyard 1905/06b; Tod, *et al.* 1906/07; Woodward 1907/08; Woodward 1908/09a; Woodward 1909/10a.

[233] Loring 1890.

[234] Hogarth 1899/1900c.

[235] Bosanquet 1909/10.

[236] Hogarth 1888b.

[237] Loring 1895a.

[238] Forster 1903/04a; Forster 1905.

[239] Woodhouse 1893.

[240] Wace and Thompson 1910/11. For further inscriptions observed by Wace in Macedonia: Tod 1922, 180-81.

[241] Wace and Woodward 1911/12.

[242] Woodward 1913. See also Woodward 1911/12.

[243] Baker-Penoyre and Tod 1909.

[244] Tod 1904.

[245] Tod 1905.

[246] Heath 1912/13.

[247] Hutton 1914/16b.

The development of the Asia Minor Exploration Fund saw the recording of large numbers of new texts. These included ones from eastern Anatolia,[248] Pontus and Pisidia,[249] Pisidian Antioch,[250] Mysia,[251] Caria,[252] Pamphylia,[253] and Lycia.[254] Such epigraphical studies were not confined to Greece (or Anatolia) and included Droop's work on Messapian inscriptions.[255] Cheesman published an inscription observed by Henry Reitlinger, at Gerasa in Syria.[256] Former BSA students also turned their skills to Graeco-Roman Egypt: Milne on Greek inscriptions,[257] and Edgar on newly recognised Greek inscriptions and papyri.[258]

Students also worked on historic collections of inscriptions: Hutton worked on the Greek inscriptions from Petworth House in Sussex,[259] and Ormerod on the Liverpool Royal Institution.[260] Tod's work on epigraphy developed during his time as a student at the BSA, and this evolved into regular epigraphic surveys.[261] Woodward was involved with the preparation of the catalogue of the Acropolis Museum and made a number of epigraphic studies.[262]

History of Christianity

One of the driving forces for the work in Asia Minor was the discovery of sites relating to the early church. Several students from Scotland, reflecting Ramsay's influence, were admitted to the BSA to work on early Christianity. This change took place at the end of Gardner's directorship, perhaps in response to his desire to broaden the appeal of the BSA. The first two students admitted for this area of study were John Duncan and Adam F. Findlay.[263] While Duncan worked on Modern Greek before joining Petrie in Egypt,

---

[248] Yorke 1898.

[249] Cumont and Anderson 1912; Woodward 1910/11a. See also Munro 1900.

[250] *E.g.* Anderson 1913; Cheesman 1913.

[251] Munro 1897.

[252] Paton and Myres 1896.

[253] Ormerod and Robinson 1910/11; Ormerod 1912.

[254] Ormerod and Robinson 1914.

[255] Droop 1905/06b.

[256] Cheesman 1914.

[257] Milne 1901.

[258] Edgar 1925; Edgar 1928;Edgar 1937.

[259] Hutton 1914/16a.

[260] Ormerod 1914.

[261] *E.g.* Tod 1901/02; Tod 1902/03b; Tod 1903/04; Tod 1904/05; Tod 1911/12; Tod 1913. For his surveys: Tod 1914; Tod 1915b. The surveys had originally appeared in *The Year's Work in Classical Studies* from 1906 to 1910.

[262] Woodward 1908; Woodward 1908/09b; Woodward 1909; Woodward 1909/10b; Woodward 1910; Woodward 1911.

[263] British School at Athens 1894/95, 26.

Findlay 'worked at N. T. criticism and antiquities, and Modern Greek … made special study of the question of St. Paul and the Areopagus'.[264] This area of study continued the followed year with the admission of Archibald Paterson from Edinburgh, working on Christian antiquities.[265]

Modern Greece

John Ellingham Brooks worked on 'early Italian travellers in Greece, with the Greek teachers in Italy at the time of the Renaissance, and with the records and doings of the French and English travellers at the end of the last and the beginning of the present century' (sc. late 18th and early 19th centuries).[266] R. A. H. Bickford-Smith was admitted to work on a history of Greece; he subsequently prepared a study of Crete at the end of its period under Ottoman rule.[267] Arnold Toynbee was also influenced in his study of history by his time in Greece.[268]

Folklore was an element of student research. The Cambridge emphasis can probably be traced back to J. G. Frazer (himself a student at the BSA) and to William Henry Denham Rouse (1863-1950). One of the earliest discussions is by Edward E. Sikes of St John's, who worked on folklore elements in Hesiod in the early 1890s. Sikes drew on contemporary folklore studies and interpretations.[269] John C. Lawson of Pembroke College was interested in the traditions of Skyros, and studied 'folk-lore and traditional beliefs of the Greek people' drawing on 'oral as well as literary sources'.[270] F. W. Hasluck of King's College collected folklore traditions in Anatolia.[271] R. M. Dawkins of Emmanuel College recorded folk-tales and noted carnivals.[272] A. J. B. Wace also collected folk-tales and reworked them in a series of short stories.[273] One of the few non-Cambridge students to work in this area was Mary Hamilton of St Andrews, who researched Greek saints and explored continuity from pre-Christian times.[274]

Philology

Students at the BSA usually had developed ancient language skills and this is reflected in the study of historical texts for topography. Yet few chose to work on literary texts. An

---

[264] Findlay 1894/5.

[265] British School at Athens 1895/96, 4.

[266] British School at Athens 1894/95, 26.

[267] Bickford-Smith 1893; Bickford-Smith and Prior 1898.

[268] Clogg 2000, 21-26. See also Clogg 1986.

[269] Sikes 1893. He acknowledged the influence of Frazer and Rouse. See also Sikes 1909.

[270] British School at Athens 1899/1900, 129; Lawson 1899/1900; Lawson 1910.

[271] Hasluck 1911/12b; Hasluck 1912/13; Hasluck, et al. 1926.

[272] Dawkins 1904; Dawkins 1904/05g; Dawkins and Rouse 1906; Dawkins 1906; Dawkins 1951; Dawkins 1953.

[273] Wace 1964.

[274] Hamilton 1906; Hamilton 1906/7; Hamilton 1910.

exception was J. G. Frazer who worked on his commentary on Pausanias.[275] The study of modern Greek dialects was one of the interests of BSA students. In 1896/7, W. W. Reid, a graduate of Aberdeen and Edinburgh, was admitted as a BSA student and 'worked at Modern Greek, and proceeded to Asia Minor and Cyprus'.[276] While some students were interested in developing their language skills, several made specific philological studies. One of the most gifted linguists was Richard M. Dawkins.[277] He had been admitted to the BSA in 1902 and seems to have developed an interest in language during his visit to Karpathos; by the following year (while he was also engaged in excavating in eastern Crete) he was working on 'the dialects of Carpathos and Palaikastro'.[278] Dawkins and Hasluck travelled through the islands and into Anatolia. One of the key travels was in the May and June of 1906 just before Dawkins took up office as Director of the BSA.[279] They started at Smyrna, using the railway as a way of visiting a number of sites as far as Soma, and then continued by road to Balukiser, Brusa and Nicaea.[280]

After his appointment as Director, Dawkins made three main journeys through Cappadocia in 1909, 1910 and 1911 that provided him with the research material for his main study of Greek dialects.[281] In the last of these journeys he was accompanied by the Oxford-educated William R. Halliday, Craven Fellow at the BSA, and later Professor of Ancient History at Liverpool. In 1914 Dawkins travelled in the Pontus to work on the dialects of the Greek communities on the Black Sea shore, but the outbreak of war and subsequent events meant that his study of the dialect of the region never came to fruition.[282]

Dawkins was not alone in studying Greek dialect. During his directorship Wace and Thompson visited Rhodes 'with a view to studying both ancient sites and modern dialects'.[283] Wace and Thompson then worked in northern Greece where Thompson made a study of 'the Vlach language'.[284] Arnold Toynbee described their methods from his time as a student in 1911/12:

> Wace used to accompany his Vlachs on their migrations between their summer and their winter pastures. In most of these varied pursuits, Thompson was Wace's partner. They hunted together like a couple of hounds; and, like hounds on the scent,

---

[275] Frazer 1898.

[276] British School at Athens 1897/98, 121.

[277] Mackridge 1990; Gill 2004g.

[278] Dawkins 1902/03e; Dawkins 1903/04i. See also British School at Athens 1903/04, 245.

[279] Dawkins and Hasluck 1905/06.

[280] See *BSA Annual Report* 1905/6, 483.

[281] Dawkins 1908/09c; Dawkins 1910c; Dawkins 1910b; Dawkins and Halliday 1916; Dawkins 1934. See also, Mackridge 1990, 203-04.

[282] Mackridge 1990, 206.

[283] British School at Athens 1907/08, 426.

[284] British School at Athens 1910/11, 287. See also Wace and Thompson 1914.

they were indifferent, while chasing their quarry, to heat, cold, hunger, or exposure to the elements. They set one an exacting standard of physical endurance.[285]

Cecil A. Scutt, admitted to the BSA under Dawkins, made a study of Tsakonian dialect in the communities of the Argolic gulf to the north-east of Sparta.[286] It is likely that this was an area of interest to Dawkins, emanating from his time excavating at Artemis Orthia; Dawkins and Scutt visited Naxos in December 1912 to study the dialect of the island.[287]

Textiles

Louisa Pesel, the Director of the Royal Hellenic School of Needlework, was admitted as an associate of the BSA in 1902/03, the year in which Alan Wace was admitted. Bosanquet, the Director, also had an interest in textiles and this may have encouraged Wace to collect embroidery on his various travels. By 1905 he was an authority on the subject and prepared a *Catalogue of a collection of Modern Greek Embroideries* for an exhibition at the Fitzwilliam Museum.[288] Wace and Dawkins made a specific study of embroidery in the southern Sporades in the summer of 1906, and they collaborated on a study for the *Burlington Magazine*.[289] Wace and Dawkins lent their collection of textiles for an exhibition of textiles at the Burlington Fine Arts Club in 1914.[290] After Wace's term of office as Director at the BSA came to end, he was appointed Deputy keeper in the Department of Textiles at the Victoria and Albert Museum.[291]

Other projects

Students had a wide range of interests beyond the core areas. In the area of Greek religion, E. F. Benson worked on the cult of Asclepius,[292] and A. P. Oppé on Delphi.[293] L. B. Tillard studied Greek fortifications,[294] a topic that was continued immediately after the First World War by Lilian Chandler.[295] W. M. Calder researched Seleucid history.[296] One of the more unusual topics was undertaken by Pirie-Gordon, who was making 'a study of the mediaeval

[285] Toynbee 1969, 22.

[286] Scutt 1912/13; Scutt 1913/14.

[287] British School at Athens 1912/13, 269.

[288] Wace 1905a.

[289] British School at Athens 1905/06, 484; Dawkins and Wace 1905/06; Wace and Dawkins 1914. For work in the Sporades: Wace 1906b.

[290] Wace and Lawrence 1914.

[291] For this aspect of his career with bibliography: Gill 2004q.

[292] British School at Athens 1894/95, 25.

[293] Oppé 1904.

[294] British School at Athens 1910/11, 287.

[295] Chandler 1926. For the context for her work: Gill 2007.

[296] British School at Athens 1907/08, 425.

castles of Cyprus and Syria'.[297] In fact he was making a general tour of the eastern Mediterranean with his friend Harry Luke.[298]

Conclusion

The students of the BSA worked on a wide range of topics from the core areas of classical archaeology, such as pottery and sculpture, to dialects and textiles. Some specialized areas, such as epigraphy, reflected their own educational backgrounds. This combined research was written up and appeared largely in articles in the School's *Annual*.

---

[297] British School at Athens 1907/08, 426.

[298] Gill 2006a.

CHAPTER 5:

WOMEN AT THE BRITISH SCHOOL AT ATHENS

By 1910, David G. Hogarth could observe, 'The search for ancient things below ground appeals to most minds, but especially to those of women, who are moved even more than men by curiosity and the passion of hazard'.[1] The focus for the lecture was his excavations in Egypt; Egyptology had particularly drawn the interest of women since the publication of Amelia Edwards' *A Thousand Miles up the Nile* (1877).[2] Women had even started to conduct fieldwork and excavate in Egypt, including Margaret Benson (sister of E. F. Benson, a BSA student) at the temple of Mut at Thebes.[3] Hogarth had observed the growing number of women who wished to participate in the life of the BSA and was anticipating the expectation that women would wish to be involved in British archaeological excavations in Greece. Yet he had his reservations: 'Not too nice a trade, you see, dear lady. Best let it be!'[4]

By the time that Hogarth's essay reappeared in *The Wandering Scholar* (1925), British women were making an important contribution to the archaeology of the Greek world. The work of British women in Greece during the 1920s and 1930s is relatively well documented. Women participated in excavations at Mycenae and Sparta, as well as in Macedonia.[5] Near all-women teams were to be developed by Winifred Lamb working on Lesbos, Chios and later in mainland Anatolia at Kusura.[6] Edith Eccles was to work on Chios, as well as on Crete with Mercy Money-Coutts, Hilda Pendlebury and John

---

[1] Hogarth 1910, 142 (Chapter VII: 'Digging'). The chapter is reproduced in Hogarth 1925, esp. p. 231 (with slightly different wording): 'The search for ancient things below ground appeals strongly to many minds, but especially to those of women, which are moved most readily by curiosity and the passion of hazard'.

[2] See Rees 1998.

[3] Benson 1917.

[4] Hogarth 1910, 159; Hogarth 1925, 250 (without '!').

[5] For Sparta see Hood 1998, nos. 11 (Ursula Dorothy Hunt), 12 (Winifred Lamb), 13 (Margaret Blanche Hobling) and 15 (Elaine Tankard). Winifred Lamb and May Herford participated in the Mycenae excavations. Lamb also joined the School excavations in Macedonia.

[6] For Lamb's work in Anatolia: Gill 2000b. For full details of Lamb's teams see Gill 2004r.

Pendlebury.[7] No longer were women confined to the library or museum: they were taking an active part in the fieldwork that had been considered the domain of men.[8]

Although this growth in archaeological work by women can be explained in part by the death during the First World War of many promising young men who had been students at the BSA,[9] a small number of British women had already paved the way in working at the BSA, touring the sites and museums of Greece, and taking part in excavations. Their achievements have been eclipsed by those of some of their male counterparts who gained a high profile in the archaeological world: men like Ernest Gardner, Yates Professor of Classical Archaeology in the University of London,[10] John H. Marshall, Director General of Antiquities in India,[11] and Richard M. Dawkins, Bywater and Sotheby Professor of Byzantine and Modern Greek Language and Literature in Oxford.[12] It is true that British women were not as prominent in the field as their American counterparts, but they were to make a significant contribution to the interpretation of the Greek world in late Victorian and Edwardian Britain. Women's visibility in Britain was increasing at the same time through the growing movement for women's suffrage, notably the National Union of Women's Suffrage Societies (1897) and later Emmeline Pankhurst's Women's Social and Political Union (1903).[13]

This was also a period of change in the political map of Greece. Thessaly had only been incorporated as part of Greece in 1881, Crete (still part of the Ottoman Empire) had been occupied by international forces in the wake of the 1897 war between Greece and Turkey (and was not ceded to Greece until 1913), Salonica was captured in November 1912 during the First Balkan War, and Macedonia was partially acquired after the Second Balkan War of the summer of 1912. In 1912 Chios, Lesbos and Samos were seized by the Greeks, and the Dodecanese was occupied by the Italians.[14] Thus the Aegean was not perceived as a 'safe' place for women to visit.

British Women in Greece

The BSA admitted its first male students for the 1886-87 session. Although women were not to be admitted as students until the 1890-91 session, women had long travelled in Greek lands. In the eighteenth century Lady Mary Wortley Montagu had travelled through

---

[7] Pendlebury, *et al.* 1937/38; Seiradaki 1960; Eccles, *et al.* 1934. For the background to this period: Huxley 2000; Grundon 2007.

[8] For the useful identification of areas of study suitable for women in the period before the First World War: Melman 1995, 38-39.

[9] The death of Guy Dickins was a particularly serious loss. For the British School's war memorial: *BSA* 24 (1919-20; 1920-21), 212.

[10] Gill 2004j.

[11] Gill 2000a.

[12] Jenkins 1955; Gill 2004g. For an assessment of his work: Mackridge 1990.

[13] For a perspective from an archaeologist's viewpoint: Murray 1963, 167-73 ('The suffrage movement'). For the growing number of women travelling abroad in this period: Birkett 1989.

[14] For a convenient history of modern Greece: Clogg 1992. For an assessment by a former student of the British School at Athens who had worked on material from Praisos and had participated in the Laconia survey: Forster 1941.

the Aegean islands, although she had not visited Athens itself.[15] The establishment of women's colleges in both Cambridge and Oxford during the nineteenth century opened up the possibility of higher education for women and developed an informed interest in classical ruins. In Cambridge, Girton College was founded in 1869, followed in 1871 by Newnham.[16] Those women choosing to read classics had not been drilled in the classical languages to the same extent as the men, and so the archaeological options within the degree scheme were particularly attractive.[17] An exception would be women trained at schools like Wycombe Abbey – where Dorothy Lamb was educated – which deliberately tried to emulate boys' public schools and included Latin and Greek in the curriculum.[18]

Jane Harrison, one of the first students to read classics at Newnham (1874-79), made regular trips to Greece, though she was never a student of the BSA. For example, she visited the temple of Apollo at Bassai in the spring of 1888 with D. S. MacColl.[19] Harrison also accompanied her Newnham student, Jessie Crum (later Stewart), to Greece in the Easter vacation of 1901.[20] Crum was in her final year of studies and thus was not in a position to be admitted to the BSA as a student at this stage. Her trip, however, provided her with first-hand observations that helped her to obtain a First in Part II of the Classical Tripos. Mabel Winkworth, daughter of early benefactors of Newnham, spent a year at Newnham (1880-81); and although she did not follow classics specifically, she combined her studies with a tour of Greece.[21] Almost certainly, like Jane Harrison, she had been influenced by the Cambridge lectures of Sidney Colvin, the Slade Professor of Fine Art and Director of the Fitzwilliam Museum.[22] Winkworth's year at Newnham would have coincided with the first year in Cambridge for Charles Waldstein, who lectured on classical archaeology. It was also the first year that the College had its own classics lecturer, Margaret Merrifield.[23] Winkworth's love of Greece was later to be passed on to her daughter, Winifred Lamb, who excavated widely in Greece, the Aegean Islands and in mainland Anatolia during the 1920s and 1930s.[24]

Women students from Oxford also travelled to Greece. Maria Millington Lathbury, stepmother to Sir Arthur Evans, read classics at Somerville College, although she did not apply until she was thirty.[25] She had been influenced in her interest in classical archaeology by Jane Harrison's 'Extension Lectures in the suburbs', and subsequently in

---

[15] Grundy 1999.

[16] See Tullberg 1998.

[17] Breay 1999.

[18] Gill 2004i.

[19] Stewart 1959, 90; Peacock 1988; Beard 2000, 70-71; Robinson 2002, 99-100. See also Harrison 1888a.

[20] Stray 1995; Beard 2000, 131; Robinson 2002, 133-38.

[21] Winifred Lamb's letters home from Greece refer to Mabel's travels in the Peloponnese.

[22] For Colvin's influence see Cook 1931, 46. See also Colvin 1921.

[23] Breay 1999, 57; Robinson 2002, 54.

[24] Gill 2004r.

[25] Evans 1964, 21. See also MacGillivray 2000, 101.

Oxford by Percy Gardner, the Lincoln and Merton Professor of Classical Archaeology.[26] With Harrison's help, she developed her own course of lectures on classical archaeology. She was subsequently invited to travel to Greece 'as companion to a younger woman', and in the early summer of 1892 they joined one of Dörpfeld's organised tours of the islands, in addition to travelling round the Peloponnese.[27]

Gertrude Bell, a student at Lady Margaret Hall during the 1880s, was a contemporary and friend of Janet Hogarth,[28] sister of David Hogarth, one of the first students at the BSA and subsequently Director (1897-1900).[29] In early 1889, soon after finishing in Oxford, Bell visited Constantinople.[30] In 1899 she travelled to Athens, in the company of her father and uncle (the classicist, Thomas Marshall), and joined one of Dörpfeld's parties.[31] However, Bell was to be drawn to Arabia rather than to the Aegean, though she did work with Hogarth again as a member of the Arab Bureau during the First World War.[32]

American Precedents

By the time that Eugénie Sellers was admitted as a student to the BSA, women had already joined the ASCSA. Annie S. Peck, a graduate of the University of Michigan, had been the first in 1885-86;[33] she then returned to Smith College, the institution attended by so many American women who were to go out to Athens. She may have been an influence on Harriet Boyd, although Boyd dropped Latin, Peck's subject, after her first year.[34] Boyd first went to Greece in 1896-97, and subsequently as a Fellow of the Archaeological Institute of America (1898-99) and as Agnes Hoppin Memorial Fellow (1899-1900).[35]

When Boyd arrived in Greece, ASCSA was mainly excavating at Corinth. In 1897 Rufus B. Richardson, the Director of ASCSA, had only conducted a very limited excavation at Corinth, but in both 1899 and 1900 there were full seasons.[36] Boyd's first year at the School was interrupted by uprisings on Crete and the Greek-Turkish 'Thirty Day War' which brought about the defeat of Greece.[37] Boyd herself served as a nurse at

---

[26] Evans 1964, 21-22.

[27] Evans 1964, 22-23.

[28] Winstone 1993, 16.

[29] Waterhouse 1986, 9. For details of Hogarth's career: Lock 1990; Ryan 1995; Perry 2000; Gill 2004l. For obituaries and other biographical studies: Breasted 1928; Fletcher 1928; Hall 1928; Sayce 1927.

[30] Winstone 1993, 24.

[31] Winstone 1993, 66.

[32] Westrate 1992.

[33] Lord 1947, 15.

[34] Allsebrook 1992, 11.

[35] Lord 1947, 370.

[36] Lord 1947, 298. The excavation dates were: 14-23 April 1897; 27 March-27 May 1899; 30 March-28 May 1900.

[37] Clogg 1992, 70.

Volos during the conflict.[38] In 1899, as a Fellow of the Archaeological Institute of America, Boyd had hoped to 'try to find tombs in the neighbourhood of Corinth, where the American School was digging'.[39] She had envisaged using part of her Fellowship money towards such work, but 'the Director did not approve'.[40] Boyd was determined, as the official history of ASCSA presented it, to disprove 'Richardson's dictum that a woman could not endure the hardship of active excavation by conducting at her own expense an excavation in Crete'.[41] Encouraged by both David G. Hogarth, BSA Director (1897-1900), and Arthur J. Evans, excavator of Knossos,[42] Boyd looked to Crete, supported both by Richardson and the President of the Archaeological Institute of America.[43] Boyd set off for Crete accompanied by Jean Patten, an old friend and student of botany,[44] in what has been described as 'the first expedition in the Mediterranean directed by a woman'.[45] There she conducted excavations at Kavousi.[46] The following year, now holding a post at Smith College, Boyd returned to Crete with Blanche Wheeler,[47] which resulted in her excavation of Gournia.[48] By the next year, Boyd's contribution to archaeology had been noted in the *Philadelphia Public Ledger* of 5 March 1902:

> A woman has shattered another tradition and successfully entered unaided a field hitherto occupied almost exclusively by men, namely archaeological exploration. Special skill and training, infinite patience and executive ability, much courage, power of endurance and force of will are required for this work, besides other qualifications supposedly possessed only by men.[49]

Boyd's contribution to archaeology was praised in *The Times Weekly Edition* of 6 August 1909 which recorded:

> In these days of woman's emancipation there should be nothing surprising in the success-ful conduct of a scientific excavation in the Near East by a lady, and least of all by an American lady; but, as a matter of fact, Mrs Hawes [Boyd had married Charles Hawes] comes before us as actually the first of her sex who has both directed in person a scientific excavation in classical soil and edited in chief the scientific statement of its results.[50]

[38] Allsebrook 1992, 44-55.

[39] Quoted in Allsebrook 1992, 85.

[40] Allsebrook 1992, 85.

[41] Lord 1947, 95. See Bolger 1994, esp. 44.

[42] See MacGillivray 2000, 180 for her visit to Knossos in April 1900.

[43] Allsebrook 1992, 85.

[44] Allsebrook 1992, 80, 85.

[45] Bolger 1994, 44. This claims excludes the work of women like Maggie Benson in Egypt.

[46] Boyd 1901. See also MacGillivray 2000, 188. For the site: Myers, *et al.* 1992, 120-23.

[47] Allsebrook 1992, 99.

[48] Hawes, *et al.* 1908. For the site: Myers, *et al.* 1992, 104-11.

[49] Quoted in Allsebrook 1992, 110-11.

[50] Quoted in Allsebrook 1992, 134.

Boyd's excavations on Crete seem to have caused a change of attitudes at ASCSA. In 1908 Elizabeth Gardiner, a graduate of Radcliffe and Wellesley Colleges,[51] was allowed to join the American excavations at Corinth, now under the direction of Bert Hodge Hill, where she worked on the sculptures.[52] The first all-women excavation was conducted by Alice Walker Kosmopoulos, of Vassar College, and Hetty Goldman,[53] of Bryn Mawr and Radcliffe Colleges, at Halae in Locris from the spring of 1911.[54] The remote location of the site – reminiscent of Boyd's distant dig at Kavousi in Crete – may have been deliberately out of the way of the 'male dominated' ASCSA.[55] It is against such a background that British women started to be allowed to participate in fieldwork in Greek lands.

Women at the British School at Athens

It is noticeable that most of the women who became students of the BSA had been educated at Cambridge. One possible influence on women at Cambridge was the presence of Charles Waldstein, who had served as Director of ASCSA (1888-92) and who placed an emphasis on 'fine art'.[56] Waldstein influenced Cambridge men as well; for example, Alan J. B. Wace, a future Director of the BSA, studied Hellenistic sculpture almost certainly at Waldstein's prompting.[57] Archaeology had a particular appeal to women in Cambridge as it gave a non-linguistic option in their studies.[58]

Girton College seemed to encourage its graduates to complete their studies in Athens. Eugénie Sellers had studied at Girton from 1879 to 1882, though achieving poor marks in her final examinations.[59] Among the archaeological influences on her was Sidney Colvin, the Slade Professor of Fine Art.[60] Sellers was not admitted to the BSA for another eight years, although once the precedent had been set, a series of Girton women were to follow her to Athens: Caroline Amy Hutton (1896-97), Olivia C. Köhler (1899-1900), Hilda L. Lorimer (1901-02) and Gisela M. A. Richter (1904-05).[61] Julia Katherine Wickes of Girton, a student of Jane Harrison, had applied to be admitted as a student to work on Greek mythology, but

---

[51] Lord 1947, 377.

[52] Gardiner 1909. See also Dyson 1998, 88.

[53] For caricature and convenient short biography: Hood 1998, 48-51.

[54] Goldman 1915; Walker and Goldman 1915. For the context: Lord 1947, 119, 300.

[55] Dyson 1998, 92.

[56] Lord 1947, 51. For Waldstein's influence on Cambridge: Cook 1931, 49-52.

[57] Wace 1902/03. See also Stubbings 1958; Gill 2004q.

[58] Breay 1999, 67; Stray 1995.

[59] She was awarded a 3rd. For the Girton years: Dyson 2004, 15-25. The Classics tutor at Girton was Elizabeth Welsh (1843-1921) who had been admitted as a student to Girton in 1872: Megson 2004; see also Lindsay and Megson 1961. For the reasons behind such poor results: Beard 2000, 18-19, 176 n. 12. The statistics for these results are presented by Breay 1999, 64-66, 68-69.

[60] Dyson 2004, 21.

[61] Only Köhler and Richter were admitted to the BSA straight after their studies at Girton.

was refused as her 'standard of actual attainment was lower than that generally required of candidates for admission, and … it was undesirable to lower that standard, even in a somewhat exceptional case such as this'.[62] The exceptional circumstances were that Wickes lived in Greece as her father worked for the Lake Copais Company. Richter specifically recalled the influence of her classics tutor at Girton, Katharine ('Kits') Jex-Blake,[63] who had been a contemporary of Sellers.[64] Richter had, however, found the Cambridge lectures on archaeology 'rather elementary' after hearing Professor E. Loewy lecture in Rome when she was 14.[65] It was Loewy's influence which made her decide to 'become an archaeologist'.[66]

The place of Girton women at Athens was then taken by former students of Newnham College: Margery K. Welsh (1903/04), Dorothy Lamb (1910/11), Margaret M. Hardie (1911/12), Mary N. L. Taylor (1913/14), and Agnes Conway (1913/14).[67] This shift to Newnham may have been influenced by Jane Harrison's presence (from 1898) as Research Fellow and (from 1899) College Lecturer in Classical Archaeology (until 1922). Conway, although following the History Tripos, wrote to her parents:

> I have just been having such a nice talk with Miss Harrison about all my next year's and for ever afterwards work. … We all incline to think it would be best for me to begin Greek *at once*, and … to clear off my historical tripos next year and have a year at the end free for archaeology only …[68]

Harrison emphasised the archaeology of Greece by giving a course of lectures at Cambridge on Delphi, and another series on the topography of Athens and the Parthenon sculptures.[69]

Apart from Cambridge, only two other universities were represented by women at the BSA. Mary Hamilton (1905-06, 1906-07) had read classics at St Andrews, Scotland, and Ethel Beatrice Abrahams (Bedford College, University of London, 1902-05; University College, London, 1905-06) and Baroness E. Rosenörn-Lehn (Royal Holloway College, and University College, London, 1901-02) at the University of London. Rosenörn-Lehn was from Copenhagen and had studied the history of art for two to three years before enrolling at Royal Holloway for a year to study classics (1898-9), and then at University College, London before going out to Athens (1901-02).

---

[62] BSA Minute Book 3, Meeting of October 13, 1898. Wickes was a Girton from 1890-93. She obtained an ordinary degree.

[63] Richter 1972, 8.

[64] Beard 2000, 21; Dyson 2004, 18.

[65] Richter 1972, 4. The reference was probably to Colvin.

[66] Richter 1972, 8.

[67] Conway had studied History. However she did go and hear Gilbert Murray lecture in Cambridge, and was captivated by Jane Harrison: Evans 1966, 198-99.

[68] Quoted in Evans 1966, 199.

[69] Breay 1999, 61. Agnes Conway's father, at the time Slade Professor, was quite critical of Harrison's approach to archaeology: Evans 1966, 200.

London had become a centre for the study of archaeology in Britain. Not only were there public lectures from women like Harrison, Sellers, and Lathbury, but archaeology was becoming more prominent as a subject in the university.[70] (Sir) Charles Newton, who had excavated in the Ottoman Empire, had been appointed Keeper of Greek and Roman Antiquities at the British Museum in 1861, and Professor of Archaeology at University College, London in 1880.[71] Under the terms of Amelia Edwards' will, a chair of Egyptology was established at University College in 1892. Its first holder, Flinders Petrie, found that most of his first students were women.[72] Indeed one of them, Janet Gourlay, later directed, with Margaret Benson,[73] the first all-women excavation in Egypt. Classical archaeology also flourished in London. On Newton's retirement from the British Museum in 1889, he was followed by Reginald S. Poole, Keeper of Coins and Medals at the British Museum, who also had a strong interest in Egyptology. The appointment of Ernest A. Gardner in 1896 – Jane Harrison was the other main contender[74] – meant that the London Yates chair of classical archaeology was filled by somebody with experience of excavation in Greece (and Egypt).[75]

A number of women appear on the periphery of the BSA. Margaret Benson (1865-1914), visited during the winter of 1893-94 while her brother (and novelist) Edward Frederic was a BSA student between 1891 and 1895.[76] He recalled her 'sketching and going on expeditions, hearing lectures at the Archaeological School, helping me with German, and herself taking lessons in modern Greek'.[77] Maggie's interest in archaeology found expression not in Greece, but in Egypt, where she excavated the temple of Mut at Thebes. Christina Mackenzie, sister of Evans's future assistant Duncan Mackenzie, was granted permission to become a student of the BSA in December 1897 with the support of Jane Harrison.[78] For some reason, perhaps financial, she never became a student although she did stay in Athens. Louisa Pesel, who was in charge of the Royal Hellenic School of Needlework, became an Associate of the BSA in 1902 through the prompting of the

---

[70] Egytpology was also becoming more important with a large number of women active in London: Janssen 1992. See also Gill 2004d.

[71] Gardner 1894/5; Cook 1997. Newton was a great influence of Harrison and Sellers. Sellers performed as 'Helen' before Newton in May 1883: Dyson 2004, 33. Among the guests were Jane Harrison and Cecil Smith (Harcourt-Smith).

[72] Drower 1995, 203.

[73] Benson had been educated at Lady Margaret Hall, Oxford. For her life: Benson 1917.

[74] Drower 1995, 222. For a detailed account: Calder III 1991.

[75] One of Gardner's later pupils was the influential Sir Mortimer Wheeler: Hawkes 1982, 41.

[76] For her brother's archaeological work: Benson 1895a; Benson 1895b. He later excavated with Hogarth at Alexandria. He is better known as a novelist than as an archaeologist.

[77] Quoted in Benson 1917, 151. Her letters cover the period from November 1893 to January 1894 (pp. 155-62).

[78] Momigliano 1999, 28.

Director, Robert Carr Bosanquet, who had an interest in Greek textiles.[79] She appears to
have been a major influence on Richard M. Dawkins and Alan J. B. Wace who both
collected textiles; she later collaborated with Wace on Greek textiles when he was a
curator at the Victoria and Albert Museum in London.[80] On the fringe of the School,
though again not an official student, was Mona Wilson. She had been educated at
Newnham College (1892-96), and had then served as the secretary to the Women's
Industrial Law Committee and Women's Trade Unions League (1899-1902). Ellen
Bosanquet, wife of the BSA's Director, recalled that Wilson 'spent much of her time
travelling alone on foot through the Peloponnese'.[81]

It is noticeable that unlike many of the men who became students at the BSA directly
after leaving university, the first women tended to have followed other pursuits in the
meantime. Bosanquet, the future Director, had read classics at Trinity College in Cambridge
(1890-94), and had then travelled to Greece on the Craven Travelling Fellowship. John
Hubert Marshall, the future Director-General of Antiquities for India, had read classics at
King's College, Cambridge (1895-1900), before going out to Athens in 1900 as the
Prendergast Travelling Student.[82] In contrast, Sellers had taught at St Leonard's School in St
Andrews for a year before moving to London where she made her base, giving lectures at
the British Museum;[83] she later studied in Germany, then the centre for classical
archaeology.[84] Caroline Amy Hutton was a contemporary of Sellers at Girton, and she
achieved an only slightly better degree (1879-83).[85] She held a teaching post in classics and
had already published a study of inscriptions on Greek pottery from the British excavations
at Naukratis, the Greek trading settlement in the Nile Delta, before she went to Greece.[86]
Hilda Lorimer had taken the classical tripos in 1896 and was placed in the first class.[87] She
had then been appointed classics tutor at Somerville College in Oxford. She was not
admitted to the BSA until the 1901-2 session as Pfeiffer Travelling Student, when she was in
her late twenties.

The situation for women changed during the directorship of Bosanquet. Welsh completed
her Part II of the Classical Tripos at Newnham College in 1903, and then spent a year at

---

[79] Taylor 1998, 178. The rules and regulations of the School stated: 'The Managing committee may
elect as Associates of the School any persons actively engaged in study or exploration in Greek
lands' (XXII).

[80] Stubbings 1958, 266.

[81] Bosanquet n. d. , 61. See also Lewis 1939, 251. See British School at Athens 1903/04, 245.

[82] Gill 2000a.

[83] Dyson 2004, 24-45.

[84] Dyson 2004, 63-73. She went to Berlin in late 1892. Male students also studied in Berlin: *e.g.*
Webster (1902/03), Halliday (Hoffmeister) (1909), Calder (1909/10).

[85] Hutton was awarded a 3rd, division 2 for Part 1 (1882), as opposed to Sellers' 3rd, division 3. On
this phenomenon: Breay 1999, 62-63. Women were only allowed to take the Tripos examinations in
Cambridge from 1881.

[86] Hutton 1893.

[87] Hartley 1954; Benton 1954.

the BSA with the help of the Marion Kennedy Studentship. Richter, who followed her in the next year, decided to spend a year in Athens rather than a fourth year in Cambridge; as she was to recall, 'how much more illuminating is it to study the buildings on the Akropolis standing in front of them than in a Cambridge lecture room!'[88] Three further Newnham students, Dorothy Lamb, Margaret Hardie and Mary Taylor went out to Athens on completing their studies at Newnham (in 1910, 1911 and 1913 respectively). An exception was Agnes Conway, who was 28 when she was admitted.[89] Dorothy Lamb was awarded a studentship supplemented by Jane Harrison,[90] whereas the following year Margaret Hardie was awarded a full Cambridge studentship (1911/12).[91]

Research Topics

Many of the research topics followed by the women and men at the BSA were library and museum based, though they also involved some travel.[92] This was in part created by the restrictions on travel in Greece during the winter months. Richter later recalled how she was guided in her choice of research topic. She arrived in Athens in November 1904, and Bosanquet, the Director, advised her on choice of subject, and gave her encouragement as the research progressed. Her choice was 'The Forms of Attic vases in relation to their geographical distribution'.[93] The topic may have been partly influenced by Bosanquet's personal interest in Attic pottery, and in particular white-ground lekythoi.[94] This study was to be a piece of original research: 'Now for the first time I was engaged in formulating something new, and presenting it as best I could'.[95]

Many of the research topics in this period were linked to pottery. Even Henry Stuart-Jones, better known for his revision of the *Greek-English Lexicon*, worked on Athenian pottery when he was admitted to the BSA.[96] Sellers made a study of black-figured

[88] Richter 1972, 10.

[89] Evans 1966, 220.

[90] BSA Minute Book 6, Meetings of 21 June and 26 July 1910. The minutes record: 'Miss Harrison considered [Dorothy Lamb] the most brilliant student she had had, and confidently recommended her to the committee. The lady had little means of her own, and Miss Harrison and the Secretary thought that she could hardly go out as a student to the School with a less grant than £75'. In the end the BSA awarded her £25 with an extra £50 given by Harrison.

[91] Harrison argued that the regulation, 'a duly qualified member of the University', would exclude women who were not, at that point, full members of Cambridge University: BSA Minute Book 7, Meeting of 16 July 1912. For further details: Robinson 2002, 286-87.

[92] The Rules and Regulations stated, 'Students attached to the School will be expected to pursue some definite course of study or research in a department of Hellenic studies, and to write in each season a report upon their work. Such reports shall be submitted to the Director, shall by him be forwarded to the Managing Committee, and may be published by the Committee if and as they think proper' (XX). For further details see ch. 4.

[93] Richter 1904/5.

[94] Bosanquet 1896.

[95] Richter 1972, 10.

[96] Stuart-Jones 1891. For the context: Gill 2004m.

funerary *lekythoi* which had been excavated in 1888 at Eretria and put on display in the National Museum at Athens.[97] This material had become particularly important through the further excavations in the cemeteries at Eretria which had been conducted in the early months of 1891 by Charles Waldstein. In particular he was 'desirous … of finding some white *lekythoi*'.[98] Sellers, too, had an interest in 'white-faced ware' which she saw as significant for the study of 'Greek painting proper';[99] in other words these figure-decorated pots would provide evidence for the lost panel paintings celebrated in works such as the Elder Pliny, the focal point for her later research.[100] Her research on the *lekythoi*, completed in Berlin in January 1893, was conducted with the co-operation of the Ephors of Antiquities in Athens, and with the support of Ernest Gardner, the BSA Director. The drawings were prepared by the Swiss draughtsman Emile Victor Gilliéron.[101] Lorimer also worked on Greek pottery, with a focus on the iconography of the country-cart.[102] The starting point for her study was a red-figured *pyxis* from Eretria in the National Museum in Athens. She showed familiarity with the Boeotian black-figured pottery from the Kabeirion at Thebes which was then being prepared for publication by the German Institute.[103]

At the end of the 19th century and in the early 20th century there was a great deal of interest in the Greek theatre. Not only were Greek plays performed in London and Cambridge,[104] but in Greece there had been fierce debate about the architectural form of the ancient Greek theatre. In 1890 a Greek theatre had been created at Bradfield College, a boys' public school.[105] Archaeology was seen as a source of information about the costumes and the setting for plays as well as the costumes.[106] Charles Waldstein was to comment in connection with the Cambridge production of *Ajax* in 1882, 'The armour, properties and dress of the actors, as well as of the sailors in the Chorus, are taken from ancient monuments, chiefly statues and vase-paintings approaching the time of Sophocles and representing scenes from the Homeric poems'.[107] David Hogarth assisted with the Oxford University Dramatic Society 1892 production of Aristophanes' *Frogs.*[108] It is perhaps significant that Charles Ricketts, designer of settings and costumes for *The Persians* (1907), *Elektra* (1907), *Medea* (1907), *Oedipus Rex,* and the *Bacchae* (1916), as well as a future Cambridge benefactor of Greek antiquities, was photographed in the

---

[97] Sellers 1892/3. See also Dyson 2004, 51.

[98] Lord 1947, 75.

[99] Sellers 1892/3, 1.

[100] Sellers 1896.

[101] Richards 1892/3; Richards 1894a; Richards 1894b. See also MacGillivray 2000, 186.

[102] Lorimer 1903.

[103] Lorimer 1903, 137.

[104] Easterling 1999.

[105] Easterling 1999, 34 n. 21.

[106] Easterling 1999, 34; Beard 2000, 51.

[107] Quoted in Easterling 1999, 35.

[108] Parry, *et al.* 1890; Frere, *et al.* 1892.

theatre of Dionysos when he visited Athens with the painter Charles Shannon in 1911.[109] In 1890 the BSA, under Ernest Gardner (a performer in the 1882 Cambridge production of *Ajax*), had excavated the theatre at Megalopolis in the Peloponnese which had caused so much interest and indeed controversy.[110] Sellers, who was in Athens during 1891 working on a translation of Carl Schuchhardt's *Schliemann's Excavations*,[111] joined the debate about the raised stage as a later feature in the Greek theatre on the side of the German Dörpfeld, and against her British colleagues.[112] Such academic debates probably help to explain the American work on the theatre at Eretria in early 1891, and renewed investigation of the theatre at Sikyon later in the same year.[113]

An interest in Greek dress was encouraged by the finds of archaic *korai* during excavations on the Athenian acropolis in 1885-86, in particular fourteen in one deposit to the north-west of the Erechtheion inside the wall of the acropolis.[114] The combination of the continuing interest in Greek theatre and the appearance of new finds available for study and comment probably lay behind Abrahams' research into Greek dress during the 1905-6 session.[115] Similar research had been conducted by Maria Millington Lathbury, Sir Arthur Evans' stepmother, during her study in Greece in 1892, which was to culminate in a monograph.[116] Greek dress was also being studied in Germany by Margarete Bieber and in Austria by Ada von Netoliczka.[117]

The finds from the excavations on the Athenian acropolis provided other sources for research, such as the terracotta relief dedications and bronze statuettes studied by Hutton.[118] Following the success of the BSA's Catalogue of the Sparta Museum,[119] a second project for the Acropolis Museum, supervised by Guy Dickins, was proposed.[120] Dorothy Lamb, daughter of the mathematician Professor Horace Lamb and sister of the celebrated painter Henry Lamb, and Lilian Tennant had travelled out to Greece together specifically to work on this new catalogue.[121] They studied the material through the winter months so that by the

---

[109] For the plays: Delaney 1990, 222-23, 228, 261, 294-95. For Ricketts at Athens: Delaney 1990, 256, fig. 35.

[110] Gardner, *et al.* 1890; Gardner 1894c. For the wider context: Beard 2000, 66-68. The debate was focused on Wilhelm Dörpfeld's interpretation of the theatre of Dionysos at Athens.

[111] Schuchhardt 1891. See also Beard 2000, 68; Dyson 2004, 52.

[112] Sellers 1891a. See also Dyson 2004, 53.

[113] Lord 1947, 75-76. See also Dyson 2004, 53.

[114] Richter 1968, 5-6, pl. ii.

[115] Abrahams 1908. See also the review Hutton 1909. For the display of these statues in the 1880s see Yiakoumis 2000, 225.

[116] Millington-Evans 1894. See also MacGillivray 2000, 101.

[117] Bieber 1917; Netoliczka 1912. See also Dyson 1998, 224; Richter 1968, pl. iii, a-b.

[118] Hutton 1897; Hutton 1896/7.

[119] Tod and Wace 1906.

[120] Dickins 1912.

[121] Gill 2004i.

end of the session it could be reported that 'good progress had been made'.[122] Lamb continued the research on her return to England, stopping off to study the collection of terracottas in the Louvre.[123] The first volume of the catalogue was published in the following year,[124] and Lamb's text for the second volume was virtually complete in 1913.[125] She spent March 1914 working on the catalogue at the BSA, followed, in April, by the study of terracottas from Tiryns in the Nauplia Museum.[126] Although Lamb's manuscript was delivered to Cambridge University Press that summer, the outbreak of war, and Dickins' subsequent death on the Somme, meant that the volume was not published until 1921.[127] Lamb's project may well have influenced Mary N. L. Taylor, another Newnham student, who went to Athens to research terracottas.

Welsh's study of 'portrait and honorary statues' was largely library based,[128] although the *Annual Report of the British School at Athens* suggests that she spent the session from October to May in Athens, as well as 'making several excursions to sites in Greece'. Hamilton's time at the BSA was an extension of her research from the University of St Andrews and more recently in Italy. Her main interest was in the practice of *incubatio* in antiquity as well as in Christianity. Her three months in Greece during the spring of 1906 completed her research, which was published as a monograph.[129] She was subsequently awarded a fellowship from the Carnegie Trust for the Universities of Scotland to research 'the festivals of the Greek Church and their connection with the ceremonies of the ancient Greeks'.[130] From November 1906 to April 1907 she stayed in Athens, working in the BSA library and observing local festivals.

Life at the British School

In the early years of the BSA, both men and women had to find accommodation in hotels.[131] The situation was eased with the opening of a hostel for men in 1895.[132] Women only gained access to this facility during the autumn of 1920, when the disturbed political climate in Athens forced the situation; the absence of the then Director, Alan Wace, meant that there could be no objections.[133] Ellen Bosanquet, wife of the Director, wrote from her

---

[122] British School at Athens 1910/11, 286.

[123] British School at Athens 1910/11, 287.

[124] Dickins 1912.

[125] British School at Athens 1912/13, 271; British School at Athens 1913/14, 137.

[126] British School at Athens 1913/14, 137.

[127] Casson 1921.

[128] Welsh 1904/5.

[129] Hamilton 1906.

[130] Hamilton 1906/7; Hamilton 1910.

[131] In 1890 Sellers stayed at a pension with her friend, Mary Lowndes, who had also studied at Girton: Dyson 2004, 50.

[132] Waterhouse 1986, 13.

[133] Bernard Ashmole recalled the events of November 1920: 'The British Minister decided that all students should be moved into the British School in case they had to leave the country at short

personal experience of the difficulties of finding a suitable hotel in Athens before the First World War: 'The cost of living in Athens is relatively high, and the terms quoted by the large hotel-keepers seem exorbitant until we remember that for the moment Athens has outgrown its sources of supply'.[134] Richter, when she went out to Athens in November 1904, stayed at the Pensione Merlin, where she socialised with women from ASCSA. Her fellow guests were Edith H. Hall, a graduate of Smith College (1899) and Agnes Hoppin Memorial Fellow (1903-04); Rachel Berenson, graduate of Smith (1902) and Radcliffe (1904) colleges; and Nora C. Jenkins. The Merlin continued to be the base for women archaeologists in Athens even after the First World War.[135]

Apart from working in the BSA library – extended as 'the Penrose Library' in April 1904[136] – and visits to museums in Athens, students, men and women, attended archaeological lectures, usually on a Saturday,[137] such as those given by Wilhelm Dörpfeld, Director of the German Archaeological Institute (Deutsches-Archäologisches Institut).[138] These lectures were intended to familiarise the students with the topography of Athens, as well as with the different types of artefact which might be found on excavations.[139] The main period of residence at the BSA was deemed to be from mid-November until March when it was recommended that students should 'settle down in Hostel for 3 or 4 months of steady work on sites and in Museums, attending some of the half-dozen available courses of lectures, and making frequent short excursions into the country, by train, bicycle, carriage, or on mule-back'.[140]

Other Women at the British School

Although female students were excluded from living at the BSA, many of the early Directors, who lived in the Upper House, were married. Ernest and Mary Gardner married in 1887, the year that he was appointed Director of the BSA to succeed Francis Penrose.[141] David and Laura Hogarth had been married for three years before his appointment in 1897. It is unclear to what extent there was a tension between the male bachelors, the single women students, and the wives.[142]

notice, and this set the precedent, followed since, for wives to reside with their husbands in the School' (Kurtz 1994, 23. See also Gill 2007.

[134] Bosanquet 1914, 2-3.

[135] Gill 2007, 58. Margaret Benson resided at the Grand Hotel in the winter of 1893-94.

[136] Waterhouse 1986, 18.

[137] See Allsebrook 1992, 29. This pattern continued into the post-war period.

[138] See Lord 1947, 72, 91.

[139] See also Lord 1947, 72.

[140] Quoted in Waterhouse 1986, 153.

[141] Their first child, a son, was born in May 1888 at the house of Thomas Gardner in Hampstead (*The Times* 25 May 1888). A daughter was born in Cambridge in October 1890 (*The Times* 14 October 1890).

[142] See Stray 1995, for the tension between these groups in contemporary Cambridge.

To some extent the role of the Director's wife was a pastoral one towards the (male) students. When Bosanquet developed malaria during his study of Pylos, he was visited in the Evangelismos Hospital in Athens by the wife of the then BSA Director, Alice Edith Harcourt Smith.[143] During his subsequent convalescence at Vevey in France, he wrote to his mother:

> I shall always look back on those months with wonder at the endless kindness I received. Now that I can dress like an ordinary mortal I am constantly coming on some proof of Mrs Cecil's – or her servant Alexandri's – thoughtfulness. She had my whole wardrobe put in order, and finding that my pyjamas were old and tattered, took great pains, busy woman though she is, in choosing flannels and having them made up – *sehr billig* – by her dressmaker: whereby if I am radiant by day through having a full complement of buttons, I am gorgeous at night – in pink and white stripes.[144]

When Bosanquet was first appointed Director of the BSA he was unmarried, and so for his first two winters (1900-01, 1901-02) his sister Ellie had come out to act as his housekeeper.[145] In July 1902 he married Ellen S. Hodgkin, who had studied history at Somerville College, Oxford (1896-1900); her father was the historian, Thomas Hodgkin. In October of that year the Bosanquets returned to Athens, and on Easter Day (19 April) 1903 their first son was born at the BSA.[146] After a spell back in Britain, Ellen returned to Athens with Elisabeth Holmes as a companion. Richter recalled pushing the young Charles Bosanquet in his pram![147] Ellen remembered the way in which the male students expected to be 'mothered'. She describes one of the male students coming to see her 'as yellow as an orange and asked what treatment I prescribed, I got out my medical dictionary and read the whole paragraph on jaundice aloud to him, not sparing his blushes, and then left him to carry out the instructions as best he could'.[148] Dawkins, who was unmarried, was accompanied to Athens by his younger sister, Edith.

The presence of women at the BSA also led to romance and marriage. Mary Hamilton married her near contemporary, Guy Dickins, and they continued to visit the BSA on a regular basis to pursue their separate lines of research.[149] Margaret Hardie's marriage to F. W. Hasluck, the Assistant Director, created a dilemma for the BSA as the Assistant Director lived in the hostel with the other male students. Jane Harrison, Hardie's tutor from Newnham, urged the Managing Committee to permit this new arrangement to see

---

[143] Letter of 20 January 1897; quoted in Bosanquet 1938, 64.

[144] Letter of Friday, 26 February 1897; quoted in Bosanquet 1938, 67.

[145] Bosanquet n. d., 53, 59.

[146] Bosanquet n. d., 59.

[147] Waterhouse 1986, 134.

[148] Bosanquet n. d., 62.

[149] Hamilton 1910; Dickins 1903; Dickins 1904/05a; Dickins 1904/05b; Dickins 1904/05c; Dickins 1905/06a; Dickins 1905/06b; Dickins 1905/06c; Dickins 1905/06d; Dickins 1906/07a; Dickins 1906/07b; Dickins 1906/07c; Dickins 1910/11; Dickins 1911; Dickins 1912; Dickins 1914a; Dickins 1914b; Dickins 1914/16.

'whether the presence of ladies resident in the Hostel would not work well'.[150] However the male dominated Committee did not approve as 'in the long run the men would certainly feel less comfortable than they had hitherto'.[151] Frederick W. Hasluck remained in Athens when the First World War broke out and volunteered to work with British intelligence, specifically on an index system for assisting with counter-espionage.[152] Margaret initially worked in military intelligence in Whitehall, but then transferred to Athens when her husband's health started to fail; they eventually moved to Switzerland where Frederick died in 1920.[153]

Travels in Greece

An integral part of the year in Greece was a tour of sites and museums outside Athens. There were two possible approaches: one could either join an organised trip or travel privately. Some of the organised parties were under the auspices of Wilhelm Dörpfeld's tours of the Greek islands, 'comfortably settled on a large steamer'.[154] John W. White of the American School had even commented on the value of these Dörpfeld tours that 'it was more profitable for a student to cross the Peloponnesus or sail among the Islands than to take part in an excavation'.[155] The pattern for such trips seems to have been fixed in a scheme for students first published by Bosanquet in 1900.[156] It was suggested that in October the new student should visit 'Olympia, Delphi, Mycenae, Epidaurus, the Heraeum near Argos, before the rains begin in November'.[157] In the spring it was recommended that students 'join one of the island-cruises to which Professor Gardner and Professor Dörpfeld have hospitably admitted students in the past'.[158] This pattern lies behind the itinerary of Dorothy Lamb, who spent part of her year travelling in Euboea, Crete, Aetolia and the Peloponnese, whereas her companion Lilian Tennant only travelled 'on the mainland of Greece, among the islands and in Crete'.[159] In April 1901 Hilda Lorimer joined Dörpfeld's tour of the Peloponnese along with Jane Harrison and Jessie Crum.[160] Lorimer's subsequent independent travels in Greece were described as follows: 'Her exceptional vigour and pertinacity took her to places no matter how remote and difficult if they were thought to be of archaeological interest: days of twelve hours walking, hard lodging, unappetising food – nothing deterred her'.[161]

[150] Quoted in Waterhouse 1986, 134.

[151] Quoted in Waterhouse 1986, 134.

[152] Mackenzie 1931, 197-98.

[153] Waterhouse 1986, 25.

[154] Richter 1972, 11.

[155] Lord 1947, 91.

[156] Waterhouse 1986, 17.

[157] Quoted in Waterhouse 1986, 153.

[158] Waterhouse 1986, 153.

[159] British School at Athens 1910/11, 287.

[160] Stray 1995; Beard 2000, 131.

[161] Hartley 1954, 27.

A fuller description of one of these Dörpfeld island cruises is provided by Ellen Bosanquet who joined one in the spring of 1904 while her husband was excavating at Palaikastro in eastern Crete:

> We were a serious party. One American girl and I were the only women; the rest were all Dörpfeldt's [sic] own students from the German Archaeological School, or Professors from American and European Universities – French, Italian, Scandinavian, Russian, and Poles. Most of us could speak, and all could understand, German, but in some cases we had to communicate in a mixture of dog-Latin and modern Greek. It was glorious summer weather for sea travel but boiling on land. We toiled up the rocky slopes of Thera, Melos, Delos, Samos, Miletus, and stood in circles under large masculine umbrellas while Dörpfeldt, in his impassioned prose, lectured on the problems of each site. No wonder the students insisted on a barrel of beer being hauled up along with us, to be drunk at the end of the lecture. Then, in the late afternoon, we would return to our little Greek steamer and have dinner on deck, first in sunset and then in candlelight. Sometimes, if the climb was specially arduous, the American girl (whose name I cannot remember) and I were supplied with horses or mules. Once I remember we had two strange animals with no bits in their hard mouths; only the usual rope round the nose as a bridle. They were all right for the climb, but when it came to the descent of course we could not hold them, and so came clattering down the hillside at a tremendous pace, bringing half the rocky path with us and making a noisy triumphant finale among the hot professors. I remember one American teasing Dörpfeldt and saying: "I should like to see your Prussian cavalry do anything equal to that".[162]

The Dörpfeld tour visited Crete, and Gournia where Harriet Boyd and Edith Hall were excavating. On 11 May, the day after a visit by the Cambridge scholar Charles Hawes (Harriet's future husband), the group arrived.

> The following day started excitedly at 5 am, with news that a boat-load of archaeologists and tourists had been sighted. The little Stars and Stripes fluttered on the balcony as the rowboats brought swarms of Germans ashore. Dr Dörpfeld lectured to them on the site of Gournia, made a complimentary speech where once the palace hall stood, and then took Harriet and Edith Hall off to Palaikastro.[163]

For other independent travels in Greece, Ellen Bosanquet's advice was to engage the services of a dragoman who 'takes you wherever you wish to go, find the mules or carriages, takes beds and a cook (or cooks himself), and arranges a comfortable lodging at the end of each day's journey'.[164]

Richter made several tours during her year. The first was made 'with friends' in the spring of 1905 'to see the sites of the Peloponnese, Attica, and Euboea'.[165] This was then

---

[162] Bosanquet n. d. , 64.

[163] Allsebrook 1992, 122. See also Becker and Betancourt 1997, 39.

[164] Bosanquet 1914, 3.

[165] Richter 1972, 10. See also Bosanquet 1938, 11.

followed by a tour of the Greek islands with members of ASCSA, which consisted of her three companions from the Pensione Merlin – Berenson, Hall and Jenkins – and two men, Leslie Shear (who was to marry Jenkins)[166] and the slightly older Oliver Washburn.[167] They used local small boats, or caiques, to travel from island to island. They may have made this choice to avoid Dörpfeld's cruise that year, for it included a party of 150 who had attended the first International Congress of Classical Archaeology in Athens.[168] Richter's party, expanded by two further members of ASCSA (Gorham Stevens and Chandler Post), then travelled through western Turkey and the offshore islands (still part of the Ottoman Empire), visiting the excavations at Priene,[169] Pergamon[170] and Lesbos, before concluding the tour at Constantinople. Travel was still relatively difficult. Richter was to recall:

> We travelled on mule or donkey, slowly, able to take in our surroundings. To cross the Trojan plain, however, we had to take horses, as no other transportation was available. So I mounted my horse, a new experience for me, and was buffeted hither and yon – until by some miracle I suddenly learned to rise in my stirrups. What a joy! Horseback-riding became a passion with me for the rest of my life.[171]

Most of the party returned to Athens, though Richter and Jenkins made a trip to Broussa, where Richter's maternal grandfather had been the American consul while running a silk business.[172]

Richter's third trip was to Crete in July, where she had arranged to visit Knossos with Harriet Boyd, the excavator of Gournia.[173] They are likely to have met for the first time at the first International Congress of Classical Archaeology which was held in Athens in April 1905.[174] Together they visited the excavations, but Richter fell ill with 'gastric fever' that required care at Candia (Herakleion).[175] During her convalescence Boyd introduced her to the classification of Minoan ceramics.

Hamilton's research on *incubatio* required more extensive travelling, sometimes away from the more frequented sites. For example, she visited the island of Tenos for the Feast of the Annunciation, held on 6 April in the Greek calendar (the equivalent of 25 March in the western calendar at that time).[176] During her second year in Athens she visited the

---

[166] Hood 1998, 174.

[167] Richter 1972, 11.

[168] Allsebrook 1992, 125.

[169] See Marchand 1996, 193.

[170] See Marchand 1996, 95.

[171] Richter 1972, 11.

[172] Richter 1972, 7.

[173] Richter 1972, 11.

[174] Becker and Betancourt 1997, 57; Richter 1972, 11; Allsebrook 1992, 125; MacGillivray 2000, 233-34.

[175] Allsebrook 1992, 129.

[176] See on this festival Robert Carr Bosanquet's letter of 9 April 1893, quoted in Bosanquet 1938, 23-28.

islands of Rhodes and Thera, as well as travelling to the Peloponnese, specifically to Sparta, monasteries in Laconia, and to Mount Ithome in Messenia.

A more detailed account of travels was written by another Newnham student, Agnes Conway, on the eve of the First World War; she travelled with Evelyn Radford.[177] Apart from visits around Attica, they went to Constantinople (via Smyrna) and Salonica.[178] They then took a steamer to Litochori and headed for the Vale of Tempe.[179]

> It is extremely beautiful, but its great reputation must be due in some measure to the rarity of real rivers in Greece. Even to our eyes, with their not so very distant English background, the sight of a river full of water and filling its bed was a remarkable thing. We climbed the Pyrgos, a hill a thousand feet high or so, from which one can see the whole length of the Vale, and so get a just idea of its extraordinary narrowness. It is a ribbon's width between the mountains.[180]

They then continued through Thessaly, describing their train travels in the following terms:

> We always went third class and made tea with a spirit-lamp, to the intense delight of the people in the long corridor carriage, who clustered around us, watching our every movement. Tea-making was forced upon us because we found it impossible to preserve the Andros water, which we carried with us in a real Greek water-pouch, uncontaminated. At every station some Greek would run out and fill it up again at a poisonous station well.[181]

They visited the monasteries of the Meteora, though only two admitted women visitors. From there they visited the site of the battle of Chaeronea, and then took donkeys up to Delphi via Agios Loukas in Stiris; at Delphi they felt it was where 'Greek history becomes intensely alive'.[182] The pair returned to Athens via Itea and a steamer.

Conway and Radford then set out on their tour of the Peloponnese. The party travelled from the Piraeus to Nauplion by ship.[183] From there they walked 'in grilling sunshine through dust a foot thick' to the Bronze Age site of Tiryns.[184] They spent the night at 'La Belle Heléne' at Mycenae, which they found 'exquisitively clean'.[185] From Mycenae they headed to Nemea with half an eye on the possibility of planning an excavation there at

---

[177] Conway 1917. They arrived in Greece in late February 1914 and spent four months in the Aegean.

[178] Conway 1917, 42-55.

[179] Conway 1917, 56-62.

[180] Conway 1917, 62.

[181] Conway 1917, 63-64.

[182] Conway 1917, 82. Conway and Radford were there for Easter.

[183] Conway 1917, 93.

[184] Conway 1917, 94-95.

[185] Conway 1917, 95.

some point.[186] They were deterred by the 'prosperous vineyards, too expensive to be bought out'. On returning to Nauplion by train, they set out for Epidauros, staying at the on-site guest house.[187] After a visit to Argos, they then took the train to Kalamata: interestingly the parallels were with home, 'Bits of the oak-strewn country might have been an English park'.[188] From Kalamata they made an excursion to Mount Ithome, passing the monastery, and climbing to the summit where they were offered minor antiquities. They then descended to the ancient city of Messene: 'It is a flat area of fields and fig trees now, as green as anything in England, and the circumvallating walls and square towers might well belong to some Frankish town of the Middle Ages'.[189] From Kalamata the group took the Langada Pass to Sparta, stopping for lunch at Lada, 'unexpectedly luxuriant ... like a little Italian hill-town'.[190] They met an Olympic champion fencer, almost certainly Ioannis Georgiadis who had won gold at both the Athens (1896 and 1906) games. During a sabre lesson with Radford he noted: 'Six years ago some English ladies came through here, and one of them fenced with me'.[191] Conway recognised the name as one of her friends. After the pass they made their way to Mistra, and then to Sparta where they viewed the scant remains of the sanctuary of Artemis Orthia.[192] From the sanctuary they returned to the centre of the town. There they visited the museum, which had been catalogued by Wace and Tod.

> The sculpture was as pitifully bad as the architecture, but the ivories and vases of the seventh and sixth century BC show a delicacy of design and workmanship of which the historical Spartans had lost every vestige. What induced the change? Why was every artistic impulse suffocated in so lovely a spot, and how could a people who built like children conquer the splendid Athenians? It is all very well to consider this problem dispassionately in England, but on the spot it assumes very different proportions.[193]

From Sparta they made their way to Megalopolis, site of the BSA excavations under Ernest Gardner.

> Epidauros had, after all, not spoilt us for that, for the size of it is most impressive. It is the largest in Greece, and the great sweep of open hill-side covered with rich vegetation is very beautiful. We bought coins, which had been picked up there, from a little man; otherwise no human being came within sight.[194]

---

[186] Conway 1917, 96-97.

[187] Conway 1917, 98.

[188] Conway 1917, 104.

[189] Conway 1917, 106.

[190] Conway 1917, 111.

[191] Conway 1917, 111.

[192] Conway 1917, 119-21.

[193] Tod and Wace 1906. For description: Conway 1917, 120.

[194] Conway 1917, 126.

They climbed up into the mountains to visit the temple at Bassae,[195] and after dropping down to the coast they took the train to Olympia.[196] This in effect was the end of their tour of Greece; they made their way to Patras, Yannina and then travelled through the Balkans.

Excavations

The first British women at the BSA were not permitted to take part in fieldwork or excavations, though, as has been shown, they were encouraged to travel in Greece and to join Dörpfeld's cruises of the islands. This was in contrast to the situation in Egypt where a number of women had taken part in excavations.[197] Perhaps the earliest British woman to be involved in a field project in Greece was G. E. Holding, a graduate of the University College of South Wales at Cardiff, who participated in the excavation of the cemetery at Rhitsona in Boeotia under R. M. Burrows and Percy Ure.[198] Holding was responsible for photographing the finds in the Thebes Museum. Strictly speaking this was a project under the auspices of the BSA rather than an official excavation.

It was not until the spring (end of March to late May) of 1911 that the first women attended an excavation organised by the BSA. This took place, under the direction of Richard M. Dawkins, at Phylakopi on the island of Melos, the site of earlier British work from 1896-99.[199] Three women were involved: Dorothy Lamb and her companion Lilian Tennant, who had been working on the *Catalogue of the Akropolis Museum*, and Hilda Lorimer, a former student from the 1901-02 session and now classical tutor at Somerville College, who had come out from Oxford specially for the excavations, probably because of her expertise with pottery. Apart from Dawkins, there were three male students on the excavation: John P. Droop, William R. Halliday and Laurence B. Tillard.[200] Droop, veteran of excavations at Sparta and in Thessaly, had particular responsibility for the pottery along with Tennant.[201]

Droop's experience of the 1911 Phylakopi excavation almost certainly influenced his views on women on archaeological excavations, which were to be expressed in his handbook, *Archaeological Excavation*, a volume dedicated to Dawkins.[202] These thoughts were expounded in the handbook's Epilogue – subsequent generations of women at the British School dubbed it 'Droop's VIIth' – where he claimed that although he had

---

[195] Conway 1917, 134-35.

[196] Conway 1917, 138-40.

[197] For a summary of the situation: Melman 1995, 39.

[198] Burrows and Ure 1907/08; Burrows and Ure 1909.

[199] Momigliano 1999, 19-34.

[200] Dawkins 1910/11b, with names at p. 3. A decision to include Lorimer, Lamb and Tennant was taken at the meeting of 24 January 1911 (BSA Minute Book 6) on condition that 'suitable quarters would be procured'.

[201] Dawkins and Droop 1910/11c; Dawkins and Droop 1910/11e; Dawkins and Droop 1910/11d. For Tennant: British School at Athens 1910/11, 287.

[202] Droop 1915.

never seen a trained lady excavator at work. ... Of a mixed dig however I have seen something, and it is an experiment that I would be reluctant to try again; I would grant if need be that women are admirably fitted for the work, yet I would uphold that they should undertake it by themselves.[203]

He claimed that there were several reasons for this.

In the first place there are the proprieties; I have never had a very reverent care for these abstractions, but I think it is not everywhere sufficiently realised that the proprieties that have to be considered are not only those that rule in England or America, but those of the lands where it is proposed to dig; the view to be considered is the view of the inhabitants, Greek, Turk, or Egyptian.[204]

Secondly, the presence of women interfered, in his personal opinion, with the male camaraderie that had developed on digs.

My objection lies in this, that the work of an excavation on the dig and off it lays on those who share in it a bond of closer daily intercourse than is conceivable, except perhaps in the Navy where privacy is said to be unobtainable, except for a captain; with the right men that is one of the charms of the life, but between men and women, except in chance cases, I do not believe that such close and unavoidable companionship can ever be other than a source of irritation; at any rate I believe that, however it may affect women, the ordinary male at least cannot stand it.[205]

No doubt this male camaraderie was familiar to men educated in English public schools and the single-sex colleges of Cambridge and Oxford. The comment that even elicited mention in Droop's own obituary, not least because it seemed contradictory to his own nature, was on the use of appropriate (or inappropriate) language on an excavation:

A minor, and yet to my mind weighty, objection lies in one particular form of constraint entailed by the presence of ladies, it must add to all the strains of an excavation, and they are many, the further strain of politeness and self-restraint in moments of stress, moments that will occur on the best regulated dig, when you want to say just what you think without translation, which before ladies, whatever their feelings about it, cannot be done.[206]

The exception to Droop's rule was when husband and wife excavated together. He could 'imagine a man conducting a small excavation very happily with his wife'.[207] He perhaps had in mind the Dickinses or the Haslucks.

Margaret M. Hardie had nearly made a landmark for women when she arrived at the School in 1911. The Director, Dawkins, had been hoping to undertake an excavation at

---

[203] Droop 1915, 63.

[204] Droop 1915, 63.

[205] Droop 1915, 64.

[206] Droop 1915, 64.

[207] Droop 1915, 64.

Datcha near Knidos, and the question of 'whether ladies prudently could take part in excavations in the Ottoman Empire' was raised in the Managing Committee.[208] However the unstable political situation, which led to the outbreak of the First Balkan War in October 1912, meant that the excavation never took place. Hardie instead joined Sir William Ramsay for one of his tours in Anatolia, and worked on the extra-mural sanctuary of Mên Askaenos outside the Roman colony of Pisidian Antioch, as well as on sculpture observed in Smyrna.[209]

Life after the British School

For some of the women, the period of study at the BSA consolidated their undergraduate studies and prepared their way for future academic careers and research. Sellers went to study at Rome, and completed a number of works[210] before marrying S. Arthur Strong in 1897.[211] Following her husband's death in 1904, she concentrated on Roman art,[212] especially after her appointment in 1909 – then aged 48 – as Assistant Director and Librarian of the British School at Rome.[213] The following year she was elected a Research Fellow at Girton College.[214] Although she flourished at first under Thomas Ashby, Director of the BSR (1906-25), there was a growing tension between the two which led to their 'resignation' in 1925.[215]

Lorimer returned to Somerville where she served as a classics tutor until 1939, and university lecturer from 1929. At Oxford she was involved with the publication of the pottery from Hogarth's excavations at Naukratis in the Nile Delta in the spring of 1903,[216] and she became an authority on Protocorinthian pottery.[217] During the First World War she served as an orderly in the Scottish Women's Hospital.[218] She later developed an interest in Homer[219] and excavated in 1922 at Mycenae with Wace,[220] in the early 1930s on Ithaca with W. A. Heurtley[221] and in 1934 with Sylvia Benton on Zakynthos.[222]

---

[208] Quoted in Waterhouse 1986, 134.

[209] Hardie 1912; Hardie 1912/13.

[210] *E.g.* Sellers 1896.

[211] See Samuels 1979, 259, 271; Dyson 2004, 76.

[212] Strong 1907; Strong 1915.

[213] Beard 2000, 24; Wiseman 1990; Dyson 2004. For the context: Hodges 2000; Wallace-Hadrill 2001.

[214] Beard 2000, 26; Dyson 2004, 115-16.

[215] Beard 2000, 24-26; Smith 1931; Wiseman 1990, 15-16; Dyson 2004, 153-54.

[216] Hogarth, *et al.* 1905, esp. 118-22; Lorimer 1910. See also Waterhouse 1986, 121.

[217] Lorimer 1912.

[218] Hartley 1954, 27.

[219] *E.g.* Lorimer 1950.

[220] Wace 1921/22, 1922/23; Wace 1932.

[221] Heurtley and Lorimer 1932/33.

[222] See Benton 1954, 29.

Hutton returned to England and continued to serve the BSA by acting as Assistant to Cecil Harcourt-Smith, the Editor of the *Annual of the British School at Athens* (from 1904); she was later Joint Editor of the *Annual* from 1906 to 1926.[223] She also served as honorary secretary to the Society for the Promotion of Hellenic Studies in London. Richter went to the Metropolitan Museum of Art in New York. She seems to have been close to Richard Seager, the Cretan archaeologist, though his premature death brought any possible romance to an end.[224] Her career developed with a broad spectrum of major publications on archaic sculpture, Greek pottery, gemstones and portraiture. Certainly the richness of the collection at the Metropolitan in part reflects Richter's eye for acquisitions.

After her year in Greece Dorothy Lamb continued to work on the terracottas for the *Catalogue of the Akropolis Museum*. This was largely completed by 1912 when she took a year-long lectureship at the all women's Bryn Mawr College.[225] She was awarded the Mary Ewart Travelling Scholarship from Newnham College (1913-14), which allowed her to travel to various sites and museums in Europe.[226] She was clearly interested in both early Christian and Islamic art, studying Christian mosaics in Rome and 'paying special attention to Byzantine and Ottoman arts and architecture' in Constantinople,[227] recently the focus of study by the Byzantine Research Fund.[228] During the summer she made a second visit to Turkey to study the Seljuk buildings of Konya, in particular the Mosque of Sultan Alaeddin, the Energheh Mosque, and the Indjeh Minareli Medresseh.[229] Her career was disrupted by the outbreak of the First World War, and she returned to Britain working in the Ministry of National Service (1916-18), and then the Ministry of Food (1918-20), for which she was made a Member of the Order of the British Empire (MBE). Her active archaeological interests seems to have ended with her marriage to a career civil servant, John Reeves Brooke, although she continued her interest in the classical world with two further publications, one on Greek and Roman private correspondence, and the other on Late Antiquity.[230] Mary Taylor developed her studies of Greek terracottas by taking up the Gilchrist Studentship to study Italo-Greek terracottas at the BSR during the 1915-16 session; the School was in the process of moving into its new building in the Valle Giulia.[231] She collaborated on a publication of architectural terracottas from Falerii Veteres with her future husband Harold C. Bradshaw, who had held the Rome Scholarship in Architecture for 1913.[232]

---

[223] Waterhouse 1986, 161.

[224] See in particular Becker and Betancourt 1997, 161.

[225] Cf. Griffin 1992, 445, letter of 19 December 1912.

[226] British School at Athens 1913/14, 137.

[227] British School at Athens 1913/14, 137.

[228] George 1913.

[229] Lamb 1914/16.

[230] Brooke 1929; Brooke 1930; Brooke 1937.

[231] Wiseman 1990, 13.

[232] Taylor and Bradshaw 1916. See also Wiseman 1990, 13-14, 26.

Mary Hamilton developed her studies on the saints of Greece after her marriage to Guy Dickins; she seems to have accompanied her husband on his trips to Greece for the study of Hellenistic sculpture.[233] After Dickins' death in the First World War, she married Lacey Davis Caskey (1880-1944), curator of Classical Art at the Museum of Fine Arts in Boston; Caskey, a member of ASCA, had been Dickins' contemporary in Athens.

The Haslucks continued to travel in Greece and the Ottoman Empire.[234] During the First World War Margaret worked in Military Intelligence, first in London and then later in Greece. After her husband's death in 1920, Margaret settled in Albania where she not only prepared her husband's unpublished papers for publication but also pursued her own anthropological interests.[235]

For other women at the BSA before the First World War, their time at Athens was a prelude to marriage: Köhler married Charles Smith, Abrahams married a Mr Culley. Tennant returned to Greece during the Balkan Wars of 1912 and 1913 and 'took part in the humane task of feeding and nursing the refugees in Epeiros'.[236] Back in Britain she married F. J. Watson Taylor. In August, on her return from Greece, Margery Welsh married Augustus Moore Daniel, who had been elected an Associate of the BSA in 1903. They initially lived in Scarborough on the Yorkshire coast, where she was involved with the local Council of Social Welfare. They then moved to Rome where Augustus was librarian at the BSR (under Thomas Ashby),[237] before becoming Director of the National Gallery in London (1929-33). Welsh retained a memento from her time in Greece, a Protocorinthian sherd, which she later presented to the Fitzwilliam Museum in Cambridge in 1956.[238]

---

[233] British School at Athens 1912/13, 268. Dickins 1914/16.

[234] *E.g.* Hasluck 1912/13.

[235] For her husband's work: Hasluck 1922; Hasluck 1921; Hasluck 1923a; Hasluck 1923b; Hasluck and Hasluck 1924; Hasluck and Hasluck 1929; Hasluck, *et al.* 1926. For her own work: Hasluck 1932. See also Dawkins 1949.

[236] British School at Athens 1912/13, 266.

[237] Margery assisted with the British School at Rome's project on the sculptural collections. See Stuart-Jones 1912, iii. Stuart-Jones noted that A. M. Daniel worked on the project in his capacity as Assistant Director (1906-7) and 'was throughout assisted by Mrs Daniel'. See also Hodges 2000, 49.

[238] Cambridge, Fitzwilliam Museum acc. no. GR. 1. 1956: 'a Proto-Corinthian sherd, which may be approximately dated to the seventh century BC'.

CHAPTER 6:
OTHER STUDENTS IN ATHENS

The main body of students at the BSA consisted of individuals educated at Oxford and Cambridge. However there was a large group of architects who spent part of their year in Athens. There were also students who had been educated in Scotland. The BSA also admitted those who wanted to be in Athens for a shorter length of time to be Associates.

Architects at the School

Penrose had a long-standing interest in architecture and had made a study of the classical buildings of Athens.[1] He was the architect for the original house at the BSA which was completed in 1886 for him to take up residence as Director. Architects were soon included as key members of the BSA. As early as November 1887 the BSA and the Royal Institute of British Architects (RIBA) agreed to sponsor a 'duly qualified architectural student' to go out to Athens 'to assist upon architectural work in excavations' either in Greece or Cyprus.[2] The first person to be appointed was Ravenscroft Elsey Smith, who assisted with the excavations at Paphos, Cyprus (1887/8).[3] Smith was the son of an architect, Thomas Roger Smith, who also held the chair of architecture at University College London from 1880.[4] Father and son went into partnership together, and the son later held the chair of architecture at King's College, London.

Two of the architectural students, Robert Weir Schultz and Sidney Howard Barnsley, went out to the BSA in 1887-88 and made a study of Byzantine buildings. Schultz had been specifically sent to Athens to make 'a fairly complete set of accurate drawings to full scale of Greek mouldings of the best period'.[5] During the year the two students made a study of Byzantine churches in Athens and the immediate area including Daphnae.[6] They also worked with Ernest Gardner on the Erechtheion.[7] Schultz returned for the following two sessions, overlapping with Barnsley, who returned in 1889/90. In the autumn of 1889

---

[1] Penrose 1851.

[2] *The Times* 30 November 1887, 4. The School and the RIBA were to offer £50 each towards expenses.

[3] Gardner, *et al.* 1888.

[4] Elsey Smith's mother was the sister of the surgeon and explorer Joseph Ravenscroft Elsey (1834-57), who was a member of the North Australian Exploring Expedition. Elsey Smith's grandfather was an official of the Bank of England.

[5] Gardner 1889, 274, 277-78.

[6] Macmillan 1890b. For Daphnae: Gardner 1891, 396.

[7] Gardner and Schultz 1891; Barnsley 1891.

Schultz and Barnsley worked on the monastery of Agios Loukas in Phocis.[8] In the spring of 1890 they travelled though the Peloponnese, studying Byzantine structures, in particular at Mistra.[9] They were subsequently due to travel to Salonica and then to Mount Athos on a project funded by Dr Edwin Freshfield (subsequently a Trustee of the BSA). The plan was to publish a monograph on the monasteries of Mount Athos 'illustrative of the architecture and general decoration of these unique churches, which exist today in much the same state as when they were first built'.[10]

Macmillan made a special plea for financial support for this project, appealing 'to all lovers of Byzantine art and to all who wish to see English students take the lead in working out a somewhat neglected department of Hellenic study'.[11] The pair went to Salonica after the fire of 1890 to record some of the surviving buildings.

> We have got a permit from the Pasha to photograph and work where we like, and so anticipate no difficulty.
>
> We are working at St. Sophia, and yesterday B[arnsley] took 18 photos in one church – St. Demetrios – which is perhaps the most interesting of the many interesting ones in the town.
>
> We are taking the opportunity of St. Sophia's being in a deserted state to make new measured drawings of it – Texier's (exteriors especially) of this church being very far out, the drawings having evidently been made after a lapse of time, perhaps of years, from M. Texier's notes by people who had never seen the originals. The mosaics, although practically uninjured, are covered with a coating of smoke and dirt which makes them unfit for drawing. Careful drawings could not be made of these without expensive scaffoldings in dome and bema. The church is structurally still sound; some of the fine caps and old green marble pillars are irretrievably ruined. The dome is all right. The aisle roofs, which were wooden and modern, have been burnt, as also the Turkish colonnade in front. The first has burnt out a part of the dirtiest and thickest populated part of the town, but in proportion of the area it is, perhaps, about one-tenth or less of the enclosure within the walls. It lies close to the water and on the level. Seen from the sea the town seems as if nothing had happened, blocks along the quay, which had escaped, hiding the mass of ruins behind.[12]

Barnsley returned to Greece on his own during the session 1890/91.

The architectural students offered great assistance with the excavations. Architectural students were there 'to make the plans and measurements which are so essential a part of excavation'.[13] Gardner had seen the benefits of architects on Cyprus and at Megalopolis, where he was assisted by Schultz.[14] As a result the Managing Committee created an

---

[8] Schultz and Barnsley 1901.

[9] Macmillan 1890b.

[10] Macmillan 1890b. This is also mentioned in Gardner 1890a, 215.

[11] Macmillan 1890b.

[12] F. C. Penrose, 'The fire at Salonica', *The Times* 4 November 1890.

[13] British School at Athens 1895/96, 4.

[14] Gardner, *et al.* 1892.

architectural studentship which was first held by Charles R. R. Clark (1896/97), who had been admitted to the BSA in the preceding year as a student of the Royal Academy. Subsequent architects helped with other excavations. Rodeck assisted Cecil Smith's excavations of Kynosarges,[15] though he was also working on 'a study of the principles of Ionic architecture and of the Byzantine churches of Attica and Mount Athos'.[16] As the BSA turned to Melos, a succession of architects worked on the excavations: Charles Clark, Edward Hoare and Thomas D. Atkinson.[17] Atkinson was admitted as the BSA Architect with a stipend of £100 with the requirement that he reside in Greece for two months.[18] Atkinson was a contributor to the final report on Phylakopi.[19] Hoare had been a student at Hogarth's college, Magdalen, before turning to architecture. He was admitted in 1897/98, under Hogarth, on the newly established architectural studentship. Other architects also joined projects, such as two friends of Bosanquet's from Trinity, Fletcher and Kitson, who charted the Byzantine churches of Melos.[20]

As the BSA turned from Melos to Crete, Robert Douglas Wells, who had studied at Trinity College, Cambridge was appointed to the architectural studentship in 1900/01 helping with the excavation at Praesos;[21] Bosanquet the current Director had also been a student at Trinity though they did not overlap. The following year, Charles Heaton Comyn assisted with Bosanquet's excavations at Palaikastro from 1902.[22] Several excavations were undertaken simultaneously on Crete. David T. Fyfe, architectural student (1899/1900), worked with Evans on the Knossos excavations.[23] He also made some illustrations of the pottery,[24] in addition to preparing the architectural plans. He published a study of the church of Titus at Gortyn.[25] Fyfe was succeeded in 1905 by Christian C. T. Doll who was appointed superintending architect to the excavations at Knossos. He had been a student at Trinity College, Cambridge (1898-1901) before taking an architectural diploma at University College, London (1903).

Elsewhere Arthur E. Henderson worked with Hasluck and Bosanquet on the survey of Cyzicus.[26] Henderson later joined Hogarth on the excavation of the Artemision at

[15] Rodeck 1896/7.

[16] British School at Athens 1896/97, 230.

[17] Atkinson 1898/9.

[18] BSA Minute Book 3, Meeting of 18 August 1898.

[19] Atkinson, *et al.* 1904.

[20] Fletcher and Kitson 1895/6.

[21] Bosanquet 1901a, 339. Wells and John H. Marshall are noted as travelling together in Crete on the way to the excavations in May 1901: Bosanquet 1938, 75. Both Wells and Bosanquet had been at Trinity College.

[22] Bosanquet and Tod 1902, 384; Bosanquet 1902a; British School at Athens 1903/04, 244-45. Comyn clearly took part in the festivities of May 1902: Bosanquet 1938, 125, 127.

[23] Bosanquet 1900, 168; Bosanquet 1901a, 334; Bosanquet and Tod 1902, 384.

[24] *E.g.* Hogarth and Welch 1901, 94-95.

[25] Fyfe 1907.

[26] Hasluck and Henderson 1904.

Ephesus. Ramsay Traquair was admitted on an architectural studentship to work with the Laconia Survey in 1906. He took a particular interest in the medieval castles and churches.[27] Walter George joined the excavations, specifically at the sanctuary of Artemis Orthia, as draughtsman in 1907 and 1909; he made a special study of the architectural terracottas.[28]

Many of the architects took an interest in Byzantine architecture and indeed some used these influences to design churches back in Britain. The Byzantine Research Fund, founded in 1908, sponsored the study of Christian and Islamic buildings in Constantinople where several BSA architects had worked. Edwin F. Reynolds arrived in Greece in 1902, making a study of Byzantine architecture; he also went to Constantinople to prepare architectural drawings.[29] One of the first architects attached to the Byzantine Research Fund was Ramsay Traquair (1874-1952), who had earlier worked in Laconia.[30] In Constantinople he worked with Wace on the column of Theodosios, as well as on other Byzantine buildings in the city.[31] He was succeeded by Walter S. George (1881-1962), who came out the following year (and had been working with Dawkins at Sparta), and then for three further seasons (1908/09, 1909/10, 1912/13).[32]

The architectural students were available to play their part in the developments of the facilities at the BSA. Charles R. R. Clark (1869-1933) was admitted in two consecutive years, and prepared the plans for the hostel in conjunction with the Athenian architect Moussis.[33] Charles Heaton F. Comyn (1877-1933), who arrived in Athens in March 1904, designed the Penrose Memorial Library as well as the extension for the hostel.[34]

Other architectural students joined the BSA as part of their wider studies. James B. Fulton was admitted as a Soane Student in 1902 as part of a study tour of Egypt, Palestine, Turkey, Greece, Italy and Germany. Others combined Athens with study at the BSR: W. Harvey (1907/08; Gold Medallist and Travelling Student of the Royal Academy), Lionel B. Budden (1909/10), Harry H. Jewell (1909/10; Gold Medallist of the Royal Academy), and George E. G. Leith (1912/13; BSR 1911).

[27] Traquair 1905/06a; Traquair 1905/06b; Traquair 1906/07; Traquair 1908/09.

[28] George and Woodward 1929.

[29] These drawings are preserved in the archive of the RIBA. He visited Byzantine churches in Greece, Saint Luke of Stiris (1903); Constantinople: Church of Saint Theodore (1903), Mosque of Suleiman I (1903); Mosque of Osman III (1903); Mosque of Ahmed I (1903); Santa Sophia (1903); Kariye Jami (1903)Yeni Valideh Jami (1903); Mosque of Ruslem Pasha (1903); Palace of Belisarius (1903)Mosque of Beyazid II (1903); Church of Saint Bacchus and Saint Sergius (1903); Bursa, The Green Mosque (1903).

[30] Traquair 1905/06a; Traquair 1906/07; Traquair 1908/09. Traquair was given the architectural studentship to help van Millingen in Constantinople: BSA Minute Book 5, Meeting of 17 October 1905.

[31] Wace and Traquair 1909; Van Millingen, *et al.* 1912.

[32] Van Millingen, *et al.* 1912; George 1913.

[33] Macmillan 1910/11, xiv. See also Macmillan, *et al.* 1903/04, 236.

[34] Macmillan, *et al.* 1903/04, 236-37.

The British School at Athens and the British School at Rome

The BSR emerged after a visit to Rome by two Oxford men, Henry Francis Pelham and Francis Haverfield, in 1898.[35] The emphasis was less archaeological than that of the BSA, as the prospectus outlined:

> It is obvious, too, that in some respects the work of a School at Rome would be more many-sided than is possible in Athens. It would be less predominantly classical and archaeological, and its students would be found in the galleries, libraries, and churches, as well as in the museums, or among the monuments of the Palatine or the Forum. A School at Rome would also be a natural centre from which work could be directed and organized at Naples, Florence, Venice, and elsewhere in Italy.
>
> It is therefore not only to those who are interested in classical history or archaeology that the proposed School should be of service, but equally to students of Christian Antiquities, of Mediaeval History, of Palaeography, and of Italian Art.[36]

The first Director, Gordon McNeil Rushforth (1900-03) was appointed.[37] The School itself was based in the Palazzo Odeschali. Work of the School was published in *Papers of the British School at Rome*, published by Macmillan and taking a similar format to the *Annual of the British School at Athens*. Both Schools shared the same Honorary Secretary.

Rushforth's resignation led to the appointment of another Oxford man and former BSA student, Henry Stuart Jones, as Director (1903-05).[38] Jones had suffered from a period of ill health after returning to Oxford from Greece; and the appointment to Rome was supported by a research fellowship made by Trinity College.[39] Jones had a strong interest in classical archaeology, publishing on both Greek pottery and sculpture.[40] His interest developed under the influence of Percy Gardner. His contribution was a study of some of the sculptural collections in Rome, a project in which he was assisted by another BSA student, Alan Wace.[41] He began to prepare a catalogue of sculptures in the Capitoline, the Conservatori, and the Antiquarium on the Caelian Hill.[42] A parallel for the project could be found in Greece with the catalogues for the museums in Sparta and the Acropolis Museum in Athens.[43] Wace had completed his first year in Athens working on Hellenistic sculpture,[44] a topic that reflected the interest of Charles Waldstein. Wace fell into a pattern of working on the Rome sculpture catalogues in the autumn of each year. He

---

[35] Wallace-Hadrill 2001, 20-21.

[36] Quoted in Wallace-Hadrill 2001, 21.

[37] Wiseman 1981; Wallace-Hadrill 2001, 22-27.

[38] Gill 2004m.

[39] Gill 2004m.

[40] Stuart-Jones 1891; Stuart-Jones 1895.

[41] Stuart-Jones 1912. Wace 1906a; Wace 1907;Wace 1910.

[42] Wallace-Hadrill 2001, 27.

[43] Tod and Wace 1906; Dickins 1912; Casson 1921.

[44] Wace 1902/03.

would then spend the following spring and summer in Athens, where he would work on field projects in Laconia and Thessaly.[45]

In 1905/06 Wace was appointed Librarian in Rome, specifically to assist with the sculpture catalogue. Stuart-Jones and Wace were joined by Guy Dickins, who had already been in Athens for a year, to work on sculpture collections. He published a fragment in the Terme Museum in Rome, and collaborated on the sculpture catalogue publishing material from the Conservatori.[46] Dickins had been working on a sculptural project on Damophon of Messene, following the Greek finds at Lykosura.[47] Henry J. W. Tillyard, who had been appointed assistant librarian in Athens in 1904/05, spent part of the following year (1905/06) in Rome, perhaps drawn by his friendship with Wace, with whom he collaborated in Laconia.

The foundation of the BSR in 1900 brought a change to the regulations for residence for the BSA.[48] Whereas residence in Athens had previously been set as three months, the BSR was seen as a partner institution. Special regulations were developed to allow students to move between the two institutions. The BSA regulations for students stated:

> XX. No person, other than a student of the British School at Rome, shall be admitted as a Student who does not intend to reside at least three months in Greek lands. In the case of Students of the British School at Rome, an aggregate residence of four months at the two Schools will be accepted as alternative to three months' residence in Greece.

In addition there was agreement over where research from students should be published. One of the distinctions was that projects based on the Greek colonies of southern Italy and Sicily should appear in the *Annual of the British School at Athens*.[49] One of the BSR students who was admitted under reciprocal arrangements was John D. Beazley who had been working on Athenian pottery in the collections in Rome.[50]

Other BSA students working on projects in Italy included John P. Droop who published on Messapian texts in Calabria;[51] he had already spent two years in Athens. It may have been Droop's work that made the BSA committee reflect on which School was responsible for the publication of research on 'Magna Graecia and Sicily'.[52] W. M. Calder was able to study epigraphic material in Italy in 1907 before passing through Athens to join William Ramsay's surveys of Asia Minor.[53] A. C. Sheepshanks, who was teaching at Eton, was admitted as a student in Rome and Athens in 1907 to devote 'his time to

[45] Gill 2004q.

[46] Dickins 1906; Dickins 1911.

[47] Dickins 1906.

[48] Wallace-Hadrill 2001, 30.

[49] *E.g.* Droop 1905/06b.

[50] Beazley 1911/12; Beazley 1912/13. For Beazley: Gill 2004a.

[51] Droop 1905/06b.

[52] BSA Minute Book 5, Meeting of 21 November 1905.

[53] See Wallace-Hadrill 2001, 29.

procuring that first hand acquaintance with ancient sites which does so much to give interest and freshness to historical and classical teaching'.[54] It was not specifically that 'such visits to classical sites give to the teaching of the classics in England additional reality and life'.[55]

Stuart-Jones's health started to fail and he, like Rushworth, was forced to resign in 1905; Thomas Ashby, the Oxford-educated Assistant Director, was in charge of the BSR for the year 1905/06, with Wace as Librarian.[56] Wace applied for the directorship but in 1906 was offered the post of assistant to Ashby, which he declined.[57] Ashby became the third Director, and his first assistant was Augustus Moore Daniel, an associate of the BSA.[58] Daniel was married to Margery K. Welsh, a former BSA student, who had studied honorific statues while in Athens.[59] Wace continued to work on the Rome sculpture project, publishing sculptures in Turin, the Palazzo Spada, and contributing to the section on Roman portraits in the catalogue of the Capitoline collection.[60] Among the students admitted to the BSR was Gisela M. A. Richter, a former student of the BSA, who arrived in 1906 after she had moved to New York.[61]

The BSR had restrictions on excavations. Ashby was looking for new opportunities and travelled through Sardinia with Duncan Mackenzie in the spring of 1906.[62] Mary Hamilton spend part of the session 1905/06 in Rome where she was due to work with Ashby on ethnographic aspects of his Sardinian work.[63] Hamilton's time in Rome and in Athens coincided with her future husband, Guy Dickins. The Sardinian work also involved another former Athens student, Francis B. Baker-Penoyre, in 1907.[64] During the same year T. Eric Peet was a student in Rome, investigating the 'origin of the iron age civilisation of South Italy'.[65] He was the first holder of the Pelham Studentship created in memory of Henry Pelham.[66] This western research was given a wider perspective through his work with Wace and Thompson at the BSA.[67] Peet was able to excavate on Malta with Ashby in May

---

[54] British School at Athens 1907/08, 426; Wallace-Hadrill 2001, 30.

[55] Quoted from the *Annual Report of the British School at Rome* (1907/08) in Wallace-Hadrill 2001, 30.

[56] Wallace-Hadrill 2001, 28; Hodges 2000, 48.

[57] Wallace-Hadrill 2001, 28.

[58] Hodges 2000, 49.

[59] Wallace-Hadrill 2001, 28; Gill 2002.

[60] Wace 1906c; Wace 1910; Stuart-Jones 1912.

[61] Richter was sometimes in Rome looking for potential acquisitions for the Metropolitan Museum of Art: Dyson 2004, 169-70.

[62] Wallace-Hadrill 2001, 32; Momigliano 1999, 80-83; Hodges 2000, 42-43.

[63] Momigliano 1999, 81. See also Annual Report of the British School at Rome (1905/06), 3.

[64] Wallace-Hadrill 2001, 32.

[65] Peet 1906/07; Peet 1907. See also Wallace-Hadrill 2001, 32.

[66] Wallace-Hadrill 2001, 31.

[67] Peet, *et al.* 1908.

1910.[68] W. L. H. Duckworth, a physical anthropologist, was admitted to the BSR in 1909. He had already worked with Bosanquet on human remains from excavations on Crete.

In 1909 Eugénie (Sellers) Strong, a former BSA student, moved to Rome and became involved with the publication of the city's sculpture collections. In 1911 she was appointed Assistant Director of the BSR.[69] This period is marked by the growing number of students who split their year between Athens and Rome. Arnold J. Toynbee of Balliol College (and like Ashby, a fellow Wykehamist), travelled in Lazio and Umbria in 1911: 'there is no doubt that such firsthand knowledge on the part of the teacher makes classical and historical teaching gain greatly in reality and interest'.[70] Toynbee recalled cycling with Ashby who 'travelled like the White Knight in *Alice through the Looking Glass*, except that his mount was, not a wooden horse, but a bicycle'.[71] Toynbee then went to Greece working with Wace and Thompson in Thessaly.

Some former BSA students later went out to the BSR for a specific purpose. Norman Whatley had been a student in Athens (1907/08), but was admitted to the BSR in 1910 when he had been appointed Fellow and Tutor at Hertford College, Oxford. Mary N. L. Taylor was admitted to the BSR in 1913 and later went on to Athens. In Rome she met her future husband, Harold Chalton Bradshaw, Rome Scholar in Fine Arts (1913).[72] Together they published a study of architectural terracottas from Falerii Veteres.[73] Agnes Conway, who had studied history at Newnham College, had been admitted to the BSR in 1912, two years before she went to Greece.[74] Other students who split their year between Rome and Athens included the Canadian, William A. Kirkwood (1904/05), and the numismatist, Sidney Grose (1909/10).

At least five of the BSA architects spent time in Rome.[75] Among them was Gordon Leith, who had worked with (Sir) Herbert Baker on the Union Buildings (1910-13) in South Africa. Baker had himself benefited from travels in the Mediterranean and had used classical features in his architecture.[76] He established in 1912 a scholarship to allow architects from South Africa to travel. He helped to prepare a reconstruction for the Palace of Domitian. Frank G. Orr, who had studied at the Glasgow School of Art, was admitted to the BSR (1904/05), and then spent the following year in Athens (1905/06). The other three architects (two of them Royal Academy Gold Medallists), W. Harvey (1907/08), Lionel Budden (1909/10), and Harry H. Jewell (1909/10), split the year between Athens and Rome.

---

[68] Peet 1910; Ashby, *et al.* 1913. See also Hodges 2000, 44.

[69] Dyson 2004, 111-27; see also Hodges 2000, 50.

[70] Quoted from the Annual Report of the British School at Rome (1911/12) in Wallace-Hadrill 2001, 30. See also Toynbee's own recollections: Toynbee 1969, 18.

[71] Toynbee 1969, 22-23.

[72] Wallace-Hadrill 2001, 53. See also Dyson 2004, 125.

[73] Taylor and Bradshaw 1916.

[74] Her visits to Rome are briefly mentioned: Conway 1917, 14.

[75] The first four were: Frank George Orr (BSR 1904), W. Harvey (BSR 1908), Lionel B. Budden (BSR 1909), Harry H. Jewell (BSR 1910).

[76] Wallace-Hadrill 2001, 36. See also Abramson 2004.

Students from Scotland at the School

Apart from Oxford and Cambridge, one of the main groups of students admitted to the BSA in the period up to 1914 consisted of Scots. A key influence was William Ramsay, a graduate of the university of Aberdeen, who had continued his studies at St John's College, Oxford (Literae humaniores 1876). Ramsay had travelled widely in Asia Minor and was elected a research fellow at Exeter College in 1882. He was appointed to the Lincoln and Merton Chair of Classical Archaeology at Oxford in 1885, before moving back to Aberdeen in 1886, where he was Regius Professor of Humanity.

At least three of Ramsay's students completed their studies at Aberdeen and then continued their studies in England. One of the first students was John G. C. Anderson, son of the Rev. Alexander Anderson, from Morayshire. On completing his studies in Aberdeen he went to Christ Church as an exhibitioner (1891-96) aged 20, and then out to the BSA as Craven University Fellow. He was involved with the publication of epigraphic material from the BSA's excavation at Kynosarges.[77] He went on to travel in Anatolia, making a special study of Phrygia.[78] One of Anderson's achievements was the plotting of a map of Asia Minor. William Moir Calder, the son of a farmer, went to Robert Gordon College, Aberdeen (1894-99), then to Aberdeen University, where he obtained a first class degree in classics (1903). Like Anderson, he studied at Christ Church as an Exhibitioner (1903), aged 22. On completing his degree in 1907, he was admitted first to the BSR under Thomas Ashby.[79] The third student was Margaret Masson Hardie, the daughter of a farmer from Chapelton, Drumblade near Elgin, who had been educated at Elgin Academy before moving to Aberdeen University, where she obtained a first class degree in classics. She then continued her studies at Newnham College, obtaining a first in classics. She was admitted to the BSA in 1911/12 and assisted with Ramsay's epigraphic survey of the sanctuary of Mên Askaenos at the Roman colony of Pisidian Antioch.[80]

Students from Glasgow and Dundee followed this pattern of continuing their studies in England. Two of the BSA students had previously studied at Glasgow. James George Frazer had been at Larchfield Academy, Helensburgh, and then at the University of Glasgow (1869-74). Among the influences there was George Gilbert Ramsay, Professor of Humanity, who had been educated at Trinity College, Oxford. Aged 20, Frazer went to Trinity College, Cambridge (1874-78), where he obtained a first class in the Classical Tripos (1878). Frazer was admitted to the BSA as a mature student to work on Pausanias. One of G. G. Ramsay's other pupils was Campbell Cowan Edgar, from Tongland, Kirkcudbrightshire. He was educated at Ayr Academy, then Glasgow University (1887-91). For part of this time Edgar studied under Richard Claverhouse Jebb (1875-89) and Gilbert Murray (1889-99), consecutive holders of the chair of Greek at Glasgow.[81] Jebb had been one of the key people

---

[77] Anderson 1896/7.

[78] Anderson 1897a; Anderson 1897b.

[79] Wallace-Hadrill 2001, 29.

[80] Hardie 1912.

[81] Murray's assistant (1891-97) was Ronald Montagu Butler, who was later to excavate in Boeotia. However at this stage in his career he did not have an interest in archaeology.

behind the newly formed BSA. After Glasgow Edgar became Bible Clerk at Oriel College (1891) at the age of 20, continuing his study of classics (1891-95). The award of a Craven Fellowship allowed him to study in Athens, where he gained archaeological experience on the BSA excavations at Kynosarges[82] and on Melos.[83] Anderson was his contemporary at Oxford and the BSA. Edgar gained further experience of excavation under David Hogarth at Naukratis and shortly afterwards joined the catalogue commission in Cairo.[84]

Hilda Lorimer, the daughter of Rev. Robert Lorimer, was educated at Dundee High School, and then at the University College, Dundee (1889-93) where she obtained a first class in Classics. At the age of 20 she obtained a scholarship to continue her studies at Girton College, Cambridge, obtaining a first (1896). She was admitted to the BSA as Pfeiffer Travelling Student (1901-02), and was able to work with W. Dörpfeld of the German School.

Duncan Mackenzie, who had studied in Edinburgh (1882-90), chose to study on continental Europe. He completed a doctorial thesis on Lycian sculpture from the University of Vienna (1895). His experience of continental archaeological training soon come into its own in the BSA excavations on Melos,[85] and then with Evans at Knossos.[86] Harcourt-Smith wrote to George Macmillan about his arrival in Athens:

> Mackenzie is a good deal with us, and we like him very much. He is of course socially a little untrained, but with excellent instinct and altogether a very nice fellow. He comes with the best reputation from Wenndorf, and gives me the impression of being a thorough going and capable man: I am sure he will prove a valuable acquisition to the School.[87]

Few Scottish students were admitted directly from Scotland. During the session 1894/95 two theology students from Aberdeen were sent out: John Garrow Duncan from Aberdeen, by the Church of Scotland, and Adam Fyfe Findlay, by the United Presbyterian Church of Scotland. Both worked specifically at modern Greek. Duncan became interested in Egyptian antiquities and worked with Petrie in Egypt and Palestine.[88] Findlay worked specifically on the account of Paul at Athens in the Acts of the Apostles.[89]

In 1895 there was a concerted move to improve the financial situation of the BSA. The appeal to the treasury was supported by academics from several universities in Scotland: St Andrews, Glasgow, Aberdeen and Edinburgh.[90] This seems to have encouraged the admission of a number of students who came straight from Scotland. One of the first was Archibald

---

[82] Edgar 1897.

[83] Edgar 1896/7; Edgar 1897/8; Edgar 1898/9c; Atkinson, *et al.* 1904.

[84] Edgar 1898/9a; Edgar 1898/9b.

[85] Mackenzie 1896/7.

[86] Mackenzie 1903.

[87] Letter, December 30, 1895 (Macmillan archive). I am grateful to Christopher Stray for drawing my attention to this.

[88] Petrie and Duncan 1906; Duncan 1908.

[89] Findlay 1894/5.

[90] Macmillan 1910/11, xii. A list of universities appears in *BSA* 1 (1894-95) xv-xvi.

Paterson, an Edinburgh graduate, who went to Athens 1895/96 to work on Christian antiquities. W. W. Reid was a student of Ramsay in Aberdeen, who was admitted to the BSA on a Blackie Travelling Studentship (1896-97).[91] He travelled through Asia Minor and Cyprus. He was later ordained as a minister in the Church of Scotland. William Alexander Curtis, who had studied theology at Edinburgh, went to Athens at the age of 21 (1897-98); he went on to become a colleague of Ramsay at Aberdeen when he took up an appointment as Professor of Systematic Theology (1903-15) before returning to Edinburgh. Mary Hamilton, a Classics graduate of the University of St Andrews, was admitted to the BSA as a holder of a Research Fellowship under the Carnegie Trust (1905-06, 1906-07).[92] She was also working at the interface of theology and the classical world, and in particular on the custom of incubation.[93]

John Arnott Hamilton, an ordained minister and Edinburgh graduate, was admitted to the BSA at a mature student (1913-14). He had a long-standing interest in church architecture,[94] and went out to Athens as a holder of the Blackie Scholarship to study Byzantine architecture, completing a work on the church at Kaisariani.[95] Several of the architects admitted to the BSA had trained at the Glasgow School of Art: David Theodore Fyfe (1899/1900), who became architect to the excavations at Knossos, and Frank G. Orr (1905/06), to name but two. Other Scots studied in England. Harry Pirie-Gordon, son of the 12th Laird of Buthlaw, was a student in Oxford before being admitted to the BSA.

Wales and the British School at Athens

It is noticeable that one of the obvious gaps in the profile of students was Wales. This is in spite of the contribution made by George Chatterton Richards (1867-1951). Subsequent to being a student of the BSA (1889-91), he became Professor of Greek at the University College of South Wales and Monmouthshire (1891-98). During this period he was not only ordained, but also serviced as Assistant Director of the BSA under David Hogarth (1897). He was succeeded in Cardiff by Ronald Montagu Burrows (1867-1920), who held the post until 1908 when he moved to Manchester. Cardiff had a succession of Greek archaeologists including Percy Neville Ure (1879-1950) who was lecturer in Greek from 1903 until his move to Leeds. G. E. Holding, a Cardiff student, may hold the honour of being the first British woman to work on a field-project in Greece, Rhitsona in Boeotia, although it was not an official excavation of the School.

Associates of the School

The Rules and Regulations of the BSA allowed for the election of Associates who consisted of 'persons actively engaged in study or exploration in Greek lands' (XXIII). The reason was explained in the Annual Meeting of July 1896:

[91] Reid subsequently studied at Edinburgh.

[92] The Carnegie Trust had been asked to support students from Scotland in 1902: BSA Minute Book 4, Meeting of 6 March 1902. However the Trust took the view that it could use its funds to support either the BSA or the BSR (Meeting of 3 July 1902).

[93] Hamilton 1906; Hamilton 1906/7; Hamilton 1910.

[94] Hamilton 1890.

[95] Hamilton 1916.

In the case of mature scholars who might thus visit Athens and avail themselves of the conveniences of study afforded by the School, the Committee has for some time past had in contemplation the possibility of attaching them directly to the School without laying upon them the obligations of an ordinary Student. The problem has been solved during the past session by the creation of a new class of Associates, who are to enjoy the privileges of membership *honoris causa*.[96]

The first three associates were elected in 1896: Rev. Alfred Hamilton Cruikshank (1862-1927), Assistant Master at Winchester (1894-1910); Professor John Bagnell Bury (1861-1927), Trinity College, Dublin; and Arthur J. Evans (1851-1941), Keeper, The Ashmolean Museum, Oxford. Evans had been travelling through Crete since 1894 and had recently investigated the cave at Psychro.[97] Bury had by this stage had two periods of study in Athens (in 1894/95 and 1895/96) and had gone on to work on 'Greek history and topography'; he published two studies on the topography of the battlefields of the Persian wars.[98] Cruikshank was an Assistant Master at Winchester (from 1894), and prior to that a teacher at Harrow (1891-94). He had been educated at Winchester (a contemporary of David Hogarth, and two years below Cecil Harcourt-Smith) and then New College, Oxford, where he had also been a Fellow (1885) and Tutor (1889-91). His interest in Greece was the Meteora.[99] Cruickshank made use of the new railways in Thessaly and his published account was more of a travelogue.

> On emerging from the station we were confronted by the usual assembly of screaming men and boys with mules. After effecting a bargain we mounted, the stirrups here being of rope, an uncomfortable device too common in Greece. My guide was an elderly person of unprepossessing appearance, with no hair on his head, parchment skin and an evil eye. Baedeker announces that the most interesting of the monasteries is Hagios Barlaam, and thither I was bent on going, but our muleteers took advantage of our slight acquaintance with the language and ignorance of the geography to take us in an entirely opposite direction. Perhaps it was as well, for we were late as it was, not arriving at Kalabaka till four pm.[100]

Three more Associates were appointed in the following session. The architect Ambrose M. Poynter (1867-1923) was working on Roman mosaics in early 1897.[101] These included the pavements in the theatre of Dionysos at Athens, in the temple of Zeus at Olympia, and in the Odeion of Herodes Atticus at Athens. The other two Associates were both former

---

[96] British School at Athens 1895/96, 5.

[97] Brown 1993; Brown 2000; Brown and Bennett 2001. See also MacGillivray 2000. For Evans' work in the *Annual*: Evans 1895/96.

[98] Bury 1894/5; Bury 1895/6.

[99] Cruickshank 1895/6.

[100] Cruickshank 1895/6, 107.

[101] Poynter 1896/7. His father, Sir Edward Poynter, chaired the annual meeting of Subscribers on July 15, 1897: British School at Athens 1896/97, 221. He was a contemporary of several BSA students at Eton. Poynter had hoped to be admitted as a student but could only stay in Greece for six weeks: BSA Minute Book 2, Meeting of October 26, 1896.

students: John Linton Myres (1869-1954) had previously worked with William Roger Paton on a topographical survey of the Bodrum peninsula, and had subsequently travelled with Evans through Crete. He was now a Student of Christ Church. John Ellingham Brooks (1863-1929) had been admitted to the BSA in 1894/95.

Some of the Associates were placed in this category because they were not staying in Greece for a sufficient length of time. For example Alfred E. Zimmern, fellow of New College, was working on the Greek economy.[102] However in the case of George Kennedy of Balliol College, Oxford, and the Slade School of Art it was felt that he 'had had no archaeological training in Oxford'.[103]

1895/96: Rev. Alfred Hamilton Cruikshank (1862-1927). Assistant Master at Winchester (1894-1910); Durham.

1895/96: Professor John Bagnell Bury (1861-1927). Trinity College, Dublin.

1895/96: (Sir) Arthur J. Evans (1851-1941). Keeper, The Ashmolean Museum, Oxford.

1896/97: Ambrose M. Poynter (1867-1923). Eton. Royal Academy.

1896/97: John Ellingham Brooks (1863-1929). Peterhouse, Cambridge. Former student.

1896/97: John Linton Myres (1869-1954). Student of Christ Church, Oxford. Former student.

1897/98: Professor Ernest A. Gardner (1862-1939). University College London. Former Director.

1902: Louisa Pesel (c. 1870-1947). Directrice of the Royal Hellenic School of Needlwork and Laces at Athens.

1902: John Foster Crace (d. 1960). Classical master at Eton (1901-35).

1903: Mona Wilson (1872-1954). Newnham College, Cambridge (1892-96).

1903: J. S. Carter

1903: B. Townsend

1903: (Sir) Augustus Moore Daniel (1866-1950). Trinity College, Cambridge. Assistant Director of the British School at Rome; Director of the National Gallery.

1906: H. W. Allen

1906: William Miller (1864-1945). Hertford College, Oxford. Journalist and historian.

1906: George Kennedy. Balliol College, Oxford; Slade School of Art.

1910: (Sir) Alfred Eckhard Zimmern (1879-1957). Winchester; New College, Oxford. Fellow and tutor of New College (1904-09); Inspector, Board of Education (1912-15).

1912: Mary B. Negreponte

1913: C. J. Ellingham. St John's College, Oxford.

1913: Capt. H. M. Greaves, R. A. Keble College, Oxford.

Table 12. Associates of the British School at Athens

---

[102] BSA Minute Book 6, Meeting of 13 July 1909. Zimmern 1909; Zimmern 1911.

[103] BSA Minute Book 5, Meeting of 8 January 1907.

PART 3:
FIELDWORK

CHAPTER 7: CYPRUS

One of the aims of the BSA had been to establish a programme of archaeological fieldwork.[1] Members took part in the already existing projects: the work of the Asia Minor Exploration Fund and the Cyprus Exploration Fund. The BSA went on to develop official excavations with the controversial, and not altogether successful, work at Megalopolis. Cecil Harcourt-Smith improved the work with his training dig at Kynosarges and the development of a major project on Melos (notably at Phylakopi). The changing political situation in the Aegean with the opening of Crete led to the formation of the Cretan Exploration Fund with the major excavations by Evans, Hogarth, Bosanquet and Dawkins at Knossos, the Dictaean Cave, Kato Zakro, Praesos and Palaikastro. Bosanquet refocused the work in Laconia which continued under Dawkins as the work of the Laconia Exploration Fund; this included the excavation of the sanctuary of Artemis Orthia and the Menelaion.

Alongside these major projects were exploratory excavations including Aegosthena, and work in Boeotia. It is striking that excavations were often accompanied by regional surveys. Hogarth travelled widely in Cyprus alongside the excavations. The travels of Evans and Myres on Crete suggested the sites that they considered to be worth exploring by digging. Surveys in Thessaly and Macedonia led to concerted series of excavations.

Cyprus

Britain obtained the administration of Cyprus in 1878 from the Ottoman Empire.[2] There had been a growing interest in the archaeology of the island, in part generated by investigations of the American consul General Luigi Palma di Cesnola.[3] The establishment of the BSA in 1886 allowed British archaeologists to consider excavating on Cyprus.

The inspiration for the project in fact had, in fact, come from Francis H. H. Guillemard, a fellow of Caius College. He had been travelling on Cyprus in early 1887 and observed 'continual discoveries, legitimate and illegitimate', and this led to the suggestion that there should be a Cambridge based expedition to Cyprus.[4] The British High Commissioner on the island, Sir Elliott Bovill, was keen to see excavations backed by a body, and so the Hellenic Society was approached and the Cyprus Exploration Fund (CEF) was formed. The CEF was chaired by Sidney Colvin; the secretary was George Macmillan and the treasurer Walter Leaf.[5] These events coincided with the appointment of Ernest Gardner,

---

[1] For a useful survey of archaeological discoveries in 'Greek lands' (including Cyprus and Anatolia) see Marshall 1920.

[2] For the history of British excavations on Cyprus: Megaw 1988; Cadogan 2005; Challis 2008, 160-75.

[3] Karageorghis 2000.

[4] Gardner, *et al.* 1888, 149.

[5] The full committee is given at Colvin, *et al.* 1888.

also at Caius, as BSA Director in the autumn of 1887. Indeed part of the BSA's commitment to the CEF was the agreement that the Director would superintend the excavations and that students of the BSA would participate in the work.[6] That same October the Hellenic Society created the Cyprus Exploration Fund for work on the island.[7] The circular made the case:

> It has long been felt by students that systematic archaeological researches ought to be undertaken in Cyprus and it has often been made a subject of reproach against this country that no such researches have been attempted since the island came under English government. Private and casual excavations at various sites have already yielded results of the greatest importance for the study both of Greek art itself and of the foreign influences which surrounded its cradle. Such excavations have lately been prohibited by authority, but not until their fruits had convinced those interested in the subject that regular and scientifically-conducted researches should, if possible, be set on foot under official sanction without delay.[8]

The Hellenic Society made an initial grant of £150 towards the project, which was matched by Oxford, Cambridge and the BSA. Clearly it was envisaged that the Cyprus Exploration Fund would be similar to the Funds for work in Asia Minor, Egypt and Palestine.[9]

Gardner and Guillemard arrived on Cyprus in November 1887 and immediately travelled in the western parts looking for possible sites.[10] There were three possibilities: near Lapithos, Poli tes Chrysochou (thought to be the ancient Arsinoë), and the temple of Aphrodite near Old Paphos. The ambitions of the team guided them towards the temple of Aphrodite due to 'the historical importance of the site'.[11] The rest of the team arrived in Cyprus in December: David Hogarth; the architect R. Elsey Smith (supported by a £50 grant from the Royal Institute of British Architects); and Montague Rhodes James, then a Fellow of King's College, Cambridge, who had been awarded £40 for archaeological work on Cyprus.[12] James was immediately assigned a preliminary excavation at Leontari Vouno near Nicosia.[13] The team then moved to Old Paphos, assisted by Gregori Antoniou as foreman, establishing a long tradition with the BSA.[14] The work was initially restricted by the lack of equipment.[15] Apart from some work on a few tombs, the main excavation

---

[6] 'Archaeological research in Greece and Cyprus', *The Times* 20 July 1888, 13.

[7] Macmillan 1910/11, x.

[8] Quoted in Colvin, *et al.* 1888.

[9] Colvin, *et al.* 1888. For the Asia Minor Exploration Fund: Gill 2004c. For the Egypt Exploration Fund: James 1982.

[10] Gardner, *et al.* 1888, 150-51.

[11] Gardner, *et al.* 1888, 151.

[12] *The Times* 20 January 1888, 10.

[13] Gardner, *et al.* 1888, 152-58. The excavation took place 7-24 January 1888, with 7 to 15 men.

[14] Gardner, *et al.* 1888, 158.

[15] Gardner, *et al.* 1888, 159. Work started on 1 February, but the full set of tools and wheelbarrows had not arrived until March 9.

concentrated on the sanctuary, with a workforce of up to 230.[16] Among the finds was a head of a young boy.[17] Gardner himself had to leave the excavation in mid-March due to illness and he returned to Athens; James had to return to England in April.[18]

Before the end of the excavating season, and before the local workforce had to tend to crops and other agricultural activities, the team turned to excavate at Amargetti, twelve miles away from Kouklia.[19] They were rejoined by Gardner, as well as by Malcolm Macmillan and Louis Dyer of Harvard. Inscribed material suggested that it was a sanctuary of Opaon Melanthios. There was a special interest in the inscribed material; for example, an inscribed statue to Opaon Melanthios, from Amargetti.[20] The finds from the excavations were divided up; a selection was shipped to England to be divided between the British, Ashmolean and Fitzwilliam museums.[21] After the excavations had been completed in May, Hogarth travelled through the island in the summer of 1888 and investigated the site of Lapithos, where he felt there was little depth for excavation.[22] He also made two trips to Poli, which he felt was bound to provide 'museum objects'.[23]

As the work progressed there was growing support in Britain. An appeal was launched in March 1888 which had a distinctly nationalistic tone stating that it was imperative: 'to carry out these excavations in a manner worthy of English achievements in the past, and with results comparable to those obtained by the Germans at Olympia and at Pergamos, by the French at Delos, and by the Austrians in Lycia'.[24] The fund was even the subject of an editorial in *The Times*.

> The time has come, perhaps, when it behoves us to take a broader view of our responsibilities in Cyprus than is involved in the measures we have adopted for promoting the material welfare of its inhabitants. A civilized community is not merely concerned with the present and the future. The past has claims on it as well. It is impossible to measure the loss which the human race at large, and especially that chosen portion of it whose civilization is progressive, would suffer if the whole of its past were plotted out. Modern civilization has its roots in the life and thought of the races which once occupied the countries surrounding the Mediterranean. We cannot completely recover and reproduce the living lineaments of their daily existence. Their surviving literature will help us in the effort, but it needs to be interpreted and vivified by the material remains of their art and culture. In the abstract we all

---

[16] Gardner, *et al.* 1888, 164. for other discussions of the excavations: Hogarth 1888a; Hogarth 1888d.

[17] Gardner 1890c.

[18] Gardner, *et al.* 1888, 165-66.

[19] Gardner, *et al.* 1888, 169-74. The work concluded on 23 May 1888.

[20] Mitford 1946, 36-39. Some of the inscribed objects were presented to the Fitzwilliam Museum.

[21] Gardner, *et al.* 1888, 174. For a discussion of one of the inscriptions from Paphos in the British Museum: Paton 1890.

[22] Gardner, *et al.* 1888, 151; Hogarth 1889.

[23] Gardner, *et al.* 1888, 174.

[24] Colvin, *et al.* 1888.

recognize this. We are proud of the noble specimens of Greek art which adorn the British Museum, and we watch with envy the efforts made of late years by foreign nations to recover the remains of Hellenic antiquity. Germany has been searching for years at Troy, and the results of its searches have been of incalculable moment to the history of Greek art and life. France is pursuing similar researches in Delos, and Austria in Lycia. These excavations have been conducted on soil in which the respective nations engaged in them have no more than a historical and archaeological interest. Germany, France, and Austria have merely presented and acknowledged the common heritage of Europe in the remnants of Hellenic antiquity, though in so doing they have manifested a true and genuine sense of the continuity of European civilization. It surely cannot be supposed that England, which has ruled for ten years in Cyprus, is less interested than other European nations in racing the origin of our common civilization in the antiquities of the Hellenic world.[25]

It was perceived that Cyprus stood at the meeting point between the Levant and Egypt, and the Aegean world. Darwinism already had its impact on thought.

The idea of evolution has invaded and permeated the study of archaeology as it has every other department of human inquiry. Our forefathers were content to study the art of PHIDIAS or PRAXITELES and to admire it. It is our task to explain it, to trace it to its *origines*, to investigate the intellectual and spiritual atmosphere which nourished it, to study the convergent streams of thought and tendency which engendered its ideas, and to observe the slow and tentative processes of material embodiment which gave substance to those ideas, and in the end achieved so consummate a perfection of executive skill as might seem almost to render the idea material and matter ideal. From this point of view, the exploration of Cyprus is as important as the exploration of Olympia. Even if we cannot hope to find works of art equal to the ELGIN marbles, the Hermes of PRAXITELES or the Victory of PAEONIUS, we can at any rate be sure of finding many things which will throw invaluable light on the history and development of the art which produced those incomparable relics. Here, then, is an admirable opportunity for the wealthy learned classes of this country to show how much they really care for the study of that civilization which has inspired and enriched all Europe with its ideas.[26]

The editorial, after explaining about the established of the CEF, then closed with the words, 'the whole civilized world may well say to Englishmen, *Cyprum nactus es, hanc explora'.*[27]

News of the work was consolidated by reports presented at the annual meetings of the Hellenic Society in June and the joint meeting of the BSA and CEF in July.[28] George

---

[25] *The Times* 3 March 1888, 11.

[26] This is clear from the later work of the 'Cambridge Ritualists' and their circle. See, for example, Robinson 2002; Gill 2004f.

[27] This is clear from the later work of the 'Cambridge Ritualists' and their circle. See, for example, Robinson 2002; Gill 2004f.

[28] For the announcement of the meeting of the Cyprus Exploration Fund: *The Times* 12 July 1888, 10 (for the meeting on 18 July).

Macmillan, secretary of the Hellenic Society, reported on the first season of excavations in the summer of 1888. He explained the situation:

> The [British] High Commissioner of Cyprus, who had recently forbidden any further private excavations on the island, expressed his willingness to give proper facilities, in accordance with the laws of the island, to a comprehensive scheme of excavation on a scientific basis. In the end a Cyprus Exploration Fund was instituted with a strong Committee, representing the leading Archaeological Societies, the Universities of Oxford and Cambridge, and the British Museum.[29]

Ernest Gardner was back in London to report on the work in Cyprus for the July meeting. The note is slightly apologetic:

> Of the general results of the work in Cyprus it is enough to say that, if not quite as brilliant as might have been hoped for, they have amply justified the undertaking. That it has been a gain to the school to be associated with such an enterprise cannot be doubted, while its assistance was, in fact, essential to the success of the scheme, as providing the services of such efficient explorers as Messrs. Gardner and Hogarth and of a thoroughly trained architect in Mr Elsey Smith.[30]

Colvin presented a report on the Fund itself, followed by Gardner on details of the excavations. Colvin reported that Hogarth 'is still in Cyprus, and proposes to spend this summer in travelling for the purpose of completing an archaeological survey of the island – a work very much needed', before turning to the excavations themselves:

> If they cannot boast of artistic spoils such as have rewarded the labours of the Germans at Olympia and at Pergamon, the thorough laying bare of so famous a centre of worship as the great temple of Aphrodite at Paphos is in itself a noteworthy achievement, and one, moreover, which so competent authority as Dr Dörpfeld, now director of the German Institute at Athens, had long regarded as of first rate importance. The harvest of inscriptions will throw much light upon the history of Cyprus. At least one object of art, a beautiful head of Eros, will be a valuable acquisition to the treasures of Greek art in this country.[31]

Gardner stressed the importance of the inscriptions found at the site. Further publicity to the Fund and its work was provided in September when *The Times* published a long report on 'Excavations in Cyprus', along with Elsey Smith's plan of the sanctuary, and concluding with an appeal for further funding as a new site had been selected 'which is confidently expected to yield a rich harvest of antiquities'.[32]

The second season's work concentrated at Marion and Limniti.[33] This was conducted by Gardner, and two BSA students, John Arthur Ruskin Munro (Fellow of Lincoln

---

[29] Hellenic Society 1888, xxxviii-xxxix.

[30] 'Archaeological research in Greece and Cyprus', *The Times* 20 July 1888, 13.

[31] 'Archaeological research in Greece and Cyprus', *The Times* 20 July 1888, 13.

[32] 'Excavations in Cyprus', *The Times* 24 September 1888, 4.

[33] Munro and Tubbs 1890.

College, Oxford) and Henry Arnold Tubbs (Craven Travelling Fellow). Marion had been selected as a possible site during the preliminary survey in 1887, and then by Hogarth's two visits in the summer of 1888. It had already been the subject of preliminary excavations under J. W. Williamson.[34] The planned director was unable to take charge of the work, and Gardner was released to take his place.[35] Gardner and Munro arrived on the island in February and after securing the necessary permits made their way to the site, where Gregori was to be their foreman. Work started on excavating in the cemeteries, and the team was shortly joined by Tubbs. Gardner left Munro and Tubbs at the end of February. They devised a system of 'spade-men' to clear the shafts to the tombs, 'knife-men' to extract the finds, and women were employed to remove the soil.[36] They also discovered late classical funerary *stelai*.[37] By the end of March Munro and Tubbs had to review the situation as Easter would soon disrupt excavations, and their workers would turn to their fields.[38] They decided to close the excavation at Poli and to excavate at Limniti, a site also owned by Williamson, and close enough to Poli to allow the relatively easy transfer of materials. Munro was due to leave the island towards the end of April, so Tubbs was given the sole responsibility of excavating at Limniti.[39] This was a sanctuary site that included a number of bronzes and terracotta figurines.

The results were reported at the joint meeting of the BSA and the CEF in July 1889. Lord Carnarvon, who chaired the meeting, allowed a note of disappointment to creep into his presentation.

> The results of the excavation have hardly been so striking as those that were obtained last year at Paphos, but, taken as a whole, the finds in Cypriote inscriptions and in works of art of various styles and periods – more especially in pottery and terra-cotta – are of very considerable interest.[40]

Colvin, as chairman of the CEF then presented a report:

> Mr Williamson's vineyard, which was first tried, proved unproductive. Excavations were then begun on a site south-east of the village, and about 20 tombs were opened. In those were found a great quantity of Cypriote pottery, black glazed ware, terra cotta figures, mostly of poor workmanship, objects of bronze and iron, such as strigils, knives, and mirrors, alabastra, vases of various styles, glass, a little jewelry, and two inscriptions in Cypriote character.[41]

---

[34] Herrmann 1888.

[35] Munro and Tubbs 1890, 3. The director was presumably to have been Hogarth.

[36] Munro and Tubbs 1890, 9.

[37] Munro and Tubbs 1890, 14, fig. 2. This was presented to the Fitzwilliam Museum, inv. GR. 6. 1890: Budde and Nicholls 1964, 14-15, pl. 7, no. 31. For other finds: Tubbs 1890.

[38] Munro and Tubbs 1890, 16.

[39] Munro and Tubbs 1890, 82. Hogarth had surveyed the site in the previous year. Work started on 23 April.

[40] 'The British School at Athens', *The Times* 11 July 1889, 6.

[41] 'The British School at Athens', *The Times* 11 July 1889, 6.

He noted that the fund was down to £175, and that the High Commissioner for the island had suggested that they move their attention to Salamis for a third season. Colvin explained:

> Salamis was beyond questions by far the largest and most important city in Cyprus, for, if the many references of ancient authors were not sufficient, the great extent of ruin still existing would attest this fact. … From the excavator's point of view the site is promising – more so, possibly than any other in the island. The villagers of Agios Sergios, Limnia, and Enkomi find upon the site, and in the tombs about the monastery of St. Barnabas, more coins, gems, and miscellaneous treasure-trove than is gathered from all the rest of the island; and Alexander di Cesnola, when his excavations were stopped by the British government in the first year of the occupation, was finding a large number of unrifled tombs, extending inland from the city, and containing very fine specimens of western and native art. Large numbers of such tombs remain still unopened; indeed, no systematic excavation of them has ever been attempted.[42]

It was proposed that Munro should direct a third season of work, assisted by Tubbs.[43] It was considered that a sum of £1,000 be required to conduct the work.

The third season's work in 1890 took place at Salamis and Marion.[44] Charles Newton had encouraged work at Salamis soon after the British had acquired control of Cyprus.[45] Work started in January 1890 under Munro and Tubbs. They recovered a series of sculptures from one of the gymnasia; these included a Zeus Serapis.[46] Further funding was obtained to continue the work at Marion, left unfinished from the previous season.[47] This was directed by Munro as Tubbs had returned to England. Tubbs presented the results of his excavations at the annual meeting of the BSA in July.[48] Further work was carried out at Salamis in 1891; this included the discovery of terracotta figures with painted decoration.[49]

Work then ground to a halt. The *Birmingham Daily Post* reported in 1892, 'The Cyprus Exploration Fund is doing what it can with meagre resources to wipe out by private effort the public blot, but large sums are needed, and scarcely likely to be forthcoming before the excavations can be in an adequate way completed'.[50] In 1894 the balance of the Fund

[42] 'The British School at Athens', *The Times* 11 July 1889, 6.

[43] Colvin 1889.

[44] Munro, *et al.* 1891; Munro 1891.

[45] Munro, *et al.* 1891, 59. Hogarth had visited the site in 1888: Hogarth 1889, 61.

[46] Cambridge, Fitzwilliam Museum GR. 1. 1891. Budde and Nicholls 1964, 31-32, pl. 18, no. 56. The statue was probably originally displayed in the theatre.

[47] Munro 1891. Funding had been secured by Cecil Smith of the British Museum.

[48] 'British School at Athens', *The Times* 3 July 1890, 6.

[49] Hellenic Society 1891, xliv. For some examples presented to the Fitzwilliam Museum: Vassilika 1998, 48-49, no. 22.

[50] 'Relics of ancient Cyprus', *Birmingham Daily Post* 23 May 23 1892.

was offered to Myres, who had developed a strong interest in the island.[51] He conducted a series of excavations at Agia Paraskevi near Nicosia, Kalopsida and Turbai Tekke. He also prepared catalogues for the antiquities in the Nicosia Museum,[52] as well as the Cesnola collection.[53]

Alexander Stuart Murray (1841-1904), Keeper of Greek and Roman Antiquities at the British Museum from 1886, had a long-standing interest in Cyprus and had served on the committee of the CEF.[54] He used the Miss Emma Turner bequest to start excavations in the cemeteries at Amathus (the work was observed by Myres) during 1894.[55] The following year Henry Beauchamp Walters (1867-1944), an assistant keeper, directed the Museum's work at Curium.[56] In 1896 new work was opened at Enkomi, initially directed by Murray, and then under Arthur Hamilton Smith (1860-1914), also of the British Museum.[57] Francis B. Welch, a student of the BSA and a member of Magdalen College (like Hogarth the BSA Director), was invited to direct the British Museum's excavations in 1899.[58]

Markides, who had spent two years in Oxford, was appointed Director of Antiquities on Cyprus.[59] The Managing Committee seriously considered a proposal to work on Cyprus again under Dawkins as it was considered an easier option given British control of the island.[60] In the end it was decided to excavate at Datcha and to restart work at Phylakopi. Markides was invited to publish in the *Annual*.[61] Myres conducted further investigations on the island in 1913.[62]

The BSA has continued to work on Cyprus especially after the Second World War, especially at Old Paphos.[63]

[51] Myres 1897.

[52] Ohnefalsch-Richter and Myres 1899.

[53] Myres 1914. For the Cesnola collection: Karageorghis 2000.

[54] Murray 1877; Murray 1887.

[55] Gardner 1894a, 232; Hellenic Society 1894, v-vi. For the British Museum excavations on Cyprus: Murray, *et al.* 1900.

[56] Gardner 1895, 210; 'Excavations in Cyprus', *The Times* 6 January 1896, 14. See also Walters 1897.

[57] 'British Museum excavations in Cyprus', *The Times* 13 July 1896, 4; Murray 1899.

[58] Hogarth and Bosanquet 1899, 322. The request for the BSA to support the British Museum's work on Cyprus had been made by Harcourt-Smith: BSA Minute Book 3, Meeting of 19 January 1899.

[59] BSA Minute Book 6, Meeting of 8 February 1910.

[60] Dawkins presented a report on Cyprus to the Managing Committee on 30 March 1909 (BSA Minute Book 6). See also meeting of 19 October 1909.

[61] Markides 1911/12.

[62] Myres 1940/45a.

[63] Iliffe and Mitford 1952.

CHAPTER 8: MAINLAND GREECE

Members of the BSA were involved in a number of projects on mainland Greece. These ranged from formal BSA excavations, such as Megalopolis, Kynosarges, and Sparta, to regional projects and surveys in Aetolia, Laconia, Thessaly and Macedonia, and smaller excavations. Some of the regions considered here were first explored when they were part of the Ottoman Empire. The BSA's work in the Peloponnese was dominated by the two excavations at Megalopolis and at Sparta. Both were accompanied by regional surveys. However the Peloponnese was on the regular route of the students in their travels; Bosanquet in his 'Suggested Plan of Study' proposed that students should visit Olympia, Mycenae, Epidauros and the Argive Heraion in October. John Baker-Penoyre made a study of Lake Pheneus at the foot of Kyllene after a visit there in July 1901 as part of one these student itineraries.[1] After the First World War the BSA developed a major excavation at Mycenae under the direction of Alan Wace.[2]

Attica

The Temple of Olympian Zeus

During the first year of the BSA, Penrose was invited to take part in the excavation of the north propylon for the temple of Olympian Zeus.[3] Remains of the Peisistratid temple were recovered and Penrose proposed a possible reconstruction. The excavation was supported by the Society of Dilettanti.

Kynosarges

Harcourt-Smith directed the excavations of the Kynosarges gymnasium during the session 1895/96; it was seen as training for excavations at Phylakopi later in the session.[4] Duncan Mackenzie, newly arrived at the BSA, was part of the team.[5] The gymnasium, which lay outside the walls of the city, had been destroyed by Philip V of Macedon in 200 BC.[6] The first excavations in 1895/6 were reported:

> The site of the ancient Athenian suburb called Kynosarges, known chiefly for its gymnasium, was for a long time thought to lie at the foot of Mount Lykabettos, on the south-eastern side. This was Leake's view, and was not disputed till recently,

[1] Baker-Penoyre 1902. These walking routes became well-trodden: Conway 1917; Gill 2007.

[2] Wace 1919/20, 1920/21a; Wace 1919/20, 1920/21b; Wace 1921/22, 1922/23.

[3] Penrose 1887, 272-73.

[4] Waterhouse 1986, 14.

[5] Momigliano 1999, 19-20.

[6] Livy 31. 23-26. See Camp II 2001, 168-69.

when Professor Doerpfeld made it clear, from a comparison of the testimonials of ancient authors, that the Kynosarges must have lain further to the south, along the banks of the Ilissus. In pursuance of this view, Mr Cecil Smith, director of the British School, had his attention attracted to a spot on the south bank of the river, several hundred yards below the Stadion, where the ground falls away from a small plateau in remarkably abrupt and perpendicular manner, indicating the presence of hidden walls. As on either side of this plateau are two prominent hills, which might well be those mentioned by ancient authors in connexion with the Kynosarges, it was decided to dig a trench through this plateau. The trench, at a depth of a few inches, brought to light numerous walls, chiefly of the Roman period; and one of the first constructions whose outline could be traced exactly was that of a Roman *calidarium*. This would seem to point to the existence of a gymnasium, and this fact, if proved, would go far towards settling the question of the Kynosarges site, provided that the remains of the classic period can be found beneath or beside these Roman remains. Numerous interesting fragments of ancient Greek vases and various metal objects have been found in the rubbish excavated; the remains of a huge vase of Melian type, as it seems, deserve especial mention, as this would be almost a unique find in Attica. The wide extent of the ruins and the solid character of the masonry discovered thus far make it evident that this is the site of a large public building or group of buildings – a very significant fact for a spot so far outside the ancient city walls. The British School are to be congratulated on having secured a piece of work which promises to be of such importance for the study of ancient Athenian topography; and if it should prove at length to be the site of Kynosarges, it will be a source of special satisfaction to Englishmen that the site, which was eagerly sought by two English excavators at the beginning of this century, and for whose discovery Lord Byron once planned excavations, should have been brought to light by the British School at Athens.[7]

Harcourt-Smith then reported the finds as follows in 'Archaeology in Greece':

The excavation is still proceeding, and it is sufficient here to say that we have found the foundation walls of a large public building which appears to date from the sixth century BC, and to be, in plan, suitable for a gymnasium. It lay in the midst of a necropolis of tombs, dating from the seventh century BC downwards, and, subsequently to the third century BC, was used partly as the site of a Roman bath, partly as a graveyard. Adjoining it are the remains of a larger building which seems to have been a gymnasium of the time, perhaps, of Hadrian.[8]

It was communicated to the July 1897 annual meeting:

In the winter and spring the excavations begun last season on the supposed site of the gymnasium of Kynosarges in Athens were carried to completion. The cost of this undertaking had been met by funds provided by private friends.[9]

---

[7] 'British excavations at Athens', *The Times* 26 March 1896, 4. The piece was also published in *The Academy*.

[8] Smith 1896, 337-38.

[9] 'British School at Athens', *The Times* 17 July 1897, 18.

Rodeck, the architect on the excavation, made a study of the Ionic capital from the gymnasium,[10] and the inscriptions were studied by Anderson.[11] Among the finds was a lead tablet which appears to be the record of the transaction of a slave, Ophelion, a *lithologos*. A number of funerary *stelai*, some of the Roman period, were also identified; two were published by C. C. Edgar.[12] Harcourt-Smith published the Proto-Attic pot fragments that were found set in the mortar of a large Roman bath-house complex.[13]

Megalopolis

The BSA's first major excavation in mainland Greece was at Megalopolis in the central Peloponnese. Ernest Gardner had earlier been working on Cyprus through the Cyprus Exploration Fund. The choice of excavation may, in part, have been influenced by the Greek excavations at nearby Lykosoura. The focus of the Megalopolis work was on the theatre, in part to explore issues over 'the Greek stage' and its bearing on performance.[14] This focus on the archaeology of Greek drama linked to work by ASCSA at Eretria and Phlius.[15] Gardner quickly reported, 'the stage was in very fair preservation, and had not, like so many, been tampered with in Roman times'.[16] The work, which started in 1890/91 and continued to 1893/94, was directed by Gardner, who was keen to demonstrate the importance of the BSA and its contribution to classical archaeology.[17] He was joined by several students including William Loring, George C. Richards and William J. Woodhouse, assisted by Joseph G. Milne and Arthur George Bather. The results were published as a direct challenge to W. Dörpfeld, who had suggested that in the classical theatre the actors and chorus were placed at the same level.[18]

The BSA's interpretations were controversial and sparked a major debate. Eugénie Sellers, a BSA student, wrote a letter in support of Dörpfeld (and critical of Gardner) to the *Athenaeum* ('The Theatres of Megalopolis', July 4, 1891).[19] In addition, a short note from her, dated 29 March 1891, was published by the *Classical Review* along with a summary of Dörpfeld's comments summarised by Louis Dyer.[20] Sellers' letter, and the wider dispute, was noted in the weekly theatrical newspaper *The Era*.

[10] Rodeck 1896/7.

[11] Anderson 1896/7, 112-20.

[12] Edgar 1897.

[13] Smith 1902, 30-31, pls. ii-iv.

[14] Gardner, *et al.* 1890; Gardner, *et al.* 1892; Gardner 1894c. The issue was over the place of the 'raised stage': Macmillan 1910/11, xi. For summaries: Gardner 1891, 395-96.

[15] Lord 1947, 297; see also Dyson 2004, 53.

[16] Gardner 1890a, 214.

[17] Gill 2004j. For a summary: Gardner 1890a, 214-15.

[18] Gardner, *et al.* 1890, 297, where the School's work was described as 'fatal' to Dörpfeld's theory.

[19] Sellers 1891b.

[20] Sellers 1891a. The letter was dated 29 March [1891] and the note was published in the May number.

A quarrel is a capital thing in a family, but, like all other good things, it should come to an end some time or other. There was a theatre built several hundred years BC, of which a good deal still remains to be quarrelled over; but we must say that we think it would show better taste if people just dropped the subject now. The theatre (or its ruins) is at Megalopolis; but it is quite a long time since there were any performances there – a thousand years, very likely. Probably the Megalopolitan Lord Chamberlain would insist on its being relicensed if they wanted to play the Agamemnon or the Seven Against Thebes there now; and, anyhow, we think Mr Gardner and Dr Dörpfeld might leave off squabbling about it in the highly respectable page of the *Athenaeum*. No doubt the point they are fighting over is one of supreme importance. Dr Dörpfeld says that the lower steps could not possibly, any more than the wall at the back, belong to the original structure, and Mr Gardner says contrariwise. But, after a thousand years or so, even a subject like this palls, unless, indeed, it is treated by Mr Rider Haggard; and Mr Gardner's obstinacy has actually brought a pretty girl into the controversy. Miss (or Mrs) Eugénie Sellers – we do not know her, but she must be pretty with that name – has only last week written a letter to say that Mr G. is a bold, bad man and has no right to chaff Dr D. about the *scaenae frons* when he makes such gross errors himself about the *logeion*. Eugénie even goes so far as to say some very cross things about certain *Skenengebäude* mentioned by Mr G.[21]

This response had probably emerged from the public statement made by Gardner at the July 1891 annual meeting of the BSA. He commented that:

he was glad to say that any misunderstanding which might have existed between Dr Dörpfeld and himself and colleagues had been removed, and that they were now all working together in harmony. (Hear, hear.) As to the difference of opinion on matters of detail between Dr Dörpfeld and the British School, he would ask for a suspension of judgment until a later date.[22]

Dörpfeld, Gardner and Loring published a joint statement in May and reissued in the *Classical Review* in June acknowledging 'the evidence is extremely difficult and complicated'.[23] The arguments presented by Dörpfeld were strong and Loring was won over.[24] Over the summer *The Times* reported that the work at Megalopolis had 'yielded results of the highest interest and importance'.[25] This focused on the theatre:

… a large theatre in good preservation was partially dug out, the front row of seats … bearing inscriptions of the classical period; and an elevated stage was laid bare, the construction of which appears to determine in the affirmative the long-debated

[21] 'Theatrical Gossip', *The Era* 11 July 1891.

[22] 'The British School at Athens', *The Times* 6 July 1891, 13.

[23] Dörpfeld, *et al.* 1891.

[24] Loring 1892/1893.

[25] 'British Archaeology in Greece', *The Times* 11 August 1891, 14.

controversy as to whether the Greeks used the proscenium for the purposes of a stage.[26]

Gardner wrote to *The Times* in August 1891, correcting the views on the layout of the stage.[27] A more measured account was given in Gardner's account of 'Archaeology in Greece'.

> Complete plans of the theatre are now being prepared by Mr Schultz, and with their help we shall be able to publish the whole of the evidence in a form that will enable even those who have not seen the site to judge for themselves as to the correctness of our conclusions. This seems most desirable in a case where it is probable that the views of those most competent to decide seem likely to differ widely from one another as to the inferences to be drawn from the architectural evidence. As to the facts on which these inferences are based, I do not now think that there will be any room for difference of opinion; and so it is most desirable that they should be placed before the public in an intelligible form.
>
> The preliminary plan of the theatre … has been shown by a more complete excavation of the site to be in some respects misleading; we wish to acknowledge the help of Dr Dörpfeld, in pointing out this fact during his visit to Megalopolis last April while our excavations were going on. It now appears that the wall with the three thresholds resting upon it is of later construction, and has bases of the portico built into its foundations; it cannot therefore have been the back wall (scena) of the original stage. The broad foundation in front of this was a stylobate, and probably carried the columns and entablature of which fragments are lying about. This structure consists of five steps, the two upper ones having actually been discovered; but the three lower ones are not part of the original plan. The inferences from these facts are very important, but it seems better to reserve them for the present; without the evidence upon which they are based, they could only awake controversy without offering materials for its decision.[28]

The excavation was deemed to be significant enough to launch the supplementary series for the Society for the Promotion of Hellenic Studies.[29] Further work was conducted on the Thersilion, adjacent to the theatre,[30] and the excavations recovered a fragment of the Edict of Diocletian.[31]

Gardner continued to present a brave face on the work at Megalopolis in 1893. At the Annual Meeting of the BSA it was reported:

> The excavation of Megalopolis was a work about which our fathers would have gone wild with delight. It was a vast city, and embodied one of the most perfect theoretical constitutions which ever existed. The theory was translated into the

---

[26] 'British Archaeology in Greece', *The Times* 11 August 1891, 14.

[27] 'The British Archaeological School at Athens', *The Times* 13 August 1891, 6.

[28] Gardner 1891, 395-96.

[29] Gardner, *et al.* 1892.

[30] Benson 1892; Bather 1892c.

[31] Loring 1890.

most magnificent stone and marble which even Greece ever produced. The city had a strange fate. The magnificent hall with the bases of its columns was still there, and we could realize the space and traverse the area in which 10,000 Greeks used to assemble.[32]

Other work was conducted as a result of the excavations. A survey of the hinterland of Megalopolis was conducted in the spring of 1892.[33] Bather and Vincent W. Yorke conducted excavation work on the possible sites of Bathos and Basilis on the slopes on Mount Lykaion. Both sites were mentioned by Pausanias.[34] At the first site, in a gorge of the Alpheios, a mass of terracotta dedications, a small number of bronzes, black-figured pottery and lamps were found. The presence of sows among the dedications was deemed to support the identification with a sanctuary of Demeter and Kore mentioned by Pausanias. The second site was located near the modern village of Kiparissia. Here Bather and Yorke discovered what appeared to be a road flanked with statue bases. Loring continued the survey work of the area plotting ancient routes in the region of Mantinea, Tegea, Megalopolis and down to Sparta.[35] As part of this study Loring published a number of inscriptions from the site of Tegea,[36] and Richards published reliefs that had been found at Dimitsana.[37]

Laconia

The BSA did not return to mainland Greece for a major excavation for some years. After productive work on Melos and on Crete, supporters at home were keen that the BSA should start work on a historical site on the mainland. Kavvadias, the Ephor-General, assigned the province of Laconia to the BSA.[38] Edward S. Forster, who had worked with Bosanquet at Praesos, made a preliminary study of sites in south-western Laconia, noting extant inscriptions.[39] This prepared the way for a concerted search. In April 1905 Bosanquet set up his camp at Koutiphari on the eastern Messenian Gulf to start work at the site of Thalamai.

We are in clean roomy quarters in the Editor's house, but shall move to an empty school close to the site to-morrow. This is in the midst of the village, among closely packed houses and noisy little lanes, and, although it is taller than most, so that our bedroom has a view, we shall be better off in the empty Girls' School and Mistress's house. They are within a stone's throw of the spring which is said by

---

[32] 'The British School at Athens', *The Times* 20 July 1893, 12.

[33] Bather and Yorke 1892, 228.

[34] Paus. 8. 29.

[35] Loring 1895b.

[36] Loring 1895a.

[37] Richards 1891.

[38] Macmillan 1906.

[39] Forster 1903/04b; Forster 1903/04a. For his publication of a fragmentary version of the Edict of Diocletian from Gythium: Forster 1905.

tradition to be the spring of the ancient oracle. Any way, we shall have lots of trees and water near – but no mosquitoes, it's said.[40]

This was Bosanquet's first visit to the Mani. He then turned to the site.

As to prospects. This site has been occupied continuously. Maina as a whole remained pagan, but this district seems to have been Christianised; there are numerous little churches and Byzantine inscriptions. The churches contain many ancient blocks, and the area where the ancient remains have been found has been ransacked for building material. So I am not hopeful.

Yesterday, in a little church, we came on a fine fragment of a marble screen, Frankish work, like some found at Geraki. We dug away a mass of plaster and uncovered a charming little crouching lion, evidently one of two placed on either side of the central cross. The man who guided us, an eccentric amateur antiquary whom his fellow villagers regard as a lunatic, was radiantly happy over the discovery of this 'cat', as he called it. Our arrival seems to fulfil the dream of his life. He has shown a succession of travellers over the site, and knows every ancient stone by heart; among other things he's wonderfully handy, and we made him useful yesterday in hafting our picks and shovels, under Michael's direction which he did very cleverly.[41]

The finds from Thalamai were published by Guy Dickins.[42]

The second site selected by the BSA was at Geronthrae (Geraki) to the east of the Eurotas.[43] The site was occupied from the Early Bronze Age and later became a Byzantine settlement. Hasluck and Wace directed the excavations and Henry J. W. Tillyard assisted with the study of the inscriptions. Wace made a study of the prehistoric finds. The third site was at Angelona on the Malea peninsula which was excavated by Hasluck and Wace.[44] They discovered a site of a Classical-Hellenistic *heroön*. Alongside these three sites, there was also a survey of the north-east frontier of Laconia.[45] In addition to the fieldwork, Tod and Wace worked on a catalogue for the Sparta Museum.[46] The project also allowed members of the BSA to develop an interest in Byzantine Greece. In 1906 W. Sejk, the project surveyor, and Ramsay Traquair, the architect, continued a survey of Byzantine remains in Laconia, including the remains at Geraki, Monemvasia,

---

[40] Bosanquet 1938, 158-60. For detailed bibliography: Cavanagh, *et al.* 1996, 299-300, LL150.

[41] Bosanquet 1938, 158-60. For detailed bibliography: Cavanagh, *et al.* 1996, 299-300, LL150.

[42] Dickins 1904/05b; Dickins 1904/05c.

[43] Wace and Hasluck 1904/05b; Wace 1904/05a; Tillyard 1904/05; Wace 1904/05b; Van De Put 1906/07; Wace 1909/10. See also Macmillan 1910/11, xx. For bibliography: Cavanagh, *et al.* 1996, 291, GG103.

[44] Wace and Hasluck 1904/05a. For bibliography: Cavanagh, *et al.* 1996, 310, NN232.

[45] Romaios 1904/05.

[46] Tod and Wace 1906. Tod had to take over responsibility when Wace was appointed Librarian at the BSR: BSA Minute Book 5, Meeting of 30 January 1906. The museum was expanded in 1907: Dawkins 1906/07a, 1.

the Frankish castles at Passava, Maina and Kelephá.[47] Traquair later made a survey of churches in the Mani in 1909.[48]

Following the earlier work at Thalamai and Geraki, students engaged in the excavations at Sparta made a series of surveys of Laconia. Forster explored Gythium and sites on the north-west coast of the Laconian gulf in 1907.[49] He had visited the area before and published a fragmentary inscription of the Edict of Diocletian from Gythium.[50] He visited the remains of a Roman bridge and aqueduct at Petrina,[51] and the Spartan fort at Trinisia,[52] as well as Gythium itself.[53]

Wace and Hasluck, who had worked at Geraki, studied the topography of south-eastern Laconia, Wace publishing sites in the east coast of the Laconian gulf, and Hasluck the Malia peninsula and the area round Epidauros Limera.[54] Wace and Hasluck conducted further work in east-central Laconia, the area of western Parnon.[55] Arthur M. Woodward continued the earlier BSA work by a study of the Mani.[56] Henry A. Ormerod travelled through Vardoúnia and the north-east Maina in 1910.[57] He noted a Late Bronze Age tomb at Krikiles, a Roman *verde antico* quarry at Psiphi, the church at Vigla, and the Roman remains at Petrina.[58]

Sparta

The excavations in Laconia had started to draw wider attention. In February 1906 George Macmillan announced the creation of a Laconian Fund to support the work.[59] One of the reasons for this push was that the other foreign schools had prominent and prestigious excavations on the mainland: the Germans at Olympia, the French at Delphi, and the Americans at Corinth. Charles Waldstein and ASCSA had conducted some preliminary

---

[47] Traquair 1905/06a. See also Macmillan 1910/11, xxi. For Passava: Cavanagh, *et al.* 1996, 300, LL153. For Kelephá: Cavanagh, *et al.* 1996, 300, LL155. For Monemvasia: Cavanagh, *et al.* 1996, 311, NN237.

[48] Traquair 1908/09.

[49] Forster 1906/07. Arthur M. Woodward had made a proposal to excavate at Gythium: BSA Minute Book 5, Meeting of 8 October 1907.

[50] Forster 1905.

[51] See also Cavanagh, *et al.* 1996, 295, JJ123.

[52] See also Cavanagh, *et al.* 1996, 296, JJ126.

[53] See also Cavanagh, *et al.* 1996, 296-97, JJ128.

[54] Wace and Hasluck 1907/08. See also Cavanagh, *et al.* 1996, 307-13.

[55] Wace and Hasluck 1908/09. See also Cavanagh, *et al.* 1996, 285-87.

[56] Woodward 1906/07. See also Cavanagh, *et al.* 1996, 299-307.

[57] Ormerod 1909/10.

[58] See also Cavanagh, *et al.* 1996, 295, sites JJ120, JJ121, JJ345, and JJ123.

[59] Macmillan 1906. The fund had been discussed at the meeting of 30 January 1906 (BSA Minute Book 5).

work at Sparta in the spring of 1892 and 1893.[60] The British proposal was for the start of a major project at Sparta, with outlying survey and excavations.

> … the committee have decided to make a detailed survey of the site of ancient Sparta, the principal object of this season's operations. In conjunction with the survey trial excavations will be made with a view to ascertaining the extent of the remains, their general character and state of preservation, and the prospects of an excavation on a larger scale. When the heat brings work at Sparta to an end the excavations at Geronthrae will be continued, and possibly other sites may be tests. Serious attention will be given also to the remains of the Byzantine and Frankish periods, in which the Province of Laconia is so rich. For this work the committee have secured the services of an able architect, Mr Ramsay Traquair, of Edinburgh.[61]

There was great anticipation for the work, Bosanquet describing the Sparta excavations as 'what seems likely to be the most extensive and productive piece of work yet undertaken by the British School at Athens'.[62] The initial work was on the Roman *stoa*, the late antique defences of the Acropolis, and the theatre.[63] Bosanquet started work in March the same year (1906) at Sparta itself.

> Here all is going well. We have found several inscriptions and are on the line of one of the main roads, which may guide us to some of the ninety or more buildings enumerated by Pausanias. The site is a group of low hills, covered with olives and sown with corn, now green. Two of the larger hills were enclosed in late Roman times, after a Gothic invasion, within a massive wall largely composed of architectural blocks and inscribed or sculptured monuments. One hopes that at some distance from this wall the destruction may not have been so great as it certainly was in the neighbourhood of this line of defence. We are getting a plan of the "Kastro", with its towers, and disentangling the walls of a big *Stoa*, a portico with 23 vaulted shops or offices along its front. Under 30 workmen still, for we are making trials rather than excavating any one building. We have some trouble with the landowners, who are distressed by the damage caused to crops by the spectators who flock to look on, and we have had to post very inefficient policemen to protect their interests. In this country they are all afraid of one another and I am amused to find how much more easily I can make myself obeyed than the local authorities, who don't like to speak out or use their powers. Dickins, who is with me, is a tower of strength, and Gregori, our Cyprus foreman, a master of his art …[64]

---

[60] Lord 1947, 77-78, 297.

[61] Macmillan 1906.

[62] Bosanquet 1905/06a.

[63] Traquair 1905/06b; Dickins 1905/06c.

[64] Bosanquet 1938, 162-63.

Among the other work was Wace's survey of the city walls.[65] Bosanquet had to return to Athens for the start of the Olympic Games and Dickins took over as director of the excavations. In April the sanctuary of Artemis Orthia was identified; Wace excavated a nearby *heroön*, and Dickins an archaic altar.[66] Wace also studied the extant Roman baths.[67]

Excavations were resumed in March the following year.[68] In April 1907 Vincent Yorke, the treasurer to the BSA, announced that Dawkins had 'discovered the site of the Sanctuary of Athene Chalkioikos' on the acropolis at Sparta.[69] He was keen to stress the significance of the find and the need for financial support:

> It is difficult to over-estimate the importance of the discovery last year of the Temple of Artemis Orthia, and now of this sanctuary; but the new "find" will entail fresh demands upon the slender fund available for the excavations.
>
> The appeal for £1,500 issued last autumn has only brought in £500, and it is most necessary that further support should now be forthcoming.[70]

Yorke's appeal was boosted by the donation of £1,000 by William Waldorf Astor, the proprietor of the *Pall Mall Gazette* and the *Pall Mall Magazine*.[71] The sanctuary itself revealed 'a few bronze nails and some bronze plates', but little that was spectacular.[72] The same season Wace was able to trace the line of the largely demolished city wall through his identification of the stamped roof tiles; he made a study of some 500 stamped examples.[73] In addition to the sanctuary of Athena Chalkioikos and Artemis Orthia, a further sanctuary was identified by Dickins on the Megalopolis road.[74] Dickins discovered a Hellenistic cemetery; the pottery was published by Wace.[75]

Work was continued on the sanctuary of Athena Chalkioikos in 1908,[76] and in the following year most of the activity was concentrated here and in the Menelaion.[77] The

---

[65] Wace 1905/06a. See also Wace 1905/06c.

[66] Wace 1905/06b; Dickins 1905/06b.

[67] Wace 1905/06d.

[68] Dawkins 1906/07a.

[69] Yorke 1907. The inscribed roof tile identifying the sanctuary was found on 4 April: Macmillan 1910/11, xxii. Dawkins also stressed the sanctuary was 'the most important of the whole campaign': Dawkins 1906/07a, 3.

[70] Yorke 1907. The inscribed roof tile identifying the sanctuary was found on 4 April: Macmillan 1910/11, xxii. Dawkins also stressed the sanctuary was 'the most important of the whole campaign': Dawkins 1906/07a, 3.

[71] Donation reported in *The Times* 27 June 1908, 12.

[72] Macmillan 1910/11, xxiii. For the report: Dickins 1906/07b.

[73] Wace 1905/06a; Wace 1906/07a. For the tiles: Wace 1905/06c; Wace 1906/07b.

[74] Dickins 1906/07c.

[75] Wace and Dickins 1906/07.

[76] Dickins 1907/08.

[77] Dawkins 1908/09a.

Menelaion, on the east side of the Eurotas, had been explored by Wace in 1909.[78] In 1910 Dawkins continued exploration in the area of the Menelaion to try and identify Late Bronze age remains.[79] The work at Sparta was concluded in 1910 as trial excavations suggested that 'no site of importance remained to be excavated'.[80]

The excavations themselves had produced a mass of new material that was parcelled out to the students. John P. Droop worked on the pottery and bronzes;[81] Wilfrid J. Farrell on the archaic terracottas;[82] Henry J. W. Tillyard, Marcus N. Tod and later Arthur M. Woodward on the inscriptions;[83] and Alan Wace on the coins.[84] The BSA returned to Sparta after the First World War in excavations under the directorship of Woodward.

The Sanctuary of Artemis Orthia

After the work on the acropolis at Sparta, Bosanquet returned to Athens for the Olympic Games. In early April archaic deposits were discovered near the Eurotas.[85] Dickins and Wace supplemented the team, and in June 1906 Bosanquet was back excavating at the sanctuary of Artemis Orthia, identified by an inscription from the site. The work entailed constructing a new water-channel for a nearby mill. Bosanquet wrote home:[86]

> The heat lasted until Monday evening, and now we have had two much cooler days; Taygetus wrapped in clouds again at sunset this evening. We are finding masks in great numbers, lead figurines, and all the early offerings. We are also building a house for the watchman.
>
> Sunday evening.
>
> All day long the house has been strewn with fragments of masks which are being pieced and mended. Some lovely ones among them – some terrible monsters. Trays of noses of every conceivable and inconceivable shape, trays of ears and so on, covering all our tables and beds. It has been a big haul this last week.

Bosanquet rapidly published the initial finds from Artemis Orthia.[87] At the annual Meeting on October 1906 it was announced:

---

[78] Wace, *et al.* 1908/09. See also Cavanagh, *et al.* 1996, 401-06, Q360.

[79] Dawkins 1909/10a.

[80] Macmillan 1910/11, xxv.

[81] Droop 1906/07a; Droop 1906/07b; Droop 1907/08; Droop 1908/09.

[82] Farrell 1907/08.

[83] Tillyard 1905/06a; Tillyard 1905/06b; Tod, *et al.* 1906/07; Woodward 1907/08; Woodward 1907/08; Woodward 1908/09a; Woodward 1909/10a. Woodward was responsible for publishing the inscriptions when the BSA resumed excavations at Sparta after the First World War: Woodward 1923/24, 1924/25; Woodward 1925/6; Woodward 1927/8.

[84] Wace 1907/08.

[85] Bosanquet 1905/06a, 278.

[86] Bosanquet 1938, 165 (Sparta, 6 June 1906).

[87] Bosanquet 1905/06b; Bosanquet 1905/06c.

The most important archaeological find of the year has been the discovery, near the bank of the river Eurotas, of the Shrine of Artemis Orthia, the savage goddess at whose altar the Spartan youths underwent the ordeal of scourging. In the trial trenches which had been sunk a greater mass of the remains of the archaic period of Greek art had been found than had ever been found at any site, and that included thousands of votive offerings of various materials, and a series of painted terra-cotta masks. The masks might have been used in some ritual mystery-play, and thus had important bearings on the earliest history of the drama in Greece.[88]

Work was resumed at Artemis Orthia the following year.[89] A plan of the Roman theatre was made by Walter George.[90] The deeper levels suggested that occupation went back into the archaic period, with well over one metre of stratigraphy. This included imported ivories, as well as representations of the deity. The mudbrick altar of the sanctuary was found in the 1908 season.[91] The fourth season at the sanctuary of Artemis Orthia produced a plan of the earliest sanctuary and this was put into public circulation through *The Times*.[92] A short campaign was conducted in 1910.[93]

The site was overgrown by 1914 when it was visited by Agnes Conway in her tour of the Peloponnese.

As for the excavations of the precinct of Artemis Orthia, which have yielded the British archaeologists objects of great importance in an unbroken succession from the tenth century BC downward, we could scarcely believe that the rubbishy foundation walls had not been built the other day by peasants. Had we come upon such things ourselves, we should have shamefacedly covered them up again and said nothing about them! A shepherd's hut on the edge of the enclosure was infinitely better built.[94]

Although interim reports had appeared, the pressure of publishing Paliakastro as well as the intervening war years, meant that the final report did not appear until 1929.[95]

Megarid

The fortified town of Aegosthena lies on one of the bays on the eastern side of the Corinthian Gulf. The BSA, under Edward F. Benson, conducted a survey of the

[88] 'British School at Athens', *The Times* 31 October 1906, 11.

[89] Dawkins 1906/07b.

[90] Macmillan 1910/11, xxii. See Dawkins 1906/07b, pls. II, III.

[91] 'The Excavations at Sparta', *The Times* 10 June 1908, 10.

[92] 'Excavations at Sparta', *The Times* 25 September 1909, 4.

[93] Dawkins 1909/10b; Dawkins 1909/10c. See also Lamb 1926/27.

[94] Conway 1917, 119-20.

[95] Dawkins 1929. It included a posthumous chapter from Guy Dickins: Dickins 1929.

outstanding remains in the spring of 1893.[96] The excavations were reported at the Annual Meeting of the BSA that July:

> … towards the end of the season a preliminary trial was made on the site of Aegesthena, at the extreme east corner of the Corinthian Gulf. Though little was known of this city in ancient times, the extant walls, which presented a remarkably perfect example of the fortifications of probably the fifth century, sufficed to show that it was a place of no little importance.[97]

A number of inscriptions were found including one relating to Hadrian. Sample work was carried out in four cemeteries surrounding the city. Among the students was Bosanquet who described the detail of the excavation in a letter to his sister Amy. The equipment included 24 spades and picks, one wheelbarrow, and one theodolite.[98]

Henry J. W. Tillyard, assisted by Christian C. T. Doll, conducted a study of two watch towers between Megara and Thebes in May 1905.[99] A short topographical study of Megara was prepared by Stanley Casson, student in 1912/13.[100] This related to interpretation of the Athenian attack on the city in 424 BC. An inscription was observed *in situ* as part of the foundations of the medieval fortifications at Minoa, the more westerly of the two coastal sites and this was published by Roger M. Heath, admitted to the BSA in 1913/14.[101] This text displayed three proxeny decrees relating to the period after 307 BC when the city was captured by Demetrius Poliorcetes. The individuals honoured were citizens of Iasos, Halikarnassos and Elis.

Boeotia

William Loring was doing survey work in the region of Livadia in 1891 when he was shown a newly discovered inscription.[102] Ronald M. Burrows, who had succeeded G. C. Richards with the chair of Greek at Cardiff (1897-1908), developed an interest in Boeotia, and on one of his trips identified an inscription built into the walls of the church of Agios Demetrios near Tanagra, the supposed site of Delium.[103] German work at Orchomenos by Fürtwangler discovered (what are now recognised as) Linear B texts in 1903.[104] One of the first BSA excavations in Boeotia was conducted by Alexander C. B. Brown at the sites of Shimatari and Dilesi in 1905/06.[105]

---

[96] Benson 1895a. He was accompanied by Mayor and Bosanquet. The excavations were described as a 'trial' at the Annual Meeting: 'The British School at Athens', *The Times* 20 July 1893, 12.

[97] British School at Athens 1893.

[98] Bosanquet 1938, 28-29.

[99] Tillyard 1905/06c. The towers were revisited in March 1907.

[100] Casson 1912/13b.

[101] Heath 1912/13.

[102] Loring 1895a, 92, no. iv.

[103] Burrows 1904/05.

[104] Reported in *The Times* 13 April 1903, 4.

[105] Brown 1905/06. See also Macmillan 1910/11, xxi.

More sustained work was conducted as sponsored, rather than official, excavations on the cemetery of Rhitsona, the presumed site of Mykalessos, from 1907 to 1909.[106] This fieldwork was carried out by Burrows and Percy N. Ure, assistant lecturer (and then lecturer) in Greek at Cardiff (1903-08).[107] The final publication was delayed by the outbreak of the First World War. Ure, with his wife Annie, returned and conducted two further seasons in 1921 and 1922. Results of the excavations were finally published in 1927 and 1934.[108]

In addition to these formal excavations, Gomme made a study of Thebes through the literary sources.[109] He continued this interest in the topography of Boeotia until the outbreak of the First World War.[110] Edward S. Forster, whose main work was on Crete and in Laconia, also published Boeotian terracottas that were in his possession.[111]

Phokis

In 1894 Bather and Yorke conducted excavations at two sites in Phokis: Abae and Hyampolis.[112] Abae was a site of oracle of Apollo mentioned by Herodotus.[113] Bather and Yorke revealed the foundations of a small sanctuary, within which were two small temples and a stoa. A cemetery was discovered on the slopes; the graves contained large numbers of terracotta figurines. Hyampolis lies just to the north of Abae, and was marked by remains of fortifications. Remains of a stoa were discovered outside the walls. Traces of what appeared to be the theatre were also observed. Inscriptions from the site include signatures by the Athenian sculptor, Euboulides son of Eucheir, part of a Hellenistic dynasty of sculptors. A further site to the west of Abae and Hampolis was identified at Smixi, and this yielded a number of inscriptions which mention Artemis. Thus this may be the site of the extra-mural temple of Artemis for Hyampolis.

Laurence B. Tillard made a study of the fortifications of Phokis in May 1911.[114] This included topographical studies at Tithorea, Charadra, Erochos, Patronis, and Aiolidai. He noted that many of the walls could be dated to a single period with 'a uniform type of masonry', perhaps to the period after Chaironeia.

---

[106] The proposed excavation appears in BSA Minute Book 5, Meeting of 8 October 1907.

[107] Burrows and Ure 1907/08; Burrows and Ure 1909; Ure 1910; Ure 1913.

[108] Ure 1927; Ure, *et al.* 1934.

[109] Gomme 1910/11.

[110] Gomme 1911/12; Gomme 1913a; Gomme 1913b.

[111] Forster 1907. Note the sale of Boeotian terracottas from the Ionides collection at Christie's, London, in December 1912.

[112] Yorke 1896a. Gardner was present for a time.

[113] Herodotus 1. 46.

[114] Tillard 1910/11.

Aetolia

Woodhouse conducted a survey of Aetolia in 1892 and 1893.[115] He recovered a number of inscriptions from the region of Naupaktos, including some from the Asklepieion.[116] He identified a further sanctuary at Palaoskala. Ernest Gardner, who had worked with Woodhouse at Megalopolis, cited the work as an example of archaeological geography pioneered by William Ramsay for Anatolia.[117] Gardner saw his approach as a model for 'other districts of Greece'. Certainly in subsequent decades there were surveys of Laconia, Thasos, Thessaly, and Macedonia. Dawkins also prepared a study of Aetolia, although it was never published.[118] After the First World War Winifred Lamb travelled through Aetolia in the hope of identifying a possible prehistoric site, but in the end she chose to excavate on Lesbos.[119]

Thessaly

The growing interest in the prehistory of Greece encouraged the study of the links between northern and southern Greece. Thessaly had become part of Greece in 1881, and one of the earliest BSA excavations here was undertaken by Charles Douglas Edmonds at Pilaf Tepe in 1899.[120]

Thessaly was brought to the attention of the archaeological community in Greece by the excavations of Staes and Tsountas at Dimini and Sesklo in 1901.[121] Alan Wace and A. W. van Buren of the American School at Rome made a survey of the Magnesian peninsula to the south-east of Volos in April 1905.[122] Wace planned to excavate at Kato Georgi, opposite Skiathos and near Cape Sopias, where there were column drums.[123] They also noted a number of inscriptions and coins.[124] The site, next to the church of the Theotokos near Bromyri, was excavated by Wace and John P. Droop in 1907; they found some architectural fragments as well as Early Iron Age graves.[125]

---

[115] Woodhouse 1893; Woodhouse 1897; see also Gardner 1892/3, 150. The Hellenic Society awarded him a grant of £30 towards the cost of illustrations: *The Times* 9 July 1897, 4.

[116] Woodhouse 1893.

[117] Gardner 1899.

[118] Archive material in the Taylorian Institute, University of Oxford (4 leaves).

[119] Gill 2006b.

[120] Edmonds 1900. See also Edmonds 1898/9. The excavations were also reported in *The Times* 26 May 1899.

[121] For Bosanquet's interest in the work: Bosanquet 1902b.

[122] Wace 1906d; Wace 1908. Wace combined this trip with a tour of Skiathos and Skopelos.

[123] Wace 1906d, 147-48. Expenses of £25 were set aside for the excavation: BSA Minute Book 5, Meeting of 26 February 1907.

[124] The coins appeared in an appendix: Wace 1906d, 165-68.

[125] Wace and Droop 1906/07. See also Macmillan 1910/11, xxiii.

Although the finds from Theotokou were disappointing, Wace and Droop decided to search for further prehistoric sites – 'maghoula-hunting' as they described it. Droop described the technique they used:

> Maghoula-hunting … was an excellent sport in which I indulged with Mr Wace … "Maghoula," signifying a mound, is a modern word that is applied to the gentle swellings on the Thessalian plain left by the *debris* of prehistoric settlements. Enquiry often gave us the direction, and we tramped the plain until we came to them, when the sherds and stone implements that we picked up gave a good indication of what lay beneath. These sites were the easiest of any to find and the least disappointing when found that my experience has met with.[126]

One of the sites identified was at Zerelia near Alymro in southern Thessaly, which Wace and Droop excavated in 1908.[127] The excavation, supported by the Cambridge Worts Fund, was joined by another BSA student, Maurice S. Thompson. The team found eight superimposed settlements including Late Bronze Age in the final layer. Wace and Thompson were joined in their Thessalian work by T. Eric Peet, who had been working on prehistoric settlements in Italy through the BSR.[128] Two further sites were excavated in 1909: Palaeomylos near Lianokladi, in the Spercheios Valley, and Tzani Maghoula near Sophades, in western Thessaly.[129] They also excavated a cave on Mount Ossa.[130]

Wace, Thompson and Peet were soon using the evidence of the lack of Aegean pottery in early layers at the site to break the link between a unified Crete, mainland Greece, and central Europe.[131] Indeed they suggest that 'there is a strong case against any attempt to unify the early pottery of the Central European, Balkan and Aegaean areas, and that these attempts have been based on general resemblances of decorative types much too superficial to carry conviction'.[132] A response to their suggestion was made by M. M. Vassits, who argued for links with Serbia.[133] Wace and Thompson responded, and while accepting possible connections between Thessaly and Serbia, rejected the main thesis that Serbia was linked to the main cultures of the Aegean.[134]

In 1910 Wace and Thompson excavated the burial mound at Tsangli between Pharsala and Velestino.[135] The mound itself was some 10 metres high. Among the finds was a batch of sling-bullets. Wynfrid Duckworth studied a skull from one of the Neolithic levels

---

[126] Droop 1915, 32-33.

[127] Wace, *et al.* 1907/08. The site is noted: Macmillan 1910/11, xxiv.

[128] Peet 1906/07; Peet 1907.

[129] For a summary: Macmillan 1910/11, xxv.

[130] Wace and Thompson 1908/09.

[131] Peet, *et al.* 1908.

[132] Peet, *et al.* 1908, 238.

[133] Vassits 1907/08.

[134] Thompson and Wace 1909.

[135] Wace and Thompson 1910. See also Dawkins 1910a, 360.

at Tsangli.[136] Wace and Thompson investigated a second mound at Rachmani, to the north-east of Larisa, and as a result of these excavations they started to develop a fourfold division for prehistory in Thessaly identified by the pottery types: two divisions of Neolithic, sub-Neolithic and Chalcolithic.[137]

In April 1911 Wace and Thompson, as part of their new study of Macedonia, visited a number of sites in Thessaly, including Tsaritsena and Magoula.[138] They were by this time writing up their study of their work that appeared the following year.[139] Arthur M. Woodward later published inscriptions noted by Wace and Thompson.[140]

Macedonia

The first archaeological work in Macedonia by a member of the BSA was by David Hogarth in the spring of 1887, during his first few months at the School.[141] Many of the inscriptions were observed in the Jewish quarter of the city, and others were to be reused for modern gravestones.[142] Another epigraphic survey of eastern Macedonia was made by John A. R. Munro and William C. F. Anderson in the autumn of 1896.[143] Munro had been admitted to the BSA in 1888/89 to work on Cyprus, and had subsequently worked with Hogarth on some of the surveys of Asia Minor. Anderson, of Firth College, Sheffield, had not been admitted as a student of the BSA, but had worked with members of the School. He took part in the 1893 Oxford excavations at Doclea in Montenegro with Munro,[144] and had collaborated with Munro on the epigraphic surveys of Mysia in 1894 and 1896.[145]

In Macedonia Anderson and Munro had noted an inscription from Hierissos on Akanthos, and a graffito from Stageira (Lympiada).[146] At Amphipolis (Yeni keui; Paleokomi) they noted a number of inscriptions including a fragmentary Latin gravestone; some had previously been copied by P. Perdrizet of the École française in 1894.[147] Heading east, they observed a Roman milestone from the Via Egnatia at Provista, dating to the reign of Caracalla. They also noted one inscription from Philippi. There was little

---

[136] Duckworth 1911.

[137] Wace and Thompson 1910; Macmillan 1910/11, xxvi.

[138] British School at Athens 1910/11, 288. See also Wace 1912/13, based on travels in Macedonia and Thessaly in 1910-12.

[139] Wace and Thompson 1912. See also Wace and Thompson 1911.

[140] Woodward 1913.

[141] Hogarth 1888b.

[142] Mazower 2005.

[143] Munro 1896. For an obituary of Anderson: *The Times* 9 October 1935. He had been educated at Queen's College, Belfast (1878-81), Durham University, and Oriel College, Oxford.

[144] Munro, *et al.* 1896. Freeman 2007, 298-99. Freeman suggests that Haverfield did not travel to the Balkans at this time.

[145] Munro and Anthony 1897b; Munro and Anthony 1897a; Munro 1897.

[146] Munro 1896.

[147] Perdrizet 1894.

British research in Macedonia following these surveys; an exception was the ethnographic work of H. Triantaphyllides encouraged by Cecil Harcourt-Smith.[148]

Research on Macedonia resumed after the conclusion of fieldwork in Thessaly by Wace and Thompson.[149] They made their first tour in 1909,[150] initially studying the mounds in the vicinity of Salonica and in the western part of the Chalkidiki.[151] In 1911 a Macedonian Exploration Fund was formed with Arthur J. Evans as the chairman and Vincent Yorke as the treasurer.[152] The main support had come, in part, from Liverpool where Myres held a chair (until 1910 when he moved back to Oxford). The aim of the Fund was 'for the promotion of research in the Balkan lands', and its scope was wide:

> Covering not only the excavation of sites, but the study of political, social, and economic customs and institutions which have survived from earlier times, the detailed surface exploration (geographical and topographical) of the district, and the investigation of monuments of all periods.[153]

Wace and Thompson started work in Macedonia in the spring of 1911 on their return from England. The Fund's committee had announced:

> Preliminary journeys in Macedonia have shown that local conditions are exceptionally favourable to more systematic work and it has been decided to form a committee of Oxford and Cambridge scholars to conduct research in the history, archaeology, and anthropology of these Balkan lands.[154]

Money was not forthcoming, and a further announcement was made:

> Macedonia, as well as Thrace, has hitherto been a terra incognita, though affording a most promising field for research in prehistoric, classical, Byzantine, and medieval archaeology.[155]

Wace and Thompdon travelled through southern Macedonia towards Veria,[156] and then along the Aliakmon valley to Velvendos and Servica (Turkish, Serfije), before heading south to Elassona.[157] At Velvendos 'they found two unpublished inscriptions, a cemetery of *pithos* burials, and a prehistoric site'. They explored a prehistoric mound at Serfije.[158] Between Servia and Elassona they discovered a Trajanic inscription, dating to AD 101,

---

[148] Triantaphyllides 1896/7.

[149] Wace and Thompson 1912.

[150] Wace 1913/14.

[151] Wace 1913/14, 124-32.

[152] 'Macedonian Exploration Fund', *The Times* 15 March 1911, 5.

[153] 'Macedonian Exploration Fund', *The Times* 15 March 1911, 5.

[154] 'Macedonian Exploration Fund', *The Times* 15 March 1911, 5.

[155] 'Archaeological research in Greece', *The Times* 31 July 1911, 3.

[156] The inscriptions were offered to Woodward for publication: Woodward 1911/12.

[157] British School at Athens 1910/11, 288. See Wace 1912/13, 250.

[158] Wace 1913/14, 123-24.

which defined the boundaries between Macedonia and Thessaly.[159] One of the inscriptions had been seen by Evans in his travels in 1885, but he had lost the squeeze and had asked Wace to return to the site.[160] It had probably come from Nestorio to the west of Kastoria. Tod also commented on an epitaph from near Elassona.[161]

Wace and Thompson returned to Macedonia in the summer, leaving Athens for Salonica in June. Over a three month period they visited a wide range of towns. One of their interests was in the Vlach population, and they made their base in the town of Samarina in the slopes of Mount Smolikas in the Pindos.[162] They noted that they had 'obtained a quantity of ethnographical, anthropological, and philological material'.[163] The hope was to conduct an excavation at 'an early site near Salonica, in a district where historic and prehistoric settlements are contiguous'.[164] However this 'had to be postponed for the present owing to the ravages of cholera in Macedonia and the recent outbreak of war between Italy and the Ottoman Empire'.[165] Wace and Thompson had hoped to excavate a prehistoric site at Sedes (Thermae) near Salonica in the spring of 1912, but due to the shortage of workers, they had to postpone the work.[166] In October 1912 the First Balkan War broke out and in November Salonica was captured and became part of Greece.

Wace took up office as Director of the BSA in the autumn of 1914. He had been planning to survey Olynthus as a possible site for excavation.[167] He spent some three weeks in Macedonia looking for possible prehistoric sites in January 1915.[168] The trench systems in Macedonia constructed during the First World War had revealed much about the potential for work in the region,[169] and excavations continued in Macedonia after the First World War under the direction of Walter Heurtley.[170]

Thrace

Thrace formed part of the Ottoman Empire in the period before the First World War. John A. R. Munro and William C. F. Anderson included a tour of Thrace as part of their

[159] For inscriptions from these surveys: Wace and Woodward 1911/12; Woodward 1913.

[160] Woodward 1913, 337, no. 17.

[161] Tod 1915a.

[162] Wace and Thompson 1914.

[163] British School at Athens 1910/11, 288. At the end of the trip they had to be in quarantine at Velemishti.

[164] British School at Athens 1910/11, 288. The site was at Sedes.

[165] British School at Athens 1910/11, 288.

[166] See British School at Athens 1911/12, 318.

[167] Wace 1914/16. See also Wace 1913/14, 127 and 132 for his visit in 1909.

[168] British School at Athens 1914/15, 187.

[169] Casson 1916; Casson and Gardner 1918/19.

[170] Heurtley 1923/24, 1924/25 1924/25; Heurtley 1939. For Winifred Lamb's involvement with Heurtley's excavations: Gill 2004r.

epigraphic survey of eastern Macedonia.[171] They noted inscriptions from sites such as Maronia. Dawkins and Hasluck studied the inscriptions of Biyze between Constantinople and Adrianople (Edirne);[172] they were present for the carnival of 1906.[173] They appear to have been hoping to identify a site that could be excavated by the BSA. Hasluck also visited the tomb at Kirk Kilisse, south-east of Adrianople (Edirne).[174] The finds in Constantinople appeared to be Hellenistic in date. However due to the threat of war, the excavations were never carried out.

[171] Munro 1896.

[172] Dawkins and Hasluck 1905/06.

[173] Dawkins 1906. Dawkins noted the predominantly Greek population of the city.

[174] Hasluck 1910/11.

CHAPTER 9: THE ISLANDS

The islands had attracted interest from the period before the foundation of the BSA. J. Theodore Bent had investigated tombs containing early Bronze Age Cycladic figures that subsequently went on display in the British Museum.[1] William R. Paton had close links with Kalymnos and had made studies of the inscriptions of some of the islands.[2] Students of the BSA frequently passed through the islands on their travels. The excavations on Melos encouraged more exploration of the Cyclades: Bosanquet made a collection of Cycladic figures during his travels in the 1890s,[3] and Mackenzie travelled in the Cyclades in the summer of 1897.[4] The inscriptions of Kos had been the subject of a study by Paton in the early 1880s.[5] Mackenzie visited the island in September 1898 to make a study of the topography.[6] He observed terracotta fragments of what he assumed were sixth century BC, as well as Roman architectural remains. He noted the remains of a cemetery at Skourdoulariés. Dawkins and Wace also travelled in the Sporades.[7]

Thasos

J. Theodore Bent made a survey of inscriptions on Thasos in the winter of 1886.[8] John Baker Penoyre revisited the island in June 1907 to complete the epigraphic survey, take photographs and make squeezes.[9] He also noted Thasian amphora stamps. Marcus Tod helped prepare Penoyre's notes for publication. This work was followed by a topographical survey of the island.[10] Baker Penoyre included detailed plan and sketches of the acropolis at Limena, as well as of the Cave of Pan, and he prepared a chronological scheme for the development of the walls based on the different styles. As the island was still part of the

---

[1] Bent 1884; Bent 1885. For the context of these finds: Gill and Chippindale 1993. For the British Museum figures: Fitton 1995.

[2] Gill 2004n.

[3] Bosanquet 1896/7b; Bosanquet 1896/7e; Bosanquet 1896/7d; Bosanquet 1896/7c; Bosanquet 1896/7a. These will be discussed in Arnott and Gill forthcoming. For a piece purchased by the Ashmolean Museum: Sherratt 2000, 160-62, no. III. 7. 31.

[4] British School at Athens 1897/98, 102; Momigliano 1999, 26. For Cycladic finds from Mackenzie's travels: Sherratt 2000, 3, 413 (Concordance).

[5] Gill 2004n.

[6] Mackenzie 1897/8b. See also Momigliano 1999, 27.

[7] Dawkins and Wace 1905/06; Wace 1906b.

[8] Hicks and Bent 1887; Hicks 1887b.

[9] Baker-Penoyre and Tod 1909.

[10] Baker-Penoyre 1909.

Ottoman Empire, the survey was undertaken with a *firman* issued by Hamdi Bey, and Baker Penoyre notified the authorities of an especially fine relief that was transferred to Constantinople.[11]

Melos

One of the most long-lasting sites linked to the BSA was at Phylakopi on Melos. Harcourt-Smith made an exploratory visit to the island in January 1896.[12] He was accompanied by his assistant John G. Smith and Vincent Corbett, secretary of the British Legation.[13] Harcourt-Smith noted:

> Our stay in Melos was unintentionally prolonged to nearly ten days, owing to violent storms, which made it impossible to leave the island; the discomforts, however, which we must otherwise have suffered during this enforced detention, were of a certain extent minimised by the hospitality of Mr Gielarakis, the British Consular Agent, who not only entertained us most generously, but facilitated our task by every means in his power.[14]

Harcourt-Smith's concern was that the island could have been over-explored:

> the principal drawback lay in the fact that for nearly a century it has served as the happy hunting ground for collectors, scientific and otherwise; it was scarcely to be expected that the locality which had produced the famous Aphrodite, not to speak of the Blacas Asklepios, the Apollo of Melos, and the Poseidon in the Athenian Museum, should have remained unexplored. But, from what we could discover, most of the previous excavations had been unsystematic, and there was still plenty of room, and indeed, much need for a more complete and systematic undertaking. On the strength of our report the Committee decided that the excavation of Melos should be begun in the middle of March.[15]

Mackenzie was assigned the task of studying the island of Melos.[16] Harcourt-Smith made the point at the Annual Meeting of Subscribers:

> The antiquities of the islands are in many instances still comparatively unexplored, and are subject to the caprice, or even the trafficking, of the ignorant peasantry, and it is therefore highly desirable that, before it is too late, everything that can be done

[11] Baker-Penoyre 1909, 250. See Ridgeway 1967.

[12] Letter to George Macmillan, 8 January 1896 (Macmillan Archive). He had to postpone the trip due to snow storms. I am grateful to Christopher Stray for drawing my attention to this letter.

[13] British School at Athens 1895/96, 21.

[14] British School at Athens 1895/96, 21-22.

[15] British School at Athens 1895/96, 22.

[16] British School at Athens 1896/97, 230. Mackenzie 1896/7. For Mackenzie on Melos: Momigliano 1999, 20-26.

should be done to place on record their valuable but steadily disappearing remains of art and history.[17]

Work started in the spring of 1896 to the end of May.[18] The initial work was at Klima, the ancient polis centre. Smith recalled the choice:

> Our first researches were directed to the shore of the little bay of Klima, which lies at the foot of the hill on which the theatre and many other traces of the old town are still distinguishable. The fact that part of this ground (the property of the Government) was said to have yielded the celebrated statue of Poseidon, now in the National Museum, as well as other statues (one of which is still lying *in situ*), and was otherwise said to be unexcavated, seemed to warrant our choice; the more so as the government had made this excavation a condition of their permission.[19]

The statue of Poseidon and one of Amphitrite had been found on Melos in 1877.[20] However little of significance was found except a paved area. Bosanquet joined the team writing of his experience:

> The Adamantines greeted us effusively, and Cecil Smith was down to meet us, having rowed round from Klima where the dig is in progress.
>   Then came a mule-ride – that is to say our luggage rode and we walked – of three quarters of an hour up to Trypiti. As the luggage included a bath, 2 cameras, 2 large portmanteaux, 1 Gladstone, 1 hold-all, 1 big roll, 1 bag and 117 small paper parcels, it was rather hard to arrange them all on 2 mules. The one that carried the bath looked like a new kind of tortoise.[21]

Harcourt-Smith then started work at Site B on the other side of the village of Klima.[22] They discovered the remains of a *stoa*. Site C was opened above Klima and remains of a Late Antique house were discovered.[23] Harcourt-Smith also investigated traces of the mole in the harbour and made observations about the change in sea-level.[24] Below the theatre (Site D) they found evidence for Late Antique housing and an inscription recording the erection of a sun-dial.[25]

---

[17] British School at Athens 1895/96, 230.

[18] Smith 1896, 347. The work started on 20 March 1896.

[19] Smith 1896, 347-48. The account also appears in Smith 1895/6b.

[20] Athens, NM 235 and NM236: Kaltsas 2002, 290-91, nos. 611-612.

[21] Bosanquet 1938, 53 (April 8, 1896; 'the house of Soulios, Trypiti, which is a village in Melos').

[22] Smith 1895/6b, 65-66. Cherry and Sparkes 1982, 54, fig. 5. 3 (W).

[23] Smith 1895/6b, 66-67.

[24] Evidence now suggests that there has been a change of some 2 metres since the classical period: Renfrew and Wagstaff 1982, 91.

[25] Smith 1895/6b, 69.

Mackenzie and Bosanquet conducted excavations in 'a field adjoining one called the Three Churches' lying at the south-east corner of the supposed agora area (Site E).[26] An inscription suggested the presence of a cult of Zeus Katabaites. Other material included the base of a portrait of Agrippina, and a colossal statue of Apollo. They also discovered the remains of a Byzantine baptistery. Again Bosanquet felt this was a great 'success'.

> … we persevered and behold the field is almost paved with marble bases and great blocks of trachyte, limestone and other commoner stones: a hotch-potch of ancient material dating from early Christian times. We got a few inscriptions, statue bases with honorary decrees, but things were dull until one evening I had a slab heaved up to examine a cavity that we saw through its joint. We cleared along the joint and found it wedged tight with a fragment of marble drapery. When we got the great slab up, under it were two marble bases and a sherd of drapery from a statue, 4 feet long. Went on digging a few minutes and came on a grand torso, the upper half of a colossus: when complete he was 12 feet high – his body, made in a separate piece from the legs which we may yet find, and headless, is 5 ½ ft. high. Our time for stopping is 6 but we toiled till 8 to get him out. A big crowd gathered as the news spread: I only had four men at work in that field and it was good when we were reinforced by men from the other sites and could work rapidly. They are splendid fellows, the best lot I ever had to deal with.[27]

He then mentioned the discovery of a tomb in the church. He continued:

> apparently in his honour they made a holocaust of all the statues – 'idols' – that they could lay hands on. Each statue was planked down in the foundation with a big stone on top to keep him quiet.[28]

In 1896 Bosanquet also searched for the east gate of the city, which was found on the line of a modern track and adjacent to a circular bastion (Site F).[29] This excavation was partly done through the use of tunnelling, to avoid the need to purchase the field, which was under cultivation. Bosanquet found some archaic pottery and suggested that the walls were constructed, or perhaps strengthened during the Peloponnesian War.[30] In the spring of 1897 Crowfoot continued Bosanquet's excavations on the Demarch's Fields, in the hope of identifying public buildings.[31] This location was particularly significant as it was

---

[26] Mackenzie 1897; Smith 1895/6b, 70. The map was mapped by Charles Clark, the architect. For the location: Cherry and Sparkes 1982, 54, fig. 5. 3 (Q). Mackenzie notes the use of Bosanquet's 'day book' to record finds. For inscriptions from the site: Smith 1897.

[27] Bosanquet 1938, 56 (April 26, 1896, to his sister Caroline).

[28] Bosanquet 1938, 56 (April 26, 1896, to his sister Caroline).

[29] Bosanquet 1938, 57 (April 25, 1896; to his sister Caroline). Bosanquet 1895/6a; Smith 1895/6b, 70. For a plan: Renfrew and Wagstaff 1982, 54, fig. 5. 3 (East Gate = L).

[30] Bosanquet 1895/6a; followed by Cherry and Sparkes 1982, 56. Bosanquet considered it to be the setting for Thucydides 5. 115.

[31] Crowfoot 1896/7. The Demarch's Field is clearly adjacent to the East Gate and note located by the 'Three Churches': Cherry and Sparkes 1982, 56.

close to where the statue of Aphrodite (subsequently removed to the Louvre) was found, which was thought to have been located within a gymnasium complex.[32] Bosanquet had previously given his reasons for thinking that the *agora* lay in this area, not least the foundations of a Roman temple with portrait statues.[33] In less than a week work was brought to a halt as it was perceived as a 'tentative' excavation. A tank, possibly containing fuller's earth, came to light, and the small finds including *terra sigillata* suggest a Roman period date.

A cemetery probably lay outside this east gate, and it was here that an archaic *kouros* had been found in 1891.[34] The British team identified further disturbed Early Iron Age ("Diplyon period") tombs covered with tiles. The team then investigated tombs around the modern village of Trypiti.[35] A further archaic cemetery was explored on the east side of Trypiti.[36]

Attention, at this point, turned to the far side of the ancient acropolis in the area around Tramythia. In the spring of 1896 Bosanquet , Mackenzie and Harcourt-Smith worked on the excavation on the 'Hall of the Mystae' in the Tramythia valley, on the slopes of the ancient city.[37] Bosanquet described to his sister Caroline the excavations at 'the Hall of the Mystae' on Melos.

> The first was an inscription about a sun-dial of which I told you, and an inscribed dedication to Dionysos. A few days later we found a statue, headless alas, lying on its back on the mosaic pavement that I mentioned. It represents a *hierophant* – a kind of high priest – of Dionysos, probably, and was set up by the Mystae or Initiates. The mosaic is an unusually large one, some 40 feet in length, and 10 feet wide, and on the whole well preserved. Yesterday we finished clearing away the stone dykes and soil that overlay the upper end and were overwhelmed by the beauty of the upper compartment: it has a vine in each corner whose branches spread over the field: among them are birds of gorgeous plumage, pheasants and peacocks, at one side a deer or goat lying down. The colouring is very rich and the design good. It is probably the best mosaic that has been discovered in Greece. I am anxious to arrange for its preservation and am wiring to Cecil Smith, whom I suppose to be in Athens, to that effect. He has left me in charge for over 3 weeks and I have only heard from him once, so I am anxiously awaiting his coming.[38]

---

[32] Bosanquet 1895/6a, 79. The stadium was located below the find-spot of the Aphrodite. Renfrew and Wagstaff 1982, 54, fig. 5. 3, S.

[33] Bosanquet 1895/6a, 81. Location: Cherry and Sparkes 1982, 54, fig. 5. 3 (P).

[34] Athens, NM 1558: Holleaux 1892, pl. xvi; Kaltsas 2002, 50, no. 48. See also Smith 1895/6b, 70; Cherry and Sparkes 1982, 57.

[35] Smith 1895/6b, 71-72.

[36] Smith 1895/6b, 75.

[37] Bosanquet 1898a; see also Smith 1895/6b, 72-74. For location: Cherry and Sparkes 1982, 54, fig. 5. 3 (U).

[38] Bosanquet 1938, 55-56 (April 26, 1896; to his sister Caroline).

The drawing was made by Charles Richmond Rowland Clark, the excavation's architect. Among the finds was a herm of M. Marius Trophinus, that fitted a head found on Melos in the 1880s.[39] An inscribed bust of Aurelia Euposia, probably third century AD in date, was dedicated by the *peribomioi.*[40] The mosaic itself had to be recovered for protection. Above this they found a small Roman bath-house complete with caldarium (Site H).[41] They then investigated the area round the retaining wall of the stadium (Site I).[42] Bosanquet described the work:

> We have been driving tunnels into a terrace of soil, above a plateau which we have trenched, and have found one tomb and a big fine cave in which was a wall built of marble fragments from some Roman building. The men love this mining; it is the way they have always carried out their secret diggings. To-day we had work going on in three tunnels and two very deep trenches. It was rather haggard work – I live in fear of an accident, but they are skilful and comparatively careful. Many have worked in mines at Laurium or here.[43]

Bosanquet felt that the success of the excavations changed in mid-April, and noted the finds. During the 1896 season Bosanquet was joined by fellow Trinity students, Henry (Harry) Martineau Fletcher (b. 1870) and Sydney Decimus Kitson (1871-1937) who were travelling through Italy and Greece as part of their early stages of architectural training.[44] They made a study of the churches on Melos.[45] After the 1896 season excavations had been completed, Mackenzie conducted a survey of the island to expand on early trips he had made with Charles Clark, the architect.[46]

Another small excavation was started by Hercules West in the cemetery at Petralonia to the east of Trypiti in 1897 but had to be abandoned after one day. He discovered 'deep rectangular sinkings' for tombs that had been long-ago looted. He found one unopened tomb containing:

> three small lekythi, black glaze with bands left unpainted around the body – these were near the head of the skeleton; two small rough oinochoae, a small terra-cotta lamp, and an alabaster pyxis supported on three feet'.[47]

No more than a short report was generated.

---

[39] Bosanquet 1898a, 74, fig. 6. Harcourt-Smith made a cast to check the fit for the head which was in Athens.

[40] Bosanquet 1898a, 77, fig. 8. Now Athens, NM 424: Kaltsas 2002, 371, no. 791.

[41] Smith 1895/6b, 74; see also Cherry and Sparkes 1982, 54, fig. 5. 3 (H).

[42] Smith 1895/6b; see also Cherry and Sparkes 1982, 54, fig. 5. 3, (S). It was Bosanquet who suggested that this was a stadium.

[43] Bosanquet 1938, 54 (April 14, 1896; to his sister Frances).

[44] Bosanquet 1938, 57 (April 25, 1896; to his sister Caroline).

[45] Fletcher and Kitson 1895/6. See also Casson 1912/13a.

[46] Mackenzie 1896/7. See also Momigliano 1999, 26.

[47] Smith 1896/7, 5-6 (containing West's report).

Pelos

In the first season of work on Melos the team's attention was drawn to the possibility of a small cemetery at Pelos.[48] Mackenzie noted,

> The tomb region, chiefly to the left of the road-way before it descends to the plain, is at the foot of the white tufa hills bounding Palaeachora on the east. Our attention had been attracted towards the site at the close of the excavation season by the proprietor, who brought us two small vases from a tomb which he came upon while digging his fields. On my visit the proprietor was unfortunately absent, and the site was shown to us by his son. The vases themselves … were purchased by us …[49]

The cemetery was excavated by Edgar and eight tombs were opened.[50] The excavation was brought to an abrupt close after the intervention of Kavvadias.[51]

Phylakopi

The site of Phylakopi had been identified in the first season. In early April 1896 Bosanquet noted,

> … We had a long day yesterday, and discovered a Mycenaean fortress, as we believe, with several contemporary cemeteries and one great hill, probably an artificial grave mound, gable-shaped and full of obsidian knives. Obsidian was no doubt exported in early times; it is abundant on the island. We also found some Greek tombs and explored a catacomb, probably Christian. The place retains the name of (A)-Pollonia, which no doubt is ancient, tho' not known in history.[52]

The site was 'partly investigated' for a short time at the end of the season.[53] Harcourt-Smith noted: 'we have already found enough to show that the mound covered the remains of a prehistoric fortress or palace of the utmost importance'.[54]

The excavations at Phylakopi were handed over to Duncan Mackenzie under the overall supervision of the new BSA Director, David Hogarth. The second season of 1897 saw a more sustained work at the site.[55] Mackenzie took the main charge for the excavation with Charles R. R. Clark as the architect.[56] This season's work was restricted

---

[48] Edgar 1896/7; Mackenzie 1896/7, 73-74. See Renfrew and Wagstaff 1982, 298, site 39.

[49] Mackenzie 1896/7, 73-74.

[50] Edgar 1896/7.

[51] Smith 1896/7, 5-6 (including text of telegram).

[52] Bosanquet 1938, 53-54 (8 April 1896; 'the house of Soulios, Trypiti, which is a village in Melos'; to his mother).

[53] Smith 1896, 342; Smith 1895/6b, 76.

[54] Smith 1895/6b, 76.

[55] Smith 1896/7, 6-30.

[56] Smith 1896/7, 10. Mackenzie was given funding 'on condition of his placing his services at the disposal of the Director for the current season': Momigliano 1999, 21 (BSA Meeting of 18 November 1897).

due to issues over the ownership of the land, and had the fortifications as the main focus. Evidence was found for the creation of obsidian tools. The third season was conducted in 1898 by Hogarth, assisted by Mackenzie, and with Edward B. Hoare as architect.[57] Hogarth avoided using Petrie's methods on the site as he found that the quantities of fine pottery required careful supervision.[58] This is likely to have been on the advice of Mackenzie who noted in the excavation day-book:

> As regards the pottery it was made a rule from the beginning that all fragments should be kept for my personal examination. ... As I was alone at the excavation throughout its duration I had to undertake the examination of the pottery on the spot as it turned up.[59]

In particular they found inscribed material. Mackenzie was responsible for making sense of the stratigraphy, and differentiating the different settlements. He drew on his knowledge of other Bronze Age settlements in the Cyclades, drawing relevant comparisons.[60] He even went to describe the fourth, or Late Bronze Age settlement as 'a walled city'. The team also discovered fragments of painted wall plaster, including a 'flying fish' fresco.[61] Edgar, who was responsible for the pottery, had also devised a chart to try and date the different types of pottery.[62] By the end of the second season in 1898 it could be reported that 'a second Troy has been found'. Richards, the BSA's Assistant Director, reported:

> Nowhere else, except at Hissárlik, have the Mycenaean and pre-Mycenaean strata been discovered in so little disturbed a condition. Three distinct strata representing different settlements have been found practically undisturbed, and the finds of pottery especially will when worked up throw much light on Aegean civilization. It may be fairly said that no excavations of the past year in Greece have been more interesting or valuable.[63]

The BSA returned to Melos in 1899 under the direction of Mackenzie.[64] He was assisted by the Thomas D. Atkinson as the architect, and Edgar once again worked on the pottery.[65] Among their finds was a structure that they supposed to be a 'Mycenaean' *megaron*. Apart

---

[57] Hogarth 1897/98; Mackenzie 1897/8a; Edgar 1897/8. Mackenzie was again given a grant 'on the understanding that he takes part in the excavations in Melos': Momigliano 1999, 21 (BSA Meeting of 18 September 1898).

[58] Hogarth 1897/98, 3-4.

[59] 12 May 1896: quoted in Momigliano 1999, 21.

[60] Momigliano 1999, 26-27.

[61] Mackenzie 1897/8a, 26-27, pl. III. For a recent discussion: Morgan 2007, 381-83.

[62] Edgar 1897/8, 47-48, fig. 3.

[63] Richards 1898, 337.

[64] Mackenzie 1898/9.

[65] Atkinson 1898/9; Edgar 1898/9c.

from digging in the settlement they extended the work to the cemetery.[66] The team was proud of its results, announcing:

> Phylakopi has already been laid bare to at least as great an extent as Mycenae, Tiryns, or any other site of the same description. Though it can hardly claim to view with these in romantic interest, its archaeological importance, as an epitome of the 'Mycenaean' and earlier periods on the coasts and islands of the Aegean, is scarcely inferior to theirs.[67]

With the start of work on Crete, excavations on Melos concluded in 1899 and a final report was published in 1904.[68]

By the autumn of 1910 with the work in Laconia drawing to a close, Dawkins was looking for a new site to excavate.[69] The political situation was such that he decided to resume work at Phylakopi in 1911.[70] Since the closure of the original excavations at Phylakopi, the Cretan Exploration Fund had been working on Crete, in particular at Knossos and so Bronze Age Crete was better understood.[71] In addition there had been further work by members of the BSA on the prehistory of mainland Greece, notably by Alan J. B. Wace and M. S. Thompson in Thessaly.[72] Dawkins had gained experience of Bronze Age Crete from Bosanquet's excavations at Palaikastro.[73] As the possibility of excavating at Datcha had to be rested due to hostilities, it was decided that a limited excavation at Phylakopi would give a timely reassessment. Dawkins was assisted by W. J. P. Jones as architect; and for the first time women, Dorothy Lamb and Lilian Tennant, were admitted on a BSA excavation.[74] Special emphasis was placed on the stratigraphic sequence of pottery which was published by Dawkins and Droop.[75] The excavations also found remains of infant burials in pithoi.[76]

This pre-First World War work on Melos conducted by Harcourt-Smith, Mackenzie and Dawkins laid the foundations for the future survey of the island as well as resumption of work at Phylakopi.[77] Stanley Casson made a brief visit to the island in April 1913.[78]

---

[66] Hogarth and Bosanquet 1899, 319-20.

[67] British School at Athens 1898/99, 101-02.

[68] Atkinson, *et al.* 1904.

[69] BSA Minute Book 6, Meeting of 4 October 1910. Datcha or Phylakopi were the main contenders.

[70] Dawkins 1910/11a; Dawkins 1910/11b.

[71] Cadogan 2000. Harriet Boyd had also been excavating at Gournia: Hawes, *et al.* 1908.

[72] *E.g.* Wace, *et al.* 1907/08; Wace and Thompson 1908/09.

[73] *E.g.* Dawkins 1902/03a; Dawkins 1903/04a; Dawkins 1904/05a; Dawkins 1905/06.

[74] Gill 2002. This was probably the setting for Droop's (in)famous comments about women on archaeological excavations: Droop 1915.

[75] Dawkins and Droop 1910/11b; Dawkins and Droop 1910/11c; Dawkins and Droop 1910/11d; Dawkins and Droop 1910/11e.

[76] Dawkins 1910/11c.

[77] Renfrew and Wagstaff 1982; Renfrew 1985; Renfrew 2007.

[78] Casson 1912/13a.

Naxos

In the autumn of 1912 the BSA was considering a number of sites for excavation.[79] The Datcha excavation was no longer feasible, and the limited excavations at Phylakopi were complete. By early February 1913 Dawkins had investigated a site on Naxos, though he was considering a site on Crete. Droop recalled the investigation of the site:

> For the season of 1913 the British School at Athens wished to find a prehistoric town to dig, and a party visited Naxos in search of one. We had a very pleasant tour round the island, but we had no luck, finding nothing of sufficient promise to justify an expedition. One particularly bitter disappointment we met with there, on visiting a site known to us as having been partially worked a few years before. The undug portion was fairly extensive and looked very hopeful with traces of walls appearing and with prehistoric island pottery lying thickly over a good area, but our hopes were dashed by the discovery of one of those round spaces where the Greeks of today use the ox, unscripturally muzzled, to tread out their corn; often these floors are paved, but this one was cut down to the living rock only six inches below the surface.[80]

It was decided to look elsewhere for a site and the BSA did not return to Naxos. Dawkins himself donated material from Naxos to the Ashmolean.[81]

Crete

Prospecting for archaeological sites on Crete was begun by British scholars in the nineteenth century. Cambridge students would have been familiar with the marbles and inscriptions presented to the university by Captain Spratt and displayed in the Fitzwilliam Museum.[82] Arthur J. Evans made his first trip to the island in the spring of 1894, and visited the site of Knossos. He quickly made a report on 'primitive pictographs' that he had observed.[83] He returned to the island in 1895 with John L. Myres, and travelled through the island, crossing the Lassithi plateau, making detailed notes of the antiquities and forming a limited collection.[84] He published a report on Lato in the *Annual*.[85] He made a further tour in 1896, acquiring an inscribed offering table at Psychro. He also visited the site of Karphi on the north side of the Lassithi plateau; this was to be excavated by John D. S. Pendlebury in the 1930s.[86]

The Cretan revolt of 1897 brought about the intervention of the Great Powers and the loss of Ottoman control. Evans revisited the island in 1898 and crossed from Khania,

---

[79] BSA Minute Book 7, Meeting of 22 October 1912.

[80] Droop 1915, 32. See also British School at Athens 1912/13, 267.

[81] *E.g.* Sherratt 2000, 139, no. III. 7. 1.

[82] Budde and Nicholls 1964. For a discussion of one of the inscriptions from Lebena: Gill 2004p.

[83] Evans 1894. For the subsequent reading of some of these texts: Robinson 2002.

[84] Brown 1993; Brown 2000; Brown and Bennett 2001.

[85] Evans 1895/96.

[86] Pendlebury, *et al.* 1937/38. See also Grundon 2007.

along the north coast, to make a circuit of the eastern part of the island. This allowed him to develop his plans to excavate at Knossos and as a result the Cretan Exploration Fund was formed, with Evans and Hogarth as directors, Macmillan as honorary treasurer and Myres as honorary secretary.[87] Even in the summer of 1899 there appears to have been a tension between the BSA and Evans. Loring, as Honorary Secretary, asked for the link between the Fund and the BSA to 'be more precisely defined' and 'to determine at starting what proportion of the sums raised would be at the disposal of the Committee for the excavation of sites reserved for the School, and what proportion would be at the personal disposal of Mr Evans'.[88] The time was right as the BSA's excavations at Phylakopi were coming to a close. Evans and Hogarth, the BSA's Director, searched for possible sites in the eastern part of the island. Their plans were revealed at the Annual Meeting in October 1899:

> The new conditions in which Crete has recently been placed, and the final emancipation of the island from Turkish rule, have at last rendered it possible to organize a serious effort to recover the evidences of her early civilization.[89]

Indeed the Managing Committee 'think it may be found desirable to concentrate on Crete, for several years to come, all the energies and funds available for excavation'.[90]

Archaeological work started at Knossos on 13 March 1900 with Hogarth's search for 'Mycenaean' graves and excavating houses.[91] The reason for this was the adoption of techniques learned from Petrie, and he made this clear in a letter to Evans.[92] After two months Hogarth reported, 'I fear I leave the solution of the Knossian cemetery problem but little advanced'.[93] Ten days later Evans, assisted by Mackenzie, started excavations on the site of the Bronze Age palace.[94] Francis B. Welch, like Hogarth from Magdalen College, Oxford, worked on the pottery; he had gained archaeological experience in the previous year, directing work for the British Museum on Cyprus.[95] Theodore Fyfe acted as the project architect.

After the search for the cemeteries, Hogarth turned his attention to the excavation of the Dictaean Cave near Psychro on the Lassithi plateau which Evans and Myres had

---

[87] Cadogan 2000, 15, fig. 12 (for brochure). Bosanquet became one of the three directors of the Fund once he had been appointed Director of the BSA. The Fund is mentioned in BSA Minute Book 3, Meeting of 3 July 1899.

[88] BSA Minute Book 3, Meeting of 3 July 1899.

[89] British School at Athens 1898/99, 102.

[90] British School at Athens 1898/99, 102.

[91] Hogarth 1899/1900b.

[92] Written in the spring of 1899; quoted in Momigliano 1999, 39.

[93] Hogarth 1899/1900b, 85.

[94] Evans 1899/1900. See Momigliano 1999, 37.

[95] Welch 1899/1900b. Welch had assisted Edgar in Athens in the previous year and was later responsible for publishing some of the pottery from Phylakopi: Atkinson, *et al.* 1904.

visited earlier.[96] The layers of deposit were removed by the use of explosives, a technique he was also to use at Carchemish on the Roman concrete layers.[97] He employed some 70 people for the three-week excavation that lasted until mid-June. Hogarth observed the presence of Kamares ware, a type that was being used to relate the chronologies of Middle Kingdom Egypt with Crete. He later described the effect of the excavation:

> The digger's life is a surfeit of surprises, but his imagination has seldom been provoked so sharply as in that dim chasm. One seemed to come very near indeed to men who lived before history. As we saw those pillared isles, so with little change had the last worshipper, who offered a token to Zeus, seen them three thousand years ago. No later life had obliterated his tracks; and we could follow them back into the primaeval world with such stirring of fancy as one feels in the Desert, which is the same today as it was yesterday, and has been since the beginning of things.[98]

Animal remains from the excavations were sent to Professor Boyd Dawkins (1837-1929), a physical anthropologist, at Manchester.[99]

While Evans continued the work at Knossos until 1910,[100] other members of the Fund turned to other parts of the island. Hogarth had resigned as Director of the BSA to concentrate on the work on Crete; Bosanquet succeeded him. For the 1901 season Hogarth excavated at Kato Zakro in the eastern part of the island, a site visited by Evans.[101] Human skulls from the Minoan burials in the caves lining the side of the gorge behind the site were studied by Boyd Dawkins, who had worked with Hogarth on the material from the Dictaean Cave.[102] The pottery was studied by John Marshall, but after his move to India, this work was continued by Richard M. Dawkins.[103] Hogarth was unable to discover the palace (which was not to be uncovered until 1961) and the excavation had to abandoned after torrential rainfall.[104] Seal-stones from the site were considered to be evidence for possible commercial relations.[105]

[96] Hogarth 1899/1900a.

[97] Hogarth 1910, 73.

[98] Hogarth 1910, 77.

[99] Boyd Dawkins 1902. See also 'Excavations in Crete', *The Times* 28 May 1902, 13. Boyd Dawkins had excavated prehistoric caves in Britain notably Wookey Hole and Cresswell Crags.

[100] Evans 1900/1; Evans 1901/02; Evans 1902/03; Evans 1903/04; Evans 1904/05. There was a break in 1906 due to a shortage of financial support: see also Momigliano 1999, 75. It is from 1906 that Evans chose to publish outside the *Annual*. For the start of the 1907 season: MacGillivray 2000, 239.

[101] Hogarth 1900/01; Hogarth 1901.

[102] Boyd Dawkins 1900/01.

[103] Dawkins 1903.

[104] Hogarth 1910, 80-84.

[105] Hogarth 1902; Hogarth 1910/11.

In the spring of 1901 Bosanquet also started work at the site of Praesos in eastern Crete, assisted by John H. Marshall and Robert D. Wells.[106] One of the reasons given by Bosanquet was the discovery of an 'Eteocretan' inscription.[107] In May Bosanquet wrote home to his mother about the find of 'a first-rate Mycenaean gem, representing a hunter seizing a couchant bull by his horns'.[108] He also looked for burial sites, using Hogarth's technique of explosives to remove calciferous deposits.[109] This cave system was revisited the following year with Bosanquet making records of the burial caves.[110] They also discovered a Minoan burial with clay *larnax*.[111] At the end of the season he conducted a short excavation at Petras near Sitia.[112] Work at Praesos continued in subsequent seasons.[113]

Archaeologists were beginning to look for other sites. The heavy rainfall in eastern Crete that had disrupted the work at Kato Zakro had uncovered the remains of a prehistoric cemetery near Palaikastro which was examined by John H. Marshall.[114] In spite of Hogarth's concern that this was treading on the feet of the German School, the site was assigned to Bosanquet, now Director of the BSA; he started the excavations in April of 1902. Bosanquet described one of his earliest pieces of digging:

> This morning I got word of a cottage floor through which, for a whole generation, fragments of pottery had from time to time protruded – went and dug; in half-an-hour unearthed half a Mycenaean vase – best yet seen here – and a large Triton (trumpet) shell, besides minor pottery. At first it looked tomb-like, then prowling round outside I found that part of the wall of the cottage is a bit of original megalithic masonry. Sticking up in the mud floor bits of pebble concrete of 3,000 years ago – this was a farmhouse then, a trifle more well-to-do than nowadays.[115]

There was an awareness of the importance to study human remains and Bosanquet despatched thirteen human skulls to Candia for study there by Boyd Dawkins who was visiting Evans.[116] Bosanquet showed a sense of humour when writing about his finds. He described the excavation of a Bronze Age house:

---

[106] Bosanquet 1901b; Bosanquet 1901/02b. See also Conway 1901/02; Forster 1901/02; Forster 1904/05; Marshall 1905/06; Bosanquet 1909/10.

[107] Bosanquet 1901a, 340.

[108] Bosanquet 1938, 81 (letter of 23 May 1901, from Praesos).

[109] Bosanquet 1938, 83 (letter of 23 July 1901, from Candia).

[110] Bosanquet 1938, 124 (letter of 30 April 1902).

[111] Hopkinson 1903/04.

[112] Bosanquet 1901/02a.

[113] *E.g.* Bosanquet 1938, 154 (letter of 9 June 1904).

[114] Gill 2000a. The possibility at excavating at the site was discussing at the meeting of 10 October 1901 (BSA Minute Book 4). It was noted that Dörpfeld was willing to let the BSA excavate at the site.

[115] Bosanquet 1938, 118 (letter of 16 April 1902).

[116] Bosanquet 1938, 119 (letter of 21 April 1902).

It was called 'Minos house' probably, and was let as lodgings to respectable slave merchants from Cnossos in the summer'.[117]

He also observed the use of bricks that had been noted in Hogarth's excavations at Zakro, and by Harriet Boyd at Gournia. At the end of May he wrote to his father-in-law, Thomas Hodgkin, about the season's work:

> At Palaikastro we have what looks like the centre of a rich agricultural district of the same period. … One can only suppose that the proprietors of olive-groves and vineyards in the eastern province had made this warm bay their winter rendezvous. … the number of the comfort and refinement of these houses at P. K. shows that there must have been a considerable upper class.[118]

Members of the 1903 team included Marcus N. Tod, and Richard M. Dawkins.[119] The Canadian Charles T. Currelly worked on the pottery, and Wynfrid Duckworth, Cambridge University lecturer in Physical Anthropology, on the human remains.[120] The team continued to work on houses and quantities of fine pottery.[121] Bosanquet noted:

> We have Houses B, Γ, Δ, E, now, all respectable big South Audley St. houses; and the pot I wrote to thee about so happy-like, has the most gorgeous design of lilies in groups of three: it couldn't be better.[122]

Tod was given the task of excavating at Ayios Nikolaos, where Bosanquet suspected the remains of the Dictaean temple.[123] In April John L. Myres joined the excavation and worked on the sanctuary of Petsophas.[124] Bosanquet and Currelly also visited the island of Kouphonisi where they found crushed murex shells and associated Kamares ware pottery, providing evidence for a purple-dye workshop in the Bronze Age.[125]

Excavations at Palaikastro were resumed in 1904. Dawkins continued the excavations of the housing in the town and Currelly studied the *larnax* burials.[126] Among the finds

---

[117] Bosanquet 1938, 121 (letter of 23 April 1902).

[118] Bosanquet 1938, 132-34 (letter of 30 May 1902).

[119] Bosanquet 1902/03a.

[120] Duckworth 1902/03a; Duckworth 1902/03b.

[121] Bosanquet 1902/03b; Bosanquet 1902/03c; Bosanquet 1902/03d; Dawkins 1902/03a; Dawkins 1902/03b; Dawkins 1902/03c; Dawkins 1902/03d; Dawkins and Tod 1902/03.

[122] Bosanquet 1938, 138 (letter of 2 April 1903). South Audley Street is near Bond Street in London's west end.

[123] Tod 1902/03a. See also Bosanquet 1938, 136 (letter of 23 March 1903).

[124] Myres 1902/03.

[125] Bosanquet 1903. See also Bosanquet 1938, 138 (letter of 23 May 1903). For a discussion and images of the site: Stieglitz 1994.

[126] Dawkins 1903/04a; Dawkins 1903/04b; Dawkins 1903/04c; Dawkins 1903/04d; Dawkins 1903/04e; Dawkins 1903/04f; Dawkins 1903/04g; Dawkins 1903/04h; Currelly 1903/04.

were small ivories. Bosanquet joined the excavations in early May.[127] Charles Comyn, the architect, was present to prepare the plans. Towards the end of May the team discovered a double-sided hymn related to Dictaean Zeus.

> The hymn is full of problems; the copy on one side apparently reproduces the same hymn as the other, but in a very corrupt version, as though cut by a workman who had no Greek and copied mechanically, making amazing blunders. Each verse has the same refrain or chorus, "hail, mighty Child, all hail, in all the power of thy beauty art thou come. … Lover of Dicte speed hither and be gladdened by our song".
>
> It is the Child Zeus, born and bred in a cave on Dicte who is addressed, no doubt. Even if we find no more we have enough to reconstruct several stanzas, and to form a most important literary document.[128]

A further fragment was found and Bosanquet quickly translated it, noting that it confirmed the location as the classical Heleia.[129] The find was timely as funds were low for the work on Crete. Bosanquet sent a telegram to Macmillan who included it in a letter to *The Times*:

> Important discoveries. Doric inscription [with] ritual hymn to infant Zeus, locating sanctuary [of] Dictaean Zeus here. Also two exquisite ivory statuettes of children in Minoan house.[130]

The 1905 excavations, essentially with Dawkins taking the lead, continued on the site of the temple of Dictaean Zeus, and remains of some of the sacrificed oxen were found.[131] A final season was conducted in the spring of 1906, and work started on the final report.[132]

By 1905 attention was switching to Laconia, and in 1906 Evans was unable to excavate at Knossos due to lack of funds.[133] The Annual Meeting of 1906 even expressed the hope that 'the School's long connexion with Crete will not be altogether broken'.[134] Evans, from this point, ceased to publish his reports from Knossos in the *Annual*.

The BSA did however return to Crete with a formal excavation. In 1913 Dawkins had been hoping to excavate at Datcha, but due to the outbreak of hostilities had been unable to start. He had recently completed the re-excavation of Phylakopi, where he had been exploring the influence of Crete on Melos.[135] One of the other sites initially marked for

---

[127] Bosanquet 1938, 146 (letter of 9 May 1904). He noted an accident in which one of the trenches, supervised by Currelly, had collapsed injuring one of the workmen.

[128] Bosanquet 1938, 147-48 (letter of May 25, 1904).

[129] Bosanquet 1938, 148-49 (letter of May 29, 1904).

[130] Macmillan 1904. See also Hogarth 1904.

[131] Dawkins 1904/05a; Dawkins 1904/05b; Dawkins 1904/05c; Dawkins 1904/05d; Dawkins 1904/05e; Dawkins 1904/05f; Hawes 1904/05; Bosanquet 1904/05a; Bosanquet 1904/05b; Bosanquet 1904/05c. See also Bosanquet 1939/40.

[132] Dawkins 1905/06. Final report: Bosanquet and Dawkins 1923. See also: Hutchinson, *et al.* 1939/40.

[133] Macmillan 1906.

[134] British School at Athens 1905/06, 493. Quoted in Cadogan 2000, 26.

[135] Dawkins and Droop 1910/11b. For the earlier significance of the Kamares Cave: Myres 1895.

excavation had been Lyttos in eastern Crete, and this was reconsidered as a possibility in 1913.[136] In the end the excavation was not possible as Halbherr had applied for the permit, so it was decided to dig in the Kamares Cave.[137] Dawkins and Max Laistner thus excavated at the Kamares Cave, a site that held significance for cross-chronology with Middle Kingdom Egypt.[138] In the spring of 1914 Dawkins excavated at a Late Minoan settlement at Plati. He also explored a Late Minoan *tholos* tomb on the Lasithi plateau.[139] The excavation took place from the end of April for one month and three students took part: John P. Droop, Roger M. Heath, and Max L. W. Laistner.

With the outbreak of war excavations came to a close. However Dawkins, John C. Lawson and William R. Halliday were posted to the island as intelligence officers with the Royal Navy Volunteer Reserve (RNVR). The BSA renewed its work on the island after the war and John Pendlebury prepared a definitive overview of Cretan archaeology.[140]

---

[136] British School at Athens 1898/99, 102. See Xanthoudidis 1898. BSA Minute Book 7, Meeting of 4 February 1913. The cave at Arkalokhóri, south-west of Lyttos, was explored by J. Hazzidakis: Hazzidakis 1912/13.

[137] BSA Minute Book 7.

[138] Dawkins and Laistner 1912/13. They were joined by Richard Lambert who was due to go up to Wadham College for the Michaelmas Term: British School at Athens 1912/13, 269.

[139] Dawkins 1913/14. See also: Cadogan 2000, 27. The site had been suggested to him by Hatzidakis. For more recent work: Watrous 1982.

[140] Pendlebury 1939. See also Grundon 2007.

CHAPTER 10: ANATOLIA

As plans were being made for the opening of the BSA there were suggestions that the School would be better placed in Smyrna than Athens so that advantage could be taken of the untapped archaeological sources in Anatolia.[1] In spite of the Athens location, students of the BSA were almost immediately plunged into projects in Anatolia.

Travellers to Anatolia since the Renaissance had noted the remains and collected the antiquities which they encountered. Fragments of the altar of Zeus at Pergamon formed part of the 'Arundel marbles' that are now, in part, displayed in the Ashmolean Museum in Oxford.[2] During the 19th century there was a renewed interest in Anatolia by British scholars. Charles Fellows travelled widely through Asia Minor in 1838, and his tour led directly to the acquisition of sculptures for the British Museum from the site of Xanthos in Lycia.[3] Charles Newton, an employee of the British Museum, worked at Bodrum from where in 1856 he was able to extract sculptural reliefs and free-standing sculpture from the great Mausoleum of Halikarnassos.[4] Newton also visited other important sites in the region including Didyma and Knidos. Edward Falkener first conducted research at Ephesus in 1845,[5] to be followed in 1863 by J. T. Wood.[6] Wood's work, which led to the identification of the Artemision, continued until 1874. R. P. Pullan, supported by the Society of Dilettanti, worked at Priene in the same period (1868-69), and fragments of the temple of Athena Polias were subsequently presented to the British Museum.[7] In June 1868 George Dennis, best known for his surveys of Etruria, settled in Smyrna where he resided until 1870. He explored several sites in the hinterland, and he excavated at Sardis.[8] In this same period, Frank Calvert was working alongside Heinrich Schliemann at Troy in a major series of excavations (1871, 1878, 1890).[9]

British archaeologists had long been active on Greek sites lying within the jurisdiction of the Ottoman Empire. Auguste Salzmann and Alfred Biliotti conducted relatively scientific excavations in the cemeteries of Kameiros on Rhodes; the finds from the 1864 were

---

[1] See chapter 1.

[2] Vickers 1985.

[3] Jenkins 1992, 140-45; Challis 2008, 23-39.

[4] Challis 2008, 55-76.

[5] Falkener 1862.

[6] Wood 1877.

[7] Jenkins 1992, 212.

[8] Rhodes 1973, 100-09.

[9] Allen 1999.

despatched to the British Museum, although there has never been a systematic publication of the grave-groups.[10] John Ruskin also explored the site of Ialysos on Rhodes in 1870.

The British exploration of sites in Anatolia needs to be seen against the work of other foreign archaeological schools.[11] New antiquities laws had been passed by the Ottoman government in February 1884 in the wake of Schliemann's excavations at Troy. In October 1886 the Rev. Joseph Hirst of Smyrna commented in a letter read to the Royal Archaeological Institute in London that the Ottoman government had 'withdrawn all permission given to Englishmen and other foreigners to excavate ancient sites within the Sultan's dominions, and also that large quantities of finely sculpted pillars, walls, and stones are being sold and utilized for modern building purposes'.[12] Such pillaging was observed by William R. Paton at Iasos, and linked to Ottoman construction works in Constantinople.[13] The growing interest in archaeology is reflected by the opening of the Archaeological Museum in Constantinople in 1891.[14]

The Germans had excavated at Pergamon from 1878 to 1886, and then from 1900 to 1908.[15] Interest in the region was developed by the formation of the Comité behufs Erforschung der Trümmerstätten des Alten Orients ('Orient-Comité') in 1887.[16] This was followed by work at Magnesia on the Maeander (1890, 1891-93),[17] and then at Miletus (1899-1907). Miletus was chosen 'because here is perhaps the last point where sizeable art treasures in the area in question [Greek settlements on the Turkish coast] are to be found'.[18] German relations with the Ottoman authorities were not always good, and a crisis in 1905 led to the suspension of some archaeological activity.[19] The French excavated at Myrina, where notably they found a large number of fine terracotta figures that became highly prized (1880-82). The Austrians were equally active, exploring Lycia (1881-82) and working at sites previously explored by the British, notably Priene (1895-99) and Ephesus (1896-1907).[20]

The Archaeological Institute of America had been founded in 1879 and the first organised American excavation in Turkey was conducted at Assos (1881–83).[21] Joseph T. Clarke and Francis H. Bacon were joined by Frank Calvert, who had been

---

[10] Some of the finds feature in the permanent catalogues of the British Museum: Higgins 1954; see also Johnston 1975.

[11] *E.g.* Le Roy 1996; Marchand 1996; Wiplinger and Wlach 1996.

[12] Quoted from 'Archaeological News', *AJA* 2 (1886) 477, in Allen 1999, 215.

[13] Paton 1887; see also Hicks 1887a.

[14] Gates 1996.

[15] For a convenient summary: Kunze 1995.

[16] Marchand 1996, 193.

[17] Marchand 1996, 193.

[18] Letter of July 17, 1894, quoted in Marchand 1996, 194.

[19] Marchand 1996, 212.

[20] Wiplinger and Wlach 1996, 8-9; Marchand 1996, 193. For concern that Austria was working in areas which should have been explored by British archaeologists: Macmillan 1891.

[21] Gates 1996.

associated with the excavations at Hisarlik.[22] The Americans under Howard Crosby Butler (1872-1922) of Princeton excavated the temple of Artemis at Sardis (1910-14), but the work was interrupted by the outbreak of the First World War.[23] Charles Eliot Norton had also hoped to excavate there.[24] The delicacy of archaeological excavation and survey in Anatolia in this period before the First World War is drawn out by the following tribute to Butler:

> It was the sterling integrity, as well as the consummate skill of Butler's work there which led to the highest distinction ever offered to an American and Christian explorer by a Mohammedan government, namely, the unsolicited invitation to enter and take command of the excavation of Sardis. The Turks knew they could trust Butler; they knew he was absolutely honorable.[25]

Asia Minor Exploration Fund

Students of the BSA had joined parties reaching deep inland from the very first session (1886/87), often using Smyrna as the starting-point. In some ways these expeditions find a parallel in the tours of the Austrians Otto Benndorf and Count Carl Lanckoronsky (1881-92).[26] David G. Hogarth, a future Director of the BSA, made the following observation: 'for the Ottoman Empire has been shut against the West so long and so closely that in many parts he [sc. 'The Scholar'] will find himself a pioneer breaking new ground for every science'.[27] The early British travellers were certainly penetrating what was still a closed country.

The search for new classical texts was one of the driving forces for archaeological surveys in the Ottoman Empire. A. H. Sayce had resigned his fellowship at Oxford in 1879 to allow him to travel in the countries bordering the eastern Mediterranean. He was able to visit the Troad, where he was shown round the excavations of Hisarlik by Frank Calvert,[28] before moving to Smyrna, where he met George Dennis.[29] Sayce travelled through Lydia making notes on Hittite monuments.[30]

Sayce had been instrumental in appointing William Mitchell Ramsay to an Oxford studentship which would allow him to conduct this archaeological work: 'I already saw in him [sc. Ramsay] a possible recruit for a scheme of exploration in Asia Minor which was already beginning to take shape in my own mind'.[31] This exploration was to be an extension of the work of the newly formed Society for the Promotion of Hellenic Studies;

---

[22] Allen 1999, 214-15.

[23] King 1983, 146.

[24] Dyson 1998, 166.

[25] *Dictionary of American Biography.*

[26] Wiplinger and Wlach 1996, 2.

[27] Hogarth 1925, 4.

[28] Sayce 1880; Sayce 1923, 161.

[29] Sayce 1923, 167.

[30] Sayce 1880.

[31] Sayce 1923, 158.

Sayce even had a vision for a British Archaeological School in Smyrna, a plan thwarted by the establishment of the BSA in 1886.[32] Ramsay's first trip to Anatolia was in May 1880,[33] and he reported on sites near Smyrna in the first volume of the *Journal of Hellenic Studies*.[34] Another British archaeological enterprise was the early systematic survey of eastern Cilicia by J. Theodore Bent, one of the pioneers of Aegean archaeology and a future member of the BSA's Managing Committee.[35] The inscriptions he noted were published by Hicks.[36]

Archaeological activity in Anatolia increased, and supported by the Asia Minor Exploration Fund founded in the summer of 1882.[37] Ramsay was joined by the Munich-educated J. R. Sitlington Sterrett, secretary of ASCSA (1883-84).[38] Sterrett made two important journeys, noting new inscriptions in 1884 and 1885;[39] in later life he recognised the importance of Anatolia as a source for new epigraphic material.[40] Ramsay was joined by Arthur Hamilton Smith (1860-1941), the future Keeper of Greek and Roman Antiquities at the British Museum in the summer of 1884;[41] Smith was supported by the Cambridge Worts Fund.[42] The *firman* had been awarded for work in Phrygia.[43]

The Asia Minor Exploration Fund also enabled students from the BSA to operate in Anatolia. One of the first BSA students was David G. Hogarth. In mid-May 1887, after working on Greek inscriptions at Salonica, he joined Ramsay and H. A. Brown ('an adventurous fellow who had spent part of his youth in Albania and Montenegro') for a journey across Anatolia.[44] Hogarth admitted: 'Our main purpose was to find inscriptions, and I was taught by precept and example how a villager may be induced to guide an inquisitive *giaur* into the recesses of his *haremlik*, or grub up the headstone of his forefather, or even saw away the floor of his mosque'.[45] The party equipped themselves with 'a single tent and a few pots and pans, but no canned stores; and two simple villagers

---

[32] Sayce 1923, 173.

[33] Rhodes 1973, 138; see also Sayce 1923, 173.

[34] Ramsay 1880.

[35] Bent 1890.

[36] Hicks 1890b.

[37] Sayce 1923, 173. The date is provided in Fergusson, *et al.* 1884. There was mention of the formation of the Fund at the Hellenic Society meeting of April 1882: Hellenic Society 1882, xxxviii. The initial sum raised was £520: Hellenic Society 1883b, xl; Fergusson, *et al.* 1884. George Macmillan was the honorary Treasurer and Secretary.

[38] Dyson 1998, 66-67; Lord 1947, 17, 358, 392.

[39] Sterrett 1888a; Sterrett 1888b.

[40] Sterrett 1911.

[41] Smith 1887.

[42] Hellenic Society 1884, xli.

[43] Ramsay 1883; Ramsay 1887.

[44] Hogarth 1910, 5; see also Hogarth 1888c.

[45] Hogarth 1910, 8.

were hired to serve us'.[46] The party took the train to Seraikeuy (Saraköy), exploring the site of ancient Mastaura near Nazli for an inscription, and riding along the Lycus valley to Hierapolis. The party then travelled up the Maeander valley: 'The land flowed with milk and honey if not much else, and I learned the grave courtesy of the Anatolian peasant'.[47] By mid-June they arrived as Afium Kara Hissar,[48] from where they were able to explore Phrygia. Hogarth described their work at Metropolis (Ayazini) and Kümbet (Meros):

> The haunted valley of Ayazin, where we grubbed mole-like under the face of a fallen tomb, and, prone in the shallow pit we had made, sketched the most curious of Phrygian reliefs: the sheer acropolis of Kumbet, where we planned a mysterious rock-house which may be of any antiquity; the gorges of Bakshish and Yapuldak, whose sculptured tombs, fashioned like houses of the living, are seen suddenly through the pines: that stupendous curtain of carved and written stone hung before the gate of death by which Midas the King passed to the Great Mother; all his desolate, impregnable city above it, with inscribed altars and rock reliefs.[49]

At the beginning of July Hogarth and Brown decided to travel to Cilicia while Ramsay returned home.[50] Their 'object was to reach Cilicia Tracheia by way of Phrygia Paroreus, and the Melas valley, pursuing in the former district a new route and especially selecting the unmapped and undescribed hill path from Ilghin to Konia'.[51] They travelled over the Taurus in a wagon and left by sea from the port of Akliman for Smyrna, via Castellórizo.[52]

Hogarth's Second Trip: 1890

Hogarth did not return for Anatolia for three years, although he was working on Cyprus as a member of the Cyprus Exploration Fund.[53] In 1890 he formed a group with Ramsay and the newly ordained Arthur C. Headlam (1862-1947), the future Bishop of Gloucester.[54] The plan was to strike further east and to explore some of the Hittite monuments. They took advantage of the extended Aydin railway line and travelled to Dineir (Dinar).[55] Their travels lasted for three months.

They travelled through Pisidia, revisiting sites familiar to Ramsay, and passed by the lake of Egerdir (Egirdir Gölü).[56] They then headed southwards, arriving at the ancient site

---

[46] Hogarth 1910, 5-6.

[47] Hogarth 1910, 7.

[48] Hogarth 1910, 9.

[49] Hogarth 1910, 9-10; see also Ramsay 1888; Ramsay 1889.

[50] Hogarth 1910, 11.

[51] Hogarth 1890, 151.

[52] Hogarth 1890, 157; see Hogarth 1910, 44.

[53] Plans for the trip were well developed by mid-January 1890: Macmillan 1890a.

[54] Hogarth 1910, preface for the mention of Headlam; see also Headlam 1892.

[55] Hogarth 1910, 12.

[56] Hogarth 1910, 13.

of Adada.[57] In spite of Hogarth's illness, they pressed on, crossing the Eurymedon,[58] and after making for Anamás Dagh and Beysehir Gölü,[59] they arrived at Konya. The party headed southwards into Cilicia, travelling down the Calycadnus valley,[60] visiting the Corycian cave. While Headlam stayed at Talas with American missionaries to recover his health,[61] Hogarth and Ramsay continued over the anti-Taurus to Gurun, where they were to study the Hittite material and 'discovered the Hittite relief of Fraktin'.[62] Ramsay returned westwards with the wagon containing the antiquities that they had acquired on their travels, while Hogarth and Headlam pressed on, studying the Hittite inscriptions of Bulgar Maden, before returning to Dineir.

Hogarth's Third Trip: 1891

Hogarth arrived at Mersina in June 1891 hoping to make a third trip with Ramsay.[63] Ramsay had already departed, but Hogarth and John A. R. Munro, along with Gregorios Antoniou, crossed the Aleian plain for the Taurus.[64] All three had worked on the excavations of the Cyprus Exploration Fund. They passed through Hajin, and then headed towards the region of Comana to make a study of the Roman road (and its milestones) that ran eastward to Melitene from Caesarea Mazaca.[65]

After completing the study of the Roman remains (at Arabissos), they were able to concentrate on Hittite relics. They went on to visit Albistan, and passed southwards through the Taurus via Zeitun to Marash in Commagene. Unfortunately the Hittite remains that they had hoped to see had been 'spirited away' to North America.[66] In spite of an injury sustained from falling from a horse, Hogarth and the rest of the party headed across the Taurus through the Pyramus gorge.[67] They were detained for a while at Derendeh due to a cordon to prevent the spread of cholera. The party travelled to Sivas, and followed the Halys valley to Zara, and north-eastwards to Nicopolis.[68] They headed along the Lycus valley reaching Neocaesareia, travelling south-westwards to Comana Pontica, following the Iris valley to Amaseia.[69] They then followed the Roman road north-westwards passing the baths of Phazemon and thence to the Black Sea. This visit through Pontus inspired Munro to return to make a study of the road

---

[57] Hogarth 1910, 13-14.

[58] Hogarth 1910, 14.

[59] Hogarth 1910, 15.

[60] Hogarth 1910, 15.

[61] Hogarth 1910, 15.

[62] Hogarth 1910, 15-16.

[63] Hogarth 1910, 16. For the appeal for this project: Macmillan 1891.

[64] See also Yorke 1898.

[65] Hogarth 1910, 16-17; Munro and Hogarth 1893.

[66] Hogarth 1910, 17.

[67] Hogarth 1910, 17.

[68] Hogarth 1910, 18.

[69] Hogarth 1910, 18.

system.[70] The Hittite 'finds' were quickly publicised in *The Times*.[71] The report also draws attention to the travellers' keenness to acquire finds along the way.

Hogarth on the Upper Euphrates

After excavating in Egypt, and preparing a survey on the possibility of work in Alexandria, Hogarth left for eastern Turkey in the spring of 1894.[72] He had hoped to excavate at either Lystra or Derbe, 'the examination of which may be expected to throw light on problems of early Christianity'.[73] His aim was to return to England in time for his marriage in November. The party, consisting of Hogarth, Vincent W. Yorke (in his second year at the BSA), Vicount Encombe and Lt. F. W. Green, arrived by sea at Mersina and travelled by the newly constructed railway line to Adana.[74] The group headed eastwards first to Aintab (Gaziantep),[75] reaching the river Euphrates, then in spate over the melt of the winter snows, near the town of Khalfat 'an hour' downstream from Rumkale.[76] This part of the journey had already been documented by the Germans Carl Humann, Otto Puchstein and Felix Von Luschan in their 1883 expedition to Nemrud Dagh; indeed the Asia Minor Exploration Fund was concerned that this British project could be 'transferred to foreign hands'.[77]

The party recrossed the river at Samsat, noting the start of the great route to India.[78] Hogarth commented on the remains of the ancient Samosata:

> Hardly a hundred huts huddle in one corner of the old site, marked now by the line of the Roman fosse, by a ruined wall and by gaunt fragments of rubble. A black stone with Hittite inscription, defaced even more hopelessly than other monuments of its class, lies face downwards where the flocks are milked; two tiles of the 'Steadfast Flavian Legion XVI' and a soldier's dedicatory altar were disinterred for us from heaps of kitchen refuse; there are some trivial Greek inscriptions in mud walls and in the castle ruins.[79]

[70] Munro 1900; Munro 1901; see also Anderson 1900; Cumont and Anderson 1912.

[71] 'Hittite discoveries in Asia Minor', *The Times* 25 July 1891, 5; 28 July 1891, 13.

[72] The appeal for funds went out in November 1893: 'Asia Minor Exploration Fund', *The Times* 15 November 1893, 14.

[73] Macmillan 1893.

[74] Yorke 1896b, 318. The journey was described in Hogarth's chapter, 'The great river Euphrates': Hogarth 1925, 66-96; see also Yorke 1896b; Yorke 1898.

[75] Yorke 1896b, 320.

[76] Hogarth 1925, 69; Yorke 1896b, 321.

[77] 'Asia Minor Exploration Fund', *The Times* 15 November 1893, 14. See also Marchand 1996, 92-94.

[78] Hogarth 1925, 71.

[79] Hogarth 1925, 72; see Yorke 1896b, 322; Yorke 1898, nos. 14-18.

At this point the party split in two. Beyond Samsat, Hogarth noted remains of an aqueduct crossing the tributaries of the Euphrates.[80] The party was prevented from following the course of the river as the road had been eroded away, and so decided to head north.[81] Near Nemrud Ddagh, the group came across a Roman bridge at Kiakhta (now the Cendere Köprüsü over the Cendere Çay),[82]

> with hardly a stone displaced. The single arch spans one hundred and twelve feet, and the keystone is fifty-six feet above mean water-level. Three columns are erect at the ends of the balustrade, graven by the four cities of Commagene with dedications to the Emperor Septimius Severus, his wife, and his son Caracalla: the fourth column, which bore Geta's name, was removed after his murder.[83]

Hogarth then took a difficult path through the Taurus mountains rather than taking the advice of his Cilician muleteers, who preferred the road along the river.[84] The party arrived at Malatya, quarantined because of a cholera outbreak just to the north.[85] The Arapkir (Arabkir) road was to the north was still open, and so they pressed on, rejoining the Euphrates near the fords of the Kuruchai.[86] Hogarth caught site of the Dersim massif, where only a year before a Turkish army unit from Erzincan had been annihilated by the local people.[87] The party proceeded to follow the northern stream of the Euphrates, known as the Murad, above the Keban Maden (now under the Keban Dam).[88] They thus made their way to Erzincan, observing the occasional piece of Roman paved road and two bridges.[89]

After Erzincan, the party made its way through the pass of Sipikor, recalling 'a little of the sense of escape which made Xenophon's weary Greeks raise their shout from a point a little further north on this same road'.[90] They passed through Sadagh (Satala), which according to the extant inscriptions was the fortress of the XV Legion Apollinaris:[91] 'the ground-plan of the wall with its square towers remains on the north and the east, and in the modern hamlet of Sadagh were preserved half a dozen tiles of LEGIO XV

---

[80] Hogarth 1925, 72-73.

[81] Hogarth 1925, 73.

[82] See also Sanders and Gill 2004.

[83] Hogarth 1925, 75; Yorke 1896b, 322-23.

[84] See also Yorke 1896b, 324.

[85] Hogarth 1925, 79-80.

[86] Hogarth 1925, 82.

[87] Hogarth 1925, 82-83. The defeat had been at the hands of the Kurds.

[88] Hogarth 1925, 85.

[89] Hogarth 1925, 87-88.

[90] Hogarth 1925, 94-95; see also Yorke 1896b, 459.

[91] Yorke 1896b, 460; Yorke 1898, no. 36.

APOLLINARIS'.[92] The trip ended in mid-June at Trebizond, where the party then boarded a ship that took them to Constantinople.[93]

Surveys with Students of the British School

Following the journeys of Hogarth and Munro, there seems to have been a concerted effort to make studies of specific areas of Anatolia. Pairs of travellers, often students at the BSA, would make sweeps though the countryside, making special note of inscriptions. The ancient routes across Asia Minor that were known from historical accounts were plotted.[94] The knowledge gained from such travels was brought together in John G. C. Anderson's *Map of Asia Minor*.[95]

Phrygia

Phrygia had been one of the areas explored by Ramsay.[96] John G. C. Anderson initiated a study in 1897, during his first year as a student at the BSA.[97] Among the sites he visited was Altyn Tash on the road to Kutahya. In 1898 Anderson and John W. Crowfoot, both Oxford-educated, revisited the area to make a study of two inscriptions located on the north side of Mount Dindymos (Murad Dagh = now Kartal T.).[98] On their way to Galatia they stopped at Böyuk Tchobanlar (Çobanlar) on the north side of the Akkar Tchai (Kaystros).[99] By the river they recorded an inscription of Marcus Aurelius erected by the demos of Eulandra, thus fixing the location of the city known from a fifth century AD bishopric.[100]

After passing through Afyon Kara Hissar, Anderson and Crowfoot visited Aï-kürük, just to then north-west of Altintas, where new discoveries had been reported. They noted that an ancient cemetery had been uncovered and stones were being removed for the construction of a mosque.[101] They explored the region to the south of ancient Aezani. At Ören they found some late antique remains including inscriptions.[102] At Aezani they noted architectural fragments, and made a study of the Steunos cave, sacred to Cybele.[103] They travelled to Kutahya, recording previously identified inscriptions.[104]

---

[92] Hogarth 1925, 88.

[93] Hogarth 1925, 88; Yorke 1896b, 318, 462.

[94] *E.g.* Anderson 1897a.

[95] See Calder and Bean 1958.

[96] *E.g.* Ramsay 1888; Ramsay 1889; Hogarth 1890.

[97] Anderson 1897b; Anderson 1898a; Anderson 1898b.

[98] Anderson 1898b; Anderson 1897/8, 49-50.

[99] Anderson 1897/8, 50.

[100] Anderson 1897/8, 50-51.

[101] Anderson 1897/8, 51-52.

[102] Anderson 1897/8, 54.

[103] Paus. 8. 4. 3 and 10. 32. 3; Anderson 1897/8, 55.

[104] Anderson 1897/8, 57.

Galatia

After the exploration of Phrygia in 1897, Anderson and Crowfoot set off for Galatia in 1898 as part of the project supported by the Asia Minor Exploration Fund.[105] Crowfoot had been admitted for a second year at the BSA, and had spent part of his time excavating on the British Museum's excavation near Larnaka. Together they set out from Smyrna in mid-May, taking the railway to Dinêr (presumably Dinar), the site of ancient Apameia.[106]

After a detour to Phrygia, the pair set out in a south-easterly direction from Afyon Kara Hisar towards Aksheir. Anderson noted: 'This district is practically a complete blank in the maps and many parts of it have never been trodden by any traveller, so that we take the chance of describing our routes here in detail'.[107] They skirted the 'Salt Desert', and noted a third century AD dedication to Mên at Selmea. They journeyed on to Angora (Ankara) in order to meet H. S. Shipley, the British Consul who was leaving, so that they could obtain the necessary permits. From Ankara they turned westwards towards Juliopolis to locate towns along its way,[108] then to the south in the region of Mihaliçcik. Anderson and Crowfoot separated in order to cover more ground. On returning to Angora they set out for Pessinus, and south-eastwards to Late Tatta (Tuz Gölü), previously visited by W. F. Ainsworth (1839) and F. Sarre (1895). Anderson later made a study of cult in the Roman province of Galatia.[109]

Pisidia

Expeditions to Pisidia and Pamphylia were mounted by the Austrians in 1884 and 1885.[110] A party led by Ramsay and including H. S. Cronin and G. A. Wathen travelled through Pisidia, Lycaonia and Pamphylia in the summer of 1901.[111] Arthur M. Woodward noted a number of inscriptions in the summer of 1911.[112] That same summer Ramsay made a study of the Roman colony of Pisidian Antioch and the extra mural sanctuary of Mên Askaênos.[113] Anderson made a special study of the agonistic festival attached to the sanctuary,[114] though he probably dated the festival later than was necessary. The survey noted a large number of inscriptions from the colony that provided rich material for further epigraphic work,[115] some of which has continued since the Second World War.[116]

[105] Anderson 1899; Crowfoot 1899.

[106] Anderson 1897/8.

[107] Anderson 1897/8, 58-59.

[108] See Crowfoot 1897/8.

[109] Anderson 1910.

[110] Wiplinger and Wlach 1996, 10.

[111] Cronin 1902; Ramsay 1902/03.

[112] Woodward 1910/11a.

[113] Hardie 1912. For a more recent assessment: Mitchell and Waelkens 1998.

[114] Anderson 1913.

[115] *E.g.* Cheesman 1913; Ramsay 1916' see also Cumont and Anderson 1912.

[116] *E.g.* Levick 1958. For the colony now see Mitchell and Waelkens 1998.

Pamphylia

Ramsay travelled to Pamphylia in 1880.[117] Subsequently there had been two Austrian expeditions to the region, made via Antalya, in 1884 and 1885.[118] Ramsay revisited the area in the summer of 1901,[119] and Hogarth landed there in the cruise of the 'Utowana'.[120] Minor work was conducted as an adjunct to the more detailed work of Lycia.[121]

Caria

Thanks to an inheritance, William Roger Paton (1857-1921) was able to travel to the Mediterranean in 1880 after reading classics at Magdalen College, Oxford.[122] Part of the reason for his travels was the search for new inscriptions. His most substantial epigraphic study was that of material from the island of Kos, co-written by Edward Lee Hicks, which appeared as *Inscriptions of Cos* (1891).[123] During a stay on the island of Kalymnos, then part of the Ottoman Empire, he had fallen in love with Irene, the daughter of Emanuel Olympitis, mayor of the island. They married, and one of their married homes was at Gumishlu on the Bodrum peninsula and near the site of ancient Myndus.

Iasos was one of the sites that interested Paton, and some of the epigraphic material was studied by E. L. Hicks.[124] However the site was being looted, and Paton turned his attention to Assarlik, presenting some of the finds to the British Museum. Paton then turned his attention to Ceramus on the north coast of the Gulf of Kos.[125] He was able to make copies of a number of inscriptions, which were published by E. L. Hicks.[126]

Although Paton was never an official student of the BSA, he is listed as a subscriber. In 1893 Ernest Gardner, BSA Director, arranged for John L. Myres to work with Paton on a survey of the Bodrum peninsula.[127] Paton continued his surveys and visited Grion and Latmos in September and October 1893,[128] the Latomos range in the summer of 1896, and later eastern Caria and southern Lydia.[129]

---

[117] Ramsay 1880.

[118] Wiplinger and Wlach 1996, 10.

[119] Cronin 1902.

[120] Hogarth 1910, 115.

[121] Ormerod and Robinson 1910/11; Ormerod 1912; Robinson 1914.

[122] Gill 2004n.

[123] See also Hicks 1888.

[124] Paton 1887; Paton 1889; Hicks 1887a.

[125] Paton 1888.

[126] Hicks 1890a.

[127] Paton and Myres 1896; Paton and Myres 1897; Paton and Myres 1898.

[128] Paton and Myres 1897, 53.

[129] Paton 1900.

Mysia

Munro turned his attention away from eastern Anatolia to Mysia. His first trip was made in the autumn of 1894,[130] accompanied by Professor William C. F. Anderson of Firth College, Sheffield, and H. M. Anthony of Lincoln College, Oxford. The party headed westwards from Brusa (Bursa) to the city of Apollonia (by Ulubat Gölü), where a number of inscriptions were observed.[131] Munro noted:

> Apollonia is full of relics of antiquity. Every second house has its "ancient stone", either built into the wall or put to some base purpose, and numerous coins and gems are offered for sale.[132]

The party recorded boundary stones (*horoi*) near the lake,[133] and where the road crossed the river Rhyndacus they could see the old bridge.[134] At Omar Keui they observed a Roman milestone marked VIII, presumably the distance from Cyzicus.[135] They reached Panderma (Panormus) and visited the site of Cyzicus (discussed below).[136]

The party then headed southwards round the lake of Manias (Kus Gölü). In the midst of a Byzantine fortress, they noted an honorific inscription probably dating from 42 BC.[137] As there was no obvious local source for the inscriptions, they speculated that the inscriptions may have been brought from Cyzicus, and that the fortress was that of Lentiana.[138] The party followed the Macestus valley southwards towards Balukiser (Balikesir), noting a series of milestones on the road from Miletopolis to Balikesir.[139] Munro commented that the natural route formed by the valley: 'It is even proposed to extend the Soma branch of the Smyrna and Kassaba railway by this route to the north coast'.[140] A ten or twelve arched Roman bridge between Susurlu (Susurluk) and Sultan Chair (Sultançayiri) seemed to them to indicate a branch of the road, guarded by a Byzantine fort. In the region of Balikesir they searched for traces of the settlement of Hadrianutherae, known from the Peutinger Table. The third part of their journey explored 'The Hill Country between the Rhyndacus and the Macestus', reaching as far as Tavshanli (Tavsanli) just to the west of Kütahya. Munro and W. C. F. Anderson made a further trip to Mysia in September 1896.[141]

---

[130] Munro and Anthony 1897b; Munro and Anthony 1897a; Munro 1897.

[131] Munro and Anthony 1897b, 152.

[132] Munro and Anthony 1897b, 154.

[133] Munro and Anthony 1897b, 154.

[134] Munro and Anthony 1897b, 156.

[135] Munro and Anthony 1897b, 158.

[136] Munro and Anthony 1897b, 158.

[137] Munro and Anthony 1897b, 160.

[138] Munro and Anthony 1897b, 160-61.

[139] Munro and Anthony 1897b, 163.

[140] Munro and Anthony 1897b, 163.

[141] Munro 1897.

Prospecting for Excavations

The idea of excavating in Anatolia coincided with a growing general interest in the region. The interest is reflected by the preparation of the Murray *Handbook*, with contributions by D. G. Hogarth and W. M. Ramsay.[142]

Colophon

At some point under Ernest Gardner, Hamdi Bey, Director of the Imperial Museums in Constantinople, had offered Colophon as a potential site to excavate.[143] Edwin Egerton, the British Minister at Athens, announced to the Annual Meeting of the BSA in July 1895 'that in Asia Minor Hamdi Bey would gladly see the British School working on a promising site'.[144] It was suggested in October 1896 that Colophon be considered as a site to excavate after the completion of Melos, and Harcourt-Smith was asked to enquire about a *firman* and to inspect the site. As Harcourt-Smith's term of office drew to a close in the spring of 1897, he joined the steam yacht *Rona,* belonging to Baron Ferdinand de Rothschild, a major donor to the BSA.[145] Rothschild had left Marseilles with Christopher Sykes, 'for Naples, on the way to Palermo, Corfu, and Athens'.[146] Harcourt-Smith is likely to have joined the *Rona* in Athens and then sailed to Salonica, Athos, Samos, and Patmos. In particular Harcourt-Smith visited Colophon in western Anatolia and prepared a report on the potential for excavation; by April he was keen for the BSA to excavate there.[147] Indeed it was clear that this was a project for Hogarth alongside his Lydian work.[148] An approach was made to Hamdi Bey and a *firman* obtained.[149] In June 1897 there was still a keenness to excavate at Colophon but no decision was taken.[150] Despite the fact that the excavation never started, Hogarth pressed to work there in 1910.[151] The Americans also considered Colophon a suitable site to excavate though the work did not start until after the First World War in 1922, and quickly came to a halt due to events in Anatolia.[152]

[142] Wilson 1895.

[143] BSA Minute Book 2, Meeting of 30 October 1896. It mentions the offer had been made 'some years ago'. For an obituary of Hamdi Bey: *The Times* 26 February 1910, 13.

[144] 'The British School at Athens', *The Times* 10 July 1895, 10.

[145] BSA Minute Book 2, Meeting of 15 March 1897.

[146] Reported in the *Pall Mall Gazette* 2 January 1897. The *Rona* had been built in 1896.

[147] BSA Minute Book 2, Meeting of 8 April 1897.

[148] BSA Minute Book 2, Meeting of 17 June 1897.

[149] BSA Minute Book 2, Meeting of 24 June 1897. See also Waterhouse 1986, 22.

[150] BSA Minute Book 2, Meetings of 17 and 24 June 1897.

[151] BSA Minute Book 6, Meeting of 25 October 1910. Sir Frederic Kenyon was still pressing for the British to excavate at Colopon in June 1921: 'Hellenic research', *The Times* 29 June 1921, 7.

[152] Lord 1947, 142-43; Dyson 1998, 82, 92-93.

Lycia

British interest in Lycia can be traced back to the travels of (Sir) Charles Fellows (1799-1860), who first arrived in Smyrna in 1838.[153] After raising funds from the British Government, Fellows and George Scharf returned to Lycia in 1839. A major expedition, including British sailors, arrived at Xanthos in the spring of 1842. A fourth visit to Xanthos took place in late 1843. The sculptures were arranged in a 'Lycian Gallery' at the British Museum which opened to the public in December 1847.[154]

Lycia was considered as a possible location for an excavation by the BSA in October 1896.[155] Hogarth was requested to make a survey of possible sites, which might lead to the formation of an excavation fund.[156] He formed a party including the Oxford-educated John G. C. Anderson, then Craven Fellow at the BSA.[157] This expedition took place in the late spring of 1897, coinciding with the thirty day war between Greece and Turkey following uprisings on Crete.

The party set out from Smyrna, and sailed to the island of Castellórizo to the east of Rhodes, and just off the coast of Lycia. Its members hired a fishing-boat to take them across the mainland, landing near the Lycian cemetery of Aperlae.[158] On visiting Myra, Hogarth observed, 'we roamed about the vaults and horseshoe of the great Theatre, and climbed unwatched the rock-cut stairway which leads to the great carved cliff of tombs'.[159] The party hired horses and were able to visit Patara and Xanthos.[160] At the latter Hogarth was able to observe the stakes that Fellows had used on the Harpy tomb after removing the frieze.[161] Hogarth felt Xanthos was 'the most promising & most practicable' of the sites he examined,[162] and it was ear-marked for future excavation: 'Some day a digger will get a rich booty at Xanthus'.[163] In the end excavations did not take place, though the offer for funding had remained.[164]

There was a proposal to excavate at Xanthos or another site in Lycia in 1901, a time that coincided with the other British exploration at Cyzicus, but the planned excavations never came to fruition due to the new access to sites on Crete following the occupation by the international powers. Hogarth's party concluded its expedition to Lycia by returning to

---

[153] Jenkins 1992, 140-53; Challis 2008, 23-39.

[154] Jenkins 1992, 152; Challis 2008, 40-54.

[155] BSA Minute Book 2, Meeting of 30 October 1896. The BSA was offered £200 towards the excavation of Xanthus 'or any other important city in Lycia' by W. Arkwright of Newbury.

[156] Hogarth 1910, 43.

[157] Hogarth 1910, preface.

[158] Hogarth 1910, 47-48.

[159] Hogarth 1910, 49.

[160] Hogarth 1910, 53.

[161] Hogarth 1910, 62, and pl.

[162] BSA Minute Book 2, Meeting of 27 May 1897.

[163] Hogarth 1910, 63.

[164] BSA Minute Book 2, Meeting of 15 March 1897.

Rhodes. Hogarth returned to Lycia in the spring of 1904 aboard the yacht *Utowana*, owned by Mr Allison V. Armour.[165] Other members of the party included Richard Norton (a former student at ASCSA), A. W. van Buren and C. D. Curtis. The party started on the west coast of Anatolia, visiting Didyma, Iasus, Bargylia, Bodrum, Knidos, Loryma and Rhodes.[166] The *Utowana* travelled along the coast of Lycia, visiting some of the major cities, and on to Pamphylia.[167] At the Eurymedon they landed to see the ruins of Aspendos, where Hogarth observed the theatre had 'the grandeur of scale which excites fancy, and that perfection in survival which, lulling the sense of strangeness, allows fancy to leap unastonished across the centuries'.[168] They sailed eastwards to Old Adalia, finding Cretan refugees camped out among the ruins of Side.[169] After sailing on to Cilicia and Cyprus, the party headed for Cyrenaica.[170]

Cyzicus

The excavating strategy of the BSA changed in 1900. David Hogarth resigned as BSA Director, and joined the Cretan Exploration Fund as one of the Directors. Crete, now protected by international forces, was open for excavations, though, for the British, this meant under the patronage of Arthur Evans. The main British excavations at Phylakopi on the island of Melos had been concluded, and so Anatolia was considered as a possible area for future work. Munro's expedition to Mysia in 1894 had observed Cyzicus:

> The site of Cyzicus … has been for so many centuries a quarry for building-stone that little is now standing above ground. The level ground is one big garden of vines and fruit-trees – olives, walnuts, peaches, and cherries. The bay tree grows wild in such profusion that the air is scented with its perfume. Inscribed or carved stones, plundered from the site, are to be found in most of the neighbouring villages. At Edinjik especially there are many inscriptions, and the wooden columns which support the upper chambers over the public "exchange" rest upon inverted capitals.[171]

The BSA had been approached by R. de Rustafjaell in the spring of 1901 to see if they would be willing to work with him at Cyzicus.[172]

In early December 1901 a small party from the BSA set sail on the SS *Electra* as part of an expedition to explore Cyzicus. Bosanquet, the Director, observed 'swarms of interesting deck passengers, Albanians and Bosniaks, mainly Moslem lads going to work

---

[165] Hogarth 1910, preface, 108.

[166] Hogarth 1910, 108.

[167] Hogarth 1910, 115.

[168] Hogarth 1910, 118-19.

[169] Hogarth 1910, 121.

[170] Hogarth 1910, 122.

[171] Munro and Anthony 1897b, 158.

[172] BSA Minute Book 3, Meeting of 25 April 1901.

at Constantinople'.[173] The party formed at the Pera Palace hotel in Constantinople, consisting of Bosanquet, R. de Rustafjaell, F. W. Hasluck, Amadura ('a clean English-bred Italian'), and Thompson ('speaks Turkish fluently and knows all the ropes and remains pleasantly British in spite of it'). Bosanquet described Hasluck as 'splendid and sticks to his business in spite of all temptations to consort with other nations – Italian concessionaires with diamond studs and "that lot"'.[174] They boarded the SS *Volga*, a 'steamer even smaller and more squalid than the Greek coasters; like them, Clyde-built'. Bosanquet and Hasluck travelled light, 'in the hardy Athenian plan … a kitbag and holdall apiece'.[175] They travelled via Bandirma, where Bosanquet was identified as a spy, and on by sailing caique.[176]

Bosanquet made the observation: 'The peninsula is a big hilly region, looking much bigger than it did on the map …'.[177] The expedition set up base in the village of Yenikeni, in 'a trim clean timber-house, with glass sash windows and spotless lilac cotton curtains, chairs and floor rugs and divans and all manner'.[178] The stores were 'Armier and Navier even than the stock we took to Praesos' (Bosanquet's excavation in eastern Crete), and Bosanquet bewailed the fact that the marmalade 'isn't a patch on our own British School Home-made'.[179] The team was assisted by a Kurd, Ali, 'a handsome honest active man, in the richly embroidered khaki livery these Constantinople servants delight to wear – lots of black braid, relieved with touches of gold'. Hasluck and Bosanquet made an initial survey: '[we] walked over part of the site before luncheon and we have all spent a long afternoon there'.[180] One of the first monuments to be studied was the theatre. Bosanquet observed, 'Its outline is clear, but like all the other heaps of ruins it is a mass of undergrowth, chiefly bay trees'.[181] Elsewhere on the site, there was 'Marble everywhere, mutilated fragments of architecture and sculpture in the walls, strewn about the fields, even embedded in the roads.'

The following day they looked 'at the great sarcophagus', and rode on to the ancient Artake (modern Erdek), to the west, to observe ancient marble quarries.[182] On the Saturday Bosanquet and Hasluck studied 'the Poseidon monument, a pedestal or altar with tridents and fish and galleys thereon'. Hasluck and Bosanquet

> took the village watchman, a Tcherkess from the Caucasus, who patrols the fields armed with an old musket, and went to the amphitheatre, a most beautiful spot outside the walls. A stream has burst through the mighty fence and careers through

---

[173] Bosanquet 1938, 92.

[174] Bosanquet 1938, 94, 4 December 1901.

[175] Bosanquet 1938, 94, 4 December 1901.

[176] Bosanquet 1938, 95, 5 December 1901.

[177] Bosanquet 1938, 95, 5 December 1901.

[178] Bosanquet 1938, 95.

[179] Bosanquet 1938, 98.

[180] Bosanquet 1938, 96.

[181] Bosanquet 1938, 96, 5 December 1901.

[182] See Munro and Anthony 1897b, 158.

the arena; a great part of the walls has fallen; but great piles of masonry still tower
to heaven, and the hillsides are full of overgrown vaults; the whole hollow is a
mass of luxuriant thickets, bay, arbutus, ivy and honeysuckle; sprays of unripe
blackberries hang over the water.[183]

A full report was prepared by Bosanquet for the meeting of the Managing Committee in
January 1902.[184] The main sticking point was clearly de Rustafjaell; Bosanquet wrote:

> The real difficulty is that of exporting antiquities. ... This contravention of the
> *firman* is an essential part of his (Mr de R's) scheme.

The committee was reluctant to move ahead with de Rustafjaell as a partner if the export of
antiquities was being considered. Although he was given an opportunity to respond to the
concerns, de Rustafjaell failed to comment.[185] In spite of this Hasluck and Arthur E.
Henderson went to Cyzicus to make a systematic study of the city.[186] De Rustafjaell also
published on the topography site as well as the inscriptions;[187] his rights to excavate the site
came to an end in February 1903.[188] The Managing Committee decided not to pursue any
excavations at Cyzicus, in part because Bosanquet was heavily committed in eastern Crete.

Hasluck continued to visit Mysia after the Cyzicus expedition. He travelled through the
area with Dawkins in the summer of 1906,[189] noting a bridge on the Aesepus,[190] and in
1907 Hasluck visited the Marmara islands.[191] This research came to fruition in a
monograph on the city of Cyzicus.[192] The area was also visited by E. L. Hicks in April
1907 as part of a party from the *Argonaut* (with F. G. Harman and J. Alison Glover).[193]
The party started at Troy and then moved to Brusa.

The growing interest in Anatolia

The possibility of excavating at Cyzicus had reminded the BSA of the potential of Anatolia.
In 1903, Alan J. B. Wace observed in a report on 'Recent excavations in Asia Minor',

---

[183] Bosanquet 1938, 98, 7 December 1901.

[184] BSA Minute Book 4, Meeting of 30 January 1902.

[185] BSA Minute Book 4, Meeting of 6 March 1902.

[186] Hasluck 1901/02; Hasluck 1902; Hasluck 1903; Hasluck and Henderson 1904; Hasluck 1904;
Hasluck 1904/05.

[187] Rustafjaell 1902; Smith and de Rustafjaell 1902.

[188] BSA Minute Book 4, Meeting of 12 February 1903.

[189] Dawkins and Hasluck 1905/06; Hasluck 1906b; Hasluck 1906a; Hasluck 1907.

[190] Hasluck 1905/06.

[191] Hasluck 1909.

[192] Hasluck 1910.

[193] Hicks 1907.

> I should like in particular to direct the attention of English archaeologists to Western Asia Minor as a field of research that is practically untouched, especially as regards the remains of the Hellenistic period.[194]

Wace was observing the large-scale excavations by the German and Austrian Schools of Archaeology at major classical sites like Miletus, Didyma, Ephesus, and Pergamum. In contrast the excavations of the BSA were on less spectacular sites, with the exception of Knossos. Wace, who had a major interest in Hellenistic sculpture, no doubt had in mind large-scale excavations on prestige sites. Alexander Stuart Murray, Keeper of the Department of Greek and Roman Antiquities at the British Museum, had been keen to re-open the Museum's excavations at Ephesus, work that went ahead under the direction of David G. Hogarth a year after Murray's premature death in 1904.[195] Yet this lack of organized British excavations disguises the regular expeditions by British archaeologists to different parts of Anatolia.

David Hogarth and Ephesus

British excavations at Ephesus had been suspended in 1874, but A. S. Murray, the Keeper of Greek and Roman Antiquities at the British Museum, had hopes of resuming the work.[196] In spite of Murray's untimely death in March 1904, Hogarth resumed the excavation of Ephesus in the September of that year.[197] The time was right as the British Museum had been supporting excavations on Cyprus (again using students from the BSA). Working on the flooded excavations brought its own problems, and Hogarth looked enviously at the concession made to the Austrian archaeological mission.[198] At the end of the year Hogarth dug through the structure known as the 'Great Altar', discovering some gold offerings and even electrum coins.[199] Hogarth reckoned that he transferred 'more than half a thousand jewels' to the museum in Constantinople by the middle of December.[200]

Hogarth returned to excavate in the spring of 1905. Among his team was A. E. Henderson who had worked with Hasluck at Cyzicus in 1904, and before that at Carchemish from 1878 to 1881.[201] Finding the site flooded, Hogarth borrowed a steam engine and pump from the Ottoman Railway Company.[202] In spite of illness, Hogarth pressed on with the excavations, finding a series of archaic objects in the lower levels, notably a pot containing nineteen electrum coins.[203] The finds were removed to London

---

[194] Wace 1903, 335.

[195] Thompson 1903/4.

[196] Thompson 1903/4. For the earlier work: Challis 2008, 117-39.

[197] Hogarth 1925, 232.

[198] Hogarth 1925, 236.

[199] Hogarth 1925, 237-38.

[200] Hogarth 1925, 240.

[201] Hogarth 1910, preface; Winstone 1990, 26-27.

[202] Hogarth 1925, 240-41.

[203] Hogarth 1925, 243.

for a year for study purposes.[204] Publication of the excavation followed soon after, and Hogarth's interest in the Greeks in western Anatolia was presented in a series of lectures to the University of London and appeared as *Ionia and the East*.[205] Further work in Ionia was clearly envisaged by the BSA.

Lycia

British interest in Lycia was renewed with a visit by Arthur M. Woodward in 1909 in a search for new inscriptions. In May 1910 Woodward, now the Assistant Director of the BSA, and Henry A. Ormerod set out for Lycia via Smyrna and Adalia.[206] One of the main aims of the expedition was to look for prehistoric sites; and Ormerod had gained experience, working with Wace and Thompson in northern Greece. While at Antalya they identified an inscription recording the capture of Antalya in 1361.[207] Woodward and Ormerod headed westwards for Termessos, though they made no detailed study as they felt that since it was in easy reach of Antalya, others could do the work. They followed the road westwards to Isinda, and then struck south-westwards to Elmali, north past Lake Karalitis, and north-westwards to Denizli. After visiting Hierapolis, they took the train to Smyrna. They were able to identify some twenty prehistoric mounds, plus a number of historic sites.[208] Ormerod continued to take an interest in Lycia,[209] especially as his research into pirates developed.[210]

Datcha

After the success of the excavations in Laconia, Dawkins was considering new possibilities. One of the sites considered was at Datcha near Knidos. The site had been explored by Captain T. A. B. Spratt RN on his survey of western Anatolia.[211] One of the people behind the proposed Datcha excavation was William R. Paton, who lived nearby and who had discovered some terracotta relief pithoi at the site during the 1880s.[212] Theodore Bent had an agent operating at Datcha who brought a number of inscriptions to his attention.[213] Datcha was considered to be the site of the ancient city of Stadia.[214]

In the autumn of 1907, Paton wrote to the BSA committee about the possibility of excavating at Datcha:

---

[204] Hogarth 1925, 244.

[205] Hogarth 1908; Hogarth 1908; Hogarth 1909.

[206] Woodward and Ormerod 1909/10.

[207] Hasluck 1909/10.

[208] *BSA Annual Report* for 1909/10, 295

[209] Ormerod 1911/12; Ormerod 1912/13; Ormerod and Robinson 1914; see also Robinson 1914.

[210] Ormerod 1922; Ormerod 1924.

[211] Noted by Hasluck 1911/12a, 211.

[212] Reported in *AJA* 6, 4 (1890), 551. For Paton: Gill 2004n.

[213] Hicks 1889, 234.

[214] Hasluck 1911/12a.

Mr Paton has written to urge the necessity of excavating, or at least of preventing piracy, in Kalymnos & the Knidian Chersonese. Some of the inhabitants have got a permit for excavation and Mr Paton suggests that the School might work, for the present, under the same permit. The Secretary has guaranteed "a small sum" for immediate expenses. Mr Paton wants someone to come at once from the BSA to view the site and see what can be done.[215]

Hasluck had hoped to visit the site with Paton in the autumn of 1907 but due to serious illness was unable to go.[216] Dawkins went instead and a report was considered at the January 1908 meeting of the Managing Committee:

The Director, accompanied by Mr M. S. Thompson, explored the site identified with Akanthos, on the S. side of the Cnidian peninsula. Some digging has already been done there by Panaghiotis Polemitios.

A walled acropolis can be plainly seen and a "Sacred" Way can be traced. There are also fragments of various ruined walls visible and some stray carvings and inscriptions. The finds of Polematios' consist of small pottery, (figurines and Vases) and of bronze and stone objects.

The Director considers this a good site, which would repay excavation. It would be necessary to build a house, and all communication would be by sailing boats to Syme.[217]

Nothing more was done while the Laconian excavations continued. The possibility of excavating at Datcha resurfaced in October 1910, when the Managing Committee was looking for a new site.[218]

Dawkins revisited the site and prepared a report that was considered at a meeting of the Managing committee in January 1911.[219] A decision was taken to excavate, a budget set at £100 and an application for a *firman* was made.[220] The start of the excavation was delayed 'owing to the political situation' which led to the outbreak of the First Balkan War in October 1912.[221] Dawkins hoped to recruit Gregori, who was working with Hogarth at Carchemish. He also hoped that Leonard Woolley would join the team.[222] This decision was reported at the Annual Meeting of Subscribers in November 1911:

---

[215] BSA Minute Book 5, Meeting of 29 October 1907. For Paton: Gill 2004n.

[216] BSA Minute Book 5, Meeting of 17 November 1907.

[217] BSA Minute Book 5, Meeting of 21 January 1908.

[218] BSA Minute Book 6, Meeting of 4 October 1910. The other possibilities included work on Cyprus, North Africa or to return to Phylakopi. See also Hasluck 1911/12a.

[219] BSA Minute Book 6, Meeting of 24 January 1911.

[220] BSA Minute Book 6, Meeting of 28 February 1911. The *firman* was discussed at the meeting of 2 May 1911 (BSA Minute Book 7).

[221] BSA Minute Book 7, Meeting of 10 October 1911.

[222] The recommendation is likely to have come from Hogarth. Lord Carnarvon had hoped to recruit Woolley to work in Egypt in August 1911. For this period: Winstone 1990, 23-25. Datcha was also discussed at the Meeting of October 24, 1911 (BSA Minute Book 7).

Now that the excavations at Sparta are successfully over, the Committee and the Director have made a careful search for a new field for the activities of the School. After protracted negotiations they have the pleasure to announce that the Imperial Ottoman Government has just granted a *firman* for excavations on a promising site on the Dorian promontory, to the east of ancient Knidos. The spot, which once bore the Greek name Akanthos, is now known by the modern Turkish name of Datcha. Mr Dawkins has twice visited the site and reports that there is reason to suppose that this is an archaic Greek sanctuary with votive offerings. The remains of the ancient city are extensive, but it is only proposed to excavate this sanctuary, which lies in a small valley near the sea. Mr Dawkins will go out specially to take charge of the excavation.[223]

An appeal for funds was launched in December 1911.[224] There was concern that the *firman* would lapse if excavation had not started by May 14, 1912.[225] Although it had been hoped that work would start, the 'state of war' meant that nothing happened.[226] Hasluck continued:

The disturbed state of the Aegean has been responsible for the postponement of the British School's excavation at Datcha, which is unfortunately in the area immediately affected.[227]

At the Annual Meeting of Subscribers in October 1912 it was reported that Dawkins

was very kindly received at the Imperial Ottoman Museum at Constantinople by the Director, H. E. Halil Bey, who promised to have the permission for the Datcha excavation deferred in the event of the war preventing work this year, and this was the course finally adopted. On the way to Athens he called at Smyrna and visited the Consulate, the consul General kindly writing to the Vali of the province to learn his opinion as to the possibility of the excavation, which was distinctly unfavourable. He then went to Athens for a short stay, and then again to Smyrna, where the Consul General finally informed him that, owing to the state of war in the islands any work at Datcha would be impossible. …

He very much regrets that political events made excavation at Datcha impossible, but there is no reason to suppose that the site has suffered in any way. The most cordial thanks are due to the kind support of the authorities of the Imperial Museum at Constantinople, to the continuous assistance of Sir Edwin Pears, and lastly to the British Consular authorities at Constantinople and Smyrna.[228]

In April 1913 Dawkins visited Constantinople and 'secured the consent of the Direction of the Imperial Museum to defer the excavation of Datcha until more favourable

---

[223] British School at Athens 1910/11, 284.

[224] BSA Minute Book 7, Meeting of 5 December 1911.

[225] BSA Minute Book 7, Meeting of 20 February 1912.

[226] BSA Minute Book 7, Meeting of 21 May 1912.

[227] Hasluck 1912, 385.

[228] British School at Athens 1911/12, 315.

circumstances'.[229] However the possibility of excavating there was still being considered in October 1913 and the spring of 1914.[230] Though Droop noted:

> As the state of war was a new bar to the proposed excavation at Datcha on the Cnidian promontory.[231]

Excavation was not possible in Anatolia, and as a result a short excavation was conducted on Crete.[232]

Conclusion

By the outbreak of the First World War, members of the BSA had made tours of most corners of Anatolia. Part of the driving force behind such work was the desire to discover new inscriptions and possible sites to excavate, though some members of the School were also interested in the Greek dialects and folklore to be found in Anatolia. In addition, former members of the BSA, such as Hogarth, did conduct major excavations at Ephesus. There is no indication that members of the BSA were deliberately gathering intelligence, especially in the tense years before the outbreak of World War One, although this is a possibility.[233] Members of the BSA were not the only travellers in the region; Captain W. H. Shakespear drove along the Black Sea coast in 1907, during his epic drive from the Persian Gulf to England.[234]

---

[229] British School at Athens 1912/13, 267.

[230] BSA Minute Book 7, Meetings of 14 October 1913, 24 March 1914.

[231] Droop 1913, 361.

[232] Dawkins and Laistner 1912/13.

[233] See Winstone 1982.

[234] Winstone 1976, 47-48.

CHAPTER 11: NORTH AFRICA
AND OTHER PROJECTS

Egypt

Ernest Gardner had worked with Flinders Petrie at Naukratis before being admitted as the first student of the BSA.[1] He assisted with the publication of the Greek epigraphy. Hogarth, the first Oxford student, had worked in Egypt at Deir-el-Bahari.[2] One of his long-standing interests was in Alexander the Great, and the establishment of the Graeco-Roman Museum in Alexandria in 1892 gave him the opportunity to excavate in the city with Edward F. Benson, a student of the BSA, in April 1895.[3]

In the winter of 1898 Bernard P. Grenfell contacted Hogarth about the state of the site of Naukratis. Grenfell and Hogarth had worked together in the Faiyum (1895-96).[4] The Managing Committee was alerted:

> The mounds there were about to be brought under cultivation by Hussein Pasha, the proprietor, who was willing however that there should be final exploration before the water was brought to them. Mr Hogarth proposed to go over for a week to examine the site & report, and asked whether funds could be provided up to about £100.[5]

The Ashmolean Museum, or rather Evans as the Keeper, offered to find some money in return for a share of the finds; it was suggested that the Fitzwilliam should also be approached.[6] The Society of Dilettanti also contributed a £100 towards the project.[7] Altogether some £187 was raised.

Hogarth discovered major changes to the site, not least because 'hundreds of natives were employed daily in digging *sebakh* (*i.e.* virgin earth for top-dressing the cotton fields) all over the mound'.[8] Work was conducted from February to March 1899 and Hogarth was joined by C. C. Edgar and C. D. Edmonds.[9] Hogarth claimed to have found the site of the Hellenion. By early May a share of the finds were 'lying at the Albert Docks', waiting

---

[1] Gardner 1886b; Gardner 1888.

[2] Gill 2004l.

[3] Hogarth and Benson 1896.

[4] Gill 2004l.

[5] BSA Minute Book 3, Meeting of 15 December 1898.

[6] BSA Minute Book 3, Meeting of 19 January 1899.

[7] British School at Athens 1898/99, 100.

[8] Hogarth 1898/9, 26-27.

[9] Edgar 1898/9a; Edgar 1898/9b.

to be shared between the Ashmolean and the Fitzwilliam museums as part of the Naucratis Excavation Fund.[10]

Hogarth conducted a further excavation at Naukratis in 1903, supported by the Craven Fund of the University of Oxford.[11] In 1905 the British School of Archaeology in Egypt was opened, which meant that the BSA no longer needed to take responsibility for work on Greco-Roman sites there.[12]

North Africa

At the same time that the BSA was considering excavating at Datcha, there was a proposal to work at Leptis Magna in Tripolitania.[13] Myres had a long-standing interest in North Africa.[14] This would be a collaborative excavation with the BSR, then under Thomas Ashby, and a *firman* had been requested from Constantinople.[15]

Byzantine Research and Publication Fund

The School had supported work on Byzantine monuments from the earliest years.[16] Under Ernest Gardner, a special fund, supported by Dr Edwin Freshfield, had assisted the work of the architectural student, Weir Schultz, to map Byzantine churches in Athens, Agios Loukas in Stiris in Phocis, and Salonica.[17] This work continued under subsequent directors. Byzantine churches featured in the project by Melos;[18] and, under Bosanquet, Heaton Comyn made a study of the church of Dauo-Mendeli in Attica.[19] On Crete Theodore Fyfe studied the church of Titus at Gortyn,[20] and Ramsay Traquair worked on the church in Laconia.[21] Harry Pirie-Gordon visited Athos with Harry Luke.[22]

Members of the BSA were also involved with the documenting of Constantinople. Arthur E. Henderson, the Owen Jones student of the Royal Institute of British Architects at the School for 1897/98, was 'wholly occupied in drawing and painting details of Byzantine

[10] BSA Minute Book 3, Meeting of 4 May 1899. The finds were distributed in December 1899. For the Fitzwilliam finds: Gill 1992b. A selection of Naukratis finds appear in Möller 2000.

[11] Hogarth, *et al.* 1905.

[12] Noted in BSA Minute Book 5, Meeting of 21 November 1905.

[13] BSA Minute Book 6, Meeting of 4 October 1910.

[14] Myres 1896/7.

[15] Wallace-Hadrill 2001, 33.

[16] See the emphasis placed by Ernest Gardner in his first report on 'Archaeology in Greece': Gardner 1889, 277-78.

[17] For an appeal for funds in May 1890: Macmillan 1890b. Schultz and Barnsley 1901. For their work at Salonica, contained in a letter from Penrose: Penrose 1890.

[18] Fletcher and Kitson 1895/6.

[19] Comyn 1902/03. See also Bosanquet 1903/04.

[20] Fyfe 1907.

[21] Traquair 1908/09.

[22] For the background: Gill 2006a.

buildings in Constantinople'.[23] In May 1904 the BSA was approached by Professor Alexander van Millingen (1840-1915), of Robert College in Constantinople, to see if it would co-operate in a scheme to plot Byzantine architecture.[24] However there was concern from the Managing Committee that the proposed work would overlap with work by German and Russian scholars. It was suggested that Henderson should be the architect for the project.

In 1906/07 Walter S. George was admitted as an architectural student and prepared architectural drawings of the church of Ayios Demetrios in Salonica in April 1907.[25] Later that year a Byzantine Research and Publication Fund was established, with Schultz Weir as the honorary secretary.[26] The honorary treasurer was H. A. Cruso, who had read classics at Balliol College, Oxford.[27] The Fund was also supported by Arthur Hamilton Smith, Keeper of Greek and Roman Antiquities at the British Museum (1909-25). Its launch was described by Edwin Freshfield in a letter to *The Times*:

> The object of it [sc. the Fund] means research into the effect of the introduction of Christianity into the history and art of the Roman Empire of Constantinople.
>
> It is only within the last 50 years that intelligent interest has been directed to this period; but within the last few years the increase in the interest has been so general and so rapid that there is great need of an English society to collect, sift, and classify the vast amount of information that has gradually been collected, not only in England, but on the Continent, upon the subject, and to induce something like order into it, and also, as a branch of it, the collecting of funds to permit the society to investigate on its own account.[28]

Freshfield was impressed with the Austrian excavations at the Byzantine church of St John the Divine at Ephesus. His appeal was soon followed by a letter by Robert Weir Schultz, secretary of the Fund:

> One of the objects of the fund is to collect reliable *data* of existing architectural remains of all buildings erected between the time of Constantine and the fall of the Eastern Empire. Almost every traveller nowadays carries a camera and there must, therefore, be numerous photographs in existence of otherwise unrecorded buildings. The committee of the fund are arranging for a permanent collection of such photographs which will be accessible to students; and we should be glad if any one possessing photographs of little-known buildings of the Christian era, especially in remote parts of the East, would contribute copies of same to be added to the collection of the fund.[29]

---

[23] British School at Athens 1897/98, 102.

[24] BSA Minute Book 4, Meeting of 17 May 1904. For van Millingen: *The Times* 17 September 1915, 11.

[25] See also Cormack 1969.

[26] Macmillan 1910/11, xxiv-xxv. See also Waterhouse 1986, 56, 129.

[27] *The Times* 26 June 1908, 11.

[28] Freshfield 1908.

[29] Schultz 1908.

A meeting of the fund was held in November of 1908.[30] It specifically mentioned a special fund which had passed through the BSA 'for Frankish studies'. Frederic Harrison also placed the fund in a wider political context:

> The prejudice, ignorance, and apathy of the old Turkish *regime* had made investigations in the sultan's dominions somewhat slow and troublesome, but from the Young Turk party, many of whose members were men of culture, Byzantine research might look for encouragement.[31]

The Fund itself was seen as recording monuments rather than primarily excavating. Harrison continued:

> In commending antiquarian research he was not confining his attention to the spade, as the ladder, the electric lamp, the camera, and the magnifying or telescopic glass skilfully used might do as much as the spade in expert hands. History, architecture, numismatics, palaeography, sculpture, painting, and ancient literature might all be enriched by systematic research in such a vast virgin museum of antiquities as Stambul.[32]

It is clear that the Fund was to promote 'Turkish art' as much as classical or Byzantine art.

Work in Constantinople continued under Walter S. George, which brought about a major study of the church of Saint Eirene,[33] and other Byzantine churches.[34] Other members of the BSA, notably Alan J. B. Wace, Ramsay Traquair and F. W. Hasluck, were involved in recording other Late Antique and Islamic remains in the city.[35] Among the other Byzantine monuments studied was the obelisk of Theodosios (by Wace),[36] and the monument of Porphyrios (by Woodward).[37] This British interest in Islamic architecture was continued by Dorothy Lamb's study of the Seljuk buildings in Konya immediately prior to the First World War.[38]

The Fund also supported Jewell's work on Paros,[39] as well as the publication of the Church of the Nativity at Bethlehem.[40] Studies of Byzantine aspects of work by BSA students are apparent in other areas: Byzantine pottery from Sparta, Byzantine emperors,

[30] 'Byzantine Research Fund', *The Times* 19 November 1908, 13.

[31] 'Byzantine Research Fund', *The Times* 19 November 1908, 13.

[32] 'Byzantine Research Fund', *The Times* 19 November 1908, 13.

[33] George 1913.

[34] Van Millingen, *et al.* 1912.

[35] Wace and Traquair 1909; Hasluck 1916/17, 1917/18.

[36] Wace and Traquair 1909.

[37] Woodward 1910/11b.

[38] Lamb 1914/16.

[39] Jewell and Hasluck 1920.

[40] Schultz 1910; see also Cruso 1910.

and Tillyard's major work on Byzantine music, to name but three.[41] John A. Hamilton, who had a long-standing interest in church design, was admitted in 1913/14 to work on the architecture of the church at Kaisariani in Attica.[42]

---

[41] Dawkins and Droop 1910/11a; Tillyard 1911/12; Tillyard 1914/16; Tillyard 1916/18; Tillyard 1918/19.

[42] Hamilton 1916.

PART 4
AFTER THE BRITISH SCHOOL AT ATHENS

CHAPTER 12: FURTHER EXCAVATIONS

The BSA was intended as a training ground for archaeologists in general. Flinders Petrie influenced the way in which Ernest A. Gardner and David G. Hogarth had been taught to excavate, and several students, notably T. Eric Peet, developed their interests in Egypt. John H. Marshall, who had worked with Robert C. Bosanquet on Crete, left to become Director-General of Antiquities in India.[1] Several other BSA students worked on sites in Britain.[2]

It should also be remembered that the directors and assistant directors of the BSA largely comprised former students who had learned their craft in Greece. Robert C. Bosanquet had first been admitted as a student under Ernest Gardner, but seems to have flourished under Cecil Harcourt-Smith and Hogarth before becoming Director in his own right. Richard M. Dawkins, Frederick W. Hasluck and Alan J. B. Wace in turn were trained by Bosanquet. Arthur M. Woodward, who became Assistant Director under both Dawkins (1909/10) and later Wace (1922/23), was trained by Dawkins at Sparta; Woodward later excavated as Director at Sparta (1923-29).

Excavating in Egypt

The contribution of students of the BSA to Egyptology has largely been overlooked.[3] An exception would be their work on the excavation of the Greek settlement of Naukratis.[4] At least thirteen of the students admitted to the BSA before the First World War – out of 115 men – were involved in archaeological work in Egypt.[5] In the late nineteenth and early twentieth centuries scientific archaeology was in its early infancy.[6] The boundaries between disciplines such as Classical Archaeology and Egyptology were not as closely drawn as they can be today. Most, though not all, of the BSA's students had studied classics at either Oxford or Cambridge.[7] Some seem to have developed research interests in Greek, Ptolemaic or Roman remains in Egypt, but others embraced earlier periods of Egyptology.

---

[1] Gill 2000a.

[2] For the history of archaeology in Britain, though overlooking the contribution of Aegean-trained archaeologists: Hingley 2000.

[3] Few of the students appear in Fagan 2004.

[4] Waterhouse 1986, 120-21.

[5] Only six of the thirteen appear in Bierbrier 1995.

[6] For a convenient summary of developments in this period: Bahn 1996.

[7] Slightly more Oxford (7) than Cambridge (4) students were involved with work in Egypt but this need not be significant.

The classical in Egypt

One clear strand of the work by Aegean trained archaeologists was to look at the classical sites and artefacts found in Egypt. One of the first students to be admitted to the BSA was Ernest A. Gardner. Gardner had an interest in Greek epigraphy,[8] and Flinders Petrie used this expertise during his excavation of Naukratis in the Nile Delta.[9] Gardner himself continued the Naukratis excavations during the 1885/86 season and then excavated at Nebeira in early 1886 under the direction of Petrie.[10] At the December meeting of the Egypt Exploration Fund, Gardner presented the work at Naukratis, though his inexperience showed: a contemporary letter from Mrs Benest commented, 'on the whole, one felt glad when he sat down – he seemed to stand with much difficulty and be much embarrassed by his hands and feet'.[11] Petrie's friendship with Gardner continued. When Gardner was appointed Director of the BSA in 1887, Petrie came to visit him specifically to look at the prehistoric pottery found in Greece, that seemed to be similar to material from Middle and New Kingdom sites in Egypt.[12] Gardner and Petrie were later to become colleagues at University College London when Gardner accepted the Yates chair in 1896.[13]

Interest in the Greek and Roman aspects of Egypt continued to attract attention from members of the BSA. Gardner's fellow student at the British School in 1886/7 had been David G. Hogarth.[14] In 1894 Hogarth visited Petrie's excavations at Koptos, and was invited to publish the Greek and Latin texts. He then joined the EEF excavations at Deir el-Bahari. In the following year he undertook exploratory excavations from February to April 1895 at Kom al-Dikka at Alexandria on behalf of the Hellenic Society.[15] In this task he was accompanied by two BSA students, Edward F. Benson of King's College, Cambridge, and Edwyn R. Bevan of New College, Oxford.[16] Benson's sister, Margaret, who had studied in Oxford at Lady Margaret Hall, travelled in Egypt at this time and was involved with the excavation of the temple of Mut at Thebes.[17] Hogarth returned to the

[8] Gardner 1885a; Gardner 1885b; Gardner 1885c; Gardner 1886c; Gardner 1887a.

[9] Petrie 1885. See also Drower 1995, 92. Other classicists were involved with the interpretation of the finds: Barclay Head for the coins, and Cecil Harcourt-Smith (a future director of the British School at Athens) for the Greek pottery. For Petrie's influence: Fagan 2004, 235.

[10] For the Naukratis excavations: Gardner 1888. For the excavations at Nebeira see Drower 1995, 96.

[11] Quoted in Drower 1995, 110.

[12] Petrie 1890. See also Waterhouse 1986, 10-11; Fagan 2004, 226-27.

[13] Janssen 1992, 12.

[14] Gill 2004l.

[15] Hogarth and Benson 1896.

[16] Bevan developed a strong interest in Hellenistic, and especially Seleucid, history: *e.g.* Bevan 1900a; Bevan 1900b; Bevan 1902b; Bevan 1902a. He later prepared a history of the Ptolemies: Bevan 1927.

[17] Benson 1917. See also Gill 2004d.

theme of Alexander in Egypt for a lecture given to the Egypt Exploration Fund in December 1914.[18]

Joseph Grafton Milne, who had studied at Corpus Christi College, Oxford, had been admitted to the School in 1890.[19] He subsequently taught at Mill Hill School (1891-93), before becoming an examiner in the Board of Education. He had been introduced to classical archaeology at Oxford by Percy Gardner, and had excavated at Doclea in Montenegro.[20] His growing interest in Greco-Roman Egypt led him to work with Petrie in 1895-96.[21] He was soon involved with the task of preparing work on the monumental catalogue of the Cairo Museum, publishing studies on Greek epigraphy (1905).[22] Among his other interests were Greek sealings,[23] numismatics,[24] papyri,[25] and other aspects of Greco-Roman Egypt.[26] He later became Reader in Numismatics in Oxford, and Deputy Keeper of Coins in the Ashmolean Museum.

Hogarth continued to work in Egypt from December 1895 to February 1896 by looking for classical papyri in the Faiyum with Bernard P. Grenfell.[27] After his appointment as BSA Director in 1897, he returned to Egypt from February to May 1899 by working at Naukratis on behalf of the Society of Dilettanti.[28] His work there was supported by two BSA students, Campbell C. Edgar, of Oriel College, Oxford, and Clement Gutch, of King's College, Cambridge.[29] Edgar was admitted to the BSA in 1895 and for the subsequent three years. He worked on the ill-fated BSA excavation at Kynosarges, publishing stelai from the site,[30] before joining Hogarth for the season of work at Naukratis in 1899. Edgar was appointed Inspector of Antiquities for Lower Egypt and later became a major contributor to the catalogue of the Cairo Museum, publishing studies that included the Greek sculpture (1903), Greek bronzes (1904), glass (1905), and Greco-

---

[18] Hogarth 1915.

[19] Last 1952.

[20] Munro, *et al.* 1896.

[21] Drower 1995, 218-19.

[22] Milne 1901.

[23] Milne 1906; Milne 1916.

[24] Milne 1916b; Milne 1917; Milne 1918; Milne 1920; Milne 1922a; Milne 1929; Milne 1933; Milne 1935; Milne 1937; Milne 1938a; Milne 1938b; Milne 1941; Milne 1943; Milne 1945; Milne 1950; Milne 1951. For other Egyptological publications: Baker-Penoyre 1910/11, xlviii-xlix.

[25] Milne 1924; Milne 1925b; Milne 1925a; Milne 1928a; Milne, *et al.* 1928; Milne 1934.

[26] Milne 1914b; Milne 1914c; Milne 1914a; Milne 1916a; Milne 1922b; Milne 1928b; Milne 1930; Milne 1939.

[27] Grenfell, *et al.* 1900. See also Montserrat 1996. For Grenfell: Milne 1926.

[28] Hogarth 1898/9.

[29] Edgar 1898/9a; Edgar 1898/9b; Gutch 1898/9. Edgar had earlier worked at Phylakopi on Melos, where he had been responsible for the pottery: Edgar 1897/8; Edgar 1898/9c. See also Macmillan 1910/11, xv.

[30] Edgar 1897. The author appears as C. E. Edgar in *The Journal of Hellenic Studies* but the article is listed as one of Edgar's publications in Baker-Penoyre 1910/11, xliii.

Egyptian coffins and mummies (1905).[31] He continued to publish classical material from Egypt.[32] Hogarth himself was to conduct a final season of excavations at Naukratis in 1903 after he had resigned from directorship of the British School.[33] His work in Syria also allowed him to develop an interest on the Egyptian in Asia.[34]

Non-classical sites in Egypt

Hogarth, whose Oxford fellowship had ended, joined the EEF excavation at Deir el-Bahari in 1894 as an experienced excavator.[35] He conducted a final excavation season in Egypt in the winter of 1906/07 in the cemeteries of Asyut.[36] The reason for this return to Egyptology is not clear, although it coincides with the time that Petrie was proposing a formal British School of Archaeology in Egypt along the lines of the BSA.

Other BSA students went to Egypt to gain more experience of excavation. Rev. J. Garrow Duncan had been admitted to the BSA in 1894-95 after being sent out from Aberdeen by the Church of Scotland. During his year at the BSA he visited Petrie's excavations.[37] He excavated in Egypt with Petrie in 1905,[38] and then published a study of the Hyksos.[39] One of Duncan's strong interests was the link between the discovery of new finds in Egypt and its impact on the interpretation of the Old Testament.[40] This explains his work in the cemeteries of Saft el Hinna, that had been identified as Goshen.[41] This experience prepared him for a developing research interest in the archaeology of the Levant, especially Palestine.[42]

The Canadian Charles Trick Currelly of Toronto met Petrie in London in 1902 while he was preparing for the ordained ministry.[43] Petrie invited him to excavate in Egypt: as a member of the BSA, Currelly excavated at the Bronze Age site of Palaikastro in eastern Crete,[44] and then excavated at Abydos until 1910.[45] Margaret Murray recalled that

---

[31] Edgar 1903a; Edgar 1903b; Edgar 1904a; Edgar 1905a; Edgar 1905b; Edgar 1906a; Edgar 1911; Edgar 1925. For other Egyptological publications: Baker-Penoyre 1910/11, xliii. For Edgar's involvement with the Cairo Museum: Hankey 2001, 146.

[32] Edgar 1904b; Edgar 1905c; Edgar 1906b; Edgar 1917; Edgar 1928.

[33] Hogarth, *et al.* 1905.

[34] Hogarth 1914.

[35] Gill 2004l.

[36] Hogarth 1910. See also Ryan 1995. Hogarth returned to Egypt to take charge of the Arab Bureau: see Westrate 1992. For further links between the Arab Bureau and former students of the British School at Athens: Gill 2006a.

[37] Drower 1995, 214.

[38] Drower 1995, 298.

[39] Petrie and Duncan 1906.

[40] Duncan 1908.

[41] Drower 1995, 301-02.

[42] *E.g.* Duncan, *et al.* 1930.

[43] Drower 1995, 267.

[44] Currelly 1903/04.

Currelly 'was a great asset that year at Abydos for he was always ready to help any of us'.[46] Currelly worked with Petrie at Ehnasya and on the survey of Sinai, and later published a catalogue of stone implements in the Cairo Museum.[47]

One of the last BSA students to join work in Egypt before the First World War was (Thomas) Eric Peet. He had taken classical and mathematical moderations (1903) and Literae Humaniores (1905) at The Queen's College, Oxford. At Oxford he was influenced by David Randall-MacIver (1873-1945), who was Lacock student of Egyptology at Worcester College.[48] Randall-MacIver had also studied classics at The Queen's College, and had subsequently excavated with Petrie at Abydos (1899-1901). He also had a strong interest in the prehistory of Italy and in the island of Malta. This may explain why Peet was drawn to the prehistory of Italy and Egypt.[49] He started his Mediterranean experience at the BSR, before moving to east to Athens and then on to Egypt where he excavated with John Garstang at Abydos (1909).[50] Another BSA student who worked at Abydos was John P. Droop (1911): he assisted with the pottery.[51] He had taken the Classical Tripos at Trinity College, Cambridge, and had been admitted to the BSA on a regular basis from 1905. He had excavated at Phylakopi on Melos (1906, 1911),[52] Sparta (1906),[53] and in Thessaly (1907). After working in Egypt he excavated at the Kamares Cave on Crete with Richard Dawkins,[54] a site significant for the type of Middle Minoan pottery found in Middle Kingdom deposits at Ilahun. Droop's experiences of excavating were brought together in a small handbook, *Archaeological Excavation* (1915), now notorious for its attitudes towards women on excavations.[55]

A final student was Walter S. George, a trained architect. He had worked with the Byzantine Research Fund through the BSA on the project to record the churches of Constantinople. He assisted John Garstang with his work at Meroë in the Sudan.[56]

---

[45] Ayrton, *et al.* 1904. See also Currelly 1965. A share of the finds was given to the Royal Ontario Museum in Toronto.

[46] Murray 1963, 115.

[47] Petrie and Currelly 1905; Petrie and Currelly 1906; Currelly 1913.

[48] Hencken and Stoddart 2004.

[49] Peet 1906/07; Peet 1907. For Peet's work with Thomas Ashby: Hodges 2000, 43-44.

[50] Peet 1914a; Peet 1914b.

[51] For Peet's observations on Droop's approach to the classification of pottery clearly derived from his work in Greece: Peet 1933.

[52] Dawkins and Droop 1910/11d.

[53] Droop 1906/07b; Droop 1907/08; Droop 1908/09.

[54] Dawkins and Laistner 1912/13.

[55] Droop 1915. For the context and Droop's excavating experiences: Gill 2002.

[56] Garstang and George 1913.

Excavating in the Levant

A small number of former BSA students went on to work in Palestine. One of the earliest was John Garrow Duncan, an ordained minister of the Church of Scotland, who went to Athens in 1894/95. From there his interests turned to Egypt, where he worked with Flinders Petrie. His particular area of study was the Hyksos period and links between Egypt and the Old Testament.[57] Francis B. Welch explored the linked between the Levant and the Aegean.[58]

One of the most experienced BSA excavators, Duncan Mackenzie, joined the Palestine Exploration Fund (PEF) in December 1909.[59] He succeeded R. A. S. Macalister as 'Explorer' for the PEF.[60] One of his first projects was at Ain Shems (Beth-shemesh).[61] Shortage of funds, however, led to the dismissal of Mackenzie and the cessation of the work.

British work continued in the Levant with David Hogarth's work at Carchemish, which had started back in 1911.[62] One of the team, T. E. Lawrence, was later recruited, on the eve of the First World War, to take part in the survey of the Sinai peninsula ('the Wilderness of Zin'), a project initiated by Hogarth through the PEF. Other former BSA students continued to make their mark in the Levant. Crowfoot, who had worked in Egypt, was elected Director of the British School of Archaeology in Jerusalem (1927-35). Agnes Conway, who had been admitted to the BSA on the eve of the First World War, later married George Wilberforce Horsfield, Director of Antiquities in Trans-Jordan (1924-36),[63] and they participated in field-work together. Duncan returned to Palestine after the War and excavated at the Ophel Quarter in Jerusalem on behalf of the PEF, and under the overall auspices of Crowfoot at the British School in Jerusalem.[64] Duncan became well known for his writing on archaeological developments in the Levant, as well as for his contributions to studies of ceramics on Levant sites.[65]

Excavating in Britain

From the 1890s there was a growing interest in Romano-British archaeology, in part fostered by Francis J. Haverfield at Oxford, who was the Camden Professor from 1907.[66] Haverfield encouraged Oxford undergraduates to take an interest in Romano-British archaeology, in particular the Roman frontiers and military installations of the province.

---

[57] Petrie and Duncan 1906; Duncan 1908.

[58] Welch 1899/1900a.

[59] Momigliano 1999, 85-115.

[60] King 1983, 23. Macalister had moved to the University of Dublin.

[61] King 1983, 90-91.

[62] Gill 2004l.

[63] King 1983, 200.

[64] 'The tomb of David: New Discoveries at Jerusalem', *The Times* 27 July 1925, 12; E. W. G. Masterman, 'Excavations at Jerusalem', *The Times* 28 July 1927, 17.

[65] Duncan, *et al.* 1930; Duncan 1930; Duncan 1931.

[66] Macdonald 1919/20; Anderson 1919; Craster 1920; Bosanquet 1920; Freeman 2007. For his publications: MacDonald 1918.

Some of the earliest work was conducted in north-west England. Among Haverfield's students was John Garstang who excavated at Ribchester in Lancashire in 1895.[67] Garstang moved on to excavate at the site of the Roman fort of Melandra Castle in Derbyshire in 1899.[68] When Garstang joined Petrie to excavate in Egypt in 1900,[69] the work was taken over by the Manchester and District branch of the Classical Association.[70] Members of the Classics department at the Victoria University of Manchester were involved with the project, and two had been students at the BSA. Particularly, John H. Hopkinson, lecturer in classical archaeology at Hulme Hall, Manchester (1904-14), contributed a chapter on the pottery.[71] He had been admitted to the BSA under Hogarth. The final report was edited by Robert S. Conway, Professor of Latin at Manchester.[72]

Attention turned to the Roman fort at Manchester, which was excavated in 1906/7.[73] Hopkinson again contributed to the study of Roman pottery. Work resumed in 1907 at Ribchester to continue Garstang's earlier excavations. This was a joint venture between the Manchester Branch of the Classical Association, and the Lancashire and Cheshire Society of Antiquaries, under the direction for the first year of Thomas May.[74] The project was strongly supported by Haverfield, who visited the site for a short spell. In the second season (1908), Leonard Cheesman, fresh from the BSA, directed the excavations; he had been at the site in the previous year. Two other former members of the BSA were involved: Hopkinson and Robert C. Bosanquet, Professor of Classical Archaeology at Liverpool. The results were published in a volume edited by Hopkinson.[75]

The northern frontier zone of Hadrian's Wall was also important. One of the first BSA students to excavate in Britain was Bosanquet, who took charge of the work at the Roman fort of Housesteads on Hadrian's Wall in 1898 on behalf of the Society of Antiquaries of Newcastle upon Tyne.[76] Bosanquet had been forced to return to Britain following a bout of malaria contracted during travels in the Peloponnese. He had previously excavated at Aegosthena, Kynosarges and on Melos.

---

[67] Garstang 1898. See Freeman 2007, 375. Freeman notes that it was this excavation that brought Garstang to Haverfield's attention.

[68] Garstang 1901. See Freeman 2007, 375.

[69] Gurney and Freeman 2004.

[70] Conway 1906; Bruton 1909.

[71] Hopkinson 1906.

[72] Although Conway had not been a student at the BSA he had assisted with School projects on Crete: Conway 1901/02; Conway 1903/04.

[73] Bruton and Conway 1909. See Freeman 2007, 416-17.

[74] Conway 1908. The Manchester Branch of the Classical Association resumed work at Ribchester in 1927: 'Roman Finds at Ribchester', *The Times* 16 April 1927, 13. See also Freeman 2007, 300.

[75] Hopkinson 1911; and for later editions, Hopkinson 1916; Hopkinson and Atkinson 1928. Haverfield was critical of the supervision of the excavation: Haverfield 1911; see Freeman 2007, 416-17.

[76] Bosanquet 1904; see also Bosanquet 1922; Freeman 2007, 414.

In 1907 large scale excavations were commenced at Corbridge, the Roman site of Corstopitum, to the south of Hadrian's Wall. These were to continue until the outbreak of the First World War. Haverfield was a member of the excavation committee and contributed to the publications.[77] He was accompanied by his Oxford students. Among them was Cheesman who had graduated with a first in 1907 and was to continue his interest in Roman archaeology as a student at the BSA and by working at Pisidian Antioch.[78]

The growth of the Institute of Archaeology at Liverpool University had an influence on excavations in Wales. In 1906 Bosanquet was appointed to the chair of Classical Archaeology at Liverpool;[79] among his colleagues were Myres and Garstang. In the 1908 a Committee was formed for Excavation and Research in Wales and the Marches, supported by Haverfield in Oxford. The committee recognised that:

> very few of the Roman sites in Wales and the Marches have been explored in the past, and this perhaps is fortunate; for within the last 15 years systematic excavation in other parts of Britain and Germany, and the study of Roman pottery of the south of France, have furnished new means for interpreting plan and construction, and made it possible to assign dates with increasing confidence.[80]

Among the first projects was work on the Roman legionary bases at Caerleon and Chester in the summer of 1908.[81] The committee members proceeded to turn their attention to smaller sites such as the fort of Caersws in mid-Wales, where the Roman baths had been uncovered in 1855.[82] This initiative from Liverpool was strengthened by the creation of the Royal Commission of Ancient Monument of Wales and Monmouthshire; Bosanquet was one of the first commissioners. Excavations continued at several Roman sites across Wales, and Bosanquet and Haverfield sometimes travelled together.[83]

This tradition of Mediterranean archaeologists continued after the First World War with Arthur Woodward's excavations at Ilkley and Rudston.[84]

---

[77] Craster 1920, 66. For Haverfield's published contributions on Corbridge: MacDonald 1918.

[78] Cheesman 1913. For Cheesman at Corbridge: Freeman 2007, 364.

[79] Gill 2004b.

[80] Bosanquet and Myres 1909. See also Freeman 2007, 414.

[81] Evelyn-White 1909.

[82] Bosanquet and Myres 1909. A further report appeared in 'Ancient Monuments in Wales', *The Times* 11 August 1910, 5. See also Freeman 2007, 384.

[83] Freeman 2007, 414-15.

[84] Woodward 1925; Woodward 1934; Woodward 1935; Woodward and Steer 1936. See also Freeman 2007, 382-83, 452.

CHAPTER 13: STUDENTS AT WAR:
ARCHEOLOGUES EN PEAU DE LOUP

In the summer of 1916 a steamer travelling along the coast of Crete was stopped and a British naval officer boarded it to inspect the passengers' papers. Much to the surprise of a French archaeologist the 'spectacled and studious' officer was 'a former pupil whom he had last seen attending a lecture on Delphic capitals in Athens many years before the war'.[1] The officer, probably either John C. Lawson, BSA student in the years 1898/99 and 1899/1900, or William R. Halliday, student in the years 1910/11, 1912/13, was one of a number men who had been admitted to the BSA and who had been recruited, in part, for intelligence roles.

This aspect of the careers of former BSA students in the First World War has largely been forgotten.[2] The School remembered its dead, and lamented the loss to scholarship notably by the death of Guy Dickins on the Western Front.[3] The escapades of high profile members such as John L. Myres with his cattle raids on the Anatolian mainland were retold. David G. Hogarth had a pivotal role in the Arab Bureau with its associations with T. E. Lawrence. Richard M. Dawkins, John C. Lawson and William R. Halliday served as RNVR officers on Crete, monitoring German submarines and involving themselves with counter-espionage. The BSA's role in intelligence activities has not been widely publicised, though it has been framed in a more humorous context by Compton Mackenzie.[4]

One of the main contributions made by members of the BSA was in the area of intelligence. This has yet to be the subject of detailed study.[5] At least eight Cambridge students held military commissions and were involved in intelligence,[6] two more were in civilian roles,[7] and ten Oxford students held military intelligence posts.[8] This does not

---

[1] 'En peau de loup. Professors as cattle lifters', *The Times* 2 August 1916, 9.

[2] For the roll of honour: British School at Athens 1918/19. For Cambridge students: Carey 1921. For Oxford students: Craig and Gibson 1920. Other universities also prepared lists of war service.

[3] Dickins' death on the Western Front was also lamented in *The Times* 26 July 1916, 7 ('Waste of material'). It was suggested that those with an expertise should be used in more appropriate ways. Dickins had been working on the catalogue of the Acropolis Museum: Dickins 1912; and see also Gill 2004i.

[4] Mackenzie 1931.

[5] Clogg notes, 'At least four members of the School served in naval intelligence in Greek waters and a further dozen or so on the Salonica front': Clogg 2000, 31. For other work in intelligence: Gill 2006a.

[6] *E.g.* Farrell, Dawkins, Gardner, Gomme, Kaines Smith, Lawson, Scutt, Tillyard.

[7] *E.g.* Hasluck and Wace, both in Athens. Hasluck's health was failing.

include other intelligence work by civilians in London.[9] Margaret Hasluck was involved in intelligence work both in London and in Athens. Not all students were active in the Aegean or eastern Mediterranean. The size of this aspect of the work is striking when it is considered in the light of the fact that there had only been 115 male students admitted in the period up to the outbreak of war, and by 1914 some had already died.[10] At least nine former students, predominantly from Oxford, were ordained members of the clergy, either in the Church of England or in various churches in Scotland.[11] Another two students had been interned,[12] and other former students were serving in the armed forces. Thus intelligence work counted for perhaps some 15% of the students who had been admitted up to 1914.

One of the reasons for this was that BSA members not only had a knowledge of modern Greek, but also a range of languages found around the eastern Mediterranean, notably Arabic and Turkish.[13] Their knowledge of these languages had been derived from fieldwork and surveys conducted not only in Greece, but also on Cyprus, throughout Anatolia (including a survey of the Euphrates) and from excavations in Egypt. In some ways the pattern for former BSA students is no different from that of their peers from Oxford and Cambridge; although in some areas it seems that particular expertise was being exploited, and that friendships and associations made at the BSA were used.

At one level there is a noticeable emphasis on officers in the Royal Navy Volunteer Reserve (RNVR), though many were serving in an intelligence role that was dominated by the Admiralty. Many of the intelligence officers on the Salonica front were in the army and were either commissioned onto the general list or transferred from other fronts. There is also a

[8] *E.g.* Casson, Forster, Halliday, Hogarth, Pirie-Gordon, Thompson, Tod, Welch, Whatley, and Woodward.

[9] *E.g.* J. A. R. Munro, 'intelligence work for the Admiralty and the War Office' in London; Hilda Lorimer, 'Intelligence Dept. of Admiralty' (1917); Droop in the Admiralty; E. R. Bevan and A. J. Toynbee with Political Intelligence in the Foreign Office; J. K. Fotheringham was 'Clerk in the War Trade Intelligence Department' (1917); Mary Dickins (Hamilton), 'Military Translation Bureau, War Office' (1916-17), and 'Reader for the Review of the Foreign Press, Military Intelligence Dept. , War Office' (1917-19). Ernest Gardner went from Salonika to the Intelligence Department of the Admiralty in October 1917.

[10] At least four former Students had died from natural causes: F. A. C. Morrison died in 1899; Clement Gutch died in 1908 aged 33; Rupert Charles Clark died in 1912 aged 45; Bickford-Smith died in 1916 aged 57.

[11] Rev. William A. Wigram, Rev. J. H. Hopkinson, Rev. C. C. Inge, Rev. O. H. Parry, Rev. G. C. Richards, Rev. A. G. Bather. There were also a number of ministers from Scotland: Rev. J. G. Duncan, Rev. A. F. Findlay, Rev. W. W. Reid. Rev. R. C. Clarke had died before the outbreak of war.

[12] Tillyard in Germany and Wigram in Constantinople.

[13] See Lawson 1920, 4: 'being competent to discourse in Modern Greek and French, and possessing withal some insight into the Greek mind and character, acquired in travel some twenty years ago, I had placed these assets at the disposal of the Admiralty, War Office, or other unnamed department'. See also 'En peau de loup. Professors as cattle lifters', *The Times* 2 August 1916, 9: 'many of them had been there before and spoke the languages of the local Turks and Dagoes'. See also Sheffy 1998, 45, for the deployment of Turkish speakers to the eastern Mediterranean in late 1914.

clear distinction between those former students who were serving in the Mediterranean where their linguistic skills were employed, and those who served on the Western Front in a way paralleled by countless other graduates who had been commissioned as officers in the army.

Boer War

BSA students had served in the armed forces before the First World War. Vincent W. Yorke was commissioned as Lieutenant in the Gloucestershire Yeomanry in 1894, after his period of study in Greece. He had travelled with David Hogarth, in the spring and summer of 1894, in the Upper Euphrates.[14] Yorke's unit, the Royal Gloucestershire Hussars, left for South Africa in February 1900, returning to England in June the following year. In June Yorke was Lieutenant in A Squadron. He was promoted to Captain (1904), and continued to serve until 1907.

William Loring volunteered for service in the Boer War while serving as an examiner for the Ministry of Education and Honorary Secretary for the BSA. He served as a corporal in the 19th (Lothians and Berwickshire) Company, which formed part of the 6th (Scottish) Battalion of the Imperial Yeomanry (1900-01). Loring was awarded the DCM.[15] He was then commissioned as a Lieutenant in the newly-formed Scottish Horse (1901-02), and was twice mentioned in despatches. He was seriously wounded at Moedwill.

The Mediterranean

Members of the BSA had considerable first-hand knowledge not only of the Aegean but also of the Ottoman Empire.[16] They were involved in a range of activities across a wide span of the eastern Mediterranean that included Cairo, Syria, Gallipoli, Macedonia, Crete and Athens.

The Levant, Cairo and the Arab Bureau

Intelligence work had been conducted in the regions bordering the eastern Mediterranean in the years leading up to the First World War.[17] In 1906 the Director of Military Operation in London commissioned a report on Syria through its intelligence unit MO2.[18] Francis Richard Maunsell travelled in the Levant, preparing a report, *Reconnaissance of Syria from the Coast Eastwards* (1908), which laid a special emphasis on possible coastal landings.[19]

Archaeological excavation and survey had been undertaken by British teams in eastern Turkey and the Levant from the late 19th century onwards.[20] David Hogarth, who had travelled along the Euphrates, returned to the Levant in the spring of 1908, visiting the site

---

[14] Yorke 1896b. See also Yorke 1898.

[15] The 19th Company was raised in 1900.

[16] Gill 2004c.

[17] Sheffy 2002.

[18] Winstone 1982, 7.

[19] Sheffy 1998, 25-27; Sheffy 2002, 34-35.

[20] Gill 2004c.

of Carchemish; he initiated excavations there in the spring of 1911, accompanied by Reginald Campbell Thomson and T. E. Lawrence.[21] The work was later supervised by C. Leonard Woolley.[22]

Harry Pirie-Gordon, who had read History at Magdalen College, Oxford (Hogarth's college), had been admitted as a BSA student for the 1907-8 session. In the spring of 1908 he travelled through Syria in part as a study of Crusader castles in the Levant.[23] Pirie-Gordon supplied maps for Lawrence on his trip to the Levant in the summer of 1909.[24] That autumn both Lawrence and Pirie-Gordon were in Urfa, to the east of the Euphrates.[25] Pirie-Gordon later became associated with Hogarth's excavations at Carchemish.[26] There has been speculation that this survey and excavation work was part of intelligence gathering. Winstone has suggested that Pirie-Gordon was working for naval intelligence but reported to Colonel Francis Maunsell, the military attaché at the British embassy in Constantinople.[27] There is, however, no clear evidence that this was the case at this stage in Pirie-Gordon's career.[28]

It does become evident that Pirie-Gordon's knowledge of the Levant started to be useful to naval intelligence. In 1911 Pirie-Gordon seems to have been travelling in the Near East, passing through Aleppo, Urfa and Beredjik on the Euphrates, where he noted destruction of the castles.[29] In 1911-12 Pirie-Gordon and Captain Ian M. Smith, RE, travelled around Alexandretta, making detailed notes of the coastline.[30] A parallel can be found with Captain Stewart F. Newcombe, also of the Royal Engineers, who was working in Damascus in the autumn of 1910,[31] and later collaborated in the archaeological survey of the Wilderness of Zin of 1913.[32] Pirie-Gordon's credentials were supported by his appointment as a foreign correspondent of *The Times*.[33]

[21] Gill 2004l; see also Lock 1990.

[22] Winstone 1990, 23-48.

[23] The date is given in *The Times* 10 Dec 1969. The obituary notes that prior to the trip Pirie-Gordon studied at the Vatican Library. See also Pirie-Gordon 1912; Gill 2006a.

[24] Winstone 1982, 43-44. For Lawrence and Wooley using Pirie-Gordon's map: Winstone 1990, 63.

[25] Winstone 1982, 45. Pirie-Gordon was attacked during this trip.

[26] Winstone 1990, 63.

[27] Winstone 1982, 7-8.

[28] I am grateful to Yigael Sheffy for his cautionary advice. See also Sheffy 2002, 36-37, for caution over T. E. Lawrence's associations with espionage at this early date.

[29] Letter, 'Vandalism in upper Syria and Mesopotamia', *The Times* 8 August 1911, 10; see also the response form T. G. Jackson, 'Young Turks and old buildings', *The Times* 11 August 1911, 3.

[30] Winstone 1990, 63. For Pirie-Gordon's knowledge of the area: Pirie-Gordon n. d., a-d. Winstone surely mistakenly places one survey of Alexandretta in 1906: Winstone 1990, 73.

[31] Winstone 1982, 63.

[32] Winstone 1990, 50. For the intelligence aspects of the survey: Sheffy 2002, 36; Winstone 1982, 108-09.

[33] In 1910 he had married Mabel Alicia Buckle, daughter of the editor of *The Times*.

Once war had broken out, Naval Intelligence in the Near East was focused on Cairo, especially with Turkey's declaration in November 1914. Naval Intelligence had sent a small group of experts to Egypt, among them David Hogarth, an expert on the Near East.[34] Hogarth had excavated at Carchemish, and had been instrumental in setting up a survey of the Sinai peninsula on the eve of war; his main employment was as Keeper in the Department of antiquities at the Ashmolean Museum, Oxford. In December 1914 Hogarth passed through Athens and the BSA on his way out to Cairo.[35] His contacts in Athens were Alan J. B. Wace, the Director, and John Linton Myres.[36]

Pirie-Gordon was commissioned as Lieutenant in the RNVR in November 1914, and by December was in Cairo.[37] There were plans afoot for the Near East that projected an invasion of the Ottoman Empire in the region of Alexandretta, the port investigated by Pirie-Gordon and Ian Hall.[38] One of incidents with which Pirie-Gordon was involved was the landing of troops near Alexandretta from HMS *Doris*.[39] The railway, which ran along the coast, was attacked by a party under Captain Larken from the *Doris* and a train was derailed. Pirie-Gordon destroyed the locomotive using guncotton 'borrowed' from a Royal Navy warship.[40] The Turkish authorities refused to blow up their own train; and with the threat of the *Doris* bombarding Alexandretta, Pirie-Gordon was 'appointed' a Turkish officer for the day in order to complete the destruction. Pirie-Gordon was subsequently awarded the Distinguished Service Cross 'for services while attached to the landing parties on the Syrian coast'.[41] The Alexandretta plan was discarded and it was decided to make for Constantinople, and for the allies to land at Gallipoli.[42]

During 1915 the Arab Bureau in Cairo took shape under the instigation of Captain William Reginald ('Blinker') Hall, head of Naval Intelligence.[43] Among Pirie-Gordon's tasks in Cairo was a report on the caliphate, prepared in March 1915, which recommended a move towards an Arabian identity.[44] In the background lay another former BSA student, J. Milne Cheetham in the Embassy at Cairo (1911-19), who was party to the intelligence

---

[34] Gill 2004l. For Hogarth's earlier work in the Near East: Gill 2004c.

[35] Winstone 1990, 61.

[36] Winstone 1990, 61.

[37] Winstone 1990, 63. For the date of his commission see *The Times* 10 December 1969, 13. Yigal Sheffy informs me that Pirie-Gordon's original role was as press censor.

[38] Alexandretta was also under observation by Woolley when his ship the *Zaida* was sunk by a mine in 1916: Winstone 1982, 79-80.

[39] The *Doris* bombarded Alexandretta on 15 December 1914. For the role of the *Doris*, Usborne 1933; Hoyt 1976.

[40] Reported in *The Times* 10 December 1969, 13.

[41] Reported in *The Times* 30 June 1915, 8.

[42] James 1999, 16: 'This *opera bouffe* episode understandably persuaded many people – including Churchill – that Turkish military competence was not very highly developed'.

[43] O'Halpin 2004.

[44] Westrate 1992, 145.

gathering.[45] With the Gallipoli campaign underway, Hogarth passed through Athens in July 1915, giving Compton Mackenzie the impression that he was looking for a job, when it is clear that Hogarth was part of Hall's plans for the Near East.[46] Hogarth's linguistic expertise was required, and in August 1915 he was interrogating Turkish soldiers captured at Gallipoli.[47]

In October 1915 Hogarth's role was made official when he was appointed Lt.-Commander in the RNVR, based in Cairo. In November 1915 Pirie-Gordon was back in Cairo working on the 'Alexandretta Project', which under the Sykes-Picot agreement was to make Alexandretta a port open for British trade.[48] He was promoted to Lt.-Commander RNVR on 2 December 1915.[49] On 30 November 1915 Gertrude Bell was working with Hogarth in the Arab Bureau: 'For the moment I am helping Mr Hogarth to fill in the intelligence files with information as to tribes and sheikhs. It's great fun and delightful to be working with him'.[50] Hogarth continued to serve in the Near East, visiting Arabia (June 1916), and then following the campaign through Palestine from the attack on Gaza in November 1917. He took part in the peace conferences at Versailles and Sèvres in the spring of 1919, before being formally released from service in July of that year.

Gallipoli

The Gallipoli campaign, with its intention to capture Constantinople, required the support of Turkish speakers to act in an intelligence role. At least two former BSA students, Hogarth and Pirie-Gordon, were active in the campaign; both of them were based in Cairo. Both had travelled widely in the Ottoman Empire and were fluent speakers of Turkish. In April 1915 Pirie-Gordon was assigned to the Middle East Force (MEF) and was sent to the Dardenelles. He served under Lt.-General William R. Birdwood as part of the ANZAC force at Helles.[51] On 24 May, the day of the armistice to bury the dead,[52] Pirie-Gordon was evacuated from ANZAC cove suffering from 'ptomaine poisoning'.[53] Hogarth seems to have been in

---

[45] Winstone 1982, 172-73. Later in the war he was based in Alexandria: Gertrude Bell Archive, Newcastle: 29 September 1919. In her diary entry for 30 September 1919 Gertrude Bell noted: 'He is a typical F. O. man of the bloodless type'. Cheetham was British High Commissioner in Egypt (1914-15). The Gertrude Bell letters and diaries are available on-line at www. gerty. ncl. ac. uk.

[46] Mackenzie 1931, 254-55.

[47] Gill 2004l.

[48] I am grateful to Yigal Sheffy for drawing my attention to the 'Alexandretta Project'.

[49] *The London Gazette* 7 December 1915, 12193 (as from 2 December 1915).

[50] Gertrude Bell Archive, letters, 30 November 1915. In a letter of 6 December 1915 Bell indicated that Hogarth was leaving Cairo on the following day and was clearly in London until early 1916.

[51] For Birdwood's landings at Helles on 25 April 1915: James 1999, 102-03.

[52] James 1999, 185-87.

[53] Mackenzie 1929, 79. Ptomaine poisoning is a term that has been replaced by food-poisoning. For Pirie-Gordon at Gallipoli: *The Times* 10 December 1969, 13. Pirie-Gordon's departure was noted by Audrey Herbert, who was also an intelligence officer at Gallipoli: Herbert 1919.

Gallipoli during the early part of August interviewing Turkish prisoners.[54] Pirie-Gordon, now a Lieutenant in the RNVR, returned and worked with Captain Ian Smith of the Royal Engineers (who had worked with Pirie-Gordon in the Levant) on interrogation.[55] Among them was Sharif Muhammad al Faruqi, an officer of the Ottoman army, who was interviewed in October 1915.[56] Faruqi was recruited for the Arab Bureau operating as 'G', and serving as a go-between for Cairo and the Sharif of Mecca.

Other former BSA students were serving in the army. G. Leonard Cheesman had enlisted in the army on 26 August 1914, and was a Lieutenant in the 10th Battalion of the Hampshire Regiment. The Hampshires formed part of the 10th (Irish) Division that landed at Suvla Bay on the morning of 7 August 1915.[57] Cheesman's unit was part of a post on the front line at The Farm, part of the allied line on Chunuk Bairun under Brigadier-General A. H. Baldwin.[58] On the morning of 10 August 1915, Mustafa Kemal (Ataturk) led a surprise attack on the British.[59] Baldwin and more than 1000 British troops died, Cheesman among them.[60]

Another former student was William Loring, who had served as a Lieutenant in the Scottish Horse during the Boer War. Holding the rank of Captain, he rejoined his old regiment, which was initially allocated to coastal defence in the north-east of England. In August the regiment, the 2nd Scottish Horse, became an infantry unit as part of the 2nd Mounted Division and was sent to Gallipoli,[61] landing at Suvla Bay on 2 September 1915.[62] Loring was wounded, as well as mentioned in despatches. However during October he was seriously wounded, evacuated and subsequently died at sea on the hospital ship *Devanha* from his wounds on 24 October 1915.[63]

[54] Gill 2004l.

[55] Mackenzie 1929, 180: 'Ian Smith had been appointed Military Consul at Van just when the war broke out. He was a delightful fellow, whose pronunciation of Turkish was probably the most acute hardship that [Wyndham] Deedes had to endure at Gallipoli. While 'Jan' Smith was interrogating prisoners, I have watched Deedes sitting in a corner of the tent with an expression on his face such as you may see on a musical aunt listening to a piano solo being played by an unmusical niece'. Smith was appointed to the intelligence work at Gallipoli in March 1915: Sheffy 1998, 103.

[56] Winstone 1982, 190. Interrogation was the normal function of intelligence units: Sheffy 2002, 37.

[57] James 1999, 280.

[58] James 1999, 297.

[59] James 1999, 298-300.

[60] Cheesman is listed on the Helles Memorial, Gallipoli.

[61] See Kitchener's allocation of the unit to the campaign: James 1999, 83.

[62] James 1999, 308.

[63] Loring is listed on the Helles Memorial, Gallipoli. Two of his brothers, Lt.-Col. Walter Latham Loring, Royal Warwickshire Regiment, and Major Charles Buxton Loring, 37th Lancers (Baluch Horse) had been killed on the Western Front in October and December 1914. A third brother, Captain (and later Rear-Admiral) Ernest Loring commanded HMS *Albion* and had served at Gallipoli.

The Aegean

With the Gallipoli campaign abandoned in January 1916, and Salonica occupied by troops of the entente in October 1915, operations continued in the Aegean. The Anatolian coast was seen as vulnerable to attack and raiding British forces could tie up large numbers of troops. Moreover ports such as Smyrna could be used to threaten entente supply lines to Salonica.[64]

Several former students were operating in this area. One of the least celebrated concerns the exploits of Pirie-Gordon, now promoted to Lt.-Commander, in the Gulf of Smyrna. It seems that the strategic port of Smyrna became the focus of British attention from the early months of 1916. A report dated 17 February noted that 'Vurla and the Turkish batteries in the Gulf of Smyrna have again been heavily bombarded'.[65] At the same time a British force landed on Chios, which faces the Çesme peninsula.[66] Details of the action were kept secure. In mid-June *The Times* notes, 'though there have been no British reports on the subject the Turks have frequently over a long period reported the bombardment of points, which are presumably fortified, near the entrance to the Gulf of Smyrna'.[67] It seems that there was a specific objective to set up a British base on the island of Makronisi (Chustan) in the Gulf of Smyrna. This was intended as a base, supported by an aerodrome, from which to enforce the blockade of Smyrna. The island had been occupied by a small British Naval force in April 1916, and renamed 'Long Island'. This force, consisting of men from the Royal Naval Division, included two 12-pounder guns which were placed on board the light cruiser HMS *Lowestoft* on 12 April.[68] The attack seems to have been successful and Pirie-Gordon was the technical civil administrator of the island. One of the more bizarre occurrences concerns his design for a new stamp for 'Long Island' on a typewriter, which he issued on 7 May 1916.[69] Some stamps were typed on plain paper, others overtyped on Ottoman issues.[70] For this

---

[64] See for example the report that 'Two German submarines, which have been brought overland, are now known to be ready for service in the Gulf of Smyrna': 'Ammunition for the Turks', *The Times* 30 July 1915, 6. The same report notes, 'Anglo-French aeroplanes have again attacked Smyrna, destroying the gasworks and the petrol depôt'. For earlier British naval attacks in this area: 'Smyrna bombarded', *The Times* 22 May 1915, 7. For the British blockade and the use of Smyrna as a base for Turkish torpedo boats: 'The pursuit of the raider', *The Times* 19 April 1915, 8. For the proposed feint on Smyrna in July/August 1915: Mackenzie 1929, 231.

[65] *The Times* 21 February 1916, 7. Vurla (the modern Urla) lies at the southern end of the Gulf of Smyrna.

[66] 'British landing at Chios', *The Times* 21 February 1916, 7. The report noted the arrest of the German and Austrian consuls. Chios had been captured by the Greeks in November 1912. The plan to arrest 'enemy agents' including consular agents in the islands off the Anatolian coast had been prepared by Compton Mackenzie in early August 1915: Mackenzie 1929, 280-83.

[67] 'Smyrna coast bombarded', *The Times* 17 June 1916, 5.

[68] Royal Naval Division War Diary, PRO ADM/3084. The *Lowestoft* was part of the 8th Light Cruiser Squadron in the Mediterranean from 1916. The Division had two 12-pounder guns at the start of the Gallipoli campaign: James 1999, 78.

[69] Noted in *The Times* 10 December 1969, 13.

[70] A convenient selection can be found in the archive of Spinks, London: www. spink. com.

undertaking Pirie-Gordon was threatened with court martial, but he saved himself by sending a set to the philatelist, King George V. The island itself had to be abandoned in the face of Turkish attack. The Royal Navy monitor, the M30, which was supporting the force was sunk on 14 May 1916 by Turkish fire.[71] Pirie-Gordon reportedly destroyed the remaining stamps on the island on 26 May, presumably when the force left. These events seem to be reflected by the Ottoman *communiqués* which appeared through June: 'North of the isle of Keusten [Makronisi] an enemy monitor was driven off by our artillery, which shelled enemy depôts on this isle and on the Isle of Hakin'.[72] This seems to place British ('enemy') bases on Makronisi (Uzun Ad.) and Hakin (Hekim Ad.). Ottoman reports noted 'an enemy [British] monitor, assisted by two airmen, fired without result some 20 shells against Beaih, south of Fotcha (Phokia), and then withdrew. Another monitor near Makronisi was driven off to the high seas by our artillery fire'.[73] Ottoman reports of activity in the area continued in the summer. They included the shelling of Makronisi by a monitor and attempted attacks by a torpedo-boat on Phokia (Foça) at the mouth of the Gulf of Smyrna.[74]

John Linton Myres was the Wykeham Professor of Ancient History at Oxford.[75] Myres, then in his mid-40s, arrived in Athens in 1915 and was initiated into intelligence work through the British Refugee Relief Office.[76] Tasks included looking for bases used by German submarines, and for monitoring the movement of Turkish forces.[77] Myres was initially based on Samos and was nominally a civilian, though he moved to Kalmynos early in 1916.[78] He was appointed Lt.-Commander in the RNVR, which he suggested was to protect him should he be captured.[79] In his new role Myres commanded the *Syra* until August 1916. During this period he raided the Turkish mainland, which drew Turkish troops away form other theatres of war.[80] Myres had gained a reputation by the summer of 1916. He knew the Anatolian coast well from his work with William R. Paton when he had first gone out to Greece.[81] *The Times* described 'a professor of archaeology' who 'perpetrate[d]

[71] The M30 had been commissioned on 23 June 1915. The M30 was commanded by Edmund Lawrence Braithwaite Lockyer.

[72] 'Monitor's attack near Smyrna', *The Times* 16 June 1916, 7. The *communiqué* was issued through Amsterdam on 15 June.

[73] 'Smyrna coast bombarded', *The Times* 17 June 1916, 5. The Ottoman report originated in Constantinople on 16 June.

[74] *The Times* 11 July 1916, 5, noted from an Ottoman *communiqué* received in Amsterdam on 9 July.

[75] Boardman 2004.

[76] Myres 1980, 12.

[77] Myres 1980, 12.

[78] Myres 1980, 13.

[79] Myres 1980, 14.

[80] Halpern 1987a, 292. For examples of raids: Halpern 1987b, 159, reporting a raid of 20 July 1916 in which Myres took '150 large cattle, 300 sheep and goats and 50 horses and asses'.

[81] Gill 2004n.

one of those cattle-lifting expeditions against the coast of Anatolia which have alike made his name famous as the Black Beard of the Aegean and provided HM ships with many a welcome head of stolen cow or sheep'.[82] Myres is reported to have opened fire on a French torpedo boat based at Mudros and this may have been at this point in time.[83]

In August 1916, after the *Syra* required repairs following a cattle-raiding exploit, Myres took charge of the caique *St Nikolas*.[84] Raids continued, though in late September in the gulf of Oassus he destroyed a house owned by the wife of Paton, which led to official complaints.[85] Damage to Greek interests on the mainland seems to have led to the cessation of the hostilities.[86] Myres was in charge of the *St Nikolas* until March 1917. He was eventually posted to the *Aulis* at Syra under Compton Mackenzie's overall control. Mackenzie described him in this manner:

> A scholar of mundane reputation before the war, Professor J. L. Myres was now a Lieutenant-Commander in the RNVR. In appearance he resembled some Assyrian king with more than a suggestion of the pirate Teach, and to such an outward form were added the passionate ubiquity of the Flying Dutchman and the fierce concentration of Captain Ahab.[87]

The *Aulis* had been the private yacht of Prince George of Greece.[88]

Mackenzie and Myres then toured the Dodecanese in April 1917.[89] Myres later replaced Mackenzie in Athens working as an intelligence officer through the International Passport Control Office.[90] Mackenzie clearly had a low opinion of his abilities, writing in August 1917:

> [Myres] cannot act as active counter-espionage officer unless you want him to run a third show. None of my officers will work under him, or if they are made to, will do their best work. He cannot manage subalterns. He thinks they're all stupid and noisy undergraduates. I understood he was to act as liaison officer with the Greek General Staff, but General Beaumont seems to think he's to be *his* active Intelligence Officer. ... Myres is running about Athens as fast as one of the cockroaches that used to eat

---

[82] 'En peau de loup. Professors as cattle lifters', *The Times* 2 August 1916, 9. In case there is any doubt about the identification, it is qualified by the description: 'once a model Proctor of Oxford University'.

[83] Woolley 1954.

[84] Myres 1980, 18. The caique had been at Kalymnos.

[85] Documentation for the raid is provided in Halpern 1987b, 175-78.

[86] Gill 2004n; Halpern 1987a, 293; Halpern 1987b, 182 (26 October 1916, 'I have given orders to discontinue the operations of raiding cattle on the Anatolian Coast').

[87] Mackenzie 1940, 136.

[88] Mackenzie 1940, 131.

[89] Mackenzie 1940. 185-87. Mackenzie noted that Myres was anti-Italian: Mackenzie 1931, 254.

[90] Mackenzie 1940, 352 (August 1917); Myres 1980, 22.

his moustache in the tug *Syra*. General Fairholme on being told of his arrival nearly had an apoplexy and ejected him from his room.[91]

Myres was appointed to the Greek Order of George I for his work in the Aegean.

Aegean and Crete

One of the serious threats to Allied activities in the Aegean, not least the supply of troops in Salonica, was the activity of German and Austrian submarines. There was considerable concern about the number of ships lost and a number of strategies, including naval intelligence, were deployed to meet the challenge.[92] Stanley Casson recalled seeing the wreck of a beached Allied merchantman as he sailed to Salonica,[93] and later coming across the crew of a German submarine, whose vessel had been sunk off the western Peloponnese, and who had been interned at Tripolitsa in the Peloponnese.[94] Even at the end of the war there were intelligence reports suggesting continued activity.[95] In 1920 Winifred Lamb and May Herford observed the roads that had been built from the Gulf of Corinth to allow troops to be moved overland in order to avoid the Aegean.[96]

One of the responses was to post officers to monitor any such activity in the Greek islands, and in particular, to try to identify possible refuelling stations.[97] Among these officers was Richard M. Dawkins, a former BSA Director, who had resigned thanks to a large legacy. Dawkins was in his mid 40s and a Fellow of Emmanuel College, Cambridge; he had been in Anatolia on the eve of the outbreak of war.[98] John Cuthbert Lawson had also been involved in censorship prior to Venizelos' move to Salonica.[99] He was in his early 40s and a Fellow and Senior Proctor of Pembroke College, Cambridge. Both Dawkins and Lawson had a detailed knowledge of modern Greek.

Lawson was commissioned in the RNVR and was allocated to the Diadem Class cruiser, HMS *Europa* based at Mudros.[100] He travelled out from Liverpool on the *Cameronian*, a former German ship captured in west Africa. At Mudros Lawson was assigned to the First Detached Squadron, and the Edgar Class cruiser HMS *Edgar*. The squadron's area of responsibility was defined as 'an area comprising Crete and the coast of Asia Minor from

[91] Mackenzie 1940, 364.

[92] Marder 1965, 334-36; Halpern 1987a, 243-59. The figures are: August 1915, British 54, Allied and Neutral 38; January-March 1916, British 13, Allied and Neutral 9; April 1916, 16; May 1916, 37; June 1916, 43; July 1916, 33, August 1916, 77, September 1916, 39.

[93] Casson 1935, 96. See, for example, the sinking of the troopship, *Marquette*, in the Gulf of Salonica on 23 October 1915: Halpern 1987a, 178, 191.

[94] Casson 1935, 165.

[95] Mackenzie 1940, 144.

[96] Gill 2007.

[97] Sheffy 2002, 38.

[98] Gill 2004g.

[99] Lawson 1920, 3.

[100] Lawson 1920, 10.

the south of Samos to Rhodes, together with any islands'.[101] Lawson was based at Suda Bay in western Crete. He was involved with counter-espionage, and was greatly exercised by the ability of the German consuls to report British shipping movements through the British-owned cable network.

One of the key events was in August 1916 when Venizelos, the former prime minister of Greece, left Crete for Salonica and formed a provisional government.[102] The crucial role of Crete and its relationship with the provisional government under Venizelos brought additional staff to assist Lawson, Richard M. Dawkins and William Reginald Halliday.[103] While Lawson remained at Suda, Dawkins was assigned to eastern Crete, and Halliday to western; Halliday later worked at Suda with Lawson.

Halliday joined the RNVR in May 1916, and was sent to Crete that year. Dawkins was commissioned as Lieutenant in the RNVR in 1917.[104] The Royal Navy was an obvious place for Dawkins to serve as the son of a former Rear-Admiral. He had been working in Turkey when war broke out, and in the early years he had served in a volunteer corps in North Wales. After an initial period working on press censorship at the British Legation in Athens from December 1915,[105] he had been engaged with cable censorship on Syra.[106] Myres took him to Astypalaia on his trawler.[107] One of Dawkins' tasks was to observe the movements of German submarines in the Aegean.

A further aspect of their work was to prepare and disseminate anti-German propaganda. Lawson played a key role in Venizelos' visit to Crete in September 1916, that confirmed the island's support for Venizelos. Lawson wrote specifically about his role as a Naval Intelligence officer.

> He must secure native agents ashore along coastlines of many hundred miles to report sightings of submarines, and movements of ships or persons suspected of communicating with or re-victualling them, and devise codes for the passing of such information. He must direct the tracking and procure the arrest of spies and enemy agents in general.[108]

---

[101] Lawson 1920, 23.

[102] Clogg 1992, 89-93. For Lawson's part: Lawson 1920, 2-3.

[103] Lawson 1920, 154: 'there were two Greek-speaking English officers now associated with me in Crete, formerly members like myself of the British Archaeological School in Athens'. The Cretan group was due to be supported by a Sub-Lietenant Henty on his reallocation from the intelligence group at Salonica to Crete in February 1917: Mackenzie 1940, 99, and 356.

[104] Dawkins famously refused to shave off his moustache or to grow a beard: Mackenzie 1940, 102 (with poem addressed to Dawkins).

[105] Mackenzie 1939, 6, 'to check the local activities of the hostile propaganda'. Dawkins was reported to be in Malta in November 1915: BSA Minute Book 8, Meeting of November 23, 1915.

[106] Mackenzie 1939, 437; Mackenzie 1940, 100-01.

[107] Dawkins 1954.

[108] Lawson 1920, 4-5. For the discovery of an apparent supply of fuel on the island of Gaulis off the southern coast of Crete: 'Allied police measures in Greece', *The Times* 1 March 1916, 7 (reported from Canea, Lawson's base, via Athens).

Lawson himself began to suspect that Kythera had become a base for German submarines that were supported by the Royalist cause in the Peloponnese in late 1916.[109] As a result he arranged for the Venizelists on Crete to annexe the island in January 1917,[110] though it was soon handed back to the Royalist cause. Not all in the intelligence community appreciated his actions. Basil Thomson, in London, commented on 'a "stunt" of a British Naval Intelligence officer, a Mr Lawson, in private life a Fellow of Pembroke College, Cambridge, whose irresponsible action had jeopardized the honour of his country'.[111] The key issue in these criticisms was that Lawson, a fluent Greek speaker, and observer of the situation on the ground, was better placed to assess the threat to Allied shipping. Thomson also accused Lawson of 'submarinitis', in spite of the heavy shipping losses that were taking place in the Aegean.[112] Lawson subsequently rose to be Lt.-Commander RNVR.

The work of Lawson and Dawkins was surprisingly highlighted in a light-hearted article in *The Times* of August 1916:

> we find that a former senior proctor of Cambridge University has for some months been in charge of our activities directed against miscreants in Western Crete – a task in which his colleague at the other end of the island is a former Director of the School at Athens, a master of arts of the same university. As to their precise functions a discreet censorship will allow no reference.[113]

Although most of the work was linked to intelligence, Dawkins clearly took an interest in archaeological work in Greece. In a report in *The Times* of May 1918, 'a former Director of the British Archaeological School at Athens' (surely Dawkins), had reported to 'a friend' in Athens 'that certain famous medieval monuments in Candia and Canea in Crete are in danger of destruction', and in particular the fortifications of Candia.[114]

Salonica

In October 1915 Britain and France opened up a front at Salonica as part of a response to aggression towards Serbia.[115] Greece was at the time still technically neutral, though with

---

[109] Lawson 1920, 242-43. Behind this may have been the sinking of the *Gallia* on 4 October 1916 off Cape Matapan: see Halpern 1987a, 258.

[110] Lawson 1920. See also Mackenzie 1940, 53.

[111] Thomson 1931, 204-05. Thomson continued, 'It was irresponsible and foolish meddling of this kind that complicated the difficulties of the Allied Governments and injured their prestige in Greece'. For an assessment of Thomson: Rutherford 2004.

[112] Thomson 1931, 155.

[113] 'En peau de loup. Professors as cattle lifters', *The Times* 2 August 1916, 9.

[114] 'Cretan monuments in danger', *The Times* 30 May 1918, 5.

[115] Clogg 1992, 89. For a discussion of events written by a former BSA student who served as an Intelligence Office in Macedonia: Forster 1941, 89. The first British and French troops landed in Macedonia on 5 October 1915.

leanings towards Germany. Cairo decided to locate an intelligence unit in Salonica,[116] and by the end of the year a group of former BSA students was based there. Among them was the newly-promoted Lt.-Commander Pirie-Gordon, who apparently in January 1916 was attached to the battleship HMS *Exmouth,* which was with the Detached Squadron at Salonica.[117] The group in Salonica was known by the acronym EMSIB, Eastern Mediterranean Special Intelligence Bureau.[118] This body, formed in March 1916, had emerged from earlier intelligence gathering groups in Greece.[119]

It is possible to identify members of EMSIB in Salonica. Ernest Gardner, Yates Professor of Classical Archaeology at the University of London and a former BSA Director, was 53 when, in 1915, he was commissioned as Lieutenant-Commander in the RNVR.[120] He had been a student at the BSA in its opening year of 1886/7, along with Hogarth. Marcus Niebuhr Tod, university lecturer in Greek epigraphy at Oxford,[121] joined the group in a civilian capacity in 1915, though he was later commissioned in the Intelligence Corps. Tod initially worked through the YMCA on the western front (1915), but his skills in Greek led to his recruitment as an interpreter in Macedonia.[122] He was commissioned as a 2nd Lieutenant, and worked in Salonica from November 1915. His initial task, working with Ernest Gardner, was 'reading the Greek daily news and translating anything that affected the Allied armies'.[123] Gardner's work is satirised in *The Times*:

> consider the labours of that other professor, who for months interpreted the oracles of the Athenian Press for the benefit of our forces in Salonika, and found that the pure fount of prophecy is defiled in the very shadow of the Parthenon by barbarian gold in a manner quite unknown to the Pythia of Delphi. Later he wrestled with the innate Byzantinism of the modern Hellene, and became consultant archaeologist to the army and took charge of the multitudinous treasures of gold, marble, and pottery dug up by the industrious trench-builders in Macedonia, tiding over a delicate diplomatic situation and reconciling the jealousies of three nations.[124]

[116] Compton Mackenzie implies that the EMSIB unit in Salonica came under EMSIB in Cairo: Mackenzie 1940, 77. The Greek intelligence operation had been relocated to Egypt after Gallipoli: Sheffy 2002, 38. For Hogarth's knowledge of Salonica: Hogarth 1888b.

[117] The appearance of a 'first day cover' franked 25 January 1916 and addressed to Pirie-Gordon is perhaps significant (auctioned Shreves Philatelic Galleries Inc, Addison TX, 27 June 2003, lot 691). Stamps for the projected Monastic Republic of Mount Athos were used on the envelope. These are reported to have been prepared on board the HMS *Ark Royal.* Given Pirie-Gordon's interest in stamps at Markonisi (Long Island) in May 1916, it is not unreasonable to link him with this project.

[118] Mackenzie called it the V Bureau: Mackenzie 1931, 340.

[119] Sheffy 2002, 38-39, 45; see also Mackenzie 1939, 7. The decision to form EMSIB was apparently taken in June 1915.

[120] Gill 2004j.

[121] Crawford 2004.

[122] Tod apparently volunteered to be an interpreter: Meiggs 1974, 490.

[123] Meiggs 1974, 490.

[124] 'En peau de loup. Professors as cattle lifters', *The Times* 2 August 1916, 9.

The British archaeologists in Macedonia found time to study the inscriptions and antiquities that were coming to light during operations.[125] Gardner ensured the protection of the objects by forming a collection based in the White Tower.

A number of other former BSA students also arrived in Salonica in November 1915. It is not always clear whether they were members of EMSIB or attached to military units of the Salonica Expeditionary Force. Edward Seymour Forster, who had studied at Oriel College and was Lecturer in Greek at Bangor, was commissioned 2nd Lieutenant in Special Lists in November 1915, and served in the Intelligence Corps in Salonica from 24 November 1915 until 1918.[126] Arthur Maurice Woodward, who had studied at Magdalen College, Oxford, and had served as Assistant Director of the BSA, was then Assistant Lecturer at the University of Leeds.[127] He not only had travelled in Turkey (with Ormerod), but had also worked on Greek epigraphy from Thessaly and Macedonia.[128] He served as Officer Interpreter and subsequently Intelligence Officer with British Salonika Force, from November 1915 to January 1919.[129] Francis Bertram Welch, Headmaster of Wadham House School Hall, Cheshire, was recruited at the age of 40 and joined the intelligence team at Salonica as a Lieutenant in February 1916.[130] Welch had not only studied at Magdalen College, Oxford, Hogarth's college, but had also been a student at the BSA under Hogarth. During their time at the BSA they had worked on Phylakopi together, as well as on various projects on Crete.[131] During this period Welch was based in the Strymon valley, for part of the time in charge of a Turkish labour battalion.[132] A further possible member of EMSIB was Arnold Wycombe Gomme, who had studied at Trinity College, Cambridge, and was Lecturer in Greek and Roman History at the University of Glasgow.[133] He had made a study of Boeotia while a BSA student.[134] He was in his early 30s when he enlisted, initially serving in the Army Service Corps in France; due to poor eyesight he was unsuitable for combat duties. He then worked for Intelligence at Salonica.

---

[125] Casson and Gardner 1918/19; Casson 1916; see also Tod 1919; Tod 1922. Tod cites material noted by Captain A. E. W. Salt, Base Censor in Salonica. For French archaeological work in Macedonia: Picard 1918/19.

[126] Forster 1941. He rose to the rank of temporary Major. Forster's record card states that he arrived in Salonica on 24 November 1915.

[127] Hood 1998, 60-64, no. 10.

[128] Woodward and Ormerod 1909/10; Woodward 1910/11a; Woodward 1913. Woodward had published material from Constantinople, but had clearly not been there at the time of his research: Woodward 1910/11b. For the context of the work in Anatolia: Gill 2004c.

[129] According to his service record, Woodward arrived at Salonika on 23 January 1916. During this period he was promoted from 2nd Lieutenant to Lieutenant in the Intelligence Corps.

[130] Welch's war record shows that he was initially a staff appointment and was later transferred to the Intelligence Corps.

[131] Hogarth and Welch 1901; Atkinson, et al. 1904.

[132] Welch 1918/19b; Welch 1918/19c; Welch 1918/19a.

[133] Kitto 1959.

[134] Gomme 1910/11; Gomme 1911/12.

At the start of 1916 Forster described Salonica as 'a hot-bed of *espionnage* and intrigue, and every movement of the allied armies was reported to the enemy'.[135] The neutral position of Greece allowed diplomatic staff from Germany, Austria, Bulgaria and Turkey to observe the situation and so counter-espionage became key. Events took a dramatic turn when on 23 May 1916 the strategic Fort Rupel was surrendered by the Greek forces to the Bulgarians.[136] This led to the declaration of martial law in Salonica, and the opening of an entente offensive in August.

This new situation in Macedonia saw a change in the deployment of intelligence personnel.[137] In mid-1916 Tod was commissioned as a Captain in the Intelligence Corps and was assigned to the French Sector of the Macedonian front, where he was involved with censorship and the decoding of German ciphers.[138] Stanley Casson left Britain for Salonica in February 1916.[139] He had responded to a request for officers who had personal knowledge of Greece and the Balkans in addition to linguistic ability.[140] In Salonica he was a member of the Intelligence Corps, attached to the 10th Irish Division.[141] Eustace M. W. Tillyard had served in France from 1915 as a Captain in the 4th Royal Lancashire Regiment. However in 1916 he was seconded to Salonica, specifically working with the Intelligence Corps. Maurice S. Thompson, who had studied at Corpus Christi College, knew northern Greece, and especially Thessaly, extremely well.[142] He had served in the Durham Light Infantry in France before transferring to the Macedonian front in 1916 as an intelligence officer, apparently as part of EMSIB. Cecil Allison Scutt's knowledge of modern Greek brought him a commission in February 1916 and an appointment in Macedonia.[143] His obituary noted that he worked in 'intelligence and outpost work', and that 'he commanded a mixed band of Macedonian irregulars in the roughest of guerrilla conditions. A born leader of men where only manhood counted, he retained this quality throughout his life and stood firmly to his judgement of what was real and what was trivial, in human affairs'.[144] Scutt transferred to become an intelligence officer to a division in 1917. EMSIB in Salonica was not composed entirely of former BSA students. Among the Slavonic scholars in EMSIB was Nevill Forbes, of Balliol College, Oxford, who was appointed Lieutenant in the RNVR.[145] Another former BSA student was Solomon Charles Kaines Smith, who was a Major in the

---

[135] Forster 1941, 100.

[136] For Lawson's analysis of the background to the incident and the possible go-between: Lawson 1920, 68.

[137] For Army Intelligence at Salonica in 1916: Mackenzie 1939, 10.

[138] Meiggs 1974, 490; Waterhouse 1986, 25. For French intelligence: Sheffy 2002, 48.

[139] Casson 1935, 94.

[140] Casson 1935, 92.

[141] Casson 1935, 100.

[142] Wace, *et al.* 1907/08; Wace and Thompson 1912; Wace and Thompson 1914.

[143] Scutt was appointed a temporary 2nd Lieutenant on 13 February 1916: *The London Gazette* suppl. 16 February 1916, 1780.

[144] *Clare College*, 93.

[145] Stone 2004.

Censor's Department of the General Staff at Salonica from 1916 working as the Aegean Postal Censor. He had studied at Magdalene College, Cambridge, and had been admitted to the BSA under Hogarth. He also served as Advisory Officer to the Greek Government.[146]

In August 1916 Pirie-Gordon was posted from Cairo to Salonica to take charge of EMSIB activities there, though he apparently did not arrive until September.[147] This is against the background of the Bulgarian occupation of eastern Macedonia in August 1916; and on 30 August significant elements of the Greek garrison in Macedonia offered to support the entente.[148] Venizelos left Crete on 25 September and arrived in Salonica on 9 October, thus creating a rival government in Greece.[149] One of Pirie-Gordon's tasks was to strengthen the work with French intelligence, and it is likely that Tod was a key component in this strategy.[150] In this period there was a growing tension in Salonica between the work of EMSIB and the intelligence work of Army GHQ. Compton Mackenzie described the issue as follows:

> … the anxiety of Army Headquarters at Salonica to be completely independent of either control or advice by General Headquarters of the Mediterranean Expeditionary Force at Imbros led the Intelligence there to hinder and oppose in every conceivable way the work of the V Bureau in Salonica, and thus equally in Athens, both of which had been to some extent dependent on the good will of the GHQ. … Later on, relations between the branch of the V Bureau in Salonica and the Intelligence of Army Headquarters became so strained that no efforts from Athens to bring about a better understanding could accomplish anything, while they were regarded with suspicion by both sides.[151]

This came to a head in the autumn of 1916, when the GHQ in Salonica carried out a 'purge' of the EMSIB, 'which lost them the services of the two best Intelligence officers in the Eastern Mediterranean'.[152] One of the tensions was over liaison with French intelligence, and Mackenzie recalled,

> GHQ had forbidden them [EMSIB] to communicate directly with the French Intelligence Service, except through GHQ, and consequently work which in the ordinary way would be accomplished in half an hour often took as much as five days.

---

[146] Wace expresses strong views on Kaines Smith in a review in *JHS* 44, 1 (1924) 138.

[147] Mackenzie 1931, 341. Dates for these events are recorded in the Magdalen College, Oxford archive. I am grateful to Robin Darwell-Smith for providing me the information.

[148] Forster 1941, 111.

[149] Forster 1941, 111-12.

[150] For this co-operation: Sheffy 1998, 156-57.

[151] Mackenzie 1931, 340-41. See also Mackenzie 1939, 10, 'Army Headquarters at Salonica resented the B branch of the EMSIB almost as much as Army Headquarters itslf resented not being General Headquarters'.

[152] Mackenzie 1940, 51, and see 77, 'GHQ had expelled two invaluable officers of the EMSIB from Salonica'.

The result was that the French Intelligence officers met Pirie-Gordon and [Captain Eustace] Barker secretly at night to discuss matters and exchange ideas.[153]

Pirie-Gordon, who was sick in hospital at the start of the year, gave up his position in Salonica in January 1917 and served the rest of the war in the Palestine campaign.[154] There was pressure from the Foreign Office to make Pirie-Gordon a Military Control Officer at Athens,[155] though this did not happen.[156] In early February 1917 EMSIB Salonica was ordered by the GHQ 'to suspend work', and Mackenzie was asked to withdraw the staff to Syra as part of a newly designed 'Aegean Intelligence Service'.[157] By this time the staff comprised Captain Eustace Barker, Lieutenant N. Dewhurst and Sub Lt. Henty RNVR.[158]

Those members of EMSIB who remained in Salonica were now required to operate through the GHQ. Tillyard was transferred to the Intelligence Corps in 1917, and in 1918 became the British Liaison Officer with Greek GHQ (until 1919). Tod continued to work in Macedonia (until February 1919), except for a period between January and March 1918. Thompson, who had returned to England in the autumn of 1917 to marry, returned to Salonica to find both a promotion to the rank of Major, and transfer to GHQ under Sir George Francis Milne, commander of the British forces.[159] In 1918 he worked in the front lines collecting intelligence. Casson was attached to the General Staff as an intelligence officer at the end of 1917.[160] Part of his brief was to monitor for a possible Bulgarian attack which would mirror the large German push on the western front in the spring of 1918.[161] Gardner, whose role in Salonica was little more than supervisor of antiquities, returned to London where he worked in naval intelligence at the Admiralty from the autumn of 1917 to 1919. Welch, who had served in the intelligence team in Salonika, was moved to Athens in 1918. In 1917 the Allied offensive on the Macedonia front in April failed to make gains, although the entente position in northern Greece was enhanced by the occupation of Thessaly in June. There was also the Great Fire in Salonica in August 1917.[162]

Other former members of the School were engaged in the Salonica force. Thomas Eric Peet, who had studied at The Queen's College, Oxford, was a Lecturer in Egyptology at Manchester.[163] He was in his mid-30s when he was commissioned in the Royal Army

---

[153] Mackenzie 1940, 51.

[154] There was an attempt to make Mackenzie responsible for the Salonica operation: Mackenzie 1940, 77. For Compton Mackenzie's role in intelligence work: Sheffy 2002, 44.

[155] Mackenzie 1940, 103-04, 107, 140-41.

[156] Mackenzie 1940, 158.

[157] Mackenzie 1940, 77; Sheffy 1998, 151.

[158] Mackenzie 1940, 78, 130-31. Barker was second-in-command in Salonica: Mackenzie 1940, 51. The party arrived at Syra in early March.

[159] Hood 1998, 113. For Milne: Reid 2004.

[160] Casson 1935, 192.

[161] Casson 1935, 194-95.

[162] Casson 1935, 184-89. Mackenzie noted the fire as 19 August: Mackenzie 1940, 364.

[163] Gunn 2004.

Service Corps (1915), and was responsible for the support of the British forces in Macedonia while based in Salonica. He was then transferred to the King's Liverpool Regiment in France (1918).[164] Hilda Lorimer, who had studied at Girton College before being admitted to the BSA, and was classical tutor at Somerville College, Oxford, worked at the Scottish Women's Hospital in Salonica from 1917.[165] Henry Arderne Ormerod, who like Peet had studied at The Queen's College, was Assistant Lecturer in Greek at Liverpool and in his late twenties. Although there are no clear indications that he served in Macedonia after his time in France, he was awarded the Chevalier of Order of King George I of Greece. His unit, the 148th Battery (of the 20th Brigade) of the Royal Field Artillery, moved to Macedonia in November 1915 as part of the 27th Division.[166] In March 1917 he succeeded to the care of the museum of antiquities, which had been looked after by Gardner.[167]

One of the former students who was in Salonica in a civilian capacity was Robert Carr Bosanquet, the former BSA Director. Already in his mid-40s, he applied to the War Office to aid the war effort, but it seems that his health was seen as an impediment.[168] Instead he was asked to go and help with Serbian refugees. He left London on 1 January 1916, and later that month was at Medua in Albania. Part of his task was to deliver supplies, which had been collected by the American Harriet Boyd Hawes, whom he had known when excavating at Crete and who was married to a former BSA student.[169] From February to April 1916 Bosanquet was in Corfu, which had been occupied by the French on 10 January 1916.[170] In August he went out to Macedonia, working with the Serbian Relief Fund. In a letter home he cryptically notes: 'I rode two or three evenings a week, thanks to the kindness of one of our Intelligence officers who got me a mount, and that kept me fit'.[171] Like many of the British troops in Salonica, Bosanquet suffered from malaria and 'enteric'. As a result he was forced to return to England in September 1917.

Following the September 1918 entente offensive, Bulgaria arranged a truce at the end of the month, followed by Turkey on 30 October. The GHQ for the British Army in Salonica was transferred to Constantinople. In November 1918 Casson was working on a scheme for the occupation of Constantinople.[172] Casson was based in the city as part of the Army of the Black Sea, which covered the region from Syria (now under French control) to Russia.[173]

---

[164] The transfers of men from Macedonia took place through the summer of 1918.

[165] Waterhouse 2004. See also Waterhouse 1986, 24; Gill 2002. For the hospital: Bosanquet 1938, 203.

[166] In December 1916 his battery was broken up and men deployed to the 67th and 99th Battery within the same Brigade.

[167] Casson and Gardner 1918/19, esp. p. 27 for Ormerod's dates in Salonika. Ormerod left for England in Autumn 1917.

[168] Bosanquet 1938, 181.

[169] Bosanquet 1938, 184; Allsebrook 1992, 143.

[170] Bosanquet 1938, 190. See also Forster 1941, 101; Allsebrook 1992, 144-45; Clogg 1992, 89.

[171] Bosanquet 1938, 197.

[172] Casson 1935, 214.

[173] Casson 1935, 217.

The Bolshevik Revolution of 1917 led to a number of areas declaring independence, notably Transcaucasia on 22 April 1918. British forces were sent to support these newly established states, arriving at Baku on 4 August 1918. Other British troops were sent to southern Russia in December 1918. At least three former BSA members were involved in these campaigns. Casson was posted to British forces in Turkestan,[174] Wilfrid Farrell in Transcaucasia, and Forster worked in Constantinople and then in the Black Sea region until 1919. It is clear from his later publications that Forster was a fluent Turkish speaker. Thompson also worked in Constantinople from November until he returned to England in March for demobilisation. Woodward seems to have moved forward with the British troops in the September offensive as he served in Bulgaria at the end of his career. British forces withdrew from Transcaucasia on 19 August 1919 and from southern Russia in November 1920.

Athens

See under Wace in Chapter 2.

Palestine and Mesopotamia

Pirie-Gordon had been removed from Salonica in January 1917. He returned to his work with the Arab Bureau and was a member of the Political Mission in Palestine (1917-19). The latter part of 1917 saw manoeuvring between Hogarth and Sykes over the degree to which France would have future influence in the Middle East. Both Hogarth and Pirie-Gordon were involved in Allenby's push from Gaza (November 1917) northwards through Palestine.[175] Pirie-Gordon appears to have returned to London, but was recalled to the Arab Bureau in Cairo in early 1918, apparently at the request of Mark Sykes.[176] Pirie-Gordon was given the rank of Lt.-Colonel and in January 1918 prepared a report on the future role of the Arab Bureau.[177] One of his achievements was the creation of a series of detailed maps of the Levant that were made available to the public after the war.[178] As Allenby pressed into Palestine, Pirie-Gordon edited the *Palestine Times*, which provided news for the Egyptian Expeditionary Force.

Among the British forces was the Rev. Adam F. Findlay, a military chaplain, who served in Egypt, finally attached to the 1/6 Highland Light Infantry of the 52nd Division in Palestine. On the Mesopotamian front, Wilfrid Farrell served in the Intelligence Corps in both Egypt and Iraq.[179]

---

[174] Casson 1935, 236.

[175] Pirie-Gordon 1919.

[176] Westrate 1992, 111. For the intervention of Sykes: *The Times* 10 December 1969, 13.

[177] Westrate 1992, 195. For Pirie-Gordon's new rank and service: *The London Gazette* suppl. 6 February 1918, 1712. His commission dated from 16 January 1918.

[178] Pirie-Gordon n. d., a-d.

[179] Unpublished memoir, 'Pedagogue's progress: reminiscences of Mesopotamia, Transcaucasia, and Palestine' (photocopy at St Anthony's College, Oxford, Middle East Centre Archive, GB165-0104).

Western Front

Former BSA students were in action within weeks of the declaration of war. Among the first casualties was Kingdon Tregosse Frost.[180] Frost had joined the Officers' Training Corps when he became lecturer at Queen's, Belfast. He was associated with the Cheshire Regiment, which was garrisoned in Londonderry; and in 1912 he was an officer in the 3rd Battalion. At the outbreak of war he seems to have transferred to the 1st Battalion, which was sent to Belgium as part of the British Expeditionary Force. He was involved in the Battle of Mons and was killed on 24 August near Elouges 'fighting like a demon, having refused to surrender'.[181] It was not immediately noted that Frost had been killed as he was officially part of the 3rd Battalion.[182] He was buried at Wihéries Communal Cemetery, Hainault.

Other members of the School were soon in action in France. At least three served in France before being transferred to Macedonia. Eustace M. W. Tillyard was commissioned in the 4th Royal Lancaster Regiment and by 1915 held the rank of Captain.[183] He served in France from 1915-16 before being seconded to Salonica in 1916. Stanley Casson served in Flanders with 1st Battalion East Lancashire Regiment during 1915. His Battalion, part of the 11th Brigade, 4th Division, took part in the battles of St Julien, Frezenberg, and Bellewaarde (24 April – 25 May 1915), which formed part of the Second Battle of Ypres. He was seconded to staff duties in Salonica on 1 March 1916.[184] Maurice S. Thompson was commissioned on 19 September 1914 in the 14th (Service) Battalion Durham Light Infantry.[185] The choice of unit may have been influenced by Thompson's lectureship at Armstrong College in Newcastle upon Tyne. Cyril Bertram Moss-Blundell, a fellow Oxford classicist, who had been due to be a BSA student for the academic year 1914-15, was commissioned as Lieutenant to the same battalion in January 1915.[186] The Battalion initially formed part of 64th Brigade, 21st Division. On arriving in France on 11 September 1915, Thompson and Moss-Blundell found their unit engaged in the Battle of Loos as one of the reserve units brought into action on 26 September.[187] There were significant losses, with the Division suffering some 3800 casualties, among them Moss-Blundell who was killed in action on 26 September.[188] On 28 November 1915 the Battalion was transferred to 18th Brigade, 6th Division, and Thompson found himself at Ypres. Just after Christmas he was

---

[180] Dunlop 2000.

[181] Quoted by Dunlop 2000, 8.

[182] This explains why Frost's date of death was sometimes given as 4 September 1914 (as it is on the BSA's war memorial).

[183] The Battalion was formed in 1915.

[184] *London Gazette* suppl. 27 March 1916, 3271.

[185] Hood 1998, 112. Thompson was mentioned five times in despatches.

[186] *The London Gazette* suppl. 22 January 1915, 793, lists him as temporary Lieutenant with the 14th Battalion.

[187] Thompson's Medal Record Card in the National Archives gives 11 September 1915 as the date he entered France.

[188] The Commonwealth War Graves Commission lists the date of death as 27 September 1915. Moss-Blundell is listed on the Loos Memorial.

sent home after being gassed. He did not return to France and was instead posted to Salonica.

Other members of the School fared less well. Guy Dickins, Fellow of St John's College, Oxford, had joined the King's Royal Rifle Corps, the 13th (Service) Battalion (part off 111th Brigade, 37th Division), in November 1914. Erwin W. Webster, Fellow of Wadham College, had received his commission on the same day and in the same battalion as Dickins. Webster had been unsuccessful in trying to become an interpreter: his mother was German (and he was Taylorian Scholar in German and had studied in Berlin), he had been brought up in France, and his father was a noted Hispanist. Webster's attempt to become an airman was thwarted by an accident. Both Dickins and Webster, now Captains (February 1915), went with their battalion to France in July 1915. Dickins, a company commander, was wounded on 13 July 1916 during the Somme offensive, and died of wounds in hospital on 17 July.[189] Webster was wounded at the end of 1915, and in the autumn of 1916 was seriously ill as a result of trench fever (caused by lice). Webster was killed on 9 April 1917 leading his company into action on the first day of the Battle of Arras (First Battle of the Scarpe).[190]

Other former BSA students serving in France included Edward S. G. Robinson, a 2nd Lieutenant in the Norfolk Regiment (1915-16), who was severely wounded in the legs during the Somme offensive.[191] Roger M. Heath had enrolled in September 1915, serving as a private in the Royal Fusiliers. He was commissioned as 2nd Lieutenant in the 9th (Reserve) Battalion of the Somerset Light Infantry. However with the pressure on troops following the Somme offensive, he was attached to the 3rd Battalion in France, serving as the Adjutant. He was posted to a position near Delville Wood, which had just been captured as part of the Somme offensive. On his first day in the trenches, 16 September 1916, he was killed in action.[192]

Another member of the BSA who served in France was Lawrence B. Tillard, who had studied classics at St John's College, Cambridge. He was gazetted 2nd Lieutenant in the 6th (City of London) Battalion, The London Regiment (City of London Rifles) in September 1914, rising to Captain in June 1916 when the battalion became part of the King's Royal Rifle Corps.[193] A. C. Sheepshanks was commissioned in the 8th (Service) Battalion of the Rifle Brigade in 1914. The Battalion was attached to 41st Brigade, 14th (Light) Division. His

---

[189] Casson recalled that it had been Dickins 'who had been mainly instrumental in my ever going to Greece at all, whose scholarship and archaeological learning had helped and guided me, was dead, shot through the head': Casson 1935, 266-67. Dickins is buried in the St Pierre Cemetery, Amiens. This cemetery was used at that time for the dead from the 56th (South Midland) Casualty Clearing Station. Information from the Commonwealth War Grave Commission. A short obituary appeared in *The Times* 22 July 1916, 9.

[190] Webster is listed on the Arras Memorial. Edward Thomas, the poet, was killed on the same day in the same battle.

[191] Sutherland 1977. Robinson wrote two poems which reflect on his wounds (reproduced at pp. 427-28). Robinson's obituary states that he served in the Northamptonshire Regiment, but his military record shows that he was in fact in the Norfolk Regiment.

[192] Casson 1935, 266. Casson and Heath had travelled through Greece in the winter of 1913-14 when both were School students. Heath is listed on the Thiepval Memorial on the Somme.

[193] *London Gazette* 13 October 1914; 1 August 1916; 7 March 1917; 14 November 1917.

unit took part in the action of the Battle of Hooge on 30 July 1915, when German forces first used flame-throwers in action. For this he was awarded the DSO, for which the citation stated:

> For conspicuous gallantry in a counter-attack on 30th July, 1915, when he continued to advance with his company till only he and 6 riflemen were left standing. He then checked a bomb attack by the enemy, and held on to his trench till late in the evening. He was wounded in the head early in the day, but returned to duty with his Company after the wound had been dressed.[194]

Sheepshanks eventually ended up as Lt.-Colonel (1918). He served with his battalion until February 1918, when he became an Assistant Instructor at the Army Infantry School.

At least two former members of the BSA served in the Royal Field Artillery. Henry A. Ormerod won the Military Cross while serving as a temporary Lieutenant in the 148th Battery, Royal Field Artillery. His Battery formed part of 20th Brigade of the Royal Field Artillery, serving in France in September 1915. His citation stated:

> For conspicuous gallantry during operations. As FOO he directed fire for 39 hours after the occupation of a village, under constant shell fire. Next day his information regarding a heavy counter-attack by the enemy was most valuable. Though wounded he continued to observe from a spot where he was constantly sniped at. He did other fine work.[195]

It is not clear where this action took place, though France is likely.[196] Ormerod was also mentioned in despatches in 1917. Wilfrid Farrell, who was teaching at Haileybury until July 1915, was transferred from the territorial force to the Royal Field Artillery with effect from 11 September 1915.[197] He served with the Royal Field Artillery in France from the summer of 1916,[198] before transferring to the Intelligence Corps in the Middle East.

Other BSA members who served in France included Thomas Eric Peet, who had earlier served on the Salonica front, and was transferred to the King's Liverpool Regiment in France (1918). Norman Whatley, Fellow of Hertford College, had been a member of the Oxford University OTC from 1909. He served in France as Captain and then Brevet Major with the Intelligence Corps. Charles Heaton Comyn, the architect, had initially enrolled in the Artists Rifles, but received a commission in the Royal Garrison Artillery. He served with 284 Siege Battery in Flanders from March 1917 to November 1918.[199] His unit saw action in the battle of Passchendaele. Harry H. Jewell, another architect, served in the Royal West

---

[194] *The London Gazette* 3 September 1915, 8840.

[195] *The London Gazette* suppl. 26 September 1916, 9429.

[196] One possibility is the action at St Eloi, as part of the battle of Neuve Chapelle, 14-15 March 1915. The events could have taken place during the Second Battle of Ypres in April-May 1915. If the Military Cross was awarded for action in 1916, the events must have taken place in Macedonia.

[197] *The London Gazette* suppl. 15 September 1915, 9195.

[198] Farrell's Military records seem to suggest that he went to France on 9 May 1916.

[199] This was part of the 84th Heavy Artillery Group from September to October 1917.

Surrey Regiment (1916) as a Lieutenant, until he was transferred to the 139th Company of the Labour Corps, working on advanced roads.

Two non-combatants worked in France before being recruited for military intelligence due to their linguistic skills. William R. Halliday had worked for the Red Cross in France during 1915 before being commissioned in the RNVR and serving on Crete. Marcus Tod had worked with the YMCA in France during 1915, before transferring to intelligence in Salonica. Max Laistner, who had been appointed lecturer at Queen's University, Belfast in 1915 as a successor to Frost, enlisted as a private in the 29th (Works) Battalion of the Middlesex Regiment in 1916,[200] and rose to the rank of CQM Sergeant. The unit served in the United Kingdom throughout the war. On demobilisation in 1919 he became an Assistant Lecturer in Classics at Manchester University.

Other War Service

Two former BSA students were in the Royal Army Medical Corps. Wynfrid Laurence Henry Duckworth was University Lecturer in Physical Anthropology at Cambridge.[201] He had trained as a doctor and was commissioned Captain in the RAMC; he was not sent to the front due to injuries sustained earlier in his life. John Henry Hopkinson had read classics at University College, Oxford, and had been a Craven University Fellow at the BSA. He had become a lecturer in Classical Archaeology in the University of Manchester, and warden of Hulme Hall (1904-14). He was ordained in the Church of England in 1914, but served as a private in the Royal Army Medical Corps. In 1915 he became vicar of Holy Trinity, Colne, Lancashire.

The architect, Edward Barclay Hoare, had studied at Magdalen College, Oxford, and then went to Athens as an architectural student. He was working in New Delhi at the outbreak of war, and served with the Indian Defence Force. John Frederick Randall Stainer, the son of the composer Sir John Stainer, was in his late 40s when wore broke out. He had read classics at Magdalen College, Oxford and had been admitted to the BSA for the session 1889-90. He served as a sergeant with the East Surreys (1914-19).[202]

Non-combatant roles

A number of former BSA members were active in non-combatant roles. Halliday and Tod had worked on the western front for the Red Cross and YMCA, and Bosanquet for the Serbian Relief Fund in 1916 and 1917. Sidney Barnsley had also worked as a VAD in a Red Cross Hospital in England. Henry J. W. Tillyard had married Wilhelmina Kaufmann, of Lahr, Baden in 1913. At the beginning of the war he was interned in the Ruhleben concentration camp (1914-15), before being allowed to return to his lectureship in Greek at Edinburgh University.[203]

---

[200] The battalion was formed in June 1916 in Mill Hill. In April 1917 it became part of the Labour Corps, 5th Battalion.

[201] Boyd 2004.

[202] He does not seem to have left the UK.

[203] For Ruhleben: Stibbe 2008.

A number of former students were members of government departments. Edwyn R. Bevan worked for the Political Intelligence Bureau of the Foreign Office. E. F. Benson also worked on propaganda for the Foreign Office. Arnold Joseph Toynbee, who had studied classics at Balliol, had been excused war service on the grounds of a bout of dysentery that he had picked up in his travels in the Mediterranean.[204] He concentrated instead on working on anti-Turkish propaganda;[205] but after resigning his Oxford fellowship, he worked for the intelligence department of the Foreign Office from May 1917. Henry Stuart-Jones, along with Robert M. B. McKenzie of Trinity College, Oxford, was employed by the Foreign Office and undertook 'confidential work in London and Geneva, in which their knowledge of eastern European languages was of great value'.[206] This seems to have been in the academic year 1917/18 when Stuart-Jones served as a member of the Intelligence Department of the War Office.[207] Sir Milne Cheetham was based in the British Embassy in Cairo. Adolph Paul Oppé worked in the Ministry of Munitions, which was formed in 1915; and Dorothy Lamb worked in the Ministry of National Service (1916-18) and Ministry of Food (1918-20), and was awarded the MBE in 1919.[208]

Some former students were clearly involved with intelligence work, not least Alan Wace, F. W. Hasluck, and his wife Margaret Hasluck, at Athens. Gardner returned from Salonica in 1917, and that autumn joined naval intelligence at the Admiralty where he served until 1919. John A. R. Munro, bursar of Lincoln College, Oxford, worked in intelligence for both the Admiralty and the War Office.[209] Arnold W. Gomme joined the intelligence section of the Admiralty when he was invalided out of Salonica. William J. Woodhouse acted as an interpreter in the Censor's Office, in Sydney, Australia. Mrs Culley (formerly E. B. Abrahams) worked as an examiner for postal censorship.

Charles Douglas Edmonds was around 40 when war broke out. He had read classics at Emmanuel College, Cambridge, and had been teaching at the Royal Naval College, Osborne from 1905.[210] Osborne was in effect the preparatory school for Dartmouth, the Royal Navy's Training Establishment, taking boys at 13. John P. Droop had been declared unfit for military service at the start of the war. He initially started work for the long-established Society of Friends of Foreigners in Distress, but by September 1915 was involved with Lady

---

[204] Millar 2004.

[205] Toynbee 1915; Toynbee 1916.

[206] Gill 2004m. Henry Stuart-Jones is listed in the 1st Battalion Pembrokeshire Volunteer Regiment as a temporary 2nd Lieutenant (from 26 March 1917), and as a temporary Lieutenant as from 12 October 1917: *London Gazette* suppl. 2 May 1917, 4193; suppl. 7 January 1918, 428. From December 1905 Stuart-Jones had made his second home at Saundersfoot in Pembrokeshire. Mackenzie served as a Sub-Lt. in the RNVR. For intelligence work in Switzerland: Sheffy 1998, 152-53.

[207] Annual Report for Trinity College. I am grateful to Clare Hopkins for this information.

[208] Gill 2004i.

[209] Munro had worked with Hogarth in Anatolia: Munro and Hogarth 1893. See also Gill 2004c.

[210] The College had opened in 1903.

Roberts' Field Glass Fund, which worked to obtain optical equipment for military purposes. In October 1917 he was employed as a Higher Division clerk in the Admiralty.[211]

Decorations

Students of the School were decorated for their service in Macedonia and on the Western Front. Of the British military awards, Pirie-Gordon was awarded the Distinguished Service Cross (DSC) for his role in the *Doris* attacks on Alexandretta. A. C. Sheepshanks was awarded the DSO (1915). Several students were awarded the Military Cross: Farrell,[212] Ormerod, Scutt and Thompson. Several former students were mentioned in despatches, among them Forster (twice), Hogarth (three times), Kaines Smith, Lawson,[213] Myres,[214] E. M. W. Tillyard (three times), Woodward (twice), Thompson (four times), and Ormerod. Hogarth was made a Commander of the Order of St Michael and St George (CMG) in 1918 for his work with the Arab Bureau. Several students were awarded the Order of the British Empire, either as Officers (OBE), Lawson,[215] Myres, E. M. W. Tillyard, Tod,[216] or as Members (MBE), Forster, Dorothy Lamb, and Kaines Smith (1919).

Students were also awarded foreign decorations. Hogarth was decorated for his war services. He received the Egyptian Order of the Nile (2nd class), which was instituted in 1915, and the Sherifician Order (2nd Class), both for his work with the Arab Bureau. Several students were awarded Greek decorations.[217] The most prestigious was the Order of the Redeemer, first awarded in 1833. There are five classes. The Gold Cross was awarded to Gardner, and the Silver Cross to Lawson and Dawkins. Other members of the school – Bosanquet, Casson, Halliday, Kaines Smith, Woodward (1924) – were awarded the order though the class is not clear. The second most prestigious was the Royal Order of George I, instituted in January 1915. There were two recipients, Myres (Commander) and Ormerod (Chevalier). Kaines Smith and Lawson were awarded the Greek Medal of Military Merit, and E. M. W. Tillyard the Greek Military Cross. Farrell's General Service Medal had clasps for Iraq and Palestine.[218]

Three former students received Serbian awards. Bosanquet and Evelyn Radford received the Order of St Sava for their work with the Serbian relief fund. Forster received the Order

---

[211] Though there is no record that Droop worked in intelligence, many classicists were in the Admiralty for this purpose: Gill 2004r, 426-27. See also Beesly 1982. I am grateful to Adrian R. Allan (Liverpool University) for clarifying this part of Droop's career.

[212] *The London Gazette* suppl. 12 December 1919, 15446.

[213] *The London Gazette* suppl. 20 July 1917, 7424.

[214] *The London Gazette* suppl. 20 July 1917, 7424.

[215] 'For valuable services with the British Naval Mission to Greece': *The London Gazette* suppl. 17 July 1919, 9109.

[216] *The London Gazette* suppl. 15 March 1918, 3289. Tod's rank is given as Captain in the Intelligence Corps.

[217] Details of these awards can be found on the website of the Presidency of the Hellenic Republic, www. presidency. gr/en/tagmata. htm (accessed on 11 August 2005).

[218] The information is recorded on Farrell's record card in the National Archives.

of St Sava (5th Class), presumably for his work alongside Serbian forces in Macedonia. Tod was awarded the *Croix de Guerre (avec palmes)* for deciphering enemy signals during his time attached to the French forces in Macedonia.[219]

Conclusion

The carnage of the First World War brought about major changes to the BSA. During the 1920s significant numbers of women were admitted to the School, notably Winifred Lamb and May Herford in 1920. Secondly students who had served in the war were being admitted as students. Bernard Ashmole had fought in France in the Royal Fusiliers and had been decorated with the Military Cross.[220] Frank Laurence Lucas had served on the western front in the Royal West Kent Regiment, and then later in the Intelligence Corps.[221] Walter A. Heurtley, a Cambridge classicist who had served in Macedonia in the East Lancashire Regiment, became Assistant Director of the BSA in 1923.[222] Heurtley returned to Macedonia excavating prehistoric mounds.[223]

Casson returned as Assistant Director. He was later to excavate in Constantinople, where he had served at the end of the war.[224] For some the war did not end with the Armistice in November 1918. Pirie-Gordon was transferred to the Gulf of Finland and served on a torpedo boat in 1919 in the wake of the Russian revolution. In August 1919 he was part of the military mission in northern Russia.[225] This is likely to have been the period when he made the claim of commanding 'The smallest flagship' in the Royal Navy.[226]

The contributions made by members of the BSA played a significant part in the British war effort, not least in the Aegean, Macedonian and indeed Ottoman spheres. An Aegean-based correspondent for *The Times* – one suspects the hand of Compton Mackenzie – made the point in 1916: 'many members of the British School of Archaeology in Athens have earned the confidence of multitudinous naval and military superiors, and have won, by their industry and adaptability, coupled with their local knowledge, positions of importance'.[227]

---

[219] *The London Gazette* suppl. 25 September 1917, 9946.

[220] Kurtz 1994.

[221] Cohen and Pottle 2004.

[222] Hood 1998, 147. Heurtley had been the Deputy Governor of the Military Prison in Salonika.

[223] Heurtley 1923/24, 1924/25; Heurtley and Hutchinson 1925; Heurtley and Hutchinson 1925/26; Heurtley 1926/27; Heurtley and Davies 1926/27; Heurtley 1927; Heurtley 1931; Heurtley 1939.

[224] Jones, *et al.* 1928; Rice, *et al.* 1929; Macridy Bey and Casson 1931.

[225] 'To rescue Petrograd. New government formed, British mission at work, Yudenitch's bold move', *The Times* 16 August 1919, p. 10. *The London Gazette* suppl. 18 August 1919, 10450 noted that temporary Lt.-Col. Pirie-Gordon was 'specially employed' on the General List (as of 14 May 1919).

[226] *The Times* 24 April 1967, 9 (letter). Although Pirie-Gordon does not identify the officer, the reference to the command of a Motor Torpedo Boat (MTB) in Portsmouth is likely to be to himself.

[227] 'En peau de loup. Professors as cattle lifters', *The Times* 2 August 1916, 9.

EPILOGUE

The BSA changed enormously in the thirty or so years from its opening in 1886. Archaeology as a discipline had been in its infancy and there were still hints of antiquarianism in the early days of the School. Yet the influences of the new scientific approaches of Flinders Petrie started to alter the work of Ernest Gardner and, more significantly, the energetic research of David Hogarth. Cecil Harcourt-Smith started to develop the concept of training for students by assigning them specific projects as well as by introducing a training excavation. The idea of a 'curriculum' was reflected in Robert Carr Bosanquet's scheme for the session that he presented in February 1901. The BSA had struggled with its finances from the very beginning and its income was too low to sustain active field work; Ernest Gardner's salary as Director was in effect subsidised by his Cambridge college. Cecil Harcourt-Smith, with his secondment from the British Museum, transformed the administrative structures of the School and managed to establish a regular government income to pay for the Director.

The research conducted by members of the BSA influenced the way in which archaeology could be seen as a tool for understanding the ancient world in general. This was part of a new methodological approach that had its roots in Oxford. Henry Francis Pelham had a vision for the way in which physical remains of the past could be used alongside ancient history as a means of understanding the ancient world. Pelham, a member of the managing committee of the BSA until his death in 1907, was a moving force behind the establishment of the British School at Rome. Francis Haverfield was another key presence in Oxford; many of his students were admitted to the BSA and became involved in archaeological work in Britain. Skills honed in the Mediterranean were put to good use on the remains of the Roman occupation of Britain.

The BSA managed to establish itself with an expertise for regional surveys as a means of exploring and recording the prehistory of the Aegean. The surveys of Laconia, Thessaly and Aetolia were innovative and also more cost effective than labour-intensive digs.[1] The prehistoric excavations at Phylakopi, Knossos and Palaikastro have had lasting influence on the study of the Bronze Age Aegean. Yet despite these developments there were less than perfect excavations: Megalopolis, Kynosarges, and the sanctuary of Artemis Orthia at Sparta. There were also frustrations: noticeably the cancelled BSA dig at Datcha.

Former students of the BSA pursued a wide range of careers and vocations. Some followed an academic pathway, and at the Silver Jubilee Year of the BSA, Macmillan summed up one of the benefits of the School in terms of an institution that prepared

---

[1] Surveys have continued to be an important fieldwork strategy for members of the BSA: *e.g.* Bintliff and Snodgrass 1985; Cavanagh, *et al.* 1996; Mee and Forbes 1997.

individuals for subsequent academic life.[2] Some 15 students were awarded college fellowships at Cambridge, and 18 at Oxford. The period coincided with the expansion of university education in Britain. Former students became members of departments across England, Wales, Scotland and Ireland. The presence of former students at Birmingham, Liverpool (with its newly established Institute of Archaeology) and Manchester is particularly striking. The students' firsthand experience of Greece, the islands and Anatolia helped to foster a British interest in the archaeology of the Greek world, though some of the promising students died during the First World War.

Among the former students who were to influence future generations was John L. Myres in both Oxford (as Wykeham Professor of Ancient History from 1910) and Liverpool. At Oxford, Henry Stuart-Jones, who was appointed Camden Professor of Ancient History (1919), was one of the key influences; he was succeeded in 1927 by John G. C. Anderson. Marcus N. Tod was University Lecturer in Greek Epigraphy, and Stanley Casson was University Lecturer in Classical Archaeology. John A. R. Munro became Rector of Lincoln College (1919). Three Oxford men were poised to make a major impact but were killed during the War: G. Leonard Cheesman, Fellow of New College, Guy Dickins as University Lecturer in Classical Archaeology, and Erwin W. Webster as Tutor at Wadham College. At Cambridge Alan Wace was appointed Laurence Professor in Classical Archaeology (1934) and encouraged the study of the prehistory of the Aegean. Montague Rhodes James was elected Provost of King's College in 1905, and Eustace M. W. Tillyard later became Master of Jesus College (1945-59).

Academic careers were not confined to Britain. Charles H. Hawes held the post of Lecturer in Anthropology at the University of Wisconsin, and then at Dartmouth College, before becoming Associate Director of the Museum of Fine Arts in Boston. Max Laistner held a series of posts in Britain before being appointed Professor of Ancient History at Cornell (1925). Some students went to universities in what was then the British Empire. William John Woodhouse was elected to the chair of Greek at the University of Sydney (1901), and Cecil A. Scutt Professor of Classical Philology at the University of Melbourne (1920). H. Arnold Tubbs held the post of Professor of Ancient History at University College, Auckland, New Zealand (1894), although he was dismissed in 1907. Henry J. W. Tillyard was appointed Professor of Latin at University College, Johannesburg (1919-21).

Several students helped to develop archaeology abroad: John W. Crowfoot as Director of the British School of Archaeology in Jerusalem, Campbell C. Edgar as Inspector of Antiquities for Lower Egypt, John H. Marshall as Director-General of Antiquities in India, and Henry Stuart-Jones as Director of the British School at Rome. Others pursued careers in museums by working in national collections such as the British Museum and the Victoria and Albert Museum, and in university museums such as the Fitzwilliam and the Ashmolean.[3] Three students worked for museums in North America: the Museum of

---

[2] Macmillan 1910/11, xxx.

[3] Edward S. G. Robinson became Keeper of the Department of Coins and Medals at the British Museum (1949). Alan Wace was Deputy Keeper at the Victoria and Albert Museum (1924-34). Montague Rhodes James was Director of the Fitzwilliam Museum in Cambridge (1893-1908), and David Hogarth was Keeper of the Ashmolean Museum (1908).

Fine Art in Boston, the Metropolitan Museum of Art in New York, and the Royal Ontario Museum in Toronto.[4] Campbell C. Edgar rose to be Keeper at the Cairo Museum.[5]

At least 15 former students pursued careers as schoolmasters. Several taught at Winchester, among them Arthur George Bather who created a school museum, giving 'much time and thought to classifying the exhibits of Greek and Roman Art', as well as contributing to the collection.[6] Two, Herbert Awdry and Arthur Charles Sheepshanks, were admitted to the BSA while they teaching to enable them to benefit from a period of study in Greece.[7] Following Awdry's trip to Greece he published on the topography of Pylos and Sphacteria.[8] Both Percy Gardner and John L. Myres had a vision for including classical archaeology in the school curriculum.[9] Other former students held senior positions in the Board of Education. William Loring was involved with the preparation for the 1902 Education Act, and later held the position of Warden of Goldsmith's College, New Cross.

Many of the BSA students in this period were clergy sons – and in at least one case, a daughter of the manse.[10] It is therefore unsurprising that some of the male students followed their fathers' vocation. Most of the BSA students who were ordained in the Church of England were from Oxford. Several were involved in the Church of England's attempts to foster links with the Orthodox churches of the east.[11] Oswald H. Parry,

---

[4] Charles Henry Hawes in Boston, Gisela Richter in New York, and Charles Currelly in Toronot.

[5] For his earlier work on the catalogue commission: Edgar 1903a; Edgar 1903b.

[6] 'Arthur George Bather', *The Wykemist* 699 (29 March 1928) 486-87.

[7] British School at Athens 1894/95, 26: 'the Committee were very glad to admit Mr. Awdry as a regular student in order to emphasise the usefulness of the School as an adjunct to the ordinary classical education at home'.

[8] Awdry 1900; Compton and Awdry 1907. For work on Sicily: Awdry 1909.

[9] Myres and Gardner 1902; Myres and Gardner 1905.

[10] For the Cambridge men: M. R. James, son of Rev. Herbert James, rector of Goodnestone, Kent; J. C. Lawson, son of Rev. Robert Lawson, rector of Camerton, Bath; W. Loring, son of Rev. Edward Henry Loring, rector of Gillingham, Norfolk; R. J. G. Mayor, son of Rev. Joseph Bickersteth Mayor of Kingston-upon-Thames, headmaster; E. E. Sikes, son of Rev. Thomas Burr Sikes, vicar of Burstow, Surrey; J. L. Stokes, son of Rev. Augustus Sidney Stokes, vicar of Elm, Cambridgeshire; H. H. West, son of the Very Rev. John West, Dean of St Patrick's Cathedral, Dublin; W. A. Wigram, son of Rev. Woolmore Wigram, vicar of Brent Pelham with Furneaux Pelham, Hertfordshire. For the Oxford men: J. G. C. Anderson, son of Rev. Alexander Anderson, of Edinkillie, Morayshire; A. C. B. Brown, son of Rev. George Bolney Brown, rector of Aston-by-Stone; J. W. Crowfoot, son of John Henchman Crowfoot, Wiggington, Oxfordshire; D. G. Hogarth, son of Rev. George Hogarth, vicar of Barton upon Humber, Lincolnshire; C. C. Inge, son of Rev. William Inge, Provost of Worcester College; H. Stuart-Jones, son of Rev. Henry William Jones, vicar of St Andrew's Church, Ramsbottom, Lancashire; J. L. Myres, son of Rev. William Miles Myres, vicar of Swanbourne; O. H. Parry, son of Rev. Edward St John Parry; John Ff. Baker Penoyre, son of Rev. Slade Baker Penoyre; E. W. Webster, son of Rev. Wentworth Webster. The single woman was Hilda Lorimer, daughter of Rev. Robert Lorimer of Dundee.

[11] Coakley 1992.

formerly Archbishop's Missioner to the Nestorian Christians, was consecrated Bishop of Guiana (1921). Three of the BSA students from Scotland were ordained ministers.

In 1919 the BSA started to look ahead. Alan Wace, who had been appointed as Director on the eve of the First World War, was able to develop his interest in the prehistoric Aegean through his work at Mycenae.[12] However the spirit of rivalry emanating from Sir Arthur Evans effectively brought Wace's fieldwork career in the Mediterranean to a close; it restarted at Mycenae on the eve of the outbreak of the Second World War.[13] As the First World War erupted, the BSA had been looking at Macedonia as a possible area for fieldwork and Wace had investigated the site of Olynthus. The military campaigns round Salonica revealed numerous archaeological sites and Ernest Gardner, serving in naval intelligence, established a small museum to bring the finds together.[14] Walter Heurtley, who had served on the Macedonian front, worked after the war on a series of excavations in the area.[15] There was also a return to Sparta with Arthur M. Woodward's series of excavations.[16] Long-standing interest in the prehistory of the Aegean would be reflected through the work on Ithaca.[17]

A new generation of students was admitted to the BSA from 1920/21, including growing numbers of women.[18] Winifred Lamb pioneered the search for prehistoric sites in the Aegean and links with Anatolia. She excavated at Thermi on Lesbos and later in Turkey.[19] John Pendlebury became Knossos Curator and excavated at Amarna in Egypt.[20] Humfry Payne, an authority on Corinthian pottery, opened the BSA's excavation at Perachora.[21]

The pre-First World War influences remained on the BSA. John L. Myres was the chair of the Managing Committee (1933-47) and Evans continued to be an important voice. However the relatively weak financial position was not addressed and consequently remained unresolved. Yet as far as research was concerned new areas were being explored. Pendlebury pioneered the links between the Aegean and Egypt in the Bronze Age, and Payne gave a focus to the archaic period.

By 1936, the Golden Jubilee of the BSA, it was recognised that British archaeologists had made a major contribution to the study of the Aegean world. The students of the pre-war generation had laid some solid foundations.

[12] Wace 1919/20, 1920/21a; Wace 1919/20, 1920/21b; Wace 1921/22, 1922/23.

[13] Wace 1939.

[14] Casson and Gardner 1918/19.

[15] Heurtley 1923/24, 1924/25; Heurtley 1939.

[16] *E.g.* Woodward 1923/24, 1924/25; Woodward 1928/30.

[17] *E.g.* Heurtley and Lorimer 1932/33; Benton 1934/35; Benton 1938/39; Heurtley 1939/40.

[18] Gill 2007.

[19] Lamb 1936; Gill 2000b. See also Gill 2004r.

[20] Grundon 2007.

[21] Blakeway, *et al.* 1940.

APPENDIX I TRUSTEES

AGG-GARDNER, JAMES TYNTE (SIR) (1846-1928)

Born, 25 November 1846, Cheltenham; son of James Agg-Gardner (1804-58) and his wife
Eulalie Emily (1819-1901).

Educ. Harrow (1861).

Camb. Trinity Coll.; matric. 1865; no degree.

Parliamentary candidate, Cheltenham, 1868.

Inner Temple, 1868; called to the bar, 1873.

Conservative MP, Cheltenham, 1874-80, 1885-95, 1900-06, 1911-28.

Mayor of Cheltenham, 1908-09, 1912-13.

Chairman, the Cheltenham Original Brewery Company Ltd.; the Cheltenham Newspaper
Company.

BSA Founding Trustee.

Died, 9 August 1928, at the Carlton Club, London.

Obituaries, memoirs and studies

J. Agg-Gardner, *Some Parliamentary Recollections* (London: Burrow & Co. , 1927); *The
Times* 10 August 1928, 14 August 1928; Richard Davenport-Hines, 'Gardner, Sir
James Tynte Agg- (1846-1928)', in *ODNB*, vol. 21, 460-61.

FRESHFIELD, EDWIN (C. 1827-1918)

Born, c. 1827, Reigate, Surrey; son of James William Freshfield (1801-57), solicitor, and
his wife Mary Anne (1800-75).

Educ. Winchester.

Camb. Trinity Coll.; matric. 1850; BA (1854) MA (1857); LL. D. (1884).

Solicitor, Freshfields (1858); senior partner (1903-18).

Byzantine Research Fund, President.

Winchester Coll., Fell. (1888-95).

Knight of Justice of Order of St John of Jerusalem in England.

BSA Trustee.

FSA.

Married, Zoe Charlotte Hanson, dau. of J. F. Hanson, of the Levant Company, Smyrna, 12
September 1861.

Died, 1 September 1918, Chipstead, Surrey.

Publications

'The Christian Antiquities of Constantinople', *The Times* 25 January 1881, 4.

'The Christian Antiquities of Constantinople', *The Times* 17 March 1881, 6.

'The Mosque of Hagia Sofia at Salonica', *The Times* 8 September 1890, 7.

'Byzantine Research Fund', *The Times* 25 June 1908, 9.

Obituaries, memoirs and studies

The Times 2 September 1918; J. Slinn, *A History of Freshfields, the Firm* (London: Freishfields, 1984); Judy Slinn, 'Freshfield Family (per. 1800-1918)', *ODNB*, vol. 20, 993-95.

JEBB, RICHARD CLAVERHOUSE (SIR) (1841-1905)

Born, 27 August 1841, Claverhouse; son of Robert Jebb, barrister, and his wife Emily Harriet.

Educ. St Columba's College, Rathfarnham; Charterhouse.

Camb. Trinity Coll.; matric. 1858; grad. Senior Classic (1862); Porson Prize (1859); Craven Scholarship (1860); First Chancellor's Medal (1862).

Fell. Trinity Coll. (1863).

Cambridge, Public Orator (1869).

Glasgow Univ. Chair of Greek (1875).

Cambridge, Regius Chair of Greek (1889).

Conservative MP for Cambridge Univ. (1891, 1892, 1895, 1900).

BSA Trustee.

FBA (1902).

Royal Academy, Prof. of Ancient History.

British Mus. Trustee.

Married, Caroline Lane Slemmer (née Reynolds), widow of General Adam Slemmer, 18 August 1874.

Died, 9 December 1905, at Cambridge.

Publications

'Archaeology at Athens and Rome', *The Times* 18 September 1878, 11.

'Delos', *JHS* 1 (1880) 7-62.

'Homeric and Hellenic Ilium', *JHS* 2 (1881) 7-43.

'The Ruins at Hissarlik and Their Relation to the Iliad', *JHS* 3 (1882) 185-217.

(and A. H. Sayce) 'The ruins of Hissarlik', *JHS* 4 (1883) 142-55, 436.

'The Homeric House, in Relation to the Remains at Tiryns', *JHS* 7 (1886) 170-88.

'Sir C. T. Newton', *JHS* 14 (1894) xlix-liv.

'Sir C. T. Newton', *CR* 9 (1895) 81-85.

'Meeting in Celebration of the Twenty-Fifth Anniversary of the Society for the Promotion of Hellenic Studies', *JHS* 24 (1904) l-lxxiii.

Obituaries, memoirs and studies

The Times 11 December 1905; C. Jebb, *Life and Letters of Sir Richard Claverhouse Jebb* (Cambridge: Cambridge University Press, 1907); Hugh Lloyd-Jones, Jebb, Sir Richard Claverhouse (1841-1905)', *ODNB*, vol. 29, 850-53; *DBC*.

LEAF, WALTER (1852-1927)

Born, 28 November 1852, Upper Norwood; son of Charles John Leaf, businessman, and his wife Isabella Ellen Tyas.

Educ. Harrow (1866).

Camb. Trinity Coll.; Class. schol. (1869); matric. 1870; Senior Classic (1874). Craven schol. (1873).

Camb. Trinity Coll. Fell. (1875).

Leaf, Sons, and Co., partner (1877).

London and Westminster Bank, Director (1891); Chairman (1918).

Institute of Banker, Chairman (1919).

BSA Trustee (from 1906).

Married, Charlotte Mary Symonds, 1894.

Died, 8 March 1927, Torquay.

Publications

(Trans.) *The Iliad Translated into English* (London: Macmillan, 1882).

'Some Questions Concerning the Armour of Homeric Heroes', *JHS* 4 (1883) 73-85.

'Notes on Homeric Armour', *JHS* 4 (1883) 281-304.

'The Homeric Chariot', *JHS* 5 (1884) 185-94.

(ed.), *The Iliad* (London: Macmillan, 1886, 1888).

'The Trial Scene in *Iliad* XVIII', *JHS* 8 (1887) 122-32.

'The Codex Wittianus of the *Iliad*', *CR* 3, 9 (1889) 417.

'Nero', *CR* 5, 7 (1891) 338.

A Companion to the Iliad for English Readers (London: Macmillan, 1892).

'Horace, *Carm.* IV. II', *CR* 21, 4 (1907) 104-05.

'Hesiod and the Dominions of Aias', *CR* 24, 6 (1910) 179-80.

'The Topography of the Scamander Valley – I', *ABSA* 17 (1910/11) 266-83.

'The Topography of the Scamander Valley – II', *ABSA* 18 (1911/12) 286-300.

'Trade Routes and Constantinople', *ABSA* 18 (1911/12) 301-13.

'Notes on the Troad', *Geographical Journal* 40, 1 (1912) 25-45.

Troy: A Study in Homeric Geography (London: Macmillan, 1912).

'Some Problems of the Troad', *ABSA* 21 (1914/16) 16-30.

'The Lokrian Maidens', *ABSA* 21 (1914/16) 148-54.

Homer and History (London: Macmillan, 1915).

'Rhesos of Thrace', *JHS* 35 (1915) 1-11.

'On a History of Greek Commerce', *JHS* 35 (1915) 161-72.

'The Commerce of Sinope', *JHS* 36 (1916) 1-15.

'The Military Geography of the Troad', *Geographical Journal* 47, 6 (1916) 401-16 (with discussion, 416-21).

'Strabo, and Demetrios of Skepsis', *ABSA* 22 (1916/18) 23-47.

'Notes on the Text of Strabo XIII. I', *JHS* 37 (1917) 19-30.

'Mr Maury on Achaian Greece', *CJ* 13, 1 (1917) 66-69.

'Paraphrases', *CR* 32, 1/2 (1918) 47.

'The Homeric Catalogue of Ships', *CR* 36, 3/4 (1922) 52-57.

Strabo on the Troad (Cambridge: Cambridge University Press, 1923).

'The Homeric Catalogue of Ships', *CR* 37, 1/2 (1923) 27.

'Corinth in Prehistoric Times', *AJA* 27, 2 (1923) 151-56.

'Prehistoric Corinth', *CR* 37, 3/4 (1923) 65-66.

'Tragic and Homeric Cryptograms', *CJ* 20, 6 (1925) 364.

Obituaries, memoirs and studies

DBC; Charlotte M. Leaf, *Walter Leaf 1852-1927: Some Chapters of Autobiography with a Memoir* (London: J. Murray, 1932); William C. Lubenow, 'Leaf, Walter (1852-1927)', *ODNB*, vol. 32, 967-68.

MACMILLAN, GEORGE AUGUSTIN (1855-1936)

Born, 1 August 1855, Cambridge; son of Alexander Macmillan (1818-96).
Educ. Eton; King's Schol.
Publisher (1874); partner (1879).
BSA, Hon. Sec. (1886-98); trustee (1900).
Hellenic Society, Hon. Sec. (1879); Hon. Treas. (to 1934).
BSA Trustee (from 1900).
Died, 3 March 1936, Danby-in-Cleveland, Yorkshire.

Publications

'A Ride Across the Peloponnese', *Edinburgh Monthly Magazine* (1878), 551-52, 61, 63.
'The British School at Athens', *The Times* 10 February 1885, 6.
'Byzantine Architecture in Greece', *The Times* 28 May 1890, 13.
'Asia Minor Exploration Fund – Proposed Expedition for 1890', *The Times* 18 January 1890, 10.
'Exploration in Asia Minor', *The Times* 12 May 1891, 12.
'Asia Minor Exploration Fund', *The Times* 21 November 1893, 3.
(*et al.*) 'The Penrose Memorial Library', *ABSA* 10 (1903/04) 232-42.
(and Cecil Harcourt-Smith) 'Penrose Memorial Fund', *The Times* 3 November 1904, 10.
'Discoveries in Crete', *The Times* 31 May 1904, 8.
'The British School at Athens - Survey at Sparta', *The Times* 6 February 1906, 8.
'A Short History of the British School at Athens. 1886-1911', *ABSA* 17 (1910/11) ix-xxxviii.
'Excavations at Sparta', *The Times* 27 June 1923, 13.
'An Outline of the History of the Hellenic Society', *JHS*, 49, 1 (1929) i-li.
'M. Jean Gennadius', *JHS* 52, 2 (1932) 297.
(and Cecil Harcourt-Smith) *The Society of Dilettanti: its Regalia and Pictures* (London: Macmillan, 1932).

Obituaries, memoirs and studies

The Times 4 March 1936; Charles Morgan, *The House of Macmillan (1843-1943)* (London: Macmillan, 1943); Rosemary T. Van Arsdel, 'Macmillan Family', ODNB, vol. 35, 863-76; *DBC*.

RALLI, PANDELI (1845-1928)

Born, 1845, Marseilles; son of Thomas Ralli of London (b. c. 1802, Greece) and his wife Mary (Marie; b. c. 1818, Greece), daughter of M. Pandeli Argenti of Marseilles.
Educ. London Univ. (BA 1866).
Fell. Royal Geographical Soc. (1870).
Founder member of the Hellenic Soc.; Council (1882).
Trustee, BSA (to 1900).
Private sec. to George J. Goschen at the Admiralty (c. 1871-74).

Liberal MP for Bridport, 1875-80.

Deputy-Lieutenant for Dorset.

Liberal MP for Wallingford, 1880-85.

Liberal parliamentary candidate for Wells, 1885; Unionist candidate for Gateshead, 1891, and Gloucester, 1900.

President, East Finsbury Conservative Association (by 1901).

BSA Founding Trustee (replaced in 1900).

Residence, Belgravia Square, London.

Died, 1928, Brighton.

Obituaries, memoirs and studies

The Times 23 August 1928, 14.

WARING, CHARLES (C. 1827-87)

Born, c. 1827, Eccleshall, Yorkshire.

'Civil engineer', York (1841).

Partner of Waring Brothers, railway contractors (with his brothers William, b. c. 1821, and Henry, b. c. 1823).

Waring Brothers and Shaw: Central Pensinular Railway Company, Portugal (1853); Dorset Central (1858); Ceylon (1859); the Pernambuco, Recife and San Francisco Railway (1860); Sicily (1862); the East Indian Railway (1862); the Bristol Port Railway (1863); the Honduras Railway (1870); the Uruguay Central Railway (1871).

Contractor for St Pancras terminus, London (1868).

Liberal MP, Poole 1865, 1868; disqualified 1874.

Liberal parliamentary candidate, Poole 1885.

BSA Founding Trustee.

Residence, Grosvenor Gardens, London; Wycombe Abbey (rented from Charles Robert Carrington).

Married, Eliza.

Died, 26 August 1887, Wycombe Abbey.

Obituaries, memoirs and studies

Pall Mall Gazette 1 September 1887.

APPENDIX II MANAGING COMMITTEE

Former Directors were members of the Managing Committee: for details see Directors and Students.

ALLBUTT, THOMAS CLIFFORD (SIR) (1836-1925)
Born, 20 July 1836, Dewsbury, Yorkshire; son of the Rev. Thomas Allbutt, and his wife Marianne.

Educ. St Peter's School, York.

Camb. Gonville and Caius; matric. 1885; class. schol.; Nat. Sci. Trip. 1st (1860); MB (1861).

London, St George's Hospital.

Camb. Regius Prof. of Physic.

BSA Managing Committee (1895/96).

KCB 1907.

Married, Susan England, 15 September 1869.

Died, 22 February 1925, Cambridge.

Obituaries, memoirs and studies

H. D. Rolleston, *The Right Honorable Sir Thomas Clifford Allbutt KCB: a Memoir* (London: Macmillan, 1929); H. D. Rolleston (rev. Alexander G. Bearn), 'Allbutt, Sir (Thomas) Clifford (1836–1925)', *ODNB*, vol. 1, 764-65.

BENT, JAMES THEODORE (1852-97)
Born, 30 March 1852, Baildon, Yorkshire; son of James Bent, and his wife Margaret Eleanor.

Educ. Malvern Wells; Repton Sch.

Oxf. Wadham Coll.; matric. 1871; BA 1875.

Lincoln's Inn, 1874.

BSA Managing Committee (1896/97).

Married, Mabel Virginia Anna Hall-Dare, 2 August 1877.

Died, 5 May 1897, London.

Publications

'Researches Among the Cyclades', *JHS* 5 (1884) 42-58.

The Cyclades, or Life Among the Insular Greeks (London: Longmans, 1885).

'On the Gold and Silver Mines of Siphnos', *JHS* 6 (1885) 195-98.

'On Insular Greek Customs', *JRAI* 15 (1886) 391-403.

'An Archaeological Visit to Samos', *JHS* 7 (1886) 143-47.

'King Theodore of Corsica', *English Historical Review* 1, 2 (1886) 295-307.

(and E. L. Hicks) 'Inscriptions from Thasos', *JHS* 8 (1887) 409-38.

'Discoveries in Asia Minor', *JHS* 9 (1888) 82-87.

'The Lords of Chios', *English Historical Review* 4, 15 (1889) 467-80.

'The Ancient Home of the Phoenicians', *CR* 3, 9 (1889) 420-21.

'The Bahrein Islands, in the Persian Gulf', *Proceedings of the Royal Geographical Society and Monthly Record of Geography* 12, 1 (1890) 1-19.

'Recent Discoveries in Eastern Cilicia', *JHS* 11 (1890) 231-35.

'Cilician Symbols', *CR* 4, 7 (1890) 322.

'Explorations in Cilicia Tracheia', *Proceedings of the Royal Geographical Society and Monthly Record of Geography* 12, 8 (1890) 445-63.

'The English in the Levant', *English Historical Review* 5, 20 (1890) 654-64.

'A Journey in Cilicia Tracheia', *JHS* 12 (1891) 206-24.

'The Ruins of Mashonaland, and Explorations in the Country', *Proceedings of the Royal Geographical Society and Monthly Record of Geography* 14, 5 (1892) 273-98.

The Ruined Cities of Mashonaland: Being a Record of Excavation and Exploration in 1891 (London: Longmans, Green, 1893).

'On the Finds at the Great Zimbabwe Ruins (With a View to Elucidating the Origin of the Race that Built Them)', *JRAI* 22 (1893) 123-36.

'The Ancient Trade Route Across Ethiopia', *Geographical Journal* 2, 2 (1893) 140-46.

'The Ruins in Mashonaland', *Geographical Journal* 2, 5 (1893) 438-41.

'Expedition to the Hadramut', *Geographical Journal* 4, 4 (1894) 315-31.

'Exploration of the Frankincense Country, Southern Arabia', *Geographical Journal* 6, 2 (1895) 109-33.

'A Visit to the Northern Sudan', *Geographical Journal* 8, 4 (1896) 335-53.

Obituaries, memoirs and studies

The Times 7 May 1897; Elizabeth Baigent, 'Bent, (James) Theodore (1852–97)', *ODNB*, vol. 5, 209-10.

BLOMFIELD, REGINALD THEODORE (SIR) (1856-1942)

Born, 20 December 1856; son of the Rev. George John Blomfield (d. 1900), and his wife Isabella.

Educ. Haileybury, 1869-75.

Oxf. Exeter Coll.; Stapledon Schol. (1875); Lit. Hum. 1st (1879); Hon. Fell. (1906).

Liverpool Univ. Hon. LittD (1920).

Architectural office of his uncle, Sir A. W. Blomfield (1881).

BSA Managing Committee (1903-05).

Knighted, 1919.

Married, Anne Frances May Burra, 1886.

Died, 27 December 1942, at Frognal, Hampstead.

Publications

(and Percy Gardner) *Greek Art and Architecture: Their Legacy to Us* (The World's Manuals; London: Oxford University Press, 1922).

Obituaries, memoirs and studies

Memoirs of an Architect (London: Macmillan, 1932); M. S. Briggs (rev. Richard A. Fellows), 'Blomfield, Sir Reginald Theodore (1856–1942)', *ODNB*, vol. 6, 262-64.

COLVIN, SIDNEY (SIR) (1845-1927)

Born, 18 June 1845, Norwood, Middlesex; son of Bazett David Colvin (1805-71), and his wife Mary Steuart Bayley (1821-1902).

Educ. at home.

Camb. Trinity Coll.; matic. 1863; 1st Class. Trip. (1867); Fell. (1868).

Camb. Slade Prof. of Fine Art (1873-85); Dir. Fitzwilliam Mus. (1876-84).

London, British Mus. Keeper of Prints and Drawings (1884).

Hellenic Soc. inaugural vice-president (1879)

Society of Dilettanti, secretary (1891-96).

Literary Society, treasurer, president.

BSA Managing Committee (from 1895).

Knighted, 1911.

Married, Frances Jane Sitwell (née Fetherstonhaugh), 7 July 1903.

Died, 11 May 1927, Kensington.

Publications

'On Representations of Centaurs in Greek Vase-Painting', *JHS* 1 (1880) 107-67.

'A New Diadoumenos Gem', *JHS* 2 (1881) 352-53.

'Paintings on the Amazon Sarcophagus of Corneto', *JHS* 4 (1883) 354-69.

'An Undescribed Athenian Funeral Monument', *JHS* 5 (1884) 205-08.

(and Walter Leaf, George A. Macmillan) 'Exploration in Cyprus', *The Times*, 3 March 1888, 6.

'Cyprus Exploration Fund', *The Times*, 29 July 1889, 6.

(ed.) *History of the Society of Dilettanti* (London: Society of Dilettanti, 1898).

(and L. Cust) *History of the Society of Dilettanti* (London: Society of Dilettanti, 1914).

Memories & Notes of Persons & Places 1852-1912 (London: Edward Arnold, 1921).

Obituaries, memoirs and studies

Ernest Mehew, 'Colvin, Sir Sidney (1845–1927)', *ODNB*, vol. 12, 837-39; *DBC*.

DROOP, JOHN PERCIVAL

See Directors and Students.

ELLIOT, FRANCIS EDMUND HUGH (SIR) (D. 1940)

Born 24 March 1851, The Hague; son of Right Hon. Sir Henry Elliot (1817-1907), British Ambassador to Vienna, and his wife Anne Antrobus (d. 1899).

Educ. Eton (1864-69).

Oxf. Balliol Coll.

Diplomatic Service (1874).

Constantinople (1874-78); Vienna (1878); Rio de Janeiro, Second Secretary; Stockholm; Lisbon; Cairo; Paris, First Secretary and Head of the Chancery (1885-90); Athens, Secretary of Legation (1890-95); Sofia, agent and Consul-General (1895-1903); British Minister in Athens (1903-17).

Foreign Office, Deputy Controller of the Foreign Trade Department.

GCVO (1903); GCMG (1917); KCMG.

BSA Managing Committee (1917/18).

Anglo-Hellenic League, joint president (1919).

Married, Marie Ford (d. 1938), daughter of Francis Clare Ford, British Envoy at Athens,
    25 October 1881.
Died, 20 January 1940, Oxford.
Obituaries, memoirs and studies
The Times 22 January 1940, 6 and 9.

EVANS, ARTHUR JOHN (SIR) (1851-1941)

Born, 8 July 1851; son of Sir John Evans (1823-1908), and his wife Harriet Ann
    Dickinson (1823-58).
Educ. Harrow.
Oxf. Brasenose Coll.
Oxf. Ashmolean Mus., Keeper (1884-1908).
Society of Antiquaries, London, president (1914-19).
British Association, president (1916-19).
BSA Managing Committee (from 1903/04).
British Museum, trustee.
Died, 11 July 1941, Youlbury.
Publications

The Ashmolean Museum as a Home of Archaeology in Oxford (Oxford: Parker, 1884).
'Recent Discoveries of Tarentine Terracottas', *JHS* 7 (1886) 1-50.
'Primitive Pictographs and Prae-Phoenician Script from Crete and the Peloponnese', *JHS*
    14 (1894) 270-372.
(and John L. Myres) 'A Mycenaean Military Road', *The Academy* 1204 (1895) 469.
'Goulas: the City of Zeus', *ABSA* 2 (1895/96) 169-94.
'Knossos. I. The Palace', *ABSA* 6 (1899/1900) 3-70.
'The Palace of Knossos in its Egyptian Relations', *Archaeological Report of the Egyptian
    Exploration Fund* (1900) 60-66.
'The Palace of Knossos, 1901', *ABSA* 7 (1900/1) 1-120.
'The Palace of Knossos: Provisional Report of the Excavations for the Year 1902', *ABSA*
    8 (1901/2) 1-124.
'The Palace of Knossos: Provisional Report for the Year 1903', *ABSA* 9 (1902/3) 1-153.
'The Palace of Knossos', *ABSA* 10 (1903/4) 1-62.
'The Palace of Knossos and its Dependencies: Provisional Report for the Year 1905',
    ABSA 11 (1904/5) 1-26.
*Scripta Minoa: The Written Documents of Minoan Crete with Special Reference to the
    Archives of Knossos* I (Oxford: Clarendon Press, 1909).
*The Palace of Minos: a Comparative Account of the Successive Stages of the Early Cretan
    Civilization as Illustrated by the Discoveries at Knossos* 4 vols (London: Macmillan,
    1921, 1928, 130, 1935).
'On a Minoan Bronze Group of a Galloping Bull and Acrobatic Figure from Crete', *JHS*
    41 (1921) 247-59.
'The Early Nilotic, Libyan and Egyptian Relations with Minoan Crete', *JRAI* 55 (1925)
    199-228.

(ed. John L. Myres) *Scripta Minoa: the Written Documents of Minoan Crete with Special Reference to the Archives of Knossos II. The Archives of Knossos* (Oxford: Clarendon Press, 1952).

Obituaries, memoirs and studies

Casson, Stanley (ed.), *Essays in Aegean Archaeology Presented to Sir Arthur Evans in Honour of his 75th Birthday* (Oxford: Clarendon Press, 1927); Ann Brown, *Before Knossos . . . Arthur Evans's Travels in the Balkans and Crete* (Oxford: Ashmolean Museum, 1993); ead., 'Evans in Crete before 1900', in Davina Huxley (ed.), *Cretan Quests: British Explorers, Excavators and Historians* (London: British School at Athens, 2000) 9-14; ead. and K. Bennett (eds.), *Arthur Evans's Travels in Crete 1894-99* (BAR International Series, 1000; Oxford: Archaeopress, 2001); J. A. MacGillivray, *Minotaur: Sir Arthur Evans and the Archaeology of the Minoan Myth* (New York: Hill and Wang, 2000) [with biography]; J. L. Myres (rev. A. M. Snodgrass), 'Evans, Sir Arthur John (1851–1941)', *ODNB*, vol. 18, 663-66; *DBC*.

FYFE, THEODORE

See Directors and Students.

GARDNER, PERCY (1846-1937)

Born 24 November 1846, Hackney, Middlesex; son of Thomas Gardner, and his wife Ann Pearse.

Educ. City of London Sch.

Camb. Christ's Coll.; matric. 1865; 1st Class. Trip. (1869); 1st Moral Sci. Trip. (1869); Fell. (1872); Hon. Fell. (1897).

London, British Mus. Dept. of Coins and Medals, assistant (1871).

Camb. Disney chair of archaeology (1880).

Journal of Hellenic Studies, editor (1880-96).

Oxf. Lincoln and Merton chair of classical archaeology (1887).

BSA Managing Committee (from 1905).

FBA (1903).

Married, Agnes Reid, 1874.

Died, 17 July 1937, Oxford.

Publications

'On Some Coins with the Inscription ΤΡΙΗ', *NC* 11 (1871) 162-65.

'On an Unpublished Coin of Artavasdes II, King of Armenia', *NC* 12 (1872) 9-15.

'A Coin of Heraus, Saka King', *NC* 14 (1874) 161-67.

'Thasian Manubria', *NC* 14 (1874) 268-76.

'Plautiana, a Rectification', *NC* 15 (1875) 34-40.

'Sicilian Studies', *NC* 16 (1876) 1-44.

'The Date of King Mostis, and of Certain Later Coins of Thasos', *NC* 16 (1876) 299-306.

'A Monetary League on the Euxine Sea', *NC* 16 (1876) 307-14.

(and R. S. Poole, B. V. Head) *Catalogue of Greek Coins: Sicily*, (London: The Trustees of the British Museum, 1876).

'On an Inscribed Greek Vase with Subjects from Homer and Hesiod', *Journal of Philology* 7 (1876) 215-66.

The Parthian Coinage (London: Trübner, 1877).
'Macedonian and Greek Coins of the Seleucidae', *NC* 18 (1878) 90-102.
'Numismatic Reattributions. Phanes, Lamia, Electryona', *NC* 18 (1878) 261-72.
'New coins from Bactria', *NC* 19 (1879) 1-12.
'Coins from Kashgar', *NC* 19 (1879) 274-79.
'Ares as a Sun-god, and Solar Symbols on the Coins of Macedon and Thrace', *NC* 20 (1880) 49-61.
'Stephani on the Tombs at Mycenae', *JHS* 1 (1880) 94-106.
'The Pentathlon of the Greeks', *JHS* 1 (1880) 210-23.
'On Some Coins of Syria and Bactria', *NC* 20 (1880) 181-91.
'Boat-races Among the Greeks', *JHS* 2 (1881) 90-97.
'Boat-races at Athens', *JHS* 2 (1881) 315-17.
'Statuette of Pallas from Cyprus', *JHS* 2 (1881) 326-31.
'Floral Patterns on Archaic Greek Coins', *NC* 1 (1881) 1-7.
'Coins from Central Asia', *NC* 1 (1881) 8-12.
'Pollux' Account of Ancient Coins', *NC* 1 (1881) 281-305.
'The Palaces of Homer', *JHS* 3 (1882) 264-82.
'Samos and Samian Coins', *NC* 2 (1882) 201-90.
The Types of Greek Coins: an Archaeological Essay (Cambridge: Cambridge University Press, 1883).
'Votive Coins in Delian Inscriptions', *JHS* 4 (1883) 243-47.
'A Statuette of Eros', *JHS* 4 (1883) 266-74.
'A Sepulchral Relief from Tarentum', *JHS* 5 (1884) 105-42.
'Coins Struck by Hannibal in Italy', *NC* 4 (1884) 220-24.
(and F. Imhoof-Blumer) 'Numismatic Commentary on Pausanias', *JHS* 6 (1885) 50-101.
'Amphora Handles from Antiparos', *JHS* 6 (1885) 192-94.
'Zacynthus', *NC* 5 (1885) 81-107.
'Inscriptions from Samos', *JHS* 7 (1886) 147-53.
'Greek Coins Acquired by the British Museum in 1885', *NC* 6 (1886) 249-64.
Faith and Conduct: an Essay on Verifiable Religion (London: Macmillan, 1887).
Classical Archaeology: Wider and Special. Introductory Lecture, Oxford, October 19, 1887 (London: Oxford University Press, 1887).
'New Greek Coins of Bactria and India', *NC* 7 (1887) 177-84.
'The Exchange-value of Cyzicene Staters', *NC* 7 (1887) 185-90.
'Hector and Andromache on a Red-figure Vase', *JHS* 9 (1888) 11-17.
'Countries and Cities in Ancient Art', *JHS* 9 (1888) 47-81.
'A Vase of Polygnotan Style', *JHS* 10 (1889) 117-25.
Classical Archaeology at Oxford (Oxford: Printed for private circulation, 1889).
'A Stele Commemorating a Victory in a Boat-race', *JHS* 11 (1890) 146-50.
New Chapters in Greek History: Historical Results of Recent Excavations in Greece and Asia Minor (London: J. Murray, 1892).
'Cacus on a Black-figure Vase', *JHS* 13 (1892/93) 70-76.
'Tithonus on a Red-figure Vase', *JHS* 13 (1892/93) 137-38.
'The Chariot-group of the Mausoleum', *JHS* 13 (1892/93) 188-94.

Catalogue of the Greek Vases in the Ashmolean Museum (Oxford: Clarendon Press, 1893).

The Origin of the Lord's Supper: a Historical Inquiry (London: Macmillan and Co., 1893).

'Diogenes and Delphi', *CR* 7, 10 (1893) 437-39.

'The Origin of the Lord's Supper: a Reply', *CR* 8, 6 (1894) 267-70.

(and F. B. Jevons) *A Manual of Greek Antiquities* (London: C. Griffin, 1895; 2nd ed. 1898).

'A Marble Head Perhaps from Sunium', *JHS* 15 (1895) 188-91.

'Two Sepulchral Lekythi', *JHS* 15 (1895) 325-29.

Sculptured Tombs of Hellas (London: Macmillan and Co., 1896).

'A Stone Tripod at Oxford, and the Mantinean Basis', *JHS* 16 (1896) 275-84.

'The Coins of Elis', *NC* 19 (1897) 221-73.

'Boreas and Oreithyia on a Late Attic Vase', *JHS* 18 (1898) 136-40.

'A Themistoclean Myth', *CR* 12, 1 (1898) 21-23.

'The Scenery of the Greek Stage', *JHS* 19 (1899) 252-64.

Exploratio Evangelica: a Brief Examination of the Basis and Origin of Christian Belief (London: A. and C. Black, 1899).

'A New Pandora Vase', *JHS* 21 (1901) 1-9.

A Historic View of the New Testament: the Jowett Lectures Delivered at the Passmore Edwards Settlement in London, 1901 (London: A. and C. Black, 1901).

'Two Heads of Apollo', *JHS* 23 (1903) 117-31.

Oxford at the Crossroads: a Criticism of the Course of Litterae Humaniores in the University (London: A. and C. Black, 1903).

'Vases Added to the Ashmolean Museum', *JHS* 24 (1904) 293-316.

Professor Seeley and the Methodical Study of Man: Address Delivered to the Social and Political Education League on May 2nd, 1904 (London: Social and Political Education League, 1904).

(and J. L. Myres) *Classical Archaeology in Schools* (2nd edn.; Oxford: Clarendon Press, 1905).

'Vases Added to the Ashmolean Museum. Part 2', *JHS* 25 (1905) 65-85.

'The Apoxyomenos of Lysippus', *JHS* 25 (1905) 234-59.

A Grammar of Greek Art (Handbooks of Archaeology and Antiquities; London: Macmillan & Co., 1905).

'A Note on the Cacus Vase of the Ashmolean Museum', *JHS* 26 (1906) 226-28.

The Growth of Christianity: London Lectures (London: Adam and Charles Black, 1907).

'Adolf Furtwängler', *CR* 21, 8 (1907) 251-53.

'The Gold Coinage of Asia Before Alexander the Great', *PBA* 3 (1907/08) 107-38.

Modernity and the Churches (Crown Theological Library, 29; London; Williams & Norgate, 1909).

'Some Bronzes Recently Acquired for the Ashmolean Museum', *JHS* 30 (1910) 226-35.

'The Coinage of the Ionian Revolt', *JHS* 31 (1911) 151-60.

The Religious Experience of Saint Paul (Crown Theological Library, 34; London: Williams & Norgate, 1911).

'The Earliest Coins of Greece Proper', *PBA* 5 (1911/12) 161-201.

'Note on the Coinage of the Ionian Revolt', *JHS* 33 (1913) 105.

'Coinage of the Athenian Empire', *JHS* 33 (1913) 147-88, pls. xiii-xiv.

The Principles of Greek Art (2nd edn.; New York: The Macmillan Company, 1914).

'A Silver Dish from the Tyne', *JHS* 35 (1915) 66-75.

The Ephesian Gospel (Crown Theological Library, 40; London: Williams and Norgate, 1915).

'Professor Wickhoff on Roman Art', *JRS* 7 (1917) 1-26.

'A Female Figure in the Early Style of Pheidias', *JHS* 38 (1918) 1-26.

A History of Ancient Coinage 700-300 BC (Oxford: Clarendon Press, 1918).

Evolution in Christian Doctrine (Crown Theological Library, 41; London: Williams and Norgate, 1918).

Evolution in Christian Ethics (Crown Theological Library, 42; London: Williams and Norgate, 1918).

'A Bronze Head of the Fifth Century BC ', *JHS* 39 (1919) 69-78.

'Postscript to Paper on Diadumenos Head', *JHS* 39 (1919) 39, 232.

Recent Discovery in Classical Archaeology: a Paper Communicated to the Leeds Branch at its Fifth Annual General Meeting, 25th January, 1919 (Cambridge: Cambridge University Press, 1919).

(and Guy Dickins) *Hellenistic Sculpture* (Oxford: Clarendon Press, 1920).

'The Financial History of Ancient Chios', *JHS* 40 (1920) 160-73.

'A Numismatic Note on the Lelantian War', *CR* 34, 5 /6 (1920) 90-91.

(and Reginald Theodore Blomfield), *Greek Art and Architecture: Their Legacy to Us* (The World's Manuals; London: Oxford University Press, 1922).

'A New Portrait of Livia', *JRS* 12 (1922) 32-34.

'A Statue from a Tomb', *JHS* 43 (1923) 53-54.

'A Female Head of the Bologna Type', *JHS* 43 (1923) 50-52.

The Practical Basis of Christian Belief: an Essay in Reconstruction (London: Williams & Norgate, 1923).

'Ancient Sparta', *The Times* 28 June 1923, 13.

The Principles of Greek Art (New York: The Macmillan Company, 1926).

New Chapters in Greek Art (Oxford: Clarendon Press, 1926).

Modernism in the English Church (London: Methuen & Co., 1926).

The Principles of Christian Art (London: J. Murray, 1928).

The Interpretation of Religious Experience (London: William & Norgate, 1931).

Autobiographica (Oxford: B. Blackwell, 1933).

Obituaries, memoirs and studies

J. M. C. Toynbee and H. D. A. Major (rev. John Boardman), 'Gardner, Percy (1846–1937)', *ODNB*, vol. 21, 464-65; *DBC*.

GENNADIOS, JOHN (1844-1932).

Born, 20 January 1844, Athens; son of George Gennadios, from Epiros, and his wife Artemis Venizelos.

Educ. English Coll. Malta.

Worked for the Ralli Brothers, London.

Greek Diplomatic Service (1872): Washington, attaché; Constantinople, second secretary; London, first secretary (1875); Constantinople (1881); London, Chargé d'Affaires (1882), Minister Resident (1885); Washington (1888); London (1890); recalled 1892.

Greek Minister in London (1910; resigned December 1916); London representative of the National Government (1917-18); Hon. Greek Minister for Life.

BSA Managing Committee (from 1886).

Benefactor of the Library at the American School of Classical Studies at Athens.

Hon. GCVO.

Married, Florence Laing, 1902, daughter of Samuel Laing, MP (1812-97).

Died, 7 September 1832, East Molesey.

Obituaries, memoirs and studies

The Times 8 September 1932; G. A. Macmillan, 'M. Jean Gennadius', *JHS* 52, 2 (1932), 297; W. Miller, 'The "Gennadeion": Dr Gennadius' Monument at Athens', *JHS* 52, 2 (1932) 297-302.

GEORGE, WALTER SYKES

See Directors and Students.

HARRISON, JANE ELLEN (1850-1928)

Born, 9 September 1850, at Cottingham, Yorkshire; daughter of Charles Harrison, and his wife Elizabeth Hawksley Nelson.

Educ. by governesses.

Cheltenham Ladies' Coll. (1868).

London Univ. exam. for women (1870).

Camb. Newnham Coll. (1874); school.; Class. Trip. 2nd.

Newnham Coll. Research Fell. (1898).

BSA Managing Committee (from 1895).

Died, 15 April 1928, Bloomsbury.

Publications

'Archaeology and School Teaching', *Journal of Education* 2 (1880) 105-6.

Myths of the Odyssey in Art and Literature (London: Rivingtons, 1882).

'Monuments Relating to the Odyssey', *JHS* 4 (1883) 248-65.

Introductory Studies in Greek Art (London: T. Fisher Unwin, 1885).

'Odysseus and the Sirens-Dionysiac Boat-races-A Cylix by Nikosthenes', *JHS* 6 (1885) 19-29.

'The Judgment of Paris: Two Unpublished Vases in the Graeco-Etruscan Museum at Florence', *JHS* 7 (1886) 196-219.

'Archaeology in Greece, 1887-1888', *JHS* 9 (1888) 118-33.

'Some Fragments of a Vase Presumably by Euphronios', *JHS* 9 (1888) 143-46.

'Two Cylices Relating to the Exploits of Theseus', *JHS* 10 (1889) 231-42.

'The Central Slab of the E. Parthenon Frieze', *CR* 3, 8 (1889) 378.

'The Festival of the Alora', *CR* 3, 8 (1889) 378-79.

(and Margaret de G. Verrall) *Mythology and Monuments of Ancient Athens: Being a Translation of a Portion of the 'Attica' of Pausanias, with an Introductory Essay and Archaeological Commentary* (London: Macmillan, 1890).

'Dr Dörpfeld on the Greek Theatre', *CR* 4, 6 (1890) 274-77.

'Mythological Studies', *JHS* 12 (1891) 350-55.

(and D. S. MacColl) *Greek Vase Paintings: a Selection of Examples* (London: T. Fisher Unwin, 1894).

'Athene Ergane', *CR* 8, 6 (1894) 270-71.

'Some Points in Dr Furtwaengler's Theories on the Parthenon and its Marbles', *CR* 9, 1 (1895) 85-92.

'The Central Group of the East Frieze of the Parthenon peplos or στρωμνη?', *CR* 9, 8 (1895) 427-28.

'Notes Archaeological and Mythological on Bacchylides', *CR* 12, 1 (1898) 85-86.

'Delphika. (A) The Erinyes. (B) The Omphalos', *JHS* 19 (1899) 205-51.

'Pandora's Box', *JHS* 20 (1900) 99-114.

'Is Tragedy the Goat-song?', *CR* 16, 6 (1902) 331-32.

Prolegomena to the Study of Greek Religion (Cambridge: Cambridge University Press, 1903).

'Mystica Vannus Iacchi', *JHS* 23 (1903) 292-324.

'Mystica Vannus Iacchi (Continued)', *JHS* 24 (1904) 241-54.

'Note on the Mystica Vannus Iacchi', *ABSA* 10 (1903/04) 144-47.

The Religion of Ancient Greece (London: Constable, 1905).

Primitive Athens as Described by Thucydides (Cambridge: Cambridge University Press, 1906).

'Helios-Hades', *CR* 22, 1 (1908) 12-16.

'The Kouretes and Zeus Kouros. A Study in Pre-historic Sociology', *ABSA* 15 (1908/09) 308-38.

Themis, a Study of the Social Origins of Greek Religion: With an Excursus on the Ritual Forms Preserved in Greek Tragedy by Gilbert Murray and a Chapter on the Origin of the Olympic Games by F. M. Cornford (Cambridge: Cambridge University Press, 1912).

Ancient Art and Ritual (Home University Library of Modern Knowledge; London: Williams & Norgate, 1913).

Alpha and Omega (London: Sidgwick & Jackson, 1915).

'The Head of John the Baptist', *CR* 30, 8 (1916) 216-19.

Aspects, Aorists and the Classical Tripos (Cambridge: Cambridge University Press, 1919).

Epilegomena to the Study of Greek Religion (Cambridge: Cambridge University Press, 1921).

Obituaries, memoirs and studies

J. Stewart, *Jane Ellen Harrison: a Portrait from Letters* (London: The Merlin Press, 1959); S. J. Peacock, *Jane Ellen Harrison: the Mask and the Self* (New Haven: Yale University Press, 1988); S. Arlen, *The Cambridge Ritualists: an Annotated Bibliography of the Works by and about Jane Ellen Harrison, Gilbert Murray, Francis M. Cornford, and Arthur Bernard Cook* (Metuchen, N. J., and London: Scarecrow Press, 1990); W. M. Calder III, 'Jane Harrison's Failed Candidacies for the Yates Professorship (1888, 1896): What Did Her Colleagues Think of Her?', in W. M. Calder III (ed.), *The Cambridge Ritualists Reconsidered* (Atlanta: Illinois Classical

Studies, 1991), 37-59; M. Beard, *The Invention of Jane Harrison* (Revealing Antiquity vol. 14; Cambridge (Mass.): Harvard University Press, 2000); A. Robinson, *The Life and Work of Jane Ellen Harriso*n (Oxford: Oxford University Press, 2002); Hugh Lloyd-Jones, 'Harrison, Jane Ellen (1850–1928)', *ODNB,* vol. 25, 504-07; *DBC.*

HAVERFIELD, FRANCIS JOHN (1860-1919)

Born, 8 November 1860, at Shipston-on-Stour; son of the Rev. William Robert Haverield, and his wife, Emily Mackarness.

Educ. Winchester; senior schol. (1873).

Oxf. New Coll. (1879); 1st Class mod.; 2nd class in Lit. Hum.

Lancing Coll. sixth-form master.

Oxf. Christ Church, senior student and tutor (1892).

Oxf. Camden Prof. of Ancient History (1907); Brasenose Coll.

BSA Managing Committee (1900-02).

Married, Winifred E. Breakwell, 1907.

Died, 1 October 1919, Oxford.

Publications

'Zu Aurelius Victor', *Hermes* 20, 1 (1885) 159-60.

'Cavillor', *CR* 1, 8 (1887) 244.

'Roman Dacia', *English Historical Review* 2, 8 (1887) 734-36.

'Discoveries of Roman Remains in Britain. I', *CR* 7, 9 (1893) 430-31.

'Discoveries of Roman Remains in Britain. II', *CR* 8, 5 (1894) 227-28.

'Tacitus, "Agricola" 24', *CR* 9, 6 (1895) 310-11.

'English Topographical Notes', *English Historical Review* 10, 40 (1895) 710-12.

(and J. A. R. Munro, W. C. F. Anderson, J. G. Milne) 'On the Roman Town of Doclea in Montenegro: Communicated to the Society of Antiquaries', *Archaeologia* 55 (1896) 33-92.

'Discoveries of Roman Remains in Britain. III', *CR* 10, 1 (1896) 73-74.

'Early British Christianity', *English Historical Review* 11, 43 (1896) 417-30.

'Tacitus, "Agricola" XXIV', *CR* 11, 9 (1897) 447.

'Discoveries of Roman Remains in Britain. IV', *CR* 12, 1 (1898) 83-84.

'Roman Shoe Found at Birdoswald', *CR* 12, 2 (1898) 142.

'Did Agricola Invade Ireland?', *CR* 13, 6 (1899) 305-06.

'The Last Days of Silchester', *English Historical Review* 19, 76 (1904) 625-31.

'Notes on Roman Britain', *CR* 19, 1 (1905) 57-58.

'The Ordnance Survey Maps from the Point of View of the Antiquities on Them', *Geographical Journal* 27, 2 (1906) 165-72.

(and J. L. S. Davidson, E. R. Bevan, E. M. Walker, D. G. Hogarth, and L. Cromer) 'Ancient Imperialism', *CR* 24 (1910) 105-16.

(and D. G. Hogarth, D. Strathan, A. Stein, J. L. Myres, E. A. Gardner, W. A. Cannon, M. M. Allorge, W. N. Shaw, and J. W. Gregory) 'The Burial of Olympia: Discussion', *Geographical Journal* 36 (1910) 675-86.

'An Inaugural Address Delivered Before the First Annual General Meeting of the Society, 11th May, 1911', *JRS* 1 (1911) xi-xx.

(and J. G. C. Anderson) 'Trajan on the Quinquennium Neronis', *JRS* 1 (1911) 173-79.

The Study of Ancient History in Oxford. A Lecture, etc. (London: Henry Frowde, 1912).

(and H. Stuart-Jones) 'Some Representative Examples of Romano-British Sculpture', *JRS* 2 (1912) 121-52.

'Four Notes on Tacitus', *JRS* 2 (1912) 195-200.

'Notes on the Roman Coast Defences of Britain, Especially in Yorkshire', *JRS* 2 (1912) 201-14.

Ancient Town Planning (Oxford: Clarendon Press, 1913).

'Ancient Rome and Ireland', *English Historical Review* 28, 109 (1913) 1-12.

An Account of the Roman Remains in the Parish of Corbridge-upon-Tyne (Newcastle-upon-Tyne: Andrew Reid, 1914).

'Leonard Cheesman', *CR* 29 (1915) 222-23.

'Obituary: Leonard Cheesman', *JRS* 5 (1915) 147-48.

'Tacitus During the Late Roman Period and the Middle Ages', *JRS* 6 (1916) 196-201.

'Centuriation in Roman Britain', *English Historical Review* 33, 131 (1918) 289-96.

(rev. G. MacDonald) *The Roman Occupation of Britain, Being six Ford Lectures* (Oxford: Clarendon Press, 1924).

Obituaries, memoirs and studies

G. MacDonald, 'Professor Haverfield: A Bibliography', *JRS* 8 (1918) 184-98; 'Obituary: Prof. F. J. Haverfield', *Geographical Journal* 54 (1919) 395; J. G. C. Anderson, 'Obituary: Professor F. Haverfield', *CR* 33 (1919) 165-66; G. Macdonald, 'F. Haverfield: 1860-1919', *Proceedings of the British Academy* 9 (1919/20) 475-91; R. C. Bosanquet, 'Francis John Haverfield, FSA, a Vice-President', *Archaeologia Aeliana* 17 (1920) 137-43; H. H. E. Craster, 'Francis Haverfield', *English Historical Review* 35 (1920) 63-70; George Macdonald (rev. P. W. M. Freeman), 'Haverfield, Francis John (1860–1919)', rev. P. W. M. Freeman, *ODNB*, vol. 25, 856-57; *DBC*; P. W. M. Freeman, *The Best Training Ground for Archaeologists: Francis Haverfield and the Invention of Romano-British Archaeology* (Oxford: Oxbow, 2007).

HUTTON, CAROLINE AMY
See Directors and Students.

JEBB, RICHARD CLAVERHOUSE
See Trustees.

JEWELL, HARRY HERBERT
See Directors and Students.

LEAF, WALTER
See Trustees.

LEIGHTON, FREDERIC (SIR) (BARON) (1830-96).

Born, 3 December 1830, at Scarborough, Yorkshire; son of Dr Frederic Septimus Leighton, and his wife Augusta Susan.

Educ. University College School.

Berlin, Academy of Art (1842-43); Frankfurt am Main, Stellwag's Academy (1843); Florence, Accademia de Belle Arti (1845); Frankfurt, Städelesches Kunstinstitut (1846, 1850).

Royal Academy, member (1868).

BSA Managing Committee (1886).

Died, 25 January 1896, Leighton House.

Obituaries, memoirs and studies

Christopher Newall, 'Leighton, Frederic, Baron Leighton (1830–1896)', *ODNB,* vol. 32, 258-66.

LORING, WILLIAM

See Directors and Students.

MACMILLAN, GEORGE AUGUSTIN

See Trustees.

MAYOR, ROBERT JOHN GROTE

See Directors and Students.

MONRO, DAVID BINNING (1836-1905)

Born, 16 November 1836, at Edinburgh; son of Alexander Binning Monro, and his wife Harriet.

Educ. privately.

Glasgow Univ. logic and mathematics (1851); LLD (1883).

Oxf. Brasenose Coll. (1856); schol.; 1st final class. school; 2nd final mathematical schools (1858); Ireland Schol. (1858); Hon. DCL (1904).

Oxf. Oriel Coll. Fell. (1859), lecturer (1862), tutor (1863), vice-provost (1874), provost (1882).

Lincoln's Inn, student.

Oxf. Vice-Chancellor (1901-04).

Oxf. Philological Soc. (1870).

Hellenic Soc., vice-president.

Classical Association, vice-president.

BSA Managing Committee (1895-1905).

FBA.

Died, 22 August 1905, Heiden, Switzerland.

Publications

'The Homeric Question', *The Quarterly Review* 125, no. 250 (1868) 440-73.

Homer: Iliad, Book 1, With an Essay on Homeric Grammar and Notes (Oxford: Clarendon Press, 1878).

A Grammar of the Homeric Dialect (Oxford: Clarendon Press, 1882; 2nd edn. 1891).

'On the Fragment of Proclus' Abstract of the Epic Cycle Contained in the Codex Venetus of the Iliad', *JHS* 4 (1883) 305-34.

(ed.) *Homer: Iliad, Books I-XII, with an Introduction, a Brief Homeric Grammar, and Notes* (Oxford: Clarendon Press, 1884; 2nd edn. 1890; 3rd edn. 1893; 4th edn. 1897).

'The Poems of the Epic Cycle', *JHS* 5 (1884) 1-41.

(and J. Fergusson, H. F. Pelham, and G. A. Macmillan) 'Exploration in Asia Minor', *The Times* 21 March 1884, 3.

'Homer and the Early History of Greece', *English Historical Review* 1, 1 (1886) 43-52.

(ed.) *Homer: Iliad, Books XIII-XXIV, with Notes* (Oxford: Clarendon Press, 1889; 2nd edn. 1890; 3rd edn. 1893; 4th edn. 1899).

'On Pindar, *Nem.* II. 14', *CR* 6, 1 / 2 (1892) 3-4.

(and James Adam) 'Mr Adam and Mr Monro on the Nuptial Number of Plato', *CR* 6, 6 (1892) 240-44.

The Modes of Ancient Greek Music (Oxford: Clarendon Press, 1894).

'The Modes of Greek Music', *CR* 9, 1 (1895) 79-81.

(ed.) *Homeri Opera et Eeliquiae*, 3 vols. (Oxford: Clarendon Press, 1896).

'Mr Agar's Review of the Oxford Homer', *CR* 10, 9 (1896) 455.

(ed.) *Homer's Odyssey, Books XIII-XXIV* (Oxford: Clarendon Press, 1901).

(ed. with T. W. Allen) *Homeri Opera* vols. 1-2 (Oxford: Clarendon Press, 1902).

'The Place and Time of Homer', *CR* 19, 5 (1905) 239-41.

Obituaries, memoirs and studies

Phelps, L. R., and R. Smail, 'Monro, David Binning (1836-1905)', in *ODNB*, vol. 38, 646-47; *DBC*.

MYRES, JOHN LINTON

See Directors and Students.

PELHAM, HENRY FRANCIS (1846-1907)

Born, 19 September 1846, at Bergh Apton, Norfolk; son of John Thomas Pelham, bishop of Norwich, and his wife, Henrietta Tatton.

Educ. Harrow.

Oxf. Trinity Coll. (1865-69); 1st Class. mod; 1st Lit. Hum.; BA (1869); MA (1872).

Oxf. Exeter Coll. Fell. (1869-73).

Oxf. Reader in Ancient History (1887).

Oxf. Camden Prof. of Ancient History (1889); Fell. Brasenose Coll.

Oxf. Trinity Coll. President (1897-1907).

BSA Managing Committee (from 1895).

Married, Laura Priscilla Buxton, 30 July 1873.

Died, 12 February 1907, Oxford.

Publications

(and J. Fergusson, D. B. Monro, and G. A. Macmillan) 'Exploration in Asia Minor', *The Times* 21 March 1884, 3.

Outlines of Roman History (London: Percival & Co., 1893).

Essays, Collected and ed. by F. J. H. Haverfield (Oxford: Clarendon Press, 1911).

Obituaries, memoirs and studies

F. Haverfield (ed.), *Essays by Henry Francis Pelham* (Oxford: Clarendon Press, 1911); F. J. Haverfield (rev. Roger T. Stearn), 'Pelham, Henry Francis (1846–1907)', *ODNB*, vol. 43, 467-68; *DBC*.

PENOYRE, JOHN FFOLIOT BAKER

See Directors and Students.

REID, JAMES SMITH (1846-1926)

Born, 3 May 1846, Sorn, Ayrshire; son of John Reid, schoolmaster, and his wife, Mary
Smith.

Educ. City of London Sch.

Camb. Christ's Coll.; schol. (1865); Browne Medal for a Latin epigram; Chancellor's
Medallist (1869); Fell. (1869); LLM (1872).

Camb. Pembroke Coll. classical lecturer (1880-85).

Camb. Gonville & Caius, Fell. (1878); Prof. of Ancient History (1899-1925).

BSA Managing Committee (from 1903).

FBA (1917).

Married, Ruth Gardner, 1872 (sister of Percy and Ernest Gardner).

Died, 1 April 1926, Cambridge.

Publications

Passages for Practice in Translation at Sight (London: Daldy, Isbister & Co., 1877).

(ed.) *Cicero: Academica* (London: Macmillan, 1874; 2nd ed. 1885).

(ed.) *Cicero: Pro Sulla* (Cambridge: Cambridge University Press, 1882).

(trans.) *The Academics of Cicero* (London: Macmillan, 1885).

'Note on Cic. 'de Fin. ' ii. 56', *CR* 10, 3 (1896) 155.

'Note on Cicero, 'Ad Fam. '. 1, 2, 2 and 1, 1, 2', *CR* 11, 5 (1897) 244-46.

'Notes on Some Passages in Cicero's Letters ad Familiares', *CR* 11, 7 (1897) 350-51.

'Note on the Roman Portoria', *CR* 18, 1 (1904) 44.

'The Plural of res publica', *CR* 18, 3 (1904) 159.

'On the Fragments of an Epitome of Livy Discovered at Oxyrhynchus', *CR* 18, 6 (1904)
290-300.

'Note on the Introductory Epistle to the Eighth Book of Caesar's Gallic War', *Classical
Philology* 3, 4 (1908) 441-45.

'Lucretiana: Notes on Books I and II of the De Rerum Natura', *Harvard Studies in
Classical Philology* 22 (1911) 1-53.

'On the Questions of Roman Public Law', *JRS* 1 (1911) 68-99.

'Note on Lucretius, V. 311, 312', *CR* 25, 7 (1911) 202-03.

'Human Sacrifices at Rome and Other Notes on Roman Religion', *JRS* 2 (1912) 34-52.

The Municipalities of the Roman Empire (Cambridge: Cambridge University Press, 1913).

'Problems of the Second Punic War', *JRS* 3, 2 (1913) 175-96.

'Problems of the Second Punic War: III. Rome and her Italian Allies', *JRS* 5 (1915)
87-124.

'The So-called 'Lex Iulia Municopalis', *JRS* 5 (1915) 207-48.

'Roman Ideas of Deity', *JRS* 6 (1916) 170-84.

'Tacitus as a Historian', *JRS* 11 (1921) 191-99.

'Some Aspects of Local Autonomy in the Roman Empire', *Cambridge Historical Journal*
1, 2 (1924) 121-25.

(ed.) Cicero: De Finibus Bonorum et Malorum, Books 1 and 2 (Cambridge: Cambridge
University Press, 1925).

Obituaries, memoirs and studies
F. E. Adcock (rev. R. Smail), 'Reid, James Smith (1846-1926)', in *ODNB*, vol. 46, 392-93; *DBC*.

RIDGEWAY, WILLIAM (SIR) (1858-1926)
Born, 6 August 1858, at Ballydermot, Ireland; son of the Rev. John Henry Ridgeway, and Marianna Ridgeway.

Educ. Portarlington School.

Trinity Coll. Dublin.

Camb. Peterhouse (1876); Gonville & Caius (1878); schol.; Class. Trip. (BA, 1880); MA (1883); Fell. (1880); ScD (1909).

Univ. Coll. Cork, chair of Greek (1883-94).

Camb. Disney Prof. of Archaeology (1892-1926); Brereton Reader in Classics (1907-26).

Royal Anthropological Institute, President (1908-10).

BSA Managing Committee (1896-1904).

FBA (1904).

Classical Association, President (1914).

Knighted, 1919.

Married, Lucy Samuels, 1880.

Died, 12 August 1926, Fen Ditton, Cambridgeshire.

Publications
'The Homeric Land System', *JHS* 6 (1885) 319-39.

'The Homeric Talent, its Origin, Value, and Affinities', *JHS* 8 (1887) 133-58.

'Pindar, Nem. VII. 17', *CR* 1 (1887) 313.

'Metrological Notes', *JHS* 9 (1888) 18-30.

'Contributions to Strabo's Biography', *CR* 2 (1888) 84.

'Thucydides VI. 2', *CR* 2 (1888) 180.

'Euripides, Ion. 576-80', *CR* 2 (1888) 225.

'Metrological Notes', *JHS* 10 (1889) 90-97.

The Origin of Metallic Currency and Weight Standards (Cambridge: Cambridge University Press, 1892).

'Reply to Mr Torr', *CR* 9 (1895) 378-79.

'What People Made the Objects Called Mycenaean?', *JHS* 16 (1896) 77-119.

'Bassareus', *CR* 10 (1896) 21-22.

'What Led Pythagoras to the Doctrine that the World was Built of Numbers?', *CR* 10 (1896) 92-95.

'The Game of Polis and Plato's Rep. 422 E', *JHS* 16 (1896) 288-90.

The Early Age of Greece, I (Cambridge: Cambridge University Press, 1901).

'The Early Age of Greece', *CR* 16 (1902) 135-36.

The Origin and Influence of the Thoroughbred Horse (Cambridge Biological Series; Cambridge: Cambridge University Press, 1905).

'The Genealogy of the Thoroughbred Horse: a Reply to Mr W. S. Blunt', *Cambridge Review* (1906) 254-55.

'The Supplices of Aeschylus', in *Praelections Delivered before the Senate of the University of Cambridge, 25, 26, 27 January 1906* (Cambridge: Cambridge University Press, 1906) 141-64.

(and Duckworth, W. L. H., A. C. Haddon, W. H. R. Rivers) 'Anthropology at the Universities', *Man* 6 (1906) 85-86.

'Who Were the Romans?', *PBA* 3 (1907) 17-60.

'The Origin of the Turkish Crescent', *JRAI* 38 (1908) 241-58.

'Presidential Address. The Relation of Anthropology to Classical Studies', *JRAI* 39 (1909) 10-25.

'Minos: the Destroyer Rather than the Creator of the So-called 'Minoan' Culture of Cnossus', *PBA* 4 (1909/10) 97-129.

The Origin of Tragedy, with Special Reference to the Greek Tragedians (Cambridge: Cambridge University Press, 1910).

'Presidential Address. The Influence of Environment on Man', *JRAI* 40 (1910) 10-22.

The Dramas and Dramatic Dances of Non-European Races: in Special Reference to the Origin of Greek Tragedy with an Appendix on the Origin of Greek Comedy (Cambridge: Cambridge University Press, 1915).

'The Relation of Archaeology to Classical Studies', *Proceedings of the Classical Association* 12 (1915) 19-31.

'The President's Speech', *Proceedings of the Classical Association* 12 (1915) 19-36.

The Supplices of Aeschylus (Cambridge: Cambridge University Press, 1916).

'Niall "Of the Nine Hostages" in Connexion with the Treasures of Traprain Law and Ballinrees, and the Destruction of Wroxeter, Chester, Caerleon and Caerwent', *JRS* 14 (1924) 123-36.

'Euripides in Macedon', *CQ* 20 (1926) 1-19.

The Early Age of Greece II (Cambridge: Cambridge University Press, 1931).

Obituaries, memoirs and studies

E. C. Quiggin (ed.), *Essays and Studies resented to William Ridgeway on his Sixtieth Birthday, 6 August, 1913* (Cambridge: Cambridge University Press, 1913); R. S. Conway, 'Sir William Ridgeway 1853-1926', *PBA* 12 (1926) 327-36; R. S. Conway (rev. A. M. Snodgrass), 'Ridgeway, Sir William (1858–1926)', rev. A. M. Snodgrass, *ODNB*, vol. 46, 931-33; *DBC*.

SANDYS, JOHN EDWIN (SIR) (1844-1922)

Born, 19 May 1844, at Leicester; son of the Reverend Timothy Sandys, Church Missionary Society, and his wife, Rebecca Swain.

Educ. Church Missionary Society School, Islington; Repton.

Camb. St John's Coll. (1863); schol.; Browne Medal for Greek Ode (1865); senior classic (1867); tutor (1870); LittD (1886); hon. LLD (1920).

Camb. Public Orator (1876).

BSA Managing Committee (1886; from 1904).

FBA (1909).

Knighted 1911.

Married, Mary Grainger Hall, 1880.

Died, 6 July 1922, Cambridge.

Publications

Isocrates ad Demonicum et Panegyricus (London: Rivingtons, 1868; 2nd ed. 1872).

(ed. with F. A. Paley) *Select Private Orations of Demosthenes* (Cambridge: Cambridge University Press, 1874; rev. ed. 1896).

The Bacchae of Euripides with Critical and Explanatory Notes and with Numerous Illustrations from Works of Ancient Art (Cambridge: Cambridge University Press, 1880; rev. ed. 1892, 1900).

Ad M. Brutum Orator (Cambridge: Cambridge University Press, 1885).

The Speech of Demosthenes Against the Law of Leptines (Cambridge: Cambridge University Press, 1890).

Aristotle's Constitution of Athens (London: Macmillan, 1893).

First Greek Reader and Writer (London: Swan Sonnenschein, 1896).

The First Philippic and the Olynthiacs of Demosthenes (London: Macmillan, 1897).

Demosthenes, On the Peace, Second Philippic: On the Chersonesus, and Third Philippic (London: Macmillan, 1900; rev. ed. 1913).

A History of Classical Scholarship, 3 vols. (Cambridge: Cambridge University Press, 1903-08).

Harvard Lectures on the Revival of Learning (Cambridge: Cambridge University Press, 1905).

Orationes et Epistolae Cantabrigienses (1876-1909) (London: Macmillan, 1910).

Orationes et Epistolae Cantabrigienses (1909-1919) (Cambridge, 1921). [Compiled from *Cambridge University Reporter.*]

Obituaries, memoirs and studies

E. E. Sikes (rev. Richard Smail), 'Sandys, Sir John Edwin (1844–1922)', *ODNB,* vol. 48, 932; *DBC.*

TOD, MARCUS NIEBUHR

See Directors and Students.

WALDSTEIN, CHARLES (SIR CHARLES WALSTON) (1856-1927)

Born, 30 March 1856, in New York City; son of Henry Waldstein, and his wife, Sophie Srisheim.

Columbia Coll. New York.

Heidelberg Univ.

Camb. lecturer in the Classics Faculty (1880); Reader in classical archaeology (1883-1907); director of the Fitzwilliam Mus. (1883-89); Slade Prof. of Art (1895-1901; 1904-11).

American School of Classical Studies at Athens, director (1889-93).

BSA Managing Committee (from 1895).

British citizenship (1899).

Knighted, 1912.

Married, Florence Seligman, 1909.

Name changed to Walston (1918).

Died, 21 March 1927, Naples.

Publications

'Pythagoras of Rhegion and the Early Athlete Statues', *JHS* 1 (1880) 168-201.

'Pythagoras of Rhegion and the Early Athlete Statues (Continued)', *JHS* 2 (1881) 332-51.

'Notice of a Lapith-head in the Louvre, from the Metopes of the Parthenon', *JHS* 3 (1882) 228-33.

'Views of Athens in the Year 1687', *JHS* 4 (1883) 86-89.

'A Ring with the Inscription "Attulas"', *JHS* 4 (1883) 162-63.

'The Hesperide of the Olympian Metope and a Marble Head at Madrid', *JHS* 5 (1884) 171-75.

'The Eastern Pediment of the Temple of Zeus at Olympia and the Western Pediment of the Parthenon', *JHS* 5 (1884) 195-204.

Essays on the Art of Pheidias (Cambridge: Cambridge University Press, 1885).

'The Panathenaic Festival and the Central Slab of the Parthenon Frieze', *American Journal of Archaeology and the History of the Fine Arts* 1, 1 (1885) 10-17.

'Notes on the Collection of Ancient Marbles in the Possession of Sir Charles Nicholson, Bart', *JHS* 7 (1886) 240-50.

'Pasiteles and Arkesilaos, the Venus Genetrix and the Venus of the Esquiline', *American Journal of Archaeology and the History of the Fine Arts* 3, 1 / 2 (1887) 1-13.

'The Newly Discovered Head of Iris from the Frieze of the Parthenon', *American Journal of Archaeology and the History of the Fine Arts* 5, 1 (1889) 1-8.

'Report on Excavations near Stamata in Attika', *American Journal of Archaeology and the History of the Fine Arts* 5, 4 (1889) 423-25.

(J. C. Rolfe, F. B. Tarbell) 'Report on Excavations at Plataia in 1889', *American Journal of Archaeology and the History of the Fine Arts* 5, 4 (1889) 439-42.

'Trapezó and Kosmó in the Frieze of the Parthenon', *JHS* 11 (1890) 143-45.

'Discoveries at Plataia in 1890. I. General Report on the Excavations', *American Journal of Archaeology and the History of the Fine Arts* 6, 4 (1890) 445-48.

'The Mantineian Reliefs', *American Journal of Archaeology and the History of the Fine Arts* 7, 1 / 2 (1891) 1-18.

'Excavations by the School at Eretria. Introductory Note', *American Journal of Archaeology and the History of the Fine Arts* 7, 3 (1891) 233-35.

(and H. S. Washington) 'Excavations by the American School at Plataia in 1891. Discovery of a Temple of Archaic Plan', *American Journal of Archaeology and the History of the Fine Arts* 7, 4 (1891) 390-405.

Excavations of the American School of Athens at the Heraion of Argos, 1892 (Boston: Williams and Norgate, 1892).

(and C. L. Meader) 'Reports on Excavations at Sparta in 1893', *American Journal of Archaeology and the History of the Fine Arts* 8, 3 (1893) 410-28.

(and J. M. Paton) 'Report on Excavations Between Schenochori and Koutzopodi, Argolis, in 1893', *American Journal of Archaeology and the History of the Fine Arts* 8, 3 (1893) 429-36.

'Preliminary Report from Prof. Waldstein on the Excavations at the Argive Heraeum in 1893', *American Journal of Archaeology and the History of the Fine Arts* 9, 1 (1894) 63-67.

'A Head of Polycletan Style from the Metopes of the Argive Heraeum', *American Journal of Archaeology and the History of the Fine Arts* 9, 3 (1894) 331-39.

'The Circular Building of Sparta', *American Journal of Archaeology and the History of the Fine Arts* 9, 4 (1894) 545-46.

The Study of Art in Universities: Inaugural Lecture of the Slade Professor of Fine Art in the University of Cambridge (London: Osgood, McIlvaine & Co., 1896).

(and T. D. Seymour, R. B. Richardson, J. R. S. Sterrett) 'Sixteenth Annual Report of the Managing Committee of the American School of Classical Studies at Athens', *AJA* 1, 2 (1897) 91-122.

(and J. C. Hoppin) 'Terra-cotta Reliefs from the Argive Heraeum', *AJA* 2, 3 / 4 (1898) 173-86.

'The Earliest Hellenic Art and Civilization and the Argive Heraeum', *AJA* 4, 1 (1900) 40-73.

'The Argive Heraeum and Bacchylides XI. 43-84', *CR* 14, 9 (1900) 473-74.

'The Argive Hera of Polycleitus', *JHS* 21 (1901) 30-44.

The Argive Heraeum I (Boston: Houghton, Mifflin, 1902).

(and G. A. Macmillan, HRH The Crown Prince of Greece, C. Harcourt-Smith, M. T. Homolle, A. Conze, J. R. Wheeler, R. C. Bosanquet) 'The Penrose Memorial Library', *ABSA* 10 (1903/04) 232-42.

'The Bronze Statue from Cerigotto and the Study of Style', *JHS* 24 (1904) 129-34.

'Damophon', *JHS* 24 (1904) 330-31.

'Some Notes on the Ancient Greek Sculpture Exhibited at the Burlington Fine Arts Club', *CR* 18, 2 (1904) 133-37.

'On the Ancient Sculptures Exhibited at the Burlington Fine Arts Club. Corrections in Professor Furtwängler's reply (C. R., Nov. pp. 419 sq.)', *CR* 18, 9 (1904) 470-74.

The Argive Heraeum II (Boston: Houghton, Mifflin, 1905).

'Professor Furtwängler, Ageladas and Stephanos', *CR* 19, 4 (1905) 234-35.

(and L. Shoobridge) *Herculaneum: Past, Present and Future* (London: Macmillan, 1908).

'A Head of Aphrodite, Probably from the Eastern Pediment of the Parthenon, at Holkham Hall', *JHS* 33 (1913) 276-95.

Greek Sculpture and Modern Art, Two Lectures Delivered to the Students of the Royal Academy of London (Cambridge: Cambridge University Press, 1914).

'The Holkham Head: a Reply', *JHS* 34 (1914) 312-20.

'The Establishment of the Classical Type in Greek Art', *JHS* 44, 4 (1924) 223-53.

(and The Early of Ronaldshay, M. Conway, J. L. Myres) 'Recent Researches on the Peninsula of Carthage: Discussion', *Geographical Journal* 63, 3 (1924) 187-89.

'Addendum to J. H. S., XLIV. pp. 223-253. The Establishment of the Classical Type in Greek Art', *JHS* 45, 2 (1925) 179.

Alcamenes and the Establishment of the Classical Type in Greek Art (Cambridge: Cambridge University Press, 1926).

Notes on Greek Sculpture I. The Constantinople Pentathlete and Early Athletic Statues; II. A Marble Draped Female Figure in Burlington House (Cambridge: Cambridge University Press, 1927).

Obituaries, memoirs and studies

Nigel Spivey, 'Walston, Sir Charles (1856–1927)', *ODNB,* vol. 57, 155-56; *DBC*.

WHIBLEY, LEONARD (1863-1941)

Born, 20 April 1863, at Gravesend; son of Ambrose Whibley, and his wife Mary Jean Davy.

Educ. Bristol Grammar School.

Camb. Pembroke Coll.; schol. (1882); 1st Class. Trip. Pt 1 (1885), 1st Pt 2 (1886); Fell. (1889).

Camb. univ. lecturer in Ancient History (1899-1910).

BSA Managing Committee (from 1910).

Married, Henrietta Leiningen Barwell, 17 February 1920.

Died, 8 November 1941, Frensham, Surrey.

Publications

Political Parties in Athens during the Peloponnesian War (Cambridge: University Press, 1889).

Greek Oligarchies: Their Character and Organisations (London: Methuen, 1896).

(ed.) *A Companion to Greek Studies* (Cambridge: Cambridge University Press, 1905; 2nd edn. 1906; 3rd edn. 1906; 4th edn. 1931).

'The Bronze Trumpeter at Sparta and the Earthquake of 464 BC ', *CQ* 3, 1 (1909) 60-62.

Obituaries, memoirs and studies

S. C. Roberts (rev. M. Pottle), 'Whibley, Leonard (1863-1941)', in *ODNB*, vol. 58, 471; *DBC*.

YORKE, VINCENT WODEHOUSE

See Directors and Students.

ZIMMERN, ALFRED ECKHARD (1879-1957)

Born, 26 January 1879, at Surbiton, Surrey; son of Adolf Zimmern, and his wife, Matilda Sophia Eckhard.

Educ. Winchester Coll.

Oxf. New Coll.; 1st class Class. mod. (1900), Lit. Hum. (1902); lecturer in Ancient History; Fell. and tutor (1904-09).

Univ. Coll. of Wales, Aberystwyth, Prof. of International Relations (1919-21).

Oxf. Montague Burton Prof. of International Relations (1930-44).

Chatham House, Deputy Director (1943-45).

Trinity Coll. Hartford, Connecticut, visiting Prof. (1947); director, Centre for World Affairs (1948).

BSA Managing Committee (from 1912).

Married, Lucie Anna Elisabeth Olympe Barber, 31 March 1921.

Died, 24 November 1957, Avon, Connecticut.

Publications

Translation of G. Ferrero, *The Greatness and Decline of Rome* (London: Heinemann, 1907).

'Was Greek Civilization Based on Slave Labour?', *Sociological Review* 2 (1909) 2-19.

The Greek Commonwealth: Politics and Economics in 5th century Athens (Oxford: Clarendon Press, 1911).

Solon and Croesus, and Other Greek Essays (London: Oxford University Press, 1928).

Obituaries, memoirs and studies

D. J. Markwell, 'Zimmern, Sir Alfred Eckhard (1879-1957)', in *ODNB*, vol. 60, 993-95; *DBC*.

APPENDIX III

DIRECTORS AND STUDENTS
OF THE BRITISH SCHOOL AT ATHENS
(1886-1919)

Abbreviations

adm. = admitted
Asst. = Assistant
BSR = British School at Rome
Camb. = Cambridge
Class. mod. = Classical moderations
Class. Trip. = Classical Tripos
Coll. = College
dau. = daughter
Dir. = Director
Educ. = Educated
Exhib. = Exhibitioner or Exhibition
Fell. = Fellow
hons. = honours
Lect. = Lecturer
Lit. Hum. = Literae Humaniores
matric. = matriculated
Oxf. = Oxford
pens. = pensioner
Schol. = Scholar or Scholarship
Soc. = Society
UCL = University College London
Univ. = University

ABRAHAMS, ETHEL BEATRICE (1881-1956) (MRS CULLEY)

Born, c. 1881, Clerkenwell; dau. of Phineas Abrahams, upholsterer (1881) and 'house furnisher' (1891).

Bedford College, University of London (1901-04); BA Classics, 2nd; pupil of A. B. Cook; MA in Archaeology (1905-07) ('Greek Dress'); London Diploma in teaching (1908-09); re-enrolled (January-June 1911) for inter-collegiate MA in Classical Archaeology.

Fellowship from the Reid Trustees, Bedford College, University of London (1905).

BSA adm. 1905-06.

War service, Examiner for Postal Censorship (1916-June 1919).

Married, Walter Willoughby Basil Culley (1887-1978) (1916), who served in the 28th London Regiment, Royal Garrison Artillery.

Died, April 1956.

Publications

Greek Dress: a Study of the Costumes Worn in Ancient Greece. London: John Murray, 1908.

ANDERSON, JOHN GEORGE CLARK (1870-1952)

Born, 6 December 1870; son of Rev. Alexander Anderson, of Edinkillie, Morayshire.

Aberdeen Univ. (under W. M. Ramsay).

Oxf. Christ Church; Exhib. (1891-96), Lit. Hum. 1st; MA (1899).

BSA adm. 1896-97 (Craven Univ. Fell.)

Fell. Lincoln Coll., Oxf.

Student, Tutor and sometime Senior Censor of Christ Church (1900-27); Univ. Lect. (1919-27); Reader in Roman Epigraphy (1927); Camden Prof. of Ancient History and Fell. Brasenose Coll. (1927-36).

War service, Labour Regulations Dept., Wages Section, Ministry of Munitions (1916-18); Chief of Section, Wages and Arbitration Dept., Ministry of Labour (1918-19).

Died, 31 Oxford 1952, Oxford.

Publications

'The Campaign of Basil I. Against the Paulicians in 872 AD ', *CR* 10 (1896) 136-40.

'An Epigraphic Miscellany', *ABSA* 3 (1896/7) 106-20.

'The Road-system of Eastern Asia Minor with the Evidence of Byzantine Campaigns', *JHS* 17 (1897) 22-44.

'A Summer in Phrygia: I', *JHS* 17 (1897) 396-424.

'Exploration in Asia Minor during 1898: First Report', *ABSA* 4 (1897/8) 49-78.

'A Summer in Phrygia: Part II', *JHS* 18 (1898) 81-128.

'A Summer in Phrygia: Some Corrections and Additions', *JHS* 18 (1898) 340-44.

'Exploration in Galatia cis Halym, Part II', *JHS* 19 (1899) 52-164.

'Pontica', *JHS* 20 (1900) 151-58.

'A New Hittite Inscription', *JHS* 21 (1901) 322-24.

'A Journey of Exploration in Pontus', in *Studia Pontica* 1. Brussels: H. Lamertin, 1903.

'A Celtic Cult and Two Sites in Roman Galatia', *JHS* 30 (1910) 163-67.

(and F. Cumont, H. Gregoire) 'Receuil des inscriptions Grecques et Latines du Pont et de l'Armenie', in *Studia Pontica* 3. Brussels: H. Lamertin, 1910.

(and F. Haverfield) 'Trajan on the Quinquennium Neronis', *JRS* 1 (1911) 173-79.

(and F. Cumont) 'Three New Inscriptions from Pontus and Pisidia', *JRS* 2 (1912) 233-36.

'Festivals of Mên Askaênos in the Roman Colony at Antioch of Pisidia', *JRS* 3 (1913) 267-300.

'Obituary: Professor F. Haverfield', *CR* 33 (1919) 165-66.

'When Did Agricola Become Governor of Britain?' *CR* 34 (1920) 158-61.

'A Correction: When Did Agricola Become Governor of Britain?' *CR* 35 (1921) 44.

'Pompey's Campaign Against Mithradates', *JRS* 12 (1922) 99-105.

Cornelii Taciti de vita Agricolae, ed. H. Furneaux. Oxford: Clarendon Press, 1922.

'Augustan Edicts from Cyrene', *JRS* 17 (1927) 33-48.

'The Genesis of Diocletian's Provincial Re-organization', *JRS* 22 (1932) 24-32.

'An Imperial Sstate in Galatia', *JRS* 27 (1937) 18-21.

Corneli Taciti de origine et situ Germanorum. Oxford: Clarendon Press, 1938.

'Sir George MacDonald: A Bibliographical Supplement', *JRS* 30 (1940) 129-32.

Obituaries, memoirs and studies

The Times 22 April 1952; *The Brazen Nose* 9 (May 1952) 236-37; *DBC*.

Archive material

Sackler Library, Oxford.

ATKINSON, THOMAS DINHAM (1864-1948)

Born, 1864, Sheffield; son of the Rev. George Barnes Atkinson, Rector of Swanington, Norfolk, and Schoolmaster in Sheffield.

Educ. Rossall School.

UCL.

Articled to Sir Arthur Blomfield, ARA; architect with William Milner Fawcett, Trumpington Street, Cambridge (resident in Cambridge as architect in 1891).

BSA adm. 1898-99 (Architectural Student).

Surveyor to the Dean and Chapter of Ely; surveyor to the Dean and Chapter of Winchester (from 1918) and to the Warden and Fellows of Winchester Coll. (1919-46).

ARIBA (1889), FRIBA (1910).

Hon. Sec. Cambridge Antiquarian Soc.

Married, Annie Gertude Chataway (1907), dau. of Rev. J. Chataway, Rector of Rotherswick, Hampshire.

Died, 29 December 1948.

Publications

Cambridge Described & Illustrated: Being a Short History of the Town and University. London: Macmillan and Co., 1897.

'Excavations in Melos, 1899. B. The structures', *ABSA* 5 (1898/9) 10-14.

English Architecture. London: Methuen, 1904.

A Glossary of Terms Used in English Architecture. London: Methuen, 1906.

(and R. C. Bosanquet, C. C. Edgar, A. J. Evans, D. G. Hogarth, D. Mackenzie, C. Harcourt-Smith, and F. B. Welch) *Excavations at Phylakopi in Melos*. Society for the Promotion of Hellenic Studies, Occasional Paper 4. London, 1904.

Obituaries, memoirs and studies

The Times 1 Jan 1949; *Builder* 176 (7 Jan 1949) 18; *RIBA Journal* 56 (1949) 143; *DBA*; The Incorporated Church Buildings Society (www. churchplansonline. org).

Archive material
Hampshire Record Office; Society of Antiquaries, London; Norfolk Record Office.

AWDRY, HERBERT (1851-1909)
Born, 20 October 1851, at Notton House, near Chippenham, Wiltshire; 3rd son of Sir John
    Wither Awdry.
Educ. Winchester Coll.; Commoner (Sept. 1865).
Oxf. New Coll.; matric. Winchester Schol. (14 Oct 1870); Lit. Hum. 2nd (1874); MA (1877).
Taught at Hurstpierpoint (1872-74); Asst. Master, St Paul's Coll., Stony Stratford (1875-81);
    Asst. Master, Wellington Coll. (1881-1908); Tutor of the Hardinge and Combermere
    (1884-1904); Librarian (1904-08).
BSA adm. 1894-95.
Died, 6 December 1909.
Publications
'Criticism of Grundy's Plataea', *ABSA* 1 (1894/5) 90-98.
'Pylos and Sphacteria', *JHS* 20 (1900) 14-19.
'Note on the Walls on Epipolae', *JHS* 29 (1909) 70-78.
(and W. C. Compton) 'Two Notes on Pylos and Sphacteria', *JHS* 27 (1907) 274-83.
Obituaries, memoirs and studies
Wellington Year Book (1908), 62; (1909), 64; *JHS* 30 (1910) lii.

BAKER, FRANCIS BRAYNE (BRAYNE-BAKER) (B. 1868)
Born, 19 September 1868, at Wychwood, Oxon.; son of William Baker, farmer.
Educ. Cheltenham Coll.
Camb. Christ's Coll.; adm. pens. (14 January 1887); Schol. (1887); Exhib. (1891); Class.
    Trip. Pt 1, 2. 1 (1890); Pt 2, 2nd (1891); BA (1890); MA (1896).
BSA adm. 1891-92. Craven Fund (£40): 'for archaeological study in connexion with the
    British School at Athens' (1891).
Asst. Master at Malvern Coll. (1893-1928).
War service, agricultural work in connection with Malvern Coll.
Married, Dorothea Mary Porcher (9 August 1904), Cheltenham.
Later changed name to Francis Brayne-Baker.
Date of death unknown; alive in 1944, living in Minehead.
Publications
'Coin-types of Asia Minor', *NC* 12 (1892) 89-97.
'Some Rare or Unpublished Greek Coins', *NC* 13 (1893) 21-35.
Obituaries, memoirs and studies
Venn.

BARNSLEY, SIDNEY HOWARD (1865-1926)
Born, 25 February 1865, Birmingham; son of Edward Barnsley (d. 1881), builder and
    partner of John Barnsley & Sons, and his wife Amelia.
Birmingham School of Art.
Worked in office of Richard Norman Shaw (1885-88).
BSA adm. 1887-88 (Student of the Royal Academy); re-adm. 1889-90, 1890-91.

Co-founder of Kenton & Co. (1890/91-92).

War service, VAD in Red Cross Hospital (England).

Married, Lucy Morley (1895).

Died, 25 September 1926.

Publications

'The North Doorway of the Erechtheum', *JHS* 12 (1891) 381-83.

(and R. W. Schultz) *The Monastery of Saint Luke of Stiris, in Phocis: and the Dependent Monastery of Saint Nicolas in the Fields, near Skripou, in Boeotia.* London: Macmillan, 1901.

Obituaries, memoirs and studies

N. Jewson, *By Chance I Did Rove*. Cirencester: Earle & Ludlow, 1952; Alan Crawford, 'Barnsley family (*per.* 1885-1987)', in *ODNB*, vol. 4, pp. 4-7; *DBA*.

BATHER, ARTHUR GEORGE (1868-1928)

Born, 5 August 1868, at Dayhouse, Meole Brace, Shrewsbury; 5th son of John Bather (1837), J. P., deceased, late of Meole Brace, Shrewsbury.

Educ. Rossall; Exhib.

Camb. King's Coll.; adm. schol. (8 Oct. 1887); Class. Trip. Pt 1, 1st (1889); Pt 2, 1st (1891); BA (1891); MA (1895).

BSA adm. 1889-90; re-adm. 1891-92 (Cambridge Studentship); 1892-93 (Prendergast Greek Student); 1893-94 (Cambridge Student); Hellenic Soc. student (1893); Craven student (1894).

Fell. King's Coll. (1894).

Asst. Master at Winchester Coll. (1894-1928); Commander of the Corps (1895-1902); Housemaster, Sunnyside (1903-20).

Ordained Deacon (1896); Priest (Winchester) (1897).

War service, Captain of Winchester Coll. OTC.

Married, Lilian Dundas Firth (1875-1957) (1895), dau. of Charles H. Firth, steel manufacturer, of Upper Hallam, Yorkshire.

Died, 18 March 1928, at Winchester.

Publications

'The Bronze Fragments of the Acropolis', *JHS* 13 (1892) 124-30.

'The Bronze Fragments of the Acropolis. II. Ornamented Bands and Small Objects', *JHS* 13 (1892) 232-71.

'The Development of the Plan of the Thersilion', *JHS* 13 (1892) 328-37.

(and V. W. Yorke) 'Excavations on the Probable Sites of Basilis and Bathos', *JHS* 13 (1892) 227-31.

'The Problem of the Bacchae', *JHS* 14 (1894) 244-63.

Obituaries, memoirs and studies

The Times 25 March 1928; *The Wykehamist* 699 (29 March 1928) 486-87; Venn.

BENSON, EDWARD FREDERIC (1867-1940)

Born, 24 July 1867, at Wellington Coll., Berks.; 3rd son of Edward White (1829-96), Headmaster of Wellington Coll, and later Archbishop of Canterbury.

Educ. Marlborough Coll. (September 1881-July 1887); B1 house; Foundation School.

Camb. King's Coll.; adm. (4 October 1887); Exhib. (1888); Schol. (1890); Prizeman; Class. Trip. Pt 1, 1st (1890); Pt 2, 1st (1891); BA (1890); MA (1938).

BSA adm. 1891-92 (with grant of £100 from the Worts Fund); 1892-93 (Cambridge Studentship); 1893-94 (Craven Student); 1894-95 (Prendergast Student); excavated in Egypt for the Hellenic Soc. (1895).

War service, propaganda work for the Foreign Office and Ministry of Information.

Novelist; Mayor of Rye (1934-37).

Hon. Fell. Magdalene (1938).

Died, 29 Feb. 1940, University College Hospital, London.

Publications

'The Thersilion at Megalopolis', *JHS* 13 (1892) 319-27.

'Two Epidaurian Cures by Asclepius', *CR* 7 (1893) 185-86.

'Aegosthena', *JHS* 15 (1895) 314-24.

'A Fourth Century Head in Central Museum, Athens', *JHS* 15 (1895) 194-201.

(and D. G. Hogarth) *Report of Prospects of Research in Alexandria.* London: Macmillan, for the Society for the Promotion of Hellenic Studies, 1896.

The Life of Alcibiades. London: E. Benn, 1928.

As We Were. A Victorian Peep-show. London: Longmans, Green and Co., 1930.

Obituaries, memoirs and studies

Venn; *WWW*; Brian Masters, *The Life of E. F. Benson* (London: Chatto & Windus, 1991); *DBC*; Sayoni Basu, 'Benson, Edward Frederic (1867-1940)', in *ODNB*, vol. 5, 172-73.

Archive material

Oxf. Bodleian Lib.; Cambridge UL; UCLA Lib.

BEVAN, EDWYN ROBERT (1870-1943)

Born, 15 Feb 1870, London; son of Robert Cooper Lee Bevan (1809-90), a banker, and Emma Frances Shuttleworth (1827-1909), poet, of Trent Park, New Barnet.

Educ. Cheam and Monkton Combe (Summer term 1885-Summer term 1888).

Oxf. New Coll.; Open Classical Schol.; Class. mod. 1st (1890); Lit. Hum. 1st (1892).

Travelled to India (1892-93).

BSA adm. 1893-94; excavated with Hogarth at Alexandria.

Lived on private means.

War service, work in the Dept. of Information and in the Political Intelligence Dept. of the Foreign Office (1915-19).

Lect. in Hellenistic History and Literature, King's Coll. London (1922-33).

FBA (1942).

Married, Mary Waldegrave (d. 1935) (25 April 1896), dau. Granville Augustus William Waldegrave, third Baron Radstock.

Died, 18 Oct 1943.

Publications

'A Note on Antiochos Epiphanes', *JHS* 20 (1900) 26-30.

'Note on the Command Held by Seleukos, 323-321 B. C', *CR* 14 (1900) 396-98.

'"Ἀκραγῆ and Agrigentum', *CR* 16 (1902) 200.

'Antiochos III and his Title "Great-King"', *JHS* 22 (1902) 241-44.

The House of Seleucus. London: E. Arnold, 1902.

Jerusalem Under the High-priest: Five Lectures on the Period between Nehemiah and the New Testament. London: E. Arnold, 1904.

(and F. Haverfield, J. L. S. Davidson, E. M. Walker, D. G. Hogarth, and L. Cromer) 'Ancient Imperialism', *CR* 24 (1910) 105-16.

Stoics and Sceptics: Four Lectures Delivered in Oxford During Hilary Term 1913 for the Common University Fund. Oxford: Clarendon Press, 1913.

Hellenism and Christianity. New York: Books for Libraries Press, 1921.

A History of Egypt Under the Ptolemaic Dynasty. London: Methuen, 1927.

Later Greek Religion. London: J. M. Dent, 1927.

Sibyls and Seers, a Survey of Some Ancient Theories of Revelation and Inspiration. London: G. Allen & Unwin, 1928.

Christianity. London: T. Butterworth, 1932.

Symbolism and Belief: the Gifford Lectures, 1933-4. London, 1938.

Holy Images: an Inquiry into Idolatry and Image-worship in Ancient Paganism and in Christianity. London: G. Allen & Unwin, 1940.

Obituaries, memoirs and studies

Gilbert Murray, *PBA* 26 (1943) 411-20; *DBC*; Gilbert Murray and Clement C. J. Webb (revised Michael H. Crawford), 'Bevan, Edwyn Robert (1870-1943)', in *ODNB*, vol. 5, 575-76.

Archive material

Oxf. Bodleian Lib.

BICKFORD-SMITH, ROANDEU ALBERT HENRY (1859-1916)

Born, 3 May 1859, at Camborne, Cornwall; son of William, of Trevarno, Cornwall, MP for Truro Division of Cornwall (1885-92), and Margaret Leaman Venning (d. 1868).

Educ. Marlborough Coll. (February 1871-December 1874), Littlefield House; Leys, Cambridge.

London Univ. hons. in Mathematics (1876).

Camb. Trinity. Coll.; adm. pens. (1 June 1878); Law 2nd (1882); BA (1883); MA (1886).

Adm. at the Inner Temple (1882); called to the Bar (1886); barrister.

BSA adm. 1889-90.

Captain in the Royal Cornwall Rangers Militia.

FSA.

Married, Caroline Louisa Marianne Skinner (b. 1873) (1891).

Died, 13 December 1916.

Publications

Greece under King George. London: R. Bentley, 1893.

(and M. Prior) *Cretan Sketches.* London: R. Bentley, 1898.

Obituaries, memoirs and studies

Venn; Walford County Families.

BOSANQUET, ROBERT CARR (1871-1935)

Born, 7 June 1871, London; son and heir of Charles Bertie Pulleine Bosanquet (1834-1905), and his wife Eliza Isabella Carr (1838-1912), of Rock Hall, Alnwick, Northumberland.

Educ., Eton (1883-90), King's Schol.; Latin Prose Prize (1889).

Camb. Trinity Coll.; adm. pens. (17 June 1890); Schol. (1891); Class. Trip. Pt 1, 1ˢᵗ (1892); Pt 2, 1ˢᵗ (1894); BA (1894); MA (1898). Athletics 'blue', (1891, 1894).

BSA adm. 1892-93; re-adm. 1894-95 (Craven Univ. Student); 1895-96, 1896-97 (Craven Student); Asst. Dir. (1899-1900); Dir. (1900-06).

Excavated Housesteads, Hadrian's Wall (1898).

Prof. of Classical Archaeology at Liverpool Univ. (1906-20).

Member of the Royal Commission on Ancient Monuments (Wales), and of the Advisory Board on Ancient Monuments in England.

War service, officer of British Red Cross Soc.; a representative for the Serbian Relief Fund on the Adriatic Coast and Corfu (January-March 1916); Dir. of Serbian Relief Fund in Macedonia (August 1916-August 1917). Orders of the Redeemer of Greece, and St Sava of Serbia.

J. P. for Northumberland (1927).

Married, Ellen Sophia Hodgkin (1875-1965) (8 July 1902), dau. of Thomas Hodgkin, the historian, of Northumberland.

Died, 21 April 1935.

Publications

'The Latest Discoveries at Hissarlik', *ABSA* 1 (1894/5) 101-09.

'Excavations at Melos: the East Gate', *ABSA* 2 (1895/6) 77-82.

'Prehistoric Graves in Syra', *ABSA* 2 (1895/6) 141-44.

'On a Group of Early Attic Lekythoi', *JHS* 16 (1896) 164-77.

'Notes from the Cyclades: a Pre-Mycenaean Wrist-guard', *ABSA* 3 (1896/7) 67-70.

'Notes from the Cyclades: Pre-Mycenaean Pottery from Melos', *ABSA* 3 (1896/7) 52-57.

'Notes from the Cyclades: Stone Dishes or Troughs', *ABSA* 3 (1896/7) 64-67.

'Notes from the Cyclades: Textile Impressions on Aegean Pottery', *ABSA* 3 (1896/7) 61-63.

'Notes from the Cyclades: the So-called Kernoi', *ABSA* 3 (1896/7) 57-61.

'Excavations of the British School at Melos. The Hall of the Mystae', *JHS* 18 (1898) 60-80, pls. i-iii.

'Notes on Pylos and Sphacteria', *JHS* 18 (1898) 155-59.

'Some Early Funeral Lekythoi', *JHS* 19 (1899) 169-84, pls. ii-iii.

(and D. G. Hogarth) 'Archaeology in Greece, 1898-99', *JHS* 19 (1899) 319-29.

'Archaeology in Greece, 1899-1900', *JHS* 20 (1900) 167-81.

'Archaeology in Greece, 1900-1901', *JHS* 21 (1901) 334-52.

'Crete: Excavations. Report on Excavations at Praesos in Eastern Crete', *Man* 1 (1901) 187-89.

'Excavations at Palaikastro. I', *ABSA* 8 (1901/02) 286-316.

'Excavations at Petras', *ABSA* 8 (1901/02) 282-85.

'Excavations at Praesos. I', *ABSA* 8 (1901/02) 231-70, pls. vii-xii.

(and M. N. Tod) 'Archaeology in Greece, 1901-1902', *JHS* 22 (1902) 378-94.

'Crete. A Mycenaean Town and Cemeteries at Palaiokastro', *Man* 2 (1902) 170-72.

'A Mycenaean Town and Cemeteries in Crete', *Biblia* 15 (1902) 278-82.

'Thessaly. Prehistoric Villages in Thessaly', *Man* 2 (1902) 106-07.

'Excavations at Palaikastro. II. § 1. The Second Campaign - Outlying Sites', *ABSA* 9 (1902/03) 274-77.

'Excavations at Palaikastro. II. § 2. The Town', *ABSA* 9 (1902/03) 277-80, pl. vi.

'Excavations at Palaikastro. II. § 3. The Chronology of Palaikastro and Zakro', *ABSA* 9 (1902/03) 281-87.

'Excavations at Palaikastro. II. § 4. The Houses. Block β', *ABSA* 9 (1902/03) 287-89.

'Church of the Ruined Monastery at Daou-Mendeli', *ABSA* 10 (1903/04) 190-91.

(and T. D. Atkinson, C. C. Edgar, A. J. Evans, D. G. Hogarth, D. Mackenzie, C. Harcourt-Smith, and F. B. Welch) *Excavations at Phylakopi in Melos*. Society for the Promotion of Hellenic Studies, Occasional Paper 4. London, 1904.

'Excavations on the Line of the Roman Wall in Northumberland. 1: The Roman Camp at Housesteads', *Archaeologia Aeliana* 25 (1904) 193-300.

'Some "Late Minoan" Vases Found in Greece', *JHS* 24 (1904) 317-29, pls. xi-xiv.

'Excavations at Palaikastro. IV. § 8. The Temple of Dictaean Zeus', *ABSA* 11 (1904/05) 298-300.

'Excavations at Palaikastro. IV. § 9. The Architectural Terracottas', *ABSA* 11 (1904/05) 300-05.

'Excavations at Palaikastro. IV. § 10. The Pottery and the Bronzes', *ABSA* 11 (1904/05) 305-08.

'Laconia II. Excavations at Sparta, 1906. § 1. The Season's Work', *ABSA* 12 (1905/06) 277-83.

'Laconia II. Excavations at Sparta, 1906. § 5. The Sanctuary of Artemis Orthia', *ABSA* 12 (1905/06) 303-17.

'Laconia II. Excavations at Sparta, 1906. § 7. The Cult of Orthia as Illustrated by the Finds', *ABSA* 12 (1905/06) 331-43.

'The Palaikastro Hymn of the Kouretes', *ABSA* 15 (1908/09) 339-56, pl. xx.

'Inscriptions from Praesos', *ABSA* 16 (1909/10) 281-89.

'Greek and Roman Towns I. Streets', *Town Planning Review* 5 (1915) 286-93.

'Greek and Roman Towns II. Town Planning in Syria', *Town Planning Review* 6 (1915) 101-13.

'Francis John Haverfield, FSA, a Vice-President', *Archaeologia Aeliana* 17 (1920) 137-43.

'A New Roman Inscription from Hexham', *Archaeologia Aeliana* 18 (1921) 117-20.

'A Newly Discovered Centurial Stone at Housesteads', *Archaeologia Aeliana* 19 (1922) 198-99.

'On an Altar Dedicated to the Alaisiagae', *Archaeologia Aeliana* 19 (1922) 185-97.

'The Realm of Minos', *Edinburgh Review* 236 (1922) 49-70.

(and R. M. Dawkins) *The Unpublished Objects from Palaikastro Excavations, 1902-1906*. British School at Athens supplementary papers, vol. 1. London: British School at Athens, 1923.

'The Realm of Minos', *Edinburgh Review* 248 (1928) 212.

'A Roman Bronze Patera from Berwickshire, with Notes on Similar Finds in Scotland', *Proceedings of the Society of Antiquaries of Scotland* 62 (1927/28) 246-54.

'Dr John Lingard's Notes on the Roman Wall', *Archaeologia Aeliana,* 4th ser., 6 (1929) 138-62.

'Memoir of Alan Ian, Eighth Duke of Northumberland, K.G., President of the Society', *Archaeologia Aeliana,* 4th ser., 8 (1931) 1-5.

'Cavaliers and Covenanters: the Crookham Affray of 1678', *Archaeologia Aeliana,* 4th ser., 9 (1932) 1-49.

'John Horsley and His Times', *Archaeologia Aeliana*, 4th ser., 10 (1933) 58-81.

(and J. Charlton) 'Excavations at Dunstanburgh Castle in 1931', *Archaeologia Aeliana*, 4th ser., 13 (1936) 179-292.

(and I. A. Richmond) 'A Roman Skillet from South Shields', *Archaeologia Aeliana*, 4th ser., 13 (1936) 139-51.

'Dicte and the Temples of Dictaean Zeus', *ABSA* 40 (1939/40) 60-77.

(and J. D. Cowen) 'A Bone Weaving-frame from South Shields in the Black Gate Museum', *Archaeologia Aeliana* 26 (1948) 89-97.

Obituaries, memoirs and studies

The Times 23 Apr. 1935; Venn; R. H. Hodgkin, 'Robert Carr Bosanquet', *Archaeologia Aeliana* 13 (1936) 1-8; E. S. Bosanquet, *Days in Attica*. New York: Macmillan Company, 1914; ead. (ed.), *Robert Carr Bosanquet: Letters and Light Verse*. Gloucester: John Bellows Ltd., 1938; ead., *Late Harvest: Memories, Letters and Poems*. London: Chameleon Press, n.d.; *DBC*; D. W. J. Gill, 'Bosanquet, Robert Carr (1871-1935)', in *ODNB*, vol. 6, pp. 695-96.

Archive material

National Library of Wales; Cambridge Univ. Lib.; Oxf. Bodleian Lib.

BOXWELL, J.

Trinity College, Dublin; Schol.
Univ. of Cape Colony, BA. Travelling Schol. of Union of South Africa.
BSA adm. 1913-14.

BRADSHAW, MARY N. L.

See Taylor, Mary N. L.

BRAYNE-BAKER, FRANCIS

See Baker, Francis Brayne.

BROOKE, DOROTHY

See Lamb, Dorothy.

BROOKS, JOHN ELLINGHAM (1863-1929)

Born, 3 June 1863; son of Charles Brooks, farmer, of Winslow, Bucks.
Educ. St Paul's Coll., Stony Stratford, Bucks.
Camb. Peterhouse; adm. pens. (1 Oct. 1883); BA (1886).
Adm. Lincoln's Inn (28 Jan. 1887); Roman Law exam. (1889).
BSA adm. 1894-95; re-adm. as associate 1896-97.
Resident on Capri.
Married, (Beatrice) Romaine Mary Goddard (1874-1965), an American citizen, on Capri (13 June 1903); the marriage lasted about one year.
Died, May 1929.

Obituaries, memoirs and studies

Venn; Diana Souhami, *Wild Girls: Paris, Sappho, and Art - the Lives and Loves of Natalie Barney and Romaine Brooks*. New York: St Martin's Press, 2005.

BROWN, ALEXANDER CRADOCK BOLNEY (1882-1942)

Born, 17 July 1882, Aston Vicarage, Stone, Staffordshire; son of the Rev. George Bolney Brown, Rector of Aston-by-Stone.

Educ. Winchester Coll. (Sept. 1895-1901); Schol.

Oxf. New Coll.; Winchester Schol. (11 October 1901); Class. Mod. 1st (1903); Lit. Hum. 2nd (1905); BA (1905); MA (1909).

BSA adm. 1905-06.

Asst. Lect. in Classics, Manchester Univ. (1906-08).

Asst. Master at Marlborough Coll. (1908-42).

Fereday Fell. St John's Coll., Oxford (1908-15); non-residential fellowship.

Died, 21 October 1942.

Publications

'Excavations at Schimatari and Dilisi in Boeotia', *ABSA* 12 (1905/06) 93-100.

Selection from the Latin Literature of the Early Empire. Oxford: Clarendon Press, 1910.

The Shorter Tacitus. Annals XI-XVI. Arranged and Edited for the Use of Schools by A. C. B. Brown. Bell's Shorter Classics, 1924.

The Shorter Livy. Books XXXI-XXXV. Arranged and Edited for the Use of Schools by A. C. B. Brown. Bell's Shorter Classics, 1927.

The Shorter Livy. Books XL-XLV. Arranged and Edited by A. C. B. Brown. Bell's Shorter Classics, 1929.

Obituaries, memoirs and studies

The Marlburian (December 1942) 100-02.

BUDDEN, LIONEL BAILEY (1887-1956)

Born, 1887, Lancashire.

Educ. Merchant Taylors' School, Crosby.

Liverpool School of Architecture (1905); BA (1909); MA (1910).

BSA adm. 1909-10.

BSR adm. 1909.

Lect. (1910), Associate Prof. (1924 -33), and Roscoe Prof. of Architecture (1933 - 52), Univ. of Liverpool; one of the designers for the Leverhulme Building, Univ. of Liverpoool.

ARIBA.

War service, voluntary part-time munition and canteen work.

Married, Dora Magdalene Fraser (1921), in Liverpool.

Died, July 1956.

Publications

(ed.) *The Book of the Liverpool School of Architecture*. Liverpool: University Press of Liverpool, 1932.

Obituaries, memoirs and studies

The Times 23 July 1956; *Builder* 191 (27 July 1956) 149; Peter Shepheard, *JRIBA* 63 (September 1956) 11; WWW.

CALDER, WILLIAM MOIR (SIR) (1881-1960)

Born, 2 July 1881, Presley, Morayshire; son of George McBeth Calder, a farmer.

Educ. Robert Gordon's Coll., Aberdeen (1894-99).

Aberdeen Univ., Classics, 1st (1903).

Oxf. Christ Church (1903); Exhib. (1903); Schol. (1906). Class. Mod. 1st (1905); Lit. Hum. 1st (1907); BA (1907).

Research Student, Brasenose Coll.

Wilson Travelling Fell. Aberdeen Univ.

Craven Fell. 1907.

BSA adm. 1907-08.

BSR adm. 1907.

Studied in Berlin (1909-10) and Paris (1910-11).

Hulme Prof. of Greek in Victoria Univ., Manchester (1913); Lect. in Christian Epigraphy.

Chair in Greek, Edinburgh Univ. (1930-51).

Knighted 'for services to Greek scholarship' (1954); FBA.

Married, Isabel Watt Murray (1910), dau. of F. R. Murray of Aberdeen.

Died, 17 Aug 1960.

Publications

Bibliography in J. M. R. Cormack, *PBA* 47 (1961) 358-60.

'The Eastern Boundary of the Province Asia', *CR* 22 (1908) 213-15.

'A Cult of the Homonades', *CR* 24 (1910) 76-81.

'Militia', *CR* 24 (1910) 10-13.

(and W. H. Buckler) (ed.), *Anatolian Studies Presented to Sir William Mitchell Ramsay.* Manchester: Manchester University Press, 1923.

Some Monuments of the Great Persecution. Manchester: Manchester University Press, 1924.

Eastern Phrygia. MAMA 1. Manchester: Manchester University Press, 1928.

(and W. H. Buckler, W. K. C. Guthrie) *Monuments and Documents from Eastern Asia and Western Galatia.* MAMA 4. Manchester: Manchester University Press, 1933.

(and W. H. Buckler) *Monuments and Documents from Phrygia and Caria.* MAMA 6. Manchester: Manchester University Press, 1939.

(and J. Keil) (ed.) *Anatolian Studies Presented to William Hepburn Buckler.* Manchester: Manchester University Press, 1939.

'Obituary: James O. Ewart', *ABSA* 41 (1940/45) 8-9.

Monuments from Eastern Phrygia. MAMA 7. Manchester: Manchester University Press, 1956.

(and G. E. Bean) *A Classical Map of Asia Minor, Being a Partial Revision, by Kind Permission of Messrs. John Murray, of J. G. C. Anderson's Map of Asia Minor.* London: British Institute of Archaeology at Ankara, 1958.

(and J. M. R. Cormack) *Monuments from Lycaonia, the Pisido-Phrygian Borderland, Aphrodisias.* MAMA 8. Manchester: Manchester University Press, 1962.

Obituaries, memoirs and studies

The Times 19 August 1960; J. M. R. Cormack, *PBA* 47 (1961) 346-60; *DBC.*

Archive material

Aberdeen Univ.

CARY, MAX
See Caspari, Max Otto Bismarck.

CASPARI, MAX OTTO BISMARCK (MAX CARY) (1881-1958)

Born, 6 August 1881 in Liverpool; 3rd son of Otto Caspari, corn-broker and merchant, of
　　Liverpool.

Educ. Liverpool Coll.

Oxf. Corpus Christi Coll.; Schol.; Class. Mod. 1st (1901); Lit. Hum. 1st (1903); D. Litt.
　　(1922).

Ireland and Craven Schol. (1900); Hertford Scholar (1901); Taylor (German) Scholar 1903.

BSA adm. 1903-04 (School Student.).

Dip. Ed. Liverpool Univ. (1905).

Lect. in Greek, Univ. of Birmingham (1905-08).

Reader in Ancient History (1908-37), Prof. of Ancient History (1937-46), Univ. of London
　　(University and Bedford Colls.).

War service, special constable Metropolitan Area (1915); enlisted as private in Royal
　　Fusiliers (1916); Middlesex Regiment; service in BEF, France (1917-19).

Married, Mary Goodrick Swann (1913), dau. of J. Spencer Swann, of Edgbaston.

Died, 2 Jan 1958 in London.

Publications

'On the Γῆς Περίοδος of Hecataeus', *JHS* 30 (1910) 236-48.

'The Etruscans and the Sicilian Expedition of 414-413 BC ', *CQ* 5 (1911) 113-15.

'Stray Notes on the Persian Wars', *JHS* 31 (1911) 100-09.

'On the Egyptian Expedition of 459-4 BC ', *CQ* 7 (1913) 198-201.

'On the Revolution of the Four Hundred at Athens', *JHS* 33 (1913) 1-18.

'On the Long Walls of Athens', *JHS* 34 (1914) 242-48.

'The Ionian Confederacy', *JHS* 35 (1915) 173-88.

'The Ionian Confederacy-Addendum', *JHS* 36 (1916) 102.

'A Survey of Greek Federal Coinage', *JHS* 37 (1917) 168-83.

(and H. E. Butler) *M. Tullii Ciceronis de provinciis consularibus oratio ad Senatum.*
　　Oxford: Clarendon Press, 1924.

(and H. E. Butler) *C. Suetoni Tranquilli Divus Iulius.* Oxford: Clarendon Press, 1927.

The Documentary Sources of Greek History. Oxford: B. Blackwell, 1927.

(and E. H. Warmington) *The Ancient Explorers.* London: Methuen, 1929.

A History of Greek World from 323 to 146 BC London: Methuen, 1932.

(and T. J. Haarhoff) *Life and Thought in the Greek and Roman World.* London: Methuen,
　　1940.

The Geographic Background of Greek & Roman History. Oxford: Clarendon Press, 1949.

A History of Rome Down to the Reign of Constantine. London: Macmillan 1954.

Cicero ad Brutum. Loeb Classical Library, 1953.

Obituaries, memoirs and studies

The Times 3 January 1958; V. Ehrenberg, 'Max Cary', *Gnomon* 30 (1958) 319-20; *DBC*.

CASSON, STANLEY (1889-1944)

Born, 7 May 1889; son of William Augustus Casson, a barrister, and Kate Elizabeth Casson. Educ. Merchant Taylors' School.

Oxf. Lincoln Coll.; matric. (1908); Lit. Hum. 2nd (1912); MA (1919).

Senior Scholar, St John's Coll., Oxford.

BSA adm. 1912-13 (School Student), re-adm. 1913-14.

WW1, enlisted 6 August 1914, 3rd Battalion East Lancashire Regiment; 1st Bn East Lancashire Regiment, Flanders (1915); wounded (May 1915); General Staff, Thessaloniki (1916-18); Allied Control Commission in Thessaly (1917); General Staff, GHQ, Constantinople and Turkestan (1919); demobilised April 1919. Greek Order of the Redeemer. Mentioned in despatches.

Asst. Dir. BSA (1920-22).

Fell. New Coll. Oxf. (1920); Lect. in Classical Archaeology (1922).

WW2, Lt. -Col. Intelligence Corps.

Married, Nora Elizabeth Joan Ruddle (1924), d. of G. Ruddle, of Harewood House, Langham, Rutland.

Killed on active service in flying accident, 17 April 1944.

Publications

'The Topography of Megara', *ABSA* 19 (1912/13) 70-81.

'The Baptistery at Kepos in Melos', *ABSA* 19 (1912/13) 118-22.

'The Dispersal Legend', *CR* 27 (1913) 153-56.

'Note on the Ancient Sites in the Area Occupied by the British Salonika Force, During the Campaign 1916-1918', *BCH* 40 (1916) 293-97.

(and E. A. Gardner) 'Macedonia: Antiquities Found in the British Zone, 1915-1919', *ABSA* 23 (1918/19) 10-43.

'Excavations in Macedonia', *ABSA* 24 (1919/20, 1920/21) 1-33.

'Cornelius Nepos: Some Further Notes', *JHS* 40 (1920) 43-46.

Hellenic Studies. London: E. Mathews, 1920.

'Hera of Kanathos and the Ludovisi Throne', *JHS* 40 (1920) 137-42.

(ed.) *Catalogue of the Acropolis Museum II*. Cambridge: Cambridge University Press, 1921.

(and P. Gardner) *Rupert Brooke and Skyros*. London: E. Mathews. 1921.

Ancient Greece: a Study. London: Oxford University Press, 1922.

'Bronze Work of the Geometric Period and its Relation to Later Art', *JHS* 42 (1922) 207-19.

'Some Greek Bronzes at Athens', *Burlington Magazine* 41 (1922) 137-43.

'Mycenaean Elements in the North Aegean', *Man* 23 (1923) 170-73.

'The Bronze Age in Macedonia', *Archaeologia* 74 (1923/4) 73-88.

'Excavations in Macedonia. II', *ABSA* 26 (1923/24, 1924/25) 1-29.

'New Light on the Ruins of Troy', *Discovery* 5 (1924) 14-19.

'A Pottery Decorative Design of the Hallstatt Period', *Man* 24 (1924) 7-10.

'The New Athenian Statue Bases', *JHS* 45 (1925) 164-79.

'Etruscan Art', in *Cambridge Ancient History*, vol. 4, 421-32. Cambridge: Cambridge University Press, 1926.

'Excavations in Macedonia', *Antiquaries Journal* 6 (1926) 59-72.

Macedonia, Thrace and Illyria: Their Relations to Greece from the Earliest Times Down to the Time of Philip Son of Amyntas. London: Oxford University Press, H. Milford, 1926.

'A New Copy of a Portrait of Demosthenes', *JHS* 46 (1926) 72-79.

(ed.) *Essays in Aegean Archaeology Presented to Sir Arthur Evans in Honour of his 75th Birthday*. Oxford: Clarendon Press, 1927.

'The Growth of Legend', *Folklore* 38 (1927) 255-71.

'Some Greek Seals of the 'Geometric' Period', *Antiquaries Journal* 7 (1927) 38-43.

'Thracian Tribes in Scythia Minor', *JRS* 17 (1927) 97-101.

Some Modern Sculptors. London: Oxford University Press, H. Milford, 1928.

(and A. H. M. Jones, D. T. Rice, and G. F. Hudson) *Preliminary Report Upon the Excavations Carried Out in the Hippodrome of Constantinople in 1927*. London: The British Academy by H. Milford, Oxford University Press, 1928.

(and D. T. Rice, G. F. Hudson, and B. Gray) *Second Report Upon the Excavations Carried Out in and Near the Hippodrome of Constantinople in 1928 on Behalf of the British Academy*. London: The British Academy by H. Milford, Oxford University Press, 1929.

Archaeology. Benn's Sixpenny Library, vol. 149. London: E. Benn, 1930.

'Cretan and Trojan Emigres', *CR* 44 (1930) 52-55.

'Some Technical Methods of Archaic Sculpture', *JHS* 50 (1930) 313-26.

XXth Century Sculptors. London: Oxford University Press, 1930.

'The Hermes of Praxiteles', *AJA* 35 (1931) 262-68.

(and T. Macridy Bey) 'Excavations at the Golden Gate, Constantinople', *Archaeologia* 81 (1931) 63-84.

(and L. H. D. Buxton, J. L. Myres) 'A Cloisonne Staff-head from Cyprus', *Man* 32 (1932) 1-4.

Artists at Work: Based on a Series of Broadcast Dialogues Between the Editor and Frank Dobson, Henry Rushbury, Albert Rutherston and Edward Halliday. London: G. G. Harrap & Co., 1933.

'Battle Axes from Troy', *Antiquity* 7 (1933) 337-39.

'The Bay of Eleutherae', *Antiquity* 7 (1933) 341-44.

'Byzantium and Anglo-Saxon Sculpture', *Burlington Magazine* (1933) 265-74.

'A Greek Settlement in Thrace', *Antiquity* 7 (1933) 324-28.

The Technique of Early Greek Sculpture. Oxford: Clarendon Press, 1933.

Catalogue of the Marbles, Gems, Bronzes, and Coins of the Warren Collection of Greek and Roman Antiquities, Bowdoin Museum of Fine Arts, Walker Art Building. Brunswick: Bowdoin College, 1934.

'Correction', *JHS* 54 (1934) 78-79.

Progress of Archaeology. London: G. Bell and Sons, 1934.

'Early Greek Inscriptions on Metal: Some Notes', *AJA* 39 (1935) 510-17.

Steady Drummer. London: G. Bell & Sons, Ltd, 1935.

Ancient Cyprus: its Art and Archaeology. London: Methuen, 1937.

'A Bridge in Thrace', *Antiquity* 11 (1937) 479-80.

'The Hermes and Dionysos of Olympia', *JHS* 57 (1937) 80.

'Note on the Use of the Claw-chisel', *AJA* 41 (1937) 107-08.

Progress and Catastrophe: an Anatomy of Human Adventure. London: H. Hamilton, 1937.

'The Modern Pottery Trade in the Aegean', *Antiquity* 12 (1938) 464-73.

Murder by Burial. London: H. Hamilton, 1938.

'The Cypriot Script of the Bronze Age', *Iraq* 6 (1939) 39-44.

The Discovery of Man: the Story of the Inquiry into Human Origins. London: H. Hamilton, 1939.

'Professor Gjerstadt on Cyprus', *JHS* 59 (1939) 287-88.

'Submarine Research in Greece', *Antiquity* 13 (1939) 80-86.

Greece Against the Axis. London: H. Hamilton, 1941.

Greece. Oxford Pamphlets on World Affairs, vol. 57. Oxford: Oxford University Press, 1942.

'How Homer Wrote the Odyssey', *Antiquity* 16 (1942) 71-84.

'Rejoinder to Colin Hardie on Homer', *Antiquity* 16 (1942) 275-77.

Greece and Britain. The Nations and Britain. London: Collins, 1943.

Obituaries, memoirs and studies

The Times 24 April 1944; J. L. Myres, 'Obituary: Stanley Casson', *ABSA* 41 (1940/45) 1-4; WWW; *DBC*; Commonwealth War Graves Commission.

Archive material

Wellcome Library for the History and Understanding of Medicine; Manchester, John Rylands Lib.; Oxf. Bodleian Lib.

CHEESMAN, GEORGE LEONARD (1884-1915)

Born, 14 September 1884; son of George Cheesman, solicitor, of 36 Medina Villas, Hove, Sussex, and Mary Salisbury Cheesman.

Educ. Winchester (Sept. 1897-1903); Schol.

Oxf. New Coll.; matric. as Winchester Schol. (October 1903); Class. Mod. 1st (1905); Lit. Hum. (1907); BA (1907); MA (1910).

Christ Church (1907): teaching.

Fell. New Coll. (Elect. October 1908).

BSA adm. 1908-09.

Arnold History Essay Prize (1911), 'Auxilia of the Roman army'.

Excavated at Corbridge and Ribchester.

Soc. for the Promotion of Roman Studies, Council.

War service, enlisted Lieutenant, 10th Battalion Hampshire Regiment (26 Aug. 1914); posted, Gallipoli (1915).

Killed in action during the attack on Chunuk Bair, 10th August 1915.

Publications

'The Date of the Disappearance of Legio XXI. Rapax', *CR* 23 (1909) 155.

'Numantia', *JRS* 1 (1911) 180-86.

'The Family of the Caristanii at Antioch in Pisidia', *JRS* 3 (1913) 253-66.

The Auxilia of the Roman Imperial Army. Oxford: Clarendon Press, 1914.

'An Inscription of the Equites Singulares Imperatoris from Gerasa', *JRS* 4 (1914) 13-16.

Obituaries, memoirs and studies

F. Haverfield, 'Leonard Cheesman', *CR* 29 (1915) 222-23; id., 'Obituary: Leonard Cheesman', *JRS* 5 (1915) 147-48; *The Oxford University Roll of Service 1914-18* p. 18; A. Macdonald and S. Leeson, *Wykehamists Who Died in the War, 1914-1918* (Winchester: Warren, 1921) 240 (ill.).

Archive material

Oxf. New Coll.; Oxf. Bodleian Lib., Dept of Western MSS, MSS Eng lett d 369; Eng misc f 351; Commonwealth War Graves Commission.

CHEETHAM, J. MILNE (SIR) (1869-1938)

Born, 9 July 1869, Preston; 2nd son of Joshua Milne Cheetham, cotton manufacturer, of Eyford Park, Gloucestershire.

Educ. Rossall School.

Oxf. Christ Church; matric. as Schol. (12 October 1888); 2nd class degree (1892).

BSA adm. 1892-93 (Oxford Studentship)

Diplomatic service (1894). Served in Paris (1896), Berlin (1901), Rome (1905), Rio de Janeiro (1908-09), Cairo (1911-19); Peru and Ecuador (1919-20), Paris (1921-22), Switzerland (1922-24), Athens (1924-26); HM Envoy Extraordinary and Minister Plenipotentiary at Copenhagen (1926-28).

CMG (1912); KCMG (1915).

Married, first, Anastasia Mouravieff (1907), dau. of the Russian ambassador in Rome, divorced; second, Cynthia Seymour (1923).

Died, 6 January 1938.

Obituary

WWW.

Archive material

Cambridge Univ. Library; Oxf. St Anthony's Coll., Middle East Centre.

CLARK, CHARLES RICHMOND ROWLAND (1869-1933)

Born, 1869, Berkshire; son of Joseph H. Clark, landowner, of Bray, Maidenhead, Berks.

In 1891, 'Architectural Artist', living at Cookham, Maidenhead, Berks.

BSA, appointed 1895-96; re-appointed 1896-97 (Architectural Student).

Student of the Royal Academy.

War service, Special Constable; work at Board of Agriculture and at Office of Works.

Died, 1933.

CLARKE, RUPERT CHARLES (1866-1912)

Born, 4 July 1866, Taunton; 5th son of Frederick Ricketts Clarke, printer.

Educ. Taunton College School.

Oxf. Balliol. Coll.; matric. (15 October 1884); awarded a Stapeldon Schol. at Exeter Coll. Oxf. (8 December 1884); Class. Mods. 2nd (1886); Lit. Hum. 2nd (1888); BA (1888); MA (1892).

BSA adm. 1886-87.

Curate of St Mary's, Reading (1889); Rector of Ellesborough, Bucks, and Rural Dean of Wendover.

Died, April 8, 1912.

Obituary, memoirs and studies

The Stapeldon Magazine 3, 17 (June 1912).

COMYN, CHARLES HEATON FITZWILLIAM (1877-1933)

Born, 16 August 1877, at Satara, Bombay, India.

Educ. Dulwich College.

ARIBA (1900), FRIBA (1919).

BSA adm. 1901-02 (Architectural Student); re-adm. 1903-04; excavated in eastern Crete with J. H. Marshall.

Surveyor to the Worshipful Company of Drapers (1911).

War service, Artists Rifles (May 1916); 2nd Lt., commissioned RGA (November 1916); 284 Siege Battery, Flanders (March 1917-November 1918).

MRSanI.

Died, 25 September 1933.

Publications

'Church of the Ruined Monastery at Daou-Mendeli, Attica', *ABSA* 9 (1902/03) 388-90.

Obituaries, memoirs and studies

Builder 145 (13 October 1933) 572; *JRIBA* 41 (Nov 1933) 44.

CONWAY, AGNES ETHEL (HON. MRS HORSFIELD) (1885-1950)

Born, 2 May 1885, at Park Street, London; dau. of Prof. Sir William Martin Conway (later Baron Conway of Allington) (1856-1937), art historian, and Katrina (d. 1933), dau. of Charles Lombard of Maine, USA.

King's College, London, MA.

Camb. Newnham Coll. (1903-07); History Trip. Pt 1, 2nd (1905); Pt 2, 2nd (1906).

Institute of Historical Research (1910-12); Creighton Memorial Prizewinner (1911).

BSR adm. 1912.

BSA adm. 1913-14.

War service, co-director of Convalescent Home for Belgian Soldiers (1914); hon. Secretary Maidstone Hospital Supply Depot; Registrar of Registry of University women (1916); Hon. Sec. Women's Branch of National War Museum. Belgian Order of Queen Elizabeth.

Worked on the women's section of the Imperial War Museum (1914-21) where her father was Honorary Director-General (1917-37).

On the death of her mother in 1933 she inherited Allington Castle which her parents had bought in 1904.

MBE (1918).

Litt. D. Trinity College Dublin.

Associate of Newnham College (1930-46).

Married, George Wilberforce Horsfield, Dir. of Antiquities in Trans-Jordan (1924-36), 28 January 1932, at Jerusalem.

Died, 1 September 1950, at Hartfield, Sussex.

Publications

A Ride Through the Balkans: on Classic Ground with a Camera. London: R. Scott, 1917.

(and G. Horsfield, N. Glueck) 'Prehistoric Rock-Drawings in Transjordan', *AJA* 37 (1933) 381-86.

'Journey to Kilwa, Transjordan', *Geographical Journal* 102 (1943) 71-77.

Obituary, memoirs and studies

The Times 7 September 1950; Joan Evans, *The Conways: a History of Three Generations*. London: Museum Press, 1966; A. Robinson, *The Life and Work of Jane Ellen Harrison*. Oxford: Oxford University Press, 2002.

CROWFOOT, JOHN WINTER (1873-1959)

Born, 28 July 1873, Wigginton, Oxfordshire; son of Rev. John Henchman Crowfoot.

Educ. Marlborough College (1887-July 1892); B2 house; Foundation Schol.

Oxf. Brasenose Coll.; Somerset Thornhill Manor Scholar (1892); Class. Mod. 1st (1894); Lit. Hum. 2nd (1896); Senior Hulme Schol. of Brasenose College (Lent, 1896); BA (1896); Hon. D. Litt. (1958).

BSA adm. 1896-97 (Oxford Studentship); re-adm. 1897-98.

Resident at Brasenose College (Michaelmas, 1898).

Classical Lect., Mason Univ. College, and Univ. of Birmingham (1899-1900).

Asst. Master, Tewfikian School, Ministry of Education, Cairo (1901-03).

Asst. Dir. of Education and Acting Conservator of Antiquities, Sudan Government (1903-08)

Inspector in the Ministry of Education, Cairo (1908-14).

Dir. of Education, Sudan Government, and Principal of Gordon College, Khartoum (1914-26).

Dir. of the British School of Archaeology in Jerusalem (1927-35).

Vice-president, Soc. of Antiquaries (1941-45).

Chairman, Palestine Exploration Fund (1945-50).

CBE (1919).

Married, Grace Mary Hood (1877-1957) (1909), dau. of Sinclair Frankland Hood, of Nettleham Hall, Lincoln.

Died, 6 December 1959, Suffolk.

Publications

'Excavations on the Demarch's Fields, Melos', *ABSA* 3 (1896/7) 31-34.

'A Thracian Portrait', *JHS* 17 (1897) 321-26.

'Notes Upon Late Anatolian art', *ABSA* 4 (1897/8) 79-94.

'Exploration in Galatia cis Halym, Part I', *JHS* 19 (1899) 34-51, 318.

'The Lions of Kybele', *JHS* 20 (1900) 118-27.

'Some Portraits of the Flavian Age', *JHS* 20 (1900) 31-43.

'Survivals Among the Kappadokian Kizilbash (Bektash)', *Journal of the Anthropological Institute of Great Britain and Ireland* 30 (1900) 305-20.

'122. A Yezidi Rite', *Man* 1 (1901) 147-47.

The Island of Meroë. Archaeological Survey of Egypt, Memoirs, vol. 19. London: Egypt Exploration Fund, 1911.

'Some Red Sea Ports in the Anglo-Egyptian Sudan', *Geographical Journal* 37 (1911) 523-50.

(and F. L. Griffith) *The Island of Meroë, Part II. Napata to Philae and Miscellaneous*. Archaeological Survey of Egypt, Memoirs, vol. 20. London: Egypt Exploration Fund, 1912.

'Christian Nubia', *JEA* 13 (1927) 141-50.

'Five Greek Inscriptions from Nubia', *JEA* 13 (1927) 226-31.

'Some pot sherds from Kassala', *JEA* 14 (1928) 112-16.

'6. Pot Making in Dongola Province, Sudan', *Man* 33 (1933) 11-12.

'Churches at Bosra and Samaria-Sebaste', *JHS* 59 (1939) 139.

'Syria and the Lebanon: The Prospect', *Geographical Journal* 99 (1942) 130-41.

Obituaries, memoirs and studies

London Gazette 3 June 1919, 7272 (in letter of 5 June 1919); 5 December 1919; *The Times* 7 December 1959; *The Brazen Nose* (1960) 27-30 (TLH); WWW; Brasenose College Register (1909). See also *The Times* 25 March 1957 (Grace Mary Crowfoot).

Archive material

Oxf. Bodleian Lib.; Durham Univ. Lib.

CURRELLY, CHARLES TRICK (1876-1957)

Born, 11 January 1876, Exeter, Ontario.

Victoria College, Univ. of Toronto, BA (1898), MA (1902).

BSA adm. 1902-03; re-adm. 1903-04.

Formerly assistant to Prof. Flinders Petrie under the Egypt Exploration Fund.

Excavated at Abydos (1902/03), Ehnasyah (1903/04), Sinai (1904/05), Deir el-Bahri (1905/06, 1906/09).

Curator (1907), Dir. (1914-46) of the Ontario Museum of Archaeology (Royal Ontario Museum).

Prof. of the History of Industrial Art, Univ. of Toronto.

Died, 17 April 1957, Baltimore.

Publications

'Excavations at Palaikastro. III. § 9. The Larnax Burials', *ABSA* 10 (1903/04) 227-31.

(and E. R. Ayrton, A. Weigall, and A. H. Gardiner) *Abydos. Part III.* Egypt Exploration Fund, Special Extra Publication. London: Egypt Exploration Fund, 1904.

(and W. M. F. Petrie) *Ehnasya, 1904.* The Egypt Exploration Fund, 26th Memoir. London: The Egypt Exploration Fund, 1905.

(and W. M. F. Petrie) *Researches in Sinai.* London: J. Murray, 1906.

Stone implements. Catalogue général des antiquités égyptiennes du Musée du Caire. Le Caire: Impr. de l'Institut français d'archéologie orientale, 1913.

I Brought the Ages Home. Toronto, 1965.

Obituaries, memoirs and studies

C. T. Currelly, *I Brought the Ages Home.* Toronto, 1965.

CURTIS, WILLIAM ALEXANDER (B. 1876)

Born, 1876, Thurso, Caithness; son of John Curtis.

Univ. Edinburgh MA Class. lang. and lit., 1st class (1897). Heriot Scholar of Edinburgh Univ.

BSA adm. 1897-98.

Divinity Hall, BD (1901); D. Litt.; Hon. D. D. (Edin. 1914). Pitt Club Scholar in Theology.

Studied at Heidelberg, Leipzig, and Oxford; D. Theol. (Paris).

Prof. Systematic Theology, Univ. of Aberdeen (1903-15).

Regius Prof. of Biblical Criticism and Biblical Antiquities in the Univ. of Edinburgh (1915); Principal, New College, Edinburgh (1935).

Publications

A History of Creeds and Confessions of Faith in Christendom and Beyond. Edinburgh: T & T Clark, 1911.

Obituaries, memoirs and studies

'Scottish University Appointments', *The Scotsman* 28 August 1915, 6 (short biography); 'New Edinburgh Professor of Biblical Criticism', *The Scotsman* 22 October 1915, 9 (inaugural address).

W. D. Simpson, *The Fusion of 1860. A Record of the Centenary Celebrations and a History of the United University of Aberdeen 1860-1960.* Edinburgh and London: Oliver and Boyd, 1963, 227-28.

DANIEL, MARGERY KATHARINE

See Welsh, Margery Katharine.

DARBISHIRE, ROBERT SHELBY (1886-1949)

Born, 4 Oct 1886; son of Godfrey Darbishire (Balliol 1872), Fort Meade, Florida; great-nephew of S. D. Darbishire (Balliol 1865).

Educ. Rugby

Oxf. Balliol Coll. (1905-1909); tutor A. L. Smith (modern history, later Master of Balliol); Modern History 3rd; BA (1909); MA (1928).

BSA adm. 1911-12.

Farmed in the USA at Shelby City, Kentucky; Archaeological and Relief work in Greece and Turkey (1919); American School of Classical Studies at Athens (1926); Asst. Master in a Philhellene school at Athens (1927-29); in America (1930-31); Athens College (1932).

Residence, Stanford, Kentucky.

Married, Ruth Elizabeth Whiting (1921), of Connecticut; 1 son, 2 daughters. Died, 30 March 1949.

Obituaries, memoirs and studies

Lord, *American School*, p. 196

DAWKINS, RICHARD MCGILLIVRAY (1871-1955)

Born, 24 October 1871 Surbiton, Surrey; son of Rear-Admiral Richard Dawkins (1828-96), and his wife Mary Louisa (McGillivray) (d. 1897), of Stoke Gabriel, Totnes, Devon.

Educ. Marlborough (1884-90).

King's College London (1890-92), Electrical Engineering. Apprenticed to Cromptons, Chelmsford, Essex.

Camb. Emmanuel Coll.; adm. pens. (Oct. 1898); Scholar (1899); Class. Trip. Pt 1, div. 3 (1901); Pt 2, 1st language, distinction (1902); BA (1901); MA (1905).

BSA adm. 1902-03; re-adm. 1903-04 (Craven Student); re-adm. 1904-05. Dir. (1906-14).

Craven Student, 1902; Research Studentship, 1902.

Fell. Emmanuel College 1904; Hon. Fell. 1922.

War service, Red Cross work at Malta (1915); attached to the HBM Legation, Athens (December 1915-April 1916); Lieut., RNVR, Aegean Sea (December 1916-April 1919). Silver Cross of the Greek Order of the Saviour.

Prof. of Byzantine and Modern Greek, at Oxford (1920-39); MA Oxford. Fell. Exeter College, Oxford (1922); Hon. Fell. (1939).

FBA (1933). Hon. PhD., Univ. of Athens (1937).

Residence, Plas Dulas, Llandulas, Abergele, Denbs.

Died, 4 May 1955, Oxford.

Publications

'Aetolia', pp. 4 leaves; 29 x 23 cm. Oxford, n.d.

'Excavations at Palaikastro. II. § 5. The Houses. Block γ', *ABSA* 9 (1902/03) 290-92.

'Excavations at Palaikastro. II. § 6. Block δ' *ABSA* 9 (1902/03) 292-94.

'Excavations at Palaikastro. II. § 7. Block ε and ο', *ABSA* 9 (1902/03) 294-96.

'Excavations at Palaikastro. II. § 8. The Pottery', *ABSA* 9 (1902/03) 297-328.

(and M. N. Tod) 'Excavations at Palaikastro. II. § 9. Kouraménos', *ABSA* 9 (1902/03) 329-35.

'Notes from Karpathos', *ABSA* 9 (1902/03) 176-210.

'Pottery from Zakro', *JHS* 23 (1903) 248-60.

'Excavations at Palaikastro. III. §1. Nomenclature', *ABSA* 10 (1903/04) 192-96.

'Excavations at Palaikastro. III. § 2. Τὰ Ελληνικά and Early Minoan Discoveries', *ABSA* 10 (1903/04) 196-202.

'Excavations at Palaikastro. III. § 3. Blocks κ and λ', *ABSA* 10 (1903/04) 202-04.

'Excavations at Palaikastro. III. § 4. Block ε', *ABSA* 10 (1903/04) 204-07.

'Excavations at Palaikastro. III. § 5. Block ξ', *ABSA* 10 (1903/04) 207-12.

'Excavations at Palaikastro. III. § 6. Block π', *ABSA* 10 (1903/04) 212-14.

'Excavations at Palaikastro. III. § 7. Blocks ς and υ', *ABSA* 10 (1903/04) 214-16.

'Excavations at Palaikastro. III. § 8. Block δ, and the Shrine of the Snake-Goddess', *ABSA* 10 (1903/04) 216-26.

'Notes from Karpathos', *ABSA* 10 (1903/04) 83-102.

'Mycenaean Vases at Torcello', *JHS* 24 (1904) 125-28.

'Greek and Cretan Epiphany Customs', *Folklore* 15 (1904) 214.

'Excavations at Palaikastro. IV. § 1. The Season's Work', *ABSA* 11 (1904/05) 258-64.

'Excavations at Palaikastro. IV. § 2. The Finds', *ABSA* 11 (1904/05) 264-68.

'Excavations at Palaikastro. IV. § 3. An Early Minoan Ossuary', *ABSA* 11 (1904/05) 268-72.

'Excavations at Palaikastro. IV. § 4. Temple Site (Block χ)', *ABSA* 11 (1904/05) 272-86.

'Excavations at Palaikastro. IV. § 5. Block π', *ABSA* 11 (1904/05) 286-90.

'Excavations at Palaikastro. IV. § 6. A Larnax Burial', *ABSA* 11 (1904/05) 290-92.

'A Visit to Skyros', *ABSA* 11 (1904/05) 72-80.

'Excavations at Palaikastro. V', *ABSA* 12 (1905/06) 1-8.

'Laconia II. Excavations at Sparta, 1906. § 6. Remains of the Archaic Greek Period', *ABSA* 12 (1905/06) 318-30.

(and F. W. Hasluck) 'Inscriptions from Bizye', *ABSA* 12 (1905/06) 175-83.

(and A. J. B. Wace) 'Notes from the Sporades: Astypalaea, Telos, Nisyros, Leros', *ABSA* 12 (1905/06) 151-74.

'The Modern Carnival in Thrace and the Cult of Dionysus', *JHS* 26 (1906) 191-206.

(and W. H. D. Rouse) 'The Pronunciation of θ and δ', *CR* 20 (1906) 441-43.

'Laconia I. Excavations at Sparta, 1907. § 1. The Season's Work and Summary of Results', *ABSA* 13 (1906/07) 1-4.

'Laconia I. Excavations at Sparta, 1907. § 4. The Sanctuary of Artemis Orthia', *ABSA* 13 (1906/07) 44-108.

'Archaeology in Greece (1906-1907)', *JHS* 27 (1907) 284-99.

'Laconia I. Excavations at Sparta, 1908. § 1. The Season's Work', *ABSA* 14 (1907/08) 1-3.

'Laconia I. Excavations at Sparta, 1908. § 2. The Sanctuary of Artemis Orthia', *ABSA* 14 (1907/08) 4-29.

'Archaeology in Greece, 1907-1908', *JHS* 28 (1908) 319-36.

'Archaeology in Greece: a Correction', *JHS* 28 (1908) 153.

'Laconia I. Excavations at Sparta, 1909. § 1. The Season's Work', *ABSA* 15 (1908/09) 1-4.

'Laconia I. Excavations at Sparta, 1909. § 2. The Sanctuary of Artemis Orthia', *ABSA* 15 (1908/09) 5-22.

'The Transliteration of Modern Greek', *ABSA* 15 (1908/09) 214-22.

'Archaeology in Greece, 1908-1909', *JHS* 29 (1909) 354-65.

'Laconia I. Excavations at Sparta, 1910. § 1. The Season's Work', *ABSA* 16 (1909/10) 1-3.

'Laconia I. Excavations at Sparta, 1910. § 2. The Mycenaean City Near the Menelaion', *ABSA* 16 (1909/10) 4-11.

'Laconia I. Excavations at Sparta, 1910. § 3. The Eleusinion at Kalyvia tes Sochás', *ABSA* 16 (1909/10) 12-14.

'Laconia I. Excavations at Sparta, 1910. § 4. Artemis Orthia: the Excavation of 1910', *ABSA* 16 (1909/10) 15-17.

'Laconia I. Excavations at Sparta, 1910. § 5. Artemis Orthia: the History of the Sanctuary', *ABSA* 16 (1909/10) 18-53.

'Archaeology in Greece, 1909-1910', *JHS* 30 (1910) 357-64.

'Modern Greek in Asia Minor', *JHS* 30 (1910) 109-32, 267-91.

'The Excavations at Phylakopi in Melos, 1911. § 1. Introduction', *ABSA* 17 (1910/11) 1-2.

'The Excavations at Phylakopi in Melos, 1911. § 2. The Excavation', *ABSA* 17 (1910/11) 2-6.

'The Excavations at Phylakopi in Melos, 1911. § 3. Intramural Tombs of Infants', *ABSA* 17 (1910/11) 6-9.

(and J. P. Droop) 'The Excavations at Phylakopi in Melos, 1911. § 4. Melos and Crete', *ABSA* 17 (1910/11) 9-15.

(and J. P. Droop) 'The Excavations at Phylakopi in Melos, 1911. § 5. Melos and the Mainland', *ABSA* 17 (1910/11) 16-19.

(and J. P. Droop) 'The Excavations at Phylakopi in Melos, 1911. § 6. Native Melian Fabrics', *ABSA* 17 (1910/11) 19-21.

(and J. P. Droop) 'The Excavations at Phylakopi in Melos, 1911. § 7. Miscellaneous Finds', *ABSA* 17 (1910/11) 21-22.

(and J. P. Droop) 'Byzantine Pottery from Sparta', *ABSA* 17 (1910/11) 23-28.

'Archaeology in Greece (1910-1911)', *JHS* 31 (1911) 296-307.

'The Apollo Temple on Sikinos', *ABSA* 18 (1911/12) 30-36.

(and M. L. W. Laistner) 'The Excavations of the Kamares Cave in Crete', *ABSA* 19 (1912/13) 1-34.

'Cruciform Fonts in the Aegean Area', *ABSA* 19 (1912/13) 123-32.

'Excavations at Pláti in Lasithi, Crete', *ABSA* 20 (1913/14) 1-17.

(and A. J. B. Wace) 'Greek Embroideries', *Burlington Magazine* 26/140 (1914) 49-50, 99-107.

(and W. R. Halliday) *Modern Greek in Asia Minor: a Study of the Dialects of Silli, Cappadocia and Pharasa, with Grammar, Texts, Translations and Glossary.* Cambridge: Cambridge University Press, 1916.

(and R. M. Dawkins) *The Unpublished Objects from Palaikastro Excavations, 1902-1906.* British School at Athens supplementary papers, vol. 1. London: British School at Athens, 1923.

'Ancient Statues in Mediaeval Constantinople', *Folklore* 35 (1924) 209-48.

'Ancient Statues in Mediaeval Constantinople: Additional Note', *Folklore* 35 (1924) 380.

(and M. M. Hardie-Hasluck) *Letters on Religion and Folklore.* London: Luzac & Co., 1926.

The Sanctuary of Artemis Orthia at Sparta. Society for the Promotion of Hellenic Studies, Supplementary Paper, vol. 5. London: Macmillan, 1929.

'Presidential Address: Folklore and Literature', *Folklore* 40 (1929) 14-36.

'A Picture of the Battle of Lepanto', *JHS* 50 (1930) 1-3.

(and A. J. B. Wace, J. P. Droop) 'A Note on the Excavation of the Sanctuary of Artemis Orthia', *JHS* 50 (1930) 329-36.

'Presidential Address: Folk-memory in Crete', *Folklore* 41 (1930) 11-42.

The Vocabulary of the Mediaeval Cypriot Chronicle of Makhairas. Hertford: Stephen Austin & Sons, 1931.

'Letter-writing in Verse', *JHS* 53 (1933) 111-12.

'The Massacres of Chios', *JHS* 53 (1933) 111.

'Some Modern Greek Songs from Cappadocia', *AJA* 38 (1934) 112-22.

The Monks of Athos. London: G. Allen & Unwin, 1936.

'The Semantics of Greek Names for Plants', *JHS* 56 (1936) 1-11.

'The Process of Tradition in Greece', *ABSA* 37 (1936/37) 48-55.

'173. A Beam Oil-press in Tunisia', *Man* 38 (1938) 150-53.

'90. The Colchicum Crocus at Knossos', *Man* 39 (1939) 104-05.

'Folklore in Stories from the Dodecanese', *Folklore* 53 (1942) 5-26.

'Soul and Body in the Folklore of Modern Greece', *Folklore* 53 (1942) 131-47.

'Modern Greek Oral Versions of Apollonios of Tyre', *The Modern Language Review* 37 (1942) 169-84.

'A Modern Greek Folktale and Comments', *Folklore* 55 (1944) 150-61.

The Nature of the Cypriot Chronicle of Leontios Makhairas. Oxford: Clarendon Press, 1945.

'34. The Cultivation of the Date-palm in Minoan Crete', *Man* 45 (1945) 47.

'A Byzantine Carol in Honour of St Basil', *JHS* 66 (1946) 43-47.

'The Later History of the Varangian Guard: Some Notes', *JRS* 37 (1947) 39-46.

'Some Remarks on Greek Folktales', *Folklore* 59 (1948) 49-68.

'The Story of Griselda', *Folklore* 60 (1949) 363-74.

'Obituary: Margaret Masson Hasluck', *Folklore* 60 (1949) 291-92.

Forty-five Stories from the Dodecanese. Cambridge: Cambridge University Press, 1950.

'The Meaning of Folktales', *Folklore* 62 (1951) 417-29.

'Obituary: W. H. D. Rouse', *Folklore* 62 (1951) 269-70.

'Recently Published Collections of Modern Folktales', *ABSA* 46 (1951) 53-60.

Norman Douglas. London: R. Hart-Davis, 1952.

'The Silent Princess', *Folklore* 63 (1952) 129-42.

Modern Greek Folktales. Oxford: Clarendon Press, 1953.

'In a Greek Village', *Folklore* 64 (1953) 386-96.

'Notes on Life in the Monasteries of Mount Athos', *Harvard Theological Review* 46 (1953) 217-31.

'John Linton Myres: 1869-1954', *Man* 54 (1954) 40-41.

More Greek Folktales. Oxford: Clarendon Press, 1955.

The Chronicle of George Boustronios, 1456-1489. University of Melbourne Cyprus Expedition, 2. Carlton, Victoria: Melbourne University Press, 1964.

Obituaries, memoirs and studies

WWW; Venn; R. J. H. Jenkins, 'Richard MacGillivray Dawkins, 1871–1955', *PBA* 41 (1955) 373-88; P. Mackridge, '"Some Pamphlets on Dead Greek Dialects": R. M. Dawkins and Modern Greek Dialectology', *ABSA* 85 (1990) 201-12; *DBC*; D. W. J. Gill, 'Dawkins, Richard MacGillivray (1871-1955)', in *ODNB*, vol. 15, pp. 538-40.

Archive material

Oxf. Taylor Institution Lib.; Oxf. Bodleian Lib.; Camb. Emmanuel Coll. Lib.; National Lib. of Scotland.

DICKINS, GUY (1881-1916)

Born, 23 October 1881, Hopefield, Manchester; son of A. L. Dickins and Margaret Dickins.

Educ. Winchester (Sept. 1895-1900); Schol.

Oxf. New Coll.; Schol. (1900); Class. Mod. 2nd (1902); Lit. Hum. 1st (1904); MA (1907).

Craven Univ. Fell. (1904).

BSA adm. 1904-05; re-adm. 1905-06, 1906-07 (School Student), 1907-08, 1908-09; re-adm. 1912-13.

BSR adm. 1905.

Fell. St John's, Oxf. (1909); Lect. in Ancient History (1910), University Lect. in Classical Archaeology (1914).

Married, Mary Hamilton (St Andrews) (by 1909).

War service, commissioned November 1914; 13th (Service) Battalion, King's Royal Rifle Corps (1914); Captain (February 1915); serving in France from July 1915. Wounded on 13 July at Pozières, battle of the Somme.

Died, died of wounds in hospital, 17 July 1916.

Publications

'Some Points with Regard to the Homeric House', *JHS* 23 (1903) 325-34.

'A Head in Connexion with Damophon', *ABSA* 11 (1904/05) 173-80.

'Laconia III. Thalamae. 1. Excavations', *ABSA* 11 (1904/05) 124-30.

'Laconia III. Thalamae. 2. Inscriptions', *ABSA* 11 (1904/05) 131-36.

'Damophon of Messene', *ABSA* 12 (1905/06) 109-36.

'Laconia II. Excavations at Sparta, 1906. § 4. The Great Altar Near the Eurotas', *ABSA* 12 (1905/06) 295-302.

'Laconia II. Excavations at Sparta, 1906. § 10. The Theatre and Adjoining Area', *ABSA* 12 (1905/06) 394-406.

'Laconia II. Excavations at Sparta, 1906. § 13. Topographical Conclusions', *ABSA* 12 (1905/06) 431-39.

'A New Replica of the Choiseul-Gouffier Type', *JHS* 26 (1906) 278-80.

'Damophon of Messene. II', *ABSA* 13 (1906/07) 357-404.

'Laconia I. Excavations at Sparta, 1907. § 7. The Hieron of Athena Chalkioikos', *ABSA* 13 (1906/07) 137-54.

(and A. J. B. Wace) 'Laconia I. Excavations at Sparta, 1907. § 8. The Hellenistic Tombs', *ABSA* 13 (1906/07) 155-68.

'Laconia I. Excavations at Sparta, 1907. § 9. The Sanctuary on the Megalopolis Road', *ABSA* 13 (1906/07) 169-73.

'Laconia I. Excavations at Sparta, 1908. § 6. The Hieron of Athena Chalkioikos', *ABSA* 14 (1907/08) 142-46.

'The Art of Sparta', *Burlington Magazine* 14 (1908) 65-84.

'Damophon of Messene. III', *ABSA* 17 (1910/11) 80-87.

'The Sandal in the Palazzo dei Conservatori', *JHS* 31 (1911) 308-14.

'The True Cause of the Peloponnesian War', *CQ* 5 (1911) 238-48.

Catalogue of the Acropolis Museum I. Cambridge: Cambridge University Press, 1912.

'The Growth of Spartan Policy', *JHS* 32 (1912) 1-42.

'The Growth of Spartan Policy. A reply', *JHS* 33 (1913) 111-12.

(and G. B. Grundy) 'The True Cause of the Peloponnesian War', *CQ* 7 (1913) 59-62.

'The Holkham Head and the Parthenon Pediment', *JHS* 34 (1914) 122-25.

'Some Hellenistic Portraits', *JHS* 34 (1914) 293-311.

'The Followers of Praxiteles', *ABSA* 21 (1914/16) 1-9.

(and P. Gardner) *Hellenistic Sculpture*. Oxford: Clarendon Press, 1920.

Obituaries, memoirs and studies

The Times 22 July 1916; A. Macdonald and S. Leeson, *Wykehamists Who Died in the War, 1914-1918* (Winchester: Warren, 1921) 184 (ill.); *ABSA* 21 (1914-16) 198; *DBC*.

DOLL, CHRISTIAN CHARLES TYLER (1880-1955)

Born, 22 March 1880, Paddington, London; son and heir of Charles Fitzroy Doll (d. 1929), architect, of 86, Gower Street, Bedford Square, London, and his wife Emily Frances (d. 1938), dau. of Capt. W. G. B. Tyler of the Indian Army.

Educ. Charterhouse.

Camb. Trinity Coll.; adm. pens. (25 June 1898); BA (1901); MA (1906).

Architectural Diploma, University College, London (1903).

Articled to his father.

BSA adm. 1904-05.

Superintending architect at the excavations at Knossos (from 1905).

War service, special constable in Metropolitan Area; Hertfordshire County Constabulary.

FRIBA (1929).

Member, MCC.

Residence, Hadham Towers, Much Hadham, Herts. and 5, Southampton Row, Bloomsbury, WC

Died, 5 April 1955, Meldreth, Cambridgeshire.

Obituaries, memoirs and studies
Builder 6 May 1955, 761; Venn.

DROOP, JOHN PERCIVAL (1882-1963)

Born, 4 Oct 1882, Paddington, London; son of Henry Richmond Droop (1832-84), a
   barrister.

Educ. Marlborough.

Camb. Trinity Coll. (1900-04); Class. Trip. Pt 1, 2nd div. 1 (1904); Pt 2, 1st archaeology
   (1905); BA (1904); MA (1912).

BSA adm. 1905-06; re-adm. 1906-07 (Prendergast Student), 1907-08, 1908-09, 1910-11; re-
   adm. 1912-13, 1913-14. Worked on material from Kynosarges; excavated at Phylakopi
   (1906, 1911); Sparta (1906); Theotokou, Thessaly (1907); Abydos, Egypt (1911);
   Kamares Cave (1913).

BSR adm. 1907.

Asst. to Dr Aurel Stein, British Museum (1909-11).

Unfit for military service. The Soc. of Friends of Foreigners in Distress (1914); Lady
   Roberts' Field Glass Fund (September 1915-March 1917); Higher Division Clerk,
   Secretariat, the Admiralty (From October 1917-1921).

Charles W. Jones Prof. of Classical Archaeology, Liverpool (to 1948).

Chairman of the Liverpool University Press.

Married, Ita B. Moloney (1916), daughter of Michael Maloney, barrister, of Streatham.

Died, 26 September 1963, Vence, France.

Publications

'Dipylon Vases from the Kynosarges Site', *ABSA* 12 (1905/06) 80-92.

'Messapian Inscriptions', *ABSA* 12 (1905/06) 137-50.

'Some Geometric Pottery from Crete', *ABSA* 12 (1905/06) 24-62.

'Laconia I. Excavations at Sparta, 1907. § 5. The Early Bronzes', *ABSA* 13 (1906/07) 109-
   17.

'Laconia I. Excavations at Sparta, 1907. § 6. The Early Pottery', *ABSA* 13 (1906/07) 118-36.

(and A. J. B. Wace) 'Excavations at Theotokou, Thessaly', *ABSA* 13 (1906/07) 308-27.

'Laconia I. Excavations at Sparta, 1908. § 3. The Pottery', *ABSA* 14 (1907/08) 30-47.

(and A. J. B. Wace, M. S. Thompson) 'Excavations at Zerélia, Thessaly', *ABSA* 14
   (1907/08) 197-223.

'Two Cyrenaic Kylikes', *JHS* 28 (1908) 175-79.

'Laconia I. Excavations at Sparta, 1909. § 3. The Pottery', *ABSA* 15 (1908/09) 23-39.

(and A. J. B. Wace, M. S. Thompson) 'Laconia I. Excavations at Sparta, 1909. § 6. The
   Menelaion', *ABSA* 15 (1908/09) 108-57.

'The Dates of the Vases Called "Cyrenaic"', *JHS* 30 (1910) 1-34.

(and R. M. Dawkins) 'The Excavations at Phylakopi in Melos, 1911. § 4. Melos and Crete',
   ABSA 17 (1910/11) 9-15.

(and R. M. Dawkins) 'The Excavations at Phylakopi in Melos, 1911. § 5. Melos and the
   Mainland', *ABSA* 17 (1910/11) 16-19.

(and R. M. Dawkins) 'The Excavations at Phylakopi in Melos, 1911. § 6. Native Melian
   Fabrics', *ABSA* 17 (1910/11) 19-21.

(and R. M. Dawkins) 'The Excavations at Phylakopi in Melos, 1911. § 7. Miscellaneous Finds', *ABSA* 17 (1910/11) 21-22.

(and R. M. Dawkins) 'Byzantine Pottery from Sparta', *ABSA* 17 (1910/11) 23-28.

(and D. G. Hogarth, E. A. Gardner, J. L. Myres, B. Nopsca, A. Stein, F. R. Maunsell, M. S. Thompson, A. M. Woodward, and A. J. B. Wace) 'The Distribution of Early Civilization in Northern Greece: Discussion', *Geographical Journal* 37 (1911) 636-42.

'Archaeology in Greece, 1912-1913', *JHS* 33 (1913) 361-68.

Archaeological Excavation. The Cambridge Archaeological and Ethnological Series. Cambridge: Cambridge University Press, 1915.

(and A. J. B. Wace, R. M. Dawkins) 'A Note on the Excavation of the Sanctuary of Artemis Orthia', *JHS* 50 (1930) 329-36.

'Facts or Fancies', *ABSA* 32 (1931/32) 247-50.

'Droop Cups and the Dating of Laconian Pottery', *JHS* 52 (1932) 303-04.

Obituaries, memoirs and studies

The Times 7 October 1963, 11 October 1963; Venn; WWW; R. Koehl, 'A Letter from Evans to Droop on the "Problem" of Wace', *Classical Journal* 86 (1990) 45-52; *Faces of Archaeology* 128-31 no. 24; *DBC*.

DUCKWORTH, WYNFRID LAURENCE HENRY (1870-1956)

Born, 5 June 1870, at Toxteth Park, Liverpool; son of Henry Duckworth, JP, and his wife Mary J. Bennett, of Chester.

Educ. Birkenhead and L'École libre des Cordéliers, Dinan, Brittany, France.

Camb. Jesus Coll.; adm. Exhib. (Apr. 1889); Schol. (1890); Nat. Sci. Trip. Pt 1, 1st (1892); Pt 2, 1st (1893); BA (1892); MA (1896); MD (1905); Sc. D. (1906).

Horton Smith Prize, 1905.

Fell. Jesus Coll. (1893); Steward (1895-1920 and 1929); Senior Proctor (1904); Bursar (1933); Master (1940).

University Lect. in Physical Anthropology (1898-1920); Additional Demonstrator of Human Anatomy (1898-1907); Senior Demonstrator of Anatomy (1907-20); Reader in Human Anatomy (1920-40).

BSA adm. 1902-03.

BSR adm. 1909.

War service, Capt., RAMC

General Medical Council, representative of Cambridge University (1923-6).

Married, Eva Alice Wheeler (Cheyne) (d. 1955) (1902), widow of Charles Cheyne, dau. of Frederick Wheeler.

Died, 14 February 1956.

Publications

'Note on a Skull from Syria', *JRAI* 29 (1899) 145-51.

'Excavations at Palaikastro. II. § 11. Human Remains at Hagios Nikolaos', *ABSA* 9 (1902/03) 344-50.

'Excavations at Palaikastro. II. § 12. Ossuaries at Roussolakkos', *ABSA* 9 (1902/03) 350-55.

(and A. C. Haddon, W. H. R. Rivers, and W. Ridgeway) 'Anthropology at the Universities', *Man* 6 (1906) 85-86.

'35. Report on a Human Skull from Thessaly (Now in the Cambridge University Anatomical Museum)', *Man* 11 (1911) 49-50.

'Cave Exploration at Gibraltar in September, 1910', *JRAI* 41 (1911) 350-80.

'Cave Exploration at Gibraltar in 1911', *JRAI* 42 (1912) 515-28.

'Cave Exploration at Gibraltar in 1912', *JRAI* 44 (1914) 264-69.

Obituaries, memoirs and studies

Venn; WWW; J. D. Boyd, 'Duckworth, Wynfrid Laurence Henry (1870-1956)', in *ODNB*, vol. 17, 47.

DUNCAN, JOHN GARROW (B. C. 1873)

Born, c. 1873, Botriphnie, Banffshire.

Church of Scotland.

BSA adm. 1894-95.

Sent out from Aberdeen by the Church of Scotland. Minister of Kirkmichael, Ballindalloch, N. B.; 'Worked at Modern Greek and Egyptian antiquities. Afterwards joined Prof. Flinders Petrie in Egypt, and thence proceeded to Palestine. '

Minister at Gamrie, Banffshire (1901).

MA, BD; FSA (Scot.).

War service, work in the Huts at Barlin (Béthune) and Etaples.

Excavated for the Palestine Exploration Fund in Jerusalem with Robert Steward Macalister (1923-25).

Married, Katherine S. Duncan.

Publications

(and W. M. F. Petrie) *Hyksos and Israelite cities.* British School of Archaeology in Egypt and Egyptian Research Account, 12th year. London: Office of School of Archaeology, 1906.

The Exploration of Egypt and the Old Testament: a Summary of the Results Obtained by Exploration in Egypt up to the Present Time, with a Fuller Account of Those Bearing on the Old Testament. Edinburgh: Oliphant Anderson & Ferrier, 1908.

(and Robert Steward Macalister) 'Excavations of the Hill of Ophel, Jerusalem 1923-1925 Being the Joint Expedition of the Palestine Exploration Fund and the Daily Telegraph', *PEF Annual* 4 (1926).

The Accuracy of the Old Testament: the Historical Narratives in the Light of Recent Palestinian Archaeology. London: Society for Promoting Christian Knowledge, 1930.

(and W. M. F. Petrie, J. L. Starkey) *Corpus of Dated Palestinian Pottery, Including Pottery of Gerar and Beth-pelet, and Beads of Beth-pelet.* British School of Archaeology in Egypt, Publications of the Egyptian Research Account, no. 49. London: British School of Archaeology in Egypt, 1930.

Digging up Biblical History: Recent Archaeology in Palestine and its Bearing on the Old Testament. London; New York: Society for Promoting Christian Knowledge; Macmillan, 1931.

EARP, FRANK (FRANCIS) RUSSELL (1871-1955)

Born, 27 Mar. 1871, Matham Manor Lodge; son and heir of Russell Earp, stockbroker, of Matham Manor Lodge, East Molesey, Surrey.

Educ. Uppingham.

Camb. King's Coll.; adm. (Oct. 4, 1890); Exhib. (1892); Schol. (1893); Prizeman; Class. Trip. Pt 1, 1st (1893); Pt 2, 1st (1894); BA (1893); MA (1897).

BSA adm. 1896-97.

Craven Fund grant (1896).

Fell. King's College (1897).

Cambridge, Fitzwilliam Museum, catalogued the pictures.

Travelled unofficially in Persia with the English Mission (1902-3).

Lect. in Classics at East London College (1905-30); Prof. of Classics, and Fell. Queen Mary College, Univ. of London, (1930-6).

Residence, Hill Crest, Goring Road, Steyning, Sussex (1941).

Married, Edith Mary Purser (1906), dau. of J. E. Purser, of Dublin; one son (d. 1944 on active service) and a daughter.

Died, 14 January 1955, Steyning, Sussex.

Publications

(and S. Colvin) *A Descriptive Catalogue of the Pictures in the Fitzwilliam Museum.* Cambridge: Cambridge University Press, 1902.

Translation of *Herodotus in Vernacular Syriac.* Urni, Persia: Press of the Archbishop's Mission, 1904.

'Greek Painting', in *A Companion to Greek Studies*, edited by L. Whibley, 322-33. Cambridge: Cambridge University Press, 1905.

'Roman Painting', in *Cambridge Companion to Latin Studies*, edited by J. E. Sandys, 590-601. Cambridge: Cambridge University Press, 1910.

The Way of the Greeks. London: Oxford University Press, 1929.

The Style of Sophocles. Cambridge: Cambridge University Press, 1944.

'Some Features in the Style of Aeschylus', *JHS* 65 (1945) 10-15.

The Style of Aeschylus. Cambridge: Cambridge University Press, 1948.

Obituaries, memoirs and studies

The Times 17 January 1955; Venn; WWW.

EDGAR, CAMPBELL COWAN (1870-1938)

Born, 26 December 1870, Tongland; son of Andrew Edgar, from Tongland, Kirkcudbright.

Educ. Ayr Academy.

Glasgow Univ. (1887-91; MA 1897).

Oxf. Oriel Coll.; adm. as Bible Clerk (1891); Class. Mod. 1st (1893); Lit. Hum. 1st (1895); BA (1897).

Craven Fell. (1895); Bishop Fraser's Scholar (1895).

Munich, studying with A. Furtwängler.

BSA adm. 1895-96; re-adm. 1896-97 (Craven Univ. Fell.), 1897-98, 1898-99.

Catalogue Commission, Cairo (1900).

Inspector of Antiquities for Lower Egypt (1905-20).

Asst. Keeper (1920), Keeper (1923), Cairo Museum.

Dunblin, hon. Lit. D.

Retired, 1927.

Died, 10 May 1938, Berkhamstead.

Publications

'Prehistoric Tombs at Pelos', *ABSA* 3 (1896/7) 35-51.

'Two Stelae from Kynosarges', *JHS* 17 (1897) 174-75.

'Excavations in Melos, 1898. II. The Pottery', *ABSA* 4 (1897/8) 37-48.

'Excavations at Naukratis. B. The Inscribed and Painted Pottery', *ABSA* 5 (1898/9) 47-65.

'Excavations at Naukratis. C. A Relief', *ABSA* 5 (1898/9) 65-67.

'Excavations in Melos, 1899. C. The Pottery', *ABSA* 5 (1898/9) 14-19.

Greek Moulds. Catalogue général des antiquités égyptiennes du Musée du Caire, vol. 8. Le Caire: Imprimerie de l'Institut français d'archéologie orientale, 1903.

Greek Sculpture. Catalogue général des antiquités égyptiennes du Musée du Caire, vol. 13. Le Caire: Impr. de l'Institut française d'archéologie orientale, 1903.

Greek Bronzes. Catalogue général des antiquités égyptiennes du Musée du Caire. Le Caire: Impr. de l'Institut française d'archéologie orientale, 1904.

'An Ionian Dedication to Isis', *JHS* 24 (1904) 337.

(and T. D. Atkinson, R. C. Bosanquet, A. J. Evans, D. G. Hogarth, D. Mackenzie, C. Harcourt-Smith, and F. B. Welch) *Excavations at Phylakopi in Melos*. Society for the Promotion of Hellenic Studies, Occasional Paper 4. London, 1904.

Graeco-Egyptian Coffins, Masks and Portraits. Catalogue général des antiquités égyptiennes du Musée du Caire. Le Caire: Istitut français d'archéologie orientale, 1905.

Graeco-Egyptian Glass. Catalogue général des antiquités égyptiennes du Musée du Caire. Le Caire: Institut français d'archéologie orientale, 1905.

'On the Dating of the Fayoum Portraits', *JHS* 25 (1905) 225-33.

(and D. G. Hogarth, H. L. Lorimer) 'Naukratis, 1903', *JHS* 25 (1905) 105–36.

Sculptor's Studies and Unfinished Works. Catalogue général des antiquités égyptiennes du Musée du Caire. Le Caire: Impr. de l'Institut française d'archéologie orientale, 1906.

'Tombs at Abou Billou', *ASAE* 7 (1906) 143-44.

'Report on an Excavation at Toukh el-Qaramous', *ASAE* 7 (1906) 205-12.

'Two Bronze Portraits from Egypt', *JHS* 26 (1906) 281-82.

'Notes from the Delta, I. – Clay Sealings from Thmouis. II. – Inscribed Potsherds from Naukratis. III. – Submerged Graves. IV. – A Greek Inscription from Behera', *ASAE* 8 (1907) 154-59.

(and G. Maspero) 'The Sarcophagus of an Unknown Queen', *ASAE* 8 (1907) 276-80.

Greek Vases. Catalogue général des antiquités égyptiennes du Musée du Caire. Le Caire: Impr. de l'Institut française d'archéologie orientale, 1911.

'Greek Inscriptions from the Delta', *ASAE* 11 (1911) 1-2.

'Notes from the Delta, I. – Bouto and Chemmis. II. – The Temple of Samanoud', *ASAE* 11 (1911) 87-96.

'Report on an Excavation at Tell Om Harb', *ASAE* 11 (1911) 164-69.

'Inscribed Stones at Kom Frin and Kom Barnougi', *ASAE* 11 (1911) 277-78.

'Note on the Preceding Report', *ASAE* 12 (1912) 75-76.

'A Statue of a Hellenistic King', *JHS* 33 (1913) 50-52.

'Report on the Demolition of Tell Sheikh Nasreddin', *ASAE* 13 (1914) 122-24.

'Notes from my Inspectorate', *ASAE* 13 (1914) 277-84.

'A Building of Merenptah at Mit Rahineh', *ASAE* 15 (1915) 97-104.

'Some Greek Inscriptions', *ASAE* 15 (1915) 105-12.

'A Women's Club in Ancient Alexandria', *JEA* 4 (1917) 253-54.
'On the Dating of Early Ptolemaic Papyri', *ASAE* 17 (1917) 209-23.
'A Further Note on Early Ptolemaic Chronology', *ASAE* 18 (1919) 58-64.
'Selected Papyri from the Archives of Zenon (Nos. 1-10)', *ASAE* 18 (1919) 159-82.
'Selected Papyri from the Archives of Zenon (Nos. 11-21)', *ASAE* 18 (1919) 225-44.
'Selected Papyri from the Archives of Zenon (Nos. 22-36)', *ASAE* 19 (1920) 13-36.
'Selected Papyri from the Archives of Zenon (Nos. 37-48)', *ASAE* 19 (1920) 81-104.
'Tomb-Stones from Tell el Yahoudieh', *ASAE* 19 (1920) 216-24.
'Selected Papyri from the Archives of Zenon (Nos. 49-54)', *ASAE* 20 (1920) 19-40.
'Selected Papyri from the Archives of Zenon (Nos. 55-64)', *ASAE* 20 (1920) 181-206.
'Selected Papyri from the Archives of Zenon (Nos. 65-66)', *ASAE* 21 (1921) 89-109.
'Some Hieroglyphic Inscriptions from Naukratis', *ASAE* 22 (1922) 1-6.
'More Tombs-Stones from Tell el Yahoudieh', *ASAE* 22 (1922) 7-16.
'A Note on Two Greek Epigrams', *ASAE* 22 (1922) 78-80.
'Selected Papyri from the Archives of Zenon (Nos. 67-72)', *ASAE* 22 (1922) 209-31.
'Selected Papyri from the Archives of Zenon (Nos. 73-76)', *ASAE* 23 (1923) 73-98.
'Selected Papyri from the Archives of Zenon (Nos. 77-88)', *ASAE* 23 (1923) 187-209.
'Selected Papyri from the Archives of Zenon (Nos. 89-104)', *ASAE* 24 (1924) 17-52.
Zenon Papyri. Catalogue général des antiquités égyptiennes du Musée du Caire. Le Caire: Impr. de l'Institut francais d'archeologie orientale, 1925.
'Engraved Designs on a Silver Vase from Tell Basta', *ASAE* 25 (1925) 256-58.
'Two More Tombstones from Tell el Yahoudieh', *ASAE* 26 (1926) 102-04.
'Fragments of Papyri from Oxyrynchos', *ASAE* 26 (1926) 203-10.
'A Greek Epitaph from Saqqarah', *ASAE* 27 (1927) 31-32.
'Three Ptolemaic Papyri', *JEA* 14 (1928) 288-93.
'A Greek Inscription', *ASAE* 29 (1929) 77-80.
'On P. Lille I. 4', *JEA* 23 (1937) 261.

Obituaries, memoirs and studies

C. L. Shadwell, *Registrum Orielense, 1701-1900* (London, 1902), 677; *The Times* 14 May 1938; *JEA* 24 (1938) 133-34.

EDMONDS, CHARLES DOUGLAS (B. 1876)

Born, 1876; son of Orlando Edmonds, banker, of Northfield House, Stamford, Lincs.
Educ. Clifton College (Brown's House).
Camb. Emmanuel Coll.; adm. pens. (24 Mar. 24 1894); Schol. (1898); Class. Trip. Pt 1, 1st div. 3 (1897); Pt 2, 1st history (1898); BA (1897); MA (1901).
BSA adm. 1898-99 (Prendergast Student).
Asst. Master of Aldenham School (1899-1905); at the Royal Naval College, Osborne (1905-18); Berkhamsted School (1919-39).
Residence (in 1939), 270, High Street, Berkhamsted.
Married, Eleanor D. O'Grady (1921), Berkhamsted.
Died, *not known* (c. 1960).

Publications

'Some Doubtful Points of Thessalian Topography', *ABSA* 5 (1898/9) 20-25.
'The Tumulus of Pilaf-Tepe', *JHS* 20 (1900) 20-25.

Greek History for Schools. Cambridge: University Press, 1914.

Obituaries, memoirs and studies

Venn; *The Times* 5 September 1960 (will).

FARRELL, WILFRID JEROME (1882-1960)

Born, 29 November 1882, Hull; son of Thomas Frederick Farrell, solicitor, Hull, and Monica Farrell (née Collingwood).

Educ. Ushaw College, near Durham; Hymers College, Hull.

Camb. Jesus Coll.; adm. Schol. (October 1901); Class. Trip. Pt 1, 1st div. 2 (1904); Pt 2, 1st (1905); BA (1904); MA 1909).

BSA adm. 1906-07; re-adm. 1907-08, 1908-09.

Fell. (short-term) of Jesus College (1906).

Munich Univ. (1907).

Taught at Rugby (1911-13) and Haileybury (May 1913-July 1915).

War service, 2nd Lt., Captain, RFA (Spec. Res.) (1915); 9th Division Artillery, BEF (France) (1916); Staff-Lieutenant, GHQ, 2nd Echelon, EEF (1918); Special Service Officer, GHQ, MEF; Special Service Officer in Transcaucasia and South Anatolia (1919); Intelligence Corps, France, Egypt, Iraq, and Trans-Caucasia; 2nd Lt.; Captain; MC.

Education Service Iraq Government (1919-22); Acting Dir. and Advisor to Minister of Education (1921-22).

Education Service Palestine (1923-47); Dir. (1937-47).

OBE (1936); CMG (Jan. 1946).

Reported to Foreign Office on education in Libya (1949).

Retirement, Castle Townshend, Co. Cork.

Unmarried.

Died, 2 July 1960.

Publications

'Laconia I. Excavations at Sparta, 1908. § 4. The Archaic Terracottas from the Sanctuary of Orthia', *ABSA* 14 (1907/08) 48-73.

'Note on the Position of Rhoduntia', *CR* 24 (1910) 116-17.

'A Revised Itinerary of the Route Followed by Cyrus the Younger Through Syria, 401 BC', *JHS* 81 (1961) 153-55.

Obituaries, memoirs and studies

Jesus College, Cambridge Society Report (1960) 25-26 (obituary); WWW; Unpublished memoir [October 1918, Baghdad and Mosul military campaign], 'Pedagogue's Progress: Reminiscences of Mesopotamia, Transcaucasia, and Palestine' (photocopy at St Anthony's College, Oxford, Middle East Centre Archive, GB165-0104).

FINDLAY, ADAM FYFE (1869-1962)

Born, 1869, Johnshaven, Kincardineshire.

United Presbyterian Church.

BSA adm. 1894-95.

King's College, Aberdeen; DD and LL. D, Aberdeen; LL. D, Edinburgh

Sent out as holder of the Brown-Downie Fellowship by the United Presbyterian Church, Divinity Hall, Edinburgh; 'Worked at N. T. criticism and antiquities, and Modern

Greek; attended the University; made a special study of the question of St Paul and the Areopagus. '

War service, Chaplain to the Forces (1915-17); attached 2nd Scottish Horse Brigade (November 1915-Ocrober 1916); 24th Stationery Hospital, EEF (November 1916-February 1917); 1/6 Highland Light Infantry, 52nd Division, in Egypt and Palestine (February 1917-November 1917).

Church ministry: Whithorn, Arbroath, Edinburgh and Linlithgow.

Prof. of Church History and Christian Ethics, in the United Free Church College, Aberdeen (1924-35); Master of Christ's College, Aberdeen.

Professor of Christian Ethics and Practical Theology, Aberdeen (1935).

Married, Jeanie Macdonald (1898).

Died, January 1962, Aberdeen.

Publications

'St Paul and the Areopagus', *ABSA* 1 (1894/5) 78-89.

Byways in Early Christian Literature: Studies in the Uncanonical Gospels and Acts: the Kerr Lectures, Delivered in the United Free Church College, Glasgow During Session 1920-21. Kerr lectures, 1920-21. Edinburgh: T. & T. Clark, 1923.

Memoir and Obituary

The Scotsman 13 March 1935, 14; *The Times* 22 January 1962.

Archive material

National Lib. of Scotland.

FORSTER, EDWARD SEYMOUR (1879-1950)

Born, 16 December 1879, Crowthorne, Berkshire; son of Michael Seymour Forster, of Oswestery, Salop., and one-time Bursar of Wellington College.

Educ. Wellington.

Oxf. Oriel Coll. (1898); Bishop Frazer's Schol.; Class. Mod. 1st (1900); Lit. Hum. 2nd (1902); BA (1903); MA (1905).

BSA adm. 1902-03 (Oxford Studentship); re-adm. 1903-04 (with grants from the Craven Fund and Oriel College); excavated, Crete and Laconia.

Asst. Lect. in the Univ. College of North Wales, Bangor (1904-05).

Lect. in Greek (1905-21), Prof. of Greek (1921-45) Univ. of Sheffield.

War service, 2nd Lt. Special Lists (22 Nov 1915), temporary Major Intelligence Corps, BSF (1918). Intelligence work in Salonica (24 November 1915-18) and in Constantinople and the Black Sea region (1918-19). Mentioned in despatches twice (Salonika 1918, 1919). MBE (Mil.). Order of St Sava (5th Class).

FSA.

Residence, Greatbatch Hall, Ashford, Derbyshire.

Died, 18 July 1950, London.

Publications

'Praesos: the Terracottas', *ABSA* 8 (1901/02) 125-56.

'South-western Laconia. Inscriptions', *ABSA* 10 (1903/04) 167-89.

'South-western Laconia. Sites', *ABSA* 10 (1903/04) 158-66.

'Terracotta Plaques from Praesos', *ABSA* 11 (1904/05) 243-57.

'A Fragment of the "Edictum Diocletiani"', *JHS* 25 (1905) 260-62.

Dent's Latin Primer for Young Beginners. London: J. M. Dent, 1906.

'Laconia II. Topography. § 1. Gythium and NW Coast of the Laconian Gulf', *ABSA* 13 (1906/07) 219-37.

'Terracottas from Boeotia and Crete', *JHS* 27 (1907) 68-74.

'An Archaic Male Head from Athens', *JHS* 31 (1911) 260-62.

Isocrates. Cyprian orations: Evagoras, Ad Nicoclem, Nicocles aut Cyprii. Oxford: Clarendon Press, 1912.

'Some Emendations in the Fragments of Theophrastus', *CQ* 15 (1921) 166-68.

'The Pseudo-Aristotelian Problems: Their Nature and Composition', *CQ* 22 (1928) 163-65.

(and T. B. L. Webster) *An Anthology of Greek Prose*. Manchester: Manchester University Press, 1933.

(and T. B. L. Webster) *An Anthology of Greek Verse*. Manchester: Manchester University Press, 1935.

The Iliad of Homer, Book XI. London: Methuen, 1939.

A Short History of Modern Greece 1821-1940. London: Methuen & Co. Ltd., 1941.

For other translations see list in *DBC*.

Obituaries, memoirs and studies

C. L. Shadwell, *Registrum Orielense, 1701-1900* (London, 1902), 717; *Oriel College Roll of Service* (Oxford, 1920), 21; *The Times* 21 July 1950 (notice); WWW; *DBC*.

FOTHERINGHAM, JOHN KNIGHT (1874-1936)

Born, 14 August 1874, Tottenham Middlesex; son of David Fotheringham, a Presbyterian minister.

Educ. City of London School.

Oxf. Merton Coll.; Exhib.; Postmaster (1892-96); Class. Mod. 2nd (1894); Lit. Hum. 1st (1896); Modern History 1st (1897); BA (1896); MA (1899); D. Litt. (1909).

Senior Demy, Magdalen Coll. Oxf. (1898-1902); Research Fell. Magdalen Coll. (1909-16).

Johnson Memorial Prize (1911).

BSA adm. 1898-99 (Oxford Studentship).

Lect. in Classical Literature at King's College, London (1904-09); Lect. in Ancient History, King's College, London (1909-12); Reader in Ancient History (1912-20), Univ. of London.

Asst. in Oxford University Observatory (1918-25); Honorary Asst. (1925-at least 1934); Halley Lect. (1921); Reader in Ancient Astronomy and Chronology (1925-at least 1934).

FBA (1933).

Married, Mary Eleanor Atkinson (3 June 1903), dau. of Joseph Atkinson, of Crosby Garrett, Westmoreland.

Died, 12 December 1936.

Publications

The Bodleian Manuscript of Jerome's Version of the Chronicles of Eusebius. Oxford: Clarendon Press, 1905.

(and G. C. Broderick) *The History of England, from Addington's Administration to the Close of William IV's reign, 1801-1837*. Vol. 11. London: Longmans Green, 1906.

'On the "List of Thalassocracies" in Eusebius', *JHS* 27 (1907) 75-89.

(and L. F. Rushbrook Williams) *Marco Sanudo, Conqueror of the Archipelago*. Oxford: Clarendon Press, 1915.

'The Probable Error of a Water-Clock', *CR* 29 (1915) 236-38.

'Cleostratus', *JHS* 39 (1919) 164-84.

'Astronomical Comments on Dr Holmes's Note on the Julian Calendar', *CQ* 14 (1920) 97-99.

'Cleostratus: a Postscript', *JHS* 40 (1920) 208-09.

Historical Eclipses: Being the Halley Lecture Delivered 17 May 21. Oxford: Clarendon Press, 1921.

Eusebii Pamphili Chronici canones latine vertit, adavxit, ad sua tempora produxit S. Eusebius Hieronymus. London: H. Milford, 1923.

'The Probable Error of a Water-Clock', *CR* 37 (1923) 166-67.

'Cleostratus (III)', *JHS* 45 (1925) 78-83.

(and S. Langdon, C. Schoch) *The Venus Tablets of Ammizaduga, a Solution of Babylonian Chronology by Means of the Venus Observations of the First Dynasty*. London: Oxford UniversityPress, 1928.

Obituaries, memoirs and studies

F. R. Stephenson, 'Fotheringham, John Knight (1874-1936)', in *ODNB*, vol. 20, 539-40.

FRAZER, JAMES GEORGE (1854-1941)

Born, 1 Jan 1854. Glasgow; son of Daniel F. Frazer, partner in a firm of chemists.

Educ. Larchfield Academy, Helensburgh.

Univ. of Glasgow (1869-74).

Camb. Trinity Coll. (1874-78); Class. Trip. 1st (1878).

Fell. Trinity, Cambridge (1879).

Middle Temple, called to the bar (1882).

BSA adm. 1889-90.

Prof. of Social Anthropology, Univ. of Liverpool (1908).

Knighthood (1914).

War service, 'literary work' (translations from the French).

Married, Elisabeth Johanna de Boys (22 April 1896).

Died, 7 May 1941.

Publications

For a full list: T. Besterman, *A Bibliography of Sir James George Frazer O. M.* London: Macmillan, 1934.

The Golden Bough: a Study in Magic and Religion. London: Macmillan, 1890.

'The Pre-Persian Temple on the Acropolis', *JHS* 13 (1892) 153-87.

'Plataea', *CR* 12 (1898) 206-07.

Pausanias's Description of Greece. Translated with a Commentary by J. G. Frazer. London: Macmillan, 1898.

Obituaries, memoirs and studies

Venn; W. Ridgeway, 'The Methods of Mannhardt and Sir J. G. Frazer: as Illustrated by the Writings of the Mistress of Girton (Miss Phillpotts), Miss Jessie Weston, and B. Malinowski', *PCPS* 125 (1923) 6-19; R. Ackerman, *J. G. Frazer: his Life and Work*. Cambridge, 1987; *id.*, *The Myth and Ritual School: J. G. Frazer and the Cambridge*

Ritualists. London and New York, 1991; *DBC;* R. Ackerman, 'Frazer, Sir James George (1854-1941)', in *ODNB*, vol. 20, 892-94.

Archive material

Camb. Trinity College Lib.; Camb. King's Coll. Lib; British Lib.; London UCL; Oxf. Bodleian Lib.

FROST, KINGDON TREGOSSE (1877-1914)

Born, 12 March 1877, Launceston, Cornwall; son of Dennis Tregosse Frost, solicitor.

Educ. Bath College.

Oxf. Lincoln Coll. adm. as Classics Exhib. (1896); Junior Hume Exhib. at Brasenose Coll. Oxf. (Lent Term, 1897); Class. Mod. 2nd (1898); Lit. Hum. 3rd (1900); BA (1900); MA (1905); BLitt, 'Studies in Greek athletic art; Appendix: British Museum notes' (1909).

BSA adm. 1900-01 (Oxford Studentship).

Travelled through Mesopotamia.

Tutor and Lect. at Isleworth Training College, Middlesex (1902-04).

Excavating in Egypt with F. Petrie (1904-5); expedition to Sinai.

FRGS (1905).

Lect. in Ancient History, The Ministry of Public Instruction in Egypt (1905-08).

Bodleian Library, Oxford (November 1908-August 1909).

Lect. in Archaeology and Ancient History at the Queen's Univ., Belfast (1 October 1909).

War service, Captain in the 3rd Bn Cheshire Regiment. Gravestone (and Commonwealth War Graves Commission) suggests rank of Lt.

Killed in action, 25 August 1914 (gravestone, though reported as 4 Sept 1914). Buried at Wihéries Communal Cemetery, Hainault. [1st Bn in the Battle of Mons, 24 August 1914.]

Publications

'The Statues from Cerigotto', *JHS* 23 (1903) 217-36.

'The Navy of Tarshish', *Expository Times* (1904).

'Boats on the Euphrates and Tigris', *ABSA* 12 (1905/06) 190-95.

'Greek Boxing', *JHS* 26 (1906) 213-25.

'Strategy of the Exodus and the Siege of Jericho', *Expository Times* (1907).

'Comment on Waste and Destruction of Useful Antiquities', *CR* 22 (1908) 99-100.

'The Lost Continent', *The Times* 19 February 1909 ('From a correspondent').

Notes on Greek Sculpture: an Introduction to the Collection of Casts. Belfast: Municipal Museum and Art Gallery, 1912.

'The Critias and Minoan Crete', *JHS* 33 (1913) 189-206.

Obituaries, memoirs and studies

W. M. Dunlop, 'Kingdon Tregosse Frost: First Lecturer in Archaeology at the Queen's University of Belfast', *Ulster Journal of Archaeology* 59 (2000) 2-10; Commonwealth War Graves Commission.

FULTON, JAMES BLACK (1875-1922)

Born, 11 August 1875, Fenwick, Scotland; son of Robert Fulton.

Educ. Fenwick and Bearsden.

Articled to William Forsyth McGibbon (1890-95).

Glasgow School of Art and the Glasgow & West of Scotland Technical College.
Royal Academy Prize (1899).
Architect in London (1901).
BSA adm. 1902-03.
Soane Student (1902); study tour of Egypt, Palestine, Turkey, Greece, Italy and Germany.
ARIBA (1906).
Practiced, Bedford Row, London (from 1906).
War service, Sapper, 1st London Field Reserve Company, Royal Engineers.
Dir. of Studies at the Glasgow School of Architecture (1920-22); Prof. of Architectural Design, Glasgow School of Art.
Married, Jessie Bisset Valentine.
Died, 11 April 1922
Publications
Competition Design for the National Museum of Wales. [London]: The Architect, 1910.
Obituary
Builder 122 (12 May 1922) 727; *RIBA Journal* 29 (1921/22) 412.
Archive material
RIBA.

FYFE, DAVID THEODORE (1875-1945)
Born, 3 November 1875, Yloilo, Philippines; son of James Sloane Fyfe (d. 1884), an architect/architectural draftsman, and his wife Jane Charlotte Abercrombie Fyfe (d. 1882).
Educ. the Albany Academy, Glasgow.
Apprentice architect; articled to John Burnet (1890).
Architectural training at the Glasgow School of Art (1890-91, 1894-95, 1895-96, 1896-97); Haldane Bursary (1894).
Asst. to Arthur Beresford Pite (1897); and Aston Webb, London.
BSA adm. 1899-1900 (Architectural Studentship).
Architectural Association Travelling Student, 1899.
Appointed as architect to the Cretan Exploration Fund (to c. 1905).
Architect, based in Gray's Inn Square, Holborn (1901).
Work for John Burnet on the King Edward VII Building, British Museum (c. 1905).
FRIBA (1907).
Work included Christ Church, Spitalfields (1910-11).
War service, resident architect, HM Factory, Queensferry (Ministry of Munitions, Dept. Explosives Supply, Housing Branch).
Architect to the Dean and Chapter of Chester Cathedral (1919).
Master and then Dir., School of Architecture, Cambridge Univ. (1922-35).
Excavated, Glastonbury (1926-27).
Holder of the Henry L. Florence Bursary (1933) used to visit sites in Italy, Greece, Turkey, Syria, Palestine, Jordan and Egypt; report submitted, 'Hellenistic architecture'.
Married, Mary Nina Brown (1911).
Died, 1 January 1945 (skating accident).

Publications

'Painted Plaster Decoration at Knossos', *JRIBA* 10, 3rd series (1910) 107-31.

'The Church of St Titus at Gortyna, Crete', *Architectural Review* 22 (1907) 5-60.

Hellenistic Architecture: an Introductory Study. Cambridge: Cambridge University Press, 1936.

Obituary, memoirs and studies

The Times 5 January 1945; *Builder* 168 (19 Jan 1945) 45; DBA.

Archive material

Oxf. Sackler Lib. (Knossos notebooks).

GARDNER, ERNEST ARTHUR (1862-1939)

Born, 16 March 1862; son of Thomas Gardner, stock exchange.

Educ. City of London School.

Camb. Gonville & Caius Coll.; adm. (1880); Schol.; Class. Trip. Pt 1, 1st (1882); Pt 2, 1st (1884).

Fell. 1885-94.

Excavated at Naukratis, Egypt with the EEF (1885-86).

BSA adm. 1886-87 (Cambridge and Craven Univ. Student); Craven Student 1887-90. Dir. (1887-95); excavated Cyprus Exploration Fund; Megalopolis. Hon. Student of the School.

Yates Prof. of Archaeology (1896) and Public Orator (1910-32) in the Univ. of London.

War service, Sergeant, Metropolitan Special Constabulary (October 1914-1915); Lt.-Cmdr RNVR, Naval Intelligence Officer, Thessalonike (October 1915-17); Officer in charge of HQ Museum (December 1915-March 1917); Intelligence Dept., Admiralty (October 1917-January 1919); Military Intelligence Dept. (July, August 1919). Gold Cross of the Greek Order of the Saviour.

Married, Mary Wilson (d. 1936) (1887), dau. of Major John Wilson (d. 1923), Royal Scots Greys.

Died, 27 November 1939, Boyn Hill, Maidenhead.

Publications

'Athene in the West Pediment of the Parthenon', *JHS* 3 (1882) 244-55.

'Ornaments and Armour from Kertch in the New Museum at Oxford', *JHS* 5 (1884) 62-73.

'Inscriptions Copied by Cockerell in Greece, I', *JHS* 6 (1885) 143-52.

'Inscriptions Copied by Cockerell in Greece, II', *JHS* 6 (1885) 340-63.

'Inscriptions from Cos, &c', *JHS* 6 (1885) 248-60.

'A Statuette Representing a Boy and a Goose', *JHS* 6 (1885) 1-15.

'The Early Ionic Alphabet', *JHS* 7 (1886) 220-39.

'Excavations at Naukratis', *American Journal of Archaeology and of the History of the Fine Arts* 2 (1886) 180-81.

'An Inscription from Chalcedon', *JHS* 7 (1886) 154-56.

'An Inscription from Boeae', *JHS* 8 (1887) 214-15.

'Recently Discovered Archaic Statues', *JHS* 8 (1887) 159-93.

'Two Naucratite Vases', *JHS* 8 (1887) 119-21.

(and D. G. Hogarth, M. R. James, and R. Elsey Smith) 'Excavations in Cyprus, 1887-8. Paphos, Leontari, Amargetti', *JHS* 9 (1888) 147-271.

'Archaeology in Greece, 1888-89', *JHS* 10 (1889) 254-80.

'Early Greek Vases and African Colonies', *JHS* 10 (1889) 126-33.

'Archaeology in Greece, 1889-90', *JHS* 11 (1890) 210-17.

'The Processes of Greek Sculpture as Shown by Some Unfinished Statues at Athens', *JHS* 11 (1890) 129-42.

'Two Fourth Century Children's Heads', *JHS* 11 (1890) 100-08.

(and W. Loring, G. C. Richards, and W. J. Woodhouse) 'The Theatre at Megalopolis', *JHS* 11 (1890) 294-98.

'Archaeology in Greece, 1890-91', *JHS* 12 (1891) 385-97.

(and R. W. Schultz) 'The North Doorway of the Erechtheum', *JHS* 12 (1891) 1-16.

(and W. Dörpfeld, W. Loring) 'The Theatre at Megalopolis', *CR* 5 (1891) 284-85.

(and W. Loring, G. C. Richards, W. J. Woodhouse, and R. W. Schultz) *Excavations at Megalopolis, 1890-1891*. Society for the Promotion of Hellenic Studies, supplementary papers, no. 1. London, 1892.

'Archaeology in Greece, 1892', *JHS* 13 (1892/3) 139-52.

'Palladia from Mycenae', *JHS* 13 (1892/3) 21-24.

'Archaeology in Greece, 1893-94', *JHS* 14 (1894) 224-32.

'A Lecythus from Eretria with the Death of Priam', *JHS* 14 (1894) 170-85.

'Notes on Megalopolis', *JHS* 14 (1894) 242-43.

'The Paintings by Panaenus on the Throne of the Olympian Zeus', *JHS* 14 (1894) 233-41.

'Two Archaeological Notes', *CR* 8 (1894) 69-70.

'Archaeology in Greece, 1894-95', *ABSA* 1 (1894/5) 55-66.

'Note on the Two Temples at Rhamnus', *ABSA* 1 (1894/5) 110.

'Sir Charles Newton, K. C. B.', *ABSA* 1 (1894/5) 67-77.

'Archaeology in Greece, 1894-5', *JHS* 15 (1895) 202-10.

A Handbook of Greek Sculpture, vol. 1. Handbooks of Archaeology and Antiquities. London: Macmillan and Co., 1896.

'Caeneus and the Centaurs: a Vase at Harrow', *JHS* 17 (1897) 294-305.

A Catalogue of the Greek Vases in the Fitzwilliam Museum, Cambridge. Cambridge: Cambridge University Press, 1897.

A Handbook of Greek Sculpture, vol. 2. Handbooks of Archaeology and Antiquities. London: Macmillan and Co., 1897.

'A Head in the Possession of Philip Nelson, Esq., M. B.', *JHS* 18 (1898) 141-46.

'A Head of Athena, Formerly in the Disney Collection', *JHS* 19 (1899) 1-12.

'An Inscribed Scarab', *JHS* 19 (1899) 341.

'A Vase in Chicago Representing the Madness of Athamas', *AJA* 3 (1899) 331-44.

'The Greek House', *JHS* 21 (1901) 293-305.

'The Bronze Statue from Cerigotto', *JHS* 23 (1903) 152-56.

'The Atalanta of Tegea', *JHS* 26 (1906) 169-75.

'Note on the Atalanta of Tegea', *JHS* 26 (1906) 283.

(and R. P. Jones) 'Notes on a Recently Excavated House at Girgenti', *JHS* 26 (1906) 207-12.

'The British School at Athens', *Oxford and Cambridge Review* 1 (1907) 121-30.

'A Statue from an Attic tomb', *JHS* 28 (1908) 138-47.

Six Greek Sculptors. London; New York: Duckworth and Co.; Charles Scribner's Sons, 1910.

(and D. G. Hogarth, D. Strathan, F. Haverfield, A. Stein, J. L. Myres, W. A. Cannon, M. M. Allorge, W. N. Shaw, and J. W. Gregory) 'The Burial of Olympia: Discussion', *Geographical Journal* 36 (1910) 675-86.

A Handbook of Greek Sculpture, Revised edition. Handbooks of Archaeology and Antiquities. London: Macmillan and Co., 1911.

'A Polycleitan Head in the British Museum', *JHS* 31 (1911) 21-30.

(and D. G. Hogarth, J. L. Myres, B. Nopsca, A. Stein, J. P. Droop, F. R. Maunsell, M. S. Thompson, A. M. Woodward, and A. J. B. Wace) 'The Distribution of Early Civilization in Northern Greece: Discussion', *Geographical Journal* 37 (1911) 636-42.

'The Boston Counterpart of the Ludovisi Throne', *JHS* 33 (1913) 73-83.

'Note on the Boston Counterpart of the Ludovisi Throne', *JHS* 33 (1913) 360.

(and S. Casson) 'Macedonia: Antiquities Found in the British Zone, 1915-1919', *ABSA* 23 (1918/19) 10-43.

(and D. W. Freshfield, L. Grogan) 'A Contribution to the Geography of Macedonia: Discussion', *Geographical Journal* 55 (1920) 30-34.

'The Aphrodite from Cyrene', *JHS* 40 (1920) 203-05.

'Notes on Greek Sculpture', *JHS* 43 (1923) 139-43.

'A Reputed Fragment from the Parthenon', *Contemporary Review* 125 (1924) 319-24.

Greece and the Aegean, New revised edition. London: George G. Harrap & Co., 1938.

Obituaries, memoirs and studies

The Times 29 November 1939; *The Caian* 48 (1939-40) 72-74; Venn; *DBC*; D. W. J. Gill, 'Gardner, Ernest Arthur (1862-1939)', in *ODNB*, vol. 21, 454-55.

Archive material

British Library; UCL (diaries and notebooks, c. 1880-1916).

GEORGE, WALTER SYKES (1881-1962)

Born, 24 February 1881, Ashton-under-Lyme.

BSA adm. 1906-07; re-adm. 1908-09, 1909-10, as Student of the Byzantine Research Fund; re-adm. 1912-13.

Worked in Egypt.

Travelling Student in Architecture of the Royal College of Art.

Soane Medallist of the Royal Institute of British Architects.

Moved to India to work on the construction of New Delhi (1915).

War service, trooper, Punjab Light Horse, India Defence Force (1915-19), while acting on Imperial Delhi Secretariat.

Private practice, India.

President, Indian Institute of Archtects; Indian Institute of Town Planning.

CBE (1961).

Married.

Died, 7 January 1962, Delhi, India.

Publications

(and A. Van Millingen, A. E. Henderson, and R. Traquair) *Byzantine Churches in Constantinople: Their History and Architecture*. London: Macmillan & Co., 1912.

The Church of Saint Eirene at Constantinople. London: Oxford University Press, 1913.

(and J. Garstang) *Excavations at Meroë, Sudan, 1913, Fourth Season: Guide to the Twelfth Annual Exhibition of Antiquities Discovered*. Liverpool: Institute of Archaeology University of Liverpool, 1913.

(and A. M. Woodward) 'The Architectural Terracottas', in R. M. Dawkins (ed.), *The Sanctuary of Artemis Orthia at Sparta*, 117-43. Society for the Promotion of Hellenic Studies., suppl. papers, vol. 5. London: Macmillan, 1929.

Obituary

The Times 8 January 1962; *JRIBA* 69 (March 1962) 102, (Apr 1962) 141.

Archive material

RIBA.

GOMME, ARNOLD WYCOMBE (1886-1959)

Born, 16 November 1886, London; son of Sir (George) Laurence Gomme (see *ODNB*), an administrator of the Metropolitan Board of Works, and Alice Bertha Gomme (see ODNB), a folk-lorist.

Educ. Merchant Taylors' School.

Camb. Trinity Coll.; Class. Trip. Pt 1, 1st (1907); Pt 2, 1st with distinction in archaeology (1908).

BSA adm. 1908-09 (Prendergast Student).

Asst. Lect. in Classics, Univ. of Liverpool (1910-11); Asst. Lect. and Lect. in Greek and Roman History, Univ. of Glasgow (1911-45), reader (1945), Prof. of Greek (1946-57); LLD from Glasgow (1958).

War service, commissioned 2nd Lieutenant, Interpreters' Corps (October 1914); 8th Division, BEF (France) (November 1914-November 1915); transferred to Army Service Corps in France (June 1915); Intelligence at Thessaloniki, British Salonika force (November 1915-October 1916); promoted Lieutenant (April 1916); invalided (1916); work for admiralty (March 1917-January 1918); transferred to General List for work at Athens and Constantinople (January 1918-February 1919).

President, Society for the Promotion of Hellenic Studies (1956); Scottish Classical Association (1956-57).

FBA.

Married, Phyllis K. H. Emmerson (1917), in Chelsea.

Died, 18 Jan 1959, Long Crendon, Buckinghamshire.

Publications

Bibliography to 1960 in D. A. Campbell (ed.) and A. W. Gomme, *More Essays in Greek History and Literature*. Oxford: B. Blackwell, 1962.

'The Literary Evidence for the Topography of Boeotia', *ABSA* 17 (1910/11) 29-53.

'The Topography of Boeotia and the Theories of M. Bérard', *ABSA* 18 (1911/12) 189-210.

'The Legend of Cadmus and the Logographi', *JHS* 33 (1913) 53-72.

'The Legend of Cadmus and the Logographi. -II', *JHS* 33 (1913) 223-45.

Mr Wells as Historian, an Inquiry Into Those Parts of Mr H. G. Wells' Outline of History Which Deal With Greece and Rome. Glasgow: MacLehose, Jackson and Co., 1921.

'The Scenery of Greece', *Geographical Journal* 57 (1921) 418-27.

The Population of Athens in the Fifth and Fourth Centuries BC. Oxford: B. Blackwell, 1933.

Menander. Oxford: B. Blackwell, 1937.

Greece: History of the Economic and Social Progress of Modern Greece. London: Oxford
University Press, 1945.

A Historical Commentary on Thucydides, vols. 1-3. Oxford: Clarendon Press, 1945-56.

The Greek Attitude to Poetry and History. Sather Classical Lectures, vol. 27. Berkeley:
University of California Press, 1954.

'Notes on Greek Comedy', *CR* 8 (1958) 1-4.

(and F. H. Sandbach) *Menander: a Commentary.* London: Oxford University Press, 1973.

Obituaries, memoirs and studies

The Times 20 January 1959, 30 January 1959; Venn; WWW; H. D. F. Kitto, 'Arnold Wycombe
Gomme, 1886-1959', *PBA* 65 (1959) 335-44; 'Arnold Wycombe Gomme', *JHS* 79
(1959)1-2; A. Andrews, 'Arnold Wycombe Gomme', *Gnomon* 32 (1960) 190-91; *DBC.*

Archive material

Glasgow, Univ. Lib. Special Collections Dept.: oration on the award of LLD from Glasgow by
Norman Davies (Glasgow acc 44. 13); newspaper cuttings, memorial service (IP6/1/40); 2
photographs, one of him lecturing and one in a group in Humanity Classroom (UP1/453/1
and UP5/9/2) and a University retirement appreciation in 1957 and obit in 1959 (College
Courant).

GROSE, SIDNEY WILSON (1886-1980)

Birth: 5 January 1886, Camberwell, son of Sidney Grose, printseller (and grandson of
Frederick Grose, pawnbroker); later living in Lewisham.

Educ. St Olave's Grammar School, Southwark.

Scholar of Christ's College (1909).

Camb. Christ's Coll.; Exhib. (1905); Schol. (1907); Class. Trip. Pt 1, 1st div. 2 (1908); Pt 2,
classical archaeology, 1st, distinction (1909).

BSA adm. 1909-10 (School Student).

BSR adm. 1910.

Fell. (1919) and Senior Tutor (1922) of Christ's College, Cambridge; Praelector; Librarian;
Vice-Master (by 1943).

From 1914 cataloguing the McClean Collection of Greek Coins in the Fitzwilliam Museum.

War service, Secretariat of Central Control Board, Liquor Traffic (1915).

Hon. Keeper of Coins at the Fitzwilliam Museum (1936).

Died, 5 September 1980.

Publications

'Croton', *NC* 15 (1915) 179-91.

'A Dekadrachm by Kimon and a Note on Greek Coin Dies', *NC* 16 (1916) 113-32.

'Some Rare Coins of Magna Graecia', *NC* 16 (1916) 201-45.

'Primitiae Heracliensis', *NC* 17 (1917) 169-89.

'ΠΕΡΙΣΚΕΛΗΣ', *CR* 32 (1918) 168-69.

'The Balliol College Collection', *NC* 20, 4th ser. (1920) 117.

*Catalogue of the McClean Collection of Greek Coins [in the] Fitzwilliam Museum,
Cambridge.* Cambridge: Cambridge University Press, 1923.

Obituaries

The Times 9 September 1980.

GUILLEMARD, FRANCIS HENRY HILL (1852-1933)

Born, 12 September 1852, Eltham; 5th son of Isaac Guillemard, doctor, of Eltham, Kent.

Educ. Blackheath (Rev. Richard Cowley Powles) and Richmond (Rev. W. Hiley).

Camb. Gonville & Caius Coll.; adm. pens. (Feb. 1, 1870); BA (1874); MA (1877); M. D. (1881).

University Lect. in Geography (1888); Reader in Geography.

Naturalist and traveller, Lapland (1873); Central Africa (1876); South Africa (1877-8); yacht *Marchesa* with C. T. Kettlewell in Asia (1881-4); Cyprus (1887-8); Morocco, with Sir C. Evan-Smith (1892).

BSA adm. 1887-88 (for work in Cyprus).

General Editor, 'Cambridge Geographical Series' (1896).

Syndic of the Fitzwilliam Museum (1918); Cambridge Botanic Garden.

FLS; FZS; FRGS.

Married, Katharine Stéphanie Guillemard (1890), his cousin, dau. of the Rev. W. H. Guillemard, DD, vicar of Little St Mary's, Cambridge.

Residence, The Old Mill House, Trumpington, Cambridge.

Died, Dec. 23, 1933, Old Mill House, Trumpington.

Publications

(and Lord Lilford) 'Notes on the Ornithology of Cyprus in 1887 and 1888', *The Ibis* (1888-9) 94-124, 205-19, 305-50.

'Prehistoric Buildings in Minorca', *Proceedings of the Cambridge Antiquarian Society* 11 (1905/06) 465-79.

Obituaries

The Times 27 December 1933, 6 January 1934; E. H., 'Obituary: Francis Henry Hill Guillemard', *Geographical Journal* 83 (1934) 350-52; *Cambridge Review* 19 Jan 1934; Venn; WWW.

Archive material

Camb. Univ. Lib. (incl. memoir, 'Years that the Locust Hath Eaten'); Camb. Gonville & Caius College Lib; Oxf. Bodleian Lib.

GUTCH, CLEMENT (1875-1908)

Born, 29 Apr. 1875, Holgate Lodge; 3rd son of John James Gutch, solicitor, of Holgate Lodge, Holgate, Yorks.

Educ. Harrow (Easter 1889-Summer 1894); an entrance Schol.; Monitor (1891); a Neeld Schol. (a Classical leaving Schol.) (1893); later in The Head Master's House.

Camb. King's Coll.; adm. Schol. (Oct. 9, 1894); Schol. (1897); Class. Trip. Pt 1, 1st (1897); Pt 2, Greek and Roman archaeology, 1st (1898); BA (1897); MA (1901). Powis Medal, 1897.

BSA adm. 1898-99 (Cambridge Studentship).

Classical Lect. at Girton and Newnham Colleges, 1898-1903; at King's and St John's, 1902-3. Classical and archaeological 'Coach'.

Married, Margaret Isabella Newton (1901).

Died, 25 June 1908, Whitstead, Barton Road, Cambridge.

Publications

'Excavations at Naukratis. D. The Terracottas', *ABSA* 5 (1898/9) 67-97.

General Guide to the Art Collections. National Museum of Ireland. Dublin: His Majesty's
    Stationary Office, 1899.
Review of C. A. Hutton, *Greek Teracotta Statuettes* (1899), in *CR* 14, 6 (1900) 324-25.
The Greek Games and their Mythology, etc. Cambridge: University Press, 1900.
Review of W. H. D. Rouse, *Greek Votive Offerings. An Essay in the History of Greek
    Religion*, in *CR* 17, 7 (1903) 372-74.
Review of H. B. Walters, *Catalogue of the Terracottas in the Department of Greek and
    Roman Antiquities, British Museum*, in *CR* 19, 1 (1905) 84-85.
Obituaries, memoirs and studies
The Times 27 June 1908; Venn.

HALLIDAY (HOFFMEISTER), WILLIAM REGINALD (SIR) (1886-1966)

Born, 26 September 1886, Belize, British Honduras; son of Charles Reginald Hoffmeister
    (Halliday from 1905), barrister, and Helen Sybella, dau. of William Halliday. (New
    College Register notes Leslie Hunter Halliday, solicitor, of 131 King Henry's Road,
    London NW, presumably as guardian).
Educ. Winchester; Schol.
Oxf. New Coll.; matric. as Winchester Schol. (October 1905); Lit. Hum. 1st (1909); MA
    (1928). Hon. LLD Glasgow (1928).
Prizes: Latin Verse (1907); Gaisford Greek Prose (1908); Craven Fell. (1909); Derby
    Scholar (1909); Charles Oldham Prize (1910); Passmore Edwards Scholar (1910);
    Chancellor's Latin Essay (1910).
Studied at Berlin Univ. (1909).
BSA adm. 1910-11; re-adm. 1912-13.
Elected a Fell. New College (1912).
Lect. in Greek History and Archaeology, Univ. of Glasgow (1912-14).
Rathbone Prof. of Ancient History, Univ. of Liverpool (1914-28).
Visiting Prof., Harvard Univ. (1928).
Principal of King's College, London (1928-33); Deputy Vice-Chancellor, London Univ.
    (1932).
War service, Red Cross in France (1915); Lt. RNVR and intelligence officer on Crete (1916-
    18). Mentioned in Despatches. Chevalier of the Order of the Redeemer. Legion of
    Honour (1938).
Changed name to Halliday (1905).
Knighted (1946).
Married, Edith Hilda McNeile Dixon (22 November 1918), dau. of Prof. William Macneile
    Dixon, Prof. of English Language and Literature, Glasgow Univ. (1904-35).
Died, 25 November 1966.
Publications
'A Note on Herodotus vi. 83 and the Hybristika', *ABSA* 16 (1909/10) 212-19.
'The Force of Initiative in Magical Conflict', *Folklore* 21 (1910) 147-67.
'A Spitting Cure', *Folklore* 21 (1910) 388.
'Cenotaphs and Sacred Localities', *ABSA* 17 (1910/11) 182-92.
'A Note on the θήλεα νοῦσος of the Skythians', *ABSA* 17 (1910/11) 95-102.
'Note on Homeric Hymn to Demeter, 239 ff', *CR* 25 (1911) 8-11.

'Damis of Nineveh and Walter of Oxford: a Literary Parallel', *ABSA* 18 (1911/12) 234-38.

'A Greek Marriage in Cappadocia', *Folklore* 23 (1912) 81-88.

'Folklore Scraps from Greece and Asia Minor', *Folklore* 23 (1912) 218-20.

'Modern Greek Folk-tales and Ancient Greek Mythology', *Folklore* 23 (1912) 486-89.

'Aeschylus, *Septem*, 745 ff. (Oxford Text)', *CR* 27 (1913) 162-63.

'Cretan Folklore Notes', *Folklore* 24 (1913) 357-59.

Greek Divination: a Study of its Methods and Principles. London: Macmillan, 1913.

'Note on the Fragments of the Gypsy Carol', *ABSA* 20 (1913/14) 57-58.

(and W. R. Paton) 'Modern Greek Carols of Honour of Saint Basil', *ABSA* 20 (1913/14) 32-57.

'Modern Greek Folk-tales and Ancient Greek Mythology: Odysseus and Saint Elias', *Folklore* 25 (1914) 122-25.

(and R. M. Dawkins). *Modern Greek in Asia Minor: a Study of the Dialects of Silli, Cappadocia and Pharasa, with Grammar, Texts, Translations and Glossary*. Cambridge: Cambridge University Press, 1916.

'Obituary: F. W. Hasluck', *Folklore* 31 (1920) 336-38.

'The Story of Ali Baba and the Forty Thieves', *Folklore* 31 (1920) 321-23.

'Snake Stones', *Folklore* 32 (1921) 262-71.

'Pygmies and Cranes', *CR* 35 (1921) 27.

'Roman Burial', *CR* 35 (1921) 154-55.

Lectures on the History of Roman Religion from Numa to Augustus. The Ancient World. Liverpool: University Press of Liverpool, 1922.

'Snake Stones', *Folklore* 33 (1922) 118-19.

'Picus-Who-Is-Also-Zeus', *CR* 36 (1922) 110-12.

The Growth of the City State: Lectures on Greek and Roman History. Ancient World. Liverpool: University Press of Liverpool, 1923.

'Notes Upon Indo-European Folk-tales and the Problem of Their Diffusion', *Folklore* 34 (1923) 117-40.

'Mossynos and Mossynoikoi', *CR* 37 (1923) 105-07.

Folklore Studies: Ancient and Modern. London: Methuen, 1924.

'Passing Under the Yoke', *Folklore* 35 (1924) 93-95.

'The Mithraic Grade of "Eagles"', *Folklore* 35 (1924) 381.

'Macrobii: Aithiopians and Others', *CQ* 18 (1924) 53-54.

'Orthagoriscus', *CR* 38 (1924) 15.

'Who was the ὑπεκκαύστρια at Soli?' *Harvard Studies in Classical Philology* 36 (1925) 165-77.

'A Note upon the Sunday Epistle and the Letter of Pope Leo', *Speculum* 2 (1927) 73-78.

'"The Superstitious Man" of Theophrastus', *Folklore* 41 (1930) 121-53.

Indo-European Folk-tales and Greek Legend. Gray Lectures, 1932. Cambridge: The University Press, 1933.

'A Motif Found in Moslem Legend', *Folklore* 61 (1950) 218.

Obituaries, memoirs and studies

The Times 28 November 1966; M. S. Leigh (ed), *Winchester College 1884-1934: a Register* (Winchester 1940) 228; WWW.

Archive material

Oxf. Bodleian Lib.; London, KCL.

HAMILTON, JOHN ARNOTT

Univ. of Edinburgh. MA (1912), BD (1917).

Edinburgh, PhD (1925), 'A history of Byzantine architecture with special reference to problems of origin and evaluation of plan'.

Edinburgh OTC Infantry, Cadet (Nov. 1909-Apr. 1913).

Holder of the Blackie Schol.

BSA adm. 1913-14.

War service, Asst. Chaplain, Cromarty.

Publications

The Principles of Church Design. Edinburgh: Church of Scotland, 1890.

The Church of Kaisariani in Attica: its History, Architecture and Mural Paintings. A Study in Byzantine Art. Aberdeen: W. Jolly & Sons, 1916.

A Mediaeval City in Greece, its Churches and its Ruins. Aberdeen: W. Jolly & Sons, 1921.

Byzantine Architecture and Decoration. Batsford's Historical Architecture Library. London: B. T. Batsford, 1933.

HAMILTON, MARY BOWMAN (MRS G. DICKINS; MRS L. D. CASKEY) (1881-1962)

Born, c. 1881, Mains, Forfarshire; eldest dau. of Rev. William Hamilton, of 'Craigieside', Arbroath Road, Dundee (minister of Trinity Congregational Church).

Univ. of St Andrews. MA Classics, 1st (1902); D. Litt. (1908), on incubation.

Holder of a Research Fellowship under the Carnegie Trust (£50) (1903/04).

BSA adm. 1905-06, 1906-07.

BSR adm. 1905.

War service, Military Translation Bureau, War Office (1916-17); Reader for the Review of the Foreign Press, Military Intelligence Dept, War Office (1917-19).

Address: Oxford; from 1925, 'Riverview', Callendar.

Married, first, Guy Dickins (d. 1916), by 1909; second, Lacey Davis Caskey (1880-1944), Curator of Classical Art, Museum of Fine Arts, Boston (obit. *The Times* 14 June 1944), by 1931.

Died, Friday 21 September 1962, at 'Riverview', Callendar.

Publications

Incubation, or, the Cure of Disease in Pagan Temples and Christian Churches. London: W. C. Henderson & Son, 1906.

'The Pagan Element in the Names of Saints', *ABSA* 13 (1906/07) 348–56.

Greek Saints and Their Festivals. London: W. Blackwood & Sons, 1910.

Obituary

The Scotsman Monday 24 September 1962.

HARCOURT-SMITH, CECIL

See Smith, Cecil Harcourt.

HARDIE, MARGARET MASSON (MRS F. W. HASLUCK) (1885-1948)

Born, 18 June 1885, at Chapelton, Drumblade, near Elgin; eldest dau. of John Hardie, a farmer, of Easterton, Elgin, N. B.

Educ. Elgin Academy

Univ. of Aberdeen, Classics, 1st.

Camb. Newnham Coll.; Class. Trip. Pt 1, 1st div. 2 (1909).

BSA adm. 1911-12 (School Student).

War service, clerk in Intelligence Office, HBM Legation, Athens (1915); War Office, Intelligence Branch and HBM Legation, Athens (1915-16).

Married, Frederick W. Hasluck (26 September 1912), at Pluscarden, N. B.

Died, 18 October 1948, Dublin.

Publications

'The Shrine of Mên Askaenos at Pisidian Antioch', *JHS* 32 (1912) 111-50.

'Dionysos at Smyrna', *ABSA* 19 (1912/13) 89-94.

'The Significance of Greek Personal Names', *Folklore* 34, 2 (1923) 149-154, 249-51.

'The Evil Eye in Some Greek Villages of the Upper Haliakmon Valley in West Macedonia', *JRAI* 53 (1923) 160-72.

(and F. W. Hasluck) *Athos and its Monasteries*. London; New York: K. Paul, Trench, Trubner & Co. Ltd: E. P. Dutton & Co., 1924.

'Ramadan as a Personal Name', *Folklore* 36 (1925) 280.

'The Basil-cake of the Greek New Year', *Folklore* 38 (1927) 143-77.

(and F. W. Hasluck) *Christianity and Islam under the Sultans*. Oxford: Clarendon Press, 1929.

(and R. M. Dawkins) *Letters on Religion and Folklore*. London: Luzac & Co., 1926.

(and G. M. Morant) 'Measurements of Macedonian Men', *Biometrika* 21 (1929) 322-36.

'Oedipus Rex in Albania', *Folklore* 60 (1949) 340-48.

The Unwritten Law in Albania. Cambridge, Cambridge University Press, 1954.

Obituaries, memoirs and studies

R. M. Dawkins, 'Obituary: Margaret Masson Hasluck', *Folklore* 60 (1949) 291-92; M. Clark, 'Margaret Masson Hasluck', in J. Allcock and A. Young (eds.), *Black Lambs and Grey Falcons: Women Travellers in the Balkans* (Oxford, 2000); *DBC*; D. W. J. Gill, 'A Preliminary Bibliography of the Works of F. W. Hasluck and of M. M. Hardie (Mrs F. W. Hasluck)', in *Archaeology, Anthropology and Heritage in the Balkans and Anatolia: the Life and Times of F. W. Hasluck, 1878-1920*, vol. 2. Edited by D. Shankland, 485-90. Istanbul: The Isis Press, 2004; Roderick Bailey, 'Hasluck , Margaret Masson (1885-1948)', in *ODNB*, vol. 25, 716-17.

HARVEY, W.

Gold Medallist and Travelling Student of the Royal Academy.

BSA adm. 1907-08.

BSR adm. 1908.

HASLUCK, FREDERICK WILLIAM (1878-1920)

Born, 16 Feb. 1878, Bytham Lodge; 2nd son of Percy Pedley, of Bytham Lodge, Southgate, Middlesex ('income from houses and funds', 1881).

Educ. Leys, Cambridge.

Camb. King's Coll.; adm (Oct. 12, 1897); Schol. (1899); Class. Trip. Pt 1, 1st (1899); Pt 2, 1st (1901); BA (1901); MA (1904). Sir William Browne Medal (Latin Epig.) 1901.

BSA adm. 1901-02 (Cambridge Studentship); re-adm. 1902-03, 1904-05, 1905-06; expl.
  Cyzicus. Asst. Dir. and Librarian, 1906-15; Hon. Student.
Fell. King's College (1904).
War service, Clerk in the Intelligence Dept. of HBM Legation, Athens (1915-16).
Married, Margaret Hardie (26 September 1912), at Pluscarden, N. B.
Died Feb. 22, 1920, at Beau Reveil sanatorium, Leysin, Switzerland.

Publications

For a full list: D. W. J. Gill, 'A Preliminary Bibliography of the Works of F. W. Hasluck and
  of M. M. Hardie (Mrs F. W. Hasluck)', in *Archaeology, Anthropology and Heritage in
  the Balkans and Anatolia: the Life and Times of F. W. Hasluck, 1878-1920*, vol. 2.
  Edited by D. Shankland, 485-90. Istanbul: The Isis Press, 2004.

Obituaries, memoirs and studies

The Times 26 Feb. 1920; reproduced in *ABSA* 23 (1918-19) xvi; Venn; D. Shankland, ed.,
  *Archaeology, Anthropology and Heritage in the Balkans and Anatolia: the Life and
  Times of F. W. Hasluck, 1878-1920*, 2 vols. Istanbul: The Isis Press, 2004; *DBC*; Peter
  W. Lock, 'Hasluck, Frederick William (1878-1920)', in *ODNB*, vol. 25, 715-16.

HASLUCK, MARGARET MASSON

See Hardie, Margaret Masson.

HAWES, CHARLES HENRY (1867-1943)

Born, 30 September 1867, at New Southgate, Middlesex; son of Frederick Hawes, a com-
  mercial traveller and then a shop fitter's manager, of 'Grasmere', Torrington Park,
  Finchley, Middlesex, and his wife Mary Ann.
Educ. City of London School.
Camb. Trinity Coll.; adm. pens. (June 30, 1896); BA (1899); MA (1903).
BSA adm. 1904-05.
Lect. in Anthropology at the Univ. of Wisconsin.
Prof. of Anthropology, Dartmouth College, USA (1910).
Associate Dir., Museum of Fine Arts, Boston, Mass., USA.
Married, first wife died prior to 1896; second, Harriet Boyd (3 March 1906), St John's
  Episcopal Church, Washington.
Died Dec. 13, 1943.

Publications

'Excavations at Palaikastro. IV. § 7. Larnax Burials at Sarandari', *ABSA* 11 (1904/05) 293-
  97.
'Some Dorian Descendants?" *ABSA* 16 (1909/10) 258-80.

Obituaries, memoirs and studies

Venn; M. Allsebrook, *Born to Rebel: the Life of Harriet Boyd Hawes*. Oxford: Oxbow Books,
  1992; D. L. Bolger, 'Ladies of the Expedition: Harriet Boyd Hawes and Edith Hall at
  Work in Mediterranean Archaeology', in C. Claassen, ed., *Women in Archaeology*, 41-50.
  Philadelphia: University of Pennsylvania Press, 1994.

Archive material

Royal Anthropological Institute of Great Britain and Ireland.

HEATH, ROGER MEYRICK (1889-1916)

Born, 3 August 1889; son of Meyrick William Heath of Mortimer House, Clifton, Bristol, bank manager, and his wife Katharine Rose Heath.

Educ. Rugby.

Oxf. Oriel Coll.; Schol. (1908); Class. Mod. 1st (1910); Lit. Hum. 1st (1912); BA (1912); Diploma in Classical Archaeology, distinction. Newdigate Prize Poem, 'Achilles' (1911); Bishop Fraser Scholar (1912).

BSA adm. 1913-14. Craven Fell. (1913).

War service, enrolled September 1915, private (and promoted to corporal), Royal Fusiliers; 2nd Lt. 9th, attached 3rd, Somerset Light Infantry (Adjutant); posted to France (1916); listed as a member of the 6th Battalion.

Killed in action near Delville Wood, 16 Sept 1916, his first day in the trenches.

Publications

'Proxeny Decrees from Megara', *ABSA* 19 (1912/13) 82-88.

'A Lament', *ABSA* 21 (1914/16) 10.

Beginnings (Oxford: B. H. Blackwell, 1913) [poetry collection].

Obituaries, memoirs and studies

C. L. Shadwell, *Registrum Orielense, 1701-1900* (London, 1902), manuscript entry; *Oriel College Roll of Service* (Oxford, 1920), 23; *The Oriel Record* 2, pt 2, (March 1917); Commonwealth War Graves Commission.

HENDERSON, ARTHUR EDWARD (1870-1956)

Born, 1870, Aberdeen, Scotland; son of John S. Henderson, advocate, and his wife Emily Henderson, of Banchory Devenick from Yorkshire.

Educ. Aberdeen.

Architect's Asst. (1891), architect (1901).

BSA adm. 1897-98 (Owen Jones Student of Royal Institute of British Architects); re-adm. 1898-99, 1901-02 and 1902-03.

Remained in Constantinople until 1904; assisted with Hogarth's excavations at Ephesus.

Decorated church of Christ Church, Streatham Hill.

Member of the Royal Soc. of British Artists.

FSA; RIBA.

Married, Susannah Colier Moore (1903), in Lambeth.

Died, 8 November 1956, East Grinstead, Sussex.

Publications

(and F. W. Hasluck) 'On the Topography of Cyzicus', *JHS* 24 (1904) 135-43.

Contribution to D. G. Hogarth, *Excavations at Ephesus: the Archaic Artemisia*. London: British Museum, 1908.

(and A. Van Millingen, W. S. George, and R. Traquair) *Byzantine Churches in Constantinople: Their History and Architecture*. London: Macmillan & Co., 1912.

Obituary

The Times November 10, 1956; *Builder* 191 (16 Nov 1956) 857, 1092.

HOARE, EDWARD BARCLAY (1872-1943)

Born, 25 July 1872; son of Robert Gurney Hoare (1844-99), banker, of Jesmond Park, Newcastle upon Tyne, and his wife, Anne.

Educ. Harrow (Easter 1886-Summer 1890); The Head Master's House.

Oxf. Magdalen Coll.; Commoner (1890-94); BA (1894).

BSA adm. 1897-98 (Architectural Student)

Occupation (in 1911 and 1922), architect; firm of Hoare & Wheeler, 22 Portman Street, Portman Square, London; work included church architecture.

War servce, served with the Indian Defence Force.

Died, 13 December 1943.

Obituaries, memoirs and studies

Further information from the Incorporated Church Building Society:
www.churchplansonline.org

See also his brother: Bernard Attard, 'Hoare, Christopher Gurney (1882–1973)', in *ODNB*.

HOFFMEISTER, WILLIAM REGINALD

See Halliday, William Reginald.

HOGARTH, DAVID GEORGE (1862-1927)

Born, 23 May 1862, Barton-on-Humber; son of Rev. George Hogarth.

Educ. Winchester.

Oxf. Magdalen Coll.; Demy (1881-85); Class. Mod. 1st (1882); Lit. Hum. 1st (1885); BA (1885); MA (1888).

BSA adm. 1886-87; Craven Univ. Fell. (1886); re-adm. 1887-88 (for work on Cyprus). Dir. of the School, 1897-1900.

Fell. and tutor, Magdalen Coll. (1886-93).

Keeper of the Ashmolean Museum (1908-27).

Delegate of Oxford University Press (1912-27).

War service, Commander, RNVR, for special services (1915-19); served in Egypt, Arabia, and Palestine; Military Intelligence, Cairo (July 1915); Dir. of Arab Bureau, Residency, Cairo (March 1916); Dir. of Arab Section, G. S., GHQ, EEF (February 1918); mentioned in dispatches three times; awarded Order of the Nile (Second Class) and Sherifian Order (Second Class); CMG for war services (*The London Gazette* suppl. 1 January 1918, 82); Peace Conference, Paris (March 1919).

FBA (1905); Founder's Gold Medal.

Julia Drexel Medal, University of Pennsylvania.

Married, Laura Violet (d. 1952) (November 1894), dau. of Major George Charles Uppleby, of Burrow Hall, Lincs.

Died, 6 November 1927.

Publications

'Apollo Lermanus', *JHS* 8 (1887) 376-400.

'The Deification of Alexander the Great', *English Historical Review* 2 (1887) 317-29.

'The Army of Alexander', *Journal of Philology* 17 (1888) 1-26.

'Excavations at Old Paphos', *CR* 2 (1888) 155-57.

'Inscriptions from Salonica', *JHS* 8 (1888) 356-75.

'Notes Upon a Visit to Celaenae Apamaea', *JHS* 9 (1888) 343-49.

'The Recent Excavations at Paphos', *CR* 2 (1888) 186-88.

(and E. A. Gardner, M. R. James, and R. Elsey Smith) 'Excavations in Cyprus, 1887-8. Paphos, Leontari, Amargetti', *JHS* 9 (1888) 147-271.

Devia Cypria: Notes of an Archaeological Journey in Cyprus in 1888. London: Henry Frowde, 1889.

'Notes in Phrygia, Paroreus and Lycaonia', *JHS* 11 (1890) 151-66.

(and C. H. H. Parry, A. D. Godley) *The Music to the Frogs of Aristophanes*. Leipzig and London: Breitkopf & Hartel, 1890.

(and J. H. Frere, A. D. Godley) 1892. *The Frogs of Aristophanes: Adapted for Performance by the Oxford University Dramatic Society, 1892*. Oxford: Oxford University Dramatic Society, 1892.

(and J. A. R. Munro) *Modern and Ancient Roads in Eastern Asia Minor*. Royal Geographical Society, supplementary papers, vol. 3, part 5. London: Royal Geographical Society, 1893.

A Wandering Scholar in the Levant. London: John Murray, 1896.

(and E. F. Benson) *Report of Prospects of Research in Alexandria*. London: Macmillan, for the Society for the Promotion of Hellenic Studies, 1896.

(and W. M. F. Petrie) *Koptos*. London: Bernard Quaritch, 1896.

Philip and Alexander of Macedon. Two Essays in Biography. London: John Murray, 1897.

'Excavations in Melos, 1898. I. The Season's Work', *ABSA* 4 (1897/8) 1-16.

'Excavations at Naukratis. A. Sites and Buildings', *ABSA* 5 (1898/9) 26-46.

(ed.) *Authority and Archaeology: Sacred and Profane. Essays on the Relation of Monuments to Biblical and Classical Literature*. London: John Murray, 1899.

(and R. C. Bosanquet) 'Archaeology in Greece, 1898-9', *JHS* 19 (1899) 319-29.

'The Dictaean Cave', *ABSA* 6 (1899/1900) 94-116.

'Knossos II. Early Town and Cemeteries', *ABSA* 6 (1899/1900) 70-85.

'Knossos IV. A Latin Inscription', *ABSA* 6 (1899/1900) 92-93.

(and B. P. Grenfell, A. S. Hunt, and J. G. Milne) *Fayum Towns and Their Papyri*. Egypt Exploration Fund. Graeco-Roman Branch, Memoirs, vol. 3. London: Egypt Exploration Fund, 1900.

Scenes in Athens. London: Henry Frowde, 1900.

'Excavations at Zakro, Crete', *ABSA* 7 (1900/01) 121-49.

'Explorations at Zakro in Eastern Crete', *Man* 1 (1901) 186-87.

(and F. B. Welch) 'Primitive Painted Pottery in Crete', *JHS* 21 (1901) 78-98.

'Bronze Age Vases from Zakro', *JHS* 22 (1902) 333-38.

The Nearer East. The Regions of the World. London: H. Frowde, 1902.

'Note of Major Sykes' "Anthropological Notes on Southern Persia"', *Journal of the Anthropological Institute* 32 (1902) 349.

'The Zakro Sealings', *JHS* 22 (1902) 76-93.

The Penetration of Arabia: a Record of the Development of Western Knowledge Concerning the Arabian Peninsula. The Story of Exploration. London: Lawrence and Bullen, Ltd., 1904.

(and T. D. Atkinson, R. C. Bosanquet, C. C. Edgar, A. J. Evans, D. Mackenzie, C. Harcourt-Smith, and F. B. Welch) *Excavations at Phylakopi in Melos*. Society for the Promotion of Hellenic Studies, Occasional Paper 4. London, 1904.

'Three North Delta Nomes', *JHS* 24 (1904) 1-19.

(and H. L. Lorimer, C. C. Edgar) 'Naukratis, 1903', *JHS* 25 (1905) 105–36.

'Hierapolis Syriae', *ABSA* 14 (1907/08) 183-96.

'The Archaic Artemisia', *JHS* 28 (1908) 338.

Excavations at Ephesus: the Archaic Artemisia. London: British Museum, 1908.

Ionia and the East: Six Lectures Delivered Before the University of London. Oxford: Clarendon Press, 1909.

'Recent Hittite Research', *Journal of the Anthropological Institute* 39 (1909) 408-15.

'Recent Hittite Research', *Man* 9 (1909) 192.

Accidents of an Antiquary's Life. London: Macmillan and Co., 1910.

(and F. Haverfield, J. L. S. Davidson, E. R. Bevan, E. M. Walker, and L. Cromer) 'Ancient Imperialism', *CR* 24 (1910) 105-16.

(and D. Strathan, F. Haverfield, A. Stein, J. L. Myres, E. A. Gardner, W. A. Cannon, M. M. Allorge, W. N. Shaw, and J. W. Gregory) 'The Burial of Olympia: Discussion', *Geographical Journal* 36 (1910) 675-86.

'Note on Two Zakro Sealings', *ABSA* 17 (1910/11) 264-65.

(and E. A. Gardner, J. L. Myres, B. Nopsca, A. Stein, J. P. Droop, F. R. Maunsell, M. S. Thompson, A. M. Woodward, and A. J. B. Wace) 'The Distribution of Early Civilization in Northern Greece: Discussion', *Geographical Journal* 37 (1911) 636-42.

The Ancient East. Home University Library of Modern Knowledge. London: Williams & Norgate, 1914.

'Egyptian Empire in Asia', *JEA* 1 (1914) 9-17.

(and A. J. Toynbee, N. Forbes, and D. Mitrany) *The Balkans: a History of Bulgaria, Serbia, Greece, Rumania, Turkey*. Oxford: Clarendon Press, 1915.

'Alexander in Egypt and Some Consequences', *JEA* 2 (1915) 53-60.

Handbook of Hejaz. Cairo: Government Publications, 1916.

(and R. Curzon) *Visits to Monasteries in the Levant*. London: H. Milford, 1916.

(and K. Cornwallis) *Handbook of Yemen*. Cairo: Government Press, 1917.

Position and Prospects of King Husein. Arab Bulletin, supplementary paper, vol. 2. Cairo: Government Publicaitons, 1918.

(and T. E. Lawrence, C. E. Wilson) *Tribal Politics in Feisal's area. 'King of the Arabs'. Conversations with Dr Faris Nimr*. Arab Bulletin, supplementary paper, vol. 5. Cairo: Arab Bureau, 1918.

Hittite Seals, with Particular Reference to the Ashmolean Collection. Oxford: Clarendon Press, 1920.

Arabia. Oxford: Clarendon Press, 1922.

'Engraved Hittite Objects', *JEA* 8 (1922) 211-18.

The Wandering Scholar. London: Oxford University Press, 1925.

'George Nathaniel Curzon, Marquess Curzon of Kedleston, 1859-1925', *PBA* 11 (1924/25) 502-24.

Kings of the Hittites. Schweich Lectures, 1924. London: British Academy, 1926.

The Twighlight of History: Being the Eighth Earl Grey Memorial Lecture Delivered at King's Hall, Armstrong College, Newcastle-on-Tyne, Februaury 17, 1926. Earl Grey Memorial Lectures, vol. 8. London: Oxford University Press, 1926.

'Aegean Sepulchral Figurines', in *Essays in Aegean Archaeology, Presented to Sir Arthur Evans*, edited by S. Casson, 55-62. Oxford: Clarendon Press, 1927.

The Life of Charles M. Doughty. Oxford: Oxford University Press, 1928.

Obituaries, memoirs and studies

A. H. Sayce, 'David George Hogarth, 1862-1927', *PBA* 13 (1927) 379-83; J. H. Breasted, 'Obituary: David George Hogarth', *Geographical Review* 18 (1928) 159-61; C. R. L. Fletcher, 'David George Hogarth, President R. G. S., 1925-1927', *Geographical Journal* 71 (1928) 321-44; H. R. Hall, 'David George Hogarth', *JEA* 14 (1928) 128-30; P. Lock, 'D. G. Hogarth (1862-1927): "A specialist in the science of archaeology"', *ABSA* 85 (1990) 175-200; D. P. Ryan, 'David George Hogarth at Asyut, Egypt, 1906-7: the History of a 'Lost' Excavation', *Bulletin of the History of Archaeology* 5 (1995) 3-16; D. Montserrat, "No Papyrus and No Portraits": Hogarth, Grenfell and the First Season in the Fayum, 1895-6', *Bulletin of the American Society of Papyrologists* 33 (1996) 133-76; J. A. Perry, *Rediscovering D. G. Hogarth: a Biographical Study of Oxford's Near Eastern Archaeologist and World War I Diplomat.* MA, State University of New York at Buffalo, 2000; *DBC*; D. W. J. Gill, 'Hogarth, David George (1862-1927)', in *ODNB*, vol. 27, 537-42.

Archive material

British Library; Egypt Exploraton Society; Oxf. St Anthony's Coll., Middle East Centre; private (family).

HOPKINSON, JOHN HENRY (1876-1957)

Born, 16 December 1876 (aged 18 in 1895); 2nd son of (Sir) Alfred Hopkinson (barrister, MP, Prof. of law at Owens College, and principal of Owens College, Manchester, 1898-1913) of Dulwich, Surrey (and a former Fell. University Coll. Oxf.).

Educ. Woodlands School, Manchester (1885-89); Dulwich College (1890-July 1895).

Oxf. University Coll. (Michaelmas 1895); Schol. (1895); Class. Mod. 1st (1897); Lit. Hum. 2nd (1899); BA (1899); MA (1902).

BSA adm. 1899-1900, 1900-01 (Craven Univ. Fell.).

Lect. in Greek, Univ. of Birmingham (1901-04).

Lect. in Classical Archaeology, Victoria Univ. of Manchester (1904-14); Warden of Hulme Hall, Manchester (1905).

Ordained. Church of England, deacon (1914), priest (1915). Curate, St Bartholomew, Colne (1914); Vicar of Holy Trinity, Colne, Lancs (1915-20); Rector of Christ Church, Moss Side, Manchester (1920-21); Vicar of Burneside, Westmorland (1921-28); Canon residentiary, Carlisle Cathedral (1927-31); Vicar of Christ Church, Cockermouth (1931-36); Archdeacon of Westmoreland (1931-44); perpetual curate of Winster, near Windermere (1936-44); honorary canon, Carlisle Cathedral (1937); Asst. curate to his youngest son at Battersea (1944).

War service, Private, RAMC (July 1918-January 1919).

Westmoreland County Education Committee (1921).

Married, Evelyn Mary Fountaine (23 December 1902), dau. of Rev. Henry Thomas Fountaine, Vicar of Sutton Bridge, Lincolnshire.

Died, 22 October 1957, Kendal.

Publications

(and J. Baker-Penoyre) 'New Evidence on the Melian Amphorae', *JHS* 22 (1902) 46-75.

'Note on the Fragment of a Painted Pinax from Praesos', *ABSA* 10 (1903/04) 148-53.

'Pottery Found at Melandra', in *Melandra Castle*, edited by R. S. Conway, 77-95. Manchester: Manchester University Press, 1906.

'Pottery Found at Manchester in 1907', in *The Roman Fort at Manchester*, edited by F. A. Bruton. Manchester: Manchester University Press, 1909.

The Roman Fort at Ribchester. Manchester: Manchester University Press, 1911.

(ed.) *The Roman Fort at Ribchester*, 2nd edition. London: Sherratt & Hughes, 1916.

(and D. Atkinson) *The Roman Fort at Ribchester*, 3rd ed., 1928.

Obituaries, memoirs and studies

The Times 2 November 1957 (funeral); *Alleyn Club Yearbook* (1958); *Dulwich College Register*; WWW; *University College Record* (1958), 217. See also A. T. Davies and C. Pease-Watkin, 'Hopkinson, Sir Alfred (1851-1939)', in *ODNB*; C. Wintour, 'Hopkinson, Sir (Henry) Thomas (1905-1990)', in *ODNB*.

HORSFALL, HON. MRS.

See Conway, Agnes Ethel.

HUTTON, CAROLINE AMY (C. 1861-1931)

Born, 1861, New Zealand.

Camb. Girton Coll.; Class. Trip. Pt 1, 3rd div. 2 (1882); Pt 2, 2nd (1883).

BSA adm. 1896-97.

Joint Editor of the *Annual* 1906-26.

Hon. Acting Sec. to the Soc. for the Promotion of Hellenic Studies and the BSA (1916-19).

Elected Vice-President of the Hellenic Soc. (1931).

War service, National Registration (1915); night canteen work at Woolwich Arsenal and Paddington Free Buffet (1915-19).

Died, 6 October 1931.

Publications

'Peinture de vase représentant les Boréades', *BCH* 23 (1899) 157-64.

'Inscriptions on Pottery from Naukratis', *CR* 7 (1893) 82-83.

'On Two Terracotta Figurines', *JHS* 15 (1895) 132-35.

'On Three Bronze Statuettes', *ABSA* 3 (1896/7) 149-55.

'Votive Reliefs in the Acropolis Museum', *JHS* 17 (1897) 306-18.

Greek Terracotta Statuettes. Portfolio Monographs. London: Seeley & Co., 1899.

(and C. Harcourt-Smith) *Catalogue of the Antiquities (Greek, Etruscan and Roman) in the Collection of the Late Wyndham Francis Cook, Esquire*. London: privately printed, 1908.

'A Collection of Sketches by C. R. Cockerell, R. A. ', *JHS* 29 (1909) 53-59.

'Greek Dress', *CR* 23 (1909) 235-36.

'The Greek Inscriptions at Petworth House', *ABSA* 21 (1914/16) 155-65.

'Two Sepulchral Inscriptions from Suvla Bay', *ABSA* 21 (1914/16) 166-68.
'The Travels of "Palmyra Wood" in 1750-51', *JHS* 47 (1927) 102-28.
'Two Reliefs in the Ashmolean Museum', *JHS* 49 (1929) 240-45.
Obituaries, memoirs and studies
The Times, 9 October 1931 (funeral), 10 October 1931 (anon. tribute), 13 October 1931
    (George A. Macmillan).

INGE, CHARLES CUTHBERT (1868-1957)
Born, 2 May 1868; son of Rev. William Inge, DD., Provost of Worcester Coll.
Educ. Eton; King's Schol. (January 1883 - July 1887); in the Newcastle Select, i. e. one of
    runners-up to top Classics prize, the Newcastle Schol. (1887); Jelf Latin Verse Prize
    (1885).
Oxf. Magdalen Coll.; Demy (1887-92); Class. Mods. 1st (1889); Lit. Hum. 2nd; BA (1891);
    MA (1893); played in Varsity Lawn Tennis March, 1892;
BSA adm. 1891-92 (Oxford Studentship).
Curate, the Eton Mission, Hackney Wick (1894-6); Curate, Cranleigh, Surrey (1896-1906);
    Vicar, Holmwood, Surrey (1906-13); Vicar, St Giles, Oxford (1913-37); Rural Dean of
    Oxford (1925-37); Hon. Canon of Christ Church, (1933-48).
Married, Arabella Hamilton (October 1904), dau. of the late Lt. -Col. C. H. Sams, North
    Staffs. Regiment; three sons, two daughters.
Died, 13 April 1957.
Obituaries, memoirs and studies
The Times, 15 April 1957.

JAMES, MONTAGUE RHODES (1862-1936)
Born, 1 August 1862, at Goodnestone Rectory, Kent; 3rd son of the Rev. Herbert James
    (1842), Rector of Livermere, Suffolk.
Educ. East Sheen and Eton (1877).
Camb. King's Coll.; Schol. from Eton (Oct. 14, 1882); Carus Prize (1882); Bell Scholar
    (1883); Craven Scholar (1884); Jeremie Septuagint Prize (1884); Class. Trip. Pt 1, 1st
    (1884); Pt 2, 1st (1885); BA (1885); 1st Chancellor's medal; MA (1889); Litt. D. (1895).
BSA adm. 1887-88 (for work in Cyprus, with a grant of £100 from Cambridge Univ.);
    excavated on Cyprus (1887).
Fell. King's College (1887-1905); Dean and Tutor; Provost (1905-18); Hon. Fell. (1918).
    Sandars Reader, 1902.
Asst. Dir. of the Fitzwilliam Museum (1886-93); Dir. (1893-1908).
Vice-Chancellor (1913-14).
Trustee of the British Museum.
Hon. D. C. L., Oxford, 1927; Hon. D. Litt., Dublin; Hon. LL. D., St Andrews. FSA; FBA;
    O. M. (1930).
Unmarried.
Died, 12 June 1936, at Eton; buried there.
Publications
(and E. A. Gardner, D. G. Hogarth, and R. Elsey Smith) 'Excavations in Cyprus, 1887-8.
    Paphos, Leontari, Amargetti', *JHS* 9 (1888) 147-271, pls. vii-xi.

Obituaries, memoirs and studies

The Times 13 June 1936; *Cambridge Review* 9 October 1936; Venn; WWW; Richard W. Pfaff, 'James, Montague Rhodes (1862-1936)', in *ODNB*, vol. 29, 723-26.

Archive material

Camb. Fitzwilliam Museum; Camb. Univ. Lib.; Camb. King's Coll.

JEWELL, HARRY HERBERT (1882-1974)

Born, 1882, Wandsworth.

BSA adm. 1909-10.

BSR adm. 1910.

Royal Academy, Silver Medallist (1907); Gold Medallist (1909); and travelling studentship (£200).

War service, Lieutenant, Royal West Surrey Regiment (1916); Technical Officer to 139th Company Labour Corps working on Forward roads in France (1917-19).

Married (1911), in Billericay, Essex.

Died, 1974.

Publications

(and F. W. Hasluck) *The Church of Our Lady of the Hundred Gates: Panagia Hekatontapylian) in Paros*. Byzantine Research Fund. London: Macmillan and Co., 1920.

JONES, HENRY STUART (SIR) (1867-1939)

Born, 15 May 1867, at Moor Crescent, Hunslet, Leeds; son of Rev. Henry William Jones (1834-1909), and his wife, Margaret Lawrance Baker.

Educ. Rossall School.

Oxf. Balliol Coll.; matric. (1886). Hertford Schol. (1886); Class. Mods. 1st (1888); Ireland and Craven Schols. (1888); Lit. Hum. 1st (1890). Gaisford Prize for Greek Prose (1890).

Fell. Trinity College, Oxford (1890). Derby Scholar (1891).

BSA adm. 1890-91 (Craven Univ. Fell.); re-adm. 1892-93.

Dir. of the BSR (1903-05).

FBA (1915).

War service, Lieutenant, 1st Volunteer Battalion, The Welch Regiment (OC Detachment, Saundersfoot) (1914); special duty at the War Office (1918).

Camden Prof. of Ancient History (1919); Fell. Brasenose College, Oxford.

Principal of University College of Aberystwyth (1927-34).

Knighted (1933); changed name to Stuart-Jones (1933).

Married, Ileen Vaughan (d. 1931) (1894), daughter of Edwyn Henry Vaughan, housemaster at Harrow.

Died, 29 June 1939.

Publications

Full list in *JRS* 27 (1937) 3-11; 35 (1945) 78.

'Two Vases by Phintias', *JHS* 12 (1891) 366-80.

'The Chest of Kypselos', *JHS* 14 (1894) 30-80.

Select Passages from Ancient Writers Illustrative of the History of Greek Sculpture. London; New York: Macmillan and Co., 1895.

'A Greek Goldsmith's Mould in the Ashmolean Museum', *JHS* 16 (1896) 323-34.

'Notes on Roman Historical Sculptures', *PBSR* 3 (1905) 215-71.

'Art Under the Roman Empire', *Quarterly Review* 204 (1906) 111-37.

'The Catacomb of Commodilla', *JTS* 7 (1906) 615-20.

'The Catacomb of Priscilla and the Primitive Memorials of St Peter', *JTS* 9 (1908) 436-41.

The Roman Empire BC 29 - AD 476. The Story of the Nations 65. London: T. Fisher Unwin, 1908.

'The Remains of Ancient Painting', *Quarterly Review* 210 (1909) 429-54.

'The Historical Interpretation of the Reliefs of Trajan's Column', *PBSR* 5 (1910) 433-59.

(and C. Strong) *Classical Rome*. Grant Allen's Historical Guides. New York; London: H. Holt; Grant Richards Ltd., 1910

(and F. Haverfield) 'Some Representative Examples of Romano-British Sculpture', *JRS* 2 (1912) 121-52.

(ed.) *A Catalogue of the Ancient Sculptures Preserved in the Municipal Collections of Rome 1: the Sculptures of the Museo Capitolino*. Oxford: Clarendon Press, 1912.

Companion to Roman History. Oxford: Clarendon Press, 1912.

'The Mysteries of Mithras', *Quarterly Review* 221 (1914) 103-27.

Fresh Light on Roman Bureaucracy. Oxford: Clarendon Press, 1920.

(ed.) *A Catalogue of the Ancient Sculptures Preserved in the Municipal Collections of Rome 2: the Sculptures of the Palazzo dei Conservatori*. Oxford: Clarendon Press, 1926.

'Claudius and the Jewish Question at Alexandria', *JRS* 16 (1926) 17-35.

'A Roman Law Concerning Piracy', *JRS* 16 (1926) 155-73.

Obituaries, memoirs and studies

The Times 30 June 1939; J. L. Myres, *PBA* 26 (1940) 467-78; H. I. Bell, 'Jones, Sir Henry Stuart (1867-1939)', in *The Dictionary of Welsh Biography Down to 1940*. London: Honourable Society of Cymmrodorion, 1959; *DBC*; D. W. J. Gill, 'Jones, Sir Henry Stuart- (1867-1939)', in *ODNB*, vol. 30, 521-24.

Archive material

British Library.

KAINES-SMITH, SOLOMON CHARLES

See Smith, Solomon Charles Kaines.

KIRKWOOD, WILLIAM ALEXANDER (1873-1960)

Born, Rockside, Peel County, Ontario, 1873.

Educ. in Brampton.

University College, Toronto: BA in Classics (1895); University of Toronto, MA (1905).

Taught at Walkeerton High School (1896-97).

Classics Master, Ridley College, St Catharines (1897-1903).

Taught, International College, Smyrna, Turkey (1903-04).

BSA adm. 1904-05.

BSR adm. 1904.

Taught, St Andrew's College, Toronto (1905-06).

Studies in University of Chicago (1906).

Harvard (1906-09), AM (1907), PhD (1909), 'De oraculis ad res Graecas publicas pertinentibus'.

Toronto, Trinity College: Lect. (1909-12); Prof. of Latin (1912-39); Registrar (1914-23); Dean, Faculty of Arts (1923-43); Clerk of Convocation (from 1939); retired (1939).

Married, Mossie May Waddington (25 August 1923), Principal of St Hilda's College, Toronto, and Dean of Women; two sons and a daughter.

Died, 15 October 1960 (aged 87).

Publications

Biographical Sketches of Members of the University of Toronto Class of 1895 in Arts. Toronto, 1947.

Obituary

Globe and Mail (Toronto), 17 October 1960; *Phoenix* 14, 4 (1960) 221.

KÖHLER, OLIVIA CHRISTINA (MRS CHARLES SMITH) (1876-1923)

Born, 12 August 1876, at Leipzig; dau. of Edward Köhler, merchant, of St John's Wood, and O. C. Ashton.

Educ. Bürgerschule, Leipzig; Maida Vale High School.

Camb. Girton Coll. (1895-99); Sir Francis Goldsmid Scholar; Class. Trip. Pt 1, 3rd, div. 1 (1898), Pt 2, 2nd (1899).

BSA adm. 1899-1900.

Secretary, Morley College, London (1902-05).

Married, Charles Smith (15 April 1905); 2 sons, 2 daughters.

Died, 18 July 1923.

LAISTNER, MAX LUDWIG WOLFRAM (1890-1959)

Born, 10 October 1890, London; son of Max Laistner, Prof. of music, from Germany, resident in London.

Educ. Merchant Taylors' School.

Camb. Jesus. Coll.; adm. Senior Open Schol. (21 October 1909); Class. Trip. Pt 1, 1st (1911); Pt 2, 1st (1912); BA (1912); MA (1919); Litt. D. (by proxy, 28 April 1944).

BSA adm. 1912-13; Craven Student (1912); re-adm. 1913-14 as School Student.

Asst. Lect. in Classics, Birmingham Univ. (1914).

Lect. in Archaeology and Ancient History, Queen's Univ., Belfast (1915).

War service, Private, Middlesex Regiment (1916-19). CQM Sergeant, Details Company, Royal Fusiliers, 29th Middlesex, Eastern Labour Centre (May 1916-January 1919); Administrative Officer, Ministry of Labour (Appointments Dept.) (February-September 1919).

Asst. Lect. in Classics, Manchester Univ. (July 1919-21).

Reader in Ancient History, King's College, London (1921-25).

Prof. of Ancient History, Cornell Univ. (1925); John Stambaugh Prof. of History, Cornell Univ. (1940); Prof. emeritus.

Fell. the Royal Historical Soc. (March 1929).

Hon. Fell. Jesus Coll. Cambridge (1949).

D. Litt.

Died, 10 December 1959, Ithaca, New York.

Publications

(and R. M. Dawkins) 'The Excavations of the Kamares Cave in Crete', *ABSA* 19 (1912/13) 1-34.

'Geometric Pottery at Delphi', *ABSA* 19 (1912/13) 61-69.

'Dediticii; The Source of Isidore (Etym. 9, 4, 49-50)', *JRS* 11 (1921) 267-68.

'Isocratea', *CQ* 15 (1921) 78-84.

'The Obelisks of Augustus at Rome', *JRS* 11 (1921) 265-66.

'Candelabrvm Theodosianvm', *CQ* 16 (1922) 107.

'Two Notes from the Liber Glossarvm', *CQ* 16 (1922) 105.

'Geographical Lore in the Liber Glossarvm', *CQ* 18 (1924) 49-53.

'Floscvli Philoxenei', *CQ* 19 (1925) 192-95.

Obituaries, memoirs and studies

G. V. Carey (ed.) *The War List of the University of Cambridge* (Cambridge: CUP, 1921) 176; *The Times* 12 December 1959; *Jesus College, Cambridge Society Report* (1960) 28-29 (obituary); Venn; WWW.

LAMB, DOROTHY (MRS J. REEVE BROOKE; LADY NICHOLSON) (1887-1967)

Born, 4 October 1887, Manchester; dau. of Sir Horace Lamb, Prof. of pure mathematics at Owens College, Manchester.

Educ. Manchester High School; Wycombe Abbey School.

Camb. Newnham Coll.; Class. Trip. Pt 1, 3rd div. 2 (1909); Pt 2, 1st archaeology (1910).

BSA adm. 1910-11; re-adm. 1913-14.

War service, forewoman on inspection HE ammunition, Woolwich Arsenal (1915-16); Administrative official, recruiting dept., HQ (1916-18); Secretary of London Committee of the Supreme Economic Council and of Official Committee for Relief in Europe (1918).

OBE.

Married, first, Sir John Reeve Brooke (1880-1937) (1920); second, Sir Walter Frederic Nicholson (1876-1946) (1939).

Died, 19 September 1967, Ewhurst, Surrey.

Publications

'Notes on Seljouk Buildings at Konia', *ABSA* 21 (1914/16) 31-61.

'Terracottas', in *Catalogue of the Acropolis Museum II*. Edited by S. Casson. Cambridge: Cambridge University Press, 1921.

(ed.) *Private Letters, Pagan and Christian: an Anthology of Greek and Roman Private Letters from the Fifth Century Before Christ to the Fifth Century of Our Era*. London: Benn, 1929; New York: Dutton, 1930

Pilgrims Were They All: Studies of Religious Adventure in the Fourth Century of Our Era. London: Faber, 1937.

Obituaries, memoirs and studies

DBC; D. W. J. Gill, 'Dorothy Lamb (1887-1967): a Pioneering Mediterranean Field-archaeologist', in *Breaking Ground: Women in Old World Archaeology*, edited by M. S. Joukowsky and B. S. Lesko: Brown University, 2004. http://www. brown. edu/Research/ Breaking_Ground/

LAMBERT, RICHARD STANTON (1894-1981)

Born, 25 Aug 1894; son of R. C. Lambert JP, 101 Abbey Road, Mansions, London NW8.

Educ. Repton School (Sept 1908-July 1912).

BSA adm. 1912-13.

Subsequently Oxf. Wadham Coll.; Classical Schol. (1912); adm. (1913); B. A. (1918); involved in debating, speaking in early 1914 in favour of armaments reduction; contributor to *Oxford Poetry* (1914), 'East-End Dirge' and (1915) 'For a Folk-Song' and 'War-Time'.

War service, applied for and secured registration as a conscientious objector (1916); Friends' Ambulance Unit (1916-18); a cook in a hospital in Birmingham; at Garsington doing agricultural service (1918).

Sheffield Univ., Tutorial Class Lect. in Economics.

BBC, in charge of Adult Education (1927); Editor of *The Listener*, BBC (1929 until 1939).

Married, Elinor Klein (13 April 1918), youngest dau. of Sydney T. Klein, of Hatherlow, Reigate, at St Mark's Reigate; daughter born 25 May 1919.

Residence, 87A Lexham Gardens, London.

Died, 28 Nov 1981.

Publications

Translation (from Latin) of *Callimachus: A Play by Roswitha, The Nun of Gandersheim.* Stanton Press, 1923.

LAWSON, JOHN CUTHBERT (1874-1935)

Born, 14 Oct. 1874, Weston-in-Gordano, Somerset; 2nd son of the Rev. Robert Lawson (1865), Rector of Camerton, Bath.

Educ. Bradfield College.

Camb. Pembroke Coll.; adm. pens. (Oct. 1, 1893); Schol.; Class. Trip. Pt 1, 1st (1896); Pt 2, 1st (1897); BA (1896); Members' prize (Latin Essay) (1897); Craven Studentship (1898 and 1899); MA (1900).

BSA adm. 1898-99 (Craven Univ. Student); re-adm. 1899-1900.

Fell. Pembroke College (1899-1935); tutor and Classical Lect., Junior Proctor (1909); Senior Proctor (1912); University Lect. in Classics (1926-35).

War service, Lieutenant, RNVR (February 1916-December 1917); Acting Lieutenant commander, RNVR, British Naval Mission, Athens (January 1918-April 1919); temporary acting commander; Lieut. -Commander, RNVR, in the Naval Intelligence Branch; in Crete; O.B.E.; mentioned in despatches; Greek Order of the Redeemer and Medal for Military Merit. Silver Cross of the Greek Order of the Saviour.

Married, Dorothy Frances Holden (1900), of Lancashire.

Died Jan. 5, 1935.

Publications

'A Beast-dance in Scyros', *ABSA* 6 (1899/1900) 125-27.

Modern Greek Folklore and Ancient Greek Religion: a Study in Survivals. Cambridge: Cambridge University Press, 1910.

Tales of Aegean Intrigue. London: Chatto & Windus, 1920.

'Aeschylus, Agamemnon', *CR* 35 (1921) 100.

The Agamemnon of Aeschylus. A Revised text, With Introduction, Verse Translation, and Critical Notes by J. C. Lawson. Cambridge: University Press, 1932.

'The Agamemnon of Aeschylus', *JHS* 53 (1933) 112.

Obituaries, memoirs and studies

The Times 7 January 1935 (obit.); 19 January 1935 (memoral service at Pembroke Coll.); *Cambridge Rev.* 18 Jan. 1935; Venn.

LEITH, GEORGE ESSLEMONT GORDON (1886-1965)

Born, 1886.

Architect. Worked with Herbert Baker on the Union Buildings in South Africa.

Herbert Baker Studentship.

BSR adm. 1911; first holder of Herbert Baker Studentship.

BSA adm. 1912-13.

FRIBA (1930).

Died, 1965.

LORIMER, (ELIZABETH) HILDA LOCKHART (1873-1954)

Born, 30 May 1873, Edinburgh; dau. of Rev. Robert Lorimer, a minister of the Free Church of Scotland.

Educ. Dundee High School.

University College, Dundee (1889-93), BA, 1st.

Camb. Girton Coll.; Schol. (1893); Class. Trip. Pt 1, 1st div. 2 (1896).

Classical Tutor of Somerville College, Oxford (1896-1934); tutor in classical archaeology (1934-1939); Hon. Fell. (1939).

BSA adm. 1901-02 (Pfeiffer Travelling Student, £40).

War service, Intelligence Dept. of Admiralty (1916); Orderly in the Scottish Women's Hospital, Salonika (1917); Historical Section of the Foreign Office (1918-19).

Died, 1 March 1954.

Publications

'The Country Cart of Ancient Greece', *JHS* 23 (1903) 132-51.

(and D. G. Hogarth, C. C. Edgar) 'Naukratis, 1903', *JHS* 25 (1905) 105–36.

'A Vase Fragment from Naukratis', *JHS* 30 (1910) 35–37.

'Notes on the Sequence and Distribution of the Fabrics called Proto-Corinthian', *JHS* 32 (1912) 326–53.

'Defensive Armour in Homer: With a Note on Women's Dress', *Annals of Archaeology and Anthropology* 15 (1928) 89-130.

'Homer's Use of the Past', *JHS* 49 (1929) 145-59.

(and W. A. Heurtley). 'Excavations in Ithaca, I. LH III-Protogeometric Cairns at Aetos', *ABSA* 33 (1932/33) 22-65.

'Pulvis et umbra', *JHS* 53 (1933) 161-80.

'The Hoplite Phalanx', *ABSA* 42 (1947) 76-138.

'Dipaltos', *ABSA* 37 (1936/37) 172-86.

'Homer and the Art of Writing: a Sketch of Opinion Between 1713 and 1939', *AJA* 52 (1948) 11-23.

Homer and the monuments. London: Macmillan, 1950.

Obituaries, memoirs and studies

The Times 3 March 1954; M. Hartley, 'H. L. Lorimer', *Girton Review* 155 (1954) 26-28; S. Benton, 'H. L. Lorimer', *Girton Review* 155 (1954) 28–29; H. Wang, 'Stein's Recording Angel - Miss F. M. G. Lorimer', *Journal of the Royal Asiatic Society* 8 (1998) 207-28; *DBC*; Helen Waterhouse, 'Lorimer, (Elizabeth) Hilda Lockhart (1873-1954)', in *ODNB*, vol. 34, 446-47.

Archive material

Oxf. Bodleian Lib.

LORING, WILLIAM (1865-1915)

Born, 2 July 1865, Cobham, Surrey; 4th son of the Rev. Edward Henry Loring (1840), Rector of Gillingham, Norfolk.

Educ. Eton; King's Schol. (September 1879 - March 1884); Newcastle Select (1883); Schol. (1884).

Camb. King's Coll.; Schol. from Eton, Newcastle Schol. (1984) (Oct. 10, 1885); Bell Scholar (1886); Battie Scholar (1888); Chancellor's (Classical) medal (equal) (1889); Class. Trip. Pt 1, 1st (1887); Pt 2, 1st (1889); BA (1889); MA (1893).

BSA adm. 1889-90 (Cambridge Studentship); re-adm. 1890-91 (Craven Univ. Student), 1891-92, 1892-93. Secretary of the School, 1897-1903.

Fell. King's College (1891-7).

Called to the Bar, Inner Temple (1898).

Examiner for the Board of Education (1894-1903); Dir. of Education under the West Riding County Council (1903-05); Warden, Goldsmith's College, New Cross (1906).

Hon. Sec. of BSA and BSR.

War service, S. African War (1899-1902), corporal, 19th (Lothians and Berwickshire) Company, Imperial Yeomanry (1900-1) (DCM); Lieut. in the Scottish Horse (1901-02); twice mentioned in despatches; wounded at Moedwill; First World War, initially on home defence; Capt., 2nd Scottish Horse; Gallipoli; landed at Suvla Bay on 2 September 1915; wounded.

Married, Mary Theodosia Thackeray (1905), dau. of the Rev. F. St John Thackeray, Vicar of Mapledurham.

Died, 22 Oct. (BSA), 24 Oct. 1915 (Venn), at sea on the hospital ship *Devanha*, from wounds received at Gallipoli.

Publications

'Κανθήλη Χανδελα, Κανθήλια', *CR* 4 (1890) 424-25.

'A New Portion of the Edict of Diocletian from Megalopolis', *JHS* 11 (1890) 299-342.

(and E. A. Gardner, G. C. Richards, and W. J. Woodhouse) 'The Theatre at Megalopolis', *JHS* 11 (1890) 294-98.

'Κανθήλη', *CR* 5 (1891) 66.

(and W. Dörpfeld, E. A. Gardner) 'The Theatre at Megalopolis', *CR* 5 (1891) 284-85.

(and E. A. Gardner, G. C. Richards, W. J. Woodhouse, and R. W. Schultz) *Excavations at Megalopolis, 1890-1891*. Society for the Promotion of Hellenic Studies, Supplementary papers, no. 1. London: Society for the Promotion of Hellenic Studies, 1892.

'The Theatre at Megalopolis', *JHS* 13 (1892/93) 356-58.

'Four Fragmentary Inscriptions', *JHS* 15 (1895) 90-92.

'Some Ancient Routes in the Peloponnese', *JHS* 15 (1895) 25-89.

Obituaries, memoirs and studies

The Times Educational Supplement 7 December 1915; *Times Literary Supplement* 16 December 1915; Venn.

MACKENZIE, DUNCAN (1861-1934)

Born, 17 May 1861, at Ault-gowrie, Ross-shire, Scotland; son of Alexander Stuart Mackenzie, a gamekeeper, and his wife Margaret Kennedy.

Educ. Raining's School, Inverness (1880-82).

Arts Faculty, Univ. of Edinburgh (1882-90); MA in Philosophy.

Universities of Munich, Berlin and Vienna; Doctorate from Vienna (1895).

BSA adm. 1895-96; re-adm. 1896-97, 1897-98, 1898-99.

Excavating at Knossos (1900-).

Carnegie Fell. in History at the Univ. of Edinburgh (1903-06).

Sardinia (1906-09).

Palestine Exploration Fund (1909-12).

Sudan for Sir Henry Wellcome (1913).

Knossos Curator (1926).

Died, 25 August 1934, at Pesaro, Italy.

Publications

Bibliography in N. Momigliano, *Duncan Mackenzie: a Cautious Canny Highlander & the Palace of Minos at Knossos*. Bulletin of the Institute of Classical Studies, suppl. 72. London: Institute of Classical Studies, 1999

'Ancient Sites in Melos', *ABSA* 3 (1896/7) 71-88.

'Excavations of the British School at Melos: the Site of the "Three Churches"', *JHS* 17 (1897) 122-33.

'Excavations in Melos, 1898. II. The Successive Settlements', *ABSA* 4 (1897/8) 17-36.

'Kos Astypalaia', *ABSA* 4 (1897/8) 95-100.

'Excavations in Melos, 1899. A. The Season's Work', *ABSA* 5 (1898/9) 3-10.

'The Pottery of Knossos', *JHS* 23 (1903) 157-205.

(and T. D. Atkinson, R. C. Bosanquet, C. C. Edgar, A. J. Evans, D. G. Hogarth, C. Harcourt-Smith, and F. B. Welch) 1904. *Excavations at Phylakopi in Melos*. Society for the Promotion of Hellenic Studies, Occasional Paper 4. London, 1904.

'Cretan Palaces and the Aegean Civilization', *ABSA* 11 (1904/05) 181-223.

'Cretan Palaces and the Aegean Civilization. II', *ABSA* 12 (1905/06) 216-57.

'The Middle Minoan Pottery of Knossos', *JHS* 26 (1906) 243-67.

'Cretan Palaces and the Aegean Civilization. III', *ABSA* 13 (1906/07) 423-45.

'Cretan Palaces and the Aegean Civilization. IV', *ABSA* 14 (1907/08) 343-422.

'The East Pediment Sculptures of the Temple of Aphaia at Aegina', *ABSA* 15 (1908/09) 274-307.

Obituaries, memoirs and studies

Faces of Archaeology 15-20 no. 2; *DBC*; N. Momigliano, *Duncan Mackenzie: a Cautious Canny Highlander & the Palace of Minos at Knossos*. Bulletin of the Institute of Classical Studies, suppl. 72. London: Institute of Classical Studies, 1999; ead., "Mackenzie, Duncan (1861-1934)', in *ODNB*, vol. 35, 573.

MARSHALL, JOHN HUBERT (1876-1958)

Born, 19 Mar. 1876, at Everton House, Curzon Park, Chester; 6th son of Frederick Marshall, barrister-at-law, of The Oaks, Alleyn Park, West Dulwich, Middlesex.

Educ. Dulwich College (1887-July 1895).

Camb. King's Coll.; adm. Schol. (Oct. 9, 1895); Schol. (1898); Porson Prize (1898); Class. trip. Pt 1, 1st (1898); Pt 2, 1st (1900); BA (1898); MA (1902); Litt.D. (1913).

BSA adm. 1898-99; re-adm. 1900-01 (Prendergast Student), 1901-02 (Craven Student).

Dir. -General of Archaeology in India (1902-31); on special duty with Govt. of India, (1931-36).

Hon. Fell. King's College (1927).

CIE (1910); Knighted (1914); Commander of the Order of Leopold; Birdwood Memorial gold medallist, Royal Society of Arts (1922); Gold Medallist, Royal Asiatic Soc. (1932).

Hon. PhD; Hon. ARIBA; FSA; FBA.

Married, Florence Ellen Longhurst (1902), dau. of Sir Henry Bell Longhurst, surgeon-dentist.

Residence (in 1947), Avondale, Sydney Road, Guildford.

Died, 17 August 1958, Guildford.

Publications

Taxila: An Illustrated Account of Archaeological Excavations Carried Out at Taxila Under the Orders of the Government of India Between the Years 1913 and 1934. Cambridge: Cambridge University Press, 1951.

Studies

WWW; Venn; *DBC*; D. W. J. Gill, 'Collecting for Cambridge: John Hubert Marshall on Crete', *ABSA* 95 (2000) 517-26; *DBC*; Mortimer Wheeler (revised Jane McIntosh), 'Marshall, Sir John Hubert (1876-1958)', in *ODNB*, vol. 36, 854-56.

Archive material

Oxf. Sackler Lib.; Oxf. Bodleian Lib.

MAYOR, ROBERT JOHN GROTE (1869-1947)

Born, Aug. 20, 1869, at Twickenham, Middlesex; eldest son of the Rev. Joseph Bickersteth Mayor (1847), headmaster of Kensington School and Prof. of Classical Literature at King's College, London; of Queen's Gate House, Kingston-on-Thames, Surrey.

Educ. Eton; King's Schol. (September 1882 - December 1887); Newcastle Select (1886); Schol. (1887); Shakespeare Prize (1886); Ist Latin Prose Prize and Greek Iambics Prize (1887).

Cam. King's Coll.; Schol. from Eton (Oct. 10, 1888); Bell Scholar (1889); Craven Scholar (1891); Senior Classic, (1890); Class. Trip. Pt 2, 1st (1892); BA (1892); MA (1896).

BSA adm. 1892-93.

Fell. King's College (1894).

Called to the Bar, Lincoln's Inn (26 Jan. 1899).

Joined the Education Dept. (1896); Asst. Sec. Board of Education (1907-19); Principal Asst. Sec. (1919-26). Chairman of Committee on co-operation between Universities and Training Colleges (1926-28); and of Central Advisory Committee for certification of Teachers (1930-35).

CB (1919).

Residence (in 1946), 26 Addison Avenue, London, W.

Married, Katherine Beatrice Meinertzhagen (1912), daughter of Daniel Meinertzhagen.

Died, 19 June 1947.

Obituaries, memoirs and studies

WWW; Venn.

Archive material

Camb. Trinity Coll. Lib.; Camb. King's Coll. Archive Centre.

MILNE, JOSEPH GRAFTON (1867-1951)

Born, 23 December 1867, Bowden, near Altrincham, Cheshire; 2nd son of William Milne, yarn-supplier, and Ellen, dau. of Joseph Smith Grafton.

Educ. Manchester Grammar School (c. 1881-c. 1885); Langworthy Schol.

Oxf. Corpus Christi Coll.; Schol.; Class. Mod. 1st (1888); Lit. Hum. 2nd (1890); BA (1890); MA (1896); D. Litt. (1925).

BSA adm. 1890-91 (Oxford studentship).

Asst. Master (6th Form) at Mill Hill School (1891-93).

Junior and Senior Examiner, and Asst. Sec. to the Board of Education (1893-1926); retired.

Excavated in Egypt with Petrie (1895-96); C. T. Currelly at Deir el-Bahri (1905-06).

Reader in Numismatics, Oxf. (1930-38); Deputy Keeper of Coins, Ashmolean Museum, Oxford (1931-51); Librarian, Corpus Christi Coll., Oxf. (1933-46).

Annual Medal of the Royal Numismatic Soc. (1938); Archer M Huntingdon Medal of American Numismatic Soc. (1944).

Married, Kate Ackroyd (1896), dau. of James Edmondson Ackroyd.

Died, 7 August 1951, Oxford.

Publications

(and J. A. R. Munro, W. C. F. Anderson, and F. Haverfield) 'On the Roman Town of Doclea in Montenegro: Communicated to the Society of Antiquaries', *Archaeologia* 55 (1896) 33-92.

(and B. P. Grenfell, A. S. Hunt, D. G. Hogarth) *Fayum Towns and Their Papyri*. Egypt Exploration Fund, Graeco-Roman branch. Memoirs, vol. 3. London: Egypt Exploration Fund, 1900.

'Greek Inscriptions from Egypt', *JHS* 21 (1901) 275-92.

'Roman Coin-moulds from Egypt', *NC* 5 (1905) 342.

'A Hoard of Coins from Egypt of the Fourth Century BC ' *Revue archéologique* 5 (1905) 257-61.

'Clay-sealings from the Fayum', *JHS* 26 (1906) 32-45.

'Relics of Graeco-Egyptian Schools', *JHS* 28 (1908) 121-32.

'The Copper Coinage of the Ptolemies', *Annals of Archaeology and Anthropology* 1 (1908) 30-40.

'The Leaden Token Coinage of Egypt Under the Romans', *NC* 8 (1908) 287.

'Alexandrian Tetradrachms of Tiberius', *NC* 10 (1910) 333.

'Hoard of Silver Coins of Knidos', *NC* 11 (1911) 197.

'The Dadia Hoard of the Coins of Knidos', *NC* 11 (1911) 197.

'Two Hoards of Coins of Cos', *NC* 12 (1912) 14.

'Coutermarked Coins of Asia Minor', *NC* 13 (1913) 389-98.

'Antony and Cleopatra?' *JEA* 1 (1914) 99.

'Graeco-Roman Leaden Tesserae from Abydos', *JEA* 1 (1914) 93-95.

'The Sanatorium at Dêr-el-Bahri', *JEA* 1 (1914) 96-98.

'A Hoard of Coins of Temnos', *NC* 14 (1914) 260.

'Greek and Roman Tourists in Egypt', *JEA* 3 (1916) 76-80.

'The Organisation of the Alexandrian Mint in the Reign of Diocletian', *JEA* 3 (1916) 207-17.

'Ptolemaic Seal Impressions', *JHS* 36 (1916) 87-101.

'A Hoard of Bronze Coins of Smyrna', *NC* 16 (1916) 246.

'A Hoard of Persian Sigloi', *NC* 16 (1916) 1-12.

'Some Alexandrian Coins', *JEA* 4 (1917) 177-86.

'The Alexandrian Coinage of the Early Years of Hadrian', *NC* 17 (1917) 31.

'The Shops of the Roman Mint of Alexandria', *JRS* 8 (1918) 154-78.

'Two Roman Hoards of Coins from Egypt', *JRS* 10 (1920) 169-84.

'The Coins from Oxyrhynchus', *JEA* 8 (1922) 158-63.

'A Gnomic Ostrakon', *JEA* 8 (1922) 156-57.

'More Relics of Graeco-Egyptian Schools', *JHS* 43 (1923) 40-43.

'Aemilianus the "Tyrant"', *JEA* 10 (1924) 80-82.

'Double Entries in Ptolemaic Tax-receipts', *JEA* 11 (1925) 269-83.

'The Kline of Sarapis', *JEA* 11 (1925) 6-9.

'Bernard Pyne Grenfell: B. 16 Dec. 1869. D. 18 May 1926', *JEA* 12 (1926) 285-86.

'The Ruin of Egypt by Roman Mismanagement', *JRS* 17 (1927) 1-13.

(and H. J. M. Milne, A. D. Nock, H. I. Bell, N. H. Baynes, F. D. Zulueta, M. E. Dicker, and R. McKenzie) 'Bibliography: Graeco-Roman Egypt A. Papyri (1926-1927)', *JEA* 14 (1928) 131-58.

'Chronological Pitfalls', *JEA* 14 (1928) 20-21.

'Egyptian Nationalism Under Greek and Roman rule', *JEA* 14 (1928) 226-34.

'Ptolemaic Coinage in Egypt', *JEA* 15 (1929) 150-53.

'The Monetary Reforms of Solon', *JHS* 50 (1930) 179-85.

'The Roman Regulation of Exchange Values in Egypt: a Note', *JEA* 16 (1930) 169-70.

'Woodeaton Coins', *JRS* 21 (1931) 101-09.

'The Beni Hasan Coin-hoard', *JEA* 19 (1933) 119-21.

'Colonel T. M. Crowder's Travel Journals', *JHS* 53 (1933) 9-15.

'A Few Notes on the Currency of Britain', *JRS* 23 (1933) 221-22.

'Arthur Surridge Hunt', *JEA* 20 (1934) 204-05.

'"Phocaean Gold" in Egypt', *JEA* 20 (1934) 193-94.

'Report on Coins Found at Tebtunis in 1900', *JEA* 21 (1935) 210-16.

'Pliny on the First Coinages at Rome', *CR* 50 (1936) 215-17.

'On P. Oslo 83 and the Depreciation of Currency', *JEA* 23 (1937) 258-59.

'The Currency of Egypt Under the Ptolemies', *JEA* 24 (1938) 200-07.

'The Monetary Reform of Solon: a Correction', *JHS* 58 (1938) 96-97.

'Roman Literary Evidence on the Coinage', *JRS* 28 (1938) 70-74.

'The Silver of Aryandes', *JEA* 24 (1938) 245-46.

'Trade Between Greece and Egypt Before Alexander the Great', *JEA* 25 (1939) 177-83.

'The "Philippus" Coin at Rome', *JRS* 30 (1940) 11-15.

'The Tükh El-Karāmüs Gold Hoard', *JEA* 27 (1941) 135-37.

'The Aes Grave of Central Italy', *JRS* 32 (1942) 27-32.

'Pictorial Coin-types at the Roman Mint of Alexandria', *JEA* 29 (1943) 63-66.

'Bigati', *JRS* 34 (1944) 49-50.

'An Exchange-currency of Magna Graecia', *JRS* 34 (1944) 46-48.

'Alexandrian Coins Acquired by the Ashmolean Museum, Oxford', *JEA* 31 (1945) 85-91.

'The Problem of the Early Roman Coinage', *JRS* 36 91946) 91-100.

'Pictorial Coin-types at the Roman Mint of Alexandria: a Supplement', *JEA* 36 (1950) 83-85.

'Pictorial Coin-types at the Roman Mint of Alexandria: a Second Supplement', *JEA* 37 (1951) 100-02.

Obituaries, memoirs and studies

The Times 14 August 1951; 12 October 1951 (memorial service at Corpus Christi College, Oxford); *NC* (1951) 115-25 (with list of publications); H. Last, 'Joseph Grafton Milne', *JEA* 38 (1952) 112-14; *WWW in Egyptology*.

MORRISON, FREDERICK ARTHUR CHARLES (1872-1899)

Born, 1872; son of James. B. Morrison (from Armagh, Ireland; 1891, 'living on own means') at Belle Vue Cottage, Plumstead, Kent, and his wife, Delilah.

Educ. City of London School.

Camb. Jesus Coll.; adm. pens. (1891); Class. Trip. Pt 1, 1st (1895); Pt 2, 1st (1896); BA (1895).

BSA adm. 1896-97 (Prendergast Student).

Members' prize (1898).

Asst. Lect. at Mason College, Birmingham (1897-99).

Died, July 1899, Reigate, Surrey.

Obituaries, memoirs and studies

Venn.

MOSS-BLUNDELL, CYRIL BERTRAM (1891-1915)

Born, 12 April 1891, Seremban; youngest son of Arthur Spencer Moss-Blundell, of Sparsholt, near Winchester.

Educ. Winchester College (1904-10); King's Gold Medal, 'Hectoris Andromache' (1910).

Oxf. New Coll.; matric. as Winchester Schol. (1910); Class. Mod. 1st (1912); Lit. Hum. 1st; BA (1914); specialised in Classical Archaeology.

Hertford Schol. Examination (1912): distinction. (A one-year Oxford scholarship to encourage the study of Latin.)

BSA, student elect 1914-15.

War service, Lieutenant in the Durham Light Infantry. 14th (Service) Bn. (enlisted 23 October 1914).

Killed in action, 26 September 1915, Loos. The Commonwealth War Graves Commission states 27 September 1915.

Publications

'Correspondence (Comment on Passages in Propertius)', *CR* 26 (1912) 70-71.

Obituaries, memoirs and studies

A. Macdonald and S. Leeson, *Wykehamists Who Died in the War, 1914-1918* (Winchester: Warren, 1921) 216 (ill.); *The Oxford University Roll of Honour 1914-18,* 212; Commonwealth War Graves Commission.

MUNRO, JOHN ARTHUR RUSKIN (1864-1944)

Born, 24 February 1864; elder son of Alexander Munro, sculptor.

Educ. Charterhouse.

Oxf. Exeter Coll.; Schol. (1882-86); Class. Mod. 1st (1883); Lit. Hum. 1st (1886); BA (1886); MA.

Fell. Lincoln Coll. Oxf. (1888); Bursar (1904-19 and c. 1943-44); Lect.; Rector (6 November 1919); Hon. Fell. Exeter Coll. (1929).

BSA adm. 1888-89 (for work on Cyprus); re-adm. 1889-90 (Cyprus).

Examiner in Lit. Hum. (1894-1896); Junior Proctor (1900).

War service, intelligence work for the Admiralty and the War Office, London.

Married, Margaret Caroline Neaves Parez (1905), 2nd dau. of the Rev. C. H. Parez, inspector of schools, of Cumberland; one son, four daughters.

Died, 18 February 1944

Publications

(and H. A. Tubbs) 'Excavations in Cyprus, 1889. Second Season's Work. Polis tes Chrysochou. Limniti', *JHS* 11 (1890) 1-99.

'Excavations in Cyprus. Third Season's Work - Polis tes Chrysochou', *JHS* 12 (1891) 298-333.

(and H. A. Tubbs, and W. W. Wroth) 'Excavations in Cyprus, 1890. Third Season's work. Salamis', *JHS* 12 (1891) 59-198.

(and D. G. Hogarth) *Modern and Ancient Roads in Eastern Asia Minor*. Royal Geographical Society, supplementary papers, vol. 3, part 5. London: Royal Geographical Society, 1893.

'Epigraphical Notes from Eastern Macedonia and Thrace', *JHS* 16 (1896) 313-22.

(and W. C. F. Anderson, J. G. Milne, and F. Haverfield) 'On the Roman Town of Doclea in Montenegro: Communicated to the Society of Antiquaries', *Archaeologia* 55 (1896) 33-92.

'Inscriptions from Mysia', *JHS* 17 (1897) 268-93.

(and H. M. Anthony) 1897a. 'Explorations in Mysia', *Geographical Journal* 9 (1897) 150-69, 256-76.

'A Letter from Antigonus to Scepsis, 311 BC ', *JHS* 19 (1899) 330-40.

'Some Observations on the Persian Wars I. The Campaign of Marathon', *JHS* 19 (1899) 185-97.

'Some Pontic Milestones', *JHS* 20 (1900) 159-66.

'Gleanings from Mysia', *JHS* 21 (1901) 229-37.

'Notes on the Text of the Parian Marble. I', *CR* 15 (1901) 149-54.

'Notes on the Text of the Parian Marble. II', *CR* 15 (1901) 355-61.

'Roads in Pontus, Royal and Roman', *JHS* 21 (1901) 52-66.

'Some Observations on the Persian Wars II. The Campaign of Xerxes', *JHS* 22 (1902) 294-332.

'Some Observations on the Persian Wars III. The Campaign of Plataea', *JHS* 24 (1904) 144-65.

'Dascylium', *JHS* 32 (1912) 57-67.

'Pelasgians and Ionians', *JHS* 54 (1934) 109-28.

Obituaries, memoirs and studies

The Times 19 Feb 1944 (obit.), 24 Feb 1944 (funeral); WWW.

Archive material

Oxf. Bodleian Lib.

MYRES, JOHN LINTON (SIR) (1869-1954)

Born, 3 July 1869, Preston, Lancashire; son of Rev. William Miles Myres, vicar of St Paul's Preston, and vicar of Swanbourne, Bicks., and Jane, dau. of the Rev. Henry Linton.

Educ. Winchester.

Oxf. New Coll.; Class. Mod. 1st (1890); Lit. Hum. 1st (1892); BA (1892); MA (1895).

BSA adm. 1892-93 (Craven Fell.); re-adm. 1893-94, 1894-95. Hon. Student of the School.

Fell. Magdalen College, Oxf. (1892-94). Prize Fellowship.

Burdett-Coutts Geological Schol. (1894); Arnold Essay Prize (1899).

Student and Tutor of Christ Church (1895-1907); University Lect. in Classical Archaeology; Junior Proctor (1904-05).

Gladstone Prof. of Greek and Lect. in Ancient Geography at the Univ. of Liverpool (1907-10).

Wykeham Prof. of Ancient History and Fell. New College (1910-39).

War service, Naval Intelligence Dept. (1916-19); Military Control Office, Athens (1917-19); Commander of the RNVR, Greece; mentioned in despatches; Commander of Royal Order of George I of Greece.

FBA.

Married, Sophia Florence (25 Jul 1895), dau. of the late Charles Balance, of Clapton, Middlesex.

Died, 6 March 1954.

Publications

(and W. R. Paton) 'Three Carian Sites: Telmissos, Karyanda, Taramptos', *JHS* 14 (1894) 373-80.

'On Some Polychrome Pottery from Kamarais in Crete', *Proceedings of the Society of Antiquaries* 15 (1895) 351-56.

(and A. J. Evans) 'A Mycenaean Military Road', *The Academy* 1204 (1895) 469.

(and W. R. Paton) 'Karian Sites and Inscriptions: II', *JHS* 16 (1896) 237-71.

'A Marble Relief from the African Tripolis', *ABSA* 3 (1896/7) 170-74.

'Excavations in Cyprus in 1894', *JHS* 17 (1897) 134-73.

(and W. R. Paton) 'Researches in Karia', *Journal of the Royal Geographic Society* 9 (1897) 38-54.

(and W. R. Paton) 'Some Karian and Hellenic Oil-presses', *JHS* 18 (1898) 209-17.

(and M. H. Ohnefalsch-Richter) *A Catalogue of the Cyprus Museum: With a Chronicle of Excavations Undertaken Since the British Occupation, and Introductory Notes on Cypriote Archaeology*. Oxford: Clarendon Press, 1899.

'On the Plan of the Homeric House, With Special Reference to Mykenaian Analogies', *JHS* 20 (1900) 128-50.

(and P. Gardner) *Classical Archaeology in Schools*. Oxford: Clarendon Press, 1902.

'Ridgeway's *Early Age of Greece*', *CR* 16 (1902) 68-77, 91-94.

'Excavations at Palaikastro. II. § 13. The Sanctuary-site of Petsofà', *ABSA* 9 (1902/03) 356-87.

'The Early Pot-fabrics of Asia Minor', *Journal of the Anthropological Institute* 33 (1903) 367-400.

(and P. Gardner) *Classical Archaeology in Schools*, 2nd ed. Oxford: Clarendon Press, 1905.

'On the "List of Thalassocracies" in Eusebius', *JHS* 26 (1906) 84-130.

'A History of the Pelasgian Theory', *JHS* 27 (1907) 170-225.

'The "List of Thalassocracies" in Eusebius: a Reply', *JHS* 27 (1907) 123-30.

Greek Lands and the Greek People: an Inaugural Lecture Delivered Before the University of Oxford, November 11, 1910. Oxford: Clarendon Press, 1910.

(and D. G. Hogarth, D. Strathan, F. Haverfield, A. Stein, E. A. Gardner, W. A. Cannon, M. M. Allorge, W. N. Shaw, and J. W. Gregory) 'The Burial of Olympia: Discussion', *Geographical Journal* 36 (1910) 675-86.

The Dawn of History. Oxford: Oxford University Press, 1911.

(and D. G. Hogarth, E. A. Gardner, B. Nopsca, A. Stein, J. P. Droop, F. R. Maunsell, M. S. Thompson, A. M. Woodward, and A. J. B. Wace) 'The Distribution of Early Civilization in Northern Greece: Discussion', *Geographical Journal* 37 (1911) 636-42.

Handbook of the Cesnola Collection of Antiquities from Cyprus. New York: Metropolitan Museum of Art, 1914.

'The Plot of the Alcestis', *JHS* 37 (1917) 195-218.

Who Were the Greeks? Sather Classical Lectures, vol. 6. Berkeley: University of California Press, 1930.

'The Last Book of the Iliad', *JHS* 52 (1932) 264-96.

(and L. H. D. Buxton, S. Casson) 'A Cloisonne Staff-head from Cyprus', *Man* (1932) 1-4.

'The Amathus Bowl: a Long-lost Masterpiece of Oriental Engraving', *JHS* 53 (1933) 25-39.

'The Chronological Plan of the Iliad: a Correction', *JHS* 53 (1933) 115-17.

'The Cretan Labyrinth: a Retrospect of Aegean Research', *JRAI* 63 (1933) 269-312.

'Excavations in Cyprus, 1913', *ABSA* 41 (1940/45) 53-104.

'Obituary: D. J. Wallace', *ABSA* 41 (1940/45) 9.

'Obituary: Stanley Casson', *ABSA* 41 (1940/45) 1-4.

'Hesiod's "Shield of Herakles": its Structure and Workmanship', *JHS* 61 (1941) 17-38.

'The Minoan Signary', *JHS* 66 (1946) 1-4.

'Professor Hrozny's Table of the Minoan Signary', *JHS* 66 (1946) 129.

'Symmetry on the Chest of Cypselus at Olympia (Pausanias V. 17-19)', *JHS* 66 (1946) 122.

'The Tomb of Porsena at Clusium', *ABSA* 46 (1951) 117-21.

'The Pattern of the *Odyssey*', *JHS* 72 (1952) 1-19.

Geographical History in Greek Lands. Oxford: Clarendon Press, 1953.

'The Structure of the *Iliad*, Illustrated by the Speeches', *JHS* 74 (1954) 122-41.

Obituaries, memoirs and studies

The Wykehamist 1007 (29 March 1954), 66 (W. F. O.); L. Woolley, 'John Linton Myres: 1869-1954', *Man* 54 (1954) 40; R. M. Dawkins, 'John Linton Myres: 1869-1954', *Man*

54 (1954) 40-41; T. J. Dunbabin, 'Obituary. Sir John Myres: 1869-1954', *ABSA* 49 (1954) 311-14; id., 'Sir John Myres', *PBA* 41 (1956) 349-65; J. N. L. Myres, *Commander J. L. Myres, RNVR: the Blackbeard of the Aegean*. J. L. Myres Memorial Lecture, vol. 10. London: Leopard's Head Press, 1980; *DBC*; John Boardman, 'Myres, Sir John Linton (1869–1954)', in *ODNB*, vol. 40, 87-89.

Archive material
Oxf. Bodleian Lib.; Oxf. Ashmolean Museum; London, Society of Antiquaries.

Oppé, Adolph Paul (1878-1957)
Born, 22 Sept 1878; son of Siegmund Armin Oppé, a silk merchant, and his wife, Pauline Jaffé.

Educ. Charterhouse.

St Andrews Univ.

Oxf. New Coll.; Exhib.; Class. Mod. 1st (1899); Lit. Hum. 1st (1901).

BSA adm. 1901-02.

Lect. in Greek, St Andrews Univ. (1902).

Lect. in Ancient History, Edinburgh Univ. (1904).

Examiner in the Board of Education (1905). Retired 1938.

Secondment to Victoria and Albert Museum (1906-07, 1910-13).

War service, Ministry of Munitions (1915-17); Select Committee on National Expenditure (1917-18).

CB (1937); FBA (1952).

Married, Lyonetta Edith Regina Valentine Tollemache (23 Feb 1909), dau. of the Rev. Ralph William Lyonel Tollemache-Tollemache, Rector of South Wytham, Lincolnshire.

Died, 29 March 1957.

Publications
'The Chasm at Delphi', *JHS* 24 (1904) 214-40.

Other publications on the History of Art.

Obituaries, memoirs and studies
The Times 1 April 1957, 3 April 1957; Brinsley Ford, 'Oppé, Adolph Paul (1878-1957)', in *ODNB*, vol. 41, 897-98.

Archive material
Vaughan Williams Memorial Library.

Ormerod, Henry Arderne (1886-1964)
Born, 16 March 1886; son of J. A. Ormerod, a medical doctor, of 25 Upper Wimpole Street, London.

Educ. St George's Ascot (under Blair), Rugby (School House).

Oxf. The Queen's Coll.; Schol. to read classics; Class. Mod. 2nd (1907); Lit. Hum. 1st (1909).

BSA adm. 1909-10, 1910-11.

Asst. Lect. in Greek, Univ. of Liverpool (1911-23).

War service (WW1): 2nd Lieutenant (1915), Lieutenant (1916), Acting-Captain (June 1917), 148th Battery, Royal Field Artillery, in France (1915) and Macedonia (November 1915-19) [though BSA would suggest serving in France]; MC (1916); mentioned in despatches (1917); three times wounded; evacuated as a result of wounds (1917);

Ministry of Munitions (1917-18); War Office for special duty in Greece (1918-19); Chevalier of the Order of King George I of Greece.

Prof. of Classics, Univ. of Leeds (1923-28).

Rathbone Prof. of Ancient History, Univ. of Liverpool (1928-51).

Married, Mildred Robina Caton (1914), dau. of Dr Richard Caton MRCP.

Died, 21 November 1964 at Crookham Common, Berkshire.

Publications

'Laconia II. Topography. Bardoúnia and North-eastern Maina', *ABSA* 16 (1909/10) 62-71.

(and A. M. Woodward) 'A Journey in South-western Asia Minor', *ABSA* 16 (1909/10) 76-136.

(and E. S. G. Robinson) 'Notes and Inscriptions from Pamphylia', *ABSA* 17 (1910/11) 215-49.

'Prehistoric Remains in South-western Asia Minor. II. The Mounds at Senirdje and Bounarbashi', *ABSA* 18 (1911/12) 80-94.

'A New Astragalos Inscription from Pamphylia', *JHS* 32 (1912) 270-76.

'A Note on the Eastern Trade-route in Asia Minor', *CR* 26 (1912) 76-77.

'Prehistoric Remains in South-western Asia Minor. III', *ABSA* 19 (1912/13) 48-60.

(and E. S. G. Robinson) 'Inscriptions from Lycia', *JHS* 34 (1914) 1-35.

'Greek Inscriptions in the Museum of the Liverpool Royal Institution', *Annals of Archaeology and Anthropology* 6 (1914) 99-108.

'Towers in the Greek Islands', *Annals of Archaeology and Anthropology* 11 (1918) 31-36.

'Ancient Piracy in the Eastern Mediterranean', *Annals of Archaeology and Anthropology* 8 (1921) 105-24.

'The Campaigns of Servilius Isauricus Against the Pirates', *JRS* 12 (1922) 35-56.

Piracy in the Ancient World: an Essay in Mediterranean History. Liverpool: Liverpool University Press, 1924.

'The So-called Lex Gabinia', *CR* 39 (1925) 15-16.

The Liverpool Free School, (1515-1803). Liverpool: Liverpool University Press, 1951.

The Liverpool Royal Institution: a Record and a Retrospect. Liverpool: Liverpool University Press, 1953.

The Early History of the Liverpool Medical School from 1834 to 1877. Liverpool: Liverpool University Press, 1954.

Obituaries, memoirs and studies

The University of Liverpool Roll of Service August 1914 to November 1918 (University Press of Liverpool, 1921); *The Times* 26 November 1964; WWW; *DBC*.

Archive material

Liverpool Univ.

ORR, FRANK GEORGE (B. 1881)

Born, 10 October 1881, 7 Ashton Place, Partick; son of John Orr, a cabinetmaker and master painter, and his wife, Catherine Ross, of 14 Kelvinside Gardens, Glasgow (1898). His later address: 24 Belmont Gardens, Kelvinside.

Admitted to the Glasgow School of Art (1898-1901, 1902-03), Architecture and Modelling.

Architect.

BSR adm. 1904.

BSA adm. 1905-06.
Obituaries, memoirs and studies
DSA.

PARRY, OSWALD HUTTON (1868-1936)

Born, 18 November 1868, Tudor House, Clifton; son of Rev. Edward St John Parry; private
  school master in Stoke Poges, Bucks. (1891), and principal of Leamington Coll.;
  grandon of the Rt. Rev. Thomas Parry, Bishop of Barbados (1843-73); nephew of the
  Rt. Rev. H. H. Parry, Bishop of Perth (1876-93).
Educ. Stoke House, Slough; Charterhouse, Schol.
Oxf. Magdalen Coll.; Exhib. (1887-91); Class. Mods. 2nd (1889); Lit. Hum. 3rd (1891); BA
  (1891); MA (1895).
BSA adm. 1889-90.
Visited Jacobite Syrian Christians of Northern Mesopotamia (1892).
Theological training, Auckland Castle, Durham; Ordained, Church of England (1894); Asst.
  Curate, St Ignatius, Sunderland (1894-97); Archbishop's Missioner to the Nestorian
  Christians (1897-1907); Vicar of All Hallows, East India Dock (1908-21); Bishop of
  Guiana (1921).
War service, Palestine Relief Fund, Palestine and Egypt (1918).
Died, 28 Aug 1936, Georgetown.
Publications
*Six Months in a Syrian Monastery: Being the Record of a Visit to the Head Quarters of the
  Syrian Church in Mesopotamia, With Some Account of the Yazidis or Devil
  Worshippers of Mosul and El Jilwah, Their Sacred Book.* London: Horace Cox, 1895.
The Pilgrim in Jerusalem. London: S.P.C.K., 1920
Obituaries, memoirs and studies
The Times 31 Aug 1936; WWW.

PATERSON, ARCHIBALD (D. 1932)

Univ. of Edinburgh. MA, Classical Literature, 2nd class (1888).
Ordained.
Studied at Rome, Algiers, Constantinople, and at Berlin Univ.
BSA, 1895-96; 'worked at Christian antiquities and attended the University. '
Parish work in Richmond, Surrey (1899).
Berlin, Asst. chaplain (1908-10)
Asst. curate, St Mark's, Kennington (1914-31) under Rev. Dr Darlington.
Died, January 1932, at the Homes of St Barnabas, Dormans, Surrey.
Publications
Assyrian Sculptures: Palace of Sinacherib. The Hague: Nijhoff, 1915.
Obituaries, memoirs and studies
The Times 11 January 1932.

PEET, THOMAS ERIC (1882-1934)

Born, 12 August 1882, Liverpool; son of Thomas Peet, a corn-merchant, and his wife
  Salome Fowler.

Educ. Merchant Taylors' School in Crosby (1893).

Jodrell Scholar (1901), The Queen's College, Oxford. 2nd class in Classical Moderations (1903); 2nd class in Lit. Hum. (1905).

Officer of Egypt Exploration Fund.

BSA adm. 1906-07 (Craven Fell.), 1908-09.

BSR adm. 1909 (Pelham Student).

Lect. in Egyptology, Univ. of Manchester (1913-23).

Brunner Prof. of Egyptology, Univ. of Liverpool (1920-33).

Laycock Studentship in Egyptology, Worcester College, Oxford (1923-24).

War service, Lieutenant, Army Service Corps (1915); Macedonia (November 1915-17); Lieutenant King's (Liverpool) Regiment (1917); 18th Battalion, King's Liverpool Regiment, in BEF, France (June-December 1918).

Married, Mary Florence Lawton (1910), dau. of Richard Johnson Lawton, a civil engineer.

Died, 22 February 1934, Oxford.

Publications

'The Early Aegean Civilization in Italy', *ABSA* 13 (1906/07) 405-22.

'The Early Iron Age in South Italy', *PBSR* 4 (1907) 283-96.

(and A. J. B. Wace, M. S. Thompson) 'The Connection of the Aegean Civilization with Central Europe', *CR* 22 (1908) 233-38.

'Contributions to the Study of the Prehistoric Period in Malta', *PBSR* 5 (1910) 139-63.

'Early Egyptian Influence in the Mediterranean. Was it Responsible for the Megalithic Monuments?' *ABSA* 17 (1910/11) 250-63.

'A Possible Egyptian Dating for the End of the Third Late Minoan Period', *ABSA* 18 (1911/12) 282-85.

'Two Early Greek Vases from Malta', *JHS* 32 (1912) 96-99.

(and T. Ashby, R. N. Bradley, and N. Tagliaferro) 'Excavations in 1908-11 in the Various Megalithic Buildings in Malta and Gozo', *PBSR* 6 (1913) 1-126.

Cemeteries of Abydos. Egypt Exploration Society Memoir, vol. 34. London: Egypt Exploration Society, 1914.

'The Year's Work at Abydos', *JEA* 1 (1914) 37-39.

'Primitive Stone Buildings in Sinai', *Man* 15 (1915) 151-58.

(and T. Ashby, E. T. Leeds) 'The Western Mediterranean', in *Cambridge Ancient History*, vol. 2, 563-601. Cambridge: Cambridge University Press, 1924.

Obituaries, memoirs and studies

The Times 23 February 1934; Gardiner, A. H. 1934. 'Thomas Eric Peet', *JEA* 20: 66-70; *DBC*; Battiscombe Gunn (revised R. S. Simpson), 'Peet, (Thomas) Eric (1882–1934)', in *ODNB*, vol. 43, 435.

Archive material

Oxf. Griffith Institute; Oxf. Bodleian Lib.; Egypt Exploration Society.

PENOYRE, JOHN FFOLIOT BAKER (STALLARD-PENOYRE) (1870-1954)

Born, 10 February 1870, Clifton on Teme; son of Rev. Slade Baker Stallard-Penoyre.

Educ. Cheltenham College.

Oxf. Keble Coll.

Asst. Master, Chigwell School (1896-1900).

Oxford University Extension Lect. (classical art and archaeology).

BSA adm. 1900-01; re-adm. 1906-07, 1907-08.

Sec. and Librarian to the Soc. for the Promotion of Hellenic Studies (1903-36).

Sec. British School at Athens (1903-19); Sec. BSR (1904-12).

War service, Honorary Manager of Comforts Fund known as 'Sweaters' (1914-19); Honorary Manager of Lord Roberts' Field Glass Fund (1915-19) and of the DGVO's Fund for supplying Games, etc., to the Forces (1917-19).

CBE for his work on behalf of the armed forces.

Died, 2 January 1954.

Publications

'Pheneus and the Pheneatike', *JHS* 22 (1902) 228-40.

(and J. H. Hopkinson) 'New Evidence on the Melian Amphorae', *JHS* 22 (1902) 46-75.

'Thasos II', *JHS* 29 (1909) 202-50.

(and M. N. Tod) 'Thasos. Part I. Inscriptions', *JHS* 29 (1909) 91-102.

'Bibliography of the Work of Students, Coming Within the Scope of the School's Work but not Published in the School *Annual*', *ABSA* 17 (1910/11) xxxix-liv.

Obituaries, memoirs and studies

The Times 6 Janury 1954; WWW.

PENROSE, FRANCIS CRANMER (1817-1903)

Born, 29 October 1817, at Bracebridge, near Lincoln; son of the Rev. John Penrose, vicar of Bracebridge, and his wife Elizabeth ('Mrs Markham').

Educ. Bedford Modern Sch. (1825-29); Winchester (1829-35), schol.

Worked with the architect Edward Blore (1835-39).

Camb. Magdalene Coll.; matric. (1838); 10th senior optime, mathematics (1842); BA(1842); MA (1846); Hon. LittD (1898).

Worts Travelling Bachelor, Cambridge Univ. (1842-45): France, Italy, Greece, Switzerland, and Germany.

Hon. fell. Magdalene Coll. (1884).

ARIBA (1846); FRIBA (1848); FRAS (1867); FRS (1894); FSA (1898).

Hon. DCL, Oxford Univ. (1898).

Surveyor, St Paul's Cathedral (1852).

Director, BSA (1886-87; 1890-91, for Ernest Gardner).

Architect and antiquary, Royal Society (1898).

President, RIBA (1894-96).

Night of the order of St Saviour of Greece.

Married, Harriette Gibbs (1856), dau. of Francis Gibbs.

Died, 15 Feb. 1903, at Wimbledon.

Publications

Two letters on Certain Anomalies in the Construction of the Parthenon. London: Published for the Society of Dilettanti, 1847.

An Investigation of the Principles of Athenian Architecture, or, The Results of a Recent Survey, Chiefly Conducted with Reference to the Optical Refinements Exhibited in the Construction of the Ancient Buildings at Athens. London: Longman, 1851.

On a Method of Predicting by Graphical Construction Occultations of Stars by the Moon, and Solar Eclipses, for any Given Place, Together with More Rigorous Methods of Reduction for the Accurate Calculation of Longitude. London: Macmillan, 1869.

'Excavations in Greece, 1886-87', *JHS* 8 (1887) 269-77.

'Mycenae and Tiryns', *The Times* 31 December 1887, 4.

An Investigation of the Principles of Athenian Architecture: or, The Results of a Recent Survey Conducted Chiefly with Reference to the Optical Refinements Exhibited in the Construction of the Ancient Buildings at Athens. London: The Society of Dilettanti, 1888.

'The Fire at Salonica', *The Times* 18 November 1890, 7.

'On the Ancient Hecatompedon Which Occupied the Site of the Parthenon on the Acropolis of Athens', *JHS* 13 (1892) 32-47.

'On the Results of an Examination of the Orientation of a Number of Greek Temples, With a View to Connect These Angles With the Amplitudes of Certain Stars at the Time These Temples Were Founded, and an Endeavour to Derive Therefrom the Dates of Their Foundation by Consideration of the Changes Produced Upon the Right Ascension and Declination of the Stars Arising from the Precession of the Equinoxes', *Proc. of the Royal Society* 53 (1893) 379-84.

'On Some Traces Connected with the Original Entrance of the Acropolis of Athens', *JHS* 15 (1895) 248-50.

'The Parthenon and the Earthquake of 1894', *JRIBA* 3rd ser., 4, 14 (1897) 345-58.

'On the Orientation of Greek Temples, Being the Results of Some Observations Taken in Greece and Sicily, in May, 1898', *Proc. of the Royal Society* 65 (1900) 288-89.

Obituaries, memoirs and studies

J. D. Crace, 'Francis Cranmer Penrose', *RIBA Journal* 10 (1902/03) 339-46; Paul Waterhouse (rev. Roderick O'Donnell), 'Penrose, Francis Cranmer (1817–1903)', in *ODNB* vol. 43, 607-10; *DBC*.

Archive material

RIBA; Camb. Univ. Library; Camb. Magdalene Coll.

PIDDINGTON, JOHN GEORGE (J. G. SMITH) (B. 1869)

Born, 12 August 1869; son of J. G. Smith.

Educ. Eton (Jan. 1882 - July 1888), Mr Radcliffe's house.

Oxf. Magdalen Coll.; Commoner (1888-92); Class. Mods. 2nd (1890); Lit. Hum. 3rd (1892); BA (1892).

BSA adm. 1891-92; re-adm. 1895-96 as Asst to the Dir. .

Published "various papers in the Proceedings of the Society for Psychical Research", and he was Sec. of the same from 1900-6; hon. treasurer (in 1920).

Married, Pauline Flora (d. 1943) (1894), of North End House, Kensington, dau. of Major James St John Munro, late Consul-General at Montevideo.

Assumed surname of Piddington in 1900.

Lost touch with Magdalen Coll. c. 1920s.

Date of death unknown (still alive July 1928).

PIRIE-GORDON, CHARLES HARRY CLINTON, OF BUTHLAW (1883-1969)

Born, 12 February 1883; son of Edward Pirie-Gordon, 12th Laird of Buthlaw, Aberdeenshire.

Educ. Harrow (September 1896-Summer 1900); Grove House.

Oxf. Magdalen Coll.; Commoner (1902-05); Modern History, 3rd; BA (1905); MA (1909).

BSA adm. 1907-08.

Studied in the Vatican library before travelling through Syria (1908), ostensibly looking at Crusader Castles.

Naval Intelligence, 1909 (working with T. E. Lawrence); Autumn 1909 operating between Aleppo and Urfa where he was attacked by Kurdish tribesmen; Occupation in 1911 "Letters".

Member of the Foreign Dept. of the Times (1912-14, 1919-39).

War service, Lieutenant, RNVR (1914); served as Naval Intelligence Officer in Aegean Sea and Gallipoli campaign with ANZAC; promoted to Lt. -Commander, 2 Dec 1915; Civil Administrator, Long Island, Smyrna (April-May 1916); Dir., EMSIB, Salonika (August 1916-January 1917); Member of Political Mission attached to EEF (December 1917-February 1919); Editor of *The Palestine Times*, for the Egyptian Expeditionary Force (1918); Lt. -Col. from 16 Jan 1918; Deputy Commissioner, British Commission for the Baltic Provinces (May-Nov 1919); literary and editorial work for EEF; DSC (1915); Chevalier of the Legion d'Honneur (1918). Second world War, Temporary Civil Officer, Admiralty (1939-55).

Knight Justice of the Venerable Order of the Hospital of St John of Jerusalem; Member of the Royal Company of Archers (1911).

Residence, Gwerndale, Crickhowell, Brecon.

Married, Mabel Alicia Buckle (28 June1910), dau. of George E. Buckle, the Editor of *The Times*, with their honeymoon in Mediterranean (*The Times*, 29 June 1910, 1 July 1910); two sons.

Died, 8 Dec 1969.

Publications

Innocent the Great: an Essay on his Life and Times. London, New York: Longmans Green and Co., 1907.

'The Reigning Princes of Galilee', *English Historical Review* 27 (1912) 445-61.

(and E. H. H. Allenby) *A Brief Record of the Advance of the Egyptian Expeditionary Force Under the Command of General Sir Edmund H. H. Allenby: July 1917 to October 1918*. Cairo: The Government Press and Survey of Egypt, 1919.

A Guide-book to Southern Palestine. Vol. 1. Palestine Pocket Guide-books: Palestine News.

A Guide-book to Central Palestine. Vol. 2. Palestine Pocket Guide-books: Palestine News.

A Guide-book to Northern Palestine and Southern Syria. Vol. 3. Palestine Pocket Guide-books: Palestine News.

A Guide-book to Central Syria, Lebanon, and Phoenicia. Vol. 4. Palestine Pocket Guide-books: Palestine News.

Obituaries, memoirs and studies

The Times 10 December 1969; L. P. Kirwan, 'Obituary: Mr Harry Pirie-Gordon, OBE, DSC, FSA', *Geographical Journal* 136 (1970) 170; D. W. J. Gill, 'Harry Pirie-Gordon:

Historical Research, Journalism and Intelligence Gathering in the Eastern Mediterranean (1908-18)', *Intelligence and National Security* 21 (2006) 1045-59.

Archive material

Private; National Lib. of Scotland.

RADFORD, EVELYN (1887-1969)

Born, 21 January 1887, at Plympton St Mary, Plymouth; dau. of John Heynes Radford, business director, and Edith Mary Pinsent.

Educ. St Felix School, Southwold.

Camb. Newnham Coll. (1905-09); Class. Trip. Pt 1, 3rd div. 1 (1908); Pt 2, 1st archaeology (1909).

Creighton Memorial Prizewinner (1914).

MA (London) (1912).

BSA adm. 1913-14.

War service, Sec. and joint Resident Manager of Industrial Colony for Belgian refugees near Ely (1914-16); Manager of workrooms in Corsica for Serbian Refugees under Serbian Relief fund (1916-17); invalided (June 1917); agricultural work under food Production Dept. (1918-19). Awarded the Order of Saba from Serbian Government.

Music in Cornwall (1919) including the foundation of the Falmouth Opera Singers.

WEA Lect.

MBE for Musical Work.

Died, 30 March 1969.

Publications

'Euphronios and His Colleagues', *JHS* 35 (1915) 107-39.

Obitauries

The Times 7 April 1969 (Frank Howes).

REID, W. W.

Universities of Aberdeen and Edinburgh.

Minister of the Church of Scotland, Dumbarton, N. B.

BSA adm. as holder of Blackie Travelling Studentship (1896-97); 'Worked at Modern Greek, and proceeded to Asia Minor and Cyprus. Assisted in the excavations at Athens.'

REYNOLDS, EDWIN FRANCIS (1875-1949)

Born, 1875, Handsworth, Staffordshire; son of Alfred Reynolds, owner of cut nail manufacturing emporium, and his wife Harriet.

Kensington, Architect's Asst. (in 1901).

BSA adm. 1902-03.

Church architect.

War service, architect to Ministry of Munitions, Factory Branch.

Died, 1949.

Archive

Drawings from Greece, Constantinople and Bursa in RIBA Archive.

RICHARDS, GEORGE CHATTERTON (1867-1951)

Born, 24 August 1867 in Churchover, Warwickshire; son of John Richards, of St Keverne, Cornwall.

Educ. Rugby.

Oxf. Balliol Coll.; Class. Mods. 1st (1887); Lit. Hum. 1st (1889); MA (1892); DD (1924).

BSA adm. 1889-90 (Craven Univ. Fell.); re-adm. 1890-91; Assistant Dir. to D. G. Hogarth (1897).

Fell. Hertford Coll. Oxford (1889-91).

Formerly Prof. of Greek at Univ. College, Cardiff (1891-98); ordained and curate at St John the Baptist, Cardiff (1895-98).

Fell. and tutor of Oriel College (1899-1927); Senior Proctor (1907), Classical Moderator (1902-03, 1909-10).

War service, visitor in local hospitals.

Classical Association, sec. (1920-27).

Vicar of St Mary's, Oxf. (1923-27).

Prof. of Greek, Univ. of Durham (1927-34).

FSA.

Married (1891), in Royston.

Died, 27 January 1951, Oxford.

Publications

'Two Greek Reliefs', *JHS* 11 (1890) 284-85.

(and E. A. Gardner, W. Loring, and W. J. Woodhouse) 'The Theatre at Megalopolis', *JHS* 11 (1890) 294-98.

'Archaic Reliefs at Dhimitzana', *JHS* 12 (1891) 41-45.

(and E. A. Gardner, W. Loring, W. J. Woodhouse, and R. W. Schultz) *Excavations at Megalopolis, 1890-1891*. Society for the Promotion of Hellenic Studies, Supplementary papers, no. 1. London: Society for the Promotion of Hellenic Studies, 1892.

'Selected Vase-fragments from the Acropolis of Athens, Part I', *JHS* 13 (1892/3) 281-92.

'Selected Vase-fragments from the Acropolis of Athens, Part II', *JHS* 14 (1894) 186-97.

'Selected Vase-fragments from the Acropolis of Athens, Part III', *JHS* 14 (1894) 381-87.

'Archaeology in Greece, 1897-98', *JHS* 18 (1898) 328-39.

(and E. Herzog) *An Old-Catholic View of Confession: Being the Pamphlet "Compulsory Auricular Confession, as Practised in the Church of Rome, a Human Invention"*. Church Historical Society Tracts, vol. 83. London: S. P. C. K., under the direction of the Tract Committee, 1905.

(and C. L. Shadwell) *The Provosts and Fellows of Oriel College, Oxford*. Oxford: Blackwell, 1922.

More's Utopia. Oxford: B. Blackwell, 1923.

(and H. E. Salter) *The Dean's Register of Oriel, 1446-1661*. Oxford Historical Society, vol. 84. Oxford: Clarendon Press, 1926.

Jesus Christ Existed- and Exists. Newcastle upon Tyne: s. n., 1928.

A Concise Dictionary to the Vulgate New Testament. London: Samuel Bagster, 1934.

(and E. Clapton) *Our Prayer Book Psalter: Containing Coverdale's Version from his 1535 Bible and the Prayer Book Version by Coverdale from the Great Bible 1539-41 printed side by side*. London: S. P. C. K., 1934.

'Alfred Chilton Pearson, 1861-1935', *PBA* 21 (1935) 449-63.

Cicero: a Study. London: Chatto & Houghton, Windus, 1935.

'Gregory of Nazianzus: the Christian Scholar', *The Durham University Journal* 31 (1939).

'Dion of Prusa', *The Durham University Journal*.

'Strabo: the Anatolian who Failed of Roman Recognition', *G&R* 10 (1941) 79-90.

Baptism and Confirmation. London: Society for Promoting Christian Knowledge, 1942.

An Oxonian Looks Back (1885-1945). n.p.: n.pub., 1960.

Obituaries, memoirs and studies

The Times 30 Jan 1951; *DBC.*

Archive material

Durham Univ. Lib.; British Lib.

RICHTER, GISELA MARIE AUGUSTA (1882-1972)

Born, 15 August 1882, London; dau. of Jean Paul Richter, art historian, and his wife, the dau. of the American Consul at Broussa in Anatolia.

Educ. Florence; Maida Vale High School.

Camb. Girton Coll.; Class. Trip. Pt 1, 2nd div. 3 (1904).

BSA adm. 1904-05.

BSR adm. 1906.

Associate Curator in Dept. of Classical Antiquities, Metropolitan Museum of Art, New York.

War service, War Information Bureau, New York (American Red Cross Association); canteen work, New York (National League for Woman's Service).

Litt. D.

Died, 24 December 1972, Rome.

Publications

'The Distribution of Attic Vases', *ABSA* 11 (1904/05) 224-42.

'The Prehistoric Art of Greece in the Museum', *Bulletin of the Metropolitan Museum of Art* 3 (1908) 22-25, 27-28.

'A New Early Attic Vase', *JHS* 32 (1912) 370-84.

The Metropolitan Museum of Art. Greek, Etruscan, and Roman Bronzes. New York, 1915.

The Metropolitan Museum of Art. Catalogue of Engraved Gems of the Classical Style. New York: Metropolitan Museum of Art, 1920.

'The Subject of the Ludovisi and Boston Reliefs', *JHS* 40 (1920) 113-23.

'Dynamic Symmetry from the Designer's Point of View', *AJA* 26 (1922) 59-73.

'A Neo-Attic Crater in the Metropolitan Museum of Art', *JHS* 45 (1925) 201-09.

Ancient Furniture: a History of Greek, Etruscan, and Roman Furniture. Oxford, 1926.

'The Right Arm of Harmodios', *AJA* 32 (1928) 1-8.

'Silk in Greece', *AJA* 33 (1929) 27-33.

'The Hermes of Praxiteles', *AJA* 35 (1931) 277-90.

'The Greek Kouros in the Metropolitan Museum of Art', *JHS* 53 (1933) 51-53.

'A Roman Copy of the Eleusinian Relief', *Archaiologike Ephemeris* (1937) 20-26.

Archaic Greek Art Against its Historical Background: a Survey. New York, 1949.

'A Lost Fragment by Douris Found Again', *JHS* 69 (1949) 73.

The Metropolitan Museum of Art. The Sculpture and Sculptors of the Greeks, Rev. ed. New Haven, 1950.

'Accidental and Intentional Red Glaze on Athenian Vases', *ABSA* 46 (1951) 143-50.

Three Critical Periods in Greek Sculpture. Oxford: Clarendon Press, 1951.

The Metropolitan Museum of Art. Handbook of the Greek Collection. New York, 1953.

'The Origin of Verism in Roman Portraits', *JRS* 45 (1955) 39-46.

The Metropolitan Museum of Art. Catalogue of Engraved Gems: Greek, Etruscan, and Roman. Rome, 1956.

'Was Roman Art of the First Centuries BC and AD Classicizing?' *JRS* 48 (1958) 10-15.

Archaic Gravestones of Attica. London: Phaidon Press, 1961.

(and D. von Bothmer) *United States of America: the Metropolitan Museum of Art, New York, Attic Black-figured Kylikes*. Corpus Vasorum Antiquorum, Metropolitan Museum of Art, New York, fasc. 3. New York: Metropolitan Museum of Art, 1963.

The Portraits of the Greeks. London: Phaidon, 1965.

The Furniture of the Greeks, Etruscans, and Romans, 2nd ed. London and New York: Phaidon, 1966.

'The Pheidian Zeus at Olympia', *Hesperia* 35 (1966) 166-70.

Korai: Archaic Greek Maidens. A Study of the Development of the Kore Type in Greek Sculpture. London: Phaidon Press, 1968.

'The Department of Greek and Roman Art: Triumphs and Tribulations', *Metropolitan Museum Journal* 3 (1970) 73-95.

Kouroi: Archaic Greek Youths. A Study of the Development of the Kouros Type in Greek Sculpture, 3rd ed. New York: Oxford University Press, 1970.

Perspective in Greek and Roman Art. London and New York: Phaidon, 1970.

The Sculpture and Sculptors of the Greeks, 4th ed. edition. London and New Haven, 1970.

The Portraits of the Greeks, abridged and revised by R. R. R. Smith. London; Ithaca: Phaidon; Cornell University Press, 1984.

Obituaries, memoirs and studies

G. M. A. Richter, *My Memoirs: Recollections of an Archaeologist's Life*. Rome: R. & R. Clark Ltd., 1972; J. S. Crawford, 'Gisela Marie Augusta Richter', in *American National Biography* 18 (1999) 470-71; *DBC*.

ROBINSON, EDWARD STANLEY GOTCH (SIR) (1887-1976)

Born, 4 July 1887, Bristol; 4th son of Edward Robinson, Bristol, a paper manufacturer, and his wife Katherine Francis.

Educ. Tuition from E. J. Seltman, father of Charles Seltman; Clifton School (North Town house for day boys).

Oxf. Christ Church; Schol. (1906); Class. Mod. 1st; BA (1910); MA (1928); hon. D. Litt. (1955). Influenced by Percy Gardner. Barclay Head Prize for Ancient Numismatics.

BSA, School Student, adm. 1910-11; Craven studentship.

Asst. in the Coin and Medal Dept. British Museum (1912-1949); Keeper (1949-52).

War service, 2nd Lieutenant, 3rd Northamptonshire Regiment (March 1915); attached 1st Northamptonshire Regiment (September 1915-July 1916); wounded; temporary duty at the Home Office (April 1917-February 1919); war record indicates Norfolk Regiment.

Elected to a Honorary Studentship at Christ Church (1956).

Knighted (1972); FBA.

Residence, 23 Upper Phillimore Gardens, London W.

Married, Pamela Comfrey Horsley (1917), dau. of Sir Victor Horsley, surgeon.

Died, 13 June 1976.

Publications

(and H. A. Ormerod) 'Notes and Inscriptions from Pamphylia', *ABSA* 17 (1910/11) 215-49.

(and H. A. Ormerod) 'Inscriptions from Lycia', *JHS* 34 (1914) 1-35.

'Coins from Lycia and Pamphylia', *JHS* 34 (1914) 36-46.

Obituaries, memoirs and studies

C. H. V. Sutherland, 'Edward Stanley Gotch Robinson, 1887-1976', *PBA* 63 (1977) 423-40; N. J. Mayhew, 'Robinson, Sir (Edward) Stanley Gotch (1887–1976)', in *ODNB*, vol. 47, 407-08.

Archive material

London UCL.

RODECK, PIETER (B. 1875)

Born, 10 March 1875, Porto Rico, America; nephew of Sir Lawrence Alma-Tadema (Bosanquet, *Letter,* 66).

Educ. Clifton College.

BSA adm. 1896-97.

Travelling student and gold medallist of the Royal Academy.

Architect to Arab Monuments Committee, Cairo.

Publications

'The Ionic Capital of the Gymnasium of Kynosarges', *ABSA* 3 (1896/7) 89-105.

ROSENÖRN-LEHN, BARONESS ERIKKE (B. 1871)

Born, 23 October 1871, Hvidkilde, Denmark; dau. of Baron Erik Christian Hartvig Rosenørn-Lehn.

Royal Holloway Coll., and UCL.

BSA adm. 1901-02.

Publications

Det Nye Testamente efter Vulgata. Roskilde, 1932-33.

SCHULTZ WEIR, ROBERT WEIR (R. W. SCHULTZ) (1860-1951)

Born, 1860, Glasgow, Scotland.

BSA, Gold Medallist and Travelling Student in Architecture of the Royal Academy of Arts (1887-88); re-adm. (1888-89, 1889-90).

Architectural Asst., Edinburgh (1881).

Hon. Sec., Byzantine Research and Publication Fund.

Living in London, with Francis William Troupe, another architect (1901).

War service, Rural District Council Work, National Register, Coal Control, Chairman of Housing Committee.

Died, 1951.

Publications

(and E. A. Gardner) 'The North Doorway of the Erechtheum', *JHS* 12 (1891) 1-16, pls. i-iii.

(and E. A. Gardner, W. Loring, G. C. Richards, and W. J. Woodhouse) *Excavations at Megalopolis, 1890-1891*. Society for the Promotion of Hellenic Studies, Supplementary papers, no. 1. London: Society for the Promotion of Hellenic Studies, 1892.

(and S. H. Barnsley) *The Monastery of Saint Luke of Stiris, in Phocis: and the Dependent Monastery of Saint Nicolas in the Fields, near Skripou, in Boeotia*. London: Macmillan, 1901.

Obituary
Builder 180 (11 May 1951) 663; *The Times* 23 August 1951 (will).
Archive
RIBA.

SCHULTZ, ROBERT WEIR
See Schultz Weir, Robert Weir.

SCUTT, CECIL ALLISON (1889-1961)
Born, 30 January 1889, Wakefield, Yorkshire; son of James Duke Scutt, paper-hanger, and his wife, Emma.

Educ. Wakefield Grammar School.

Camb. Clare Coll.; adm. (1908); Class. Trip. Pt 1, 1st div. 2 (1910); Medieval and Modern Languages, 2nd (1911); Class. Trip. Pt 2, 1st (1912).

BSA adm. 1912-13 (Prendergast Student); re-adm. 1913-14.

Asst. Master, Repton (Two terms: Michaelmas 1915 and Spring 1916).

War service, with guerrillas in Macedonia; 2nd Lieutenant, Officer Interpreter, British Salonika Force (February 1916); Intelligence Officer to a Division (1917); Lieutenant (1918); invalided (1918). Special List, Interpreter, MC.

Appointed Prof. of Classical Philology, Univ. of Melbourne (1920); Dean of the Faculty of Arts (1925-28); retired 1955.

Hon. MA, Univ. of Melbourne (1925)

Married, Lilian Buckley (16 September 1918), Mirfield, Yorkshire.

Died, 26 March 1961, Great Shelford, Cambridge.

Publications
'The Tsakonian Dialect. I', *ABSA* 19 (1912/13) 133-73.

'The Tsakonian Dialect. II', *ABSA* 20 (1913/14) 18-31.

Obituaries, memoirs and studies
Clare College, 93-94; R. Clogg, *Politics and the Academy: Arnold Toynbee and the Koraes Chair*. London: Frank Cass for the Centre for the Centre of Contemporary Greek Studies, King's College, London, 1986; Diane Langmore, 'Scutt, Cecil Allison (1889 - 1961)', *Australian Dictionary of Biography*, vol. 11, Melbourne University Press, 1988, pp 558-59.

SELLERS, EUGÉNIE (MRS A. ARTHUR STRONG) (1860-1943)
Born, 25 March 1860, London; dau. of Frederick William Sellers, wine-merchant, and his wife Anna (née Oates), originally from Messina, Sicily.

Camb. Girton Coll.; Class. Trip. Pt 1, 3rd div. 3 (1882).

Private tutoring, London.

BSA adm. 1890-91.

Studied in Germany.

Librarian, Duke of Devonshire (1904-08), in succession to her husband.

BSR, Asst. Dir. (1909-25).

War service, Acting-Dir. of the BSR during the absence of the Director (1914-19).

Life Research Fell. Girton Coll. (1910).

CBE (1927); Serena Gold Medal for Italian Studies, British Academy.

Married, Sandford Arthur Strong (1863-1904) (1897), librarian to the Duke of Devonshire.

Died, 16 September 1943, Rome.

Publications

List in S. L. Dyson, *Eugénie Sellers Strong: Portrait of an Archaeologist*. London: George Duckworth, 2004.

'The Theatre at Megalopolis', *CR* 5 (1891) 239-40.

'Three Attic Lekythoi from Etretria', *JHS* 13 (1892/3) 1-12.

'Greek Head in the Possession of T. Humphry Ward, Esq', *JHS* 14 (1894) 198-205.

Commentary and Historical Introduction to the Elder Pliny's Chapter on the History of Art Translated by K. Jex-Blake. London, 1896.

Roman Sculpture from Augustus to Constantine. London, 1907.

Apotheosis and After Life: Three Lectures on Certain Phases of Art and Religion in the Roman Empire. London, 1915.

Obituaries, memoirs and studies

The Times 21 September 1943; G. Scott Thompson, *Mrs Arthur Strong: a Memoir*. London: Cohen & West, 1949; *DBC*; J. M. C. Toynbee (revised Stephen L. Dyson), 'Strong , Eugénie (1860-1943)', in *ODNB*, vol. 53, 97-98; S. L. Dyson, *Eugénie Sellers Strong: Portrait of an Archaeologist*. London: George Duckworth, 2004.

Archive material

Camb. Girton Coll.; Camb. King's Coll.; BSR; Harvard University Center for Italian Renaissance Studies; London LSE; Oxf. Bodleian Lib.

SHEEPSHANKS, ARTHUR CHARLES (1884-1961)

Born, 5 April 1884, London; son of William Sheepshanks.

Educ. Eton; Mr Vaughan's, (December 1897 - March 1901).

Camb. Trinity Coll.; adm. pens. (25 June 1903); Class. Trip. 2 div. 1 (1906); Law Special, 2nd (1906); BA (1906), MA (1920).

BSA adm. 1907-08.

BSR adm. 1907.

Asst. Master at Eton (1906-1938).

War service, commission in 8th (S.) Battalion (The Prince Consort's Own) Rifle Brigade (1914); Captain (1 November 1914 t/Captain); DSO (1915); Major (16 Dec. 1915 t/Major); Lieut. -Colonel (4 Oct. 1917 acting Lt.-Col); Asst. Instructor, Army Infantry School (24 Feb 1918); (8 Oct 1918, honorary Lt. -Col.); Twice mentioned in despatches.

OTC, Eton Coll. Contingent, Lt. -Col. (23 Sept 1919).

Deputy Lieutenant for the West Riding of Yorkshire; Chairman of Ripon Diocesan Board of Finance (1950-56); JP; County Dir. of the West Yorkshire Branch of the British Red Cross Soc. (1939-1961).

Died, 4 April 1961

Obituaries, memoirs and studies

London Gazette suppl. 25 Nov. 1914, 9962; suppl. 6 Sept. 1915, 8840; suppl. 15 April 1916, 4001; suppl. 29 Nov 1917, 12497; suppl. 27 June 1918, 7574; suppl. 6 Nov 1918, 13092; suppl. 22 Nov 1919, 11793; *The Times* 6 April 1961, 11 April 1961, 12 April 1961.

SIKES, EDWARD ERNEST (1867-1940)

Born, 26 April 1867, at Halstead, Kent; son of the Rev. Thomas Burr Sikes, Vicar of Burstow, Surrey, and his wife Frances Henrietta Alkin.

Educ. Aldenham (the Rev. J. Kennedy).

Camb. St John's Coll.; adm. pens. (May 1, 1886); Bell Schol. (1887); Schol. (1888); Class. Trip. Pt 1, 1st (1889); Pt 2, 1st archaeology (1890); BA (1889); Browne Medal (Latin Ode) (1889); MA (1893).

BSA adm. 1890-91 (Cambridge Studentship).

Asst. Master at Winchester (1890-91).

Fell. St John's Coll. (1891-1940); tutor (1900-25); President (1925-37).

President of the Univ. Philological Soc. (1920).

War service, private, CUOTC, and 1st Battalion Cambridge Volunteer Regiment (1914-19).

Visiting Prof. at Harvard Univ. (1926-7).

Donor, with his brother, Francis Henry, of the Sikes collection of British mollusca to the Natural History Museum, S. Kensington.

Resided at Newnham Grove, Cambridge.

Married, Mabel Katherine Garrett (b. 1874) (11 April 1901), in Guildford, Surrey, youngest dau. of George Mursell Garrett, Mus. D., organist of St John's.

Died, 5 Feb. 1940, at Bournemouth.

Publications

'Folk-Lore in the "Works and Days" of Hesiod', *CR* 7 (1893) 389-94.

'Further Note on Hesiod, op. et Dies. 746-7', *CR* 7 (1893) 45.

'Nike and Athena Nike', *CR* 9 (1895) 280-83.

Aeschylus, *Prometheus Vinctus*. London: Macmillan, 1898.

(and T. W. Allen) *The Homeric hymns*. London: Macmillan, 1904.

'Four-footed man: a Note on Greek Anthropology', *Folklore* 20 (1909) 421-31.

The Anthropology of the Greeks. London: D. Nutt, 1914.

(trans.) Musaeus, *Hero and Leander*. London: Methuen, 1920.

Roman Poetry. London: Methuen, 1923.

The Greek View of Poetry. London: Methuen, 1931.

Lucretius, Poet & Philosopher. Cambridge: Cambridge University Press, 1936.

'The Humour of Homer', *CR* 54 (1940) 121-27.

Obituaries, memoirs and studies

The Times 7 February 1940; Venn; WWW.

Archive material

Camb. St John's Coll. Lib.

SMITH, CECIL HARCOURT- (SIR) (1859-1944)

Born, 11 Sept. 1859, at Staines, Middlesex; son of William Smith, solicitor, and his wife
    Harriet.

Educ. Winchester (1873-78); schol.

Dept. of Greek & Roman Antiquities, British Museum (1879); assistant keeper (1896);
    keeper (1904).

Secondment, diplomatic mission to Persia (1887).

Secondment, Director BSA (1895-97).

Founder editor of *The Classical Review* (1887).

Editor, *BSA* (1895-1909).

Knighted (1909), CVO (1917), KCVO (1934).

Chairman, Committee on the Reorganization of the South Kensington Museum (1908).

Director and Secretary, Victoria & Albert Museum (1909-24).

Adviser, Royal Art Collection (1925).

Surveyor, Royal Works of Art (1928-36).

Hon. Sec. Society of Dilettanti.

Married, Alice Edith Watson (1892), dau. of H. W. Watson.

Harcourt-Smith in use by 1892; continued to publish under Smith until c. 1908.

Hon. LLD, Univ. of Aberdeen (1895); Hon. DLitt, Univ. of Oxford (1928).

Died, 27 March 1944, at Bramley, Surrey.

***Publications* (as C. Smith and C. Harcourt-Smith)**

'An Archaic Vase with Representation of a Marriage Procession', *JHS* 1 (1880) 202-09.

'Kylix with Exploits of Theseus', *JHS* 2 (1881) 57-64.

'Corrigenda: Inscriptions on Two Vases', *JHS* 2 (1881) 225-26.

'Actors with Bird-masks on Vases', *JHS* 2 (1881) 309-14.

(and D. Comparetti) 'The Petelia Gold Tablet', *JHS* 3 (1882) 111-18.

'Vase With Representation of Herakles and Geras', *JHS* 4 (1883) 96-110.

'Inscriptions from Rhodes', *JHS* 4 (1883) 136-41, 351-53.

'Amphora-stopping from Tarentum', *JHS* 4 (1883) 158-61, 436.

'Pyxis: Herakles and Geryon', *JHS* 5 (1884) 176-84.

'Four Archaic Vases from Rhodes', *JHS* 5 (1884) 220-40.

'Early Paintings of Asia Minor', *JHS* 6 (1885) 180-91.

'Vases from Rhodes with Incised Inscriptions', *JHS* 6 (1885) 371-77.

'Nike Sacrificing a Bull', *JHS* 7 (1886) 275-85.

'Two Vase Pictures of Sacrifices', *JHS* 9 (1888) 1-10.

(and E. L. Hicks) 'Theangela', *CR* 3 (1889) 139-40.

'A Protokorinthian Lekythos in the British Museum', *JHS* 11 (1890) 167-80.

'Orphic Myths on Attic Vases', *JHS* 11 (1890) 343-51.

'The Site of Olba in Cilicia', *CR* 4 (1890) 185-86.

(and F. L. Griffith) 'An Early Graeco-Egyptian Bilingual Dedication', *CR* 5 (1891) 75-77.

'Harpies in Greek art', *JHS* 13 (1892/3) 103-14.

'Deme Legends on Attic Vases', *JHS* 13 (1892/3) 115-20.

(and C. Torr) 'Egypt and Mycenaean Antiquities', *CR* 6 (1892) 462-66.

'Note on Additions to the Greek Sculptures in the British Museum', *CR* 6 (1892) 475.

(and A. S. Murray) *Designs from Greek Vases in the British Museum*. London: British Museum, 1894.

'Polledrara Ware', *JHS* 14 (1894) 206-23.

'A Vase in Form of a Bust of Athene', *JHS* 15 (1895) 184-87.

'The Myth of Ixion', *CR* 9 (1895) 277-80.

'A Kylix with a New KALOS Name', *JHS* 16 (1896) 285-87.

'Archaeology in Greece, 1895-6', *ABSA* 2 (1895/96) 47-62.

'Excavations in Melos', *ABSA* 2 (1895/96) 63-76.

Vases of the Finest Period. Catalogue of the Greek and Etruscan Vases in the British Museum, vol. 3. London: British Museum, 1896.

'Archaeology in Greece, 1895-6', *JHS* 16 (1896) 335-56.

'Excavations in Melos, 1897', *ABSA* 3 (1896/97) 1-30.

'A New Copy of the Athena Parthenos', *ABSA* 3 (1896/7) 121-48.

'Panathenaic Amphorae; and a Delos Mosaic', *ABSA* 3 (1896/7) 182-200.

'The Crucifixion on a Greek Gem', *ABSA* 3 (1896/7) 201-06.

'Inscriptions from Melos', *JHS* 17 (1897) 1-21.

'The Torch Race of Bendis', *CR* 13 (1899) 230-32.

'Trojan "Brushes"', *CR* 14 (1900) 140-41.

'A Proto-Attic Vase', *JHS* 22 (1902) 29-45.

(and R. de Rustafjaell) 'Inscriptions from Cyzicus', *JHS* 22 (1902) 190-207.

(and G. A. Macmillan, HRH The Crown Prince of Greece, M. T. Homolle, A. Conze, J. R. Wheeler, R. C. Bosanquet, and C. Waldstein) 'The Penrose Memorial Library', *ABSA* 10 (1903/04) 232-42.

(and T. D. Atkinson, R. C. Bosanquet, C. C. Edgar, A. J. Evans, D. G. Hogarth, D. Mackenzie) *Excavations at Phylakopi in Melos*. Society for the Promotion of Hellenic Studies, Occasional Paper 4. London, 1904.

'The Central Groups of the Parthenon Pediments', *JHS* 27 (1907) 242-48.

'Recent Additions to the Parthenon Sculptures', *JHS* 28 (1908) 46-48.

(and C. Amy Hutton) *Catalogue of the Antiquities (Greek, Etruscan and Roman) in the Collection of the Late Wyndham Francis Cook, Esquire*. London: privately printed, 1908.

The Collection of J. Pierpont Morgan. Paris: Librairie centrale des beaux-arts, 1913.

Inscriptions Suggested for War Memorials. London: Victoria & Albert Museum, 1919.

'Whip-Tops', *JHS* 49 (1929) 217-19.

(and G. A. Macmillan) *The Society of Dilettanti: its Regalia and Pictures*. London: Macmillan, 1932.

Obituaries, memoirs and studies

'A Great Museum Director', *The Times* 16 Jan. 1925, 8; *The Times* 29 March 1944, 7; *DBC*; James Laver (rev. Dennis Farr), 'Smith, Sir Cecil Harcourt- (1859–1944)', *ODNB*, vol. 51, 57-58.

Archive material

Royal Institute of British Architexts; Durham Univ.; Victoria & Albert Museum.

SMITH, JOHN GEORGE

See Piddington, John George.

SMITH, RAVENSCROFT ELSEY (1859-1930)

Born, 1859, Forest Hill, London; son of Thomas Roger Smith (1830-1903), architect (and Prof. of architecture at UCL from 1880), and his wife Catherine, dau. of Joseph Elsey.

Slade School, UCL (1877-78).

BSA adm. 1887-88 (RIBA studentship).

ARIBA (1889), FRIBA (1904).

Partner with his father, Thomas Roger Smith.

Prof. of Architecture, King's Coll., London (1900-13); Prof. Architecture and Construction, UCL (1913-20).

Died, 26 December 1930, Horsell, Woking, Surrey.

Publications

(and E. A. Gardner, D. G. Hogarth, and M. R. James) 'Excavations in Cyprus, 1887-8. Paphos, Leontari, Amargetti', *JHS* 9 (1888) 147-271.

'Report of a Tour in Greece and Cyprus', *Transactions of the RIBA* (1890).

Obituaries, memoirs and studies

Builder 140 (16 Jan 1931) 159; *RIBA Journal* 38 (1931) 268; *DBA*. For his father, see Paul Waterhouse (revised John Elliott), 'Smith, Thomas Roger (1830-1903)', in *ODNB*.

SMITH, SOLOMON CHARLES KAINES (1876-1958)

Born, 3 August 1876, south Australia; son of Arthur William Smith, medical doctor.

Educ. St Paul's School.

Camb. Magdalene Coll.; adm. pens. (Aug. 1, 1895); Class. Trip. Pt 2, 1st archaeology (1899); BA (1898); MA (1902).

BSA adm. 1899-1900 (Cambridge Studentship).

Official Lect. at the National Gallery (1914-16).

War service, Major; General Staff (Censor's Dept.) at Salonika and Advisory Officer to the Greek Government; MBE. (1919); mentioned in despatches; Officer of the Redeemer (Greece); Military Merit (Greece). Aegean Postal Censor.

Lect. in archaeology, Magdalene Coll., Cambridge (1922-24).

Dir. of the City Art Gallery, Leeds (1924-27).

Keeper of the City Museum and Art Gallery, Birmingham (1927-41).

Member of Advisory Council, Victoria and Albert Museum (1933-41).

Keeper, Cook Collection, Richmond, Surrey (1941-52).

Life Trustee of Shakespeare's birthplace.

FSA (1925).

Married (1910), in London; one daughter.

Died, 29 June 1958, Bath.

Publications

The Elements of Greek Worship. London: F. Griffiths, 1906.

Greek Art and National Life. London: J. Nisbet, 1913.

Looking at Pictures. London: Methuen & Co., 1913.

Obituaries, memoirs and studies

The Times 1 July 1958; Venn; WWW.

Archive material

Trinity Coll. Dublin.

SPILSBURY, ALFRED JOHN (1874-1940)

Born, 10 September 1874; son of Edward Spilsbury of 77 Graham Road, Dalston, London, N.

Educ. Hertford and Christ's Hospital (for nearly 11 years under Rev. Richard Lee); Senior Grecian.

Oxf. The Queen's Coll.; adm. schol. 12 October 1893; Jodrell Scholar (reserved for those studying Divinity, Classics, or Mathematics); Class. Mod. 1st (1895); Lit. Hum. 2nd (1897).

BSA adm. 1897-98 (Oxford Studentship).

Sixth form tutor and house tutor, Brighton Coll. (1898-1900).

Senior Classical Master, City of London School (for 16 years).

Headmaster of Haberdashers' Aske's School, Hampstead.

Head Master of Wakefield Grammar School (1917-39).

Married, Ida Kaiya Burnblum (b. 1876) (1901), of Lille and Oxford.

Died, 17 October 1940.

Obituaries, memoirs and studies

The Times October 24, 1940; WWW.

STAINER, JOHN FREDERICK RANDALL (1866-1939)

Born, 2 Oct 1866; son of Sir John Stainer, the composer.

Educ. Winchester.

Oxf. Magdalen Coll.; Exhib. (1885-9); Class. Mod. 1st (1887); Lit. Hum. 2nd (1889); BA (1889); MA; BCL (1892); Coxed Coll. First Eight (1888), when it went Head of the River.

BSA adm. 1889-90.

Barrister in 1911.

War service, served as Sergeant with the East Surreys (1914-19).

Chief Examiner, Passport Offic, (1922-31).

Hon. Sec. Musicians' Company.

MBE.

Residence, The Old Rectory, Ashstead, Surrey.

Married (1906).

Died, 6 June 1939.

STOKES, JOHN LAURENCE (1881-1948)

Born, 2 January 1881, at Garden Walk, New Chesterton, Cambridge; eldest son of the Rev. Augustus Sidney Stokes (1868), Vicar of Elm, Cambs.

Educ. Perse, Cambridge, and Charterhouse.

Camb. Pembroke Coll.; adm. (Oct. 1899); Class. Trip. Pt 1, 1st (1902); Pt 2. 2nd (1903); BA (1902); MA (1928).

BSA adm. 1903-04 (as holder of the Prior Schol. from Pembroke Coll.).

On editorial staff of Messrs Blackie and Son (in 1905).

Librarian at Charterhouse School (1905-47).

War service, harvest work.

Died, 10 Sept. 10, 1948, at Charterhouse. Benefactor to Pembroke Coll.

Publications
'Stamped Pithos-fragments from Cameiros', *ABSA* 12 (1905/06) 71-79.
Obituaries, memoirs and studies
The Times 13 September 1948 (notice); Venn.

STRONG, EUGÉNIE
See Sellers, Eugénie.

STUART-JONES, HENRY
See Jones, Henry Stuart.

TAYLOR, MARY NORAH LUTON (MRS M. N. L. BRADSHAW) (B. 1890-1967)
Born, 1890, Birmingham; dau. of Prof. John W. Taylor (1851-1910), FRCS, gynaecologist,
    and his wife, Florence Maberly Buxton.
Camb. Newnham Coll.; Class. Trip. Pt 1, 1st div. 3 (1912); Pt 2, 1st archaeology (1913).
BSA adm. 1913-14.
BSR adm. 1913; 1914 (Gilchrist Schol.).
Married, Harold Chalton Bradshaw (1893-1943) (1918), Rome Scholar in Fine Arts (1913),
    and later secretary of the Royal Fine Art Commission.
Died, 4 January 1967.
Publications
(and H. C. Bradshaw) 'Architectural Terracottas from Two Temples at Falerii Veteres',
    PBSR 8 (1916) 1-34.
Obituary
The Times 6 January 1967 (death notice). (For H. C. Bradshaw) *The Times* 16 October 1943.

TENNANT, LILIAN ELIZABETH (MRS F. J. WATSON-TAYLOR) (1884-1946)
Born, 1884, Kensington; dau. of John Tennant, barrister, hon. secretary for the Cambridge
    University Mission to Delhi, and hon. treasurer of the Institute for Massage by the
    Blind, of 19 The Boltons, London, SW.
BSA adm. 1910-11.
Married, Felix John Watson-Taylor (7 October 1913), Haughton Grove, Jamaica.
Died, 25 March 1946, at 42 Southwood Lane, Highgate.

THOMPSON, MAURICE SCOTT (1884-1971)
Born, 12 January 1884, in Upper Tooting, Surrey; son of A. Thompson, senior partner in W.
    J. & H. Thompson (brokers).
Educ. Haileybury (1898-1903).
Oxf. Corpus Christi Coll.; Class. Mod. 3rd (1905); Lit. Hum. 2nd(1907); MA (1912).
BSA adm. 1907-08 (Holder of Charles Oldham Univ. Schol.), 1908-09, 1909-10 (1908-10,
    Craven Fell.), 1910-11.
Lect. in Ancient History, Armstrong Coll., Newcastle upon Tyne (1912).
War service, commission in 14th Durham Light Infantry (1914); served in BEF, France
    (1915-16), temporary Captain; Intelligence Officer, 16th Corps, British Salonika Force

(March 1916); Major; GHQ Salonika and Constantinople (1918-19). MC. Four times mentioned in despatches.

OBE.

Married, Violette Rutledge (1917), dau. of Thomas Rutledge, at St Mary's church, Kippington.

Died, 10 March 1971, Reigate, Surrey.

Publications

(and A. J. B. Wace, J. P. Droop) 'Excavations at Zerélia, Thessaly', *ABSA* 14 (1907/08) 197-223.

(and T. E. Peet, A. J. B. Wace) 'The Connection of the Aegean Civilization With Central Europe', *CR* 22 (1908) 233-38.

(and A. J. B. Wace, J. P. Droop) 'Laconia I. Excavations at Sparta, 1909. § 6. The Menelaion', *ABSA* 15 (1908/09) 108-57.

(and A. J. B. Wace) 'A Cave of the Nymphs on Mount Ossa', *ABSA* 15 (1908/09) 243-47.

'The Asiatic or Winged Artemis', *JHS* 29 (1909) 286-307.

(and A. J. B. Wace) 'A Latin Inscription from Perrhaebia', *ABSA* 17 (1910/11) 193-204.

(and D. G. Hogarth, E. A. Gardner, J. L. Myres, B. Nopsca, A. Stein, J. P. Droop, F. R. Maunsell, A. M. Woodward, and A. J. B. Wace) 'The Distribution of Early Civilization in Northern Greece: Discussion', *Geographical Journal* 37 (1911) 636-42.

(and A. J. B. Wace) 'Excavations at Halos', *ABSA* 18 (1911/12) 1-29.

(and A. J. B. Wace) *Prehistoric Thessaly: Being Some Account of Recent Excavations and Explorations in North-eastern Greece from Lake Kopais to the Borders of Macedonia.* Cambridge Archaeological and Ethnological Series. Cambridge: Cambridge University Press, 1912.

(and A. J. B. Wace) *The Nomads of the Balkans: an Account of Life and Customs Among the Vlachs of Northern Pindus.* London: Methuen, 1914.

Obituaries, memoirs and studies

Haileybury Register; *Faces of Archaeology* 108-14 no. 20; *DBC*.

Archive material

Oxf. Bodleian Lib.

TILLARD, LAURENCE BERKLEY (1888-1943)

Born, 11 August 1888, 1 St Chad's Gardens, Headingley, Leeds; son of John Tillard, HM Inspector of Schools, and Mabel Katherine Berkley.

Educ. King Edward VI Grammar School, Norwich (1889-1902); Aldenham School (1902-06).

Camb. St John's Coll. (1906); Class. Trip. Pt 1, 1st (1909); Pt 2, 1st history (1910); BA (1909); tutor, E. E. Sikes.

Cambridge, Footlights Review (cast, 1907; Hon. Sec., 1908; president, 1909).

BSA adm. 1910-11.

Called to the Bar, Inner Temple (1914). Barrister.

War service, Captain, 6th (City of London) Battalion, The London Regiment (City of London Rifles) (1914-18); 2nd Lt. (24 September 1914); temporary Captain; Lt. (temporary Captain) (10 December 1915); Captain (1 June 1916); seconded as Asst. Instructor (3 May 1917) (*London Gazette* 13 October 1914; 1 August 1916; 7 March

1917; 14 November 1917); served in France and Belgium; in 1916 the unit became part of the King's Royal Rifle Corps.

Married, Aline Dickerson Elliott (1 June 1922), St Paul's, Knightsbridge.

Died, 12 February 1943.

Publications

'The Fortifications of Phokis', *ABSA* 17 (1910/11) 54-75.

Obituaries, memoirs and studies

Register of Twentieth-Century Johnians, Volume 1, 1900-1949; G. V. Carey, (ed.), *The War List of the University of Cambridge 1914-1918,* Cambridge: CUP, 1921.

TILLYARD, EUSTACE MANDEVILLE WETENHALL (1889-1962)

Born, 19 May 1889, Cambridge; son of Isaac Alfred Tillyard, classics master at The Leys, Cambridge, and Catherine S. Wetenhall.

Educ. College Cantonal, Lausanne; Perse, Cambridge (pupil of Dr Rouse).

Camb. Jesus Coll.; adm. Schol. (October 1908); Class. Trip. Pt 1, 1st div. 3 (1910); Pt 2, 1st (1911); BA (1911); MA (1915); Litt. D. (1933).

Craven Student.

BSA adm. 1911-12.

Prize Fellowship, Jesus Coll., Cambridge (1912-14), working on the Hope Vases.

Fell. Jesus Coll. (1913-15, 1934-45, 1959-62); Dir. of Studies in English (1934); Senior Tutor (1941); Master (1945-59). University Lect. in English (1926-54). Expert on Milton and Shakespeare.

War service, commission in 4th Royal Lancashire Regiment, Captain (1915); BEF, France (1915-16); seconded to Salonica Force (1916-19), Intelligence corps, 1917-18), British Liaison Officer with Greek GHQ (1918-19).

OBE; Greek MC; mentioned in despatches three times.

FBA (1952).

Married, Phyllis Cooke (1919), dau. of Henry M. Cooke.

Died, 24 May 1962, Cambridge.

Publications

'Theseus, Sinis, and the Isthmian Games', *JHS* 33 (1913) 296-312.

The Athenian Empire and the Great Illusion. Cambridge: Bowes & Bowes, 1914.

'A Cybele altar in London', *JRS* 7: (1917) 284-88.

The Hope Vases: a Catalogue and a Discussion of the Hope Collection of Greek Vases With an Introduction on the History of the Collection and on Late Attic and South Italian Vases. Cambridge: Cambridge University Press, 1923.

Obituaries, memoirs and studies

The Times 25 May 1962; *Jesus College, Cambridge Society Report* (1945) 80-81; (1959) 41-43; (1962) 31-33 (obituary); WWW.

Archive material

Camb. Jesus Coll. Lib.

TILLYARD, HENRY JULIUS WETENHALL (1881-1968)

Born, 18 November 1881, in Station Road, Cambridge; eldest son of Isaac Alfred Tillyard. newspaper proprietor, of Fordfield, the Avenue, Cambridge, and his wife Catharine Sarah Wetenhall.

Educ. Tonbridge School.

Camb. Gonville and Caius Coll.; adm. (1 October 1900); Schol.; Class. Trip, Pt 1, 1ˢᵗ (1902); Pt 2, 1ˢᵗ (1904); BA (1904); MA (1910).

D. Litt., Edin., 1919.

BSA, 1904-05 (Asst. Librarian); re-adm. 1905-06 (studentship), 1906-07, 1908-09; re-adm. 1912-13. Craven Fund: 1906/07.

BSR adm. 1905.

Lect. in Greek, Edinburgh Univ. (1908-17); Research Fell. Edinburgh Univ. with grant from Carnegie Trust.

Civil prisoner of war, Ruhleben concentration camp (1914-15).

Asst. Master at Tonbridge School (1918-19).

Prof. of Latin, Univ. Coll., Johannesburg (1919-21).

Prof. of Russian, Birmingham Univ. (1921-26).

Prof. of Greek, Univ. Coll., Cardiff (1926-46).

Temporary Lect. in Classics, Rhodes Univ., Grahamstown (1947-49).

Married, Wilhelmina Kaufmann (1913), of Lahr, Baden.

Residence (in 1953), 15 Brooklands Avenue, Cambridge.

Died, 2 January 1968.

Publications

'Boundary and Mortgage Stones from Attica', *ABSA* 11 (1904/05) 63-71.

'Laconia II. Geraki. 3. Inscriptions', *ABSA* 11 (1904/05) 105-12.

(and A. J. B. Wace) 'Laconia. Historical Note', *ABSA* 11 (1904/05) 112-23.

'Laconia II. Excavations at Sparta, 1906. § 9. Inscriptions from the Artemisium', *ABSA* 12 (1905/06) 351-93.

'Laconia II. Excavations at Sparta, 1906. § 14. Inscriptions from the Altar, the Acropolis, and Other Sites', *ABSA* 12 (1905/06) 441-79.

'Two Watch Towers in the Megarid', *ABSA* 12 (1905/06) 101-08.

(and M. N. Tod, A. M. Woodward) 'Laconia I. Excavations at Sparta, 1907. § 10. The Inscriptions', *ABSA* 13 (1906/07) 174-218.

'Instrumental Music in the Roman Age', *JHS* 27 (1907) 160-69.

Agathocles. Prince Consort Dissertation. Cambridge: Cambridge University Press, 1908.

'The Acclamation of Emperors in Byzantine Ritual', *ABSA* 18 (1911/12) 239-60.

'Fragment of a Byzantine Musical Handbook in the Monastery of Laura on Mt. Athos', *ABSA* 19 (1912/13) 95-117.

Greek Literature. The People's Books. London; New York: T. C. & E. C. Jack: Dodge Pub. Co., 1914

'Rhythm in Byzantine Music', *ABSA* 21 (1914/16) 125-47.

'The Problem of Byzantine Neumes', *AJA* 20 (1916) 62-71.

'The Modes in Byzantine Music', *ABSA* 22 (1916/18) 133-56.

'Some Byzantine Musical Manuscripts at Cambridge', *ABSA* 23 (1918/19) 194-205.

'The Problem of Byzantine Neumes', *JHS* 41 (1921) 29-49.

The Plays of Roswitha. London: Faith Press, 1923.

Byzantine Music and Hymnography. London: Faith Press, 1923.

'Signatures and Cadences of the Byzantine Modes', *ABSA* 26 (1923/24, 1924/25) 78-87.

'A Byzantine Musical Handbook at Milan', *JHS* 46 (1926) 219-22.

Handbook of the Middle Byzantine Musical Notation. Copenhagen: Levin & Munksgaard, 1935.

'Correction', *JHS* 56 (1936) 80.

'Keep Up Your Latin', *G&R* 16 (1947) 120-21.

'Suggestions for an Adult Beginner's Latin Reader', *G&R* 2nd series. 9 (1962) 67-71.

Obituaries, memoirs and studies

The Times 9 January 1968; Venn; WWW.

TOD, MARCUS NIEBUHR **(1878-1974)**

Born, 24 November 1878, Highgate; 2nd son of John Tod, tea marchant, and his wife Gertrude von Niebuhr.

Educ. Merchant Taylors' School, London.

Oxf. St John's Coll.; Class. Mod. 1st (1897); Lit. Hum. (1901); MA (1905).

University Lect. in Greek Epigraphy (1907); Reader (1927).

BSA adm. 1901-02 (Senior Studentship). Asst. Dir. (1902-04).

Craven Univ. Fell.

Fell. Oriel Coll. (1903); Librarian; Senior tutor; Vice-Provost (1934-45); Hon. Fell. (1947).

Hon. Fell. St John's Coll. Oxf. (1946).

War service, YMCA work in France (July-September 1915); Clerk in Ministry of Munitions (November 1915); commissioned 2nd Lieutenant, Interpreters Corps, Salonika Field Force (November 1915); 2nd Lt. in Salonika working with Ernest Gardner (end of 1915); the Intelligence Corps attached to the French Sector (August 1916); Captain (July 1917); mentioned in despatches three times; Croix de Guerre (avec palmes).

MBE; FBA (1929).

Married, Mabel Bowker Byrom (1887–1973) (1909), dau. of George F. Byrom, cotton-mill owner, of Manchester.

Died, 21 February 1974, in Sheldon Hospital, Rubery

Publications

'Some Unpublished "Catalogi Paterarum Argentearum"', *ABSA* 8 (1901/02) 197-230.

(and R. C. Bosanquet) 'Archaeology in Greece, 1901-1902', *JHS* 22 (1902) 378-94.

(and R. M. Dawkins) 'Excavations at Palaikastro. II. § 9. Kouraménos', *ABSA* 9 (1902/03) 329-35.

'Excavations at Palaikastro. II. § 10. Hagios Nikolaos', *ABSA* 9 (1902/03) 336-43.

'An Unpublished Attic Decree', *ABSA* 9 (1902/03)154-75.

'A New Fragment of the Attic Tribute Lists', *ABSA* 10 (1903/04) 78-82.

'Teams of Ball-players at Sparta', *ABSA* 10 (1903/04) 63-77.

'A New Fragment of the "Edictum Diocletiani"', *JHS* 24 (1904) 195-202.

'Inscriptions from Eumeneia', *ABSA* 11 (1904/05) 27-31.

'Notes and Inscriptions from South-western Messenia', *JHS* 25 (1905) 32-55.

(and A. J. B. Wace) *A Catalogue of the Sparta Museum*. Oxford, 1906.

(and H. J. W. Tillyard, A. M. Woodward) 'Laconia I. Excavations at Sparta, 1907. § 10. The Inscriptions', *ABSA* 13 (1906/07) 174-218.

'A Statute of an Attic Thiasos', *ABSA* 13 (1906/07) 328-38.

(and J. Baker-Penoyre) 'Thasos. Part I. Inscriptions', *JHS* 29 (1909) 91-102.

'Thoinarmostria', *JHS* 32 (1912) 100-04.

'Three Greek Numeral Systems', *JHS* 33 (1933) 27-34.

'Notes on Inscriptiones Graecae V. 1', *JHS* 34 (1914) 60-63.

'The Progress of Greek Epigraphy, 1913-14', *JHS* 34 (1914) 321-31.

'Notes on Some Inscriptions from Asia Minor', *CR* 29 (1915) 1-4.

'On an Archaic Thessalian Epigram', *CR* 29 (1915) 196-97.

'The Progress of Greek Epigraphy, 1914-15', *JHS* 35 (1915) 260-70.

'The Progress of Greek Epigraphy, 1915-1918', *JHS* 39 (1919) 209-31.

'The Macedonian Era. II', *ABSA* 24 (1919/20, 1920/21) 54-67.

'The Progress of Greek Epigraphy, 1919-1920', *JHS* 41 (1921) 50-69.

'Greek Inscriptions from Macedonia', *JHS* 42 (1922) 167-83.

'The Progress of Greek Epigraphy, 1921-1922', *JHS* 43 (1923) 11-39.

'A Survey of Laconian Epigraphy, 1913-1925', *ABSA* 26 (1923/24, 1924/25) 106-15.

'Three Notes on Appian', *CQ* 18 (1924) 99-104.

'The Progress of Greek Epigraphy, 1923-1924', *JHS* 45 (1925) 102-19, 83-200.

'Further Notes on the Greek Acrophonic Numerals', *ABSA* 28 (1926/27) 141-57.

'The Progress of Greek Epigraphy, 1925-1926', *JHS* 47 (1927) 182-217.

'A Forgotten Epigraphist', *JHS* 48 (1928) 1-6.

'Nvgae Epigraphicae', *CQ* 23 (1929) 1-6.

'The Progress of Greek Epigraphy, 1927-1928', *JHS* 49 (1929) 172-216.

'A Bronze Mirror in the Ashmolean Museum, Oxford', *JHS* 50 (1930) 32-36.

'The Progress of Greek Epigraphy, 1929-30', *JHS* 51 (1931) 211-55.

'Greek Inscriptions', *G&R* 1 (1932) 114-16.

'Greek Inscriptions', *G&R* 1 (1932) 163-65.

'Greek Inscriptions', *G&R* 2 (1932) 47-51.

'Greek Inscriptions', *G&R* 2 (1933) 108-11.

'Greek Inscriptions', *G&R* 2 (1933) 175-77.

'Greek Inscriptions', *G&R* 3 (1933) 49-52.

Selection of Greek Historical Inscriptions. Oxford: Clarendon Press, 1933.

'An Unpublished Epigram in Oxford', *JHS* 53 (1933) 54-56.

'The Progress of Greek Epigraphy, 1931-1933', *JHS* 53 (1933) 214-65.

'Greek Inscriptions at Cairness House', *JHS* 54 (1934) 140-62.

'The Progress of Greek Epigraphy,1933-1934', *JHS* 55 (1935) 172-223.

'The Progress of Greek Epigraphy, 1935-1936', *JHS* 57 (1937) 160-218.

'Notes on Attic Inventories', *JHS* 58 (1938) 97-98.

'The Progress of Greek Epigraphy, 1937-38', *JHS* 59 (1939) 241-81.

'Bithynica', *AJP* 62 (1941) 191-98.

'An Epigraphical Notebook of Sir Arthur Evans', *JHS* 61 (1941) 39.

'The Progress of Greek Epigraphy, 1939-1940', *JHS* 62 (1942) 51-83.

'A Greek Inscription from the Persian Gulf', *JHS* 63 (1943) 112-13.

(and R. P. Austin) 'Athens and the Satraps' revolt', *JHS* 64 (1944) 98-100.

'The Progress of Greek Epigraphy 1941-1945', *JHS* 65 (1945) 58-99.

'A Note on the Spelling ἐξάμου = ἐκ Σάμου', *AJP* 67 (1946) 329-33.

'The Progress of Greek Epigraphy, 1945-7', *JHS* 67 (1947) 90-127.

'Epigraphical Notes', *AJP* 70 (1949) 113-17.

'Greek Record-keeping and Record-breaking', *CQ* 43 (1949) 105-12.

'Epigraphical Notes from the Ashmolean Museum', *JHS* 71 (1951) 172-77.

'The Progress of Greek Epigraphy, 1948-9', *JHS* 72 (1952) 20-55.

(and D. E. L. Haynes) 'An Inscribed Marble Portrait-herm in the British Museum', *JHS* 73 (1953) 138-40.

'The Progress of Greek Epigraphy, 1950-51', *JHS* 74 (1954) 59-84.

'The Progress of Greek Epigraphy, 1952-53', *JHS* 75 (1955) 122-52.

'The Rhoummas Herm: a Postscript', *JHS* 75 (1955) 155.

'A New Eleusinian Title?' *AJP* 77 (1956) 52-54.

'Sidelights on Greek Philosophers', *JHS* 77 (1957) 132-41.

Obituaries, memoirs and studies

The Times 26 February 1974; R. Meiggs, 'Marcus Niebuhr Tod 1878-1974', *PBA* 60 (1974) 485-95; *DBC*; Michael H. Crawford, 'Tod, Marcus Niebuhr (1878–1974)', *ODNB*, vol. 54, 866-67.

Archive material

Oxf. Bodleian Lib.

TOYNBEE, ARNOLD JOSEPH (1889-1975)

Born, 14 April 1889; son of Harry Valpy Toynbee, secretary of the Charity Organization Soc.

Educ. Winchester; Schol. (1902)

Oxf. Balliol Coll.; matric. (October 1907); Schol.; Class. Mod.; Lit. Hum. (1911).

Jenkins Prize (1911).

BSA adm. 1911-12.

BSR adm. 1911.

Fell. and tutor, Balliol Coll. (1912).

War service, Propaganda Bureau (April 1915-April 1917); Dept. of Information, Intelligence Bureau (May 1917-May 1918); Foreign Office, Political Intelligence Dept., and British Delegation, Paris (May 1918-May 1919).

Koraes chair of modern Greek and Byzantine history, language, and literature, King's Coll., London (1919-24); reporter for the *Manchester Guardian* in the Aegean (1921).

Chair of international history, London Univ. (1925).

Dir. of studies at the Royal Institute of International Affairs (1926-55).

War service (WW2), director of the Foreign research and press Service (1939–43).

FBA (1937); Companion of Honour (1956).

Married, first, Rosalind Murray (1913; div. 1946), dau. of Gilbert Murray; second, Veronica Marjorie Boulter (1946).

Died, 22 October 1875.

Publications

Nationality and the War. London; Toronto: J. M. Dent, 1915.

(and D. G. Hogarth, N. Forbes, and D. Mitrany) 1915. *The Balkans: a History of Bulgaria, Serbia, Greece, Rumania, Turkey*. Oxford: Clarendon Press, 1915.

The Treatment of Armenians in the Ottoman Empire: Documents Presented to Viscount Grey of Fallodon. London; New York: Hodder and Stoughton, 1916.

Experiences. New York: Oxford University Press, 1969.

Obituaries, memoirs and studies

The Times 23 October 1975; W. H. McNeill, 'Arnold Joseph Toynbee, 1889–1975', *PBA* 63 (1977) 441–69; R. Clogg, *Politics and the Academy: Arnold Toynbee and the Koraes Chair*. London: Frank Cass for the Centre for the Centre of Contemporary Greek Studies, King's College, London, 1986; W. H. McNeill, *Arnold Toynbee: a Life*. Oxford: Oxford University Press, 1989; *DBC*; Fergus Millar, 'Toynbee, Arnold Joseph (1889–1975)', *ODNB*, vol. 55, 178-85.

Archive material

Oxf. Bodleian Lib.; London KCL; National Archives of Scotland.

TRAQUAIR, RAMSAY (1874-1952)

Born, 29 March 1874, at Edinburgh; son of Dr Ramsay Heatley Traquair (1840-1912), Keeper of Natural History at the Museum of Science and Art in Edinburgh, and his wife, Phoebe Anna Moss (1852-1936), the Dublin-born painter and decorative artist.

Educ. Edinburgh Academy (1884-91).

Edinburgh and Bonn Universities (1891-92), but did not graduate.

Articled to Stewart Henbest Capper (1892); Edinburgh School of Applied Art; National Art Survey Schol. (1896).

Worked for John More Dick Peddie and George Washington Browne (1897-99); assistant to Samuel Bridgman Russell, London (1899).

Survey of the Byzantine churches of Constantinople with Prof. A van Millingen.

Lect., School of Applied Art, Edinburgh (1904).

Practice (1905).

BSA adm. 1905-06 (Architectural Student).

Student of the Byzantine Fund (1908).

McGill Univ., Montreal, Prof. of Architecture (1913-39).

ARIBA (1900); FRIBA (1920/21).

Died, 26 August [October – DSA] 1952, at Guysborough, Nova Scotia.

Publications

'Laconia I. The Mediaeval Fortresses', *ABSA* 12 (1905/06) 258-76.

'Laconia II. Excavations at Sparta, 1906. § 12. The Roman Stoa and the Later Fortifications', *ABSA* 12 (1905/06) 415-30.

'Mediaeval Fortresses of the North-western Peloponnesus', *ABSA* 13 (1906/07) 268-84.

'Laconia III. Mediaeval Churches. The Churches of Western Mani', *ABSA* 15 (1908/09) 177-213.

(and A. J. B. Wace) 'The Base of the Obelisk of Theodosius', *JHS* 29 (1909) 60-69.

(and A. Van Millingen, W. S. George, and A. E. Henderson) *Byzantine Churches in Constantinople: Their History and Architecture*. London: Macmillan & Co., 1912.

Obituaries, memoirs and studies

DSA.

Archive material
Nationbal Lib. of Scotland.

TUBBS, HENRY ARNOLD (TALBOT-TUBBS) (1865-1943)
Born, 17 October 1865, Manchester; son of Henry Harmer Tubbs, bookseller (and at one stage
     a yarn agent), and his first wife, Elizabeth Notcutt (1830-70), of Crumpsall, Lancashire.
Educ. Manchester Grammar School.
Oxf. Pembroke Coll. (1883); Schol. (1883-87); Class. Mod. 1st (1884); Lit. Hum. 1st (1887);
     BA (1887); MA (1892), conferred at the University of Melbourne.
BSA adm. 1888-89 (for work on Cyprus); re-adm. (Cyprus) 1889-90. Craven Univ. Fell.
Lect. in Classics at Univ. Coll., Auckland, NZ (1890); Prof. (1894-99; 1907).
Changed name to Talbot-Tubbs (1896). Talbot was derived from his maternal grandmother.
Married, Ethel Caroline King (1870-1968) in Sydney, New South Wales (1896).
Late residence, Warringah, New South Wales, and Lilley, Queensland, Australia.
Died, 26 December 1943, Sydney, Australia.
Publications
(and J. A. R. Munro) 'Excavations in Cyprus, 1889. Second Season's Work. Polis tes
     Chrysochou. Limniti', *JHS* 11 (1890) 1-99.
'Marble Calathos-Stele from Poli', *CR* 4 (1890) 70.
'Notes on Vases', *CR* 4 (1890) 482-83.
'Wood Beams in Stone Architecture', *CR* 4 (1890) 69.
(and J. A. R. Munro) 'Excavations in Cyprus, 1890', *JHS* 12 (1891) 59-198.
(and J. A. R. Munro, W. W. Wroth) 1891. 'Excavations in Cyprus, 1890. Third Season's
     work. Salamis', *JHS* 12 (1891) 59-198.
Obituaries, memoirs and studies
Pembroke College Register; Foster's *Alumni Oxonienses*.

WACE, ALAN JOHN BAYARD (1879-1957)
Born, 13 July 1879, Cambridge; 2nd son of Frederic Charles (1836-93) and his wife Fanny,
     eldest dau. of John Campbell Bayard, J. P., of Montgomeryshire.
Educ. Shrewsbury.
Camb. Pembroke Coll.; adm. (Oct. 1898); Schol.; Class. Trip. Pt 1, 1st (1901); Pt 2, 1st
     (1902); BA (1901); Craven Student (1903); Prendergast Student (1902 and 1904); MA
     (1906).
BSA adm. 1902-03; re-adm. 1903-04, 1904-05, 1905-06, 1906-07, 1907-08, 1908-09, 1909-
     10, 1910-11. Hon. Student of the School. Dir. of the School 1914-23.
BSR adm. 1903-04; Librarian, BSR (1905-06).
Fell. Pembroke Coll. (1904-13, 1934-44); Hon. Fell. (1951).
Served in HBM Legation, Athens (1915-19).
Lect. in Ancient History and Archaeology at St Andrews Univ. (1912-14).
Dir. of the British School at Athens (1914-23).
Deputy Keeper, Victoria and Albert Museum (1924-34).
Laurence Prof. of Classical Archaeology at Cambridge (1934-44).
War service, at Athens and Cairo, G. H. Q. (1939-43).
Prof. of Classics and Archaeology, Faruq 1st Univ., Alexandria (1944-50).

Hon. Litt. D., Amsterdam and Pennsylvania; Hon. LL. D., Liverpool.

FSA (1929); FBA (1947).

Married, 1925, Helen Pence (1892-1982), dau. of Prof. W. D. Pence, of Evanston, Illinois, USA; a daughter.

Died, 9 Nov 1957, Athens.

Publications

H. Waterhouse, 'Bibliography, 1903-1950', *ABSA* 46 (1951) 232-43; ead., 'A. J. B. Wace: Supplementary Bibliography', *ABSA* 63 (1968) 327-29.

'Apollo Seated on the Omphalos: a Statue at Alexandria', *ABSA* 9 (1902/03) 211-42.

'Recent Excavations in Asia Minor', *JHS* 23 (1903) 335-55.

'Grotesques and the Evil Eye', *ABSA* 10 (1903/04) 103-14.

(and H. J. W. Tillyard) 'Laconia. Historical Note', *ABSA* 11 (1904/05) 112-23.

(and F. W. Hasluck) 'Laconia I. Excavations near Angelona', *ABSA* 11 (1904/05) 81-90.

(and F. W. Hasluck) 'Laconia II. Geraki. 1. Excavations', *ABSA* 11 (1904/05) 91-99.

'Laconia II. Geraki. 2. Sculptures', *ABSA* 11 (1904/05) 99-105.

'Laconia V. Frankish Sculptures at Parori and Geraki', *ABSA* 11 (1904/05) 139-45.

Catalogue of a Collection of Modern Greek Embroideries. Cambridge: Fitzwilliam Museum, 1905.

'Hellenistic Royal Portraits', *JHS* 25 (1905) 86-104.

'Laconia II. Excavations at Sparta, 1906. § 2. The City Wall', *ABSA* 12 (1905/06) 284-88.

'Laconia II. Excavations at Sparta, 1906. § 3. The Heroön', *ABSA* 12 (1905/06) 288-94.

'Laconia II. Excavations at Sparta, 1906. § 8. The Stamped Tiles', *ABSA* 12 (1905/06) 344-50.

'Laconia II. Excavations at Sparta, 1906. § 11. The Roman Baths (Arapissa)', *ABSA* 12 (1905/06) 407-14.

(and R. M. Dawkins) 'Notes from the Sporades: Astypalaea, Telos, Nisyros, Leros', *ABSA* 12 (1905/06) 151-74.

'Fragments of Roman Historical Reliefs in the Vatican and Lateran Museums', *PBSR* 3 (1906) 273-94.

'Skiathos und Skopelos', *Athenische Mitteilungen* 31 (1906) 129-33.

'Some Sculptures at Turin', *JHS* 26 (1906) 235-42.

'The Topography of Pelion and Magnesia', *JHS* 26 (1906) 143-68.

(and M. N. Tod) *A Catalogue of the Sparta Museum*. Oxford: Clarendon Press, 1906.

'Laconia I. Excavations at Sparta, 1907. § 2. The City Walls', *ABSA* 13 (1906/07) 5-16.

'Laconia I. Excavations at Sparta, 1907. § 3. The Stamped Tiles', *ABSA* 13 (1906/07) 17-43.

(and G. Dickins) 'Laconia I. Excavations at Sparta, 1907. § 8. The Hellenistic Tombs', *ABSA* 13 (1906/07) 155-68.

(and J. P. Droop) 'Excavations at Theotokou, Thessaly', *ABSA* 13 (1906/07) 308-27.

'Studies in Roman Historical Reliefs', *PBSR* 4 (1907) 227-76.

'Laconia I. Excavations at Sparta, 1908. § 7. A Third-century Marble Head', *ABSA* 14 (1907/08) 147-48.

'Laconia I. Excavations at Sparta, 1908. § 8. A Hoard of Hellenistic Coins', *ABSA* 14 (1907/08) 149-58.

(and F. W. Hasluck) 'Laconia II. Topography. South-eastern Laconia', *ABSA* 14 (1907/08) 161-82.

(and J. P. Droop, M. S. Thompson) 'Excavations at Zerélia, Thessaly', *ABSA* 14 (1907/08) 197-223.

'Topography of Pelion and Magnesia - Addenda', *JHS* 28 (1908) 337.

(and T. E. Peet, M. S. Thompson) 'The Connection of the Aegean Civilization with Central Europe', *CR* 22 (1908) 233-38.

(and M. S. Thompson, J. P. Droop) 'Laconia I. Excavations at Sparta, 1909. § 6. The Menelaion', *ABSA* 15 (1908/09) 108-57.

(and F. W. Hasluck) 'Laconia II. Topography. East-central Laconia', *ABSA* 15 (1908/09) 158-76.

(and M. S. Thompson) 'A Cave of the Nymphs on Mount Ossa', *ABSA* 15 (1908/09) 243-47.

(and M. S. Thompson) 'The Connection of the Aegean Culture with Servia', *CR* 23 (1909) 209-12.

(and R. Traquair) 'The Base of the Obelisk of Theodosius', *JHS* 29 (1909) 60-69.

'Laconia III. Pottery. Early Pottery from Geraki', *ABSA* 16 (1909/10) 72-75.

'North Greek Festivals and the Worship of Dionysos', *ABSA* 16 (1909/10) 232-53.

'The Reliefs in the Palazzo Spada', *PBSR* 5 (1910) 165-200.

(and M. S. Thompson) 'Excavations in Thessaly, 1910', *Man* 10 (1910) 159-60.

(and M. S. Thompson) 'A Latin Inscription from Perrhaebia', *ABSA* 17 (1910/11) 193-204.

(and D. G. Hogarth, E. A. Gardner, J. L. Myres, B. Nopsca, A. Stein, J. P. Droop, F. R. Maunsell, M. S. Thompson, and A. M. Woodward) 'The Distribution of Early Civilization in Northern Greece: Discussion', *Geographical Journal* 37 (1911) 636-42.

(and M. S. Thompson) 'The Distribution of Early Civilization in Northern Greece', *Geographical Journal* 37 (1911) 631-36.

(and M. S. Thompson) 'Excavations at Halos', *ABSA* 18 (1911/12) 1-29.

(and A. M. Woodward) 'Inscriptions from Upper Macedonia', *ABSA* 18 (1911/12) 166-88.

(and M. S. Thompson) *Prehistoric Thessaly: Being Some Account of Recent Excavations and Explorations in North-eastern Greece from Lake Kopais to the Borders of Macedonia.* Cambridge Archaeological and Ethnological Series. Cambridge: Cambridge University Press, 1912.

'Mumming Plays in the Southern Balkans', *ABSA* 19 (1912/13) 248-65.

'The Mounds of Macedonia', *ABSA* 20 (1913/14) 123-32.

(and M. S. Thompson) *The Nomads of the Balkans: an Account of Life and Customs Among the Vlachs of Northern Pindus.* London: Methuen, 1914.

(and R. M. Dawkins) 'Greek Embroideries', *Burlington Magazine* 26/140 (1914) 49-107.

(and W. M. T. Lawrence) *Catalogue of a Collection of Old Embroideries of the Greek Islands and Turkey.* London: Burlington Fine Arts Club, 1914.

'The Site of Olynthus', *ABSA* 21 (1914/16) 11-15.

'Hastings and Finlay', *ABSA* 22 (1916/18) 110-32.

(and C. W. Blegen) 'The Pre-Mycenaean Pottery of the Mainland', *ABSA* 22 (1916/18) 175-89.

'A British Officer on Active Service, 1799', *ABSA* 23 (1918/19) 126-38.

'Saint Gerasimos and the English Admiral', *ABSA* 23 (1918/19) 118-22.

'Excavations at Mycenae §I. The Campaign of 1920', *ABSA* 24 (1919/20, 1920/21) 185-87.

'Excavations at Mycenae §II. The Campaign of 1921', *ABSA* 24 (1919/20, 1920/21) 187-88.

'Excavations at Mycenae §IV. The Rhyton Well', *ABSA* 24 (1919/20, 1920/21) 200-09.

'Archaeology in Greece, 1919-1921', *JHS* 41 (1921) 260-76.

'Excavations at Mycenae V. The Campaign of 1922', *ABSA* 25 (1921/23) 3-5.

(and W. Lamb) 'Excavations at Mycenae VIII. The Palace 3. The Pithos Area', *ABSA* 25 (1921/23) 160-79.

(and W. Lamb) 'Excavations at Mycenae VIII. The Palace 6. The Court', *ABSA* 25 (1921/23) 188-204.

(and W. Lamb) 'Excavations at Mycenae VIII. The Palace 13. The Shrine and Adjoining Areas', *ABSA* 25 (1921/23) 223-32.

(and W. Lamb) 'Excavations at Mycenae VIII. The Palace 14. The Megaron', *ABSA* 25 (1921/23) 232-57.

(and W. Lamb) 'Excavations at Mycenae VIII. The Palace 15. The Ante-chamber to Domestic Quarters', *ABSA* 25 (1921/23) 257-63.

'Early Aegean Civilization', in *Cambridge Ancient History*, vol. 1, 589-615. Cambridge: Cambridge University Press, 1923.

'Prehistoric Greece', in *Cambridge Ancient History*, vol. 1, 173-80. Cambridge: Cambridge University Press, 1923.

'Crete and Mycenae', in *Cambridge Ancient History*, vol. 2, 431-72. Cambridge: Cambridge University Press, 1924.

'The Date of the Treasury of Atreus', *JHS* 46 (1926) 110-20.

A Cretan Statuette in the Fitzwilliam Museum: a Study in Minoan Costume. Cambridge: Cambridge University Press, 1927.

Old Embroideries of the Greek Islands from the Collection of George Hewitt Myers. Washington: The Century Association, 1928.

(and E. A. B. Barnard) 'The Sheldon Tapestry Weavers and Their Work', *Archaeologia* 78 (1928) 255-314.

(and L. Ashton) *Brief Guide to Persian Embroideries*. London: Victoria and Albert Museum Department of Textiles, 1929.

(and H. Wace) *Catalogue of Loan Exhibition of English Decorative Art at Lansdowne House*. London: Invalid Children's Aid Association, 1929.

(and C. W. Blegen) 'Middle Helladic Tombs', *Symbolae Osloenses* 9 (1930) 28-37.

(and J. P. Droop, R. M. Dawkins) 'A Note on the Excavation of the Sanctuary of Artemis Orthia', *JHS* 50 (1930) 329-36.

Brief Guide to the Turkish Woven Fabrics. London: Victoria and Albert Museum Department of Textiles, 1931.

Chamber Tombs at Mycenae. Archaeologia, vol. 82. London: The Society of Antiquaries, 1932.

'The Veil of Despoina', *AJA* 38 (1934) 107-11.

An Approach to Greek Sculpture. Cambridge: Cambridge University Press, 1935.

Catalogue of Algerian Embroideries. London: Victoria and Albert Museum Department of Textiles, 1935.

(and B. L. Cook) *Mediterranean and Near Eastern Embroideries from the Collection of Mrs F. H. Cook*. London: Halton & Company, 1935.

'Jericho Tomb 13', *ABSA* 38 (1936/37) 259-62.

'The Chatsworth Head', *JHS* 58 (1938) 90-95.

(and C. W. Blegen) 'The Determination of Greek Trade in the Bronze Age', *PCPS* (1938) 169-71.

'Mycenae, 1939', *JHS* 59 (1939) 210-12.

(and C. W. Blegen) 'Pottery as Evidence for Trade and Colonisation in the Aegean Bronze Age', *Klio* 32 (1939) 131-47.

'The Treasury of Atreus', *Antiquity* 14 (1940) 233-49.

(ed.) *Studies in Civilization.* University of Pennsylvania Bicentennial Conference. Philadelphia: University of Pennsylvania Press, 1941.

'Alexandrian and Roman Art: an Altar from the Serapeum', *Bulletin de la Société Archéologique d'Alexandrie* 11 (1943/4) 83-97.

'A Grave Stele from Naucratis', *Bulletin de la Société Archéologique d'Alexandrie* 11 (1943/4) 26-32.

(and E. Drioton) *Exposition d'art copte, decembre 1944: guide.* Cairo: Société d'archéologie copte, 1944.

'Recent Ptolemaic Finds in Egypt', *JHS* 65 (1945) 106-09.

(and P. Dixon) 'Obituary: John Devitt Stringfellow Pendlebury', *ABSA* 41 (1940/45) 5-8.

'The Prehistoric Exploration of the Greek Mainland', *BCH* 70 (1946) 628-38.

'The Sarcophagus of Alexander the Great', *Bulletin of the Faculty of Arts, Farouk I University* 4 (1948) 1-11.

Mycenae: an Archaeological History and Guide. Princeton: Princeton University Press, 1949.

'Prehistoric Stone Figurines from the Mainland', in *Commemorative Studies in Honor of Theodore Leslie Shear*, Hesperia suppl. 8 (1949) 423-26, 500.

'Excavations at Mycenae, 1939. Introduction, and I. The Prehistoric Cemetery', *ABSA* 45 (1950) 203-28.

'Exploring the City of Agamemnon; This Year's Excavations at Mycenae', *Illustrated London News* 207 (1950) 1041.

'Mycenae 1950', *JHS* 71 (1951) 254-57.

'Notes on the Homeric House', *JHS* 71 (1951) 203-11.

'Excavations at Mycenae, 1952', *Proceedings of the American Philosophical Society* 97 (1952) 248-53.

'The History of Greece in the Third and Second Milleniums BC ', *Historia* 2 (1953) 74-94.

'Mycenae, 1952', *JHS* 73 (1953) 131-32.

'Mycenae, 1953', *JHS* 74 (1954) 170-71.

'St George the Vampire', *Antiquity* 30 (1956) 156-62.

'The Brummagem Philhellene', *Antiquity* 31 (1957) 85-89.

'Aegean Prehistory', *Antiquity* 32 (1958) 30-34.

(and A. H. S. Megaw, and T. C. Skeat) *Hermopolis Magna, Ashmunein: the Ptolemaic Sanctuary and the Basilica.* Alexandria University, Faculty of Arts, Publications 8. Alexandria: Alexandria University Press, 1959.

(and F. H. Stubbings) *A Companion to Homer.* London: Macmillan, 1962.

(and H. Wace) *The Mycenaean Room in the National Museum, Athens.* Athens: Mrs Alan Wace, 1964.

Greece Untrodden. Athens: Mrs Alan Wace, 1964.

The Marlborough Tapestries at Blenheim Palace and Their Relation to Other Military Tapestries of the War of the Spanish Succession. London: Phaidon, 1968.

Obituaries, memoirs and studies

The Times 11 November 1957; C. W. Blegen, 'Alan John Bayard Wace (1879-1957)', *American Philosophical Society Yearbook* (1958) 162-71; S. Hood, 'Alan John Bayard Wace', *Gnomon* 30 (1958) 158-59; F. H. Stubbings, 'Alan John Bayard Wace, 1879-1957', *PBA* 44 (1958) 263-80; C. Zerner, *Alan John Bayard Wace and Carl William Blegen: a Friendship in the Realms of Bronze.* Athens: American School of Classical Studies at Athens, 1989; R. Koehl, 'A Letter from Evans to Droop on the 'Problem' of Wace', *Classical Journal* 86 (1990) 45-52; J. K. Papadopoulos, 'The Correspondence of A. J. B. Wace in the Library of the Australian Archaeological Institute at Athens', *ABSA* 88 (1993) 337-52; *DBC*; D. W. J. Gill, 'Wace, Alan John Bayard (1879-1957)', in *ODNB*, vol. 56, 632-35; Venn; WWW; *Faces of Archaeology* 41-46, no. 6.

Archive material

Camb. Pembroke Coll. Lib.; Camb. Emmanuel Coll. Lib.; London, SOAS Lib.; Oxf. Bodleian Lib.

WATSON-TAYLOR, LILIAN ELIZABETH

See Tennant, Lilian Elizabeth.

WEBSTER, ERWIN WENTWORTH (1880-1917)

Born, 9 January 1880, St Jean de Luz; son of Rev. Wentworth Webster and Thekla Laura Webster.

Educ. South Eastern Coll., Ramsgate.

Oxf. Wadham Coll.; Schol. (1898); Class. Mod. 1st; Taylorian Scholar in German (1901); Lit. Hum. 1st (1902).

BSA adm. 1902-03. In the same year he studied in Berlin for a term and travelled in Italy.

Fell. Wadham Coll., Oxford (1903); Tutor (1913).

John Locke Scholar in Mental Philosophy (1904).

Remembered as 'a fine scholar, an accomplished linguist, and a keen student of Aristotle' (*BSA* Annual Meeting of Subscribers 1918, 229).

War service, Captain in the 13th Battalion, King's Royal Rifles.

Killed in action, 9 April 1917.

Obituaries, memoirs and studies

Wadham College Gazette 60 (Summer Term 1917), 56-62, pl.

Further information

Commonwealth War Graves Commission.

WELCH, FRANCIS BERTRAM (1876-1950)

Born, 26 August 1876; son of Surg. -Col. F. H. Welch, FRCS.

Educ. Haileybury (1889-90), and Magdalen Coll. School, Oxford.

Oxf. Magdalen Coll.; Exhib. (1894-98); Class. Mod. 2nd (1896); Lit. Hum. 1st (1898); BA (1898); MA (1902).

BSA adm. 1898-99 (Craven Univ. Fell.); re-adm. 1899-1900.

Asst. Master at Pocklington (1902-9).

Headmaster of Oswestry School (1910-13), and of Wadham House School Hall, Hale, Cheshire (1913-16).

War service, Lieutenant, Intelligence Corps, Salonika (February 1916-April 1919); Asst. to Military Attaché, Athens (April-October 1919); mentioned in despatches, 1918.

Passport Control Officer and Vice-Consul at Athens (from 1919).

British Representative on the Commission mixte de l'Organisation des Populations Gréco-bulgare.

Married, Ada Annie Awburn (4 Jan 1902), dau. of Thomas Bell Awburn.

Died, 1950.

Publications

'The Influence of the Aegean Civilisation on South Palestine', *ABSA* 6 (1899/1900) 117-24.

'Knossos III. Notes on the Pottery', *ABSA* 6 (1899/1900) 85-92.

(and D. G. Hogarth) 'Primitive Painted Pottery in Crete', *JHS* 21 (1901) 78-98.

(and T. D. Atkinson, R. C. Bosanquet, C. C. Edgar, A. J. Evans, D. G. Hogarth, D. Mackenzie, and C. Harcourt-Smith) *Excavations at Phylakopi in Melos*. Society for the Promotion of Hellenic Studies, Occasional Paper 4. London, 1904.

Obituaries, memoirs and studies

Haileybury Register.

WELLS, ROBERT DOUGLAS (1875-1963)

Born, 8 July 1875, London; son of Thomas, of Randolphs, Biddenden, Staplehurst, Kent.

Educ. Uppingham.

Camb. Trinity Coll.; adm. pens. (June 13, 1893); BA (1896); MA (1907).

BSA adm. 1900-01 (Architectural Studentship).

Articled to J. J. Stephenson and Harry Redfern.

War service, work at Stratford Recruiting Station for T.S.F.A.; attached to staff of YMCA for survey work.

FRIBA.

Residence, 30, Palace Gardens Terrace, Kensington (in 1952).

Married, Madeline Rachel Holmes (1903).

Died, 28 April 1963

Obituaries, memoirs and studies

Venn; WWW.

WELSH, MARGERY KATHARINE (MRS A. M. DANIEL) (1880-1960)

Born, 1880, Altrincham, Cheshire, dau. of William Welsh, merchant (later resident at Bifrons, Fleet, Hants).

Camb. Newnham Coll.; Class. Trip. Pt 1, 1st div. 3 (1902); Pt 2, 1st archaeology (1903).

Holder of the Marion Kennedy Studentship.

BSA adm. 1903-04.

War service, work in connection with local War Charities.

Married, (Sir) Augustus Moore Daniel (1866-1950) (1904), of Saxifield, Scarborough, Asst. Dir. of the BSR (1906-07); Dir. of the National Gallery, London (1929-33); KBE (1932).

Residence, 2 Hampstead Hill Gardens, London NW3 (in 1939).

Died, 15 June 1960.

Publications
'Honorary Statues in Ancient Greece', *ABSA* 11 (1904/05) 32-49.

WEST, HERCULES HENRY (1856-1937)
Born, 6 December 1856, Dublin; youngest son of the Very Rev. John, Dean of St Patrick's
    Cathedral, Dublin.
Educ. Marlborough Coll. (August 1871-July 1875); C2 house; Foundation Schol.
Camb. Trinity Coll.; adm. pens. (May 25, 1875); Schol. (1876); Browne Medal (1877); 1st;
    BA (7th Classic) (1879); MA (1883).
Sir William Browne's Medal for Greek Epigram (1877).
BSA adm. 1896-97.
Resident, Italy (1909); Newport, Isle of Wight.
War service, work in connection with Serbian boy refugees in England.
One sister, Elizabeth Dickinson West was married to Prof. Edward Dowden (1895) of
    Trinity Coll., Dublin; a second, Caroline Amy West, was married to the Hon. Edward
    Lyttelton (1888), Master of Haileybury (1890-1905) and Headmaster of Eton (1905-16).
Died June 4, 1937, at Chandler's Ford, Hants.
Publications
(ed.), H. C. F. Mason, *Compositions and Translations*. London: C. J. Clay & Sons, 1903.
Obituaries, memoirs and studies
The Times 12 June 1937; WWW.

WHATLEY, NORMAN (1884-1965)
Born, 8 September 1884, Blackheath; son of A. T. Whatley, solicitor.
Educ. Radley.
Oxf. Hertford Coll.; Class. Mod. 1st; Lit. Hum. 1st.
Editor of *The Isis* (1904-05).
BSA adm. 1907-08.
BSR adm. 1910.
Fell. Hertford Coll., Oxf. (1907-1923); Tutor and Lect. (1908-23); Dean (1912-1920).
War service, Adjutant Oxford Univ. OTC (1914); Instructional Staff, No. 4 O. C. Battalion,
    Intelligence Corps, France (1914-19); Captain; Brevet-Major.
Headmaster of Clifton Coll. (1923-39).
Taught at St Edward's School, Oxford (1939-44).
Counciller, Oxford City Council (1919-22, 1944); mayor (1949); chairman of the education
    committee.
Married, Norah Radley Croome (16 July 1914), daughter of A. C. M. Croome; three sons.
Died, 1 April 1965, Oxford.
Publications
'On the Possibility of Reconstructing Marathon and Other Ancient Battles', *JHS* 84 (1964)
    119-39.
Obituaries, memoirs and studies
The Times 3 April 1965 (obit.), 8 April 1965 (funeral); WWW.

WIGRAM, REV. WILLIAM AINGER (1872-1953)

Born, 16 May 1872, Furneaux Pelham, Hertfordshire; son of Rev. Woolmore Wigram; brother of Sir Edgar Wigram.

Educ. King's School, Canterbury.

Camb. Trinity Hall; History Tripos, Pt 1, 2nd (1891); BA (1893).

Pupil of Bishop B. F. Westcott of Durham.

Ordained deacon (1896), priest (1897). Curate at St Barnabas, Sunderland.

Recruited by Rev. O. H. Parry for the Archbishop of Canterbury's Mission to the Assyrian Christians (1902); eastern Turkey and Persia (1902-12), Van (1907-12); Chaplaincy in Constantinople, Crimea Memorial Church (1912).

BSA adm. 1913-14.

Interned during the First World War, Constantinople and Asia Minor (1915-18).

Political Officer working with displaced persons, Mesopotamia (1918).

Working with refugees in Athens (1922); Chaplain to the British Legation, Athens (1923-26).

Associate of the BSA (1926).

Canon, the Collegiate Church of St Paul, Malta (1928-36).

Unmarried.

Died, 16 January 1953, at the Old Manor, Salisbury, Wiltshire.

Publications

An Introduction to the History of the Assyrian Church: or, the Church of the Sassanid Persian Empire, 100-640 AD London; New York: Society for Promoting Christian Knowledge; E. S. Gorham, 1910.

(and E. T. A. Wigram) *The Cradle of Mankind: Life in Eastern Kurdistan*. London: A. and C. Black, 1914.

Our Smallest Ally: a Brief Account of the Assyrian Nation in the Great War. London; New York: Society for Promoting Christian Knowledge; Macmillan, 1920.

The Assyrians and Their Neighbours. London: G. Bell & Sons, 1929.

Hellenic Travel, a Guide. London: Faber & Faber, 1947.

Obituaries, memoirs and studies

The Times 19 January 1953; J. F. Coakley, 'Wigram, William Ainger (1872-1953)', in *ODNB*, vol. 58, 861-62.

WOODHOUSE, WILLIAM JOHN (1866-1937)

Born, 7 November 1866, Clifton, Westmorland; son of Richard Woodhouse, a stationmaster, and his wife Mary.

Educ. Sedbergh Grammar School

Oxf. The Queen's Coll.; Class. Mod. 1st; Lit. Hum. 1st; BA (1889).

BSA adm. 1889-90 (Appointed to Oxford Studentship; Sir Charles Newton studentship); re-adm. 1891-92, 1892-93 (Craven Univ. Fell.). Hon. Student of the School.

Conington Prize (1894).

Asst. Lect., Univ. Coll. of North Wales, Bangor (1896-99).

Lect. in Ancient History and Political Philosophy, Univ. of St Andrews (1900).

Prof. of Greek in the Univ. of Sydney, NSW (1901); honorary curator of the Nicholson Museum of Antiquities (1903-37); Dean of the Faculty of Arts (1926-29).

War service, interpreter in the Censor's Office, Sydney.

Married, Eleanor Emma Jackson (28 March 1897), Sedbergh, Yorkshire.

Died, 27 October 1937.

Publications

(and E. A. Gardner, W. Loring, and G. C. Richards) 'The Theatre at Megalopolis', *JHS* 11 (1890) 294-98.

(and E. A. Gardner, W. Loring, G. C. Richards, and R. W. Schultz) *Excavations at Megalopolis, 1890-1891*. Society for the Promotion of Hellenic Studies, Supplementary papers, no. 1. London: Society for the Promotion of Hellenic Studies, 1892.

'Aetolian Inscriptions', *JHS* 13 (1893) 338-55.

Aetolia: its Geography, Topography, and Antiquities. Oxford: Clarendon Press, 1897.

'The Greeks at Plataiai', *JHS* 18 (1898) 33.

Cicero, De officiis, Book III. London: University Tutorial Press, 1900.

Livy, Book 9. London: University Tutorial Press, 1909.

'The Scenic Arrangements of the Philoctetes of Sophocles', *JHS* 32 (1912) 239-49.

'The Campaign and Battle of Mantineia in 418 BC', *ABSA* 22 (1916/18) 51-84.

The Composition of Homer's Odyssey. Oxford: The Clarendon Press, 1930.

The Fight for an Empire: a Translation of the Third Book of the Histories of Tacitus. Sydney: Angus & Robertson, 1931.

King Agis of Sparta and his Campaign in Arkadia in 418 BC: a Chapter in the History of the Art of War Among the Greeks. Oxford: The Clarendon Press, 1933.

'T. E. Shaw's Odyssey of Homer Translated into English Prose', *Australian Quarterly* (1934).

Solon the Liberator: a Study of the Agrarian Problem in Attika in the Seventh Century. London: Oxford University Press, H. Milford, 1938.

The Tutorial History of Greece (to 323 BC), 3rd edition. London: University Tutorial Press, 1958.

The Tutorial History of Greece (to 323 BC), 4th ed / revised by B. G. Marchant edition. London: University Tutorial Press, 1965.

Obituaries, memoirs and studies

L. F. Fitzhardinge, 'Woodhouse, William John (1866 - 1937)', *Australian Dictionary of Biography*, vol. 12, 561-62 Melbourne University Press, 1990; *DBC*.

WOODWARD, ARTHUR MAURICE (1883-1973)

Born, 29 June 1883; son of Rev. W. H. Woodward, a Church of England clergyman.

Educ. Shrewsbury.

Oxf. Magdalen Coll.; Classical Demy (1902-06); Class. Mod. 2nd (1904); Lit. Hum. 2nd (1906); BA (1906); MA (1909).

Classical Demy of Magdalen Coll.

BSA adm. 1906-07, 1907-08, 1908-09. Asst. Dir. (1909-10).

Asst. Lect. in Classics and Ancient History, Univ. of Leeds.

Asst. Lect. Liverpool Univ. (1911-12); Asst. Lect. in Classics and Ancient History (1912), Reader in Ancient History and Archaeology, Leeds Univ. (1912-22).

Dir. BSA (1923-29).

Lect. in charge of the Dept. of Ancient History, Sheffield Univ. (1931-45); Reader in
    Ancient History and Archaeology and Head of Dept. (1945-7).
War service: 2nd Lieutenant, Interpreter, British Salonika force (1915); Lieutenant (1917);
    transferred to Intelligence Corps (May 1917); served till 1919. Officer Interpreter and
    subsequently Intelligence Officer with British Salonika Force, 1915-19; Intelligence
    Corps; mentioned in despatches twice; Officer of the Redeemer of Greece.
Hon. ARIBA;
Ordinary Member of the German Archaeological Institute.
Married, Jocelyn Mary Pybus (30 October 1925), dau. of John Pybus of Newcastle-upon-
    Tyne.
Died, 12 November 1973.

Publications
A full list: D. M. Lewis, 'Bibliographic List', *ABSA* 70 (1975) 177-82.
'Laconia II. Topography. § 2. Taenarum and S. Maina', *ABSA* 13 (1906/07) 238-67.
(and M. N. Tod, H. J. W. Tillyard) 'Laconia I. Excavations at Sparta, 1907. § 10. The
    Inscriptions', *ABSA* 13 (1906/07) 174-218.
'Laconia I. Excavations at Sparta, 1908. § 5. The Inscriptions', *ABSA* 14 (1907/08) 74-141.
'Some Unpublished Attic Inscriptions', *JHS* 28 (1908) 291-312.
'Laconia I. Excavations at Sparta, 1909. § 4. The Inscriptions', *ABSA* 15 (1908/09) 40-106.
'The Quota-list of the Year 427-6 BC ', *ABSA* 15 (1908/09) 229-42.
'Three New Fragments of Attic Treasure-records', *JHS* 29 (1909) 168-91.
'Laconia I. Excavations at Sparta, 1910. § 6. The Inscriptions', *ABSA* 16 (1909/10) 54-61.
'A Panathenaic Amphora from Kameiros', *ABSA* 16 (1909/10) 206-11.
'Some New Fragments of Attic Building-records', *ABSA* 16 (1909/10) 187-205.
(and H. A. Ormerod) 'A Journey in South-western Asia Minor', *ABSA* 16 (1909/10) 76-136.
'Notes on Some Greek Inscriptions, Mainly in Athens', *JHS* 30 (1910) 260-66.
'Inscriptions From Western Pisidia', *ABSA* 17 (1910/11) 205-14.
'Some Notes on the Monument of Porphyrios at Constantinople', *ABSA* 17 (1910/11) 88-92.
'Some More Unpublished Fragments of Attic Treasure-records', *JHS* 31 (1911) 31-41.
(and D. G. Hogarth, E. A. Gardner, J. L. Myres, B. Nopsca, A. Stein, J. P. Droop, F. R.
    Maunsell, M. S. Thompson, and A. J. B. Wace) 'The Distribution of Early Civilization
    in Northern Greece: Discussion', *Geographical Journal* 37 (1911) 636-42.
'Inscriptions from Beroea in Macedonia', *ABSA* 18 (1911/12) 133-65.
(and A. J. B. Wace) 'Inscriptions from Upper Macedonia', *ABSA* 18 (1911/12) 166-88.
'Inscriptions from Thessaly and Macedonia', *JHS* 33 (1913) 313-46.
'The Antiquities from Lanuvium in the Museum at Leeds and Elsewhere. Part I. Sculpture',
    PBSR 7 (1914) 63-91.
'Notes and Queries on Athenian Coinage and Finance', *JHS* 34 (1914) 276-92.
'Hoard of Roman Coins from Halifax', *Journal of the Yorkshire Archaelogical Society* 23
    (1915) 444-51.
(and W. Cooksey) 'Macedonia. IV. Mounds and Other Ancient Sites in the Region of
    Salonika', *ABSA* 23 (1918/19) 51-60.
'Macedonia. VII. The Byzantine Castle of Avret-Hissar', *ABSA* 23 (1918/19) 98-103.
'Obituary [of Francis J. Haverfield]', *Annual Bulletin of Historical Literature* 9 (1919) 7.
(and J. J. E. Hondius) 'Laconia I. Inscriptions', *ABSA* 24 (1919/21) 88-143.

'A Decorative Bronze Silenus-mask From Ilkley', *JRS* 10 (1920) 185-88.

'Excavations at Sparta, 1924-25. § 1. Introductory', *ABSA* 26 (1923/25) 116-18.

'Excavations at Sparta, 1924-25. § 2. The Theatre', *ABSA* 26 (1923/25) 119-58.

'Excavations at Sparta, 1924-25. § 3. The Inscriptions', *ABSA* 26 (1923/25) 159-239.

(and M. B. Hobling) 'Excavations at Sparta, 1924-25. § 4. The Acropolis. 1. The Site', *ABSA* 26 (1923/25) 240-52.

'Excavations at Sparta, 1924-25. § 4. The Acropolis. 2. The Finds', *ABSA* 26 (1923/25) 253-76.

'Archaeology in Greece, 1922-1924', *JHS* 44 (1924) 254-80.

'Roman Forts at Templebrough', *Journal of the Yorkshire Archaelogical Society* 27 (1924) 112-17.

'Archaeology in Greece, 1924-1925', *JHS* 45 (1925) 210-28.

'The Roman Fort at Ilkley', *Journal of the Yorkshire Archaeological Society* 28 (1925) 137-321.

'Excavations at Sparta, 1926. ii. The Theatre', *ABSA* 27 (1925/26) 175-209.

'Excavations at Sparta, 1926. iii. The Inscriptions', *ABSA* 27 (1925/26) 210-54.

(and R. P. Austin) 'Some Note-books of Sir William Gell I', *ABSA* 27 (1925/26) 67-80.

'Archaeology in Greece, 1925-26', *JHS* 47 (1926) 223-49.

'Excavations at Sparta, 1927. ii. The Theatre', *ABSA* 28 (1926/27) 3-36.

'Some Note-books of Sir William Gell, Part II', *ABSA* 28 (1926/27) 107-27.

'Archaeology in Greece, 1926–1927', *JHS* 47 (1927) 234-63.

'Excavations at Sparta, 1924-28. The Inscriptions, Part I', *ABSA* 29 (1927/28) 2-56.

(and L. Robert) 'Excavations at Sparta, 1924-28. ii. Four Hellenistic Decrees', *ABSA* 29 (1927/28) 57-74.

'Archaeology in Greece, 1927-1928', *JHS* 48 (1928) 183-95.

'Some More Fragments of Attic Treasure-records of the Fifth Century', *JHS* 48 (1928) 159-77.

'Excavations at Sparta, 1924-28. i. The Theatre: Architectural Remains', *ABSA* 30 (1928/30) 151-240.

(and W. S. George) 'The Architectural Terracottas', in *The Sanctuary of Artemis Orthia at Sparta*, edited by R. M. Dawkins, 117-43. Society for the Promotion of Hellenic Studies, supplementary papers, vol. 5. London: Macmillan, 1929.

'The Antiquities from Lanuvium in the Museum at Leeds and Elsewhere. Part II. Sculpture (continued) and Miscellaneous', *PBSR* 11 (1929) 73-136.

'Archaeology in Greece, 1928–1929', *JHS* 49 (1929) 220-39.

'Studies in Attic Treasure-Records, I', *JHS* 51 (1931) 139-63.

'The Roman Villa at Rudston (East Yorks)', *Journal of the Yorkshire Archaeological Society* 31 (1934) 366-76.

'The Roman Villa at Rudston (E. Yorks): Second Interim Report: the Excavations of 1934', *Journal of the Yorkshire Archaeological Society* 32 (1935) 214-20.

(and K. A. Steer) 'The Roman Villa at Rudston (E. Yorks): Third Interim Report: the Excavations of 1935', *Journal of the Yorkshire Archaeological Society* 33 (1936) 81-86.

(and A. B. West) 'Studies in Attic Treasure-records, II', *JHS* 58 (1938) 69-89.

'Two Attic Treasure-records', in *Harvard Studies in Classical Philology Suppl.* vol. 1 (1940) 377-407.

'Greek History at the Renaissance', *JHS* 63 (1943) 1-14.

'*Inscriptiones Graecae* v. 1: Some Afterthoughts', *ABSA* 43 (1948) 209-59.

'The Gortyn "Labyrinth" and its Visitors in the Fifteenth Century', *ABSA* 44 (1949) 324-25.

'Some Notes on the Spartan *sphaireis*', *ABSA* 46 (1951) 191-99.

'Sparta and Asia Minor Under the Roman Empire', in *Studies Presented to D. M. Robinson*, vol. 2, 868-83. St Louis, 1953.

'Treasure Records from the Athenian Agora', *Hesperia* 25 (1956) 79-121.

'Athens and the Oracle of Ammon', *ABSA* 57 (1962) 5-13.

'Financial Documents from the Athenian Agora', *Hesperia* 32 (1963) 144-86.

(and D. M. Lewis) 'A Transfer from Eleusis', *ABSA* 70 (1975) 183-88.

Obituary

The Times 15 November 1973, 28 November 1973; *Faces of Archaeology* 60-64, no. 10; *DBC*.

YORKE, VINCENT WODEHOUSE (1869-1957)

Born, May 21, 1869, at 15, Chesham Street, Pimlico, London; 2nd son of John Reginald, of Forthampton Court, nr Tewkesbury, Gloucs. and his 2nd wife, Sophie Matilda, dau. of Baron Vincent de Tuyll de Seroskerker.

Educ. Eton; Newcastle Schol. 1888); (September 1882 - July 1888); King's Schol. after initial period in Mr Tarver's house to await a vacancy; Newcastle Select (1887); Scholar (1888); Latin Essay, Geography and Geology Prizes (1888); played in Coll. Wall (1886-87), Mixed Wall (1887).

Camb. King's Coll.; Schol. from Eton (Oct. 10, 1888); Schol. (1891); Class. Trip. Pt 1, 1st (1891); Pt 2, 1st (1892); BA (1891); MA (1895).

BSA adm. 1892-93; re-adm. 1893-94.

Fell. King's Coll. (1895).

Military service, Lieut. Gloucs. Yeomanry (1894); served in South Africa; Capt. Royal Gloucs. Hussars-Yeomanry (1904-7).

Chairman of the Mexican Railway, Ltd. (and injured in train accident, 1923); a Dir. of the Westminster Bank (from 1903); a Dir. of the Bank of Scotland; Chairman of the National Provident Institution; JP for Gloucs.

War service, engaged in the manufacture of munitions.

Residence, Forthampton Court, Gloucs.

Married, the Hon. Maud Evelyn Wyndham (24 August 1899), dau. of the 2nd Lord Leconfield; two sons.

Died, 27 November 1957.

Publications

'Newly Discovered Fragments of the Balustrade of Athena Nike', *JHS* 13 (1892) 272-80.

(and A. G. Bather) 'Excavations on the Probable Sites of Basilis and Bathos', *JHS* 13 (1892) 227-31.

'Excavations at Abae and Hyampolis in Phocis', *JHS* 16 (1896) 291-312.

'A Journey in the Valley of the Upper Euphrates', *Geographical Journal* 8 (1896) 317-35, 453-74, map.

'Inscriptions from Eastern Asia Minor', *JHS* 18 (1898) 306-27.

Obituaries, memoirs and studies

The Times 29 November 1957; WWW.

Archive material

Oxf. Bodleian Lib.

BIBLIOGRAPHY

Abrahams, E. B. 1908. *Greek dress: a study of the costumes worn in ancient Greece.* London: John Murray.

Abramson, D. M. 2004. 'Baker, Sir Herbert (1862-1946)', in *Oxford Dictionary of National Biography*, vol. 3: 380-83. Oxford: Oxford University Press.

Ackerman, R. 1987. *J. G. Frazer: his life and work.* Cambridge: Cambridge University Press.

Adams, P. 2004. 'Penrose, Dame Emily (1858-1942)', in *Oxford Dictionary of National Biography*, vol. 43: 606-07. Oxford: Oxford University Press.

Adcock, F. E., and R. Smail. 2004. 'Reid, James Smith (1846-1926)', in *Oxford Dictionary of National Biography*, vol. 46: 392-93. Oxford: Oxford University Press.

Aitchison, G., and J. Elliott. 2004. 'Pullan, Richard Popplewell (1825-1888)', in *Oxford Dictionary of National Biography*, vol. 45: 531-33. Oxford: Oxford University Press.

Aitchison, G., and R. Ward. 2004. 'Falkener, Edward (1814-1896)', in *Oxford Dictionary of National Biography*, vol. 18: 982-83. Oxford: Oxford University Press.

Allen, S. H. 1999. *Finding the walls of Troy: Frank Calvert and Heinrich Schliemann at Hisarlik.* Berkeley and Los Angeles: University of California Press.

Allsebrook, M. 1992. *Born to rebel: the life of Harriet Boyd Hawes.* Oxford: Oxbow Books.

Anderson, J. G. C. 1896/7. 'An epigraphic miscellany', *Annual of the British School at Athens* 3: 106-20.

— 1897a. 'The road-system of eastern Asia Minor with the evidence of Byzantine campaigns', *Journal of Hellenic Studies* 17: 22-44.

— 1897b. 'A summer in Phrygia: I', *Journal of Hellenic Studies* 17: 396-424.

— 1897/8. 'Exploration in Asia Minor during 1898: first report', *Annual of the British School at Athens* 4: 49-78.

— 1898a. 'A summer in Phrygia: Part II', *Journal of Hellenic Studies* 18: 81-128.

— 1898b. 'A summer in Phrygia: some corrections and additions', *Journal of Hellenic Studies* 18: 340-44.

— 1899. 'Exploration in Galatia cis Halym, Part II', *Journal of Hellenic Studies* 19: 52-164.

— 1900. 'Pontica', *Journal of Hellenic Studies* 20: 151-58.

— 1910. 'A Celtic cult and two sites in Roman Galatia', *Journal of Hellenic Studies* 30: 163-67.

— 1913. 'Festivals of Mên Askaênos in the Roman colony at Antioch of Pisidia', *Journal of Roman Studies* 3: 267-300.

— 1919. 'Obituary: Professor F. Haverfield', *Classical Review* 33: 165-66.

Arnott, R., and D. W. J. Gill. forthcoming. *Cycladica in Cambridge.*

Arsdel, R. T. V. 2004. 'Macmillan family (*per. c.* 1840-1986)', in *Oxford Dictionary of National Biography*, vol. 35: 863-76. Oxford: Oxford University Press.

Ashby, T., R. N. Bradley, T. E. Peet, and N. Tagliaferro. 1913. 'Excavations in 1908-11 in the various megalithic buildings in Malta and Gozo', *Papers of the British School at Rome* 6: 1-126.

Atkinson, T. D. 1898/9. 'Excavations in Melos, 1899. B. The structures', *Annual of the British School at Athens* 5: 10-14.

Atkinson, T. D., R. C. Bosanquet, C. C. Edgar, A. J. Evans, D. G. Hogarth, D. Mackenzie, C. Harcourt-Smith, and F. B. Welch. 1904. *Excavations at Phylakopi in Melos*. Society for the Promotion of Hellenic Studies, Occasional Paper 4. London.

Awdry, H. 1894/5. 'Criticism of Grundy's Plataea', *Annual of the British School at Athens* 1: 90-98.

— 1900. 'Pylos and Sphacteria', *Journal of Hellenic Studies* 20: 14-19.

— 1909. 'Note on the walls on Epipolae', *Journal of Hellenic Studies* 29: 70-78.

Ayrton, E. R., C. T. Currelly, A. Weigall, and A. H. Gardiner. 1904. *Abydos. Part III*. Egypt Exploration Fund: Special Extra Publication. London: Egypt Exploration Fund.

Babington, C. 1855. 'Inscriptiones Sprattianae', *Journal of Classical and Sacred Philology* 2: 98-109.

— 1865. *An introductory lecture on archaeology delivered before the University of Cambridge*. Cambridge: Deighton, Bell and Co.

— 1867. *Catalogue of a selection from Colonel Leake's Greek coins: exhibited in the Fitzwilliam Museum*. Cambridge: The University Press.

Bahn, P. G. Editor. 1996. *The Cambridge illustrated history of archaeology*. Cambridge: Cambridge University Press.

Baigent, E. 2004a. 'Bent, James Theodore (1852-1897)', in *Oxford Dictionary of National Biography*, vol. 5: 209-10. Oxford: Oxford University Press.

— 2004b. 'Pococke, Richard (1704-1765)', in *Oxford Dictionary of National Biography*, vol. 44: 667-69. Oxford: Oxford University Press.

Baker, F. B. 1892. 'Coin-types of Asia Minor', *Numismatic Chronicle* 12: 89-97.

— 1893. 'Some rare or unpublished Greek coins', *Numismatic Chronicle* 13: 21-35.

Baker-Penoyre, J. 1902. 'Pheneus and the Pheneatike', *Journal of Hellenic Studies* 22: 228-40.

— 1909. 'Thasos II', *Journal of Hellenic Studies* 29: 202-50.

— 1910/11. 'Bibliography of the work of students, coming within the scope of the school's work but not published in the School *Annual*', *Annual of the British School at Athens* 17: xxxix-liv.

Baker-Penoyre, J., and M. N. Tod. 1909. 'Thasos. Part I. Inscriptions', *Journal of Hellenic Studies* 29: 91-102.

Barnsley, S. H. 1891. 'The north doorway of the Erechtheum', *Journal of Hellenic Studies* 12: 381-83.

Bather, A. G. 1892a. 'The bronze fragments of the Acropolis', *Journal of Hellenic Studies* 13: 124-30.

— 1892b. 'The bronze fragments of the Acropolis. II. Ornamented bands and small objects', *Journal of Hellenic Studies* 13: 232-71.

— 1892c. 'The development of the plan of the Thersilion', *Journal of Hellenic Studies* 13: 328-37.

Bather, A. G., and V. W. Yorke. 1892. 'Excavations on the probable sites of Basilis and Bathos', *Journal of Hellenic Studies* 13: 227-31.

Beard, M. 1993. 'Casts and cast-offs: the origins of the Museum of Classical Archaeology', *Proceedings of the Cambridge Philological Society* 39: 1-29.

— 1999. 'The invention (and reinvention) of 'Group D': an archaeology of the Classical Tripos, 1879-1984', in *Classics in 19th and 20th century Cambridge: curriculum, culture and community*, edited by C. A. Stray, vol. 24: 95-134. Cambridge Philological Society supplementary volume. Cambridge: Cambridge Philological Society.

— 2000. *The invention of Jane Harrison*. Revealing Antiquity, vol. 14. Cambridge (Mass.): Harvard University Press.

Beard, M., and C. A. Stray. 2005. 'The Academy abroad: the nineteenth-century origin of the British School Athens', in *The organisation of knowledge in Victorian Britain*, edited by M. J. Daunton: 371-87. Oxford: British Academy and Oxford University Press.

Beazley, J. D. 1911/12. 'The Master of the Eucharides stamnos in Copenhagen', *Annual of the British School at Athens* 18: 217-33.

— 1912/13. 'The master of the Stroganoff Nikoxenos vase', *Annual of the British School at Athens* 19: 229-47.

Becker, M. J., and P. P. Betancourt. 1997. *Richard Berry Seager: pioneer archaeologist and proper gentleman*. Philadelphia: University of Pennsylvania Museum.

Beesly, P. 1982. *Room 40. British Naval Intelligence 1914-18*. San Diego: Harcourt Brace Jovanovich.

Benkovitz, M. J. 1977. *Frederick Rolfe: Baron Corvo*. London: Hamish Hamilton.

Benson, A. C. 1917. *Life and letters of Maggie Benson*. London: John Murray.

Benson, E. F. 1892. 'The Thersilion at Megalopolis', *Journal of Hellenic Studies* 13: 319-27.

— 1895a. 'Aegosthena', *Journal of Hellenic Studies* 15: 314-24.

— 1895b. 'A fourth century head in Central Museum, Athens', *Journal of Hellenic Studies* 15: 194-201.

— 1930. *As we were. A Victorian peep-show*. London: Longmans, Green and Co.

Bent, J. T. 1884. 'Researches among the Cyclades', *Journal of Hellenic Studies* 5: 42-58.

— 1885. *The Cyclades, or life among the insular Greeks*. London.

— 1890. 'Recent discoveries in eastern Cilicia', *Journal of Hellenic Studies* 11: 231-35.

Benton, S. 1934/35. 'Excavations in Ithaca, III. The cave at Polis, I', *Annual of the British School at Athens* 35: 45-73.

— 1938/39. 'Excavations in Ithaca, III. The cave at Polis, II', *Annual of the British School at Athens* 39: 1-51.

— 1954. 'H. L. Lorimer' *Girton Review* 155: 28–29.

Bevan, E. R. 1900a. 'A note on Antiochos Epiphanes' *Journal of Hellenic Studies* 20: 26-30.

— 1900b. 'Note on the command held by Seleukos, 323-321 B. C.' *Classical Review* 14: 396-98.

— 1902a. 'Antiochos III and his title "Great-King"', *Journal of Hellenic Studies* 22: 241-44.

— 1902b. *The house of Seleucus*. London: E. Arnold.

— 1927. *A history of Egypt under the Ptolemaic Dynasty*. London: Methuen.

Bickford-Smith, R. A. H. 1893. *Greece under King George*. London: R. Bentley.

Bickford-Smith, R. A. H., and M. Prior. 1898. *Cretan sketches*. London: R. Bentley and Son.

Bieber, M. 1917. 'Der schräge Mantel der archaischen Koren', *Jahrbuch des deutschen archäologischen Instituts* 32: 99-101.

Bierbrier, M. 1995. *Who was who in Egyptology*, 3rd edition. London: Egypt Exploration Society.

Bintliff, J. L., and A. M. Snodgrass. 1985. 'The Cambridge/Bradford Boeotian Expedition: the first four years', *Journal of Field Archaeology* 12: 123-61.

Birkett, D. 1989. *Spinsters abroad: Victorian lady explorers*. Oxford: Basil Blackwell.

Blakeway, A. A. A., T. J. Dunbabin, and H. G. G. Payne. 1940. *Perachora: the sanctuaries of Hera Akraia and Limenia: excavations of the British School of Archaeology at Athens, 1930-1933. 1: Architecture, bronzes, terracottas*. Oxford: Clarendon Press.

Boardman, J. 2004. 'Myres, Sir John Linton (1869-1954)', in *Oxford Dictionary of National Biography*, vol. 40: 87-89. Oxford: Oxford University Press.

Boase, G. C., and A. McConnell. 2004. 'Easthope, Sir John, baronet (1784-1865)', in *Oxford Dictionary of National Biography*, vol. 17: 590-91. Oxford: Oxford University Press.

Bolger, D. L. 1994. 'Ladies of the expedition: Harriet Boyd Hawes and Edith Hall at work in Mediterranean archaeology', in *Women in archaeology*, edited by C. Claassen: 41-50. Philadelphia: University of Pennsylvania Press.

Bosanquet, E. S. 1914. *Days in Attica*. New York: Macmillan Company.

— Editor. 1938. *Robert Carr Bosanquet: letters and light verse*. Gloucester: John Bellows Ltd.

— n. d. *Late harvest: memories, letters and poems*. London: Chameleon Press.

Bosanquet, R. C. 1895/6a. 'Excavations at Melos: the east gate', *Annual of the British School at Athens* 2: 77-82.

— 1895/6b. 'Prehistoric graves in Syra', *Annual of the British School at Athens* 2: 141-44.

— 1896. 'On a group of early Attic lekythoi', *Journal of Hellenic Studies* 16: 164-77.

— 1896/7a. 'Notes from the Cyclades: a pre-Mycenaean wrist-guard', *Annual of the British School at Athens* 3: 67-70.

— 1896/7b. 'Notes from the Cyclades: pre-Mycenaean pottery from Melos', *Annual of the British School at Athens* 3: 52-57.

— 1896/7c. 'Notes from the Cyclades: stone dishes or troughs', *Annual of the British School at Athens* 3: 64-67.

— 1896/7d. 'Notes from the Cyclades: textile impressions on Aegean pottery', *Annual of the British School at Athens* 3: 61-63.

— 1896/7e. 'Notes from the Cyclades: the so-called Kernoi', *Annual of the British School at Athens* 3: 57-61.

— 1898a. 'Excavations of the British School at Melos. The Hall of the Mystae', *Journal of Hellenic Studies* 18: 60-80, pls. i-iii.

— 1898b. 'Notes on Pylos and Sphacteria', *Journal of Hellenic Studies* 18: 155-59.

— 1899. 'Some early funeral lekythoi', *Journal of Hellenic Studies* 19: 169-84, pls. ii-iii.

— 1900. 'Archaeology in Greece, 1899-1900', *Journal of Hellenic Studies* 20: 167-81.

— 1901a. 'Archaeology in Greece, 1900-1901', *Journal of Hellenic Studies* 21: 334-52.

— 1901b. 'Crete: Excavations. Report on excavations at Praesos in eastern Crete', *Man* 1: 187-89.

— 1901/02a. 'Excavations at Petras', *Annual of the British School at Athens* 8: 282-85.

— 1901/02b. 'Excavations at Praesos. I', *Annual of the British School at Athens* 8: 231-70, pls. vii-xii.

— 1902a. 'Crete. A Mycenaean town and cemeteries at Palaiokastro', *Man* 2: 170-72.

— 1902b. 'Thessaly. Prehistoric villages in Thessaly', *Man* 2: 106-07.

— 1902/03a. 'Excavations at Palaikastro. II. § 1. The second campaign - outlying sites', *Annual of the British School at Athens* 9: 274-77.

— 1902/03b. 'Excavations at Palaikastro. II. § 2. The town', *Annual of the British School at Athens* 9: 277-80, pl. vi.

— 1902/03c. 'Excavations at Palaikastro. II. § 3. The chronology of Palaikastro and Zakro', *Annual of the British School at Athens* 9: 281-87.

— 1902/03d. 'Excavations at Palaikastro. II. § 4. The houses. Block β', *Annual of the British School at Athens* 9: 287-89.

— 1903. 'An early purple-fishery', *Man* 3: 159.

— 1903/04. 'Church of the ruined monastery at Daou-Mendeli', *Annual of the British School at Athens* 10: 190-91.

— 1904. 'Excavations on the line of the Roman Wall in Northumberland. 1: The Roman camp at Housesteads', *Archaeologia Aeliana* 25: 193-300.

— 1904/05a. 'Excavations at Palaikastro. IV. § 8. The temple of Dictaean Zeus', *Annual of the British School at Athens* 11: 298-300.

— 1904/05b. 'Excavations at Palaikastro. IV. § 9. The architectural terracottas', *Annual of the British School at Athens* 11: 300-05.

— 1904/05c. 'Excavations at Palaikastro. IV. § 10. The pottery and the bronzes', *Annual of the British School at Athens* 11: 305-08.

— 1905/06a. 'Laconia II. Excavations at Sparta, 1906. § 1. The season's work', *Annual of the British School at Athens* 12: 277-83.

— 1905/06b. 'Laconia II. Excavations at Sparta, 1906. § 5. The sanctuary of Artemis Orthia', *Annual of the British School at Athens* 12: 303-17.

— 1905/06c. 'Laconia II. Excavations at Sparta, 1906. § 7. The cult of Orthia as illustrated by the finds', *Annual of the British School at Athens* 12: 331-43.

— 1909/10. 'Inscriptions from Praesos', *Annual of the British School at Athens* 16: 281-89.

— 1920. 'Francis John Haverfield, F. S. A., a vice-president', *Archaeologia Aeliana* 17: 137-43.

— 1922. 'A newly discovered Centurial Stone at Housesteads', *Archaeologia Aeliana* 19: 198-99.

— 1939/40. 'Dicte and the temples of Dictaean Zeus', *Annual of the British School at Athens* 40: 60-77.

Bosanquet, R. C., and R. M. Dawkins. 1923. *The unpublished objects from Palaikastro excavations, 1902-1906*. British School at Athens supplementary papers, vol. 1. London: British School at Athens.

Bosanquet, R. C., and J. L. Myres. 1909. 'Roman remains in Wales', *The Times* 9 July 1909: 10.

Bosanquet, R. C., and M. N. Tod. 1902. 'Archaeology in Greece, 1901-1902', *Journal of Hellenic Studies* 22: 378-94.

Bowden, M. 1991. *Pitt Rivers. The life and archaeological work of Lieutenant-General Augustus Henry Lane Fox Pitt Rivers, DCL, FRS, FSA*. Cambridge: Cambridge University Press.

Boyd Dawkins, W. 1900/01. 'Skulls from cave burials at Zakro', *Annual of the British School at Athens* 7: 150-55.

— 1902. 'Remains of animals found in the Dictaean Cave in 1901', *Man* 2: 162-65.

Boyd, H. A. 1901. 'Excavations at Kavousi, Crete, in 1900', *American Journal of Archaeology* 5: 125-57.

Boyd, J. D. 2004. 'Duckworth, Wynfrid Laurence Henry (1870-1956)', in *Oxford Dictionary of National Biography*, vol. 17: 47. Oxford: Oxford University Press.

Breasted, J. H. 1928. 'Obituary: David George Hogarth', *Geographical Review* 18: 159-61.

Breay, C. 1999. 'Women and the Classical Tripos 1869-1914', in *Classics in 19th and 20th century Cambridge: curriculum, culture and community*, edited by C. A. Stray, vol. 24: 48-70. Cambridge Philological Society: Cambridge Philological Society.

Briggs, M. S., and R. A. Fellows. 2004. 'Blomfield, Sir Reginald Theodore (1856-1942)', in *Oxford Dictionary of National Biography*, vol. 6: 262-64. Oxford: Oxford University Press.

British School at Athens. 1893. 'The British School at Athens', *The Times* 20 July 1893: 12.

— 1894/95. 'Annual meeting of subscribers', *Annual of the British School at Athens* 1: 25-37.

— 1895/96. 'Annual meeting of subscribers', *Annual of the British School at Athens* 2: 3-27.

— 1896/97. 'Annual meeting of subscribers', *Annual of the British School at Athens* 3: 221-34.

— 1897/98. 'Annual meeting of subscribers', *Annual of the British School at Athens* 4: 101-08.

— 1898/99. 'Annual meeting of subscribers', *Annual of the British School at Athens* 5: 99-107.

— 1899/1900. 'Annual meeting of subscribers', *Annual of the British School at Athens* 6: 129-39.

— 1903/04. 'Annual meeting of subscribers', *Annual of the British School at Athens* 10: 243-51.

— 1904/05. 'Annual meeting of subscribers', *Annual of the British School at Athens* 11: 309-19.

— 1905/06. 'Annual meeting of subscribers', *Annual of the British School at Athens* 12: 481-94.

— 1907/08. 'Annual meeting of subscribers', *Annual of the British School at Athens* 14: 423-37.

— 1910/11. 'Annual meeting of subscribers', *Annual of the British School at Athens* 17: 284-94.

— 1911/12. 'Annual meeting of subscribers', *Annual of the British School at Athens* 18: 314-22.

— 1912/13. 'Annual meeting of subscribers', *Annual of the British School at Athens* 19: 266-75.

— 1914/15. 'Annual meeting of subscribers', *Annual of the British School at Athens* 21: 185-90.

— 1918/19. 'War service of students at the School, 1914-1919', *Annual of the British School at Athens* 23: viii-xiii.

Brooke, D. Editor. 1929. *Private letters, Pagan and Christian: an anthology of Greek and Roman private letters from the fifth century before Christ to the fifth century of our era.* London: Benn.

— Editor. 1930. *Private letters, Pagan and Christian: an anthology of Greek and Roman private letters from the fifth century before Christ to the fifth century of our era.* New York: Dutton.

— 1937. *Pilgrims were they all: studies of religious adventure in the fourth century of our era.* London: Faber.

Brothers, T., D. W. J. Gill, and B. Stones. 2006. *Travellers to Greece.* London: Classical Association.

Brown, A. 1993. *Before Knossos ... Arthur Evans's travels in the Balkans and Crete.* Oxford: Ashmolean Museum.

— 2000. 'Evans in Crete before 1900', in *Cretan quests: British explorers, excavators and historians*, edited by D. Huxley: 9-14. London: British School at Athens.

Brown, A., and K. Bennett. Editors. 2001. *Arthur Evans's travels in Crete 1894-1899.* BAR International Series, vol. 1000. Oxford: Archaeopress.

Brown, A. C. B. 1905/06. 'Excavations at Schimatari and Dilisi in Boeotia', *Annual of the British School at Athens* 12: 93-100.

Brown, R. N. R., and R. A. Butlin. 2004. 'Freshfield, Douglas William (1845-1934)', in *Oxford Dictionary of National Biography*, vol. 20: 995-96. Oxford: Oxford University Press.

Bruton, F. A. 1909. *Excavations at Toothill and Melandra with proceedings of the Branch.* Second annual report (Classical Association, Manchester and District Branch); Supplementary volume. Manchester: Manchester University Press.

Bruton, F. A., and R. S. Conway. Editors. 1909. *The Roman fort at Manchester.* The Classical Association. Manchester and District Branch. Second Annual Report. Manchester: Manchester University Press.

Budde, L., and R. V. Nicholls. 1964. *Catalogue of Greek and Roman sculpture in the Fitzwilliam Museum, Cambridge.* Cambridge: Cambridge University Press.

Burrows, R. M. 1896. 'Pylos and Sphacteria', *Journal of Hellenic Studies* 16: 55-76.

— 1897. 'Pylos and Sphacteria. a reply to Mr Grundy', *Classical Review* 11: 1-10.

— 1898a. 'Mr G. B. Grundy on Pylos and Sphacteria', *Journal of Hellenic Studies* 18: 345-50.

— 1898b. 'Pylos and Sphacteria', *Journal of Hellenic Studies* 18: 147-55.

— 1904/05. 'An Apollo inscription from the district of Delium', *Annual of the British School at Athens* 11: 153-72.

Burrows, R. M., and P. N. Ure. 1907/08. 'Excavations at Rhitsona in Boeotia', *Annual of the British School at Athens* 14: 226-318.

— 1909. 'Excavations at Rhitsona', *Journal of Hellenic Studies* 29: 308-53.

Bury, J. B. 1894/5. 'Marathon', *Annual of the British School at Athens* 1: 99-100.

— 1895/6. 'The campaign of Artemisium and Thermopylae', *Annual of the British School at Athens* 2: 83-104.

Butcher, K., and D. W. J. Gill. 1993. 'The director, the dealer, the goddess and her champions: the acquisition of the Fitzwilliam goddess', *American Journal of Archaeology* 97: 383-401.

Cadogan, G. 2000. 'The pioneers: 1900-1914', in *Cretan quests: British explorers, excavators and historians*, edited by D. Huxley: 15-27. London: The British School at Athens.

— 2005. 'Cyprus and the British School at Athens', in *On site: British archaeologists in Greece*, edited by E. Calligas and J. Whitley: 88-91. Athens: Motibo.

Calder III, W. M. 1991. 'Jane Harrison's failed candidacies for the Yates professorship (1888, 1896): what did her colleagues think of her?', in *The Cambridge ritualists reconsidered*, edited by W. M. Calder III: 37-59. Atlanta: Illinois Classical Studies.

Calder, W. M., and G. E. Bean. 1958. *A classical map of Asia Minor, being a partial revision, by kind permission of Messrs. John Murray, of J. G. C. Anderson's Map of Asia Minor*. London: British Institute of Archaeology at Ankara.

Calligas, E., and J. Whitley. Editors. 2005. *On site: British archaeologists in Greece*. Athens: Motibo.

Camp II, J. M. 1986. *The Athenian agora: excavations in the heart of classical Athens*. London: Thames and Hudson.

— 2001. *The archaeology of Athens*. New Haven: Yale University Press.

Capes, W. W. 1877. *University life in ancient Athens: being the substance of four Oxford lectures*. London: Longmans Green & Co.

— 1878. ''L'École française' at Athens and at Rome', *Fraser's Magazine* 103: 103-12.

Carey, G. V. 1921. *The war list of the University of Cambridge: 1914-1918*. Cambridge: The University Press.

Casson, S. 1912/13a. 'The baptistery at Kepos in Melos', *Annual of the British School at Athens* 19: 118-22.

— 1912/13b. 'The topography of Megara', *Annual of the British School at Athens* 19: 70-81.

— 1916. 'Note on the ancient sites in the area occupied by the British Salonika force, during the campaign 1916-1918', *Bulletin de Correspondance Hellénique* 40: 293-97.

— Editor. 1921. *Catalogue of the Acropolis Museum II*. Cambridge: Cambridge University Press.

— 1935. *Steady drummer*. London: G. Bell & Sons, Ltd.

Casson, S., and E. A. Gardner. 1918/19. 'Macedonia. II. Antiquities found in the British Zone, 1915-1919', *Annual of the British School at Athens* 23: 10-43, pls. i-xiii.

Cavanagh, W. G., J. Crouwel, R. W. V. Catling, and G. Shipley. 1996. *Continuity and change in a Greek rural landscape. The Laconia Survey: volume II: Archaeological Data*. London: The British School at Athens.

Challis, D. 2008. *From the Harpy Tomb to the Wonders of Ephesus: British archaeologists in the Ottoman Empire 1840-1880*. London: Duckworth.

Chandler, L. 1926. 'The north-west frontier of Attica', *Journal of Hellenic Studies* 46: 1-21.

Chandler, R. 1763. *Marmora Oxoniensia*. Oxford: Clarendon Press.

Cheesman, G. L. 1913. 'The family of the Caristanii at Antioch in Pisidia', *Journal of Roman Studies* 3: 253-66.

— 1914. 'An inscription of the Equites Singulares Imperatoris from Gerasa', *Journal of Roman Studies* 4: 13-16.

Cherry, J. F., and B. A. Sparkes. 1982. 'A note on the topography of the ancient settlement of Melos', in *An island polity: the archaeology of exploitation in Melos*, edited by C. Renfrew and M. Wagstaff: 53-57. Cambridge: Cambridge University Press.

Childe, V. G. 1915. 'On the date and origin of Minyan ware', *Journal of Hellenic Studies* 35: 196-207.

Chirol, V., and H. C. G. Matthew. 2004. 'Rumbold, Sir Horace, eighth baronet (1829-1913)', in *Oxford Dictionary of National Biography*, vol. 48: 107. Oxford: Oxford University Press.

Clogg, R. 1986. *Politics and the academy: Arnold Toynbee and the Koraes chair*. London: Frank Cass for the Centre for the Centre of Contemporary Greek Studies, King's College, London.

— 1992. *A concise history of Greece*. Cambridge: Cambridge University Press.

— 2000. 'The British School at Athens and the modern history of Greece', in *Anglo-Greek attitudes: studies in history*: 19-35. St Antony's Series. London: Macmillan.

Coakley, J. F. 1992. *The church of the East and the Church of England: a history of the Archbishop of Canterbury's Assyrian Mission*. Oxford: Oxford University Press.

Cohen, R. H. L., and M. Pottle. 2004. 'Lucas, Frank Laurence (1894-1967)', in *Oxford Dictionary of National Biography*, vol. 34: 674-76. Oxford: Oxford University Press.

Colvin, S. 1889. 'Cyprus Exploration Fund', *The Times* 29 July 1889: 6.

— 1921. *Memories & notes of persons & places 1852-1912*. London: Edward Arnold.

Colvin, S., W. Leaf, and G. A. Macmillan. 1888. 'Exploration in Cyprus', *The Times* 3 March 1888: 6.

Compton, W. C., and H. Awdry. 1907. 'Two notes on Pylos and Sphacteria', *Journal of Hellenic Studies* 27: 274-83.

Comyn, H. 1902/03. 'Church of the ruined monastery at Daou-Mendeli, Attica', *Annual of the British School at Athens* 9: 388-90.

Conway, A. E. 1917. *A ride through the Balkans: on classic ground with a camera*. London: R. Scott.

Conway, R. S. 1901/02. 'The pre-Hellenic inscriptions of Praesos', *Annual of the British School at Athens* 8: 125-56.

— 1903/04. 'A third Eteocretan fragment', *Annual of the British School at Athens* 10: 115-26.

— Editor. 1906. *Melandra Castle. With an introduction by the Rev. E. L. Hicks*. Annual Report no. 1. Manchester: University Press.

— 1908. 'Excavation at Ribchester', *Classical Review* 22: 196-97.

Cook, A. B. 1914. *Zeus: a study in ancient religion*, vol. 1. Cambridge: Cambridge University Press.

— 1931. *The rise and progress of classical archaeology with special reference to the University of Cambridge. An inaugural lecture*. Cambridge: Cambridge University Press.

Cook, B. F. 1985. *The Townley marbles*. London: British Museum Press.

— 1997. 'Sir Charles Newton KCB (1816-1894)', in *Sculptors and sculpture of Caria and the Dodecanese*, edited by I. Jenkins and G. Waywell: 10-29. London: British Museum Press.

Corbett, P. E. 1960. 'The Burgon and Blacas Tombs', *Journal of Hellenic Studies* 80: 52-60.

Cormack, R. 1969. 'The mosaic decoration of S. Demetrios, Thessaloniki: a re-examination in the light of the drawings of W. S. George', *Annual of the British School at Athens* 64: 17-52.

Cosgrove, R. A. 2004. 'Pollock, Sir Frederick, third baronet (1845-1937)', in *Oxford Dictionary of National Biography*, vol. 44: 775-77. Oxford: Oxford University Press.

Craig, E. S., and W. M. Gibson. 1920. *Oxford University roll of service*. Oxford: Clarendon Press.

Craster, H. H. E. 1920. 'Francis Haverfield', *English Historical Review* 35: 63-70.

Crawford, M. H. 2004. 'Tod, Marcus Niebuhr (1878-1974)', in *Oxford Dictionary of National Biography*, vol. 54: 866-67. Oxford: Oxford University Press.

Cronin, H. S. 1902. 'First report of a journey in Pisidia, Lycaonia, and Pamphylia', *Journal of Hellenic Studies* 22: 94-125, 339-76.

Crowfoot, J. W. 1896/7. 'Excavations on the Demarch's fields, Melos', *Annual of the British School at Athens* 3: 31-34.

— 1897. 'A Thracian Portrait', *Journal of Hellenic Studies* 17: 321-26.

— 1897/8. 'Notes upon late Anatolian art', *Annual of the British School at Athens* 4: 79-94.

— 1899. 'Exploration in Galatia cis Halym, Part I', *Journal of Hellenic Studies* 19: 34-51.

Cruickshank, A. H. 1895/6. 'Meteora', *Annual of the British School at Athens* 2: 105-12.

Cruso, H. A. A. 1910. 'The Byzantine Research and Publication Fund', *The Times* 28 December 1910: 9.

Cumont, F., and J. G. C. Anderson. 1912. 'Three new inscriptions from Pontus and Pisidia', *Journal of Roman Studies* 2: 233-36.

Currelly, C. T. 1903/04. 'Excavations at Palaikastro. III. § 9. The larnax burials', *Annual of the British School at Athens* 10: 227-31.

— 1913. *Stone implements*. Catalogue général des antiquités égyptiennes du Musée du Caire. Le Caire: Impr. de l'Institut français d'archéologie orientale.

— 1965. *I brought the ages home*. Toronto: Ryerson Press.

Curthoys, M. C. 2004. 'Hicks, Edward Lee (1843-1919)', in *Oxford Dictionary of National Biography*, vol. 27: 26-28. Oxford: Oxford University Press.

Cust, L. H., and S. J. Skedd. 2004. 'Gray, Sir James, second baronet (c. 1708-1773)', in *Oxford Dictionary of National Biography*, vol. 23: 431-32. Oxford: Oxford University Press.

Daniel, A. M. 1904. 'Damophon', *Journal of Hellenic Studies* 24: 41-57.

Davenport-Hines, R. 2004. 'Gardner, Sir James Tynte-Agg- (1846-1928)', in *Oxford Dictionary of National Biography*, vol. 21: 460-61. Oxford: Oxford University Press.

Dawkins, R. M. 'Aetolia', pp. 4. Oxford.

— 1902/03a. 'Excavations at Palaikastro. II. § 5. The houses. Block γ', *Annual of the British School at Athens* 9: 290-92.

— 1902/03b. 'Excavations at Palaikastro. II. § 6. Block δ', *Annual of the British School at Athens* 9: 292-94.

— 1902/03c. 'Excavations at Palaikastro. II. § 7. Block ε and ο', *Annual of the British School at Athens* 9: 294-96.

— 1902/03d. 'Excavations at Palaikastro. II. § 8. The pottery', *Annual of the British School at Athens* 9: 297-328.

— 1902/03e. 'Notes from Karpathos', *Annual of the British School at Athens* 9: 176-210.

— 1903. 'Pottery from Zakro', *Journal of Hellenic Studies* 23: 248-60.

— 1903/04a. 'Excavations at Palaikastro. III. §1. Nomenclature', *Annual of the British School at Athens* 10: 192-96.

— 1903/04b. 'Excavations at Palaikastro. III. § 2. Τὰ ῾Ελληνικά and Early Minoan discoveries', *Annual of the British School at Athens* 10: 196-202.

— 1903/04c. 'Excavations at Palaikastro. III. § 3. Blocks κ and λ', *Annual of the British School at Athens* 10: 202-04.

— 1903/04d. 'Excavations at Palaikastro. III. § 4. Block ϵ', *Annual of the British School at Athens* 10: 204-07.

— 1903/04e. 'Excavations at Palaikastro. III. § 5. Block ξ', *Annual of the British School at Athens* 10: 207-12.

— 1903/04f. 'Excavations at Palaikastro. III. § 6. Block π', *Annual of the British School at Athens* 10: 212-14.

— 1903/04g. 'Excavations at Palaikastro. III. § 7. Blocks ς and υ, *Annual of the British School at Athens* 10: 214-16.

— 1903/04h. 'Excavations at Palaikastro. III. § 8. Block δ, and the shrine of the snake-goddess', *Annual of the British School at Athens* 10: 216-26.

— 1903/04i. 'Notes from Karpathos', *Annual of the British School at Athens* 10: 83-102.

— 1904. 'Greek and Cretan epiphany customs', *Folklore* 15: 214.

— 1904/05a. 'Excavations at Palaikastro. IV. § 1. The season's work', *Annual of the British School at Athens* 11: 258-64.

— 1904/05b. 'Excavations at Palaikastro. IV. § 2. The finds', *Annual of the British School at Athens* 11: 264-68.

— 1904/05c. 'Excavations at Palaikastro. IV. § 3. An Early Minoan ossuary', *Annual of the British School at Athens* 11: 268-72.

— 1904/05d. 'Excavations at Palaikastro. IV. § 4. Temple site (Block χ)', *Annual of the British School at Athens* 11: 272-86.

— 1904/05e. 'Excavations at Palaikastro. IV. § 5. Block π', *Annual of the British School at Athens* 11: 286-90.

— 1904/05f. 'Excavations at Palaikastro. IV. § 6. A larnax burial', *Annual of the British School at Athens* 11: 290-92.

— 1904/05g. 'A visit to Skyros', *Annual of the British School at Athens* 11: 72-80.

— 1905/06. 'Excavations at Palaikastro. V', *Annual of the British School at Athens* 12: 1-8.

— 1906. 'The modern carnival in Thrace and the cult of Dionysus', *Journal of Hellenic Studies* 26: 191-206.

— 1906/07a. 'Laconia I. Excavations at Sparta, 1907. § 1. The season's work and summary of results', *Annual of the British School at Athens* 13: 1-4.

— 1906/07b. 'Laconia I. Excavations at Sparta, 1907. § 4. The sanctuary of Artemis Orthia', *Annual of the British School at Athens* 13: 44-108.

— 1907/08. 'Laconia I. Excavations at Sparta, 1908. § 2. The sanctuary of Artemis Orthia', *Annual of the British School at Athens* 14: 4-29.

— 1908/09a. 'Laconia I. Excavations at Sparta, 1909. § 1. The season's work', *Annual of the British School at Athens* 15: 1-4.

— 1908/09b. 'Laconia I. Excavations at Sparta, 1909. § 2. The sanctuary of Artemis Orthia', *Annual of the British School at Athens* 15: 5-22.

— 1908/09c. 'The transliteration of Modern Greek', *Annual of the British School at Athens* 15: 214-22.

— 1909/10a. 'Laconia I. Excavations at Sparta, 1910. § 2. The Mycenaean city near the Menelaion', *Annual of the British School at Athens* 16: 4-11.

— 1909/10b. 'Laconia I. Excavations at Sparta, 1910. § 4. Artemis Orthia: the excavation of 1910', *Annual of the British School at Athens* 16: 15-17.

— 1909/10c. 'Laconia I. Excavations at Sparta, 1910. § 5. Artemis Orthia: the history of the sanctuary', *Annual of the British School at Athens* 16: 18-53.

— 1910a. 'Archaeology in Greece, 1909-1910', *Journal of Hellenic Studies* 30: 357-64.

— 1910b. 'Modern Greek in Asia Minor', *Journal of Hellenic Studies* 30: 267-91.

— 1910c. 'Modern Greek in Asia Minor', *Journal of Hellenic Studies* 30: 109-32.

— 1910/11a. 'The Excavations at Phylakopi in Melos, 1911. § 1. Introduction', *Annual of the British School at Athens* 17: 1-2.

— 1910/11b. 'The Excavations at Phylakopi in Melos, 1911. § 2. The Excavation', *Annual of the British School at Athens* 17: 2-6.

— 1910/11c. 'The Excavations at Phylakopi in Melos, 1911. § 3. Intramural tombs of infants', *Annual of the British School at Athens* 17: 6-9.

— 1913/14. 'Excavations at Pláti in Lasithi, Crete', *Annual of the British School at Athens* 20: 1-17.

— 1929. *The sanctuary of Artemis Orthia at Sparta*. Society for the Promotion of Hellenic Studies, Supplementary Papers, vol. 5. London: Macmillan.

— 1934. 'Some modern Greek songs from Cappadocia', *American Journal of Archaeology* 38: 112-22.

— 1949. 'Obituary: Margaret Masson Hasluck', *Folklore* 60: 291-92.

— 1951. 'Recently published collections of modern folktales', *Annual of the British School at Athens* 46: 53-60.

— 1953. *Modern Greek Folktales*. Oxford: Clarendon Press.

— 1954. 'John Linton Myres: 1869-1954', *Man* 54: 40-41.

Dawkins, R. M., and J. P. Droop. 1910/11a. 'Byzantine pottery from Sparta', *Annual of the British School at Athens* 17: 23-28.

— 1910/11b. 'The Excavations at Phylakopi in Melos, 1911. § 4. Melos and Crete', *Annual of the British School at Athens* 17: 9-15.

— 1910/11c. 'The Excavations at Phylakopi in Melos, 1911. § 5. Melos and the mainland', *Annual of the British School at Athens* 17: 16-19.

— 1910/11d. 'The Excavations at Phylakopi in Melos, 1911. § 6. Native Melian fabrics', *Annual of the British School at Athens* 17: 19-21.

— 1910/11e. 'The Excavations at Phylakopi in Melos, 1911. § 7. Miscellaneous finds', *Annual of the British School at Athens* 17: 21-22.

Dawkins, R. M., and W. R. Halliday. 1916. *Modern Greek in Asia Minor: a study of the dialects of Silli, Cappadocia and Pharasa, with grammar, texts, translations and glossary*. Cambridge: Cambridge University Press.

Dawkins, R. M., and F. W. Hasluck. 1905/06. 'Inscriptions from Bizye', *Annual of the British School at Athens* 12: 175-83.

Dawkins, R. M., and M. L. W. Laistner. 1912/13. 'The excavations of the Kamares Cave in Crete' *Annual of the British School at Athens* 19: 1-34.

Dawkins, R. M., and J. D. Pickles. 2004. 'Giles, Peter (1860-1935)', in *Oxford Dictionary of National Biography*, vol. 22: 231-32. Oxford: Oxford University Press.

Dawkins, R. M., and W. H. D. Rouse. 1906. 'The pronunciation of θ and δ', *Classical Review* 20: 441-43.

Dawkins, R. M., and M. N. Tod. 1902/03. 'Excavations at Palaikastro. II. § 9. Kouraménos', *Annual of the British School at Athens* 9: 329-35.

Dawkins, R. M., and A. J. B. Wace. 1905/06. 'Notes from the Sporades: Astypalaea, Telos, Nisyros, Leros', *Annual of the British School at Athens* 12: 151-74.

Delaney, P. 1990. *Charles Ricketts: a biography*. Oxford: Clarendon Press.

Dickins, G. 1903. 'Some points with regard to the Homeric house', *Journal of Hellenic Studies* 23: 325-34.

— 1904/05a. 'A head in connexion with Damophon', *Annual of the British School at Athens* 11: 173-80.

— 1904/05b. 'Laconia III. Thalamae. 1. Excavations', *Annual of the British School at Athens* 11: 124-30.

— 1904/05c. 'Laconia III. Thalamae. 2. Inscriptions', *Annual of the British School at Athens* 11: 131-36.

— 1905/06a. 'Damophon of Messene', *Annual of the British School at Athens* 12: 109-36.

— 1905/06b. 'Laconia II. Excavations at Sparta, 1906. § 4. The great altar near the Eurotas', *Annual of the British School at Athens* 12: 295-302.

— 1905/06c. 'Laconia II. Excavations at Sparta, 1906. § 10. The theatre and adjoining area', *Annual of the British School at Athens* 12: 394-406.

— 1905/06d. 'Laconia II. Excavations at Sparta, 1906. § 13. Topographical conclusions', *Annual of the British School at Athens* 12: 431-39.

— 1906. 'A new replica of the Choiseul-Gouffier type', *Journal of Hellenic Studies* 26: 278-80.

— 1906/07a. 'Damophon of Messene. II', *Annual of the British School at Athens* 13: 357-404.

— 1906/07b. 'Laconia I. Excavations at Sparta, 1907. § 7. The Hieron of Athena Chalkioikos', *Annual of the British School at Athens* 13: 137-54.

— 1906/07c. 'Laconia I. Excavations at Sparta, 1907. § 9. The sanctuary on the Megalopolis road', *Annual of the British School at Athens* 13: 169-73.

— 1907/08. 'Laconia I. Excavations at Sparta, 1908. § 6. The hieron of Athena Chalkioikos', *Annual of the British School at Athens* 14: 142-46.

— 1910/11. 'Damophon of Messene. III', *Annual of the British School at Athens* 17: 80-87.

— 1911. 'The sandal in the Palazzo dei Conservatori', *Journal of Hellenic Studies* 31: 308-14.

— 1912. *Catalogue of the Acropolis Museum I*. Cambridge: Cambridge University Press.

— 1914a. 'The Holkham head and the Parthenon pediment', *Journal of Hellenic Studies* 34: 122-25.

— 1914b. 'Some Hellenistic portraits', *Journal of Hellenic Studies* 34: 293-311.

— 1914/16. 'The followers of Praxiteles', *Annual of the British School at Athens* 21: 1-9.

— 1929. 'Terracotta masks', in *The sanctuary of Artemis Orthia at Sparta*, edited by R. M. Dawkins, vol. 5: 163-86. Society for the Promotion of Hellenic Studies. Supplementary papers vol. 5. London: Macmillan.

Dodwell, E. 1819. *A classical and topographical tour through Greece during the years 1801, 1805 and 1806*. London: Rodwell & Martin.

Dörpfeld, W. 1886. 'Mycenae and Tiryns', *The Times* 29 May 1886: 5.

Dörpfeld, W., E. A. Gardner, and W. Loring. 1891. 'The theatre at Megalopolis', *Classical Review* 5: 284-85.

Droop, J. P. 1905/06a. 'Dipylon vases from the Kynosarges site', *Annual of the British School at Athens* 12: 80-92.

— 1905/06b. 'Messapian inscriptions', *Annual of the British School at Athens* 12: 137-50.

— 1906/07a. 'Laconia I. Excavations at Sparta, 1907. § 5. The early bronzes', *Annual of the British School at Athens* 13: 109-17.

— 1906/07b. 'Laconia I. Excavations at Sparta, 1907. § 6. The early pottery', *Annual of the British School at Athens* 13: 118-36.

— 1907/08. 'Laconia I. Excavations at Sparta, 1908. § 3. The pottery', *Annual of the British School at Athens* 14: 30-47.

— 1908/09. 'Laconia I. Excavations at Sparta, 1909. § 3. The pottery', *Annual of the British School at Athens* 15: 23-39.

— 1910. 'The dates of the vases called 'Cyrenaic'', *Journal of Hellenic Studies* 30: 1-34.

— 1913. 'Archaeology in Greece, 1912-1913', *Journal of Hellenic Studies* 33: 361-68.

— 1915. *Archaeological excavation*. The Cambridge Archaeological and Ethnological Series. Cambridge: Cambridge University Press.

— 1932. 'Droop cups and the dating of Laconian pottery', *Journal of Hellenic Studies* 52: 303-04.

Drower, M. S. 1982. 'The early years', in *Excavating in Egypt: the Egypt Exploration Society 1882-1982*, edited by T. G. H. James: 9-36. London: British Museum Publications.

— 1995. *Flinders Petrie: a life in archaeology*, 2nd edition. Madison: University of Wisconsin Press.

Duchêne, H., and C. Straboni. 1996. 'La conquête de l'archéologie moderne: l'histoire de l'École française d'Athènes de 1846 à 1914', CNERTA. CD-ROM.

Duckworth, W. L. H. 1902/03a. 'Excavations at Palaikastro. II. § 11. Human remains at Hagios Nikolaos', *Annual of the British School at Athens* 9: 344-50.

— 1902/03b. 'Excavations at Palaikastro. II. § 12. Ossuaries at Roussolakkos', *Annual of the British School at Athens* 9: 350-55.

— 1911. '35. Report on a human skull from Thessaly (now in the Cambridge University Anatomical Museum)', *Man* 11: 49-50.

Duckworth, W. L. H., A. C. Haddon, W. H. R. Rivers, and W. Ridgeway. 1906. 'Anthropology at the Universities', *Man* 6: 85-86.

Duncan, J. G. 1908. *The exploration of Egypt and the Old Testament: a summary of the results obtained by exploration in Egypt up to the present time, with a fuller account of those bearing on the Old Testament*. Edinburgh: Oliphant Anderson & Ferrier.

— 1930. *The accuracy of the Old Testament: the historical narratives in the light of recent Palestinian archaeology*. London: Society for Promoting Christian Knowledge.

— 1931. *Digging up Biblical history: recent archaeology in Palestine and its bearing on the Old Testament*. London ; New York: Society for Promoting Christian Knowledge: Macmillan.

Duncan, J. G., W. M. F. Petrie, and J. L. Starkey. 1930. *Corpus of dated Palestinian pottery, including pottery of Gerar and Beth-pelet, and beads of Beth-pelet*. British School of Archaeology in Egypt: Publications of the Egyptian Research Account; no. 49. London: British School of Archaeology in Egypt.

Dunlop, W. M. 2000. 'Kingdon Tregosse Frost: first lecturer in archaeology at the Queen's University of Belfast', *Ulster Journal of Archaeology* 59: 2-10.

Dyson, S. L. 1998. *Ancient marbles to American shores: classical archaeology in the United States*. Philadelphia: University of Pennsylvania Press.

— 2004. *Eugénie Sellers Strong: portrait of an archaeologist*. London: George Duckworth.

— 2006. *In pursuit of ancient pasts: a history of classical archaeology in the nineteenth and twentieth centuries*. New Haven, Conn. ; London: Yale University Press.

Easterling, P. 1999. 'The Cambridge Greek play', in *Classics in 19th and 20th century Cambridge: curriculum, culture and community*, edited by C. A. Stray, vol. 24: 27-47. Cambridge Philological Society supplementary volume. Cambridge: Cambridge Philological Society.

Eccles, E., M. B. Money-Coutts, and J. D. S. Pendlebury. 1934. *A guide to the stratigraphical museum in the Palace of Knossos*, vol. 2. Athens: British School at Athens.

Edgar, C. C. 1896/7. 'Prehistoric tombs at Pelos', *Annual of the British School at Athens* 3: 35-51.

— 1897. 'Two stelae from Kynosarges', *Journal of Hellenic Studies* 17: 174-75.

— 1897/8. 'Excavations in Melos, 1898. III. The pottery', *Annual of the British School at Athens* 4: 37-48.

— 1898/9a. 'Excavations at Naukratis. B. The inscribed and painted pottery', *Annual of the British School at Athens* 5: 47-65.

— 1898/9b. 'Excavations at Naukratis. C. A relief', *Annual of the British School at Athens* 5: 65-67.

— 1898/9c. 'Excavations in Melos, 1899. C. The pottery', *Annual of the British School at Athens* 5: 14-19.

— 1903a. *Greek moulds*. Catalogue général des antiquités égyptiennes du Musée du Caire, vol. 8. Le Caire: Imprimerie de l'Institut français d'archéologie orientale.

— 1903b. *Greek sculpture*. Catalogue général des antiquités égyptiennes du Musée du Caire, vol. 13. Le Caire: Impr. de l'Institut française d'archéologie orientale.

— 1904a. *Greek bronzes*. Catalogue général des antiquités égyptiennes du Musée du Caire. Le Caire: Impr. de l'Institut française d'archéologie orientale.

— 1904b. 'An Ionian dedication to Isis', *Journal of Hellenic Studies* 24: 337.

— 1905a. *Graeco-Egyptian coffins, masks and portraits*. Catalogue général des antiquités égyptiennes du Musée du Caire. Le Caire: Istitut français d'archéologie orientale.

— 1905b. *Graeco-Egyptian glass*. Catalogue général des antiquités égyptiennes du Musée du Caire. Le Caire: Institut français d'archéologie orientale.

— 1905c. 'On the dating of the Fayoum portraits', *Journal of Hellenic Studies* 25: 225-33.

— 1906a. *Sculptor's studies and unfinished works*. Catalogue général des antiquités égyptiennes du Musée du Caire. Le Caire: Impr. de l'Institut française d'archéologie orientale.

— 1906b. 'Two bronze portraits from Egypt', *Journal of Hellenic Studies* 26: 281-82.

— 1911. *Greek vases*. Catalogue général des antiquités égyptiennes du Musée du Caire. Le Caire: Impr. de l'Institut française d'archéologie orientale.

— 1917. 'A women's club in ancient Alexandria', *Journal of Egyptian Archaeology* 4: 253-54.

— 1925. *Zenon papyri*. Catalogue général des antiquités égyptiennes du Musée du Caire Le Caire: Impr. de l'Institut francais d'archeologie orientale.

— 1928. 'Three Ptolemaic papyri', *Journal of Egyptian Archaeology* 14: 288-93.

— 1937. 'On P. Lille I. 4', *Journal of Egyptian Archaeology* 23: 261.

Edmonds, C. D. 1898/9. 'Some doubtful points of Thessalian topography', *Annual of the British School at Athens* 5: 20-25.

— 1900. 'The tumulus of Pilaf-Tepe', *Journal of Hellenic Studies* 20: 20-25.

Étienne, R. 1996. 'L'École française d'Athènes, 1846-1996', *Bulletin de Correspondance Hellénique* 120: 3-22.

Evans, A. J. 1894. 'Primitive pictographs and prae-Phoenician script from Crete and the Peloponnese', *Journal of Hellenic Studies* 14: 270-372.

— 1895/96. 'Goulas: the city of Zeus', *Annual of the British School at Athens* 2: 169-94.

— 1899/1900. 'Knossos. I. The palace', *Annual of the British School at Athens* 6: 3-70.

— 1900/1. 'The palace of Knossos, 1901', *Annual of the British School at Athens* 7: 1-120.

— 1901/02. 'The palace of Knossos: provisional report of the excavations for the year 1902', *Annual of the British School at Athens* 8: 1-124.

— 1902/03. 'The palace of Knossos: provisional report for the year 1903', *Annual of the British School at Athens* 9: 1-153.

— 1903/04. 'The palace of Knossos', *Annual of the British School at Athens* 10: 1-62.

— 1904/05. 'The palace of Knossos and its dependencies: provisional report for the year 1905', *Annual of the British School at Athens* 11: 1-26.

Evans, J. 1964. *Prelude & fugue: an autobiography*. London: Museum Press.

— 1966. *The Conways: a history of three generations*. London: Museum Press.

Evelyn-White, H. G. 1909. 'Excavation at Caerleon', *The Times* 8 January 1909: 16.

Fagan, B. 2004. *The rape of the Nile: tomb robbers, tourists, and archaeologists in Egypt*, 3rd edition. Boulder (Co.) and Oxford: Westview Press.

Falkener, E. 1862. *Ephesus and the temple of Diana*. London: Day & Son.

Farnell, L. R. 1896. *Cults of the Greek States*. Oxford: Clarendon Press.

— 1934. *An Oxonian looks back*. London: M. Hopkinson.

Farnell, L. R., and R. Jann. 2004. 'Abbott, Edwin Abbott (1838-1926)', in *Oxford Dictionary of National Biography*, vol. 1: 43-44. Oxford: Oxford University Press.

Farrell, J. 1907/08. 'Laconia I. Excavations at Sparta, 1908. § 4. The archaic terracottas from the sanctuary of Orthia', *Annual of the British School at Athens* 14: 48-73.

— 1910. 'Note on the Position of Rhoduntia' *Classical Review* 24: 116-17.

Fearon, W. A. 1895. 'Winchester Quingentenary Memorial', *The Times* 22 November 1895: 7.

Fergusson, J., D. B. Monro, H. F. Pelham, and G. A. Macmillan. 1884. 'Exploration in Asia Minor', *The Times* 21 March 1884: 3.

Findlay, A. F. 1894/5. 'St. Paul and the Areopagus', *Annual of the British School at Athens* 1: 78-89.

Fitton, J. L. 1995. *The discovery of the Greek Bronze Age*. London: British Museum Press.

Fletcher, C. R. L. 1928. 'David George Hogarth, President R. G. S., 1925-1927', *Geographical Journal* 71: 321-44.

Fletcher, H. M., and S. D. Kitson. 1895/6. 'The churches of Melos', *Annual of the British School at Athens* 2: 155-68.

Foote, Y. 2004. 'Dodwell, Edward (1777/6-1832)', in *Oxford Dictionary of National Biography*, vol. 16: 442-44. Oxford: Oxford University Press.

Forster, E. S. 1901/02. 'Praesos: the terracottas', *Annual of the British School at Athens* 8: 125-56.

— 1903/04a. 'South-western Laconia. Inscriptions', *Annual of the British School at Athens* 10: 167-89.

— 1903/04b. 'South-western Laconia. Sites', *Annual of the British School at Athens* 10: 158-66.

— 1904/05. 'Terracotta plaques from Praesos', *Annual of the British School at Athens* 11: 243-57.

— 1905. 'A fragment of the "Edictum Diocletiani"', *Journal of Hellenic Studies* 25: 260-62.

— 1906/07. 'Laconia II. Topography. § 1. Gythium and N. W. coast of the Laconian Gulf', *Annual of the British School at Athens* 13: 219-37.

— 1907. 'Terracottas from Boeotia and Crete', *Journal of Hellenic Studies* 27: 68-74.

— 1941. *A short history of modern Greece 1821-1940*. London: Methuen & Co. Ltd.

Fraser, P. M., and E. Baigent. 2004. 'Tozer, Henry Fanshawe (1829-1916)', in *Oxford Dictionary of National Biography*, vol. 55: 192-93. Oxford: Oxford University Press.

Frazer, J. G. 1898. *Pausanias's Description of Greece*. London: Macmillan & Co.

Freeman, P. W. M. 2007. *The best training ground for archaeologists: Francis Haverfield and the invention of Romano-British archaeology*. Oxford: Oxbow.

French, E. B. 2002. *Mycenae: Agamemnon's capital. The site in its setting*. Stroud: Tempus.

Frere, J. H., D. G. Hogarth, and A. D. Godley. 1892. *The Frogs of Aristophanes: adapted for performance by the Oxford University Dramatic Society, 1892*. Oxford: Oxford University Dramatic Society.

Freshfield, E. 1881a. 'The Christian antiquities of Constantinople', *The Times* 17 March 1881: 6.

— 1881b. 'The Christian antiquities of Constantinople', *The Times* 25 January 1881: 4.

— 1890. 'The mosque of Hagia Sofia at Salonica', *The Times* 8 September 1890: 7.

— 1908. 'Byzantine Research Fund', *The Times* 25 June 1908: 9.

Frothingham, A. L., Jr. 1885. 'The British School of Archaeology at Athens', *American Journal of Archaeology and of the History of the Fine Arts* 1: 218-19.

— 1889. 'Archaeological news', *American Journal of Archaeology and of the History of the Fine Arts* 5: 358-402.

— 1890. 'Archaeological news', *American Journal of Archaeology and of the History of the Fine Arts* 6: 154-260.

Fyfe, D. T. 1907. 'The church of St. Titus at Gortyna, Crete', *Architectural Review* 22: 5-60.

Gardiner, E. M. 1909. 'A series of sculptures from Corinth: Hellenic reliefs', *American Journal of Archaeology* 13: 158-69.

Gardner, E. A. 1882. 'Athene in the west pediment of the Parthenon' *Journal of Hellenic Studies* 3: 244-55.

— 1884. 'Ornaments and armour from Kertch in the new museum at Oxford', *Journal of Hellenic Studies* 5: 62-73, pls. xlvi-xlvii.

— 1885a. 'Inscriptions copied by Cockerell in Greece, I', *Journal of Hellenic Studies* 6: 143-52.

— 1885b. 'Inscriptions copied by Cockerell in Greece, II', *Journal of Hellenic Studies* 6: 340-63.

— 1885c. 'Inscriptions from Cos, & c', *Journal of Hellenic Studies* 6: 248-60.

— 1885d. 'A statuette representing a boy and a goose', *Journal of Hellenic Studies* 6: 1-15, pl. A.

— 1886a. 'The early Ionic alphabet', *Journal of Hellenic Studies* 7: 220-39.

— 1886b. 'Excavations at Naukratis', *American Journal of Archaeology and of the History of the Fine Arts* 2: 180-81.

— 1886c. 'An inscription from Chalcedon', *Journal of Hellenic Studies* 7: 154-56.

— 1887a. 'An inscription from Boeae', *Journal of Hellenic Studies* 8: 214-15.

— 1887b. 'Recently discovered archaic statues', *Journal of Hellenic Studies* 8: 159-93.

— 1887c. 'Sculpture and epigraphy, 1886-1887', *Journal of Hellenic Studies* 8: 278-85.

— 1887d. 'Two Naucratite vases', *Journal of Hellenic Studies* 8: 119-21, pl. lxxix.

— 1888. *Naukratis II*. London: Egypt Exploration Fund.

— 1889. 'Archaeology in Greece, 1888-89', *Journal of Hellenic Studies* 10: 254-80, pl. viii.

— 1890a. 'Archaeology in Greece, 1889-90', *Journal of Hellenic Studies* 11: 210-17.

— 1890b. 'The processes of Greek sculpture as shown by some unfinished statues at Athens', *Journal of Hellenic Studies* 11: 129-42.

— 1890c. 'Two fourth century children's heads', *Journal of Hellenic Studies* 11: 100-08.

— 1891. 'Archaeology in Greece, 1890-91', *Journal of Hellenic Studies* 12: 385-97.

— 1892/3. 'Archaeology in Greece, 1892', *Journal of Hellenic Studies* 13: 139-52.

— 1893. 'The Archermus inscription', *Classical Review* 7: 140-41.

— 1894a. 'Archaeology in Greece, 1893-94', *Journal of Hellenic Studies* 14: 224-32.

— 1894b. 'A lecythus from Eretria with the death of Priam', *Journal of Hellenic Studies* 14: 170-85, pl. ix.

— 1894c. 'Notes on Megalopolis', *Journal of Hellenic Studies* 14: 242-43.

— 1894/5. 'Sir Charles Newton, K. C. B.', *Annual of the British School at Athens* 1: 67-77.

— 1895. 'Archaeology in Greece, 1894-5', *Journal of Hellenic Studies* 15: 202-10.

— 1896. *A handbook of Greek sculpture*. Handbooks of archaeology and antiquities, vol. 1. London: Macmillan and Co.

— 1897. *A handbook of Greek sculpture*. Handbooks of archaeology and antiquities, vol. 2. London: Macmillan and Co.

— 1899. 'Woodhouse's Aetolia', *Classical Review* 13: 88-89.

— 1938. *Greece and the Aegean*, New revised edition. London: George G. Harrap & Co.

Gardner, E. A., D. G. Hogarth, M. R. James, and R. Elsey Smith. 1888. 'Excavations in Cyprus, 1887-8. Paphos, Leontari, Amargetti', *Journal of Hellenic Studies* 9: 147-271, pls. vii-xi.

Gardner, E. A., W. Loring, G. C. Richards, and W. J. Woodhouse. 1890. 'The theatre at Megalopolis', *Journal of Hellenic Studies* 11: 294-98.

Gardner, E. A., W. Loring, G. C. Richards, W. J. Woodhouse, and R. W. Schultz. 1892. *Excavations at Megalopolis, 1890-1891*. Society for the Promotion of Hellenic Studies. Supplementary papers ; no. 1. London: Society for the Promotion of Hellenic Studies.

Gardner, E. A., and R. W. Schultz. 1891. 'The north doorway of the Erechtheum', *Journal of Hellenic Studies* 12: 1-16, pls. i-iii.

Gardner, P. 1933. *Autobiographica*. Oxford: B. Blackwell.

Garnett, R., and E. Baigent. 2004. 'Pashley, Robert (1805-1859)', in *Oxford Dictionary of National Biography*, vol. 42: 965-66. Oxford: Oxford University Press.

Garstang, J. 1898. *Roman Ribchester: being the report of excavations made on the site during 1898*. Preston: George Toulmin.

— 1901. 'Melandra Castle', *Journal of the Derbyshire Archaeological and Natural History Society* 23: 90-98.

Garstang, J., and W. S. George. 1913. *Excavations at Meroë, Sudan, 1913, fourth season: guide to the twelfth annual exhibition of antiquities discovered*. Liverpool: Institute of Archaeology University of Liverpool.

Gates, C. 1996. 'American archaeologists in Turkey: intellectual and social dimensions', *Journal of American Studies of Turkey* 4: 47-68.

George, W. S. 1913. *The church of Saint Eirene at Constantinople*. London: Oxford University Press.

George, W. S., and A. M. Woodward. 1929. 'The architectural terracottas', in *The sanctuary of Artemis Orthia at Sparta*, edited by R. M. Dawkins. Society for the Promotion of Hellenic Studies. Supplementary papers vol. 5: 117-43. London: Macmillan.

Gilbert, M. 1973. *Sir Horace Rumbold: portrait of a diplomat, 1869-1941*. London: Heinemann.

Giles, P., and J. Hardy. 2004. 'Neil, Robert Alexander (1852-1901)', in *Oxford Dictionary of National Biography*, vol. 40: 353-54. Oxford: Oxford University Press.

Giles, P., and M. J. Schofield. 2004. 'Adam, James (1860-1907)', in *Oxford Dictionary of National Biography*, vol. 1: 197-98. Oxford: Oxford University Press.

Gill, D. W. J. 1992a. *Donors and former owners of Greek and Roman antiquities in the Fitzwilliam Museum, Cambridge*. Cambridge: Fitzwilliam Museum.

— 1992b. *Findspots of Greek and Roman antiquities in the Fitzwilliam Museum, Cambridge*. Cambridge: Fitzwilliam Museum.

— 1999. 'Winifred Lamb and the Fitzwilliam Museum', in *Classics in 19th and 20th century Cambridge: curriculum, culture and community*, edited by C. A. Stray, vol. 24: 135-56. Cambridge Philological Society supplementary volume. Cambridge: Cambridge Philological Society.

— 2000a. 'Collecting for Cambridge: John Hubert Marshall on Crete', *Annual of the British School at Athens* 95: 517-26.

— 2000b. '"A rich and promising site": Winifred Lamb (1894–1963), Kusura and Anatolian archaeology', *Anatolian Studies* 50: 1-10.

— 2002. '"The passion of hazard": women at the British School at Athens before the First World War', *Annual of the British School at Athens* 97: 491-510.

— 2004a. 'Beazley, Sir John Davidson (1885-1970)', in *Oxford Dictionary of National Biography*, vol. 4: 683-85. Oxford: Oxford University Press.

— 2004b. 'Bosanquet, Robert Carr (1871-1935)', in *Oxford Dictionary of National Biography*, vol. 6: 695-96. Oxford: Oxford University Press.

— 2004c. 'The British School at Athens and archaeological research in the late Ottoman Empire', in *Archaeology, anthropology and heritage in the Balkans and Anatolia: the life and times of F. W. Hasluck, 1878-1920*, edited by D. Shankland, vol. 1: 223-55. Istanbul: The Isis Press.

— 2004d. 'Brodrick, Mary (1858-1933)', in *Oxford Dictionary of National Biography*, vol. 7: 791-93. Oxford: Oxford University Press.

— 2004e. 'Cook, Arthur Bernard (1868-1952)', in *Oxford Dictionary of National Biography*, vol. 13: 86-88. Oxford: Oxford University Press.

— 2004f. 'Cornford, Francis Macdonald (1874-1943)', in *Oxford Dictionary of National Biography*, vol. 13: 449-53. Oxford: Oxford University Press.

— 2004g. 'Dawkins, Richard MacGillivray (1871-1955)', in *Oxford Dictionary of National Biography*, vol. 15: 538-40. Oxford: Oxford University Press.

— 2004h. 'Disney, John (1779-1857)', in *Oxford Dictionary of National Biography*, vol. 16: 266-68. Oxford: Oxford University Press.

— 2004i. 'Dorothy Lamb (1887-1967): a pioneering Mediterranean field-archaeologist', Brown University. http://www. brown. edu/Research/Breaking_Ground/.

— 2004j. 'Gardner, Ernest Arthur (1862-1939)', in *Oxford Dictionary of National Biography*, vol. 21: 454-55. Oxford: Oxford University Press.

— 2004k. 'Harcourt-Smith, Cecil (1859-1944; Kt 1909)', in *The Dictionary of British Classicists*, edited by R. B. Todd, vol. 2: 414-15. Bristol: Thoemmes Continuum.

— 2004l. 'Hogarth, David George (1862-1927)', in *Oxford Dictionary of National Biography*, vol. 27: 537-42. Oxford: Oxford University Press.

— 2004m. 'Jones, Sir Henry Stuart- (1867-1939)', in *Oxford Dictionary of National Biography*, vol. 30: 521-24. Oxford: Oxford University Press.

— 2004n. 'Paton, William Roger (1857-1921)', in *Oxford Dictionary of National Biography*, vol. 43: 68-69. Oxford: Oxford University Press.

— 2004o. 'Richards, George Chatterton (1867-1951)', in *The dictionary of British classicists*, edited by R. B. Todd, vol. 3: 814-15. Bristol: Thoemmes Continuum.

— 2004p. 'A saviour for the cities of Crete: the Roman background to the epistle of Titus', in *The New Testament in its first century setting. Essays on context and background in honour of B. W. Winter on his 65th birthday*, edited by P. J. Williams, A. D. Clarke, P. M. Head, and D. Instone-Brewer: 220-30. Grand Rapids and Cambridge: Wm. B. Eerdmans.

— 2004q. 'Wace, Alan John Bayard (1879-1957)', in *Oxford Dictionary of National Biography*, vol. 56: 632-35. Oxford: Oxford University Press.

— 2004r. 'Winifred Lamb (1894-1963)', in *Breaking Ground: Pioneering women archaeologists*, edited by G. Cohen and M. S. Joukowsky: 425-81. Ann Arbor: University of Michigan Press.

— 2006a. 'Harry Pirie-Gordon: historical research, journalism and intelligence gathering in the eastern Mediterranean (1908-18)' *Intelligence and National Security* 21: 1045-59.

— 2006b. 'Winifred Lamb: searching for prehistory in Greece' In *Travellers to Greece*, edited by C. A. Stray: 33-53. London: Classical Association.

— 2007. 'Winifred Lamb: her first year as a student at the British School at Athens', in *Archaeology and women: ancient and modern issues*, edited by S. Hamilton, R. D. Whitehouse, and K. I. Wright: 55-75. Walnut Creek (CA): Left Coast Press.

— 2008. *Students at the British School at Athens (1886-1914)*. Swansea: Ostraka Press.

Gill, D. W. J., and C. Chippindale. 1993. 'Material and intellectual consequences of esteem for Cycladic figures', *American Journal of Archaeology* 97: 601-59.

Goldman, H. 1915. 'Inscriptions from the acropolis of Halae', *American Journal of Archaeology* 19: 438-53.

Gomme, A. W. 1910/11. 'The literary evidence for the topography of Thebes', *Annual of the British School at Athens* 17: 29-53.

— 1911/12. 'The topography of Boeotia and the theories of M. Bérard', *Annual of the British School at Athens* 18: 189-210.

— 1913a. 'The legend of Cadmus and the Logographi', *Journal of Hellenic Studies* 33: 53-72.

— 1913b. 'The legend of Cadmus and the Logographi. -II', *Journal of Hellenic Studies* 33: 223-45.

Goodwin, G., and E. Baigent. 2004. 'Cripps, John Marten (1780-1853)', in *Oxford Dictionary of National Biography*, vol. 14: 199. Oxford: Oxford University Press.

Grenfell, B. P., A. S. Hunt, D. G. Hogarth, and J. G. Milne. 1900. *Fayum towns and their papyri*. Egypt Exploration Fund. Graeco-Roman branch. Memoirs, vol. 3. London: Egypt Exploration Fund.

Griffin, N. Editor. 1992. *The selected letters of Bertrand Russell. Volume 1: the private years, 1884-1914*. London: Allen Lane.

Grose, S. W. 1916. 'A dekadrachm by Kimon and a note on Greek coin dies', *Numismatic Chronicle* 16: 113-32.

— 1923. *Catalogue of the McClean collection of Greek coins [in the] Fitzwilliam Museum, Cambridge*. Cambridge: Cambridge University Press.

Grundon, I. 2007. *The rash adventurer: a life of John Pendlebury*. London: Libri.

Grundy, G. B. 1894. 'The battle-field of Plataea', *Geographical Journal* 3: 525-26.

— 1896. 'Pylos and Sphakteria', *Classical Review* 10: 371-74.

— 1897a. 'The Pylos and Sphacteria question', *Classical Review* 11: 155-58.

— 1897b. 'Pylos. The attack on Koryphasion. A note', *Classical Review* 11: 448.

Grundy, G. B., and R. M. Burrows. 1896 and 1897. 'An investigation of the topography of the region of Sphakteria and Pylos', *Journal of Hellenic Studies* 16/17: 1-54, 55-76.

Grundy, I. 1999. *Lady Mary Wortley Montagu: comet of the enlightenment*. Oxford: Clarendon Press.

Gunn, B. 2004. 'Peet, (Thomas) Eric (1882-1934)', in *Oxford Dictionary of National Biography*, vol. 43: 435. Oxford: Oxford University Press.

Gurney, O. R., and P. W. M. Freeman. 2004. 'Garstang, John Burges Eustace (1876-1956)', in *Oxford Dictionary of National Biography*, vol. 21: 551-53. Oxford: Oxford University Press.

Gutch, C. 1898/9. 'Excavations at Naukratis. D. The terracottas', *Annual of the British School at Athens* 5: 67-97.

Hall, H. R. 1928. 'David George Hogarth', *Journal of Egyptian Archaeology* 14: 128-30.

Halpern, P. G. 1987a. *The naval war in the Mediterranean 1914 - 1918*. Annapolis: Naval Institute Press.

— Editor. 1987b. *The Royal Navy in the Mediterranean 1915-1918*. Publications of the Navy Records Society, vol. 126. Aldershot: Navy Records Society.

Hamilton, J. A. 1890. *The principles of church design*. Edinburgh: Church of Scotland.

— 1916. *The church of Kaisariani in Attica: its history, architecture and mural paintings. A study in Byzantine art*. Aberdeen: W. Jolly & Sons.

Hamilton, M. 1906. *Incubation, or, the cure of disease in pagan temples and Christian churches*. London: W. C. Henderson & Son.

— 1906/7. 'The pagan element in the names of saints', *Annual of the British School at Athens* 13: 348–56.

— 1910. *Greek saints and their festivals*. London: W. Blackwood & Sons.

Hankey, J. 2001. *A passion for Egypt: Arthur Weigall, Tutankhamun and the 'Curse of the Pharaohs'*, London: I. B. Tauris.

Harcourt-Smith, C. 1896a. 'The Parthenon and the Olympic Games', *The Times* 29 February 1896: 4.

— 1896b. *Vases of the finest period*. Catalogue of the Greek and Etruscan vases in the British Museum, vol. III. London: British Museum.

— 1896/7. 'A new copy of the Athena Parthenos', *Annual of the British School at Athens* 3: 121-48.

Harcourt-Smith, C., and G. A. Macmillan. 1932. *The Society of Dilettanti: its regalia and pictures*. London: Macmillan.

Hardie, M. M. 1912. 'The shrine of Mên Askaenos at Pisidian Antioch', *Journal of Hellenic Studies* 32: 111-50.

— 1912/13. 'Dionysos at Smyrna', *Annual of the British School at Athens* 19: 89-94.

Harrison, J. E. 1888a. 'Archaeology in Greece, 1887-1888', *Journal of Hellenic Studies* 9: 118-33.

— 1888b. 'Some fragments of a vase presumably by Euphronios' *Journal of Hellenic Studies* 9: 143-46.

Hartley, M. 1954. 'H. L. Lorimer', *Girton Review* 155: 26-28.

Hasluck, F. W. 1901/02. 'Sculptures from Cyzicus', *Annual of the British School at Athens* 8: 190-96.

— 1902. 'An inscribed basis from Cyzicus', *Journal of Hellenic Studies* 22: 126-34.

— 1903. 'Inscriptions from Cyzicus', *Journal of Hellenic Studies* 23: 75-91.

— 1904. 'Unpublished inscriptions from the Cyzicus neighbourhood', *Journal of Hellenic Studies* 24: 20-40.

— 1904/05. 'Notes on the Lion group from Cyzicus', *Annual of the British School at Athens* 11: 151-52.

— 1905/06. 'Roman Bridge on the Aesepus', *Annual of the British School at Athens* 12: 184-89.

— 1906a. 'Notes on coin-collecting in Mysia', *Numismatic Chronicle* 6: 26-36.

— 1906b. 'Poemanenum', *Journal of Hellenic Studies* 26: 23-31.

— 1907. 'Inscriptions from the Cyzicus district, 1906', *Journal of Hellenic Studies* 27: 61-67.

— 1909. 'The Marmara Islands', *Journal of Hellenic Studies* 29: 6-18.

— 1909/10. 'A French inscription at Adalia', *Annual of the British School at Athens* 16: 185-86.

— 1910. *Cyzicus: being some account of the history and antiquities of that city, and of the district adjacent to it: with the towns of Apollonia ad Rhyndoveum, Miletupolis, Hadrianutherae, Priapus, Zeleia, etc.* Cambridge archaeological and ethnological series. Cambridge: Cambridge University Press.

— 1910/11. 'Tholos tomb at Kirk Kilisse', *Annual of the British School at Athens* 17: 76-79.

— 1911/12a. 'Datcha - Stadia - Halikarnassos', *Annual of the British School at Athens* 18: 211-16.

— 1911/12b. 'Plato in the folk-lore of the Konia plain', *Annual of the British School at Athens* 18: 265-69.

— 1912. 'Archaeology in Greece 1911-1912', *Journal of Hellenic Studies* 32: 385-90.

— 1912/13. 'Studies in Turkish history and folk-legend', *Annual of the British School at Athens* 19: 198-220.

— 1916/17, 1917/18. 'Mosques of the Arabs in Constantinople', *Annual of the British School at Athens* 22: 157-74.

— 1921. 'Heterodox tribes of Asia Minor', *Journal of the Royal Anthropological Institute of Great Britain and Ireland* 51: 310-42.

— 1922. 'The caliph Mamoun and the prophet Daniel', *Journal of Hellenic Studies* 42: 99-103.

— 1923a. 'Constantinopolitana', *Journal of Hellenic Studies* 43: 162-67.

— 1923b. 'The multiplication of tombs in Turkey', *Journal of Hellenic Studies* 43: 168-69.

Hasluck, F. W., and M. M. H. Hasluck. 1924. *Athos and its monasteries*. London; New York: K. Paul, Trench, Trubner & Co. Ltd: E. P. Dutton & Co.

— 1929. *Christianity and Islam under the sultans*. Oxford: Clarendon Press.

Hasluck, F. W., and A. E. Henderson. 1904. 'On the topography of Cyzicus', *Journal of Hellenic Studies* 24: 135-43.

Hasluck, M. 1912/13. 'Dionysos at Smyrna', *Annual of the British School at Athens* 19: 89-94.

Hasluck, M. M. 1932. *Kendime Englisht-Shqip or Albanian-English Reader: sixteen Albanian folk-stories collected and translated, with two grammars and vocabularies*. Cambridge: Cambridge University Press.

Hasluck, M. M. H., R. M. Dawkins, and F. W. Hasluck. 1926. *Letters on religion and folklore*. London: Luzac & Co.

Haverfield, F. 1911. Review of J. H. Hopkinson, *The Roman Fort at Ribchester* (1911), *Journal of Roman Studies* 1: 244.

— 1915a. 'Leonard Cheesman', *Classical Review* 29: 222-23.

— 1915b. 'Obituary: Leonard Cheesman', *Journal of Roman Studies* 5: 147-48.

Hawes, C. H. 1904/05. 'Excavations at Palaikastro. IV. § 7. Larnax burials at Sarandari', *Annual of the British School at Athens* 11: 293-97.

Hawes, H. A. B., B. E. Williams, R. B. Seager, and E. H. Hall. 1908. *Gournia, Vasiliki, and other prehistoric sites on the isthmus of Hierapetra, Crete*. Philadelphia: American Exploration Society.

Hawkes, J. 1982. *Mortimer Wheeler: adventurer in archaeology*. London: Weidenfeld and Nicolson.

Hazzidakis, J. 1912/13. 'An Early Minoan sacred cave at Arkalokhóri in Crete', *Annual of the British School at Athens* 19: 35-47.

Headlam, A. C. 1892. *Ecclesiastical sites in Isauria (Cilicia Trachea)*. Society for the Promotion of Hellenic Studies: Supplementary papers vol. 2. London: Society for the Promotion of Hellenic Studies and Macmillan and Co.

Heath, R. M. 1912/13. 'Proxeny decrees from Megara', *Annual of the British School at Athens* 19: 82-88.

Hellenic Society. 1880. 'List of officers and members', *Journal of Hellenic Studies* 1: xv-xxvi.

— 1882. 'Transactions of the Society for the Promotion of Hellenic Studies. The Session of 1882', *Journal of Hellenic Studies* 3: xxxvi-lii.

— 1883a. 'The Hellenic Society. The annual meeting', *The Times* 16 June 1883: 9.

— 1883b. 'Transactions of the Society for the Promotion of Hellenic Studies. The Session of 1883', *Journal of Hellenic Studies* 4: xxxvii-lii.

— 1884. 'Transactions of the Society for the Promotion of Hellenic Studies. The Session of 1884', *Journal of Hellenic Studies* 5: xxxix-xliv.

— 1885. 'Transactions of the Society for the Promotion of Hellenic Studies. The Session of 1884-5', *Journal of Hellenic Studies* 6: xli-liv.

— 1886. 'Transactions of the Society for the Promotion of Hellenic Studies. The Session of 1885-6', *Journal of Hellenic Studies* 7: xli-lxiv.

— 1887. 'Transactions of the Society for the Promotion of Hellenic Studies. The Session of 1886-7', *Journal of Hellenic Studies* 8: xlvii-lix.

— 1888. 'Transactions of the Society for the Promotion of Hellenic Studies. The Session of 1887-88', *Journal of Hellenic Studies* 9: xxxv-xliv.

— 1891. 'Transactions of The Society for the Promotion of Hellenic Studies. Session of 1890-91', *Journal of Hellenic Studies* 12: xxxvii-xlviii.

— 1894. 'Society for the Promotion of Hellenic Studies', *Journal of Hellenic Studies* 14: i-vii+xlvii-xlviii.

Hencken, T. C., and S. K. F. Stoddart. 2004. 'MacIver, David Randall- (1873-1945)', in *Oxford Dictionary of National Biography*, vol. 35: 488-89. Oxford: Oxford University Press.

Herbert, A. 1919. *Mons, Anzac and Kut*. London: E. Arnold.

Herrmann, P. 1888. *Das Gräberfeld von Marion auf Cypern*. Programm zum Winckelmannsfeste der Archäologischen Gesellschaft zu Berlin, vol. 48. Berlin.

Heurtley, W. A. 1923/24, 1924/25. 'Pottery from Macedonian mounds', *Annual of the British School at Athens* 26: 30-37.

— 1926/27. 'A prehistoric site in western Macedonia and the Dorian invasion', *Annual of the British School at Athens* 28: 158-94.

— 1927. 'Early Iron Age pottery from Macedonia', *Antiquaries Journal* 7: 44-59.

— 1931. 'Prehistoric Macedonia: what has been and what remains to be done', *Man* 31: 216-17.

— 1939. *Prehistoric Macedonia: an archaeological reconnaissance of Greek Macedonia (west of the Struma) in the Neolithic, Bronze, and early Iron ages*. Cambridge: Cambridge University Press.

— 1939/40. 'Excavations in Ithaca, 1930-35. Summary of the work; summary of conclusions', *Annual of the British School at Athens* 40: 1-13.

Heurtley, W. A., and O. Davies. 1926/27. 'Report on excavations at the toumba and tables of Vardaróftsa, Macedonia, 1925, 1926, Part I', *Annual of the British School at Athens* 28: 195-200.

Heurtley, W. A., and R. W. Hutchinson. 1925. 'Report on an excavation at the toumba of Vardino, Macedonia', *Annals of Archaeology and Anthropology* 12: 15-36.

— 1925/26. 'Report on excavations at the toumba and tables of Vardaróftsa, Macedonia, 1925, 1926. Part I. The toumba', *Annual of the British School at Athens* 27: 1-66.

Heurtley, W. A., and H. L. Lorimer. 1932/33. 'Excavations in Ithaca, I. LH III-Protogeometric cairns at Aetos', *Annual of the British School at Athens* 33: 22-65.

Hicks, E. L. 1882. *A manual of Greek historical inscriptions*. Oxford: Clarendon Press.

— 1887a. 'Iasos', *Journal of Hellenic Studies* 8: 83-118.

— 1887b. 'A Thasian decree', *Journal of Hellenic Studies* 8: 401-08.

— 1888. 'A sacrificial calendar from Kos', *Journal of Hellenic Studies* 9: 323-37.

— 1889. 'Inscriptions from Theangela', *Classical Review* 3: 234-37.

— 1890a. 'Ceramus (*Keramos*) and its inscriptions', *Journal of Hellenic Studies* 11: 109-28.

— 1890b. 'Inscriptions from eastern Cilicia', *Journal of Hellenic Studies* 11: 236-54.

— 1907. 'Three inscriptions from Asia Minor', *Journal of Hellenic Studies* 27: 226-28.

Hicks, E. L., and J. T. Bent. 1887. 'Inscriptions from Thasos', *Journal of Hellenic Studies* 8: 409-38.

Higgins, R. A. 1954. *Catalogue of the terracottas in the Department of Greek and Roman Antiquities, British Museum I. Greek: 730-330 BC*. London: British Museum.

— 2004. 'Wood, John Turtle (1821-1890)', in *Oxford Dictionary of National Biography*, vol. 60: 121. Oxford: Oxford University Press.

Hingley, R. 2000. *Roman officers and English gentlemen: the imperial origins of Roman archaeology*. London: Routledge.

Hinings, J. 2004. 'Penrose, John (1778-1859)', in *Oxford Dictionary of National Biography*, vol. 43: 612. Oxford: Oxford University Press.

Hitchens, C. 2008. *The Parthenon Marbles: the case for reunification*. London: Verso.

Hodges, R. 2000. *Visions of Rome: Thomas Ashby, archaeologist*. London: The British School at Rome.

Hogarth, D. G. 1888a. 'Excavations at Old Paphos', *Classical Review* 2: 155-57.

— 1888b. 'Inscriptions from Salonica', *Journal of Hellenic Studies* 8: 356-75.

— 1888c. 'Notes upon a visit to Celaenae Apamaea', *Journal of Hellenic Studies* 9: 343-49.

— 1888d. 'The recent excavations at Paphos', *Classical Review* 2: 186-88.

— 1889. *Devia Cypria: notes of an archaeological journey in Cyprus in 1888*. London: Henry Frowde.

— 1890. 'Notes in Phrygia, Paroreus and Lycaonia', *Journal of Hellenic Studies* 11: 151-66.

— 1897. *Philip and Alexander of Macedon. Two essays in biography*. London: John Murray.

— 1897/98. 'Excavations in Melos 1898. I. The season's work', *Annual of the British School at Athens* 4: 1-16.

— 1898/9. 'Excavations at Naukratis. A. Sites and buildings', *Annual of the British School at Athens* 5: 26-46.

— 1899/1900a. 'The Dictaean cave', *Annual of the British School at Athens* 6: 94-116.

— 1899/1900b. 'Knossos II. Early town and cemeteries', *Annual of the British School at Athens* 6: 70-85.

— 1899/1900c. 'Knossos IV. A Latin inscription', *Annual of the British School at Athens* 6: 92-93.

— 1900/01. 'Excavations at Zakro, Crete', *Annual of the British School at Athens* 7: 121-49.

— 1901. 'Explorations at Zakro in eastern Crete', *Man* 1: 186-87.

— 1902. 'The Zakro sealings', *Journal of Hellenic Studies* 22: 76-93.

— 1904. 'The Dictaean temple', *The Times* 6 June 1904: 12.

— 1908. 'The archaic Artemisia', *Journal of Hellenic Studies* 28: 338.

— 1908. *Excavations at Ephesus: the archaic Artemisia*. London: British Museum.

— 1909. *Ionia and the East: six lectures delivered before the University of London*. Oxford: Clarendon Press.

— 1910. *Accidents of an antiquary's life*. London: Macmillan and Co.

— 1910/11. 'Note on two Zakro sealings', *Annual of the British School at Athens* 17: 264-65.

— 1914. 'Egyptian Empire in Asia', *Journal of Egyptian Archaeology* 1: 9-17.

— 1915. 'Alexander in Egypt and some consequences', *Journal of Egyptian Archaeology* 2: 53-60.

— 1925. *The wandering scholar*. London: Oxford University Press.

Hogarth, D. G., and E. F. Benson. 1896. *Report of prospects of research in Alexandria*. London: Macmillan, for the Society for the Promotion of Hellenic Studies.

Hogarth, D. G., and R. C. Bosanquet. 1899. 'Archaeology in Greece, 1898-9', *Journal of Hellenic Studies* 19: 319-29.

Hogarth, D. G., H. L. Lorimer, and C. C. Edgar. 1905. 'Naukratis, 1903', *Journal of Hellenic Studies* 25: 105–36.

Hogarth, D. G., and F. B. Welch. 1901. 'Primitive painted pottery in Crete', *Journal of Hellenic Studies* 21: 78-98.

Holleaux, M. 1892. 'Statue archaïque trouvée à Milos', *Bulletin de Correspondance Hellénique* 16: 560-67.

Hood, R. 1998. *Faces of archaeology in Greece: caricatures by Piet de Jong*. Oxford: Leopard's Head Press.

Hopkinson, J. H. 1903/04. 'Note on the fragment of a painted pinax from Praesos', *Annual of the British School at Athens* 10: 148-53.

— 1906. 'Pottery found at Melandra', in *Melandra Castle*, edited by R. S. Conway: 77-95. Manchester: Manchester University Press.

— 1911. *The Roman fort at Ribchester*. Manchester: Manchester University Press.

— Editor. 1916. *The Roman fort at Ribchester*, 2nd edition. London: Sherratt & Hughes.

Hopkinson, J. H., and D. Atkinson. 1928. *The Roman fort at Ribchester*, 3rd edition.

Hopkinson, J. H., and J. Baker-Penoyre. 1902. 'New evidence on the Melian amphorae', *Journal of Hellenic Studies* 22: 46-75.

Hopkinson, N. 2004. 'Gow, James (1854-1923)', in *Dictionary of British Classicists*, edited by R. B. Todd, vol. 2: 389-90. Bristol: Thoemmes Continuum.

Howland, R. H. Editor. 2000. *The destiny of the Parthenon marbles. Proceedings from a seminar sponsored by the Society for the Preservation of the Greek Heritage and held at the Corcoran Gallery of Art Washington, D. C. February 13, 1999*. Washington: Society for the Preservation of the Greek Heritage.

Hoyt, E. P. 1976. *Disaster at the Dardanelles*. London: Arthur Baker.

Hunt, D. 1988. 'The British School at Athens', *Classical Review* 38: 138-39.

Hutchinson, R. W., E. Eccles, and S. Benton. 1939/40. 'Unpublished objects from Palaikastro and Praisos. II', *Annual of the British School at Athens* 40: 38-59.

Hutton, C. A. 1893. 'Inscriptions on pottery from Naukratis', *Classical Review* 7: 82-83.

— 1896/7. 'On three bronze statuettes', *Annual of the British School at Athens* 3: 149-55.

— 1897. 'Votive reliefs in the Acropolis Museum', *Journal of Hellenic Studies* 17: 306-18.

— 1909. 'Greek dress', *Classical Review* 23: 235-36.

— 1914/16a. 'The Greek inscriptions at Petworth House', *Annual of the British School at Athens* 21: 155-65.

— 1914/16b. 'Two sepulchral inscriptions from Suvla Bay', *Annual of the British School at Athens* 21: 166-68.

Huxley, D. Editor. 2000. *Cretan quests: British explorers, excavators and historians*. London: British School at Athens.

Iliffe, J. H., and T. B. Mitford. 1952. 'Excavations at Aphrodite's sanctuary of Paphos, 1951: a second season's work', *Liverpool Libraries, Museums & Arts Committee Bulletin* 2: 29-66.

James, R. R. 1999. *Gallipoli*. London: Pimlico.

James, T. G. H. Editor. 1982. *Excavating in Egypt: the Egypt Exploration Society 1882-1982*. London: British Museum Publications.

Janssen, R. M. 1992. *The first hundred years: Egyptology at University College London 1892-1992*. London: University College London.

Jebb, C. 1907. *Life and letters of Sir Richard Claverhouse Jebb O. M., Litt. D.* Cambridge: Cambridge University Press.

Jebb, R. C. 1878. 'Archaeology at Athens and Rome', *The Times* 18 September 1878: 11.

— 1880. 'Delos', *Journal of Hellenic Studies* 1: 7-62.

— 1881. 'Homeric and Hellenic Ilium', *Journal of Hellenic Studies* 2: 7-43.

— 1882. 'The Ruins at Hissarlik and their relation to the Iliad', *Journal of Hellenic Studies* 3: 185-217.

— 1883. 'A tour in the Troad', *Fortnightly Review* April 1883.

— 1894. 'Sir C. T. Newton', *Journal of Hellenic Studies* 14: xlix-liv.

— 1895. 'Sir C. T. Newton', *Classical Review* 9: 81-85.

Jenkins, I. 1992. *Archaeologists & aesthetes in the sculpture galleries of the British Museum 1800-1939*. London: British Museum Press.

— 2006. *Greek architecture and its sculpture in the British Museum*. London: British Museum Press.

Jenkins, I., and K. Sloan. 1996. *Vases and volcanoes: Sir William Hamilton and his collection*. London: British Museum Press.

Jenkins, R. J. H. 1955. 'Richard MacGillivray Dawkins, 1871–1955', *Proceedings of the British Academy* 41: 373-88.

Jewell, H. H., and F. W. Hasluck. 1920. *The church of Our Lady of the hundred gates: (Panagia Hekatontapyliani) in Paros*. Byzantine Research Fund. London: Macmillan and Co.

Johnston, A. W. 1975. 'Rhodian readings', *Annual of the British School at Athens* 70: 145-67.

Jones, A. H. M., D. T. Rice, G. F. Hudson, and S. Casson. 1928. *Preliminary report upon the excavations carried out in the Hippodrome of Constantinople in 1927*. London: The British Academy by H. Milford, Oxford University Press.

Kakissis, A. 2004. 'Frederick Hasluck and the British School at Athens before World War One', in *Archaeology, Anthropology and Heritage in the Balkans and Anatolia: the Life and Times of F. W. Hasluck, 1878-1920*, edited by D. Shankland, vol. 1: 205-21. Istanbul: The Isis Press.

Kaltsas, N. 2002. *Sculpture in the National Archaeological Museum, Athens*. Los Angeles: The J. Paul Getty Museum.

Karageorghis, V. 2000. *Ancient art from Cyprus: the Cesnola Collection in The Metropolitan Museum of Art*. New York: The Metropolitan Museum of Art.

Kenyon, F. G., and B. F. Cook. 2004. 'Smith, Arthur Hamilton (1860-1941)', in *Oxford Dictionary of National Biography*, vol. 51: 41-42. Oxford: Oxford University Press.

King, P. J. 1983. *American archaeology in the Mideast: a history of the American Schools of Oriental Research*. Philadelphia: The American Schools of Oriental Research.

Kitto, H. D. F. 1959. 'Arnold Wycombe Gomme', *Journal of Hellenic Studies* 79: 1-2.

Knigge, U. 1991. *The Athenian Kerameikos. History-monuments-excavations*. Athens: Krene Editions; Deutsches Archäologisches Institut Athen.

Kunze, M. 1995. *The Pergamon altar: its rediscovery, history and reconstruction*. Mainz am Rhein: Philipp von Zabern.

Kurtz, D. Editor. 1994. *Bernard Ashmole 1894-1988: an autobiography*. Oxford: Oxbow.

Kurtz, D. C. Editor. 1985. *Beazley and Oxford. Lectures delivered at Wolfson College, Oxford on 28 June 1985*. Oxford University Committee for Archaeology Monograph, vol. 10. Oxford: Oxbow.

Laistner, M. L. W. 1912/13. 'Geometric pottery at Delphi', *Annual of the British School at Athens* 19: 61-69.

Lamb, D. 1914/16. 'Notes on Seljouk buildings at Konia', *Annual of the British School at Athens* 21: 31-61.

Lamb, W. 1926/27. 'Excavations at Sparta, 1906-1910: 6. Notes on some bronzes from the Orthia site', *Annual of the British School at Athens* 28: 96-106.

— 1936. *Excavations at Thermi in Lesbos*. Cambridge: Cambridge University Press.

— 1936/37. 'Some west Anatolian vases at Cambridge', *Annual of the British School at Athens* 37: 166-71.

Last, H. 1952. 'Joseph Grafton Milne', *Journal of Egyptian Archaeology* 38: 112-14.

Laughton, J. K., and A. Lambert. 2004. 'Spratt, Thomas Abel Brimage (1811-1888)', in *Oxford Dictionary of National Biography*, vol. 51: 984-85. Oxford: Oxford University Press.

Laughton, J. K., and R. Morriss. 2004. 'Malcolm, Sir Pulteney (1768-1838)', in *Oxford Dictionary of National Biography*, vol. 36: 301-02. Oxford: Oxford University Press.

Laver, J., and D. Farr. 2004. 'Smith, Sir Cecil Harcourt- (1859-1944)', in *Oxford Dictionary of National Biography*, vol. 51: 57-58. Oxford: Oxford University Press.

Lawson, J. C. 1899/1900. 'A beast-dance in Scyros', *Annual of the British School at Athens* 6: 125-27.

— 1910. *Modern Greek folklore and ancient Greek religion: a study in survivals.* Cambridge: Cambridge University Press.

— 1920. *Tales of Aegean intrigue.* London: Chatto & Windus.

Le Roy, C. 1996. 'L'École française d'Athènes et l'Asie Mineure', *Bulletin de Correspondance Hellénique* 120: 373-87.

Leaf, W. 1910/11. 'The topography of the Scamander Valley — I', *Annual of the British School at Athens* 17: 266-83.

— 1911/12a. 'The topography of the Scamander Valley — II', *Annual of the British School at Athens* 18: 286-300.

— 1911/12b. 'Trade routes and Constantinople', *Annual of the British School at Athens* 18: 301-13.

— 1914/16. 'Some problems of the Troad', *Annual of the British School at Athens* 21: 16-30.

Levick, B. 1958. 'Two Pisidian colonial families', *Journal of Roman Studies* 48: 74-78.

Levine, P. 1986. *The amateur and the professional: antiquarians, historians and archaeologists in Victorian England, 1838-1886.* Cambridge: Cambridge University Press.

Lewis, C. Editor. 1939. *Self-portrait taken from the letters and journals of Charles Ricketts, R. A.* London: Peter Davies.

Lindsay, J. O., and B. Megson. 1961. *Girton College, 1869-1959: an informal history.* Cambridge: Published for the Girton Historical and Political Society by W. Heffer.

Lock, P. 1990. 'D. G. Hogarth (1862-1927): "... A specialist in the science of archaeology"', *Annual of the British School at Athens* 85: 175-200.

Lord, L. E. 1947. *A history of the American School of Classical Studies at Athens 1882-1942: an intercollegiate project.* Cambridge (Mass.): American School of Classical Studies at Athens.

Lorimer, H. L. 1903. 'The country cart of ancient Greece', *Journal of Hellenic Studies* 23: 132-51.

— 1910. 'A vase fragment from Naukratis', *Journal of Hellenic Studies* 30: 35–37.

— 1912. 'Notes on the sequence and distribution of the fabrics called Proto-Corinthian', *Journal of Hellenic Studies* 32: 326–53.

— 1950. *Homer and the monuments.* London: Macmillan.

Loring, W. 1890. 'A new portion of the edict of Diocletian from Megalopolis', *Journal of Hellenic Studies* 11: 299-342.

— 1892/1893. 'The theatre at Megalopolis', *Journal of Hellenic Studies* 13: 356-58.

— 1895a. 'Four fragmentary inscriptions', *Journal of Hellenic Studies* 15: 90-92.

— 1895b. 'Some ancient routes in the Peloponnese', *Journal of Hellenic Studies* 15: 25-89.

Lubenow, W. C. 2004. 'Leaf, Walter (1852-1927)', in *Oxford Dictionary of National Biography*, vol. 32: 967-68. Oxford: Oxford University Press.

MacDonald, G. 1918. 'Professor Haverfield: A bibliography', *Journal of Roman Studies* 8: 184-98.

Macdonald, G. 1919/20. 'F. Haverfield: 1860-1919', *Proceedings of the British Academy* 9: 475-91.

MacGillivray, J. A. 2000. *Minotaur: Sir Arthur Evans and the archaeology of the Minoan myth*. New York: Hill and Wang.

Mackenzie, C. 1929. *Gallipoli memories*. London: Cassell & Co.

— 1931. *First Athenian memories*. London: Cassell & Co.

— 1939. *Greek memories*. London: Chatto & Windus.

— 1940. *Aegean memories*. London: Cassell & Co.

Mackenzie, D. 1896/7. 'Ancient sites in Melos', *Annual of the British School at Athens* 3: 71-88.

— 1897. 'Excavations of the British School at Melos: the site of the 'Three churches'', *Journal of Hellenic Studies* 17: 122-33.

— 1897/8a. 'Excavations in Melos, 1898. II. The successive settlements', *Annual of the British School at Athens* 4: 17-36.

— 1897/8b. 'Kos Astypalaia', *Annual of the British School at Athens* 4: 95-100.

— 1898/9. 'Excavations in Melos, 1899. A. The season's work', *Annual of the British School at Athens* 5: 3-10.

— 1903. 'The pottery of Knossos', *Journal of Hellenic Studies* 23: 157-205.

Mackridge, P. 1990. ''Some pamphlets on dead Greek dialects': R. M. Dawkins and modern Greek dialectology', *Annual of the British School at Athens* 85: 201-12.

Macmillan, G. A. 1878. 'A ride across the Peloponnese', *Edinburgh Monthly Magazine*: 551-52, 61, 63.

— 1885. 'The British School at Athens', *The Times* 10 February 1885: 6.

— 1890a. 'Asia Minor Exploration Fund — proposed expedition for 1890', *The Times* 18 January 1890: 10.

— 1890b. 'Byzantine architecture in Greece', *The Times* 28 May 1890: 13.

— 1891. 'Exploration in Asia Minor', *The Times* 12 May 1891: 12.

— 1893. 'Asia Minor Exploration Fund', *The Times* 21 November 1893: 3.

— 1904. 'Discoveries in Crete', *The Times* 31 May 1904: 8.

— 1906. 'The British School at Athens - survey at Sparta', *The Times* 6 February 1906: 8.

— 1910/11. 'A short history of the British School at Athens. 1886-1911', *Annual of the British School at Athens* 17: ix-xxxviii.

— 1929. 'An outline of the history of the Hellenic Society', *Journal of Hellenic Studies* 49: i-li.

Macmillan, G. A., HRH The Crown Prince of Greece, C. Harcourt-Smith, M. T. Homolle, A. Conze, J. R. Wheeler, R. C. Bosanquet, and C. Waldstein. 1903/04. 'The Penrose Memorial Library', *Annual of the British School at Athens* 10: 232-42.

Macmillan, G. A., and C. Harcourt-Smith. 1904. 'Penrose Memorial Fund', *The Times* 3 November 1904: 10.

Macridy Bey, T., and S. Casson. 1931. 'Excavations at the Golden Gate, Constantinople', *Archaeologia* 81: 63-84.

Magrath, J. R., and E. Baigent. 2004. 'Capes, William Wolfe (1834-1914)', in *Oxford Dictionary of National Biography*, vol. 9: 989-90. Oxford: Oxford University Press.

Mahaffy, J. P. 1882. 'The Site and Antiquity of the Hellenic Ilion', *Journal of Hellenic Studies* 3: 69-80.

Marchand, S. L. 1996. *Down from Olympus: archaeology and Philhellenism in Germany, 1750-1970*. Princeton: Princeton University Press.

Marder, A. J. 1965. *From the Dreadnought to Scapa Flow. The Royal Navy in the Fisher Era, 1904-1919. Volume II. The war years: to the eve of Jutland*. London: Oxford University Press.

Markides, M. 1911/12. 'A Mycenaean bronze in the Cyprus Museum', *Annual of the British School at Athens* 18: 95-97.

Markwell, D. J. 2004. 'Zimmern, Sir Alfred Eckhard (1879-1957)', in *Oxford Dictionary of National Biography*, vol. 60: 993-95. Oxford: Oxford University Press.

Marsden, J. H. 1852. *Two introductory lectures upon archaeology, delivered in the University of Cambridge*. Cambridge: Cambridge University Press.

— 1864. *A brief memoir of the life and writings of the late Lieutenant-Colonel William Martin Leake, D. C. L., F. R. S., &c. &c.* London: Whittingham and Wilkins for privately circulation.

Marshall, F. H. 1905/06. 'Tombs of Hellenic date at Praesos', *Annual of the British School at Athens* 12: 63-70.

— 1920. *Discovery in Greek lands: a sketch of the principal excavations and discoveries of the last fifty years*. Cambridge: Cambridge University Press.

Marthari, M. 2001. 'Altering information from the past: illegal excavations in Greece and the case of the Early Bronze Age Cyclades', in *Trade in illicit antiquities: the destruction of the world's archaeological heritage*, edited by N. Brodie, J. Doole, and C. Renfrew: 161-72. McDonald Institute Monographs. Cambridge: McDonald Institute.

Matthew, H. C. G. 2004. 'Stanhope, Philip Henry, fifth Earl Stanhope (1805-1875)', in *Oxford Dictionary of National Biography*, vol. 52: 149-52. Oxford: Oxford University Press.

Mauzy, C. A. 2006. *Agora excavations 1931-2006: a pictorial history*. Athens: American School of Classical Studies at Athens.

Mazower, M. 2001. *The Balkans: from the end of Byzantium to the present day*. London: Phoenix.

— 2005. *Salonica city of ghosts: Christians, Muslims and Jews 1430-1950*. London: Harper Perennial.

McConnell, A. 2004. 'Clarke, Edward Daniel (1769-1822)', in *Oxford Dictionary of National Biography*, vol. 11: 863-65. Oxford: Oxford University Press.

Mee, C. B., and H. A. Forbes. Editors. 1997. *A rough and rocky place: the landscape and settlement history of the Methana peninsula, Greece. Results of the Methana Survey Project sponsored by the British School at Athens and the University of Liverpool*. Liverpool: Liverpool University Press.

Megaw, A. H. S. 1988. 'The British School at Athens and Cyprus', *Report of the Department of Antiquities Cyprus*: 281-86.

Megson, B. 2004. 'Welsh, Elizabeth (1843-1921)', in *Oxford Dictionary of National Biography*, vol. 58: 84-85. Oxford: Oxford University Press.

Mehew, E. 2004. 'Colvin, Sir Sidney (1845-1927)', in *Oxford Dictionary of National Biography*, vol. 12: 837-39. Oxford: Oxford University Press.

Meiggs, R. 1974. 'Marcus Niebuhr Tod 1878-1974', *Proceedings of the British Academy* 60: 485-95.

Melman, B. 1995. *Women's orients: English women and the Middle East, 1718-1918: sexuality, religion and work*, 2nd edition. London: Macmillan.

Meritt, L. S. 1984. *History of the American School of Classical Studies at Athens 1939-1980*. Princeton: American School of Classical Studies at Athens.

Millar, F. 2004. 'Toynbee, Arnold Joseph (1889-1975)', in *Oxford Dictionary of National Biography*, vol. 55: 178-85. Oxford: Oxford University Press.

Millington-Evans, M. 1894. *Chapters on Greek dress*. London: Macmillan.

Milne, H. J. M., A. D. Nock, H. I. Bell, J. G. Milne, N. H. Baynes, F. D. Zulueta, M. E. Dicker, and R. McKenzie. 1928. 'Bibliography: Graeco-Roman Egypt A. Papyri (1926-1927)', *Journal of Egyptian Archaeology* 14: 131-58.

Milne, J. G. 1901. 'Greek inscriptions from Egypt', *Journal of Hellenic Studies* 21: 275-92.

— 1906. 'Clay-sealings from the Fayum', *Journal of Hellenic Studies* 26: 32-45.

— 1914a. 'Antony and Cleopatra?' *Journal of Egyptian Archaeology* 1: 99.

— 1914b. 'Graeco-Roman leaden tesserae from Abydos', *Journal of Egyptian Archaeology* 1: 93-95.

— 1914c. 'The sanatorium at Dêr-el-Bahri', *Journal of Egyptian Archaeology* 1: 96-98.

— 1916a. 'Greek and Roman tourists in Egypt', *Journal of Egyptian Archaeology* 3: 76-80.

— 1916b. 'The organisation of the Alexandrian mint in the reign of Diocletian', *Journal of Egyptian Archaeology* 3: 207-17.

— 1916. 'Ptolemaic seal impressions', *Journal of Hellenic Studies* 36: 87-101.

— 1917. 'Some Alexandrian coins', *Journal of Egyptian Archaeology* 4: 177-86.

— 1918. 'The shops of the Roman mint of Alexandreia', *Journal of Roman Studies* 8: 154-78.

— 1920. 'Two Roman hoards of coins from Egypt', *Journal of Roman Studies* 10: 169-84.

— 1922a. 'The coins from Oxyrhynchus', *Journal of Egyptian Archaeology* 8: 158-63.

— 1922b. 'A Gnomic ostrakon', *Journal of Egyptian Archaeology* 8: 156-57.

— 1924. 'Aemilianus the 'tyrant'', *Journal of Egyptian Archaeology* 10: 80-82.

— 1925a. 'Double entries in Ptolemaic tax-receipts', *Journal of Egyptian Archaeology* 11: 269-83.

— 1925b. 'The Kline of Sarapis', *Journal of Egyptian Archaeology* 11: 6-9.

— 1926. 'Bernard Pyne Grenfell: B. 16 Dec. 1869. D. 18 May 1926', *Journal of Egyptian Archaeology* 12: 285-86.

— 1928a. 'Chronological pitfalls', *Journal of Egyptian Archaeology* 14: 20-21.

— 1928b. 'Egyptian nationalism under Greek and Roman rule', *Journal of Egyptian Archaeology* 14: 226-34.

— 1929. 'Ptolemaic coinage in Egypt', *Journal of Egyptian Archaeology* 15: 150-53.

— 1930. 'The Roman regulation of exchange values in Egypt: a note', *Journal of Egyptian Archaeology* 16: 169-70.

— 1933. 'The Beni Hasan coin-hoard', *Journal of Egyptian Archaeology* 19: 119-21.

— 1934. ''Phocaean gold' in Egypt', *Journal of Egyptian Archaeology* 20: 193-94.
— 1935. 'Report on coins found at Tebtunis in 1900', *Journal of Egyptian Archaeology* 21: 210-16.
— 1937. 'On P. Oslo 83 and the depreciation of currency', *Journal of Egyptian Archaeology* 23: 258-59.
— 1938a. 'The currency of Egypt under the Ptolemies', *Journal of Egyptian Archaeology* 24: 200-07.
— 1938b. 'The silver of Aryandes', *Journal of Egyptian Archaeology* 24: 245-46.
— 1939. 'Trade between Greece and Egypt before Alexander the Great', *Journal of Egyptian Archaeology* 25: 177-83.
— 1941. 'The Tükh El-Karämüs gold hoard', *Journal of Egyptian Archaeology* 27: 135-37.
— 1943. 'Pictorial coin-types at the Roman mint of Alexandria', *Journal of Egyptian Archaeology* 29: 63-66.
— 1945. 'Alexandrian coins acquired by the Ashmolean Museum, Oxford', *Journal of Egyptian Archaeology* 31: 85-91.
— 1950. 'Pictorial coin-types at the Roman mint of Alexandria: a supplement', *Journal of Egyptian Archaeology* 36: 83-85.
— 1951. 'Pictorial coin-types at the Roman mint of Alexandria: a second supplement', *Journal of Egyptian Archaeology* 37: 100-02.
Mitchell, R. 2004. 'Penrose, Elizabeth [Mrs Markham] (c. 1779-1837)', in *Oxford Dictionary of National Biography*, vol. 43: 605-06. Oxford: Oxford University Press.
Mitchell, S., and M. Waelkens. 1998. *Pisidian Antioch: the site and its monuments*. London: Duckworth with the Classical Press of Wales.
Mitford, T. B. 1946. 'Religious documents from Roman Cyprus', *Journal of Hellenic Studies* 66: 24-42.
Möller, A. 2000. *Naukratis: trade in archaic Greece*. Oxford Monographs on Classical Archaeology. Oxford: Oxford University Press.
Momigliano, N. 1999. *Duncan Mackenzie: a cautious canny highlander & the palace of Minos at Knossos*. Bulletin of the Institute of Classical Studies supplement, vol. 72. London: Institute of Classical Studies.
Montserrat, D. 1996. ''No Papyrus and No Portraits': Hogarth, Grenfell and the First Season in the Fayum, 1895-6', *Bulletin of the American Society of Papyrologists* 33: 133-76.
Morgan, C. 1943. *The House of Macmillan (1843-1943)*. London: Macmillan.
Morgan, L. 2007. 'The painted plasters and their relation to the wall painting of the Pillar Crypt', in *Excavations at Phylakopi in Melos 1974-77*, edited by C. Renfrew, Supplementary volume 42: 371-99. London: British School at Athens.
Munro, J. A. R. 1891. 'Excavations in Cyprus. Third season's work - Polis tes Chrysochou', *Journal of Hellenic Studies* 12: 298-333.
— 1896. 'Epigraphical Notes from Eastern Macedonia and Thrace', *Journal of Hellenic Studies* 16: 313-22.
— 1897. 'Inscriptions from Mysia', *Journal of Hellenic Studies* 17: 268-93.
— 1900. 'Some Pontic milestones', *Journal of Hellenic Studies* 20: 159-66.
— 1901. 'Roads in Pontus, royal and Roman', *Journal of Hellenic Studies* 21: 52-66.

Munro, J. A. R., W. C. F. Anderson, J. G. Milne, and F. Haverfield. 1896. 'On the Roman town of Doclea in Montenegro: communicated to the Society of Antiquaries', *Archaeologia* 55: 33-92.

Munro, J. A. R., and H. M. Anthony. 1897a. 'Explorations in Mysia', *Geographical Journal* 9: 256-76.

— 1897b. 'Explorations in Mysia', *Geographical Journal* 9: 150-69.

Munro, J. A. R., and D. G. Hogarth. 1893. *Modern and ancient roads in eastern Asia Minor.* Royal Geographical Society, supplementary papers, vol. 3 part 5. London: Royal Geographical Society.

Munro, J. A. R., and H. A. Tubbs. 1890. 'Excavations in Cyprus, 1889. Second season's work. Polis tes Chrysochou. Limniti', *Journal of Hellenic Studies* 11: 1-99.

Munro, J. A. R., H. A. Tubbs, and W. W. Wroth. 1891. 'Excavations in Cyprus, 1890. Third season's work. Salamis', *Journal of Hellenic Studies* 12: 59-198.

Murray, A. S. 1877. 'On the pottery of Cyprus', in *Cyprus: its ancient cities, tombs, and temples: a narrative of researches and excavations during ten years' residence as American Consul in that island*, edited by L. P. d. Cesnola: 393-412. London: John Murray.

— 1887. 'Two vases from Cyprus', *Journal of Hellenic Studies* 8: 317-23.

— 1899. 'Excavations in Cyprus, 1896', *Journal of the Royal Institute of British Architects* 7 (ser. 3): 21-35.

Murray, A. S., A. H. Smith, and H. B. Walters. 1900. *Excavations in Cyprus: bequest of Miss E. T. Turner to the British Museum.* Reprinted 1970. London: British Museum.

Murray, M. 1963. *My first hundred years.* London: William Kimber.

Myers, J. W., E. E. Myers, and G. Cadogan. 1992. *The aerial atlas of ancient Crete.* Berkeley: University of California Press.

Myres, J. L. 1895. 'On some polychrome pottery from Kamarais in Crete', *Proceedings of the Society of Antiquaries* 15: 351-56.

— 1896/7. 'A marble relief from the African Tripolis', *Annual of the British School at Athens* 3: 170-74.

— 1897. 'Excavations in Cyprus in 1894', *Journal of Hellenic Studies* 17: 134-73.

— 1902/03. 'Excavations at Palaikastro. II. § 13. The sanctuary-site of Petsofà', *Annual of the British School at Athens* 9: 356-87.

— 1910. *Greek lands and the Greek people: an inaugural lecture delivered before the University of Oxford, November 11, 1910.* Oxford: Clarendon Press.

— 1914. *Handbook of the Cesnola Collection of antiquities from Cyprus.* New York: Metropolitan Museum of Art.

— 1940/45a. 'Excavations in Cyprus, 1913', *Annual of the British School at Athens* 41: 53-104.

— 1940/45b. 'Obituary: Stanley Casson', *Annual of the British School at Athens* 41: 1-4.

Myres, J. L., and P. Gardner. 1902. *Classical archaeology in schools.*

— 1905. *Classical archaeology in schools*, 2nd edition. Oxford: Clarendon Press.

Myres, J. N. L. 1980. *Commander J. L. Myres, R. N. V. R.: the Blackbeard of the Aegean.* J. L. Myres Memorial Lecture, vol. 10. London: Leopard's Head Press.

Neilson, K. 2004. 'Nicolson, Arthur, first Baron Carnock (1849-1928)', in *Oxford Dictionary of National Biography*, vol. 40: 883-85. Oxford: Oxford University Press.

Netoliczka, A. v. 1912. 'Die Manteltracht der archaischen Frauenfiguren', *Jahreshefte des Österreichischen Archäologischen Instituts in Wien* 15: 253-64.

Newton, C. T., E. L. Hicks, and G. Hirschfeld. 1874. *The collection of ancient Greek inscriptions in the British Museum*. Oxford: Printed by order of the Trustees.

Nicholls, R. V. 1982. 'The drunken Herakles. A new angle on an unstable subject', *Hesperia* 51: 321-28.

Nunn, P. G. 2004. 'Stillman [Spartali], Marie (1844-1927)', in *Oxford Dictionary of National Biography*, vol. 52: 800-01. Oxford: Oxford University Press.

O'Halpin, E. 2004. 'Hall, Sir (William) Reginald (1870-1943)', in *Oxford Dictionary of National Biography*, vol. 24: 646-48. Oxford: Oxford University Press.

Ohnefalsch-Richter, M. H., and J. L. Myres. 1899. *A catalogue of the Cyprus museum: with a chronicle of excavations undertaken since the British occupation, and introductory notes on Cypriote archaeology*. Oxford: Clarendon Press.

Oppé, A. P. 1904. 'The chasm at Delphi', *Journal of Hellenic Studies* 24: 214-40.

Ormerod, H. A. 1909/10. 'Laconia II. Topography. Bardoúnia and north-eastern Maina', *Annual of the British School at Athens* 16: 62-71.

— 1911/12. 'Prehistoric remains in south-western Asia Minor. II. The mounds at Senirdje and Bounarbashi', *Annual of the British School at Athens* 18: 80-94.

— 1912. 'A new astragalos inscription from Pamphylia', *Journal of Hellenic Studies* 32: 270-76.

— 1912/13. 'Prehistoric remains in south-western Asia Minor. III', *Annual of the British School at Athens* 19: 48-60.

— 1914. 'Greek inscriptions in the Museum of the Liverpool Royal Institution', *Annals of Archaeology and Anthropology* 6: 99-108.

— 1922. 'The campaigns of Servilius Isauricus against the pirates', *Journal of Roman Studies* 12: 35-56.

— 1924. *Piracy in the ancient world: an essay in Mediterranean history*. Liverpool: Liverpool University Press.

Ormerod, H. A., and E. S. G. Robinson. 1910/11. 'Notes and inscriptions from Pamphylia', *Annual of the British School at Athens* 17: 215-49.

— 1914. 'Inscriptions from Lycia', *Journal of Hellenic Studies* 34: 1-35.

Parry, C. H. H., D. G. Hogarth, and A. D. Godley. 1890. *The music to the Frogs of Aristophanes*. Leipzig and London: Breitkopf & Hartel.

Paton, W. R. 1885. 'Archaeology at Athens', *The Times* 9 February 1885: 4.

— 1887. 'Iasos', *Classical Review* 1: 176-77.

— 1888. 'Ceramic Gulf', *Classical Review* 2: 328-29.

— 1889. 'Iasos', *Classical Review* 3: 333.

— 1890. 'An inscription from Paphos', *Classical Review* 4: 283-84.

— 1894. 'Inscriptions from Kos and Halicarnassus', *Classical Review* 8: 216-18.

— 1900. 'Sites in E. Karia and S. Lydia', *Journal of Hellenic Studies* 20: 57-80.

Paton, W. R., and J. L. Myres. 1896. 'Karian sites and inscriptions: II', *Journal of Hellenic Studies* 16: 237-71, pls. x-xi.

— 1897. 'Researches in Karia', *Journal of the Royal Geographic Society* 9: 38-54.

— 1898. 'Some Karian and Hellenic oil-presses', *Journal of Hellenic Studies* 18: 209-17.

Peacock, S. J. 1988. *Jane Ellen Harrison: the mask and the self*. New Haven: Yale University Press.

Peet, T. E. 1906/07. 'The early Aegean civilization in Italy', *Annual of the British School at Athens* 13: 405-22.

— 1907. 'The early iron age in South Italy', *Papers of the British School at Rome* 4: 283-96.

— 1910. 'Contributions to the study of the prehistoric period in Malta', *Papers of the British School at Rome* 5: 139-63.

— 1914a. *Cemeteries of Abydos*. Egypt Exploration Society Memoir, vol. 34. London: Egypt Exploration Society.

— 1914b. 'The year's work at Abydos', *Journal of Egyptian Archaeology* 1: 37-39.

— 1933. 'The classification of Egyptian pottery', *Journal of Egyptian Archaeology* 19: 62-64.

Peet, T. E., A. J. B. Wace, and M. S. Thompson. 1908. 'The connection of the Aegean civilization with Central Europe', *Classical Review* 22: 233-38.

Pendlebury, H. W., J. D. S. Pendlebury, and M. B. Money-Coutts. 1937/38. 'Excavations in the plain of Lasithi. III. Karphi: a city of refuge in the Early Iron Age in Crete. Excavated by students of the British School of Archaeology at Athens, 1937-39', *Annual of the British School at Athens* 38: 57-145.

Pendlebury, J. D. S. 1939. *The archaeology of Crete*. London: Methuen.

Penrose, F. C. 1847. *Two letters ... on certain anomalies in the construction of the Parthenon*. London: Published for the Society of Dilettanti.

— 1851. *An investigation of the principles of Athenian architecture, or, The results of a recent survey, chiefly conducted with reference to the optical refinements exhibited in the construction of the ancient buildings at Athens*. London: Longman.

— 1887. 'Excavations in Greece, 1886-1887', *Journal of Hellenic Studies* 8: 269-77.

— 1887. 'Mycenae and Tiryns', *The Times* 31 December 1887: 4.

— 1888. *An investigation of the principles of Athenian architecture: or, The results of a recent survey conducted chiefly with reference to the optical refinements exhibited in the construction of the ancient buildings at Athens*. London: The Society of Dilettanti.

— 1890. 'The fire at Salonica', *The Times* 18 November 1890: 7.

— 1892. 'On the Ancient Hecatompedon Which Occupied the Site of the Parthenon on the Acropolis of Athens', *Journal of Hellenic Studies* 13: 32-47.

— 1895. 'On Some Traces Connected with the Original Entrance of the Acropolis of Athens', *Journal of Hellenic Studies* 15: 248-50.

Perdrizet, P. F. 1894. 'Voyages dans la Macédoine première', *Bulletin de Correspondance Hellénique* 18: 416-45.

Perry, J. A. 2000. Rediscovering D. G. Hogarth: a biographical study of Oxford's Near Eastern archaeologist and World War I diplomat. MA, State University of New York at Buffalo.

Petrie, W. M. F. 1885. 'The discovery of Naukratis', *Journal of Hellenic Studies* 6: 202-06.

— 1890. 'The Egyptian bases of Greek history', *Journal of Hellenic Studies* 11: 271-77.

— 1891. 'Notes on the antiquities of Mykenae', *Journal of Hellenic Studies* 12: 199-205.

Petrie, W. M. F., and C. T. Currelly. 1905. *Ehnasya, 1904*. 26th memoir of the Egypt Exploration Fund. London: The Egypt Exploration Fund.

— 1906. *Researches in Sinai*. London: J. Murray 1906.

Petrie, W. M. F., and J. G. Duncan. 1906. *Hyksos and Israelite cities*. British School of Archaeology in Egypt and Egyptian Research Account. 12th year. London: School of Archaeology in Egypt.

Petrie, W. M. F., and E. A. Gardner. 1886. *Naukratis*. 3rd memoir of the Egypt Exploration Fund. London: Trubner.

Phelps, L. R., and R. Smail. 2004. 'Monro, David Binning (1836-1905)', in *Oxford Dictionary of National Biography*, vol. 38: 646-47. Oxford: Oxford University Press.

Picard, C. 1918/19. 'Macedonia. I. Les Recherches archéologiques de l'Armée française en Macédoine. 1916-1919', *Annual of the British School at Athens* 23: 1-9.

Pirie-Gordon, C. H. C. 1912. 'The reigning princes of Galilee', *English Historical Review* 27: 445-61.

— n. d. -a. *A guide-book to southern Palestine*. Palestine Pocket Guide-books, vol. 1: Palestine News.

— n. d. -b. *A guide-book to central Palestine*. Palestine Pocket Guide-books, vol. 2: Palestine News.

— n. d. -c. *A guide-book to northern Palestine and southern Syria*. Palestine Pocket Guide-books, vol. 3: Palestine News.

— n. d. -d. *A guide-book to central Syria, Lebanon, and Phoenicia*. Palestine Pocket Guide-books, vol. 4: Palestine News.

Pirie-Gordon, H. 1919. *A brief record of the advance of the Egyptian Expeditionary Force under the command of General Sir Edmund H. H. Allenby: July 1917 to October 1918*. Cairo: The Government Press and Survey of Egypt.

Port, M. H. 2004. 'Blore, Edward (1787-1879)', in *Oxford Dictionary of National Biography*, vol. 6: 283-87. Oxford: Oxford University Press.

Poynter, A. M. 1896/7. 'Remarks on three sectile pavements in Greece', *Annual of the British School at Athens* 3: 175-81.

Purchas, A. 2004. 'Revett, Nicholas (1721-1804)', in *Oxford Dictionary of National Biography*, vol. 46: 514-15. Oxford: Oxford University Press.

Radet, G. 1901. *L'histoire et l'oeuvre de l'École française d'Athènes*. Paris: A. Fontemoing.

Radford, E. 1915. 'Euphronios and his colleagues', *Journal of Hellenic Studies* 35: 107-39.

Ramsay, W. M. 1880. 'Newly discovered sites near Smyrna', *Journal of Hellenic Studies* 1: 63-74.

— 1880. 'On some Pamphylian inscriptions', *Journal of Hellenic Studies* 1: 242-59.

— 1883. 'The cities and bishoprics of Phrygia', *Journal of Hellenic Studies* 4: 370-436.

— 1887. 'The cities and bishoprics of Phrygia (continued)', *Journal of Hellenic Studies* 8: 461-519.

— 1888. 'A study of Phrygian art. I', *Journal of Hellenic Studies* 9: 350-82.

— 1889. 'A study of Phrygian art (Part II)', *Journal of Hellenic Studies* 10: 147-89.

— 1902/03. 'Pisidia and the Lycaonian frontier', *Annual of the British School at Athens* 9: 243-73.

— 1916. 'Colonia Caesarea (Pisidian Antioch) in the Augustan age', *Journal of Roman Studies* 6: 83-134.

Randell, W. L., and A. McConnell. 2004. 'Crompton, Rookes Evelyn Bell (1845-1940)', in *Oxford Dictionary of National Biography*, vol. 14: 303. Oxford: Oxford University Press.

Rees, J. 1998. *Amelia Edwards: traveller, novelist & Egyptologist*. London: The Rubicon Press.

Reid, B. H. 2004. 'Milne, George Francis, first Baron Milne (1866-1948)', in *Oxford Dictionary of National Biography*, vol. 38: 294-98. Oxford: Oxford University Press.

Renfrew, C. 1985. *The archaeology of cult: the sanctuary at Phylakopi*. British School at Athens supplementary volume 18. London: British School at Athens.

— Editor. 2007. *Excavations at Phylakopi in Melos 1974-77*. British School at Athens supplementary volume 42. London: British School at Athens.

Renfrew, C., and M. Wagstaff. Editors. 1982. *An island polity: the archaeology of exploitation in Melos*. Cambridge: Cambridge University Press.

Rhodes, D. E. 1973. *Dennis of Etruria: the life of George Dennis*. London: Cecil & Amelia Woolf.

Rice, D. T., G. F. Hudson, S. Casson, and B. Gray. 1929. *Second report upon the excavations carried out in and near the Hippodrome of Constantinople in 1928 on behalf of the British Academy*. London: The British Academy by H. Milford, Oxford University Press.

Richards, G. C. 1891. 'Archaic reliefs at Dhimitzana', *Journal of Hellenic Studies* 12: 41-45.

— 1892/3. 'Selected vase-fragments from the Acropolis of Athens, Part I', *Journal of Hellenic Studies* 13: 281-92.

— 1894a. 'Selected vase-fragments from the Acropolis of Athens, Part II', *Journal of Hellenic Studies* 14: 186-97.

— 1894b. 'Selected vase-fragments from the Acropolis of Athens, Part III', *Journal of Hellenic Studies* 14: 381-87.

— 1898. 'Archaeology in Greece, 1897-1898', *Journal of Hellenic Studies* 18: 328-39.

Richter, G. M. A. 1904/5. 'The distribution of Attic vases', *Annual of the British School at Athens* 11: 224-42.

— 1912. 'A new early Attic vase', *Journal of Hellenic Studies* 32: 370-84.

— 1968. *Korai: archaic Greek maidens. A study of the development of the Kore type in Greek sculpture*. London: Phaidon Press.

— 1972. *My memoirs: recollections of an archaeologist's life*. Rome: R. & R. Clark Ltd.

Riddell, R. 2004. 'Parker, John Henry (1806-1884)', in *Oxford Dictionary of National Biography*, vol. 42: 697-98. Oxford: Oxford University Press.

Ridgeway, W. 1896. 'What people made the objects called Mycenaean?' *Journal of Hellenic Studies* 16: 77-119.

— 1901. *The early age of Greece, I*. Cambridge: Cambridge University Press.

— 1915. 'The relation of archaeology to classical studies', *Proceedings of the Classical Association* 12: 19-31.

Ridgway, B. S. 1967. 'The banquet relief from Thasos', *American Journal of Archaeology* 71: 307-09.

Roberts, E. S., and E. A. Gardner. 1887. *An introduction to Greek epigraphy: Part 1: The archaic inscriptions and the Greek alphabet*. Cambridge: The University Press.

Roberts, S. C., and M. Pottle. 2004. 'Whibley, Leonard (1863-1941)', in *Oxford Dictionary of National biography*, vol. 58: 471. Oxford: Oxford University Press.

Robinson, Andrew. 2002. *The man who deciphered Linear B: the story of Michael Ventris*. London: Thames & Hudson.

Robinson, Annabel. 2002. *The life and work of Jane Ellen Harrison*. Oxford: Oxford University Press.

Robinson, E. S. G. 1914. 'Coins from Lycia and Pamphylia', *Journal of Hellenic Studies* 34: 36-46.

Rodeck, P. 1896/7. 'The Ionic capital of the gymnasium of Kynosarges', *Annual of the British School at Athens* 3: 89-105.

Rolleston, H. D., and A. G. Bearn. 2004. 'Allbutt, Sir Thomas Clifford (1836-1925)', in *Oxford Dictionary of National Biography*, vol. 1: 764-65. Oxford: Oxford University Press.

Romaios, K. 1904/05. 'Laconia IV. The Hermai on the N. E. frontier', *Annual of the British School at Athens* 11: 137-38.

Rouet, P. 2001. *Approaches to the study of Attic vases: Beazley and Pottier*. Oxford Monographs on Classical Archaeology. Oxford: Oxford University Press.

Rustafjaell, R de. 1902. 'Cyzicus', *Journal of Hellenic Studies* 22: 174-89.

Rutherford, N. 2004. 'Thomson, Sir Basil Home (1861-1939)', in *Oxford Dictionary of National Biography*, vol. 54: 492-93. Oxford: Oxford University Press.

Ryan, D. P. 1995. 'David George Hogarth at Asyut, Egypt, 1906-7: the history of a 'lost' excavation', *Bulletin of the History of Archaeology* 5: 3-16.

Samuels, E. 1979. *Bernard Berenson: the making of a connoisseur*. Cambridge (Mass.): Belknap Press of Harvard University Press.

Sanders, D. H., and D. W. J. Gill. 2004. 'Theresa B. Goell (1901-1985)', in *Breaking Ground: Pioneering women archaeologists*, edited by G. Cohen and M. S. Joukowsky: 482-524. Ann Arbor: University of Michigan Press.

Sayce, A. H. 1880. 'Notes from journeys in the Troad and Lydia', *Journal of Hellenic Studies* 1: 75-93.

— 1923. *Reminiscences*. London: Macmillan.

— 1927. 'David George Hogarth, 1862-1927', *Proceedings of the British Academy* 13: 379-83.

Sayce, A. H., and R. C. Jebb. 1883. 'The ruins of Hissarlik', *Journal of Hellenic Studies* 4: 142-55, 436.

Schaus, G. P. 1985. *The East Greek, Island, and Laconian pottery. The Extramural sanctuary of Demeter and Persephone at Cyrene, Libya Final reports II*. University Museum Monograph, vol. 56. Philadelphia: The University Museum.

Schliemann, H. 1884. *Troja. Results of the latest researches and discoveries on the site of Homer's Troy, 1882*. London.

— 1887. 'Mycenae and Tiryns', *The Times* 31 December 1887: 4.

Schuchhardt, C. 1891. *Schliemann's excavations: an archaeological study*. London: Macmillan.

Schultz, R. W. 1908. 'The Byzantine Research Fund', *The Times* 3 July 1908: 11.

— 1910. *The Church of the Nativity at Bethlehem*. London: Byzantine Research Fund.

Schultz, R. W., and S. H. Barnsley. 1901. *The monastery of Saint Luke of Stiris, in Phocis: and the dependent monastery of Saint Nicolas in the Fields, near Skripou, in Boeotia.* London: Macmillan.

Scutt, C. A. 1912/13. 'The Tsakonian Dialect. I', *Annual of the British School at Athens* 19: 132-73.

— 1913/14. 'The Tsakonian Dialect. II', *Annual of the British School at Athens* 20: 18-31.

Seccombe, T. 2004. 'Ford, Sir (Francis) Clare (1828-1899)', in *Oxford Dictionary of National Biography*, vol. 20: 321-22. Oxford: Oxford University Press.

Seiradaki, M. B. 1960. 'Pottery from Karphi', *Annual of the British School at Athens* 55: 1-37.

Sellers, E. 1891a. 'The theatre at Megalopolis', *Classical Review* 5: 239-40.

— 1891b. 'The theatres of Megalopolis', *Athenaeum*.

— 1892/3. 'Three Attic lekythoi from Eretria', *Journal of Hellenic Studies* 13: 1-12.

— 1894. 'Greek head in the possession of T. Humphry Ward, Esq', *Journal of Hellenic Studies* 14: 198-205.

— 1896. *Commentary and historical introduction to the Elder Pliny's Chapter on the History of Art translated by K. Jex-Blake.* London: Macmillan.

Sheffy, Y. 1998. *British military intelligence in the Palestine campaign, 1914-1918.* Cass series. Studies in Intelligence. London: Frank Cass.

— 2002. 'British Intelligence and the Middle East, 1900-1918: how much do we know?' *Intelligence and National Security* 17: 33-52.

Sherratt, S. 2000. *Catalogue of Cycladic antiquities in the Ashmolean Museum: the captive spirit.* Oxford: Oxford University Press.

Sikes, E. E. 1893. 'Folk-Lore in the 'Works and Days' of Hesiod', *Classical Review* 7: 389-94.

— 1909. 'Four-footed man: a note on Greek anthropology', *Folklore* 20: 421-31.

Smith, A. H. 1887. 'Notes on a tour in Asia Minor', *Journal of Hellenic Studies* 8: 216-67.

— 1931. 'Thomas Ashby (1874-1931)', *Proceedings of the British Academy* 17: 515-41.

Smith, C. 1880. 'An Archaic Vase with Representation of a Marriage Procession', *Journal of Hellenic Studies* 1: 202-09.

— 1881a. 'Actors with Bird-Masks on Vases', *Journal of Hellenic Studies* 2: 309-14.

— 1881b. 'Kylix with Exploits of Theseus', *Journal of Hellenic Studies* 2: 57-64.

— 1883a. 'Inscriptions from Rhodes', *Journal of Hellenic Studies* 4: 136-41.

— 1883b. 'Inscriptions from Rhodes', *Journal of Hellenic Studies* 4: 351-53.

— 1895/6a. 'Archaeology in Greece, 1895-6', *Annual of the British School at Athens* 2: 47-62.

— 1895/6b. 'Excavations in Melos', *Annual of the British School at Athens* 2: 63-76.

— 1896. 'Archaeology in Greece, 1895-6', *Journal of Hellenic Studies* 16: 335-56.

— 1896/7. 'Excavations in Melos, 1897', *Annual of the British School at Athens* 3: 1-30.

— 1897. 'Inscriptions from Melos', *Journal of Hellenic Studies* 17: 1-21.

— 1902. 'A Proto-Attic Vase', *Journal of Hellenic Studies* 22: 29-45.

Smith, C., and D. Comparetti. 1882. 'The Petelia gold tablet', *Journal of Hellenic Studies* 3: 111-18.

Smith, C., and R. de Rustafjaell. 1902. 'Inscriptions from Cyzicus', *Journal of Hellenic Studies* 22: 190-207.

Spieser, J. -M. 1996. 'Les études byzantines à l'École française d'Athènes', *Bulletin de Correspondance Hellénique* 120: 441-49.

Spratt, T. A. B. 1865. *Travels and researches in Crete*. London: J. van Voorst.

St. Clair, W. 2004. 'Bruce, Thomas, seventh earl of Elgin and eleventh earl of Kincardine (1766-1841)', in *Oxford Dictionary of National Biography*, vol. 8: 329-31. Oxford: Oxford University Press.

Sterrett, J. R. S. 1888a. *Epigraphical journey to Asia Minor*. Boston: Damrell and Upham.

— 1888b. *Wolfe expedition to Asia Minor*. Boston: Damrell and Upham.

— 1911. *A plea for research in Asia Minor and Syria authorized by men whose high achievements and representative character make the project a call for humanity at large for light in regard to the life of man in the cradle of western civilization*. Ithaca (NY).

Stewart, A. 1990. *Greek sculpture: an exploration*. New Haven: Yale University Press.

Stewart, J. 1959. *Jane Ellen Harrison: a portrait from letters*. London: The Merlin Press.

Stibbe, M. 2008. *British civilian internees in Germany: the Ruhleben camp, 1914-1918*. Manchester: Manchester University Press.

Stieglitz, R. R. 1994. 'The Minoan origin of Tyrian Purple', *The Biblical Archaeologist* 57: 46-54.

Stillman, W. J. 1883. 'The British School at Athens', *The Times* 11 July 1883: 4.

Stokes, J. L. 1905/06. 'Stamped pithos-fragments from Cameiros', *Annual of the British School at Athens* 12: 71-79.

Stone, G. 2004. 'Forbes, Nevill (1883-1929)', in *Oxford Dictionary of National Biography*, vol. 20: 304-05. Oxford: Oxford University Press.

Stray, C. A. 1995. 'Digs and degrees: Jessie Crum's tour of Greece, Easter 1901', *Classics Ireland* 2: 121-31.

— 1998. *Classics transformed: schools, universities and society in England, 1830-1960*. Oxford: Clarendon Press.

— Editor. 1999. *Classics in 19th and 20th century Cambridge: curriculum, culture and community*. Cambridge Philological Society supplementary vol. 24. Cambridge: Cambridge Philological Society.

— 2002. 'The pen is mightier than the spade: archaeology and education in nineteenth century England', *Pharos* 10: 123-34.

— Editor. 2007. *Oxford classics: teaching and learning, 1800-2000*. London: Duckworth.

Strong, E. 1907. *Roman sculpture from Augustus to Constantine*. London: Duckworth.

— 1915. *Apotheosis and after life: three lectures on certain phases of art and religion in the Roman Empire*. London: Constable.

Stuart-Jones, H. 1891. 'Two vases by Phintias', *Journal of Hellenic Studies* 12: 366-80.

— 1895. *Select passages from ancient writers illustrative of the history of Greek sculpture*. London; New York: Macmillan and Co.

— 1905. 'Notes on Roman historical sculptures', *Papers of the British School at Rome* 3: 215-71.

— 1910. 'The historical interpretation of the reliefs of Trajan's column', *Papers of the British School at Rome* 5: 433-59.

— Editor. 1912. *A catalogue of the ancient sculptures preserved in the municipal collections of Rome 1: the sculptures of the Museo Capitolino*. Oxford: Clarendon Press.

— Editor. 1926. *A catalogue of the ancient sculptures preserved in the municipal collections of Rome 2: the sculptures of the Palazzo dei Conservatori*. Oxford: Clarendon Press.

Stubbings, F. H. 1958. 'Alan John Bayard Wace, 1879-1957', *Proceedings of the British Academy* 44: 263-80.

Sutherland, C. H. V. 1977. 'Edward Stanley Gotch Robinson, 1887-1976', *Proceedings of the British Academy* 63: 423-40.

Sutherland, G. 2004. 'Gardner, Alice (1854-1927)', in *Oxford Dictionary of National Biography*, vol. 21: 451-52. Oxford: Oxford University Press.

Taylor, M. N. L., and H. C. Bradshaw. 1916. 'Architectural terracottas from two temples at Falerii Veteres', *Papers of the British School at Rome* 8: 1-34.

Taylor, M. V. 1960. 'The Society for the Promotion of Roman Studies, 1910-1960', *Journal of Roman Studies* 50: 129-34.

Taylor, R. 1998. *Embroidery of the Greek Islands and Epirus*. Brooklyn: Interlink Books.

Thallon, I. C. 1906. 'The date of Damophon of Messene', *American Journal of Archaeology* 10: 302-29.

Thompson, E. M. 1903/4. 'Alexander Stuart Murray', *Proceedings of the British Academy*: 321-23.

Thompson, H. A., and R. E. Wycherley. 1972. *The Agora of Athens*. Athenian Agora, vol. 14. Princeton: American School of Classical Studies at Athens.

Thompson, M. S., and A. J. B. Wace. 1909. 'The connection of the Aegean culture with Servia', *Classical Review* 23: 209-12.

Thomson, B. 1931. *The allied secret service in Greece*. London: Hutchinson.

Tillard, L. B. 1910/11. 'The fortifications of Phokis', *Annual of the British School at Athens* 17: 54-75.

Tillyard, E. M. W. 1923. *The Hope vases: a catalogue and a discussion of the Hope collection of Greek vases with an introduction on the history of the collection and on late Attic and south Italian vases*. Cambridge: Cambridge University Press.

Tillyard, H. J. W. 1904/05. 'Laconia II. Geraki. 3. Inscriptions', *Annual of the British School at Athens* 11: 105-12.

— 1905/06a. 'Laconia II. Excavations at Sparta, 1906. § 9. Inscriptions from the Artemisium', *Annual of the British School at Athens* 12: 351-93.

— 1905/06b. 'Laconia II. Excavations at Sparta, 1906. § 14. Inscriptions from the altar, the acropolis, and other sites', *Annual of the British School at Athens* 12: 441-79.

— 1905/06c. 'Two watch towers in the Megarid', *Annual of the British School at Athens* 12: 101-08.

— 1911/12. 'The acclamation of emperors in Byzantine ritual', *Annual of the British School at Athens* 18: 239-60.

— 1914/16. 'Rhythm in Byzantine music', *Annual of the British School at Athens* 21: 125-47.

— 1916/18. 'The modes in Byzantine music', *Annual of the British School at Athens* 22: 133-56.

— 1918/19. 'Some Byzantine musical manuscripts at Cambridge', *Annual of the British School at Athens* 23: 194-205.

Tod, M. N. 1901/02. 'Some unpublished 'Catalogi Paterarum Argentearum'', *Annual of the British School at Athens* 8: 197-230.

— 1902/03a. 'Excavations at Palaikastro. II. § 10. Hagios Nikolaos', *Annual of the British School at Athens* 9: 336-43.

— 1902/03b. 'An unpublished Attic decree', *Annual of the British School at Athens* 9: 154-75.

— 1903/04. 'A new fragment of the Attic Tribute Lists', *Annual of the British School at Athens* 10: 78-82.

— 1904. 'A new fragment of the 'Edictum Diocletiani'', *Journal of Hellenic Studies* 24: 195-202.

— 1904/05. 'Inscriptions from Eumeneia', *Annual of the British School at Athens* 11: 27-31.

— 1905. 'Notes and inscriptions from south-western Messenia', *Journal of Hellenic Studies* 25: 32-55.

— 1911/12. 'The Greek numeral notation', *Annual of the British School at Athens* 18: 98-132.

— 1913. 'Three Greek numeral systems', *Journal of Hellenic Studies* 33: 27-34.

— 1914. 'The progress of Greek epigraphy, 1913-14', *Journal of Hellenic Studies* 34: 321-31.

— 1915a. 'On an Archaic Thessalian epigram', *Classical Review* 29: 196-97.

— 1915b. 'The progress of Greek epigraphy, 1914-15', *Journal of Hellenic Studies* 35: 260-70.

— 1919. 'The progress of Greek epigraphy, 1915-1918', *Journal of Hellenic Studies* 39: 209-31.

— 1922. 'Greek inscriptions from Macedonia', *Journal of Hellenic Studies* 42: 167-83.

Tod, M. N., H. J. W. Tillyard, and A. M. Woodward. 1906/07. 'Laconia I. Excavations at Sparta, 1907. § 10. The inscriptions', *Annual of the British School at Athens* 13: 174-218.

Tod, M. N., and A. J. B. Wace. 1906. *A catalogue of the Sparta Museum*. Oxford: Clarendon Press.

Toynbee, A. J. 1915. *Nationality and the war*. London ; Toronto: J. M. Dent.

— 1916. *The treatment of Armenians in the Ottoman empire: documents presented to Viscount Grey of Fallodon*. London; New York: Hodder and Stoughton.

— 1969. *Experiences*. New York: Oxford University Press.

Traill, D. A. 1995. *Schliemann of Troy: treasure and deceit*. London: John Murray.

Traquair, R. 1905/06a. 'Laconia I. The mediaeval fortresses', *Annual of the British School at Athens* 12: 258-76.

— 1905/06b. 'Laconia II. Excavations at Sparta, 1906. § 12. The Roman stoa and the later fortifications', *Annual of the British School at Athens* 12: 415-30.

— 1906/07. 'Mediaeval fortresses of the north-western Peloponnesus', *Annual of the British School at Athens* 13: 268-84.

— 1908/09. 'Laconia III. Mediaeval churches. The churches of western Mani', *Annual of the British School at Athens* 15: 177-213.

Triantaphyllides, H. 1896/7. 'Macedonian customs', *Annual of the British School at Athens* 3: 207-14.

Tubbs, H. A. 1890. 'Marble Calathos-Stele from Poli', *Classical Review* 4: 70.

Tullberg, R. M. 1998. *Women at Cambridge*, 3rd edition. Cambridge: Cambridge University Press.

Tzortzi, K. 2000. *The temple of Apollo Epikourios: a journey through time and space.* Athens: Committee for the Preservation of the temple of Apollo Epikourios at Bassai.

Ure, A. D. H., R. M. Burrows, and P. N. Ure. 1934. *Aryballoi & figurines from Rhitsona in Boeotia: an account of the early archaic pottery and of the figurines, archaic and classical, with supplementary lists of the finds of glass, beads and metal, from excavations made by R. M. Burrows and P. N. Ure in 1907, 1908, 1909 and by P. N. and A. D. Ure in 1921 and 1922.* Reading University studies. Cambridge: Cambridge University Press.

Ure, P. N. 1910. 'Excavations at Rhitsona in Boeotia', *Journal of Hellenic Studies* 30: 336-56.

— 1913. *Black glaze pottery from Rhitsona in Boeotia.* University College, Reading. Studies in history and archaeology. London; New York: H. Milford, Oxford University Press.

— Editor. 1927. *Sixth & fifth century pottery from excavations made at Rhitsona by R. M. Burrows in 1909 and by P. N. Ure and A. D. Ure in 1921 & 1922.* Reading University studies. London: Oxford University Press, H. Milford.

— 1932. 'Droop cups', *Journal of Hellenic Studies* 52: 55-71.

Usborne, C. V. 1933. *Smoke on the Horizon.* London: Hodder & Stoughton.

Van De Put, A. 1906/07. 'Note on the armorial insignia in the church of St George, Geraki', *Annual of the British School at Athens* 13: 281-83.

Van Millingen, A., W. S. George, A. E. Henderson, and R. Traquair. 1912. *Byzantine Churches in Constantinople: their history and architecture. ... With maps, plans, and illustrations.* London: Macmillan & Co.

Vassilika, E. 1998. *Greek and Roman Art.* Fitzwilliam Museum Handbook. Cambridge: Cambridge University Press.

Vassits, M. M. 1907/08. 'South-eastern elements in the pre-historic civilization of Servia', *Annual of the British School at Athens* 14: 319-42.

Vickers, M. 1985. 'The thunderbolt of Zeus: yet more fragments of the Pergamon altar in the Arundel Collection', *American Journal of Archaeology* 89: 516-19.

Wace, A. J. B. 1902/03. 'Apollo seated on the Omphalos: a statue at Alexandria', *Annual of the British School at Athens* 9: 211-42.

— 1903. 'Recent excavations in Asia Minor', *Journal of Hellenic Studies* 23: 335-55.

— 1904/05a. 'Laconia II. Geraki. 2. Sculptures', *Annual of the British School at Athens* 11: 99-105.

— 1904/05b. 'Laconia V. Frankish sculptures at Parori and Geraki', *Annual of the British School at Athens* 11: 139-45.

— 1905a. *Catalogue of a collection of modern Greek embroideries.* Cambridge: Fitzwilliam Museum.

— 1905b. 'Hellenistic royal portraits', *Journal of Hellenic Studies* 25: 86-104.

— 1905/06a. 'Laconia II. Excavations at Sparta, 1906. § 2. The city wall', *Annual of the British School at Athens* 12: 284-88.

— 1905/06b. 'Laconia II. Excavations at Sparta, 1906. § 3. The heroön', *Annual of the British School at Athens* 12: 288-94.

— 1905/06c. 'Laconia II. Excavations at Sparta, 1906. § 8. The stamped tiles', *Annual of the British School at Athens* 12: 344-50.

— 1905/06d. 'Laconia II. Excavations at Sparta, 1906. § 11. The Roman baths (Arapissa)', *Annual of the British School at Athens* 12: 407-14.

— 1906a. 'Fragments of Roman historical reliefs in the Vatican and Lateran Museums', *Papers of the British School at Rome* 3: 273-94.

— 1906b. 'Skiathos und Skopelos', *Athenische Mitteilungen* 31: 129-33.

— 1906c. 'Some sculptures at Turin', *Journal of Hellenic Studies* 26: 235-42.

— 1906d. 'The topography of Pelion and Magnesia', *Journal of Hellenic Studies* 26: 143-68.

— 1906/07a. 'Laconia I. Excavations at Sparta, 1907. § 2. The city walls', *Annual of the British School at Athens* 13: 5-16.

— 1906/07b. 'Laconia I. Excavations at Sparta, 1907. § 3. The stamped tiles', *Annual of the British School at Athens* 13: 17-43.

— 1907. 'Studies in Roman historical reliefs', *Papers of the British School at Rome* 4: 227-76.

— 1907/08. 'Laconia I. Excavations at Sparta, 1908. § 8. A hoard of Hellenistic coins', *Annual of the British School at Athens* 14: 149-58.

— 1908. 'Topography of Pelion and Magnesia - Addenda', *Journal of Hellenic Studies* 28: 337.

— 1909/10. 'Laconia III. Pottery. Early pottery from Geraki', *Annual of the British School at Athens* 16: 72-75.

— 1910. 'The reliefs in the Palazzo Spada', *Papers of the British School at Rome* 5: 165-200.

— 1912/13. 'Mumming plays in the southern Balkans', *Annual of the British School at Athens* 19: 248-65.

— 1913/14. 'The mounds of Macedonia', *Annual of the British School at Athens* 20: 123-32.

— 1914/16. 'The site of Olynthus', *Annual of the British School at Athens* 21: 11-15.

— 1919/20, 1920/21a. 'Excavations at Mycenae §I. The campaign of 1920', *Annual of the British School at Athens* 24: 185-87.

— 1919/20, 1920/21b. 'Excavations at Mycenae §II. The campaign of 1921', *Annual of the British School at Athens* 24: 187-88.

— 1921/22, 1922/23. 'Excavations at Mycenae V. The Campaign of 1922', *Annual of the British School at Athens* 25: 3-5.

— 1932. *Chamber Tombs at Mycenae*. Archaeologia, vol. 82. London: The Society of Antiquaries.

— 1935. *An approach to Greek sculpture*. Cambridge: Cambridge University Press.

— 1939. 'Mycenae, 1939', *Journal of Hellenic Studies* 59: 210-12.

— 1964. *Greece untrodden*. Athens: Mrs Alan Wace.

Wace, A. J. B., and R. M. Dawkins. 1914. 'Greek embroideries', *Burlington Magazine* 26/140: 49-50, 99-107.

Wace, A. J. B., and G. Dickins. 1906/07. 'Laconia I. Excavations at Sparta, 1907. § 8. The Hellenistic tombs', *Annual of the British School at Athens* 13: 155-68.

Wace, A. J. B., and J. P. Droop. 1906/07. 'Excavations at Theotokou, Thessaly', *Annual of the British School at Athens* 13: 308-27.

Wace, A. J. B., J. P. Droop, and M. S. Thompson. 1907/08. 'Excavations at Zerélia, Thessaly', *Annual of the British School at Athens* 14: 197-223.

Wace, A. J. B., and F. W. Hasluck. 1904/05a. 'Laconia I. Excavations near Angelona', *Annual of the British School at Athens* 11: 81-90.

— 1904/05b. 'Laconia II. Geraki. 1. Excavations', *Annual of the British School at Athens* 11: 91-99.

— 1907/08. 'Laconia II. Topography. South-eastern Laconia', *Annual of the British School at Athens* 14: 161-82.

— 1908/09. 'Laconia II. Topography. East-central Laconia', *Annual of the British School at Athens* 15: 158-76.

Wace, A. J. B., and W. M. T. Lawrence. 1914. *Catalogue of a collection of old embroideries of the Greek islands and Turkey*. London: Burlington Fine Arts Club.

Wace, A. J. B., and M. S. Thompson. 1908/09. 'A cave of the nymphs on Mount Ossa', *Annual of the British School at Athens* 15: 243-47.

— 1910. 'Excavations in Thessaly, 1910', *Man* 10: 159-60.

— 1910/11. 'A Latin inscription from Perrhaebia', *Annual of the British School at Athens* 17: 193-204.

— 1911. 'The distribution of early civilization in northern Greece', *Geographical Journal* 37: 631-36.

— 1912. *Prehistoric Thessaly: being some account of recent excavations and explorations in north-eastern Greece from Lake Kopais to the borders of Macedonia*. Cambridge archaeological and ethnological series. Cambridge: Cambridge University Press.

— 1914. *The nomads of the Balkans: an account of life and customs among the Vlachs of Northern Pindus*. London: Methuen.

Wace, A. J. B., M. S. Thompson, and J. P. Droop. 1908/09. 'Laconia I. Excavations at Sparta, 1909. § 6. The Menelaion', *Annual of the British School at Athens* 15: 108-57.

Wace, A. J. B., and R. Traquair. 1909. 'The base of the obelisk of Theodosius', *Journal of Hellenic Studies* 29: 60-69.

Wace, A. J. B., and A. M. Woodward. 1911/12. 'Inscriptions from Upper Macedonia', *Annual of the British School at Athens* 18: 166-88.

Wagstaff, J. M. 2004. 'Leake, William Martin (1777-1860)', in *Oxford Dictionary of National Biography*, vol. 32: 982-83. Oxford: Oxford University Press.

Waldstein, C. 1904. 'Damophon', *Journal of Hellenic Studies* 24: 330-31.

Walker, A. L., and H. Goldman. 1915. 'Report on excavations at Halae of Locris', *American Journal of Archaeology* 19: 418-37.

Walker, E. M. 2004. 'Mahaffy, Sir John Pentland (1839-1919)', in *Oxford Dictionary of National Biography*, vol. 36: 151-53. Oxford: Oxford University Press.

Wallace-Hadrill, A. 2001. *The British School at Rome: one hundred years*. London: The British School at Rome.

Walters, H. B. 1897. 'On some antiquities of the Mycenaean age recently acquired by the British Museum', *Journal of Hellenic Studies*: 63-77.

Warren, P. M. 2000. 'Early travellers from Britain and Ireland', in *Cretan quests: British explorers, excavators and historians*, edited by D. Huxley: 1-8. London: British School at Athens.

Waterhouse, H. 1986. *The British School at Athens: the first hundred years*. British School at Athens supplementary vol. 19. London: Thames & Hudson.

— 2004. 'Lorimer, (Elizabeth) Hilda Lockhart (1873-1954)', in *Oxford Dictionary of National Biography*, vol. 34: 446-47. Oxford: Oxford University Press.

Waterhouse, P., and R. O'Donnell. 2004. 'Penrose, Francis Cranmer (1817-1903)', in *Oxford Dictionary of National Biography*, vol. 43: 607-10. Oxford: Oxford University Press.

Watkin, D. 2004a. 'Cockerell, Charles Robert (1788-1863)', in *Oxford Dictionary of National Biography*, vol. 12: 355-59. Oxford: Oxford University Press.

— 2004b. 'Stuart, James (1713-1788)', in *Oxford Dictionary of National Biography*, vol. 53: 161-65. Oxford: Oxford University Press.

Watrous, L. V. 1982. *Lasithi, a history of settlement on a highland plain in Crete*. Hesperia supplement, vol. 18. Princeton, N. J.: American School of Classical Studies at Athens.

Welch, F. B. 1899/1900a. 'The influence of the Aegean civilisation on south Palestine', *Annual of the British School at Athens* 6: 117-24.

— 1899/1900b. 'Knossos III. Notes on the pottery', *Annual of the British School at Athens* 6: 85-92.

— 1918/19a. 'The folk-lore of a Turkish Labour Battalion', *Annual of the British School at Athens* 23: 123-25.

— 1918/19b. 'Macedonia. III. Prehistoric pottery', *Annual of the British School at Athens* 23: 44-50.

— 1918/19c. 'Macedonia. V. Ancient sites in the Strymon valley', *Annual of the British School at Athens* 23: 64-66.

Welsh, M. K. 1904/5. 'Honorary statues in ancient Greece', *Annual of the British School at Athens* 11: 32-49.

Westrate, B. 1992. *The Arab Bureau: British policy in the Middle East, 1916-1920*. University Park, Pennsylvania: The Pennsylvania State University Press.

White, D. M. 2004. 'Wood, Robert (1716/17-1771)', in *Oxford Dictionary of National Biography*, vol. 60: 135-37. Oxford: Oxford University Press.

Wilhelm, A. 1900/01. 'An Athenian decree', *Annual of the British School at Athens* 7: 156-62.

Williams, C. K., and N. Bookidis. Editors. 2002. *Corinth: the centenary, 1896-1996*. Corinth, vol. 20. Princeton: American School of Classical Studies at Athens.

Wilson, C. Editor. 1895. *Handbook for travellers in Asia Minor, Transcaucasia, Persia, etc.* London: John Murray.

Wilson, D. M. 2002. *The British Museum: a History*. London: The British Museum Press.

Winstone, H. V. F. 1976. *Captain Shakespear: a portrait*. London: Jonathan Cape.

— 1982. *The illicit adventure: the story of political and military intelligence in the Middle East from 1898 to 1926*. London: Jonathan Cape.

— 1990. *Woolley of Ur: the life of Sir Leonard Woolley*. London: Secker & Warburg.

— 1993. *Gertrude Bell*. London: Constable.

Wiplinger, G., and G. Wlach. 1996. *Ephesus: 100 years of Austrian research.* Vienna: Österreichisches Archäologisches Institut / Böhlau Verlag.

Wiseman, T. P. 1981. 'The first director of the British School', *Papers of the British School at Rome* 49: 144-63.

— 1990. *A short history of the British School at Rome.* London: British School at Rome.

Wood, J. T. 1877. *Discoveries at Ephesus, including the sites and remains of the great temple of Diana.* London: Longmans, Green & Co.

— 1885. 'Archaeology at Athens', *The Times* 9 February 1885: 4.

Woodhouse, W. J. 1893. 'Aetolian inscriptions', *Journal of Hellenic Studies* 13: 338-55.

— 1897. *Aetolia: its geography, topography, and antiquities.* Reprinted New York: Arno Press, 1973. Oxford: Clarendon Press.

Woodward, A. M. 1906/07. 'Laconia II. Topography. § 2. Taenarum and S. Maina', *Annual of the British School at Athens* 13: 238-67.

— 1907/08. 'Laconia I. Excavations at Sparta, 1908. § 5. The inscriptions', *Annual of the British School at Athens* 14: 74-141.

— 1908. 'Some unpublished Attic inscriptions', *Journal of Hellenic Studies* 28: 291-312.

— 1908/09a. 'Laconia I. Excavations at Sparta, 1909. § 4. The inscriptions', *Annual of the British School at Athens* 15: 40-106.

— 1908/09b. 'The quota-list of the year 427-6 B. C', *Annual of the British School at Athens* 15: 229-42.

— 1909. 'Three new fragments of Attic treasure-records', *Journal of Hellenic Studies* 29: 168-91.

— 1909/10a. 'Laconia I. Excavations at Sparta, 1910. § 6. The inscriptions', *Annual of the British School at Athens* 16: 54-61.

— 1909/10b. 'Some new fragments of Attic building-records', *Annual of the British School at Athens* 16: 187-205.

— 1910. 'Notes on some Greek inscriptions, mainly in Athens', *Journal of Hellenic Studies* 30: 260-66.

— 1910/11a. 'Inscriptions from western Pisidia', *Annual of the British School at Athens* 17: 205-14.

— 1910/11b. 'Some notes on the monument of Porphyrios at Constantinople', *Annual of the British School at Athens* 17: 88-92.

— 1911. 'Some more unpublished fragments of Attic treasure-records', *Journal of Hellenic Studies* 31: 31-41.

— 1911/12. 'Inscriptions from Beroea in Macedonia', *Annual of the British School at Athens* 18: 133-65.

— 1913. 'Inscriptions from Thessaly and Macedonia', *Journal of Hellenic Studies* 33: 313-46.

— 1923/24, 1924/25. 'Excavations at Sparta, 1924-25. § 3. The inscriptions', *Annual of the British School at Athens* 26: 159-239.

— 1925. 'The Roman fort at Ilkley', *Journal of the Yorkshire Archaeological Society* 28: 137-321.

— 1925/6. 'Excavations at Sparta, 1926. iii. The inscriptions', *Annual of the British School at Athens* 27: 210-54.

— 1927/8. 'Excavations at Sparta, 1924-28. The inscriptions, Part I', *Annual of the British School at Athens* 29: 2-56.

— 1928/30. 'Excavations at Sparta, 1924-28. i. The theatre: architectural remains', *Annual of the British School at Athens* 30: 151-240.

— 1934. 'The Roman villa at Rudston (East Yorks)', *Journal of the Yorkshire Archaeological Society* 31: 366-76.

— 1935. 'The Roman villa at Rudston (E. Yorks): second interim report: the excavations of 1934', *Journal of the Yorkshire Archaeological Society* 32: 214-20.

Woodward, A. M., and H. A. Ormerod. 1909/10. 'A journey in south-western Asia Minor', *Annual of the British School at Athens* 16: 76-136.

Woodward, A. M., and K. A. Steer. 1936. 'The Roman villa at Rudston (E. Yorks): third interim report: the excavations of 1935', *Journal of the Yorkshire Archaeological Society* 33: 81-86.

Woolley, L. 1954. 'John Linton Myres: 1869-1954', *Man* 54: 40.

Wroth, W. W., and R. D. E. Eagles. 2004. 'Chandler, Richard (bap. 1737, d. 1810)', in *Oxford Dictionary of National Biography*, vol. 11: 7-8. Oxford: Oxford University Press.

Wroth, W. W., and J. Thompson. 2004. 'Gell, Sir William (1777-1836)', in *Oxford Dictionary of National Biography*, vol. 21: 733-35. Oxford: Oxford University Press.

Xanthoudidis, S. A. 1898. 'Cretan expedition IX. Inscriptions from Gortyna, Lyttos, and Lató Pros Kamara', *American Journal of Archaeology* 2: 71-78.

Yiakoumis, H. 2000. *The Acropolis of Athens: photographs 1839-1959*. Athens: Potamos.

Yorke, V. W. 1892. 'Newly discovered fragments of the balustrade of Athena Nike', *Journal of Hellenic Studies* 13: 272-80.

— 1896a. 'Excavations at Abae and Hyampolis in Phocis ' *Journal of Hellenic Studies* 16: 291-312.

— 1896b. 'A journey in the valley of the Upper Euphrates', *Geographical Journal* 8: 317-35, 453-74, map.

— 1898. 'Inscriptions from eastern Asia Minor', *Journal of Hellenic Studies* 18: 306-27.

— 1907. 'Excavations in Laconia', *The Times* 10 April 1907: 11.

Zimmern, A. E. 1909. 'Was Greek civilization based on slave labour?' *Sociological Review* 2: 2-19.

— 1911. *The Greek commonwealth: politics and economics in 5th century Athens*. Oxford: Clarendon Press.

INDEXES

I. PEOPLE

INDEXES

II. GENERAL